The Way We Lived in North Carolina

The Way We Lived

in North Carolina

Elizabeth A. Fenn

Peter H. Wood

Harry L. Watson

Thomas H. Clayton

Sydney Nathans

Thomas C. Parramore

Jean B. Anderson

Edited by Joe A. Mobley

Maps by Mark Anderson Moore

Published in association with the

Office of Archives and History,

North Carolina Department of Cultural Resources,

by the University of North Carolina Press

Chapel Hill and London

Set in New Baskerville, Rosewood, and The Sans
by Tseng Information Systems, Inc.
Manufactured in the United States of America

The paper in this book meets the guidelines for permanence and durability of
the Committee on Production Guidelines for Book Longevity of the Council on
Library Resources.

All illustrations, unless otherwise indicated, are from the Office of Archives and History,
North Carolina Department of Cultural Resources.

Library of Congress Cataloging-in-Publication Data
The way we lived in North Carolina / by Elizabeth A. Fenn . . . [et al.] ; edited by
Joe A. Mobley.
    p. cm.
Rev. single volume ed. of the five volume series published separately in 1983 under
the titles: Natives & newcomers, An independent people, Close to the land, The quest
for progress, and Express lanes & country roads.
Includes bibliographical references (p.) and index.
ISBN 0-8078-2814-9 (cloth : alk. paper)
ISBN 0-8078-5487-5 (pbk. : alk. paper)
1. North Carolina—History.   2. North Carolina—Social conditions.   3. North
Carolina—History, Local.   4. Historic sites—North Carolina.   I. Fenn, Elizabeth A.
(Elizabeth Anne), 1959–   II. Mobley, Joe A.   III. North Carolina. Office of Archives
and History.
F254 .W35   2003
975.6—dc21   2003006428

cloth   07 06 05 04 03   5 4 3 2 1
paper   07 06 05 04 03   5 4 3 2 1

This work was previously published for the North Carolina Department of
Cultural Resources by the University of North Carolina Press as five separate
books with the collective title *The Way We Lived in North Carolina*. This edition
combines the text of those five books, with revisions, and a new selection of
illustrations and maps.

CONTENTS

FOREWORD

The year 2003 marks the one-hundredth anniversary of the founding of the North Carolina Historical Commission. The North Carolina Office of Archives and History, the agency over which the North Carolina Historical Commission presides, has chosen as the theme of the commission's anniversary observance "History for All the People." That maxim originated with Christopher Crittenden, the longtime director (1935–1968) of what was then the Department of Archives and History. Writing in 1941, Crittenden declared: "Our histories should be something of broad, general interest—not merely for the professional historians, not merely for the genealogists, not just for any other limited group, but instead for the people at large."

The publication of the revised edition of *The Way We Lived in North Carolina* in the centennial year of the North Carolina Historical Commission provides a fitting tribute to Crittenden's vision of a democratic history. Originally published for the North Carolina Department of Cultural Resources by the University of North Carolina Press in five volumes in 1983, *The Way We Lived in North Carolina* always was intended for a general audience. In the new, single-volume format, the series becomes an indispensable narrative overview of the state's history and, more specifically, of its historic places.

Twenty years ago the term "heritage tourism" probably did not exist. Entering the twenty-first century, public historical agencies such as the Office of Archives and History recognize the importance of heritage tourism to the economic vitality of communities throughout the nation. Heritage tourism, moreover, helps promote democratic values while preserving the nation's most important historic sites, museums, and places of cultural significance. Those places orient us to a landscape and time past but not forgotten. They allow us to reflect on how earlier generations met the challenges of their own time and place. They remind us of the triumphs and failures, the changes and continuities that collectively make up the fabric of our past. In a sense, *The Way We Lived in North Carolina* became a pioneering work in heritage tourism.

In particular I would like to thank Joe A. Mobley, former administrator of the Historical Publications Section in the Office of Archives and History, for his skillful editing of the revised edition. Mark Anderson Moore, a talented historian in the Research Branch of the Office of Archives and History, spent countless hours preparing the extraordinary maps in this edition. David Perry and Mark Simpson-Vos of the University of North Carolina Press demonstrated steadfast faith in this project and supplied much-needed financial and editorial support. Finally, the roles of the original authors—Peter Wood, Elizabeth Fenn, Harry Watson, Thomas Clayton, Sydney Nathans, Thomas Parramore, and Jean B. Anderson—and of William S. Price Jr. and Larry Misenheimer, both of whom are now retired from the Office of Archives and History, deserve acknowledgment and appreciation. Price and Misenheimer developed the concept for the original series.

The English novelist and short story writer L. P. Hartley observed in *The Go-Between* (1953), "The past is a foreign country: they do things differently there." With this revised edition of *The Way We Lived in North Carolina*, perhaps the past will look less foreign and more familiar to a new generation of readers.

Jeffrey J. Crow
Deputy Secretary, Office of Archives and History

PREFACE

In 1983 the Division (now Office) of Archives and History, North Carolina Department of Cultural Resources, joined with the University of North Carolina Press to publish the five-volume *Way We Lived in North Carolina.* The books covered the social history of the state from the precolonial period through 1970. *The Way We Lived in North Carolina* was based on the concept that an excellent way to comprehend the past is through the combined impact of two experiences: reading history and visiting historic places. Before the volumes recently went out of print, they received accolades from both historians and general readers. The American Historical Association honored the work with its James Harvey Robinson Prize.

Now the University of North Carolina Press and the Office of Archives and History are pleased to issue a revised edition of *The Way We Lived in North Carolina.* The new version combines the five volumes into one book composed of five parts. The original treatments by the same well-known scholars of North Carolina history remain, but some revisions have been made to the original texts, and new material has been added to the essays to bring them up to date. The marginalia prepared for the original edition by Jean B. Anderson have been blended into the main text. Many of the photographs selected by the designer of the original books, Christine Alexander, have been retained, and new ones have been added. All the illustrations, unless otherwise noted in the captions, are from the Office of Archives and History. Mark Anderson Moore of the Research Branch of the Office of Archives and History prepared the maps in the new edition.

The efforts of a number of people enhanced this work in both its original and new editions. Volunteers from local historical associations, many affiliated with the Federation of North Carolina Historical Societies, added materially to the gathering and scope of information. The staffs of various institutions aided the research. At the Office of Archives and History, the professionals who contributed their time and expertise include members of the State Archives, the Historic Sites Sections, the State Historic Preservation Office, the Office of State Archaeology, the Research Branch, the Museum of History, and Historical Publications. University repositories that provided substantial assistance were the Manuscript Department of the William R. Perkins Library, Duke University, Durham; the North Carolina Collection and the Southern Historical Collection at the Louis R. Wilson Library, University of North Carolina at Chapel Hill; and the University Archives, D. H. Hill Library, North Carolina

State University at Raleigh. A number of individuals merit specific mention for their help: Mary M. Barden, Rodney Barfield, Larry Bennett, Catherine Bishir, Paul Bock, Jean Boggs, Peggy Boswell, Mary Boyer, Gerald Brooks, Charlotte Brown, Thomas Burke, Mary Canada, Bessie Carrington, Jerry C. Cashion, William Chafe, Guy Coe, Alice Cotten, Jerry Cotten, Betty Cowan, Dennis F. Daniels, Allen de Hart, Thelma Dempsey, Margaret DeRosset, James Dorman, Mary Clare Engstrom, Bob Farrington, Gayle Fripp, Ellen Frontis, R. Neil Fulghum, L. Garibaldi, Raymond Gavins, Jay Gaynor, Brent D. Glass, Renee Gledhill-Earley, E. Franklin Grill, Philip Guy, Grace Guyer, Jacquelyn Hall, Walton Haywood, Alice Henderson, Michael Hill, Davyd Hood, Richard Hunter, H. G. Jones, Robert Kenzer, Mary Hinton Kerr, Jesse R. Lankford Jr., Jo White Linn, Sal Levi, Ruth Little-Stokes, Cici Long, Susan W. Marks, Steve Massengill, Bettie Mckinne, John A. McNeill Sr., Paulette Mitchell, Frances Moody, Malvin E. Moore, Dan L. Morrill, J. Robert Morrison, Bob Mosher, Bill Murphy, Pauline Myrick, Sylvia Nash, Marge Parker, Allan Paul, Theresa Pennington, Bob Price, Mary E. Ragsdale, Joseph Reckford, William Reddy, Lillian Robinson, Jane Rowe, Peyton Russ, Dorothy Sapp, Theresa Shipp, Marguerite Schumann, Elizabeth Smith, Judith Smith, Michael Smith, Michael Southern, Carol Spears, George Stevenson Jr., Keith Strawn, Greer Suttlemyre, Barbara E. Taylor, Gwynne Taylor, Maurice Toler, Elizabeth Turner, John E. Tyler, Susan Walker, Margaret Wall, W. Kirby Watson, Ansley Herring Wegner, Alan L. Westmoreland, Ray Whitamore, John Woodard, Ann Wortham, Kathleen B. Wyche, Ray B. Wyche, Betty O. Young, and Charlene Young.

All those who helped to produce *The Way We Lived in North Carolina* join the authors in the hope that readers—whether natives or new arrivals—will find the book to be an informative and entertaining introduction to the rich history of the Old North State.

Joe A. Mobley

Elizabeth A. Fenn & Peter H. Wood

Part I

NATIVES & NEWCOMERS
NORTH CAROLINA BEFORE 1770

North Carolina

GEOGRAPHICAL REGIONS AND COUNTIES

MAPS BY MARK ANDERSON MOORE

THE FIRST CAROLINIANS

For almost 500 years, people of European and African descent have inhabited a land now called North Carolina. Richly varied, it extends from the eastern edges of the Mississippi River basin in the Appalachian Mountains to the remarkable barrier islands known as the Outer Banks. Mount Mitchell, near the Blue Ridge Parkway in Pisgah National Forest, is the highest elevation in the eastern United States. Here northern hardwoods mingle on the steep slopes with a bewildering variety of southern flowers and shrubs. Less than 500 miles east, at Cape Hatteras, a venerable lighthouse surveys the flat but treacherous coastline. Here the warm waters of the powerful Gulf Stream bring mild, and occasionally stormy, weather to the low-lying coast. Between the rugged Blue Ridge and the broad Coastal Plain, stretching roughly from modern-day Morganton to Raleigh, lie the rolling foothills that colonial settlers called the Carolina Piedmont.

Thousands of years before settlers from Europe and Africa set foot on Carolina soil, another people inhabited the land. Termed "Indians" by Christopher Columbus, they were in fact the first Carolinians. Their history encompasses migrations the length and breadth of an immense continent, shattering invasions, and technological transformation. By the time non-Indians reached North Carolina, sound agricultural methods were well in place. Even metalworking was not unknown.

Perhaps the best way to begin the study of North Carolina Indian history is by listening to the Indians themselves. North American Indians had no written languages. They could not store their history in dusty volumes on the shelves of ancient libraries. Instead, they recorded their history orally, in the stories and legends they passed from generation to generation. It is this tradition that kept the Indian past alive.

One such story comes from the Tuscarora Indians, who lived in the vicinity of the Neuse River. The legend records a long, icy migration from a land far to the west. It was told to a modern Tuscarora man by his great-grandmother.

In the old world, the legend says, there was a long famine. Nothing would grow, and people were starving. Finally the people held a council meeting. The

Encampment of American Indians, North Carolina's earliest inhabitants. Theodore De Bry engraving of painting (ca. 1585) by John White.

council decided that the people had to leave their homeland for a new place, where they could find food.

After walking some distance, the people realized they were walking on ice. For days they walked on ice. One group got tired and decided not to go on. The other group decided to keep walking—to "where the sun rises"—until they found food. They walked during the day and at night they rested.

At last they stopped. Ahead of them was a black streak, which they thought might be a huge snake. For safety, they spread apart within hearing distance of one another. When the persons in front reached the streak, they learned it was not a snake, but a lush forest with abundant food. The message was relayed to the end of the line, and the group gathered at the forest. They found so much food that they decided to send for the others. But when they returned to the west, they discovered that the ice had melted. At the place where they had crossed, they saw only water. They had no way to reach their friends.

Another North Carolina tribe, the Cherokees, tell a similar story. Like the Tuscarora tale, it includes a long, eastward migration prompted by starvation. It even describes life in the north, wearing snowshoes and enduring the long darkness of subarctic winters.

Modern archeologists also think the ancestors of the North Carolina Indians may have migrated from the west. Although their theories vary considerably, most scholars agree on one fact: the predecessors of the American Indians at some time crossed a land bridge between Asia and America. Some say the first crossing, toward "where the sun rises," took place more than 30,000 years ago. Indeed, it could have occurred as much as 70,000 years ago, when the growing glaciers of the last ice age lowered the sea level enough to expose dry land at the Bering Strait. At the peak of the ice age's final phase, about 18,000 years ago, the land bridge from Asia to present-day Alaska may have been 1,000 miles wide. It clearly would have been possible for inhabitants of Asia to reach North America.

From the Bering Strait, the first Americans probably migrated eastward several thousand miles, crossing the northernmost extension of what we now know as the Rocky Mountains. On the eastern side of the Rockies, they found a long, narrow corridor of ice-free land. Only fifty to a hundred miles wide in places, this corridor stretched far to the south alongside the mountains. The earliest Americans followed this route, finally emerging from the ice-covered north near present-day Montana.

The first North Carolinians arrived over 10,000 years ago. Unfortunately, little evidence of these people survives. The environment they encountered was very different from what we know today. Glacial ice still lay over much of

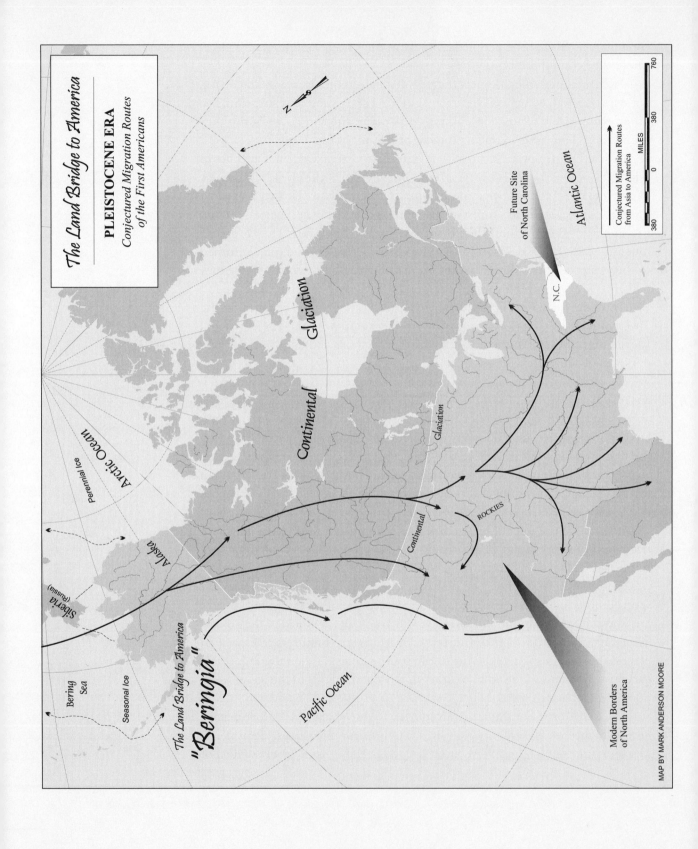

The Land Bridge to America

PLEISTOCENE ERA
*Conjectured Migration Routes
of the First Americans*

Arctic Ocean

Perennial Ice

Continental Glaciation

Glaciation

Future Site
of North Carolina

N.C.

Atlantic Ocean

Siberia
(Russia)

Alaska

Bering
Sea

Seasonal Ice

The Land Bridge to America
"Beringia"

Pacific Ocean

Continental

ROCKIES

Modern Borders
of North America

MAP BY MARK ANDERSON MOORE

Conjectured Migration Routes
from Asia to America

MILES

380   0   380   760

North Carolina's Indians made canoes from felled trees. Theodore De Bry engraving from John White painting.

North America. Although too far south to be ice-covered, the North Carolina region was nevertheless quite cold and wet. Even the animal population differed. Huge animals, such as the mastodon, roamed the land alongside more familiar game, such as deer.

These earliest North Carolinians are known as "Paleo-Indians." They lived in bands of no more than fifty people, staying in one place while they could and moving to find better food resources when necessary. With stone points bound to long wooden shafts, the Paleo-Indians hunted the large animals of the region. While Paleo-Indian hunters may have thrown their spears at animals from a distance, some scholars speculate that the hunters preferred to attack at extremely close range, where there was little chance of missing.

Not all large game hunting was done with spears. A favorite technique was to stampede a herd of animals over a cliff or other precipice, thus killing many at one time. Although these animals provided one source of food, a large part of the Paleo-Indian diet may have consisted of vegetables and small game.

The migrations of these ancient North Carolinians were not aimless. They followed herds of large animals and returned to specific sites regularly. While some areas provided seasonal food resources, other locations, like Morrow Mountain in present-day Stanly County, supplied ideal stone for projectile points. At the top of Morrow Mountain, in Morrow Mountain State Park, visitors can still see the large rhyolite outcrops where North Carolina dwellers gathered point material for over 10,000 years. Morrow Mountain and all the Uwharrie Mountains are unique for their numerous exposed deposits of rhyolite. At one time the Uwharries were volcanic mountains in a huge inland sea. The rhyolite outcrops were formed from fast-cooling lava.

As the ice age entered its last stages, North Carolina's climate warmed. By about 8000 B.C., the environment was much as it is today. In the meantime, North Carolinians had developed new ways of using the land's resources. A new tradition, called "Archaic" by archeologists, began to emerge. The people of the Archaic tradition may have been more sedentary than the Paleo-Indians. Because they relied increasingly on plant foods and small game, they did not have to follow the migrations of large animals so closely. They gathered seeds and nuts from the forest floor and developed fishing and trapping skills.

When they did hunt deer and other large animals, the Archaic people used a spear-throwing device called an "atlatl." By giving the hunter added leverage, the atlatl greatly increased the force with which the spear could be thrown. Weights of polished stone, shaped like butterflies or half-moons, were attached to the atlatl's shaft.

A great variety of projectile points and stone tools were made during the Archaic period. Many of these points had basal stems, which could be more easily bound to a shaft. Stone flakes became sharp scraping tools. Flakes and discarded points, once rechipped, served as drills. Archaic artisans carved vessels out of soapstone and ground other stones for axe heads and atlatl weights. Even without fired clay pots, they managed to boil water by placing hot rocks inside a stone or skin vessel.

Though these descendants of the first Carolinians appear to have adjusted admirably to life in southeastern North America, their culture was bound to change. New ideas and perhaps even contact with different people resulted in cultural developments. Although the changes were undoubtedly gradual, archeologists recognize the year 500 B.C. as the approximate end of the Archaic tradition. A new tradition, called "Woodland," had taken its place.

Because of the relative abundance of material remains, we know far more about the Woodland tradition than we do about its precursors. Unlike the people of the Archaic tradition, the Woodland people knew how to make pottery of clay collected from local river and stream beds. To make their clay more workable, these early potters used crushed clay grit as a tempering material. They learned to roughen the exterior of their pots with fabric-covered wooden paddles.

As ceramic techniques developed further, more vessels were made, and artisans began tempering their clay with sand. New materials adorned the paddles with which they finished their vessels. Even smoking pipes were

Tobacco plant

formed from clay. Evidence suggests that prehistoric North Carolinians smoked tobacco in their clay pipes, and they may have smoked other plants as well.

Hunting efficiency increased dramatically in the Woodland tradition as the bow and arrow replaced the atlatl. Although hunting and gathering still provided a large part of the Woodland people's dietary needs, rudimentary forms of agriculture supplemented this fare. Native plants such as the sunflower were among the earliest domesticated crops. Tobacco also may have been grown with some regularity before the time of Christ.

By A.D. 1200 North Carolinians were wholeheartedly committed to an agricultural economy. However, the serious pursuit of agriculture meant a changed way of life. Cultivated corn, beans, and squash required almost constant care during the growing season. Consumption of meat declined, and seasonal wandering dwindled. North Carolinians began to settle in permanent dwellings. The dwellings were grouped in small villages along riverbanks. A latticework of intertwined saplings covered by skins, bark, or other material formed the basic structure.

By excavating skeletal remains in ancient burial grounds, archeologists have determined that the people of the late Woodland period were the ancestors of tribes, such as the Catawba, who lived in North Carolina at the time of European contact. By this time, early in the sixteenth century, the Woodland tradition had yielded to the more modern traditions of the "Historic" period. Although they shared a common Woodland background and spoke related languages, each of the various groups across the North Carolina Piedmont had developed distinctive cultural traits. Scholars have found a great variety of linguistic traditions among North American Indians. While the Piedmont tribes spoke Siouan languages, other North Carolina tribes had Iroquoian and Algonquian linguistic heritages.

Even before the Siouan tribes of the Carolina Piedmont faced the main thrust of the European invasion, they had had to contend with another invading threat. From the region of present-day Alabama and Georgia came a group of Indians from a culture later called "Creek." Although the precise reason for their northward migration remains a mystery, it is possible that famine or other troubles had disrupted life in their home country. The Creek contingent reached North Carolina sometime near 1450. In the southern part of the state—present-day Richmond, Anson, and Montgomery Counties—they uprooted local Siouan tribes and settled in the lush Pee Dee River Valley. In this rich agricultural basin, they built dwellings, planted crops, and raised children for a hundred years. Then, just as suddenly as they had arrived, they were gone. Even before the English attempted to settle at Roanoke, the Creek invaders had been driven from North Carolina. The Siouan tribes of the Piedmont had reclaimed their homeland.

At Town Creek Indian Mound near Mount Gilead, North Carolina, visitors can view reconstructed remains of the Pee Dee Creek culture. The Creeks chose this high bluff overlooking the Little River for the site of their regional ceremonial center. Basketload by basketload, they hauled earth from nearby fields and a swampy area to the west. Finally, they completed an earthen ceremonial lodge and surrounded it with a palisade of upright logs. After much use, the earthen lodge collapsed. Once again the people of the Pee Dee collected earth, this time to cover the lodge's remains. The mound they created in covering the lodge became the foundation for their next construction: a ceremonial temple. But this building, like the first, was ill-fated. When it burned to the ground, the Creeks covered the remains as they had previously and built a third temple atop the growing earth mound.

This third and final structure is the one visitors can see reconstructed at the site today. Priests kept a sacred fire smoldering in the temple year-round. Once a year, the Creek people held their vital green corn, or "busk," celebra-

tion at the Town Creek center. The celebration, which lasted about a week, was one of renewal and purification for the year to come. Held at the first harvest of corn, the busk celebration involved fasting, ceremonial baths, and imbibing the "Black Drink," a beverage made by toasting and then boiling the leaves of various hollies, including *Ilex vomitoria*, an emetic. All the village fires and the sacred temple fire, polluted by a year's sins, were extinguished. After four days, the priests kindled a new fire. A great feast was held. Runners carried embers from the new fire to villages up and down the Pee Dee, and the Creeks reignited local fires. It was because of this ceremony that the Creeks called themselves "people of one fire."

The busk ceremony occurred only once a year. For the remainder of the year, the Town Creek Indians lived as settled farmers. Only the high priest lived within the ceremonial center's palisade. The rest of the people clustered

*Town Creek Indian
Mound and palisade*

Interior of the temple at Town Creek Indian Mound

their dwellings in small villages throughout the river valley. The women, directed by overseers, cultivated corn, tobacco, beans, squash, and pumpkins in communal fields. Children played nearby, and infants spent their earliest days bound to cradleboards, a practice that produced a unique flattening of the back of the skull among Creek and other Indians. Men practiced crafts such as woodworking.

Throughout the time they lived along the Pee Dee, the Creek Indians fought the Siouan tribes they had displaced. Intervillage rivalries and feuds, however, were settled through another sort of contest. Called "the little brother of war," Indian stickball, or lacrosse, took on a seriousness we only rarely associate with sports today. Players often suffered traumatic injuries. Broken limbs were not uncommon. Beside the temple at Town Creek, still

*Storage vessel from
Town Creek Indian Mound*

within the palisade, the ancient playing field used for lacrosse and other games is visible. A tall goalpost topped by a bear skull stands in front of the temple.

In the eighteenth century, naturalist William Bartram watched an Indian ceremony before a lacrosse game. "The people being assembled and seated in order," he observed, "and the musicians having taken their station, the ball opens, first with a long harangue or oration spoken by an aged chief in commendation of the manly exercise of the ball-play, recounting the many and brilliant victories which the town of Cowe had gained over the other towns in the nation, not forgetting or neglecting to recite his own exploits, together with those of other aged men now present, coadjutors in the performance of these athletic games in their youthful days."

By 1550 the Town Creek people were gone. The Siouan tribes of the Piedmont had returned to their homelands of old. To the east, where the powerful Powhatan confederacy of Virginia would soon be pushing its way south, European sailors had made contact with local Algonquian Indians. To the west,

Hernando de Soto, the Spanish explorer, had journeyed through the North Carolina mountains and contacted the Iroquoian-speaking Cherokee Indians. Before long the Tuscaroras, an Iroquoian tribe from the Neuse River region, would be carrying European trade goods to the Indians of the Piedmont, where Town Creek once stood.

LOST CONTINENT TO LOST COLONY

The first European explorers of North Carolina, like all early voyagers to the New World, did not find what they were actively seeking. Initially, they envisioned the discovery of an ocean pathway to the treasures of the East. It took Europeans almost a century to adjust their maps and their minds to the reality that they encountered on the Carolina coast: the sweet-scented edge of a massive continent.

In the autumn of 1492, while the men and women at Town Creek were occupied with the hard work and important rituals of the harvest season, Christopher Columbus, an Italian explorer in the service of Spain, and his crew sighted land in the Atlantic. Miscalculating, Columbus assumed that he had found the spice islands of Asia—known as the Indies. Three more voyages did not change his opinion, and he died believing that he had opened a new route to the Orient.

Those following in his wake labored to test and revise Columbus's vision. The Spaniards continued to call the local inhabitants "Indians." They extracted gold from them and demanded information of a passage farther westward to China. But they could find no western strait, only the landlocked Gulf of Mexico. Were Europeans separated from the Orient by inhabited continents they had never imagined? If so, could those lands offer up riches comparable to those of the East? Within thirty years, Spanish explorers provided all of Europe with answers to both questions. Hernando Cortez found and conquered the enormously rich Aztec Empire of central Mexico. In 1522 the ship of Ferdinand Magellan, having skirted the vast coastline of South America and crossed the Pacific, returned to Spain from its journey round the world.

The desire of rival states to emulate the Spanish discoveries brought the first Europeans to the Carolinas. The French hired their own skilled Italian navigator—Giovanni da Verrazzano—and commissioned him to explore unknown latitudes in the western Atlantic in search of a northerly route to China. In 1524 the hundred-ton ship *La Dauphine* sailed with a crew of fifty aboard, intending to reach China by sea. If blocked by "a barrier of new land," Verrazzano was to search for a "strait to penetrate to the Eastern Ocean."

*Giovanni da
Verrazzano*

After weathering a February storm "as violent as ever sailing man encountered," Verrazzano proceeded westward along the thirty-fourth degree of latitude until mid-March. Suddenly the "sweet fragrance" of large forests filled the ocean breeze, and "there appeared a new land which had never been seen before by any [European] man, either ancient or modern. At first it appeared to be rather low-lying; having approached to within a quarter of a league, we realized that it was inhabited, for huge fires had been built on the seashore."

Looking for China, the explorer had encountered what would later be North Carolina. His initial landfall was somewhere along the coast north of Cape Fear in what is now New Hanover County. But, like Columbus, Verrazzano searched for signs that he had reached some outer tip of Asia. He reported that the inhabitants "resembled the Orientals, particularly those from the farthest Sinarian regions" and that the ground was of a color that suggested gold. He noted "palms, laurel, cypress and other varieties of tree unknown in our Europe" in the fragrant forests he and his men had smelled from a hundred leagues off shore. "We think that they belong to the Orient by virtue of the surroundings, and that they are not without some kind of narcotic or aromatic liquor."

Like any newcomer in the early spring, Verrazzano was thoroughly charmed by the Cape Fear region. He named it "Forest of Laurels" and noted that it lay in the same latitude as spice-rich Damascus. He informed the king of France of the abundant game, the mild climate, the pure air, the gentle breezes, and the clear skies. "The seashore is completely covered with fine sand XV feet deep, which rises in the shape of small hills about fifty paces wide," he recounted. "Nearby we could see a stretch of country much higher than the sandy shore, with many beautiful fields and planes full of great forests, some sparse and some dense; and the trees have so many colors, and are so beautiful and delightful that they defy description."

Had *La Dauphine* arrived later in the year, the coastline might have been nearly deserted, for at that time the Cape Fear and Waccamaw Indians moved inland to harvest their crops and establish seasonal hunting camps near the numerous bay lakes in modern-day Columbus and Bladen Counties. But in March the shore was alive with local and inland groups, coming together to fish after planting their spring crops. They welcomed the first European party to come ashore, showing them where to beach their boat and offering them food. They marveled at the small stature, pale skin, and elaborate clothing of the French sailors. Verrazzano set down the earliest written description of the residents of coastal Carolina:

They go nude of everything except that at the private parts they wear some skins of little animals like martins, a girdle of fine grass woven with various tails of other animals which hang around the body as far as the knees; the rest nude; the head, likewise. Some wear certain garlands of feathers of birds. They are of dark color not much unlike the Ethiopians, and hair black and thick, and not very long, which they tie together back on the head in the shape of a little tail. As for the symmetry of the man, they are well proportioned, of medium stature, and rather exceed us. In the breast they are broad, their arms well built, the legs and other parts of the body well put together. The eyes black and large, the glance intent and quick. They are not of much strength, in craftiness acute, agile and the greatest runners.

Sailing northeastward up the Carolina coast, Verrazzano resumed his search for the Pacific, and by the end of March he thought he had found it. On 25 March he anchored off Portsmouth Bank or Ocracoke Island and sent crewmen ashore to obtain fresh water. The land appeared to be "an isthmus a mile in width and about 200 long." Looking northwest across the isthmus from the rigging, crewmen gazed at open water stretching as far as the horizon. "We could see the eastern sea from the ship," Verrazzano recorded. "This is doubtless the one which goes around the tip of India, China, and Cathay."

The water in the distance was not the Pacific, but Pamlico Sound. A drive along Route 12 through the Cape Hatteras National Seashore today explains Verrazzano's mistake. Nowhere else on the eastern seaboard does such a wide stretch of water—more than twenty-five miles in places—separate barrier islands from the mainland coast. He named the isthmus "Verrazzania" and continued along the coast, "hoping all the time to find some strait or real promontory where the land might end to the north, and we could reach those blessed shores of Cathay."

The blessed shores of China eluded Verrazzano; he was killed by Caribs in the West Indies several years later. But his suggestion of a Carolina route to China endured for generations, largely through the work of his brother, who, like Columbus's brother, was a mapmaker. The 1529 world map of Girolamo Verrazzano, which today survives in the Vatican Library, shows Pamlico Sound stretching westward all the way to the Pacific. A note on the map beside Cape Hatteras reads: "From this Eastern Ocean one sees the Western Ocean."

North Carolina, in other words, was underwater as far as the Verrazzano brothers were concerned, and it remained that way on some European charts for almost a century. Maps made by the Englishmen John Dee and John White in the 1580s showed a huge bay, "The Sea of Verrazzano," stretching from Southern California to the Carolina coast. Early in the seventeenth century, the English settlers at Jamestown were actually supplied with prefabricated boats for a possible portage to the nearby Pacific. They were instructed to probe the coastal rivers and to look beyond the adjacent mountains for some quick access to the "East India Sea."

Verrazzano had put North America on the globe for Europeans, but taken North Carolina off. Where the Town Creek Indian Mound stood, he imagined only a long finger of the Pacific. But it was the fragrant forest with its numerous inhabitants, not the Pacific Ocean, that stretched beyond the glistening waters of Pamlico Sound on the western horizon. It would take generations for Europeans to come to understand what native Americans had known for centuries about the rich landscape of North Carolina.

The quest for an "Eastern Sea" had brought the French to North Carolina. Gold brought the Spanish. Though the vast wealth of the Aztec and Inca empires preoccupied most Spaniards in the New World, a few conquistadors hoped to find comparable riches in the interior of North America. While the Spanish explorer Francisco Coronado explored the Southwest, Hernando de

Hernando de Soto

Soto led the hunt for treasure in the Southeast. His army of 600 soldiers plunged into the southern interior and became the first Europeans to see the southern Appalachian range and encounter its Indian inhabitants.

In May 1539 de Soto landed near Tampa Bay in present-day Florida. He had served under Francisco Pizarro in the conquest of Peru, and he now aspired to locate and subdue a similar empire of his own. He had received royal permission to "conquer and settle" the vast region north of Florida, including the right to build stone forts and import black slaves. His nine ships brought soldiers, servants, slaves, and camp followers, along with 220 horses, plus hogs, mules, and vicious Irish hounds.

The expedition northward took a full year. The soldiers lived off their expanding herd of hogs and food extorted from tribes along the way. Local Indians were commandeered by de Soto as burden bearers and locked in chains if they resisted. Others, forced to serve as guides, were thrown to the hounds if they displeased de Soto. By May 1540 the company had penetrated northward through modern-day Georgia and South Carolina to the Indian town of Xuala, "a village in a plain between two rivers" at the edge of the southern mountains.

Exactly how far north de Soto's expedition penetrated remains a mystery. Accepted judgments have put Xuala near the present-day intersection of the South Carolina, North Carolina, and Georgia borders, but some scholars now locate Xuala much farther north, between Marion and Old Fort in McDowell County. Whatever their exact point of departure, the Spaniards spent the last week of May crossing the high terrain of southeastern Appalachia. Mountain laurel and rhododendrons must have been coming into bloom. Except near Indian villages, the high forest of huge oak, poplar, hickory, and chestnut trees had never been cut over. Mile after mile of primeval woodlands appeared as they still do in the Joyce Kilmer Memorial Forest in Graham County.

Pushing over the steep ridges, the explorers soon encountered streams flowing north and west rather than south and east—they had crossed the Appalachian Divide. By June they had pressed into Tennessee and were moving on toward the banks of the Mississippi. A generation later, a smaller Spanish expedition under Captain Juan Pardo explored the region again, following a similar route and intending to open a pathway to the Mexican frontier as well as spread the gospel to the Indians.

The Indians encountered by Pardo's group in southern Appalachia were the Cherokees. (The word Cherokee derived from "Tsalagi," or "Tsaragi," meaning "cave people.") Their language stemmed from Iroquoian stock, and their ancestors had migrated south from beyond the Ohio River hundreds of years earlier. In the mid-sixteenth century they probably numbered well over 20,000 persons, living in scores of widely dispersed villages. The rugged mountain terrain both isolated and protected the Lower Towns below the modern South Carolina border, the Middle Towns of present-day Jackson and Macon Counties, the Valley Towns of Clay and Cherokee Counties, and the Overhill Towns of western Swain and Graham Counties. Tribesmen hunted widely beyond these core settlements for deer and also buffalo, which were plentiful in the Southeast until the eighteenth century. Agriculture in the fertile river valleys centered around corn, beans, sunflowers, and a variety of squashes, pumpkins, and gourds.

Economically self-sufficient and geographically protected, the Cherokees adapted to European colonization pressures. But their numbers were decimated by smallpox epidemics in the 1730s, and a century later the U.S. government forcibly removed the majority of the tribe to Oklahoma to make way for white land speculators. The descendants of those who remained now constitute the Eastern Band of Cherokees, living in and around the Qualla Boundary. At Oconaluftee, on U.S. 441 north of Cherokee, in Swain County, a traditional village has been reconstructed and is open to visitors every summer. Though designed to portray a later period, the village is on a site that has been used for thousands of years. Today's visitors to Oconaluftee Village can meet artisans who still know how to hollow logs with fire to make canoes; weave baskets from dried oak, river cane, and honeysuckle; and create blowguns from cane stalks for hunting small game.

Despite a half-century of overland Spanish exploration of the Southeast, nothing was known of the Cherokees or of Spanish contact with them in Elizabethan England. There the idea of Verrazzano's Sea was still widely accepted. Sir Humphrey Gilbert, given royal permission to explore and settle the American coast, possessed a chart showing the vast gulf stretching from the Pacific to the Carolina Piedmont. When Gilbert was lost at sea in 1583, his half brother, Walter Raleigh, obtained the letters patent of his deceased relative and dispatched two barks to explore the region of Verrazzano's isthmus.

Leaving Plymouth, England, on 27 April 1584, Captains Philip Amadas and Arthur Barlow reached the Outer Banks on 13 July and claimed the land for Queen Elizabeth. Unlike Verrazzano, they located an inlet through the cape and were able to drop anchor in the sound near an island that "the Indians call Roanoak." (The *Elizabeth II,* a replica of a sixteenth-century sailing vessel, can be seen today at Roanoke Island Festival Park.) After six weeks of exploration and trade, they returned to England with favorable reports and two Indians, Manteo and Wanchese, for Raleigh and Elizabeth. On 6 January 1585,

Sir Walter Raleigh

when Raleigh was knighted by the Virgin Queen and given permission to call the land Virginia in her honor, plans were already under way for a permanent settlement.

The second expedition, under Sir Richard Grenville, sailed from Plymouth with seven ships in April and reached Ocracoke Inlet on 26 June 1585. After two months of careful exploration aided by scientist Thomas Harriot and artist John White, Grenville returned to England with detailed maps, plus riches from a Spanish flagship he captured on the homeward crossing. He left behind 108 men, under Governor Ralph Lane, at a crude settlement called Fort Raleigh on Roanoke Island.

Lane's band was plagued by internal rivalries, a preoccupation with gold, and a pathetic inability to find food in an abundant region. The arrival of Francis Drake's fleet in June 1586, bringing supplies and hundreds of liberated Indians and Africans taken in raids upon Spanish strongholds in the Caribbean, perhaps could have saved the colony. But a sudden storm scattered the smaller vessels near the entrance to Roanoke Sound. Lane and his men, who had alienated local Indians and killed several of their leaders weeks before, gave up and sailed for England with Drake.

Sir Francis Drake

This was only the first of a string of losses and failures for the English. When Grenville arrived with promised supplies and reinforcements several weeks later, he found Roanoke deserted. Rather than regarrisoning Fort Raleigh with most of his 400 men, he turned his fleet toward the Caribbean in search of Spanish prizes. He left behind only fifteen soldiers, who were never heard from again. In the spring of 1587 another settlement was planned. Led by John White and including women and children, the party of 110 left the English port of Plymouth in May to establish "The Cittie of Ralegh in Virginea." They intended to settle on Chesapeake Bay, but their pilot, eager for privateering in the Caribbean, left them at Roanoke instead. In mid-August Eleanor Dare, the wife of Ananias Dare and daughter of John White, gave birth to the first American child born to English parents. On 24 August the baby was christened "Virginia" in honor of the newly claimed land, and several days later her grandfather departed for England to procure much-needed supplies for the colony.

John White's efforts to return to Roanoke the following spring were foiled by the war between Spain and England and the threatened invasion of the Spanish Armada. He did not reach the Outer Banks again until 1590. A passage once existed north of modern Oregon Inlet where Bodie Island later formed, and on 17 August a crew sought to cross the shoals in a small boat. It was tossed about in the heavy breakers and six sailors drowned in the surf. The survivors made it to the north end of Roanoke Island after nightfall, anxious to complete the long-awaited reunion. "We let fal our Grapnel neere the shore, & sounded the trumpet with a Call, & afterwardes many familiar English tunes of Songs, and called to them friendly; but we had no answere."

Before White's departure three years earlier, the colonists had discussed moving, and White had agreed with them that, should they move, "they should not faile to write or carve on the trees or posts of the dores the name of the place where they should be seated." They had also agreed that they would carve a Maltese cross above the place-name if they were in distress. The next morning, White's men went ashore and found the letters "CRO" carved on a tree in "faire Romane letters." Farther inland, they located the palisaded enclosure where the settlers had lived, now overgrown with weeds and vines. A post to the right of the entrance had had the bark removed, "and 5. foote from the ground in fayre Capotall letters was graven croatoan without any crosse or sign of distress."

White assumed his colonists had elected to migrate southward to Croatoan Island (modern-day Ocracoke south of Cape Hatteras), led by their Indian associate, Manteo. "I had found a certain token of their safe being at Croatoan," White wrote, "which is the place where Manteo was borne, and the Savages of the Iland our friends." He hoped to find them there, but bad weather, the loss of vital cables and anchors, and the fears of the sailors, six of whom had already been killed in the rescue attempt, prevented White from searching further. He had found his own books and papers that he had left at Roanoke "rotten and spoyled with rayne" and a suit of armor "almost eaten through with rust." Because the hurricane season was approaching, he had no choice but to depart for England. On 24 October White's ship, having failed in its rescue attempt, "came in safetie, God be thanks, to an anker in Plymmouth."

It seems likely that at least some of the lost colony members did go south to live and intermarry with the native people on the Outer Banks. In the mid-seventeenth century, the Hatteras (or Croatan) Indians would migrate inland, like other small coastal groups at the same time. It is possible, though not certain, that members of the Lumbee tribe now living in the Lumberton area of Robeson County are descended in part from this Outer Banks contingent of Indians and English.

Some historians now believe that another contingent from Roanoke may have gone north to Chesapeake Bay, the colony's original destination, and settled among the Chesapeake Indians near Cape Henry in present-day Virginia. The Englishman William Strachey later claimed to have reports that Pow-

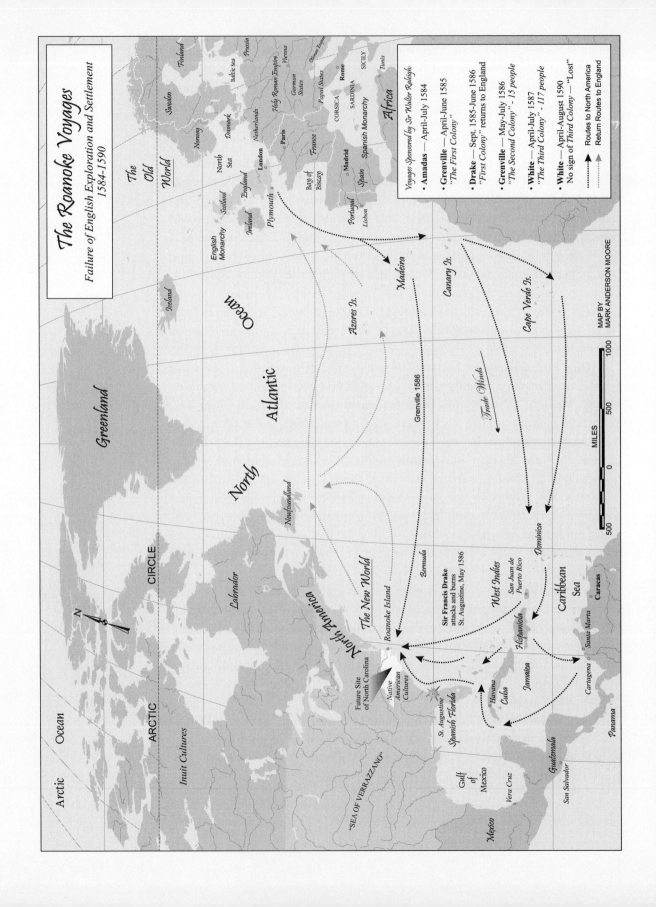

The Roanoke Voyages

Failure of English Exploration and Settlement
1584-1590

Voyages Sponsored by Sir Walter Raleigh:

- **Amadas** — April-July 1584
- **Grenville** — April-June 1585
  "The First Colony"
- **Drake** — Sept. 1585-June 1586
  "First Colony" returns to England
- **Grenville** — May-July 1586
  "The Second Colony" - 15 people
- **White** — April-July 1587
  "The Third Colony" - 117 people
- **White** — April-August 1590
  No sign of Third Colony - "Lost"

Routes to North America
Return Routes to England

MAP BY
MARK ANDERSON MOORE

MILES

500   0   500   1000

Arctic Ocean

Greenland

ARCTIC CIRCLE

Inuit Cultures

Labrador

Newfoundland

North America

The New World

Roanoke Island

Bermuda

Future Site
of North Carolina

Native
American
Cultures

St. Augustine
Spanish Florida

Sir Francis Drake
attacks and burns
St. Augustine, May 1586

West Indies

San Juan de
Puerto Rico

Hispaniola

Jamaica

Havana
Cuba

Caribbean
Sea

Santa Marta

Cartagena

Caracas

Dominica

Panama

Guatemala

San Salvador

Vera Cruz

Mexico

Gulf
of
Mexico

"SEA OF VERRAZZANO"

North Atlantic Ocean

Azores Is.

Grenville 1586

Trade Winds

Ireland

The Old World

English Monarchy

Scotland

Ireland

England

Plymouth

London

North Sea

Paris

France

Bay of
Biscay

Portugal

Lisbon

Spain

Madrid

Spanish Monarchy

Netherlands

Holy Roman Empire

German
States

Vienna

Papal States

Rome

CORSICA

SARDINIA

SICILY

Tunis

Africa

Madeira

Canary Is.

Cape Verde Is.

Norway

Denmark

Sweden

Finland

Baltic Sea

Prussia

Ottoman Empire

N

hatan, chief of an Indian confederation, advised by his counselors to destroy the Chesapeakes and the English living with them, had done so in 1607, at just the time that the Jamestown colonists arrived. The king of England had been informed, Strachey wrote, that Powhatan had "miserably slaughtered" the "men, women, and children of the first plantation at Roanoak . . . (who 20. and od yeeres had peacably lyved and intermixed with thos Savadges, and were out of his Territory)." The Jamestown colonists were specifically instructed to look for survivors from the lost colony, and two men sent to Roanoke Island in 1608 brought back crosses and letters of English origin, but no other news.

3 VIRGINIANS IN THE ALBEMARLE

After the failure of English settlement efforts at Roanoke, North Carolina Indians remained undisturbed for decades. When European intrusions finally did recur, they came not from the sea, but overland from the Virginia colony to the north. Indeed, the territory we now know as North Carolina was for years included in the tremendous Virginia Company land grant of 1606. In that year, to raise sufficient funds to finance another attempt at English colonization in the New World, King James I chartered the Virginia Company of London, a joint-stock company of merchants who hoped to make fortunes in mining and the Indian trade. Thus, the first permanent European settlements, in the far northeastern corner of North Carolina, were more an extension of the Virginia Company's colony at Jamestown, Virginia, than they were concerted efforts toward planting a new colony.

The northernmost stream feeding Albemarle Sound is the Chowan River, flowing south out of Virginia through modern Gates, Hertford, and Chowan Counties. Its westernmost tributary is the Meherrin, entering near present-day Murfreesboro, where the Chowanoc Indian town of Ramashonoc once stood. The Blackwater River intersects the Chowan from the north, after flowing parallel to the James less than twenty miles southwest of Jamestown. Whereas an expedition from Roanoke led by Ralph Lane had penetrated up the Chowan River in 1585, now Englishmen began to penetrate down the Blackwater and the Chowan toward Albemarle Sound.

As early as 1608 Captain John Smith sent two explorers from Jamestown into what would become North Carolina. Instructed to search for survivors of the Roanoke settlement, the two woodsmen probed about the Chowan River region and then returned. A year later, in May 1609, Virginia governor Sir Thomas Gates received instructions from the owners of the Virginia Company, who financed and managed the company's affairs from England. They urged him to pursue a settlement on the Chowan River, where he would find abundant "grasse silke" and would be "neere Rich Coppermines." In 1610 an expedition set out for "parts of the Chowanok," but no records of the excursion survive.

More than a decade passed before Virginians again ventured into the North Carolina swamplands. At last John Pory, former secretary of the Virginia colony, set out for the Chowan River in February 1622. Today, Pory's expedition is commemorated by a highway marker on U.S. 158, near the Chowan River bridge. In a sermon of 18 April 1622, the Reverend Patrick Copland reported that Pory had passed through a "great forest of Pynes 15. or 16. myle broad and above 60. mile long." The pines, he ventured, would "serve well for Masts for Shipping, and for pitch and tarre." Copland described the land Pory had found as "a fruitfull Countrie blessed with abundance of Corne, reaped twise a yeere." Echoing the owners of the Virginia Company, he claimed to know of "Copper Mines" and "a great deale of silke grasse" in the region. What early explorers called "silke grasse" was *Yucca filamentosa*, or bear grass. The Indians used it to make thread and string.

Although interest in the North Carolina region ran high in the years following Pory's excursion, no settlement attempts reached farther than the Virginia counties of Surry, Isle of Wight, and Nansemond, on the south shore of the James River. Then, toward the middle of the seventeenth century, Virginia's steep mortality rate—caused by disease, Indian wars, and inadequate food and housing—began to decline. The colony's population grew at an unprecedented rate. In 1644, when several hundred colonists lost their lives in the last major effort of tidewater Indians to reclaim their land, Virginia's combined white and black population was around 8,000. By 1653 it was 14,000. And by 1662 it had probably topped 25,000. As its population expanded, Virginia's supply of land grew short. Interest in the region to the south mounted and exploration intensified. Unable to move west because of powerful Indian tribes, landless Virginians looked increasingly to the Albemarle frontier for the farms they could not acquire at home.

Virginians heading southward left behind a society irreversibly committed to the production of tobacco. In fact, Virginia's commitment to this single crop was in large part what led to a "shortage" of land. Every year hundreds of indentured servants, bound to a period of unpaid labor in exchange for passage to the New World, completed their terms of service and became freedmen. Like their former masters, these freedmen sought their fortunes in tobacco.

To established planters, the sudden abundance of freedmen and the steady arrival of European immigrants posed a serious economic threat. As freedmen and new investors acquired land, tobacco production increased and the crop's market value inevitably dropped. Freedmen now competed with their former masters, and the supply of tobacco could not be restricted in order to keep prices high. Access to farmland diminished rapidly as wealthy planters began buying all the land they could, even purchasing the "head rights," or grants of land, of poorer settlers so that they could claim more acreage in the future. It was not long before most of the prime land lay in the hands of a few well-to-do owners.

As the grip on coastal farmlands tightened, driving up prices, ex-servants found it increasingly difficult to purchase land in Virginia. Many gave up hope and returned to the land of their former masters as renters. Others pushed westward up the river valleys to the backcountry frontiers, but they found themselves too far from the coastal ports and too close to local Indian tribes, as the events of Bacon's Rebellion in the 1670s revealed. Bacon's Rebellion was an abortive uprising by Virginia settlers against the colonial government. Afraid of continued Indian attacks and angered by high taxes imposed to build forts against the Indians, the colonists wanted immediate and definitive redress.

Still other poor colonists chose to migrate southward into the Albemarle region. By 1655, in the area east of the Chowan River and south of the Great Dismal Swamp, North Carolina had its first permanent English settlers. Robert Brodman, a carpenter, had spent five months building a combination house and trading post on the southwestern bank of the Pasquotank River for Virginian Nathaniel Batts. Batts, the first known permanent white settler in North Carolina, had already visited the area and established trade with local Indians. On 24 September 1660, five years after moving to the area, Batts purchased the land he lived on from its previous residents. In the first North Carolina land grant on record, King Kiscutanewh of the Weapemeoc tribe ceded to Batts, "for a valuable Consideration in hand received, viz &: all ye land on ye southwest side of Pascotank River, from ye mouth of ye sd. River to ye head of new Begin Creeke, to have & to hold to him & his heires for Ever." George Fox, founder of the Quaker faith, traveled through the Albemarle in 1672 and described Batts as a "rude, desperate man," who wondered if the Quakers had actually healed a sick woman "by our prayers and laying on of hands."

Others soon followed Batts to the promise of the Albemarle. One year after Batts received his grant, Kilcocanen, king of Yeopim, deeded to colonist George Durant "a Parcell of Land Lying & Being on Roanoke Sound & on a River Called By ye. Name of Perquimans Which Isueth out of the North Side of the aforesaid Sound." Durant's Neck, in Perquimans County today, is a modern reminder of George Durant's settlement.

Along the banks of the Pasquotank, Perquimans, and Chowan Rivers, migrants from Virginia found acres of arable land. The region, however, was not vacant; it had been settled and used for centuries. The incoming settlers all had to bargain with local Indians for the soil to plant on, just as Nathaniel Batts and George Durant had done. Sometimes they paid the Indians "a valuable consideration of satisfaction" in return for their land; other times they paid nothing at all and risked the consequences.

Many of these land transactions were founded on misunderstandings between the Indians and the English. For most southeastern tribes, the mere use of a plot of land established individual property rights. When use ceased, the land could be reclaimed by another. Europeans, however, saw no such connection between rights and use. Land was a commodity to be bought and sold. While the settlers who "acquired" Indian land undoubtedly assumed the transaction to be permanent, the Indians may have assumed it to be a temporary one based on their own traditional values.

Indian land was certainly in high demand. The North Carolina forest was known for its numerous "natural" meadows that could be quickly and easily turned to cultivation. English explorer and surveyor John Lawson described the Carolina woods at the turn of the century: "One part bearing great Timbers, others being Savanna's or natural Meads, where no Trees grow for several Miles, adorn'd by Nature with a pleasant Verdure, and beautiful Flowers, frequent in no other Places, yielding abundance of Herbage for Cattle, Sheep, and Horses." A newcomer in search of pasture and farmland could want little more.

But what John Lawson saw as the work of nature was often the work of humans. Here, as elsewhere in the eastern woodlands, many of the "natural" meadows had actually been cleared by Indians years before. On colonial maps they were occasionally designated as "Indian old fields."

James Adair, who traded and worked among southeastern Indians for over thirty-five years, observed their slow but efficient method of stripping a ring of bark from the trunk to stop the flow of sap so that huge trees died and eventually toppled. "Now, in the first clearing of their plantations," Adair explained, "they only bark the large timber, cut down the saplings and underwood, and burn them in heaps; as the suckers shoot up, they chop them off close by the stump, of which they make fires to deaden the roots, till in time they decay." Thus, even without the added clearing power of metal axes, saws, and mattocks, "the contented natives get convenient fields in a matter of time." Because Indian farmers rotated fields, not crops, large tracts of land stood uncultivated for lengthy periods of time. Such seemingly abandoned land appeared ideal to the arriving settlers.

Naturally, the commercial crop the settlers planted in these fields was tobacco. They soon found, however, that, because of obstacles of geography, North Carolina tobacco rarely yielded the profits of Virginia tobacco. The Outer Banks and the shoals of the Albemarle Sound prevented heavy commercial vessels from reaching Carolina's shores safely; as a result, farmers could not ship their tobacco directly to England. Instead, they had to haul their harvest by land to Virginia before it could be shipped overseas.

Carrying tobacco to Virginia was no small problem. In the settlement's early years, no roads existed between Virginia and the Albemarle. A map made in 1657 bears the simple inscription "This is A Swampy wilderness" across the area north of Albemarle Sound where the Great Dismal Swamp lay squarely in the path of travelers. George Fox described his route through the Albemarle as "full of great bogs and swamps; so that we were commonly wet to the knees, and lay abroad a-nights in the woods by a fire." The enormous cost of overland transit, combined with the export tax resulting from the Navigation Acts, was nearly prohibitive.

In 1663 Charles II, recently "restored" to the English throne, formally granted by charter the Province of Carolina—from present-day Florida north to the Albemarle Sound region, and from the Atlantic Ocean west to the Pacific —to eight favored courtiers. These men were known as the Lords Proprietors, and the region given to them was named Carolina (or Carolana) in honor of Charles I. By removing the Albemarle from Virginia's jurisdiction, the charter gave political definition to the geographic obstacles between the two regions. From 1679 to 1731 Virginia statutes prohibited the importation and re-exportation of Albemarle tobacco through the northern colony's ports. The Virginians claimed the Carolina product was inferior, but they were perhaps more worried about the rising competition and falling prices as tobacco exports climbed.

Some early Carolina planters evaded these restrictions by shipping their tobacco illegally. North Carolina's treacherous coastal waterways made the colony an ideal base for pirates and smugglers. It was not long before traders from New England discovered the profits to be made in North Carolina tobacco. Using shallow-draft ships, these traders carried numerous loads of tobacco from the Albemarle region to the northern colonies and Newfoundland to evade the Navigation Acts, which declared that all colonial products had to be ship directly to England. In 1673, however, England's Plantation Duty Act imposed customs duties on intercolonial shipping. This resulted in more illegal exports, and would later give rise to considerable political turmoil within North Carolina.

By 1663 the immigrant population of the tobacco-growing Albemarle region had passed 500. Scores of Virginians moved southward annually. Some years later, William Byrd, wealthy Virginia planter and surveyor of the boundary between North Carolina and Virginia, disparagingly described the migrant settlers to the Albemarle region. They were, he said, Quakers and Anabaptists,

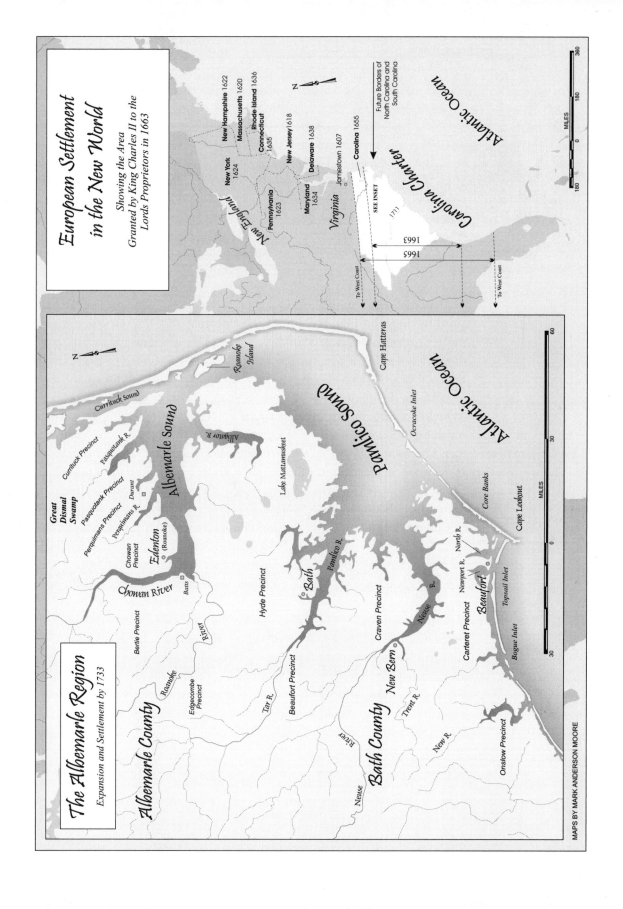

European Settlement in the New World

Showing the Area
Granted by King Charles II to the
Lords Proprietors in 1663

New Hampshire 1622
Massachusetts 1620
Rhode Island 1636
Connecticut 1635
New York 1624
New Jersey 1618
Pennsylvania 1623
Delaware 1638
Maryland 1634

New England

Virginia   Jamestown 1607

Carolina 1655

Carolina Charter

SEE INSET

1711

1663
1665

To West Coast
To West Coast

Future Borders of
North Carolina and
South Carolina

Atlantic Ocean

MILES
180   0   180   360

The Albemarle Region

Expansion and Settlement by 1733

Albemarle County

Great
Dismal
Swamp

Currituck Sound

Currituck Precinct

Pasquotank R.

Pasquotank Precinct

Perquimans Precinct

Perquimans R.

Durant

Roanoke Island

Albemarle Sound

Alligator R.

Chowan Precinct

Edenton
(Roanoke)

Chowan River

Batts

Bertie Precinct

Roanoke
River

Edgecombe
Precinct

Tar R.

Beaufort Precinct

Lake Mattamuskeet

Hyde Precinct

Pamlico Sound

Pamlico R.

Bath

Craven Precinct

New Bern

Neuse R.

Trent R.

Bath County

New R.

Neuse
River

Onslow Precinct

North R.

Newport R.

Carteret Precinct

Beaufort

Topsail Inlet

Bogue Inlet

Roanoke Island

Cape Hatteras

Ocracoke Inlet

Atlantic Ocean

Core Banks

Cape Lookout

MILES
30   0   30   60

MAPS BY MARK ANDERSON MOORE

Colonial wharf. Detail from Fry-Jefferson map, "The Most Inhabited Part of Virginia" (1775).

particularly "a swarm of Scots Quakers," who "inveigled many over [to the region] by this tempting Account of the Country: that it was a place free from those 3 great Scourges of Mankind, Priests, Lawyers, and Physicians. Nor did they tell a word of a Lye, for the People were yet too poor to maintain these Learned Gentlemen, who every where love to be paid well for what they do."

Among the immigrants was Joseph Scott, who in 1684 acquired property in a Quaker community near the Perquimans River. Scott's farm passed through several generations until Abraham Sanders, a Quaker, purchased the farm then known as Vineyard in 1727. Sanders had migrated from Virginia around 1715 and soon married Judith Pricklove, the granddaughter of Quaker leader Samuel Pricklove, one the Albemarle's earliest inhabitants. On this tract acquired from Scott, Sanders around 1730 built the dwelling now known as the Newbold-White House, one of the oldest standing buildings in North Carolina. According to architectural historians Catherine W. Bishir and Michael T. Southern, the Newbold-White House (named for later owners) "epitomizes the first generation of long lasting architecture in the Albemarle and Chesapeake regions."

The house was exceptional during the Proprietary Period (1663–1729) because it was built of brick and reflected the affluence of its owner. More characteristic of the period was the "20 foot dwelling howse" that proprietor and future Carolina governor Peter Carteret found awaiting him on Colleton Island in February 1664. Three years later, a hurricane "carried away the frame & boards of two howses." Wood, not bricks, remained the basic building material, and as tar became a staple of the colony, it was used to weatherproof dwellings. In 1737, John Brickell, a naturalist and physician who lived in North Carolina for a time, described the residences of the colonists. "Their Houses,"

Newbold-White House (ca. 1730), prior to twentieth-century restoration

he wrote in his *Natural History of North Carolina*, "are built after two different ways; viz. the most substantial Planters generally use brick, and Lime, which is made of Oyster-shells, for there are no Stones to be found proper for that purpose, but near the Mountains; the meaner Sort erect with Timber, the outside with Clap-Boards, the Roofs of both Sorts of House are made of Shingles, and they generally have Sash Windows, and affect large and decent Rooms with good Closets, as they do a most beautiful Prospect by some noble River or Creek." When traveler William Logan visited the colony in 1745, he reported: "The common peoples house here are in generall tarr^d all over to preserve y^m instead of Painting & all have Wooden Chimneys which I admire do not catch fire oftener than they do."

On Abraham Sanders's 633-acre farm, his family and a few slaves produced wheat, corn, and other crops. They also raised livestock. Animal husbandry in the Albemarle was limited primarily to hogs and cattle, which were penned occasionally but usually allowed to graze freely in surrounding woods and meadows. On occasion, settlers raised sheep. An arrogant William Byrd saw inefficiency in the way Carolinians managed their livestock. "Both Cattle and Hogs ramble in the Neighbouring Marshes and Swamps," he observed, "where they maintain themselves the whole Winter long, and are not fetch'd home till the Spring. Thus these indolent wretches during one half of the Year, lose the Advantage of the Milk of their cattle, as well as their Dung, and many of the poor Creatures perish in the Mire, into the Bargain, by this ill Management." Late in the year, when the weather was cold enough to prevent fresh meat from spoiling, Carolinians slaughtered their livestock. After slaughtering, farmers cured the meat in a smokehouse. The smoke of burning hardwood preserved beef, pork, venison, fish, and other meats while imparting a unique flavor. Considerable quantities of meat could thus be stored for year-round consumption. Pork made up a substantial portion of the colonial North Carolinian's diet. "These People live so much upon Swine's flesh," William Byrd exclaimed, "that it . . . makes them extremely hoggish in their Temper, & many of them seem to Grunt rather than to speak."

Undoubtedly the most important cultivated foodstuff was corn, the high-yield Indian grain that Europeans readily adopted throughout the New World. "Had it not been for the Fruitfulness of this Species," wrote John Lawson, "it would have proved very difficult to have settled some of the Plantations in America." For settlers in the Albemarle, corn became the staple grain to be ground into meal and baked into bread. But planters also grew garden vegetables to supplement the usual fare of bread and meat. Some planted herbs as well for seasoning and medicinal purposes.

In the early years of the Albemarle settlement, however, the raising of crops and livestock, and indeed everyday life itself, could prove difficult and precarious. Violent storms, hurricanes, and droughts destroyed crops and livestock alike, as documented by Peter Carteret, who served as governor from 1670 to 1672. He reported that in 1667 a hurricane "destroyed both corne & tob: blew downe the roof of the great hogg howse." In 1668 first drought and then torrential rains ruined crops. Another hurricane struck in 1669 and, according to Carteret, "destroyed what tob was out . . . & spoiled most of the corne this yeare." The following year, a twenty-four-hour hurricane blew down trees, houses, and the "hogg howse." Conditions were so bad that Carteret proclaimed there was bound "to bee a famine amongst us." In 1709, William Gordon, an Anglican missionary, described the poor living conditions of most Carolinians, who were "destitute of good water, most of that being brackish and muddy; they feed generally upon salt pork, and sometimes upon beef, and their bread of Indian corn which they are forced for want of mills to beat; and in this they are so careless and uncleanly that there is but little difference between the corn in the horse's manger and the bread on their tables."

He further noted that perhaps the colony was "capable of better things, were it not overrun with sloth and poverty."

Thus many of the colonists who fled south from Virginia in search of a better and more prosperous life discovered only a harsh and hostile existence in Carolina. And among the migrants, it would be the ever-increasing numbers of enslaved Africans and their descendants who would suffer the greatest hardships. In 1712, the number of enslaved blacks in the whole colony totaled only 800. But in their Fundamental Constitutions of Carolina in 1669, the Lords Proprietors made slavery an established and protected institution by emphatically declaring in Article 110: "Every Freeman of Carolina, shall have absolute Power and Authority over his Negro Slaves, of what Opinion or Religion sover." Some blacks, though, fled to the Albemarle to escape from bondage in Virginia. "It is certain," wrote William Bryd, that "many Slaves Shelter themselves in this Obscure part of the World, nor will any of their righteous Neighbors discover them." Despite the difficult circumstances that early Carolina immigrants—white and black—found awaiting them, the colony grew as new arrivals continued to spread throughout its borders and towns began to appear on the landscape.

4

EARLY COASTAL TOWNS

As colonists from Virginia first moved overland into the Albemarle region, other Englishmen and their African slaves began arriving by sea to establish settlements farther south. In the five years between 1662 and 1668, two separate expeditions would attempt to build towns in the Cape Fear region of North Carolina. Both would fail. For the remainder of the seventeenth century, and for the first quarter of the eighteenth, the European settlement of North Carolina would take place as it had started—from the north. As land ran short in the Albemarle, colonists moved into the region around Pamlico Sound, and population centers developed in both regions. Before long, towns—Edenton, Bath, New Bern, and Beaufort—would dot the Carolina coastline.

In mid-August 1662 a tiny expedition left the Massachusetts Bay Colony for Carolina, its sights set on "the discovery of Cape Feare and more South parts of Florida." Sponsored by merchants calling themselves the "committee for Cape Faire at Boston," the ship *Adventure* and its crew returned home with good news. The Cape Fear region abounded with "upland fields . . . for Catle" and an "abundance of vast meadows" for "multitudes of farms." Of course it also had swamps, but even they were "laden with varieties of great Oakes and other trees of all Sorts." The explorers noted few mosquitoes or rattlesnakes.

Encouraged by this promising description, a group of hopeful migrants sailed to Cape Fear with a supply of hogs and cattle early in 1663. Within months, the Puritan adventurers had had their fill. They soon returned to Boston, leaving their livestock behind. Tacked to a post they left a note intended for "the great discouragement of all those that should hereafter come into these parts to settle." The exact reasons for their own discouragement remain unknown.

In the same year, the proprietors received the charter to Carolina. All of these wealthy aristocrats had other interests in the expanding web of English mercantilism. Some were owners of the Royal Africa Company, and many had connections to the Caribbean island of Barbados. Sir Anthony Ashley Cooper, for instance, had invested in a Barbadian plantation in the 1640s. Sir John Colleton, described by some as "a Barbadian financier," had become a sizable planter with ties to the governor of the island. So it is hardly surprising that one of the earliest efforts to establish plantations at Cape Fear came from Barbados.

The situation on Barbados helped motivate such settlement. Barbadians, like coastal Virginians, were running out of land. During the decades after 1660, as a profitable sugar economy based on race slavery became entrenched, the island's wealthiest planters steadily enlarged their holdings. By 1680 less than 7 percent of all landowners claimed over 50 percent of the land and devoted their massive estates entirely to cash crop production. The island's timber reserve for boiling sugar and making barrels was nearly exhausted, and the local supply of foodstuffs and other staples was inadequate for the expanding workforce. It seemed only natural to turn to Carolina, a land well endowed with woods and fertile soil.

Like the Puritans before them, the Barbadians hired Captain William Hilton to undertake preliminary explorations. On 10 August 1663, Hilton once again sailed for the Cape Fear River. On his return to Barbados, he presented a glowing description much like his report to the Puritans a year before. The land, he said, was "as good land and as well timbered as any we have seen in any other part of the world, sufficient to accommodate thousands of our English nation, and lying commodiously by the said river's side." He stressed to the wine-loving planters that grape vines grew everywhere. John Lawson described the grapes that he saw on his travels in the colony. "These refuse no Ground," he reported, "swamp or dry, but grow plentifully on the Sand Hills along the Sea Coast, and elsewhere, and are great Bearers. I have seen near twelve bushels upon one vine of the black sort. Some of these, when thoroughly ripe, have a very pretty vinous Taste and eat very well, yet are glutinous. . . . Being removed by the Slip or Root, they thrive well in our Gardens, and make pleasant Shades."

The Barbadians, and likewise the Carolina proprietors, were easily convinced. Representatives of the proprietors drew up a set of proposals designed to encourage the settlement of plantations at Cape Fear. The proprietors offered a "head right," or grant of land, for every person transported to the new settlement. Thus the more laborers a planter sent to Carolina, the more land he received in return. The laborers could be men or women, European or African, enslaved or free. Knowing that black slaves had been present in Barbados for a generation, the Carolina proprietors offered "To the Owner of every Negro-Man or Slave, brought thither to settle within the first year, twenty acres; and for every Woman-Negro or Slave, ten acres of Land."

Even before they had completed arrangements with the proprietors, a party of Barbadians set sail for Cape Fear. Although the exact size of this party is unclear, it seems certain that many of the colonists were indentured white servants or African slaves. The settlers landed on the west bank of the Cape Fear River on 26 May 1664. They selected a site for the settlement of Charles Town about twenty miles upstream, two miles east of Town Creek in present-day Brunswick County.

A series of mishaps soon threatened the life of the colony. Another party of settlers arrived in 1665 after a trying voyage entailing a shipwreck and the loss of much-needed food, clothing, and other supplies. In desperation the Charles Town colonists sent a sloop to Virginia for provisions. On its return, the boat, "being ready by reason of her extreme rottenness in her timbers to Sinke," ran aground at Cape Lookout. The provisions were lost. Meanwhile, relations between colonists and the Cape Fear Indians had deteriorated. In "actuall warre with the natives," colonists killed Indian warriors, seized their children, and sold them into slavery. Unable to match the firepower of the English guns, the natives crippled the settlement by stealing its livestock. By late 1666 departing colonists outnumbered new arrivals.

Frantic efforts by the proprietors and Barbadian planters to save the colony were of no avail. No more were men drawn by the promotional claim of "good houses" and "good forts." Nor did the promoters beguile many a "Maid or single Woman" with the promise of a "Golden Age"—"for if they be but Civil, and under 50 years of Age, some honest Man or other, will purchase them for their Wives." The fact was, the governor of the colony reported in September 1666, "that thes Settlements have beene made and upheld by Negroes and without constant supplies of them cannot subsist." But more unfree labor was not to be had—it was too profitable in the Caribbean to be spared for Cape Fear. By the summer of 1667 the colony was deserted and the Indians had reclaimed their land. Until 1725 Europeans made no further attempts to settle at Cape Fear.

In the interim, the region's political status would change considerably. In

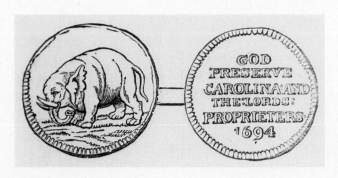

Front and back of the Carolina Half Penny ("Elephant Coin"), 1694

38 NATIVES AND NEWCOMERS

1689 the proprietors appointed Philip Ludwell as governor not just of the Albemarle, but of all Carolina "north and east of Cape Feare." In so doing, they established North Carolina and South Carolina as separate political units—a distinction that remains to this day.

Despite the failure of the best-laid plans of Boston Puritans and Barbadian proprietors, land-hungry settlers continued to stream into North Carolina. From Virginia, colonists pressed southward down the coast, past Pamlico Sound, across the Neuse, on to the North and Newport Rivers. Although most of the European settlers were yeoman farmers, the colony began to attract non-farmers as well. Settlements at the mouths of rivers became small towns and soon housed the workshops of cobblers and tanners, tailors and blacksmiths. Lawyers and officials opened offices. Merchants established stores and provided imported goods—in limited variety—for townsfolk and for farmers from the interior.

The earliest of Carolina's immigrants to settle in a town clustered in the village of Roanoke—present-day Edenton—on the northwestern shore of Albemarle Sound. The commercial center of the Albemarle, Roanoke became the region's political center as well in 1710, when it became the capital of "that part of the Province of Carolina that lies North and East of Cape Fear." Renamed Queen Anne's Town in 1715, the town acquired its final name in 1722 when it was incorporated as Edenton, honoring the memory of Governor Charles Eden. William Byrd made this observation about Edenton in 1728: "They may be 40 or 50 Houses, most of them Small, and built without Expense. A Citizen here is counted extravagant, if he has Ambition enough to aspire to a Brick-chimney. Justice herself is but indifferently Lodged, the Court-House having much the Air of a Common Tobacco-House."

The town of Edenton, in the first region of North Carolina to be permanently settled by Europeans, contains some of the colony's oldest public buildings and private residences. The first courthouse, so disparaged by Byrd and located where the village green is today, was completed in 1719. By the time of the American Revolution, the building had been replaced by a sturdy, Georgian-style brick structure. Constructed next to the green in 1767, the new building is still open to the public. In 1725, only six years after the first courthouse had been constructed, a wealthy sea captain named Richard Sanderson had the elegant Cupola House built on Broad Street. It derives its name from the octagonal cupola crowning the roof. In 1756 jurist and land agent Francis Corbin purchased the house.

In the meantime, having met with little success in establishing their colony as a profitable venture, the Lords Proprietors in 1729 surrendered their charter to the English crown. North Carolina then became a royal colony. The

Chowan County Courthouse (1767), Edenton

first royal governor was George Burrington, who took office in Edenton in 1731. But one proprietor, John Carteret, Earl Granville, refused to relinquish his interest in Carolina to the crown. He retained and sold land in the Granville District, located in the upper half of present-day North Carolina. Francis Corbin, who purchased the Cupola House, was Granville's agent for the sale of land in the district. The Granville District ended with the American Revolution.

In 1752, Bishop August Spangenburg and other Moravians visited Edenton to equip themselves for a trip into the backcountry of North Carolina, where they hoped to find land for settlement. While in Edenton, Spangenburg found Corbin to be most helpful. "He is very busy," noted the bishop, "being not only My Lord Granville's Agent but also Judge of the Court of Admiralty and of the Supreme Court, not to speak of other employment; however, almost every day I have spent some hours with him, which was to my advantage. He is a walking

encyclopedia concerning North Carolina affairs, is capable, polite, and very obliging."

Cupola House (1758–59), Edenton

While Edenton was establishing itself as the commercial and political center of the Albemarle region, land-hungry settlers from Virginia were continuing their migration southward. Small commercial and political centers soon grew up in the Pamlico region. The earliest of the Pamlico centers was Bath Town. Incorporated in 1706, Bath is situated in present-day Beaufort County on the north bank of the Pamlico River. One of the first residents and commissioners of Bath was explorer-naturalist John Lawson. In February 1701, when Lawson completed his "thousand miles travel" through the Carolinas, he emerged from the backwoods within twenty miles of the town's future location. Lawson may have chosen the site for Bath Town; it is certain that he helped lay out the town before its incorporation.

*St. Thomas Church
(1734), Bath,
Beaufort County*

In the year before Bath was incorporated, the English Parliament passed a law that gave an important new stimulus to the economy of colonial North Carolina. Wary of continued dependence on Sweden and Finland for naval stores, English mercantilists hoped the Naval Stores Act of 1705 would wean the British shipbuilding industry from its dependency upon products from the Baltic. Naval stores—tar, turpentine, pitch, and hemp—were essential materials for the construction and maintenance of wooden sailing ships. For a strong seagoing nation with growing concerns in global commerce, such supplies were of no small importance. By paying premiums on naval stores imported from British colonies, Parliament hoped to encourage production in North America. The act offered substantial subsidies of £4 per ton on tar and pitch, £6 per ton on hemp.

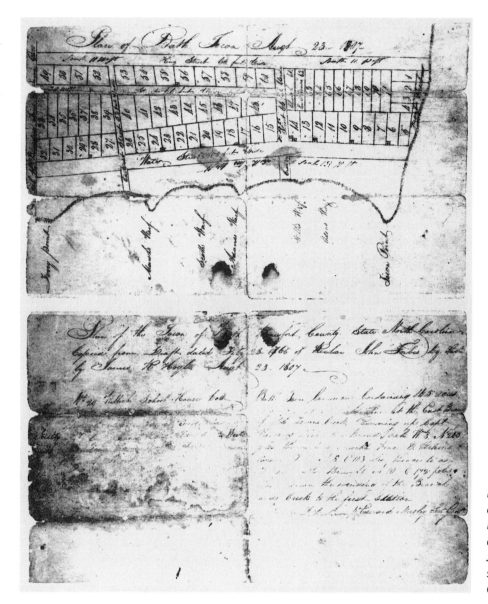

Plan of the Town of Bath. James R. Hoyle's 1807 copy of a 1766 original by John Forbis, deputy surveyor of North Carolina.

For North Carolina merchants and planters, the bounties meant that the trade in tar and pitch was suddenly profitable. Although exports of naval stores would be highest in the Cape Fear region, where production was closely tied to the availability of slaves, all of North Carolina's ports participated in the trade. Even at Port Bath, which handled fewer naval stores than any other North Carolina port, merchants were able to amass sizable fortunes through the trade in the mid-eighteenth century. One such merchant, emblem of the

Palmer-Marsh House (ca. 1750), Bath

lucrative and lively commercial enterprise that the Naval Stores Act made possible, was Michael Coutanch. His spacious house—today called the Palmer-Marsh House—survives in Historic Bath and identifies Coutanch as one of the wealthiest residents of the county. Tradition has it that Coutanch first sold his wares from a storeroom on the ground floor of the house. His ship, the *New Bern*, made regular runs to Liverpool carrying hundreds of barrels of North

Carolina tar. For the return trip, the *New Bern* took on retail merchandise for sale in Coutanch's North Carolina stores.

Council room of the Palmer-Marsh House

In 1706, while John Lawson and other colonists were founding Bath Town on the Pamlico River, settlements began springing up on the south side of the Neuse River. During the next two years, newcomers moved farther southeast toward Cape Lookout, into modern Carteret County, and constructed houses on the North and Newport Rivers. Between the two rivers, a narrow spit of land held obvious promise as a seaport. Well protected and easily accessible to the sea, the unnamed inlet drew the attention of the deputy surveyor of North Carolina in 1713, who drafted a "Plan of Beaufort Towne" that year. Named for the Duke of Beaufort, one of the eight Carolina proprietors, the town today bears much resemblance to its original design, and its street names—Queen, Ann, Orange—honor still the monarchs of the era.

Despite Beaufort's well-laid plans, the town grew little in its early years. North Carolina governor George Burrington wrote in 1731 that Beaufort had acquired "little success & scarce any inhabitants." A French visitor in 1765 found Beaufort "a Small village not above 12 houses." The "inhabitants seem miserable, they are very lasy and Indolent, they live mostly on fish and oisters, which they have in great plenty."

Indeed, for Beaufort and other coastal Carolina communities, the easy bounty of the sea put fish on the table and cash on the barrel. To John Lawson, the red drum caught off the coast provided not only "good firm meat" but an excellence of taste "beyond all the Fish I ever met." "People go down and catch as many barrels full as they please with Hook and Line." Palatable and abundant, great quantities of drumfish were "salted up and transported" from Beaufort "to the other Colonies, that are bare of Provisions."

Many residents of colonial Beaufort worked in either the fishing or forest products industries. Others labored at a trade that was actually a combination of both: shipbuilding. In 1713 George Bell, whose well-to-do family had first settled in Currituck County in the Albemarle, arranged to train two servants "in ye building of Vessells." Before long, residents of Harkers Island, just east of Beaufort, became known for their finely crafted boats. Even today the skill of Harkers Island boat builders is widely respected. By 1811 an observer in Beaufort would report: "The principle trade carried on here is Ship building in which they have acquired a very considerable reputation both on account of the solidity of the materials & the Judgement and Skill of their workmen as well as in modelling [and] in compleating their Vessels." Shipbuilding set Beaufort apart from other early Carolina towns, but by the mid-eighteenth century some of the largest fortunes there, as elsewhere along the coast, were being amassed by purchasing an African workforce and collecting the profits of its agricultural labor.

In 1996, in Beaufort Inlet, underwater archeologists discovered the wreck of an eighteenth-century vessel believed to be the *Queen Anne's Revenge*, the flagship of the infamous pirate Blackbeard, from the heyday of piracy and smuggling in North Carolina waters between 1689 and 1718. Blackbeard, also know as Edward Thatch or Teach, scuttled the *Queen Anne's Revenge* in Beaufort Inlet in the summer of 1718. He then resided for a short time in Bath, where he married a planter's daughter, his fourteenth wife according to legend. In November of that year, the notorious pirate was killed in battle near Ocracoke Inlet by Lt. Robert Maynard of the Royal Navy. The governor of Virginia had dispatched Maynard with two ships to the North Carolina coast to end Blackbeard's raids on colonial shipping. (Today, the North Carolina Office of

Blackbeard

Archives and History oversees the exploration and preservation of the wreck of the *Queen Anne's Revenge* and its artifacts.)

Edenton, Bath, and Beaufort were settled primarily by Virginians and other colonists migrating south. One Pamlico region town, however, was established in a very different manner. In 1710 over 400 immigrants from the Swiss and German Palatinate arrived in the Pamlico region to establish the town of New Bern. Famine, war, religious unrest, and economic difficulties had forced thousands of Germans out of the upper Rhine Valley after 1708. Many migrated to London and were quickly identified as potential New World colonists. In 1710 a Swiss company planning a settlement in North Carolina turned to these refugees. Baron Christoph von Graffenried, a member and representative of the company, recruited several hundred hardy colonists from the refu-

Baron Christoph von Graffenried

gees in London. After a transatlantic voyage and a difficult journey overland from the James River in Virginia, the Germans arrived at the junction of the Trent and Neuse Rivers in early September 1710. They were soon joined by a hundred impoverished Swiss immigrants. In 1711, a New Bern settler, Christen Janzen, described the area: "It is almost wholly forest, with indescribably beautiful cedar wood, poplars, oaks, beech, walnut and chestnut trees. . . . There is sassafras also, and so many other fragrant trees that I cannot describe the hundredth part. Cedar is red like the most beautiful cherry and smells better than the finest juniper. They are commonly, as well as the other trees, fifty to sixty feet below the limbs."

Despite setbacks at the start, Graffenried's colony, named after the Swiss city of Bern, quickly blossomed. Within a year, the displaced Palatines had built a thriving community. Graffenried often spoke of the residents' initiative and enterprise. For example, he noted that "since there is in the whole province only one poor water mill, the people of means have hand mills, while the poor pound their corn in a hollow piece of oak and sift the cleanest through a basket. Our people on the contrary sought out convenient water brooks and in that way, according to the condition of the water and the strength of the current, made theselves regular stamping mills by which the corn was ground, and the good man-of-the-house had time to do other work."

Talk of moving the shifting seat of government from the Albemarle to a permanent site at New Bern eventually began to circulate throughout the colony. The town would finally become the permanent seat for the colonial government, amid much controversy, when the royal governor's palace was completed there in 1770.

But, within two weeks of the settlement's first anniversary, New Bern's situation had altered considerably. On 22 September 1711 the Tuscarora War broke out in North Carolina. The creation of New Bern, where the Indian town of Chattoka had once stood, helped to precipitate a struggle that would become a major turning point in Carolina history for Indians and non-Indians alike.

5

THE TUSCARORA WAR

The tiny Algonquian tribes of the Albemarle were naturally the first to feel the effects of white settlements in North Carolina. As clapboard houses occupied old hunting grounds and cattle destroyed cornfields, the Chowanoc and Weapemeoc Indians gradually abandoned their lands. Some fled south, where they joined with the larger, more unified Tuscarora tribe. Others were bound into the colonial social structure as indentured servants or slaves. By 1700 scarcely 500 Indians remained in the Albemarle region.

For years, the Tuscaroras, an agricultural tribe related to the Iroquois, had inhabited the North Carolina Coastal Plain west of the Algonquians. According to one early eighteenth-century report, the Tuscaroras lived in fifteen different villages scattered throughout the Pamlico and Neuse River drainage basins. By the 1670s the Tuscaroras were aware that the Albemarle settlement was overspilling its bounds and the colonial government was extending its control southward. Immigrants by the hundreds invaded Tuscarora territory.

Soon traders circulated among the Tuscaroras, exchanging rum and other European goods for deerskins, furs, and Indian slaves captured from other tribes. Some Indians became addicted to liquor. Others feared enslavement themselves. Complaints of harsh treatment by traders were common. Before long the colonial population of the Pamlico region had grown enough to warrant the formation of Bath County. By 1700 settlements appeared on the Neuse River. In 1706, while the town of Bath was being incorporated, settlers crossed the Neuse and took up residence on its south shore. The Tuscarora hunting grounds shrank still further. Then in 1710 over 400 German and Swiss settlers arrived to establish the town of New Bern on the Neuse River. The beleaguered Tuscaroras became desperate. On 22 September 1711 the situation exploded. The Tuscarora War, which would nearly halve the Indian population of eastern North Carolina, had begun.

Although the circumstances leading up to the war were manifold, John Lawson put the situation quite plainly in his observation on relations with the Indians of the previous decade: "They are really better to us than we are to

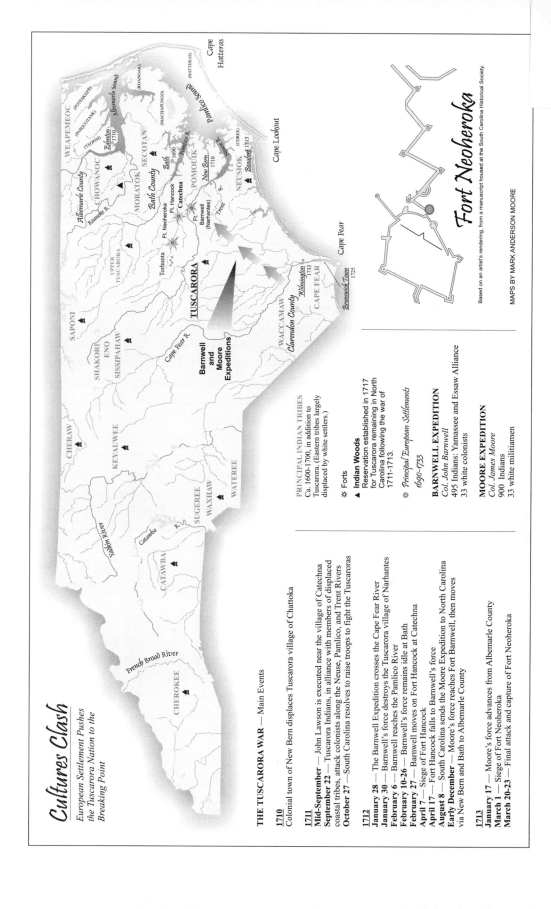

Cultures Clash

*European Settlement Pushes
the Tuscarora Nation to the
Breaking Point*

THE TUSCARORA WAR — Main Events

1710
Colonial town of New Bern displaces Tuscarora village of Chattoka

1711
Mid-September — John Lawson is executed near the village of Catechna
September 22 — Tuscarora Indians, in alliance with members of displaced coastal tribes, attack colonists along the Neuse, Pamlico, and Trent Rivers
October 27 — South Carolina resolves to raise troops to fight the Tuscaroras

1712
January 28 — The Barnwell Expedition crosses the Cape Fear River
January 30 — Barnwell's force destroys the Tuscarora village of Narhantes
February 6 — Barnwell reaches the Pamlico River
February 10-26 — Barnwell's force remains idle at Bath
February 27 — Barnwell moves on Fort Hancock at Catechna
April 7 — Siege of Fort Hancock
April 17 — Fort Hancock falls to Barnwell's force
August 8 — South Carolina sends the Moore Expedition to North Carolina
Early December — Moore's force reaches Fort Barnwell, then moves via New Bern and Bath to Albemarle County

1713
January 17 — Moore's force advances from Albemarle County
March 1 — Siege of Fort Neoheroka
March 20-23 — Final attack and capture of Fort Neoheroka

PRINCIPAL INDIAN TRIBES
Ca. 1600-1700, in addition to
Tuscarora. (Eastern tribes largely
displaced by white settlers.)

✺ Forts

▲ **Indian Woods**
Reservation established in 1717
for Tuscarora remaining in North
Carolina following the war of
1711-1713.

◉ *Principal European Settlements
1690-1733*

BARNWELL EXPEDITION
Col. John Barnwell
495 Indians: Yamassee and Essaw Alliance
33 white colonists

MOORE EXPEDITION
Col. James Moore
900 Indians
33 white militiamen

Fort Neoheroka

Based on an artist's rendering, from a manuscript housed at the South Carolina Historical Society.

MAPS BY MARK ANDERSON MOORE

them; they always give us Victuals at their Quarters, and take care we are arm'd against Hunger and Thirst: We do not do so by them (generally speaking) but let them walk by our Doors Hungry, and do not often relieve them." Specifically, the outbreak of hostilities can be narrowed down to three Indian grievances: the practices of white traders, Indian enslavement, and, most important, land encroachment.

North Carolina colonists realized the potential for profits in the fur trade even in the colony's earliest years. In 1669, only four years after their first meeting in Pasquotank County, the Albemarle County assembly passed "An Act Prohibiting Strangers Trading with the Indians." Likewise the Carolina proprietors stressed the need "to take spetiall care to prohibite all trade and commerce between the Indians and any others that are not freeholders of our Province of Carolina." Although the effort to eliminate competition in the Indian trade was not altogether successful, it certainly allowed Carolina traders to boost the price of their goods. One colonist wrote of "some turbulent Carolinians, who cheated those Indians in trading." Indeed, wrote John Lawson of the deerskin trade, "the Dealers therein have throve as fast as any Men, and the soonest rais'd themselves of any People I have known in *Carolina*." The fine for trading unlawfully with the Indians was 10,000 pounds of tobacco, half to go to the apprehender and half to the Lords Proprietors.

For the Tuscaroras, the price of European goods was doubly important. In addition to consuming such items themselves, the Tuscaroras had developed a sizable trade as middlemen carrying goods (especially rum) to the Siouan tribes in the Carolina interior. According to Lawson, the Indians of the Piedmont "never knew what it [rum] was, till within very few Years. Now they have it brought them by the *Tuskeruro's* . . . who carry it in Rundlets several hundred Miles." The sale of rum and other spirits to and among the Indians introduced a serious drunkenness among many of them. Treating with Catawba Indians in Rowan and Anson Counties in 1754, colonial officials heard King Hagler complain of the whites' selling alcoholic drink to the Indians. "Brothers," the king announced,

here is One thing You Yourselves are to Blame very much in. That is You Rot Your grain in Tubs, out of which you take and make Strong Spirits[.] You sell it to our young men and give it [to] them many times; they get very Drunk with it[.] [T]his is the Very Cause that they oftentimes Commit these Crimes that is offencive to you and us. . . . [I]t is very bad for our people, for it Rots their guts and Causes our men to get very sick and many of our people has lately Died by the Effects of that strong Drink, and I heartily wish You would do something to prevent your People from Dareing to Sell or give them any of that Strong Drink.

The Tuscaroras also traded mats, wooden bowls, and ladles for skins from inland tribes, "hating that any of these Westward *Indians* should have any Commerce with the *English* which would prove a Hinderance to their Gains." Among the goods the Tuscaroras exchanged for European wares were Indian slaves. Even before contact with Europeans, the Tuscaroras had kept captives from enemy tribes as slaves. (Though such slaves had little status in the Indian community, they had considerably more freedom than slaves in European society.) Now, however, the Tuscaroras sold their prisoners to European traders, who shipped them to the West Indies or other mainland colonies. John Lawson commented that Indian slaves "learn Handicraft-Trades very well and speedily."

But, just as the Tuscaroras captured and sold other Indians as slaves, so they also became slaves. In 1690 a Virginia colonist shipped "four of the Tuskaroro Indians out of this Country" as slaves. Meanwhile, hundreds of Indians captured in the backcountry had been exported out of the growing port of Charleston, farther south. By 1705 enslavement of Carolina Indians had become so prevalent in Pennsylvania that the colonists feared an uprising. Finally the Pennsylvania Council moved to halt further importation of Indian slaves from Carolina.

Although the Tuscarora grievances over unfair trade practices and enslavement were certainly significant, the Indians' loudest complaints were over land policy. Colonial laws validated the rights of Indians to their lands, and the courts generally upheld those laws. But settlers nevertheless transgressed against the Indians' rights to their land. For example, the minutes of the Colonial Council for November 1717 recorded: "Upon a complaint made by John Hoyter King of the Chowan Indyans that Ephraim Blanchard and Aaron Blanchard had settled upon those Indyans Lands without their leave[,] It is Ordered by this Board that the said Blanchards do attend the next Council to Shew Cause for their so doing and that in the mean time they desist from doing anything further on their Said Settlements."

As more and more settlers flocked into the Pamlico region, misunderstandings increased between planters, who claimed perpetual and exclusive ownership of property, and Indian hunters, who expected continued access to the land. According to two Tuscarora Indians John Lawson encountered at the Eno River near present-day Durham, the English settlers "were very wicked People" who "threatened the Indians for Hunting near their Plantations." A settler writing after the Tuscarora War claimed that one of its main causes was colonists who "would not allow them to hunt near their plantations, and under that pretence took away from them their game, arms, and ammunition."

Although large-scale conflict did not erupt until 1711, numerous minor incidents occurred in the years before. The Coree Indians, a tiny Algonquian tribe inhabiting what we now know as Carteret County, rose against local settlers in 1703. In 1704 other coastal Indians raided the home of a colonist named Powell. When Powell threatened to inform a nearby colonial official of the matter, the Indian leader retorted that the official "might kiss his arse." Near this time, a Bath County observer reported that "ye neighboring towns of ye Tuscororah Indians are of late dissatisfied with ye Inhabitants of this place." By 1707 Pamlico River settlers "expected ye Indians everyday to come and cut their throats."

The settlement of New Bern in 1710 pushed the Indians to the point of desperation. Over 400 Swiss and German Palatines, led by Baron Christoph von Graffenried, displaced the Indian town of Chattoka at the junction of the Neuse and Trent Rivers. Fearful of further colonial expansion, the Tuscaroras appealed to the Pennsylvania colony for asylum. In 1710, at a meeting with Pennsylvania commissioners and local Shawnee and Conestoga Indian leaders, Tuscarora emissaries proposed to relocate from North Carolina to the Susquehanna region. They sought a "lasting peace" with the Indians and government of Pennsylvania in order to "be secured against those fearful apprehensions they have these several years felt." The Pennsylvania commissioners, however, stipulated that the Tuscaroras present a certificate of good behavior from their North Carolina neighbors before they could "be assured of a favorable reception" in Pennsylvania. This demand effectively denied the Tuscarora request.

Unable to find refuge in Pennsylvania, the Tuscaroras took the offensive. In early September 1711 the Tuscaroras captured Baron von Graffenried, John Lawson, and two black slaves as they journeyed up the Neuse River. The Indians took their prisoners to the village of Catechna, about four miles north of present-day Grifton, in Pitt County. At Catechna, John Lawson quarreled heatedly with a Coree chief named Cor Tom. In response, the Indians tortured and killed Lawson. Graffenried was more diplomatic and lived to describe the experience in word and picture. Known for harboring black fugitives, the Tuscaroras spared the slaves. Lawson had been dead little more than a decade when William Byrd wrote, "they [the Indians] resented their wrongs a little too severely upon Mr. Lawson, who, under Colour of being Surveyor Gen'l, had encroacht too much upon their Territories, at which they were so enrag'd, that they . . . cut his throat from Ear to Ear, but at the same time releas'd the Baron de Graffenried, whom they had Seized for Company, because it appear'd plainly he had done them no Wrong."

On 22 September 1711 the Tuscaroras attacked European settlements along the Neuse and Pamlico Rivers. According to Baron von Graffenried, who was still a prisoner at the time, the Indians involved were "500 men strong,

The Tuscarora capture John Lawson.

well armed." At first it appeared that these Indians might repulse the settlers' invasion of their homelands. By the end of the year, 130 English and Germans were dead, and most surviving Pamlico region colonists huddled together in the town of Bath. Bitter political divisions among the settlers blocked any concerted efforts at defense.

Internal divisions split the Tuscarora tribe as well as the colonial government. The inhabitants of the northwesternmost Tuscarora villages had not felt the impact of colonial settlement as had their more southerly sisters and brothers. Because of their lucrative connections with Virginia fur traders, these villages hoped to avoid the conflict and immediately negotiated a treaty with Virginia's governor, Alexander Spotswood. Spotswood likewise wanted to protect his colony's interests in the trade. Already embroiled in disputes over the Carolina boundary line, Virginia had little sympathy for her neighbor's plight. When North Carolina appealed to Virginia for assistance, the latter sent £1,000 and some material for uniforms, but no troops.

North Carolinians next turned to South Carolina for aid. South Carolinians responded favorably—for they sensed lively profits in the making. Defeating the Tuscaroras would mean far more than helping out neighbors. Victory promised fat financial returns in the form of captured Indian slaves. On

27 October 1711 the South Carolina House of Commons resolved to raise troops to fight the Tuscaroras. Colonel John Barnwell, an Indian trader and member of the colonial Assembly later known as "Tuscarora Jack," was appointed commander-in-chief.

The makeup of Barnwell's force reflected the nature of South Carolina's commitment. Of the 528 men who marched north to Tuscarora country, 495 were Yamassee and other South Carolina Indians. Only 33 were white colonists. The pattern is a familiar one: by pitting local tribes against one another, colonists furthered their own ends at minimal cost.

By the time they neared the Neuse River, most of Barnwell's Indian troops had become disillusioned. Wisely, they were "unwilling to proceed into unknown country where they may be hem'd in by a numerous Enemy and not know how to extricate themselves." The Yamassees, who, like their commander, had high hopes for plunder in slaves, were the only group to remain in Barnwell's force.

In late January the expedition reached Narhantes, a Tuscarora stronghold on the Neuse River about twenty miles upstream from New Bern. Prompted by the anxious Yamassees, the South Carolina forces attacked almost immediately. Although the battle lasted less than half an hour, it was not without surprises for Barnwell and his men. Once inside the Tuscarora fort they found that many of the enemy's strongest warriors were women, who "did not yield until most of them were put to the sword." Although they collected numerous scalps and easily destroyed the Tuscarora village, the battle was a disappointing one for Barnwell and his few white companions. "While we were putting the men to the sword," the colonel complained bitterly, "our Indians got all the slaves and plunder, only one girl we got."

After resupplying at Bath, Barnwell and his troops set out for Catechna, the site of Lawson's execution. There they found an ingenious fort commanding Cotechney Creek. Named "Fort Hancock" for a Tuscarora king, it consisted of "a large Earthen Trench thrown up against the puncheons with 2 teer of port holes; the lower teer they could stop at pleasure with plugs, & large limbs of trees lay confusedly about it to make the approach intricate, and all about much with large reeds & canes to run into people's legs." The South Carolinians learned from prisoners that a runaway black slave named Harry had shown the Tuscaroras how to build the fort. According to Barnwell, Harry had been "sold into Virginia for roguery & since fled to the Tuscaruros." One of Barnwell's demands after the first battle at Catechna was for the return of twenty-four runaway blacks living among the Indians.

At the conclusion of the first battle, the South Carolina forces retreated seven miles downstream, where they constructed Fort Barnwell. From Fort Barnwell the colonel orchestrated a devastating ten-day siege of the Indian fort at Catechna. On 17 April 1712 Fort Hancock finally fell. The Tuscaroras consented to a humiliating surrender. But again Barnwell had very few slaves to show for his effort, "the Indians being more dextrous than us at taking slaves."

The peace was short-lived. Disappointed by the returns of the expedition, Yamassee warriors continued to forage and plunder in Tuscarora country. Settlers likewise continued penetrating Tuscarora homelands. In the summer of 1712 the beleaguered Tuscaroras rose to fight the invaders one more time.

On 8 August South Carolina again came to her neighbor's aid. As before, profit was at the heart of the matter. Desperate North Carolinians eagerly pointed out the "great advantage [that] may be made of Slaves there being hundreds of women and children, many we believe 3 or 4 thousand." Colonel James Moore would lead South Carolina's forces. This time they consisted of 900 Indians and 33 whites.

West of the present-day town of Snow Hill in Greene County the Tuscaroras' determined struggle to retain their homeland was brought to an end. Here, on 20 March 1713, Moore's forces began their attack on Fort Neoheroka. For three days the Tuscaroras withstood the South Carolina Indian onslaught.

Finally Moore's forces set fire to the bastions and to buildings within the Tuscarora stronghold. By mid-morning on 23 March they had routed the last of its Indian defenders.

The Tuscarora War was over. For the Tuscaroras the cost was bitter: 1,000 had been captured and enslaved; 1,400 were dead. A handful remained in rebellion until February 1715, when a treaty concluded the war. Most of the Tuscarora survivors migrated northward to become the sixth and smallest tribe of the powerful Iroquois League. In 1717 the few who remained in North Carolina received land on the Roanoke River near present-day Quitsna.

Ironically, the war proved as devastating for the Yamassees as for the Tuscaroras they had subdued. In 1715, when the Yamassee War broke out in South Carolina, Colonel Maurice Moore marched southward with a company of North Carolina troops that included Tuscarora warriors anxious for revenge. As the troops passed through the Cape Fear region, they destroyed local Waccamaw and Cape Fear Indians who had allied with the Yamassees. Over ten years later, a visitor to the region would comment, "there is not an Indian to be seen in the Place."

Among the first Europeans to take advantage of the removal of Indians from Cape Fear was Colonel Maurice Moore himself. Moore took up residence in the Cape Fear in 1725 and laid out the Town of Brunswick. The name evoked the German roots of England's King George I, in order to gain his favor. Only four years later, the king would purchase North Carolina from the proprietors, thus making the region a royal colony.

By July 1726 settlers were arriving in Brunswick Town and the first plot of land had been sold. In the months that followed, the Town of Brunswick and the entire Cape Fear settlement grew considerably. A ferry soon carried people and goods across the lower Cape Fear River. Upstream on the opposite bank, the village of Newton (or New Town), later called Wilmington, was established in 1733. The two towns combined to form the port of Brunswick. James Murray, a colonial official, merchant, and planter who lived for several months in Brunswick Town, was pleased with the church he found there. "We are not depriv'd of the advantages of the gospel prech'd for we have the best minister that I have heard in America to preach & read prayers to us every 2^d or 3^d Sunday at least, & in a cold day a good fire in the church to sit by. In these & many other respects this town is preferable to New town [Wilmington], & yet I believe the last will be first in a little time."

The excavated ruins of colonial Brunswick Town—which, as Murray predicted, would eventually be overshadowed in trade and activity by Wilmington—reveal the remains of Maurice Moore's old home on Front Street next to the ruins of the public house and tailor shop. Roger Moore's home stood

nearby on Second Street. A fenced-in plot marks the site of an old garden on Cross Street. Most remarkable is the ruin of St. Philip's Church, where Anglican residents of Brunswick Town worshiped. The brick walls of the church still stand tall; only the windows, roof, and worshipers are missing.

Today, a walk along the Brunswick Town nature trail reveals some of the natural environment that Maurice Moore and other early settlers found at

Ruins of St. Philip's Church (1754–68, burned 1776), Brunswick Town, Brunswick County

Cape Fear. Spanish moss hangs from the bald cypress trees in Brunswick Pond. The setting is peaceful and filled with nature's bounty—the stuff of which Carolina colonists' dreams were made. Only the carnivorous Venus's fly-trap growing nearby hints that the Cape Fear coast was also a devourer of hopes for the Tuscaroras and other native Americans—if they lingered within the range of land- and slave-hungry invaders from Europe.

PINE FOREST PLANTATIONS

6

Most of the early settlers in and around Brunswick Town came from South Carolina. By late 1726 leading South Carolina citizens were already complaining of the "Desertions from us to Cape Fear which is occasioned by the rigid usage of the merchants and lawyers." This "rigid usage" was due primarily to changes in the colony's naval-stores trade. As England's navy had expanded during the preceding half century, British officials had become increasingly anxious to obtain vital materials from their own colonies rather than from Baltic rivals. They looked to New England forests for masts and spars and to the southern colonies for the huge quantities of pitch and tar needed to protect the hulls and rigging of England's wartime and commercial fleet. Indeed, sailors applied tar with such regularity (much as modern seamen apply paint) that the men sailing before the mast became known collectively as "tars."

When Parliament began offering bounties on naval stores in 1705, many South Carolina planters made substantial investments in slaves and land. Often, these investments were on credit. The investors planned to pay off their debts with the profits they made on naval stores. But in 1725, after one extension, the Naval Stores Act expired and Parliament ceased paying bounties. A half-century of planting had pushed the pine forests back from the navigable coastal rivers, making rice more profitable than naval stores. Without the bounty, exports of tar and pitch from Charleston dropped from 60,000 barrels in 1725 to a paltry 5,000 barrels in 1728.

Caught in the shifts of the lowcountry economy, many planters found they had debts they could not pay in a colony seeking added revenues for defense. They paid their debts with a variety of currency and commodities. Because Spanish, French, and Portuguese money was far more prevalent in the English colonies than English currency, in 1704 the rate of exchange of foreign coins in English money was set by royal proclamation. In time, laws established rates of exchange as well for commodities, which were widely used in place of money. The term "proclamation money" was applied not only to the rates of exchange but to the foreign coins, the rated commodities, and to paper currency issued with these values.

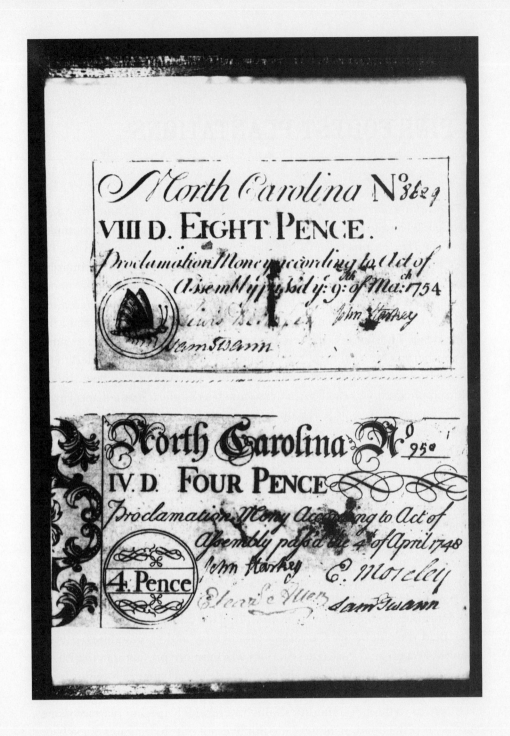

Proclamation money

Charleston officials now feared not only the Spanish in St. Augustine but also the increased number of enslaved workers. Two decades earlier, South Carolina's black population had surpassed its free white population, and, as the number and percentage of slaves increased, so did the potential for rebellion. By 1720, with the overthrow of the proprietorship and appointment of the first royal governor, blacks outnumbered whites 11,828 to 6,525—or nearly two to one—and a major slave uprising had come close to success.

In 1727 increased taxes reflected the rising cost of keeping the black workers in subjection and preventing incursions by the Catholic Spanish in St. Augustine. For indebted planters dependent on the failing naval-stores industry, these taxes proved impossible to pay. Where summonses had sufficed in the past, in 1727 a new law called for the bodily seizure of delinquent debtors. Not surprisingly, many chose to flee. Cape Fear provided asylum to debtors and offered timber-rich land, close to the coast, that could be developed for profit much as coastal South Carolina had been in preceding decades.

In December 1727 an observer described the newly arrived settlers as a "dispersed multitude of People residing up and down Cape Fear." The exact size of this "multitude" is uncertain. It seems likely, however, that many, perhaps most, of the Cape Fear settlers were in some sort of bondage. Both servants and slaves emigrated with their masters. In one attempt to slow the exodus to Cape Fear, the South Carolina Commons House considered, but then rejected, a bill restricting the transportation of indentured servants and slaves across Winyaw Bay and the Santee River. In 1742 the black population of the new settlement was estimated at 2,000 and the white population at 1,000. By 1767 the lower Cape Fear region contained 5,154 blacks and only 2,940 whites. Clearly, these numbers reflect the South Carolina society from which so many of the settlers came.

As it had been in early South Carolina, Cape Fear's chief export was naval stores. Rice exports, which soon surpassed naval-stores exports in the southern colony, were of only secondary importance at Cape Fear. Because of its great stands of longleaf pine, the Cape Fear region was ideal for naval-stores production. "Most of the Country," wrote traveler Hugh Meredith, a Welsh Pennsylvanian, to Philadelphia printer Benjamin Franklin in 1731, "is well cloathed with tall Pines, excepting the Swamps, Savanahs, and some small strips by the Side of the Rivers." Longleaf pine yields large amounts of resin, the raw material necessary for naval-stores production.

Although normally profitable, the production of naval stores could be less appealing when the price declined. As Governor Gabriel Johnston observed in 1734: "There is more pitch and tarr made in the two Carolinas than in all the other provinces on the Continent and rather more in this than in South Carolina but their two Commodities (tarr especially) bear so low a price in London (1000 Barrels scarce clearing 20ˢ sterling) that I find the Planters are generally resolved to make no more."

At the heart of the Cape Fear naval-stores industry was black labor. Skilled slaves at Cape Fear took part in every phase of naval-stores manufacture. They produced tons of tar, pitch, and turpentine annually. The extraction of resin, or crude turpentine, was the first step in naval-stores production. "The Planters," explained North Carolina naturalist John Brickell, "make their Servants or *Negroes* cut large Cavities on each side of the Pitch-Pine Tree (which they term Boxing of the Tree) wherein the Turpentine runs." The workers also peeled bark from sections of the tree so the heat of the sun could draw more turpentine to the surface. The turpentine drained into containers near the bottom of the tree, where, according to Brickell, "the Negroes with Ladles take it out and put it into Barrels." An observer in 1765 claimed "one Negro will tend 3000" boxed trees, "which will rendr about 100 Barls. terpentin."

Most turpentine was shipped from Cape Fear in its crude state. On occasion, however, planters had their slaves make oil of turpentine and its by-product, rosin, by distilling crude turpentine with water. John Brickell described the process: "The Rosin is very scarce in these parts, few giving themselves the trouble; but when made, it is done after the following manner, viz. Take Turpentine, as much as you think proper, put it into an Alembick or a Copper Vesica, with four times its weight in fair water, and distil it, which will produce a thin and clear Oil like Water, and at the bottom of the Vessel will remain the Rosin."

Each tree ran or oozed for about three years before dying and falling to the ground. The wood of these downed pines was called "lightwood." Brickell states that during the winter, when slaves could not be employed in the rice fields, planters would "make their *Negroes* gather great quantities of this *Light-Wood*, which they split about the thickness of a Man's Leg, and two or three Feet in length." Tar manufacture required a large volume of lightwood.

Slaves also built and tended the elaborate kilns in which the lightwood was fired to make tar. They selected a site, usually atop a small rise, and fashioned a concave floor. Then, according to Brickell, "they take the *Light-wood* which they pile up with the ends of each, placed slanting towards the center of the Kiln." The African American laborers covered the lightwood "with Clay Earth or Sods" and carefully set it afire through holes opened in the turf. A pipe that drained tar from the center of the floor led to a collecting barrel outside. The kiln burned continuously for several days and generally produced 160 to 180 barrels of tar. Once this difficult and sometimes dangerous job was completed,

Custom-House
Newba on Delaware } These are to certifie whom it may concern
that William Warner Master of the Sloop Betsy
and Nancy from Beaufort in North Carolina

101 Barrs Tarr.
98 Barrs Turpentine
7 Barrs Pitch.
5 Barrs Wax & Tallow.
57 sides Leather,
69 hides. 26 bundles of deer skins,
4 Cakes of Wax & Tallow

Wm Till
Collect. & Search

For the due Landing whereof in this Port Bond
was given in Beaufort aff

Given under my Hand & Seal of
Office this 21st Feby 1761

Cargo manifest for the sloop Betsy and Nancy *from the port of Beaufort, 1761, with naval stores heading the list of items aboard ship*

the workers could make pitch by burning tar in iron caldrons or pits dug into the ground.

Black laborers stored pitch, like turpentine and tar, in thirty-two-gallon barrels, which could be hauled in boats or wagons or rolled down to the docks. Because of the great volume of naval stores exported from Cape Fear, the skilled coopers who made barrels were in high demand. In early North Carolina, blacks and whites alike worked in the cooper's trade, and every plantation had a cooperage to supply casks, barrels, buckets, and hogsheads. James Murray, an early Cape Fear resident, wrote these words of advice to an aspiring planter: "If you intend to do any business here, a Cooper and a Craft that will carry about 100 barrels will be absolutely necessary."

Such small sailing craft brought the naval stores produced on Cape Fear plantations downriver to Brunswick Town or Wilmington for export. Like Michael Coutanch at the Palmer-Marsh House in Bath Town, merchants in Wilmington and Brunswick Town exported naval stores and imported English manufactured goods for local sale. Ships carried more tar, pitch, and turpentine from Brunswick than any other port in the colony. In 1768 some 63,265 barrels, or nearly half of North Carolina's naval-stores exports, departed from the port of Brunswick. Many of these barrels crossed the docks at Brunswick Town. (Today from the top of nearby Fort Anderson, visitors to the Brunswick

Town Historic Site can see the Cape Fear River and the old location of the town's wharves.)

Such trade brought considerable wealth to merchants like James Murray, who established a business and built an adjoining residence in Wilmington in the 1730s. He described to the builder how he wanted his store constructed: "[T]he 22 by 18 on the east end of the house to be lined with boards on the side & plastered on the siding, to be shelved as far as the door from the east end, & counter from side to side with a board to fold down in the middle. I hope the cellar is done underneath, and the sashes according to the dimensions I sent you by Wimble ready to put in the glass." In 1741, Murray described his house and store: "In my house there is a large Room 22 by 16 feet, the most airy of any in the Country, two tolerable lodging rooms & a Closet up stairs & Garrets above, a Cellar below divided into a Kitchen with an oven and a Store for Liquors, provisions, etc. This makes one half of my house. The other, placed on the east end, is the Store: Cellar below, the Store and Counting House on the first floor, & above it is partion'd off into four rooms, but this end is not plaister'd but only done with rough boards." On 20 November 1754 Governor Arthur Dobbs wrote to the Earl of Halifax that Wilmington had seventy families who had built "a good County House or town house, & have raised a large brick church, which is ready for the roof." The church was not finished until 1770.

Although the naval-stores industry dominated the economy of the lower Cape Fear, a small quantity of rice also passed over the docks at Wilmington and Brunswick Town. In 1768 North Carolina exported only eighty-two barrels of rice, all from Cape Fear. By comparison, South Carolina exported 132,000 barrels in the same year. Rice cultivation required even more intensive labor than naval-stores manufacture. Only a few of the most wealthy Cape Fear planters owned enough slaves to make rice growing profitable. (Large slave ships from Africa rarely, if ever, visited the North Carolina colony; the ports were too small and the coastline too treacherous. Like other imports, slaves were expensive and often entered the province overland—frequently from Charleston.) Not surprisingly, the roots of Cape Fear rice cultivation lay in slave labor.

"The best Land for Rice," wrote a South Carolinian in 1761, "is a wet, deep, miry soil; such as is generally to be found in Cypress Swamps; or a black greasy mould with a Clay Foundation." Hugh Meredith traveled a short way up the Northeast Cape Fear River in 1730 or 1731 and found that "Boggy" swamps for rice cultivation abounded in the region. After sloshing across low-lying savannahs, he reported that the "Water was mostly ancle-deep on them." It was on land like this that Maurice Moore's brother Roger settled around 1725. By 1735 Roger Moore had named his plantation "Orton" and constructed a one-and-

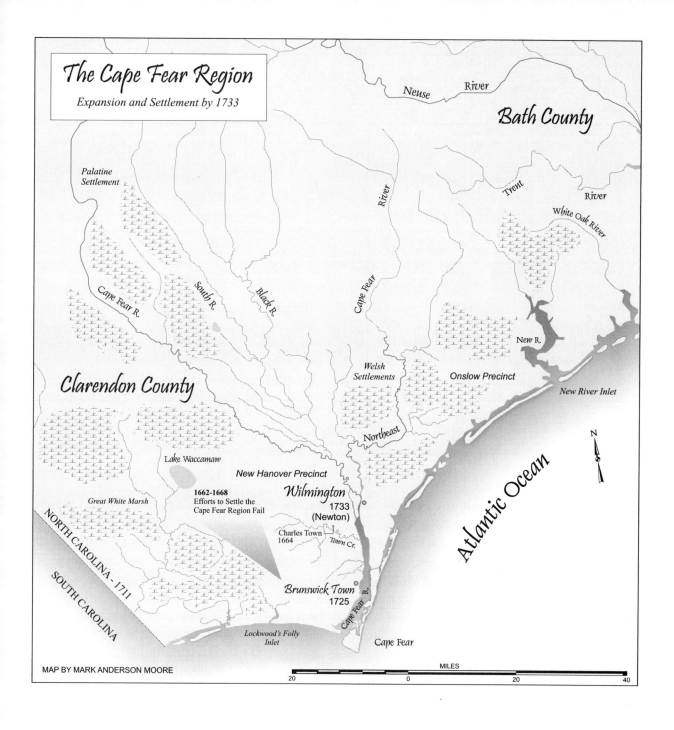

The Cape Fear Region

Expansion and Settlement by 1733

Neuse River

Bath County

Palatine Settlement

Trent River

White Oak River

South R.

Black R.

Cape Fear River

Cape Fear R.

New R.

New River Inlet

Clarendon County

Welsh Settlements

Onslow Precinct

Northeast

Atlantic Ocean

Lake Waccamaw

New Hanover Precinct

1662-1668
Efforts to Settle the
Cape Fear Region Fail

Wilmington
1733
(Newton)

N

Great White Marsh

Charles Town
1664

Town Cr.

NORTH CAROLINA - 1711

SOUTH CAROLINA

Brunswick Town
1725

Cape Fear R.

Lockwood's Folly
Inlet

Cape Fear

MAP BY MARK ANDERSON MOORE

MILES

20   0   20   40

a-half-story brick home. A visitor to Cape Fear recorded in 1734 that Roger Moore, "hearing we were come, was so kind as to send fresh horses for us to come up to his house, which we did, and were kindly received by him; he being the chief gentleman in all Cape Fear. His house is built of brick, and exceedingly pleasantly situated about two miles from the town [Brunswick], and about half a mile from the river, though there is a creek comes close up to the door, between two beautiful meadows about three miles in length. He has a prospect of the town of Brunswick, and of another beautiful brick house, a building about half a mile from him, belonging to Eleazar Allen, Esq."

Although the plantation house, now altered considerably, is the only building that has survived for two-and-a-half centuries, many more homes once existed at Orton in the form of slave quarters. When Roger Moore died in 1750, he left an estate including 250 slaves to his two sons. In fact, with so large a number of workers, Orton Plantation was more a black village than it was a white homestead. Generations of slaves cultivated rice in the field beyond the present Scroll Garden and in the great fields where flowers and shrubs now grow in front of the house. Indeed, it was their labor, in several senses, that created the opulent home of the Moores.

The black Carolinians enslaved at Orton and other Cape Fear rice plantations produced some of the highest quality rice in the North American colonies. One of the reasons rice exports from Cape Fear appear so low may be that planters shipped a great deal of the grain overland to South Carolina for seed. Like slaves in South Carolina, many black workers in the Cape Fear region may have been familiar with rice cultivation from previous experience in Africa. Those who did not bring such skills from Africa could have acquired them in South Carolina before migrating to the more northern colony.

Work toward rice cultivation at plantations like Orton began by clearing the heavy natural growth from the proposed rice fields. The swamps, wrote Hugh Meredith after his expedition, are "generally well cloathed with tall Timber, and Canes underneath; some with Trees only, others all Cane." Removing these obstacles was no small task. African American laborers "first cut down the Cane, and all the small Underbrush, and gather it in Heaps; then fall the Saplins and great Trees." The slaves burned the branches with the rest of the underbrush, but left the trunks to rot, "the Logs being little minded, because the Rice is chiefly managed with the Hoe."

Indeed, it was by the hoe and hard labor of black slaves that rice culture took hold in the Carolinas. Regulated flooding of manmade rice fields to destroy weeds became common only in the second half of the eighteenth century, and machines to help pound and clean the rice were also later innovations. Rice production in colonial Cape Fear—from planting the grain in the spring to polishing it in the fall—depended entirely upon hand labor. Many of the techniques used in the rice fields of colonial Carolina bore considerable resemblance to those used by African rice planters on the Windward Coast. African patterns are discernible throughout the stages of sowing, cultivating, and harvesting. For example, workers experienced at growing rice in western Africa continued to use the same kind of large wooden mortar and pestle when obliged to clean rice in Carolina. Once the husks had been pounded loose, they were separated from the grains by tossing the rice in large, flat, African-style winnowing baskets, woven from palmetto leaves. The wind carried away the loosened stems and husks. The workers then returned the rice to the mortar and pestle and polished the grains with the pestle's broad, blunt end. Each slave usually produced 200 to 250 pounds (about two acres' yield) of polished rice grains for market.

The prospects for exploiting Cape Fear's bountiful resources had been sensed by early European visitors long before Maurice Moore and his brothers

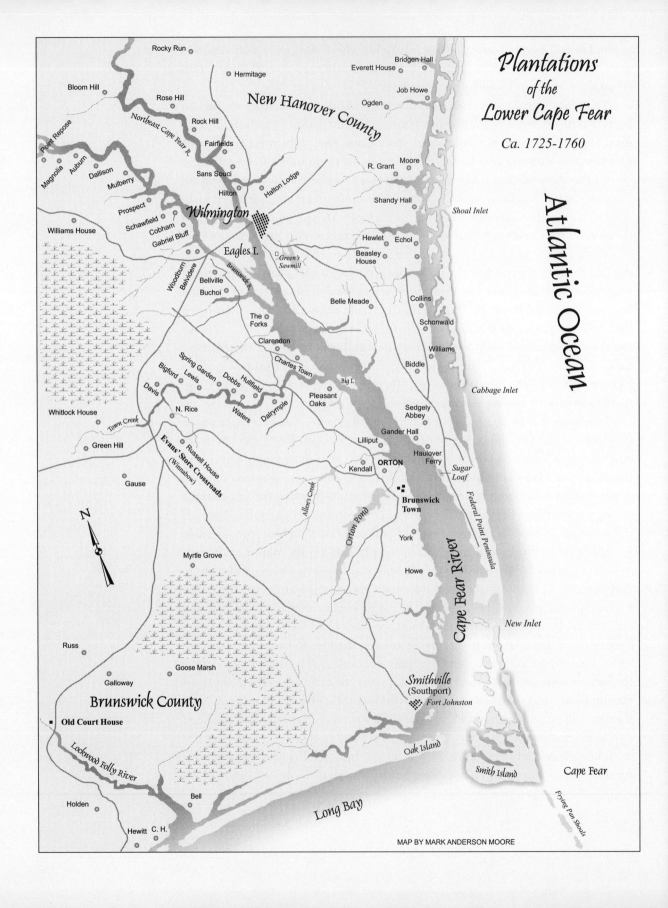

Plantations
of the
Lower Cape Fear
Ca. 1725-1760

Atlantic Ocean

New Hanover County

Rocky Run
Hermitage
Bloom Hill
Rose Hill
Point Repose
Rock Hill
Northeast Cape Fear R.
Fairfields
Magnolia
Auburn
Dallison
Sans Souci
Mulberry
Hilton
Prospect
Schawfield
Wilmington
Cobham
Gabriel Bluff
Williams House
Eagles I.
Woodburn
Belvidere
Bellville
Buchoi
Brunswick R.
The Forks
Clarendon
Charles Town
Spring Garden
Bigford
Lewis
Dobbs
Hullfield
Davis
N. Rice
Waters
Dalrymple
Whitlock House
Town Creek
Green Hill
Russell House
Evans' Store Crossroads
(Winnabow)
Gause

Everett House
Bridgen Hall
Job Howe
Ogden
Moore
R. Grant
Shandy Hall
Hewlet
Echol
Beasley House
Green's Sawmill
Belle Meade
Collins
Schonwald
Williams
Biddle
Big I.
Pleasant Oaks
Sedgely Abbey
Gander Hall
Lilliput
Haulover Ferry
ORTON
Kendall
Sugar Loaf
Brunswick Town
York
Howe

Halton Lodge
Shoal Inlet
Cabbage Inlet

Allen's Creek
Orton Pond

Cape Fear River

Federal Point Peninsula

New Inlet

N

Myrtle Grove

Brunswick County

Russ
Galloway
Goose Marsh
Old Court House

Lockwood Folly River

Holden
Hewitt
C. H.
Bell

Smithville
(Southport)
Fort Johnston

Oak Island

Smith Island

Long Bay

Cape Fear

Frying Pan Shoals

MAP BY MARK ANDERSON MOORE

arrived in the region. In 1663 William Hilton had described a land "innumerable of Pines, tall and good," and in 1666 a promoter of the Charles Town settlement lauded "The Meadows," which were "very proper for Rice." By the mid-eighteenth century, experience in South Carolina had taught profit-hungry planters that African workers enslaved for life were the cheapest form of plantation labor. By the time that the naval-stores industry was flourishing and Roger Moore was establishing his rice plantation at Orton, slavery had become entrenched in North Carolina. For many years thereafter, the economy of the colony and state would depend upon the skill and labor of enslaved persons of African descent, who often brought considerable knowledge and ability to the tasks they were forced to perform. Of these black Carolinians, Brickell observed: "There are several Blacks born here that can Read and Write, others that are bred to Trades, and prove good Artists in many of them. Others are bred to no Trades, but are very industrious and laborious in improving their Plantations, planting abundance of Corn, Rice and Tobacco, and making vast quantities of Turpentine, Tar, and Pitch being better able to undergo fatigues in the extremity of the hot weather than any Europeans."

Just before the American Revolution, one observer noted the extraordinary affluence of whites in the coastal Cape Fear region. Ignoring the harsh circumstances of the region's black majority, or perhaps not even counting them as "people," he wrote that there were "fewer of the lower class of country people than [in] any part of the whole province." Though remarkably invisible to this and other white travelers, as well as generations of historians, the African American colonists of colonial Cape Fear did fully as much as the dominant English minority to shape the region's early economic and cultural development.

7 LONG JOURNEY OF THE HIGHLAND SCOTS

In the half-century after the Tuscarora War, as Africans and Englishmen began clearing out plantations around Cape Fear, the population of colonial North Carolina became dramatically larger and more diversified. When Maurice Moore established the town of Brunswick, North Carolina was England's most thinly populated mainland colony. By the time of the American Revolution, only Virginia, Massachusetts, and Pennsylvania supported more inhabitants than North Carolina. The colony's population climbed from fewer than 35,000 in 1730 to well over 200,000 by 1775.

Beginning in the 1730s a relentless flow of immigrants poured into North Carolina. Newcomers of Welsh descent settled along the Northeast Cape Fear River in the early 1730s. Starting in 1732, Highland Scots moved into the Cape Fear backcountry. Later on, Scotch-Irish and German immigrants from Pennsylvania, Maryland, and Virginia would travel down the Great Wagon Road to the North Carolina Piedmont.

All these European immigrants came to North Carolina seeking better conditions than they had left behind. Some came for religious reasons, having heard that the Anglican Church was weak in the colony. Others came for political reasons. Most frequently, however, the settlers hoped to acquire land, inevitably a scarce and expensive resource in their homelands. Smallpox and wars had considerably diminished the Indian population of the Carolina Piedmont. The remnants of the small interior Siouan tribes had joined the Catawba Indians at such sites as Nauvasa on the Catawba River, in modern Iredell County, and Sugaree, south of present-day Charlotte. Only the Cherokees far to the west presented a significant obstacle to white expansion. Because it took the newcomers some years to reach the Cherokee country, hostilities did not break out until the 1750s. In the meantime, the situation was as Governor Burrington put it in 1733: "Land is not wanting for men in Carolina, but men for land."

Around 1730 a group of Welsh colonists from Pennsylvania arrived at Cape Fear to take up some of this abundant land. They followed the Northeast Cape Fear River northward and settled on what came to be called the "Welsh Tract" in what is now Pender County. (The general area of the Welsh tract is thought to have been about eight and half miles north of present-day Burgaw.)

Interest in the Cape Fear region was evidently quite strong among Welsh Pennsylvanians. "The new Settlement going forward at Cape Fear," Philadelphian Benjamin Franklin explained in 1731, has "for these *3* or *4* years past, been the Subject of much Discourse, especially among Country People." According to Franklin, "great Numbers" of Pennsylvanians visited the Cape Fear region annually, "that they may be capable of judging whether it will be an advantagious Exchange if they should remove and settle there." None of these travelers, Franklin complained, had "at their Return published their Observations for the Information of others." Hence he took it upon himself to print the account of his former partner, Hugh Meredith, a young Welsh Pennsylvanian, "fond of reading but addicted to drinking," who had recently traveled to the Welsh Tract.

Meredith described a land of "small Ascents and Descents, with fine Runs of Water in the Vallies, passing among Limestone Rocks." Pines abounded in the country's lower reaches, while "good Oak and Hickery" covered the land farther upstream. At one point, Meredith passed through "as fine a Wood to walk in as could be wished, of all the Sorts that are in *Pennsylvania*." Farther on he encountered "the finest Crop of Indian Corn I ever have seen; the Stalks of which measured 18 Foot long."

Despite the publication of Meredith's account in the *Pennsylvania Gazette*, Welsh migration from Pennsylvania was actually quite limited. Before long, numerous families of other descents had settled on the tract. By the time Presbyterian minister Hugh McAden visited Cape Fear in 1756, the region's ethnic makeup had broadened considerably. When he preached "to a number of Highlanders" at settler Hector McNeill's home, he noted that "some of them scarcely knew one word that I said—the poorest singers I ever heard in all my life." McAden even preached to a large group of Irish who were "very desirous of joining the Welch Tract."

Not long after the Welsh Pennsylvanians began moving to North Carolina, a group of immigrants from a much more distant land reached the colony's shores. By 1732 the first of many Highland Scots had arrived at Cape Fear. James Innes, a Highlander from the northeastern county of Caithness, received a 320-acre grant of Bladen County land in January 1732. Just over a year later, Innes acquired an additional 640 acres, and Hugh Campbell and William Forbes received 640 acres apiece. Campbell and Innes secured even more land later, as they paid for the transportation of additional settlers from the Highlands. As many as seventy Scots may have settled with these men. In the years that followed, until the outbreak of the American Revolution, thousands of Highland Scots migrated to North Carolina.

These immigrants, who made a distinctive mark on North Carolina's culture, were a small part of a larger exodus prompted by drastic economic and political changes in the Scottish Highlands. After the Jacobite uprisings of 1715 and 1745, in which several Highland clans attempted to return the Stuart line to the English throne, the crown imposed harsh punishments on all the Highland Scots. Some of these measures were designed to undermine the clan system and the power of the clan chiefs. The Highland Dress Act banned the wearing of distinctive clan attire. Military service to the clan chief—the traditional method of "paying rent" for farmland—was forbidden. As real rents inevitably climbed, many tenants were forced from their land and clan chiefs lost some of their authority.

In addition, as agricultural methods improved in the Scottish Highlands, farmers ceased choosing farmland by lottery each spring and instead worked the same plots each year. Cooperation declined as farmers strove to improve and expand their own plots. The introduction of the metal plow drastically decreased the amount of labor needed for farming. Lowlanders soon introduced sheep to the Highlands. "Enclosures" followed, as farmland was fenced in to create pastures for grazing. Finally, the spread of the new inoculation process to curb death from smallpox combined with other factors to bring about considerable population growth. There was not only less available land, but more people as well.

Before reaching the more plentiful land of Carolina, the Highland Scots, like other transatlantic migrants, had to endure a long and grueling ocean voyage. Often it was this voyage, not the actual settlement of land in Carolina, that proved most difficult for the immigrants. The journey could last from one to two months. Living quarters on shipboard were usually below deck—damp, dark, and airless. At times disease rampaged among the tightly housed Highlanders. Ship captains often violated their contracts and failed to supply the food they had promised. Mortality rates on these voyages were notoriously high. In *The Highland Scots of North Carolina*, Duane Meyer describes the experience of a shipful of Scots in 1774, journeying to North Carolina via the West Indies aboard the *Jamaica Packet*:

The settlers had been forced to leave the Highlands because of high rents. Crowded in a small compartment below deck, the passengers were once confined for a nine-day period during a sea storm. The compartment was ventilated only by the cracks in the deck above them, which also allowed the sea to run in when the deck was awash. According to contract, they were to have received each week one pound of meat, two pounds of oatmeal, a small quantity of biscuit, and some water. The provisions actually supplied them consisted of spoiled pork, moldy biscuit, oatmeal, and brackish water. The passengers were fortunate to have potatoes, which were eaten raw and used to supplement their diet. For this fare and these accommodations, they were charged double the usual transportation fees because it was late October and all the other ships had gone when they arrived. Having only enough money for the regular charges, they were forced to sell themselves to the ship owner as indentured servants in order to pay for their transportation. Poorly nourished as they were and dreading the prospect of indentured servitude, the unfortunate passengers were set upon by the crew at the crossing of the Tropic of Cancer. On threat of dragging the emigrants behind the ship with a rope, the sailors attempted to extort the little property they still possessed.

Scots bound for North Carolina almost invariably landed at Cape Fear. Unlike other North Carolina rivers, the lower Cape Fear was navigable by seagoing vessels for over twenty miles upstream. Although they disembarked at both Brunswick Town and Wilmington, the arriving Highlanders preferred the latter site because it placed them closer to the backcountry. After landing, they transferred their belongings to longboats, canoes, or other small craft and made their way up the Cape Fear River. Ninety miles upstream, at the site of present-day Fayetteville, they debarked for the last time.

For part of the eighteenth century, the city we now know as Fayetteville actually consisted of two different towns, Campbellton and Cross Creek. Cross Creek, founded about 1760, quickly became the commercial hub of the Cape Fear backcountry. The town's name derived from its location at the junction of two creeks that, according to folk tradition, crossed without mixing currents. In 1762 the colonial Assembly intended Campbellton to become the trading center of the upper Cape Fear, but because of the town's inferior location and late start, it never caught up with neighboring Cross Creek. Campbellton's deficiencies were not lost on residents of the surrounding county, a group of whom wrote: "The situation of Cross Creek is High, dry, and healthy, and accomodated with Excellent Water, & that of Campbellton, as laid out by act of Assembly, is mostly in a low, swampy situation, & the road from Cross Creek thereto is through a level clay ground, which from the constant intercourse of Wagons, is often rendered almost impassable for foot persons and extremely disagreeable to horse men." In order to allay these problems, Campbellton and Cross Creek merged in 1778 and in 1783 assumed the name of Fayetteville to honor General Lafayette, the French aristocrat who served in the patriot cause during the American Revolution.

Although those Highlanders who were merchants or artisans settled in the town of Cross Creek, most of the immigrants took up farmland in the sur-

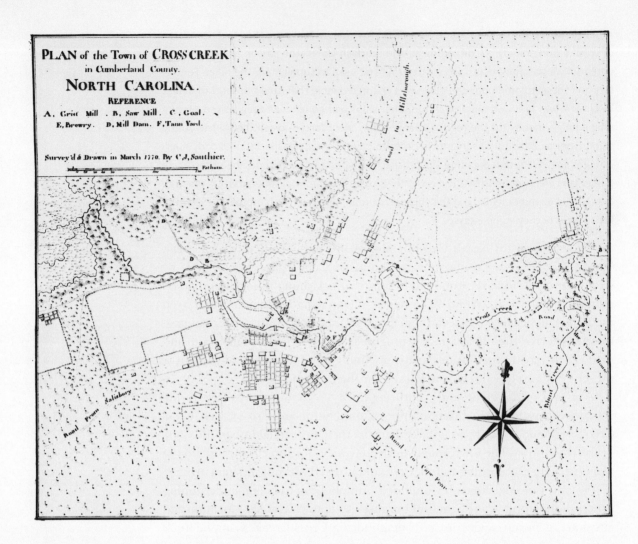

PLAN of the Town of CROSS CREEK
in Cumberland County.
NORTH CAROLINA.
REFERENCE
A. Grist Mill . B, Saw Mill . C , Goal .
E, Brewry . D, Mill Dam . F, Tann Yard .

Survey'd & Drawn in March 1770. By C J, Sauthier.

C. J. Sauthier's "Plan of the Town of Cross Creek" (1770)

rounding countryside. Some newcomers, such as those who had been aboard the *Jamaica Packet*, arrived as indentured servants and farmed the land of others. But those who could pay their transportation to the colony usually bought their own land. Fields had to be cleared and homes built before the first seeds could be sown. Like the Indians described by John Lawson years before, farmers in the Carolina backcountry cleared their land by girdling, not cutting, the trees. The stumps and trees left in the fields made plowing difficult. Most settlers relied on hoes in the early years. The crops Highland Scots produced along the upper Cape Fear were similar to those grown in the Albemarle. Corn predominated among foodstuffs. Legumes, wheat, flax, oats, potatoes, and tobacco could also be found in backcountry fields.

In the Highlands of Scotland, where wood was scarce, homes were built of stone and sod; wooden furniture was rare. Highland Scots burned peat in a central pit for heat and let the smoke rise through a hole in the roof. In North Carolina, however, wood was so abundant that settlers from the British Isles began referring to it as "lumber," their term for anything useless, cumbersome, and in the way. Highlanders on the upper Cape Fear built log homes chinked with clay. They constructed lofts, floors, and porches of wood. Hardwood logs were burned in fireplaces for warmth in winter.

By the time of the American Revolution, as many as 10,000 Highland Scots may have settled along the Cape Fear and its tributaries. There they found an abundance of land and resources unheard of in their native Scotland. But it was not just newcomers from Wales and the Scottish Highlands who swelled North Carolina's population in the mid-eighteenth century. While these settlers pushed back the Cape Fear frontier, Scotch-Irish and German immigrants poured into North Carolina by another route: the Great Wagon Road.

THE GREAT WAGON ROAD

After 1735, as the supply of land grew short in colonies farther north, numerous farmers from Pennsylvania, Maryland, and Virginia began packing their possessions and making the long journey to the North Carolina Piedmont. At first the migrants were predominantly Scotch-Irish. Then, in the mid-1700s, Pennsylvania Germans joined their neighbors on the tedious trek. As newcomers flocked southward, the population of the North Carolina backcountry grew at an unprecedented rate. The path to Carolina came to be called the Great Wagon Road. "The country," wrote colonist Nathaniel Rice in 1752, "is in a flourishing condition, the western parts settling very fast."

The diverse backgrounds of the immigrants shaped the North Carolina backcountry into a patchwork of religious and cultural enclaves. Many newcomers from Pennsylvania were Quakers. Newly arrived German families were predominantly Lutheran, with the notable exception of the Moravians. Immigrants of Scotch heritage were almost invariably Presbyterian. In addition, the Great Awakening, a tremendous religious revival that swept the English colonies in the mid-eighteenth century, resulted in the founding of several Baptist churches in the Carolina backcountry.

The Presbyterian Scotch-Irish were among the first Europeans to settle in the rolling hills of the North Carolina Piedmont. Surprisingly little is known of these early immigrants. Some of them were second-generation Americans whose parents had settled on the rich farmlands of Pennsylvania. Others were newly arrived migrants from Ulster who had landed in Philadelphia and immediately journeyed south. The Scotch-Irish appear to have taken up land throughout the North Carolina Piedmont, but, because they left so little evidence behind, the number that came to the colony is uncertain.

The Scotch-Irish were actually Lowland Scots who had moved to the region around Ulster, in northern Ireland, in the seventeenth and early eighteenth centuries. The English crown encouraged Scotch migration to Ulster in hopes that the Scots would "civilize" the Irish. Whether or not the Scots managed to alter the Irish, they certainly managed to advance themselves. By 1700 the flourishing Irish woolen industry had become a threat to the industry

Conestoga wagon. These wagons were developed in Conestoga, Pennsylvania, to transport settlers and their possessions over the rough trails to their new homes in the wilderness. The slightly up-curved ends prevented the shifting of loads going up and down hills, and the canvas hood protected the passengers from the elements.

in England. The crown soon passed the Woolen Act to protect the textile industry at home. Before long, economic depression set in around Ulster. Rents went up and crops failed. Disease destroyed numerous sheep. By 1718 the first group of Scotch-Irish immigrants had set out for North America, and further migrations followed.

Most of the early Scotch-Irish arrivals in America landed at Philadelphia and set up farms in Pennsylvania and Maryland. As these lands filled, some had to take up land in Virginia. In addition, the Scotch-Irish soon encountered competition from German immigrants (who, coming from "Deutschland," were incorrectly labeled as "Pennsylvania Dutch"). Indeed, wrote one English observer, the Scotch-Irish, "not succeeding so well in Pennsylvania as the more frugal and industrious Germans, sell their lands in that province to the latter, and take up new ground in the remote counties in Virginia, Maryland, and North Carolina." Many of the Scotch-Irish who moved to North Carolina were actually the younger children of immigrants who had settled land in Pennsylvania in earlier years. By the 1730s there was simply not enough land to go around; by 1735 the Scotch-Irish had begun entering North Carolina in significant numbers. They would continue to do so until the American Revolution.

The movement of Scotch-Irish and, eventually, of German immigrants

A wagon road

southward can be measured by the progress of the Great Wagon Road. Starting at the Schuylkill River in Philadelphia, the road would one day stretch all the way to the Savannah River at Augusta, Georgia—a distance of over 735 miles. In the 1720s, however, the road extended only to the Susquehanna River in Lancaster County, Pennsylvania. Before long it had crossed the Susquehanna, passed through the towns of York and Gettysburg, and entered the Maryland colony. From there the road took a steady course southwest, into the great Shenandoah Valley. By midcentury, the Virginia towns of Martinsburg, Winchester, and Staunton marked the road's route through the valley. Near present-day Roanoke the Great Road turned eastward and followed the Staunton River through the Blue Ridge. It then turned southward once more and entered North Carolina. By 1760 the road had passed through the Moravian settlement in Forsyth County and extended as far as the town of Salisbury,

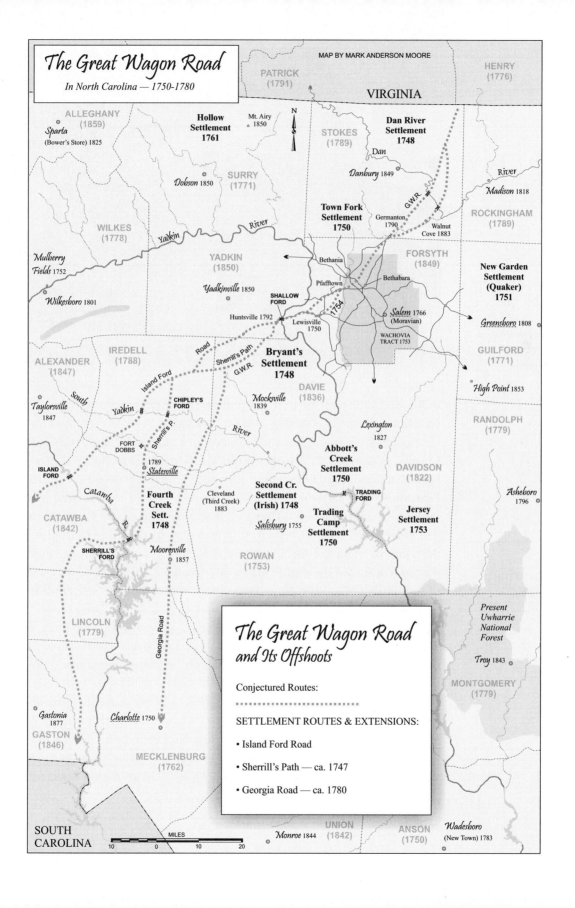

The Great Wagon Road

In North Carolina — 1750-1780

MAP BY MARK ANDERSON MOORE

VIRGINIA

PATRICK (1791)

HENRY (1776)

ALLEGHANY (1859)

Sparta (Bower's Store) 1825

Hollow Settlement 1761

Mt. Airy 1850

N

STOKES (1789)

Dan

Dan River Settlement 1748

Danbury 1849

River

Madison 1818

ROCKINGHAM (1789)

Dobson 1850

SURRY (1771)

Town Fork Settlement 1750

Germanton 1790

G.W.R.

Walnut Cove 1883

WILKES (1778)

Yadkin

River

YADKIN (1850)

Bethania

Pfafftown

Bethabara

FORSYTH (1849)

New Garden Settlement (Quaker) 1751

Mulberry Fields 1752

Yadkinville 1850

SHALLOW FORD

Salem 1766 (Moravian)

Greensboro 1808

Wilkesboro 1801

Huntsville 1792

Lewisville 1750

1754

WACHOVIA TRACT 1753

GUILFORD (1771)

IREDELL (1788)

Road

Sherrill's Path

Bryant's Settlement 1748

ALEXANDER (1847)

Island Ford

G.W.R.

DAVIE (1836)

Mocksville 1839

High Point 1853

South

Yadkin

CHIPLEY'S FORD

RANDOLPH (1779)

Taylorsville 1847

River

Lexington 1827

ISLAND FORD

FORT DOBBS

Sherrill's P.

1789 *Statesville*

Abbott's Creek Settlement 1750

DAVIDSON (1822)

Asheboro 1796

Catawba

R.

Fourth Creek Sett. 1748

Cleveland (Third Creek) 1883

Second Cr. Settlement (Irish) 1748

TRADING FORD

Salisbury 1755

Trading Camp Settlement 1750

Jersey Settlement 1753

CATAWBA (1842)

Mooresville 1857

ROWAN (1753)

SHERRILL'S FORD

Present Uwharrie National Forest

LINCOLN (1779)

Georgia Road

Troy 1843

MONTGOMERY (1779)

Gastonia 1877

Charlotte 1750

GASTON (1846)

MECKLENBURG (1762)

The Great Wagon Road and Its Offshoots

Conjectured Routes:

. . . .

SETTLEMENT ROUTES & EXTENSIONS:

• Island Ford Road

• Sherrill's Path — ca. 1747

• Georgia Road — ca. 1780

SOUTH CAROLINA

MILES

10   0   10   20

UNION (1842)

Monroe 1844

ANSON (1750)

Wadesboro (New Town) 1783

Joel McLendon House (ca. 1760), Moore County, built by a Scotch-Irish migrant and mill owner

in Rowan County. From there it continued its southerly course through South Carolina and finally ended at Augusta, Georgia.

Scotch-Irish immigrants like Mary and Francis McNairy from Lancaster County, Pennsylvania, traveled down the Great Wagon Road to make their homes in the Carolina Piedmont. Like the Highland Scots on the upper Cape Fear, most were farmers in search of land. In 1761 the newlywed McNairys bought land on Horsepen Creek in Rowan County (later Guilford County) from Hermon Husband, who would later play a major role in the Regulator uprising. By 1762 the McNairys had constructed a two-room log home and started to improve their land, which two decades later would be part of the site of the Battle of Guilford Courthouse. Though the house itself stood for generations beside the revolutionary battlefield, it has since been moved to the yard of the Greensboro Historical Museum, where it is now open to visitors. The McNairys expanded their home to its present size as the family prospered over time. "The inhabitants here and about Guilford Courthouse," wrote an observer years after the arrival of the McNairys, "are chiefly Irish, being very courteous, humane and affable to strangers, as likewise are the inhabitants of the counties of Mecklenburg and Roan." Many Scotch-Irish settlers like the McNairys would later take part in the Regulator rebellion.

During the mid-eighteenth century, Pennsylvania Germans began joining the Scotch-Irish on the long journey down the Great Wagon Road to North

Francis McNairy House (ca. 1761), Greensboro, Guilford County

Carolina. For several decades after the settlement of New Bern in 1710, few Germans had entered the colony. But, by 1748, Germans too were being forced southward by the shortage of land in Pennsylvania.

On arriving in North Carolina, the Germans tended to cluster in communities where they shared cultural traits such as language and religion with other Germans. Although they took up land throughout the Piedmont, German immigrants favored the region we know as Rowan, Cabarrus, Davidson, and Davie Counties, between the modern-day cities of Winston-Salem and Charlotte. A large number of Germans settled in Alamance, Guilford, and Orange Counties as well. Much of the land in these counties belonged to Henry McCulloh. Because of a complex set of arrangements between McCulloh and Earl Granville, settlers who bought land from McCulloh often faced a brutal succession of fees. These included paying McCulloh for the land, paying Granville's agents for recording the sale in the county courthouse, and, finally, paying annual quitrents to Granville. Many of these fees, submitted to dishonest officials like Francis Corbin, owner of the Cupola House in Edenton, were illegal and extortionate.

One settler who may have paid such fees was Michael Braun. In 1758 Braun settled in the Rowan County town of Salisbury. Rowan County had been formed only five years before, in 1753, to accommodate the numerous migrants entering northern Anson County. The county court began meeting

Michael Braun House (ca. 1766), Rowan County

regularly and soon authorized the construction of a courthouse and prison. On 11 February 1755 the town of Salisbury was officially established. Governor Arthur Dobbs visited Salisbury the following summer while touring western North Carolina. After crossing the Yadkin, "a large, beautiful river where is a ferry," Dobbs traveled about six miles to Salisbury. "The town," he wrote, "is but just laid out, the courthouse built and seven or eight log houses erected." Michael Braun, a wheelwright, must have been a valuable addition to the town when he arrived from Pennsylvania three years later.

But Michael Braun did not remain in Salisbury for long. By 1766 he had completed a great stone house that still stands in eastern Rowan County. The two-story home clearly reflects Braun's Pennsylvania German heritage. Its layout, called the "Quaker Plan," was common in Pennsylvania. The kitchen is a single-story addition off the "great hall." Braun's first wife, Margarita, and later, his second wife, Eleanor, used the kitchen's huge stone fireplace for cooking and baking. A woodstove on the hall side shares the chimney. There can be little doubt that the Braun House is more substantial than were most German homes in the Carolina backcountry.

Unique among the German settlements was the Moravian community that grew up on the Wachovia Tract in present-day Forsyth County. The United Brethren, often called the Moravians, originated in fifteenth-century Bohemia, the region we know today as the Czech Republic. After persecution and near annihilation in the early seventeenth century, the descendants of the Brethren migrated from Bohemia to Saxony, where they settled on the estate of Count Zinzendorf in 1722. There at "Herrenhut" they reorganized and revitalized the 300-year-old faith. But before long they faced persecution once again. This, in combination with an increased interest in missionary work, led the Moravians to acquire a tract of land in the new English colony of Georgia, which was seeking European migrants. From 1735 to 1740 the Brethren built a thriving communal settlement and mission in Savannah. But after five years an outbreak of hostilities between England and Spain forced the pacifist Moravians to move elsewhere. The place they chose was Pennsylvania, where they established the towns of Nazareth and Bethlehem. From these towns the United Brethren did missionary work among both Indians and whites.

Because of their success in the Georgia and Pennsylvania colonies, the Moravians quickly earned a reputation as "sober, quiet, and industrious" colonists. In fact, they were such desirable settlers that in 1749 the English Parliament passed "an act for Encouraging the People known by the Name of Unitas Fratrem, or United Brethren, to settle in His Majesties Colonies in America." This led Earl Granville to propose to the Moravians the possibility of a settlement in North Carolina. In 1752 Bishop August Gottlieb Spangenberg toured North Carolina from Edenton to the Blue Ridge in order to choose a site for the proposed community. He selected a 98,985-acre tract in Rowan (now Forsyth) County, which the church purchased for £500 and named "Wachovia," meaning "peaceful valley."

On 8 October 1753 a company of fifteen men set out for Wachovia from Bethlehem. The party included a shoemaker, a cooper, a nurse, and several farmers, millwrights, and carpenters. These men were charged with the task of preparing the site for settlers arriving the next year. They reached Wachovia on 17 November. Two days later, the Brethren began work on the town, to be called "Bethabara," or "House of Passage": "The Brn. Nathanael and Jacob Loesch measured off eight acres of land which is to be cleared at once, so that wheat can be sown. Others began to gather the dead wood and build bonfires. The grindstone was set up, a cooper's bench, and washtrough made. The Brn. Gottlob, Nathanael, and Grube laid a floor of clapboards in our cabin, for the better protection of our goods."

Bishop August Gottlieb Spangenberg

The Brethren worked all winter long; in the spring they planted potatoes, beans, corn, barley, wheat, oats, millet, tobacco, flax, and cotton. Through the summer they cleared more fields, made churns and corncribs, and built stables, fences, cow pens, and a tannery. Crops were harvested in the fall. Finally in September, "much to our joy," additional settlers from Pennsylvania began to arrive.

This first Moravian settlement is now an archeological park near present-day Winston-Salem. Although a few eighteenth-century buildings have survived intact, the ruins of many structures have been excavated and stabilized. Here visitors can see the foundation of the original Brothers' House, the first building constructed in Bethabara. Just to the west stood the first pottery shop, built in 1755, where Gottfried Aust made utilitarian ware from clay mined at Manakosy Creek. An auxiliary building was constructed in 1756. The tavern, situated well to the north of the other buildings, was erected the same year.

The Moravians also built a great palisade around the settlement in 1756. Reconstructed at the site today, it was intended as protection from the Cherokees after the outbreak of the French and Indian War on the frontier. But the Cherokees never attacked the peace-loving Moravians, probably because the Brethren at Bethabara frequently fed hungry Cherokees and even cared for Cherokee wounded. (Farther west during the same year, Fort Dobbs was constructed on a site just northwest of modern Statesville in Iredell County. The small fort, now a state historic site, was built near the foothills of the Blue Ridge to protect Piedmont settlements such as Bethabara from Indian war parties. The fort was attacked only once, and it was dismantled after the war ended in 1763.)

Other structures at Bethabara reveal more local and regional history. The Brethren built a congregation store in 1756. In order to acquire manufactured goods, the Moravians carried thousands of pounds of wheat, butter, and deerskins to Salisbury and then on to Charleston. The tailor shop, also constructed in 1756, housed Governor Tryon when he inspected the Bethabara settlement in 1767. Mrs. Tryon tested the famous Bethabara organ on the same visit. Governor Tryon stayed in the tailor's house again in 1771, after defeating the downtrodden Regulators at the Battle of Alamance.

Indians described the town of Bethabara as "the Dutch fort where there are good people and much bread." Moravian records state that around noon of 4 March 1758 some thirty Cherokees arrived in Bethabara "pretty hungry" and were given dinner at a cost of eight pence each and supper at six pence each. A month later, sixty Indians appeared in the town. The Cherokees who visited Bethabara in 1774 and heard an organ playing were certain that chil-

dren were hidden in the instrument singing. The Moravians opened it for them to see that there was no deception.

The United Brethren at Bethabara lived communally, with men and women, single and married, fulfilling separate roles in separate "choirs." Each individual worked for the good of the entire community. Decisions were made in group meetings. The United Brethren chose lifestyles, careers, and even marriage partners according to community needs, the advice of the group meeting, and the will of God as revealed in the drawing of lots. They believed in a fundamental equality among all people, perhaps most clearly expressed in the Bethabara graveyard. Here one sees identical rows of inconspicuous flat stones, each marking a seed planted in "God's Acre." With the creation of a larger, more commercial Moravian settlement at nearby Salem in the 1760s and 1770s, another "God's Acre" would be created. "It is our opinion," declared the Moravians about establishing Salem, "that Bethabara should be a farming community, not a commercial center, as otherwise there is a danger

At Fort Dobbs, built in 1756 in Iredell County, colonists fought a skirmish (1760) against Indians during the French and Indian War. The fort was abandoned in 1763. These present-day reenactors are demonstrating weapons and tactics of the period.

that building and growth there might stand in the way of the new town. . . . Furthermore, it was determined by lot that we are to let our Brethren and Sisters in America know that the Saviour wills that Salem is to be the place in Wachovia for commerce and the professions, and they are to be moved thither from Bethabara." For over two centuries, deceased members of the Salem congregation have been brought to "God's Acre" from the church in town, accompanied by a small brass band, and laid to rest on the hillside. Each departed Moravian is buried not in a family plot, but among the choir members with whom they lived and worked: single men, single women, married men, or married women.

Clearly, the United Brethren at Bethabara were different from other mid-eighteenth-century colonists in the North Carolina Piedmont. They refused to bear arms; they lived communally; they called each other "sister" and "brother." But, despite their differences, the Moravians also had much in common with the settlers around them. Like their Scotch-Irish and German neighbors, and like the Highland Scots in the upper Cape Fear region, the Moravians were first attracted to North Carolina by the availability of vast tracts of land. Also like many of their neighbors, they had migrated from Pennsylvania and did not adhere to the Anglican faith.

Benjamin Franklin estimated as early as 1763 that Pennsylvania had lost 10,000 families, or 40,000 people, to North Carolina. Certainly Maryland and Virginia lost numerous colonists as well. By the time of the American Revolution, the German population of North Carolina numbered anywhere from 8,000 to 15,000 and constituted between 10 and 30 percent of the white backcountry population. Many, perhaps even most, of the remaining white inhabitants of the backcountry were of Scotch-Irish heritage. The Great Wagon Road, more than any other route of entry, had contributed to North Carolina's phenomenal eighteenth-century growth. By 1775 the colony's population would reach 209,550, over six times what it had been in 1730.

THE RISE OF A BACKCOUNTRY ELITE

9

In the generation between 1750 and the American Revolution, settlers surged into the North Carolina backcountry. "Inhabitants flock in here daily," wrote the colony's governor in 1751. Some of these migrants stopped at the Eno River, near the site of Occaneechi, an Indian village John Lawson had visited half a century before. Here a settlement began that would soon become an economic and political center of the backcountry. Known eventually as Hillsborough, the town became a focal point for the deep-seated Regulator controversy that shook the colony in the decade before the American Revolution.

In 1752 North Carolina authorities established Orange County, reaching south from the Virginia border and embracing all of what is now Alamance, Caswell, Chatham, Durham, and Person Counties, as well as part of present Guilford, Randolph, Rockingham, and Wake Counties. For newcomers from the north and east, the locale seemed notably isolated at first. When the William Few family moved from Maryland to the banks of the Eno in 1758, eleven-year-old William Jr. was struck by the region's undeveloped state. "In that country at that time," he wrote in his autobiography many years later, "there were no schools, no churches or parsons, or doctors, or lawyers; no stores, groceries or taverns, nor do I recollect to have seen during the first two years any officer, ecclesiastical, civil, or military, except a justice of the peace, a constable, and two or three itinerant preachers. The justice took cognizance of their controversies to a small amount, and performed sacerdotal functions of uniting by matrimony. There were no poor laws nor paupers. Of the necessaries of life there were great plenty, but no luxuries."

In 1767 Governor William Tryon wrote to the Earl of Shelburne concerning Hillsborough, "I am of opinion it will be in a course of a few years the most considerable of any inland town in this province." By this time there were already more than 13,000 white inhabitants and 700 enslaved blacks in Orange County. Almost overnight, to the amazement of coastal merchants and politicians from Williamsburg to Charleston, Orange had become one of the most

Colonel William Few

populous counties in North Carolina. The county seat of Hillsborough became known as the "capital of the backwoods."

As in earlier generations, it was the prospect of land that brought rapid settlement, but most of the newcomers were yeoman farmers who differed somewhat from the dominant class farther east. They were more often Presbyterians, Baptists, Quakers, or Moravians than Anglicans. They owned fewer slaves and smaller tracts of land. In Orange County in the mid-1760s, three out of every four property holders owned between 100 and 500 acres of land. Already a few landowners—one in twenty—controlled more than 1,000 acres, but the earliest fortunes were not to be acquired by farmers.

A small network of Hillsborough merchants, lawyers, and county officials prospered first, often at the direct expense of farm families working to clear their land. A decade after its founding, the Eno River town had become the "metropolis of the county, where all the public business was done." According to William Few, the town included "two or three small stores and two or three ordinary taverns." Here newcomers from Virginia, Maryland, and Pennsylvania could obtain crucial supplies and establish credit.

Predictable frontier tensions between debtors and creditors were heightened by a severe shortage of hard currency throughout North Carolina. With little gold or silver circulating in the colony in the early 1760s, backcountry residents were hurt badly. Low prices for their crops meant little cash income. Yet, without cash, they stood to lose everything when time came to pay—in cash—their debts or taxes. Even if a person "has but one horse to plow with, one bed to lie on, or one cow to give a little milk for his children," declared an outraged George Sims in 1765, "they must all go to raise money which is not to be had."

The number of civil cases brought before the Orange County Court climbed from 223 in 1762–63 to 576 in 1764–65. In a petition to Governor Tryon, Orange County inhabitants claimed the defendants in these cases "were generally ignorant men," who were "in such necessitous Circumstances that their utmost industry could scarce afford a wretched subsistence to their Families, much less enable them to engage in uncertain Law Suits, with the rich and powerful."

When such defendants could not stave off claims or borrow money to meet them, their property was seized by the sheriff, usually at a value well in excess of the money due. Backcountry residents complained not only that "negroes, horses, cattle, hogs, corn, beds, and household furniture" were taken as recompense for debts and taxes, but also that these items were "sold for one tenth of their value" at public auctions—frequently to the friends, family, and cohorts of public officials. In the words of William Few, whose father soon lost most of his property to a Hillsborough merchant, "a fair field was opened for the lawyers."

Among the most enterprising of the lawyers to enter this "fair field" was Francis Nash, the youngest son of a Virginia planter, who became county court clerk in 1763 and was soon an adjutant in the local militia company. In the fall of 1766 Hillsborough was named the permanent seat of the county court. In the preceding eighteen months, Nash's firm had already filed more than twenty suits before the court. His older brother Abner also ventured south to share in the legal and mercantile prospects. Francis Nash established ties with Ralph MacNair, one of the town's newly arrived Scottish merchants, and obtained lots along Margaret Lane near the courthouse. (The Cameron-Nash Law Office in Hillsborough [see Part II, Chapter 4] was built in 1801 by Nash's great-nephew, Duncan Cameron.)

The opportunities for lawyers and officials in Hillsborough were in large part a result of the increased presence of merchants. William Few recalled that before long "merchants were . . . induced to establish stores that contained a good assortment of European merchandise." William Johnston, for example, arrived from Scotland around 1760 and opened a store with James Thackston across from the courthouse on the southwest corner of Churton and King Streets. He was a relation of Gabriel Johnston, the colony's former governor, and a nephew of Samuel Johnston of Edenton, who would later be North Carolina's first elected U.S. senator and one of the early governors of the state.

William Johnston did not hesitate to use his family ties to consolidate his commercial situation. In 1768 he opened a store at Snow Hill, seventeen miles northeast of Hillsborough on the road to Virginia. As a junior partner he engaged young Richard Bennehan, a Virginia native who had been selling merchandise in Petersburg and therefore had good commercial ties to Edenton, Halifax, and a number of Virginia towns as well. Bennehan managed the Snow Hill shop with such adroitness that he became a merchant in his own right. After the Revolution, he became one of the largest landowners in Orange County and founded Stagville Plantation, now a historic site north of Durham.

The handful of aspiring lawyers and prospering merchants in the backcountry consolidated their power through close association with a third, scarcely separable, category of nonfarmers: public officials. Citizens who filled such local positions as sheriff, constable, town commissioner, and overseer of the roads were appointed or nominated by justices of the county court. It was accepted practice to hold more than one public office at a time and to use all such posts for private gain. Governor Tryon himself conceded that "the sheriffs have embezzled more than one-half of the public money ordered to be raised and collected by them."

Richard Bennehan. Painting by an unknown artist, owned by Mrs. John Laborisse.

Colonel Edmund Fanning

The very tax structure that these officials enforced was itself extremely regressive. It protected the wealthy and squeezed the less affluent, giving rise to increasing demands that each individual should be allowed to "pay in proportion to the profits arising from his Estate." Residents of Anson and Mecklenburg Counties pointed out the inequity of the poll tax, which taxed everyone alike regardless of wealth. "A man that is worth 10,000£ pays no more than a poor back settler that has nothing but the labour of his hands to depend on for his daily support," explained one frustrated citizen. A county tax levied by justices of the peace supplemented the poll tax and added to the tax burden.

The same men who flaunted money acquired by openly embezzling taxes were equally flagrant in charging exorbitant fees. Tyree Harris, the Orange County sheriff between 1766 and 1768, not only collected colonial, county, and parish taxes, but he also received fees for making arrests and obtained commissions for acting as an inspector. He was a preferred customer at the Snow Hill store of Johnston and Bennehan, and when he fled the region before the Revolution he sold Richard Bennehan his home at the confluence of the Flat River and the Eno, supposedly the first brick house in Orange County.

The most notorious of the region's "designing men" was undoubtedly Edmund Fanning. A graduate of Yale who arrived in the backcountry in the early 1760s to practice law, he was what later generations would come to call a "carpetbagger." In less than ten years, according to his enemies, he "amass'd a fortune, of near ten thousand pounds Sterling, and all out of the people." Fanning served as Orange County assemblyman and justice of the Superior Court, while collecting a salary as a colonel in the militia. In addition, he turned a steady profit as the register of deeds. In 1768 local farmers protested that "We the Inhabitants of Orange County pay larger Fees for recording Deeds than any of the adjacent Counties and many other Fees more than the Law allows."

With the fees he collected, Fanning built himself an ample home on Lot 23 in Hillsborough, across from the present-day Colonial Inn. Here he lived in conspicuous splendor, purchasing goods from his associate William Johnston or ordering them from afar. A letter from Fanning to Richard Bennehan, while the latter was still in Petersburg, placed an order for a chair and gold lace from Halifax.

The pretensions of the Yale-educated lawyer soon became more than local farmers could bear. They composed a song heard at weddings and public gatherings in the area that made explicit reference to the flourish of gold lace:

> When Fanning first to Orange came
> He looked both pale and wan
> An old patched coat upon his back

An old mare he rode on.
Both man and mare warn't worth five pounds
As I've often been told
But by his civil robberies
He's laced his coat with gold.

As for the "civil robberies" of Fanning and his lawyer-merchant-officeholder coterie, the time had come for the populace to "regulate" these grievances publicly.

10 REHEARSAL FOR REVOLUTION

While Edmund Fanning was building a handsome new home in Hillsborough and trimming his coats with gold lace in the late 1760s, other newcomers to the Carolina backcountry were having trouble making ends meet. Orange County inventories from the period show that the top 10 percent of all residents holding property controlled more than 40 percent of the total wealth, while the lowest 60 percent controlled scarcely 20 percent of the wealth. Enslaved and indentured workers, with no property of their own, made up the bottom portion of backcountry society. At the top, a small elite was rapidly consolidating its wealth.

The resentment of Carolina freeholders at the rise and ostentation of a colonial elite coincided with the Stamp Act crisis that shook the British Empire in America in 1765. Public dissent swept the colonies that year in response to an imperial tax that many saw as the first step toward the subversion of their liberties as Englishmen. For some, the wave of protest promptly came to embrace the abuse of power within North Carolina itself. Citizens in Granville County petitioned the legislature for relief from the corrupt practices of local officials and were met with libel suits by the officials in return. In Orange County, resistance took root in August 1766, when a group of farmers banded together as the Sandy Creek Association and demanded—in the language of the Stamp Tax insurgency—that the North Carolina legislature hear their grievances against local officials who "carry on unjust Oppression." The association's broadside warned that power inevitably corrupts: those "set in Offices and vested with power" will always "oppress if . . . not called upon to give an account of their Stewardship." The Sandy Creek Association called on each neighborhood of Orange County to "meet together and appoint one or more men to attend a general meeting" where it could "be judiciously enquired whether the free men of this Country labor under any abuses of power or not."

The general meeting was set for Maddock's Mill, just west of Hillsborough, prior to the November court session. No liquor would be allowed; propositions would be put in writing and debated freely "and proper measures used for amendment." Following procedures similar to those being used by New England townsmen at the same time, the farmers planned "in particular to examine into the publick Tax, and inform themselves of Every Particular thereof." The association invited "Representatives, Vestry-men, and other Officers" to the meeting and requested that the officials "give the Members of the said Meeting what Information and Satisfaction they can."

Colonel Fanning rejected the association's "jurisdiction" to discuss public matters and banned the attendance of public officials at the general meeting. To join in the assembly with dissidents would give credence to their grievances, he said, charging that the movement, despite its orderliness, appeared too much "like an insurrection." Throughout the fall the situation deteriorated, as Fanning and his associates retaliated against the organized questioning of increased public fees. Hermon Husband, the prominent farmer who helped form the association and remained active throughout the ensuing controversies, recorded bitterly, "The Bombs [Bums] now grew more and more Insulting, taking Unusual Distresses for Levies; taking double, treble, and four Times the Value."

Late in 1766, while most American colonists were celebrating the repeal of the notorious Stamp Act, North Carolina's backcountry farmers were dealt a new provocation. For decades the colonial government had had no fixed seat, but had traveled up and down the seaboard with the governor. A decade earlier, Governor Dobbs had made an effort to stabilize the government and turn a profit by locating the capital upon land that he owned, but authorities in London disallowed the scheme. Already there was growing pressure from the interior to name Hillsborough the seat of government on the basis of obvious population trends. But as early as 1733, some 270 inhabitants of Craven Precinct had petitioned the royal governor to establish the capital at New Bern. "We are sensible Edenton is for many reasons a very Inconvenient Place for the Seat of Government," the petitioners claimed, "and almost as much may be said against settling it on Cape Fear River. Therefore we humbly desire and hope your Excell*ᵧ* will take proper measures for fixing the seat of Governm*ᵗ* near the Centre of the Province which we suppose is on the South side of Neuse River." In December 1766 the North Carolina Assembly, dominated by planters and merchants from the east, attempted to "settle" the controversy: it appropriated £5,000 for the construction of a permanent mansion for Governor Tryon at the coastal town of New Bern.

New Bern was an acceptable site for a colonial capital in the eyes of the powerful planter interests of the northeast and southeast, with their differing origins and economies. But for the underrepresented settlers in the western Piedmont it seemed a real and symbolic offense. The proposed dwelling, which soon came to be called "Tryon's Palace," gave added focus to the discontent

Stamps used in accordance with England's Stamp Act of 1765. The act provoked agitation and defiance among North Carolinians—as well as colonists elsewhere—by placing a tax upon newspapers, legal documents, and other items, including playing cards.

*Residents of New Bern protest
the Stamp Act.*

of backcountry taxpayers. It linked their grievances against local authorities to the colonial officials on the coast who had appointed them. Moreover, it joined the matter of how public revenues were collected with the question of how public funds were spent.

"We want no such House, nor will we pay for it," wrote William Butler of Orange County, and others in the Piedmont shared his sentiments. Nonetheless in 1767 the Assembly allocated an additional £10,000 for the project, and construction began. When the residence was completed three years later despite bitter opposition, Governor Tryon had the temerity to thank "the Country for their Gifts of this very Elegant and Noble Structure . . . A Palace that is a public Ornament and Credit to the Colony, as well as an Honor to British America."

Although it burned in 1798, Tryon's Palace was reconstructed during the 1950s and is now an historic site open to the public. Called "truly elegant and noble" by the colonial Assembly in 1770, the palace owes its grand design to the English architect John Hawks, whose own eighteenth-century home still stands only two blocks away. Hawks did not withhold care—or taxpayers' money—in creating North Carolina's first permanent capitol: the painting bill alone came to £550.

Visitors approach the palace through massive English gates and proceed

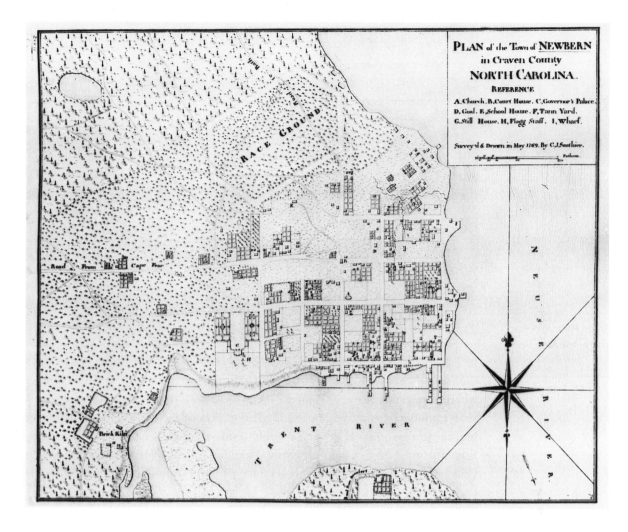

PLAN of the Town of NEWBERN
in Craven County
NORTH CAROLINA.
REFERENCE
A. Church. B, Court House. C, Governor's Palace.
D, Goal. E, School House. F, Tann Yard.
G. Still House. H, Flagg Staff. I, wharf.

Survey'd & Drawn in May 1769. By C.J.Sauthier.

C. J. Sauthier's "Plan of the Town of New Bern" (1769)

down a broad path to the elliptical front courtyard. Separate wings to the right and left contain offices and a huge kitchen, complete with a massive fireplace, a spitjack, and a beehive oven. The central building contains an opulent Council Chamber, with a mantel of sienna marble, as well as elegant living and dining quarters. As if to flaunt the colony's investment and his own ingenuity, the designer focused attention on the Great Stairs Hall, where a beautifully carved stairway ascends around three walls to the second floor without any visible support. Hawks's final bill for the entire enterprise made special mention of "Mahogany for ye Staircase."

Behind the main buildings, impressive gardens recreated in an eighteenth-century style stretch toward the meandering Trent River near its confluence with the broader Neuse. Handsome brick walls create a series of sanctuaries

*Tryon Palace
(1767–70), New Bern*

where modern visitors, like royal officials, can lose themselves in the geometric symmetries so beloved by the English gentry of the Georgian era. Discreet marble statues look out over carefully tended flowers and shrubs from both England and America. Closely clipped hedges and dwarf trees grace the Green Garden. Fragrant and savory plants once used for cooking and medicine now prosper again in the Herb Garden.

Early in 1768, as John Hawks began to lay out this elaborate complex in New Bern, "the Rumour of giving the Governor *Fifteen Thousand Pounds*, to build him a House" had reached the backcountry. What Tryon would call "a lasting Monument of the Liberality of this Country" seemed an expensive abomination to settlers in the west. Indeed, wrote a Mecklenburg County resident in a letter to the Boston *Chronicle*, "not one man in twenty of the four most populous Counties will ever see the house when built." The slaveholding planters and established merchants of the eastern counties would keep the seat of colonial government in the east and tax the more numerous backcountry farmers for its creation. Word of this decision, coming on top of harsh existing grievances in the Piedmont, simply confirmed the spreading belief that the governor and members of the Assembly were men "whose highest Study is the Promotion of their Wealth; and with whom the Interest of the Publick, when it comes in competition with their private Advantages, is suffered to Sink."

As a new wave of dissent swept the backcountry, the organizers began to call themselves "Regulators." The term had been used by farmers in England's Thames River Valley several years earlier and was in current use in South Carolina. There it was applied to the backcountry elite who wished to "regulate" their social inferiors and impose law and order in the wilderness counties. In North Carolina, in contrast, those called Regulators—following a long colonial tradition of organized public opposition to misrule—sought to regulate flagrant abuses of power by their social superiors.

As a Quaker and organizer of the now-defunct Sandy Creek Association, Hermon Husband found the new group "too hot and rash, and in some things not legal." Conditions in 1768, he wrote later, had given "rise to what was commonly called the Mob; which in a little time altered to that of the Regulators." People joined the new association "by Hundreds, and it spread every Way like Fire till it reached Sandy-Creek." Its members refused to pay taxes until "satisfied they are agreeable to Law" and proposed to "pay no Officer any more Fees than the Law allows." By these means they hoped to "bring Things to a true Regulation, according to the true Intent and Meaning hereof in the Judgement of the Majority of Us."

In this volatile atmosphere, Orange County sheriff Tyree Harris announced that during January and February he would receive taxes on two designated days at five successive places, and anyone who did not pay would be fined two shillings eight pence. "Everyone could see that this Harris' proclamation was quite insulting, as well as an Attempt to make Assess of us." wrote Hermon Husband, whose solid wealth and gift for sharp expression soon made him a strategic supporter of the movement. "This new law was calculated for the Sheriff's Ease," he said. The assessed farmers "were obliged to bring their Burdens to him" so that he and his deputies "might collect the Whole in ten Days sitting on their Greed, at Ease, in five places only."

Some citizens could not or would not meet these requirements, and in April 1768 violence flared. When the sheriff seized "a Mare, Saddle and Bridle" from an indebted farmer and put them up for sale to pay his taxes, a force of sixty or seventy Regulators gathered in Hillsborough. They reclaimed the mare and "fired a few Guns at the Roof of Colonel *Fanning's* House" on King Street. Fanning was in Halifax at the time, but he promptly commanded the arrest of Regulator William Butler and other leaders. Upon his return to Hillsborough, Colonel Fanning had Hermon Husband thrown in jail for "inciting" the band.

The arrests outraged the Regulators. Some 700 armed farmers gathered outside Hillsborough to demand the liberation of Butler and Husband. In fear for their lives, local officials released the men on bail. On the same day, Governor Tryon's personal secretary, Isaac Edwards, who lived in what is now the rear wing of the Nash-Hooper House, read a proclamation from the governor to the assembled Regulators. The governor, he said, "Would Protect and Redress them against any unlawful Extortions, or Oppressions of any Officer or Officers in the County; Provided they would disperse and Go Home." The Regulators deemed the offer a fair one. "No sooner was the Word spoke, but the whole Multitude, as with one Voice, cried out, Agreed. That is all we want; Liberty to Make our grievances known."

In a petition dated 21 May 1768, the Regulators laid out their complaints to the governor. They insisted that the root of their troubles lay in the "unequal chances the poor and weak have in contentions with the rich and powerful." But, despite the promises of his secretary, Tryon was unwilling to deal with the Regulator organization. The Regulators in turn continued to violate the law, refusing to pay taxes and exorbitant legal fees. At last, on 6 July 1768, Governor Tryon himself arrived in Hillsborough to survey the situation. To appease the Regulators he issued a proclamation ordering public officials "not to demand or receive other Fees . . . than what was established by proper authority." The insurgents responded that the proclamation had no effect whatever. Corruption seemed worse than ever.

Tensions increased in September as the trials of Husband, Butler, and two other Regulators approached. Edmund Fanning and Francis Nash were to appear before the court on charges of extortion the same day. To protect the proceedings, Governor Tryon called out the militia. But, because the sympathies of many militiamen lay with the Regulators, he could muster only 1,461 men. On the day of the trial, 3,700 Regulators gathered around Hillsborough while the militia guarded the courthouse. Although Husband was acquitted by the court, Butler and the other Regulators received fines and jail sentences. Fanning and Nash, though convicted, were merely fined "a penny each and costs" for their crimes. The Regulators were livid at the outcome of the trials, but in the face of the well-armed militia they chose to disband.

For the next year, Carolina farmers sought redress by legal means. They petitioned the governor, paid their taxes, and worked to elect sympathetic assemblymen. To a limited extent they succeeded; Hermon Husband and several like-minded men were elected to the Assembly in 1769. But even this proved futile. Governor Tryon dissolved the Assembly in November, before the body had time to address the Regulators' complaints.

Late in 1769 the Regulators once again turned to direct action. Riots or other disturbances occurred in Edgecombe, Halifax, Johnston, Anson, and Rowan Counties. In 1770 the most serious riot of the Regulation broke out in Hillsborough, where numerous Regulators faced trial in the Orange County court. On Monday, 24 September, about 150 Regulators "appeared in Hillsborough, armed with clubs, whips loaded at the ends with lead or iron, and many other offensive weapons, and at once beset the courthouse." A spokesman stated their grievances to Judge Richard Henderson, and after half an hour of discussion, angry tempers gave way to violence. The Regulators pummeled a local attorney and then turned their attention to Colonel Fanning, who had climbed high upon the judge's chair for safety. According to a newspaper account, "They seized him by the heels, dragged him down the steps, his head striking very violently on every step, carried him to the door, and forcing him out, dragged him on the ground over stones and brickbats, struck him with their whips and clubs, kicked him, and spit and spurned at him." When Fanning took refuge in Johnston & Thackston's store across Churton Street, his assailants pelted the establishment with stones. The next day, the Regulator crowd marched to the colonel's house and, after destroying its contents, "took his wearing cloaths, stuck them on a pole, paraded them in triumph through the streets, and to close the scene, pulled down and laid his house in ruins."

One traveler to North Carolina, Ebenezer Hazard, recorded in his journal the following observation about Fanning: "People in North Carolina differ much respecting Govr Tryon's Conduct in the affair of the Regulators; some blame him & some them, & some both of them; but all agree that Col. Fanning was at the Botton of it: they say that he insisted upon & took larger Fees than the Law allowed; & that when he was in the Back Country he took money from them for Lands of which he promised to procure Grants for them; & when they complained to the Govr for Redress, he told them he would believe Col. Fanning's Word sooner than their Oath."

Conditions around Hillsborough, tumultuous through the winter, exploded into warfare in the spring of 1771. In March, Superior Court judges protested to Governor Tryon that they could not hold court in the Orange County town. Determined to subdue the Regulators once and for all, Tryon called out the militia. With great difficulty he managed to muster 1,000 men and marched them into Hillsborough on 9 May. Two days later, the army proceeded west to Alamance Creek in present-day Alamance County. Five miles away, 2,000 Regulators had gathered. Though poorly organized and short on guns and ammunition, the Regulators had twice as many troops as Tryon. Regulator leaders expected the governor to negotiate rather than fight. But Tryon was determined to force the issue. On 16 May the militia moved toward the Regulator camp. Tryon gave the Regulators one hour to surrender. When the skeptical insurgents replied "Fire and be damned!" Tryon ordered the militiamen to attack their fellow North Carolinians. Reluctant to shoot at poorly armed civilians with whom they felt kinship and sympathy, the militia hesi-

Governor William Tryon confronts the Regulators.

tated. The governor stood tall in his stirrups and repeated the command. "Fire!" he shouted, daring them to disobey. "Fire on them or on me!"

The guns of the militia spoke at last, and the Battle of Alamance had begun. The Regulators were wholly unprepared for armed conflict. Many withdrew from the scene when firing started. Fighting ceased in two hours. The Regulators had been soundly defeated. Alamance Battleground State Historic Site now commemorates the Regulators' stand against Tryon.

Several dozen persons died in the encounter. Tryon's militia wounded some 200 of the local "enemies" and captured fifteen of the supposed leaders. One person was hanged on the spot. On 15 May, Tryon marched the remaining captives back to Hillsborough with the militia. There the Royal Court found twelve of the fourteen men guilty of treason and sentenced them to be executed. Six later received pardons, but on 19 June the other six were taken in carts to a hillside east of town and hanged publicly before the militia and hundreds of onlookers. One of the six hanged was James Few, brother of William Few. Though a Quaker, James proclaimed himself "sent by heaven to release the world of oppression and to begin in Carolina." The remaining Few family moved to Georgia, where William became a leader in the American Revolution. Today, a solitary marker on a grassy knoll south of St. Matthew's Episcopal Church graveyard, indicates the site where the six Regulators were hanged.

Within five years of the Battle of Alamance, major actors in the War of the

Receipt for a reward given to Thomas Sitgreaves for the capture of Regulator leader Hermon Husband after Husband's expulsion from the General Assembly on 20 December 1770.

Regulation had left the colony. Hermon Husband escaped certain execution by fleeing to Pennsylvania, where two decades later he would lead another uprising of backcountry farmers, the Whiskey Rebellion. Other Regulators dispersed to the north and west, while some of the officials whose high taxes and contempt had goaded farmers to fury also left the region. Tyree Harris moved to Caswell County; Edmund Fanning returned to the North as secretary to William Tryon, who became the last colonial governor of New York. When rebellion swept all the colonies in 1776, many such antagonists of the Regulators joined the Tory side.

Was the Regulator Movement crushed in 1771 a rehearsal for the Revolution? Colonists elsewhere were growing more shrill in their attacks on British corruption and more open in their defiance of imperial rule. By 1775 extralegal committees and conventions controlled and regulated life throughout the American colonies: they supervised courts, dictated appointments, commanded militias, and levied taxes. The goals of some of the armed and extralegal committees of the rebellion could not have displeased the Regulators. The revolutionary convention from Mecklenburg not only opposed "everything that leans to aristocracy or power in the hands of the rich . . . exercised to the oppression of the poor," but also favored the exclusion of lawyers, clerks, and sheriffs from the legislature.

Yet, for all the radicalism of their rhetoric, many who joined the independence movement against England wanted no part of a social revolution at home. An authentic civil struggle, modeled on the Regulator campaign against the "rich and powerful"—against the "designing Monsters in iniquity" who through fraud and "threats and menaces" extracted their "Fortunes . . . from others"—held no charm whatsoever for the planters and merchants who assumed the leadership of the patriots in North Carolina. In the end, neither the Regulation nor the Revolution settled the question of whether the public or the privileged would rule. A standoff in the 1770s, that battle was destined to be fought again and again by North Carolinians and Americans for generations to come.

Harry L. Watson

Part II

AN INDEPENDENT PEOPLE

NORTH CAROLINA, 1770-1820

OVERVIEW

In 1770 North Carolina sheltered a remarkable human diversity. Parts of the Albemarle Sound region had been settled by the English for more than a century. There and along the lower reaches of the Cape Fear River wealthy farmers and their African American slaves had laid the basis for a plantation society. In the western mountains, Cherokee Indians continued their traditional ways of life with little or no interference from distant whites. In between, English, Scotch-Irish, German, and Highland Scottish settlers carved out new homes in the dense forest. The inhabitants of the largest towns differed markedly from their rural neighbors in their work, their social position, and their personal opportunity. The people of North Carolina were not clearly united in politics, language, religion, or any other cultural characteristics. In many ways it would be difficult to think of them as members of the same society.

If North Carolinians shared any characteristic besides diversity, it was their basic reliance on the outside world for a variety of cultural and commercial necessities. For the most part, Carolinians supplied themselves with the corn, meat, shelter, and clothing that were necessary for simple survival, but their self-sufficiency was more a condition of wilderness isolation than true independence. Sophisticated products and ideas almost always came from elsewhere. Iron, salt, and rum came from the schooners that docked at New Bern, Edenton, and Wilmington. Fashions, furniture, and elaborate building designs came from sketches published in Europe. Religious authority came from clergymen born and trained abroad, and governmental power came from Great Britain in the person of a royal governor.

By 1820 North Carolina's diversity and dependency had begun to change. A common language and economy prevailed among most of the children of the white pioneers, regardless of their parents' ethnic origins. Assorted African tribesmen suffered a more painful process of assimilation with each other in the rigors of slavery. Considerable economic dependency on outsiders persisted, but activist citizens were pushing hard for reforms to remedy this condition. Waves of religious revivalism had brought a fundamental shift in popular worship. Most important, North Carolina had fought and won a war for po-

Harvesting wheat

litical independence and had joined the federal Union. Remnants of the older state of affairs persisted, but nineteenth-century North Carolina had become an independent society.

The changes had come about as part of an economic and political transformation. The first generation of pioneers had adopted a self-sufficient lifestyle as a necessity for survival. They built their homes from logs, fed their livestock from the forest floor, raised their own supplies of food and fiber, and sold a tiny surplus to obtain what they could not make themselves. Gradually this lifestyle had begun to give way to the widening world of the market economy. Farmers had raised more and more crops for sale and purchased increased supplies from the stores they found in growing towns and villages. As years passed and civilization developed, farmers sought ways to obtain more store-bought goods without sacrificing the cherished independence of self-sufficient freeholders.

The secret to successful commercial farming was labor, for the farmer who commanded the most laborers could raise the greatest surplus. Beyond the members of the farmer's family, almost all available workers were slaves; the institution of slavery consequently grew and strengthened as expanding farms became plantations. Formidable geographical handicaps drove up freight rates for exported plantation products and thus kept North Carolina's planters less prosperous than their counterparts elsewhere. Planters nonetheless did their best to establish the polished and genteel world of a leisured aristocracy.

Bolstered by their property, education, and personal connections, they joined with merchants, lawyers, and other urban leaders to dominate the public affairs of the colony and later the state. One visitor to North Carolina in the 1770s observed: "Almost every man in this country has been the fabricator of his own fortune, and many are very opulent. Some have obtained their riches by commerce, others by the practice of law, which in this province is peculiarly lucrative, and extremely oppressive; but most have acquired their possessions by cropping farming, and industry."

North Carolina's elite did not emerge without challenge. Slaves resisted their masters' power in a variety of ways both overt and covert. In the late 1760s, moreover, a movement of western farmers who called themselves Regulators violently protested the undemocratic features of North Carolina's economic and political order. Commanded by royal governor William Tryon, eastern militiamen crushed the Regulators in 1771 at the Battle of Alamance. During the American Revolution, westerners and smaller farmers pushed for a more democratic political system, but they achieved only limited success. For the most part, yeomen who could not match the resources of the largest slaveholders either kept silent or did their best to imitate the gentry. As they did so, society in North Carolina gradually shifted from the frontier stage and took on the contours of the antebellum South.

During this long-term process of social transformation, other developments brought North Carolina through a political revolution. British leaders sought to tax the colonies and to reduce them more directly to imperial control. These efforts sparked a bitter resistance because the colonists' intellectual heritage and their way of life had bred in them a fierce love of individual and collective liberty.

As they won their political independence, free North Carolinians sought to define the character of their new republic. Some gentlemen among the educated elite relied on human reason and the historical lessons of ancient republics as sufficient guides for the young state and its rulers. Less prominent Carolinians seemed more cautious and hearkened to Protestant evangelists who taught that personal and national salvation would come only through faith in the word of God. Less speculative political thinkers warned that new technology and improvements in transportation were vital to the state's prosperity, regardless of its ideological or theological preferences. The debate over republicanism was far from finished when the second decade of the nineteenth century ended, but all parties in the discussion still appealed to the ideal of personal independence for white freemen, in an unchanging society based on slavery and agriculture.

As they moved through half a century of social and political change, North

Carolinians left signs of their steady transformation in the buildings and other material products of their culture. Log cabins gave way to frame cottages, and changing private homes revealed a shift in ideal family arrangements. Architectural fashions from distant capitals translated themselves into appropriate forms for Carolina farmhouses. Cultural monuments like schools, churches, and public buildings displayed the tastes and ideals of an independent people.

Changes in politics, economics, religion, and ideology had an impact on Carolina lifestyles, just as the daily lives of the people exerted a pervasive pressure on the direction of larger historical events. Visitors to North Carolina's historic sites can witness the history of an era as they follow the physical evolution of the way we lived in the years that saw the establishment and early growth of the American republic.

THE FOREST, THE INDIANS, AND THE YEOMAN FAMILY

2

In the winter of 1783–84, German traveler Johann David Schöpf made a trip through the former British colony of North Carolina. In the account he later published, Schöpf searched for an image to convey his first impressions of the newly independent state. "The country . . . must be imagined as a continuous measureless forest," he began, "an ocean of trees in which only here and there cultivated spots, what are called plantations . . . are to be seen." A decade earlier, a British army officer had had a similar reaction. J. F. D. Smyth recalled "an universal gloomy shade, rendered dismal by the intermixing branches of the lofty trees, which overspread the whole country, and [which] the sun never pervades." Another voyager reported that "the mariners, going upon the coast in spring, have smelt the pines when several leagues at sea." Ebenezer Hazard, a Philadelphian, spoke more matter-of-factly. "The Country is a Pine Barren," he noted in his diary. "I have frequently rode 5 & 6 miles in this Journey without seeing any Sign of Cultivation." On another occasion, Hazard wrote a memo to himself in his diary after a hard lesson: "Take no more short cuts in North Carolina—Had to cross two Mill Dams & met with great Difficulty. Rode through a very gloomy Cypress Swamp:—lost my way—."

When they agreed on little else, travelers to North Carolina in the 1770s and 1780s concurred about the forest. Trees were everywhere: tangled oaks and cypresses where the ground was swampy in the east; stately pines where it was dry. To the west, oaks, hickories, walnuts, chestnuts, poplars, and an astonishing variety of other species took over, but always there were woods—dark, forbidding, and dense. By 1770 permanent European settlers had lived in this environment for over a hundred years, but still the wilderness felt very close. Whatever the people of North Carolina accomplished in the name of civilization—the houses they built, the fields they cleared and planted, the towns they made by the riverbanks—all took shape against a backdrop of seemingly endless forest.

The Joyce Kilmer Memorial Forest, in Graham County, is one of the very few patches of completely virgin timberland still remaining in the state today. Nourished by especially high rainfall in the area, trees in this 3,500-acre tract

Early settlers arriving in North Carolina. Courtesy of William S. Powell.

have grown to immense proportions. The tulip poplars are especially impressive, but other hardwoods and hemlocks are prevalent as well. The forests that dominated the eastern North Carolina landscape in the eighteenth century consisted of thick and lofty longleaf pines, widely spaced and bare of branches for as many as fifty feet up the trunk. Dense shade and occasional brushfires eliminated undergrowth, so the traveler could see for a mile or more beneath the deep canopy of needled branches. Some observers claimed that the forest floor was so clear and flat that a coach and four horses could travel off the road in any direction, for an indefinite distance. The steep terrain and tangled growth of the Appalachian forest creates a different effect, but the visitor in Joyce Kilmer can sense more fully than elsewhere the overpowering presence of the wilderness described by Schöpf, Smyth, and Hazard.

To a large extent, the people of North Carolina made a living from the trees around them. Pines were scarred with V-shaped notches and basins were hacked in each trunk to catch the flowing sap. When collected and poured into barrels, the sap sold well as turpentine or, when distilled, as spirits of turpentine. These tapped pines eventually died, and when the split lengths of fallen lightwood were baked in earthen ovens, black tar oozed into holes scooped out for the purpose. Tar that was boiled or burned left a residue called "pitch," an even more valuable substance. Tar, pitch, and turpentine were called "naval stores," and they found a ready market as waterproofing materials in an age of wooden sailing vessels. Water-driven sawmills also cut pine logs into planks, while oak and cypress trees were the raw materials for vast quantities of hand-made barrel staves and shingles. Skilled coopers fashioned barrels from many of these staves to hold the naval stores, while large cargoes of other staves were exported.

Lumber and naval stores were generally floated to market on rafts and flat-boats, but many North Carolinians lived too far from navigable water to make this practice feasible. These settlers exploited the forest by raising livestock, a product that carried itself to market. Cattle and hogs wandered freely in the woods and fed on nuts, roots, cane, reeds, and Spanish moss. In the fall roundup, every farmer identified his stock by the slits he had made in the animals' ears. Smyth reported on this practice of labeling livestock. "Throughout the middle and back settlements of America," he told his countrymen, "there is no other criterion to ascertain the property of black cattle, sheep, and hogs, but earmarks alone; and of horses, than brands with red hot irons, and earmarks also. Each person's mark differs from another, and they are all severally recorded by the clerk of the county courts wherein they reside." After marking the yearlings, the backcountry herdsman drove the increase of his stock to town. His market might be located in North Carolina, but it could just as easily be Charleston, Norfolk, or even Philadelphia. At the port, the animals were sometimes fattened with grain, then slaughtered and pickled in brine, packed into huge oak casks, and rolled into the hold of an oceangoing vessel. Like lumber and naval stores, beef and pork were forest-grown commodities that were crucial to export commerce and made the fortune of many an urbane merchant and courtly planter.

Passing travelers noted the economic importance of the forest eventually, but at first sight it was the scattered tiny fields and not the efficient use of forest resources that reminded observers of the presence of civilization. In the 1770s tobacco was still mostly confined to the strip of northern counties near Virginia, while rice and indigo appeared on the lower Cape Fear River. Rice had been introduced from South Carolina; indigo was the source of a dark blue dye very popular in Britain. Cotton, a staple of the nineteenth century, did not spread widely before the invention of Eli Whitney's gin in the 1790s. The most significant crop was corn, which the settlers ate themselves, fed to some of their animals, and marketed for grain. Wheat and flour were likewise important articles of trade and, like most of North Carolina's products, found their way eventually to the West Indies. These islands had been stripped of trees long before, and every foot of arable land was turned to the cultivation of sugarcane. Many of the slaves who tilled the cane fields lived on North Carolina corn, pork, and beef; slept in barracks made of North Carolina lumber and shingles; and packed the sugar, molasses, and rum into barrels made from

North Carolina staves. Of the products that were carried to Britain itself, naval stores and indigo received a government subsidy or "bounty." Remote as it sometimes seemed, the thinly settled colony was an integral unit in the British Empire.

Whether they took their living from the forest or from the fields (and most North Carolinians did some of both), a constant factor in the lives of eighteenth-century inhabitants was the importance of the land and its bounty. The shape of the terrain, the nature of the soil, the conditions of the weather— all had more direct influence on the pattern of human life than later generations would experience. The pervasive influence of the natural environment gave North Carolinians a common ground that divergent social arrangements could never entirely remove.

There were more human inhabitants than travelers often recognized at first. In 1770 an estimated 200,000 people lived in the province of North Carolina, and more newcomers were arriving every day. In the next twenty years, their numbers would nearly double, and North Carolina would rank third among the states in population. Deriving from a wide variety of ethnic and geographical backgrounds, North Carolina residents comprised a society of marked cultural diversity.

The earliest-settled section of the state was the region to the north of Albemarle Sound. Settlers from Virginia had spilled over into the region as early as the 1650s and had spread out steadily in the succeeding decades. Signs of Virginia influence persisted in the homes, speech, and customs these settlers carried from the sound region up the Roanoke, Tar, and Neuse River Valleys. To the south, newcomers from South Carolina had penetrated the Cape Fear country in the first third of the eighteenth century. Members of the lowcountry gentry, these wealthy migrants established rice and indigo plantations like the ones they had left behind and also engaged in lumber and naval-stores production. The dominant whites of both the Albemarle and Cape Fear regions were heavily dependent on the labor of black slaves and brought numbers of African Americans with them as they came.

The Cherokee Indians were the last major tribe to control a section of North Carolina. They were not forced to surrender the final remnant of their mountain homeland until 1835, but white settlement of the Piedmont—or backcountry, as it was known—proceeded very rapidly in the 1750s and 1760s. Among the multitude of immigrants who found homes there, four groups were outstanding. Probably the largest number were Scotch-Irish, the descendants of Scottish Presbyterians who had colonized northern Ireland in the seventeenth century and moved from there to Pennsylvania and Maryland in the early eighteenth century. When population growth made these colonies seem crowded, second-generation families loaded their possessions into wagons and began to follow the Shenandoah Valley southward in search of cheap and fertile land. They filled up western Virginia first and then began to flood the North Carolina Piedmont at midcentury.

A somewhat smaller group of German settlers followed the same pattern as the Scotch-Irish. Originally settled in the backcountry of Pennsylvania, where they became known as "Pennsylvania Dutch," the Germans sent new pioneers principally to the valleys of the Yadkin and Catawba Rivers. Among them was the congregation of Moravians who founded the communities of Bethabara, Bethania, and Salem in the territory they called "Wachovia." A patchwork of German and Scotch-Irish settlements soon covered the Piedmont, giving rise to alternating patterns of churches and place-names, such as Dutch Buffalo and Irish Buffalo Creeks in present-day Cabarrus County.

Unlike other backcountry settlers, the Highland Scots came directly to North Carolina from the Old World. Changing British policies in Scotland had disrupted the middle and lower ranks of highland society, and a fever for migration swept the region in the 1760s and 1770s. Disembarking at Wilmington, the Gaelic-speaking, kilt-clad strangers made for the upper reaches of the Cape Fear River, where they populated the new counties of Bladen, Cumberland, and Anson. "A North Carolina Gaelic Bard," John McCrae, came from Scotland in 1774 and wrote a lullaby in his native Gaelic, part of which, translated, says:

> Sleep softly, my darling beloved,
> Stay as you are, now that you're in a new land.
> We'll find suitors abounding in wealth and fame,
> And if you are worthy you shall have one of them.
>
> In America now are we,
> In the shade of the forest for ever unfailing.
> When the winter departs and the warmth returns,
> Nuts and apples and the sugar will grow.

The fourth body of settlers were natives of eastern North Carolina, Virginia, or colonies farther north who were mostly of English origins. They spread throughout the Piedmont without ever calling attention to themselves as a separate ethnic group. Most of these English descendants were respectable but otherwise anonymous pioneers. Some were Quakers from Pennsylvania and Nantucket. Others were wealthy and well-connected men who stepped very quickly into positions of civic, economic, and military leadership in the area.

Regardless of their origins, each divergent ethnic group had customs, manners, practices, and beliefs that distinguished it from the others. The Scots and the Germans spoke their own national languages, while the Scotch-Irish, Quakers, and Moravians each cherished a special form of worship. The Africans and Indians were both sustained and stigmatized by their non-European cultural heritage. By the first quarter of the nineteenth century, however, there was a definite tendency for many of these unique characteristics to fade. Especially among whites, the wilderness environment exerted a constant pressure on the residue of ethnic distinctiveness. An elderly grandparent or a handful of personal heirlooms was often all that kept alive the memory that identified this family as Scottish, that one as German, this other one as English by way of Virginia. Even among blacks, external conditions first broke down differences among diverse African tribesmen and then eased the distinction between "Guinea Negroes" and the "country-born" slaves who had known only life in America. A similar process seems to have occurred among many Indians, as survivors of the decimated eastern tribes banded together in swamps, with no common language but the white man's English. The ordinary business of survival brought about the creation of three distinct but overlapping southern cultures among whites, blacks, and Indians, each one centered on the land and the tasks that made it fruitful.

A harmonious relationship between human beings and nature was particularly important in the traditional culture of the American Indians. A combination of simple agriculture and hunting and gathering food from the forest environment enabled the Indians to maintain themselves comfortably without making heavy demands on the land or its resources. The Cherokees, for example, believed that disease was animals' retaliation for man's hunting them; each one contributed a specific ailment. But they also believed that plants took pity on man and each offered a cure to counteract a specific disease. Hence, the Indians depended heavily on herbal remedies.

The arrival of massive numbers of whites made the Indians' way of life increasingly precarious because the intensive land-use patterns of the Europeans were incompatible with the Indians' farming and hunting practices. Smyth noted the peril the white man posed to the Indians. "The Catawbas," he wrote, "afford a melancholy example, and striking, but insuperable proof, of the ruin and fatality brought on any Indian nation, by the intemperance and vicinity of the settlements of the whites. This astonishing havoc and depopulation . . . has been occasioned, in a great measure, by the introduction of the small-pox and spirituous liquors."

Even when the Indians showed a willingness to change their customs and to imitate the white men's economy, however, white hostility to the Indian presence ultimately drove the native Americans to the hidden, unwanted corners of the country—to the swamps of eastern North Carolina, to the peaks and valleys of the Great Smoky Mountains, or to the unsettled lands beyond the Mississippi River. In 1770, however, the grim alternatives of flight, expulsion, or extinction as a culture were still far-away threats to the Cherokees, North Carolina's largest and most powerful Indian tribe. Today, the Eastern Band of Cherokees demonstrate their eighteenth-century way of life at Oconaluftee Indian Village, a living museum of their Qualla Boundary Reservation in Swain County, close by a major entrance to the Great Smoky Mountains National Park.

Centuries before the arrival of the whites, the Cherokees had migrated to the southern Appalachians from the northern regions of what is now the United States. Like other eastern Indians, the Cherokees lived in permanent towns of twenty to sixty families. They relied on large tracts of unoccupied forest for hunting grounds and for new fields when the older plots had lost fertility. In 1735 a white trader named James Adair put their numbers at 16,000 and counted sixty-four Cherokee towns in what is now western North Carolina, Tennessee, upper South Carolina, and northern Georgia. By 1795 war and smallpox had taken a severe toll of Cherokee lives, and the tribe was reduced to forty-three towns and 2,500 warriors, or perhaps 6,700 persons altogether.

Like earlier Cherokee towns, Oconaluftee Indian Village is located beside a stream and is surrounded by a high palisade of logs and earth. Traditional Cherokee villagers had to protect themselves from a variety of enemies, both whites and other Indians. Within the walls, skilled men and women today demonstrate the crafts that were essential for tribal survival. The visitor can see pots made from coils of clay and then baked to waterproof hardness before an open fire. Traditional dyeing, weaving, basketmaking, beadwork, and food preparation are among women's other tasks, while men demonstrate how arrow points were chipped from flint and canoes were hollowed out from poplar logs. Traditional traps for bear, quail, and fish are also on display, as are a variety of artifacts pertaining to Cherokee medicine, religion, and warfare.

Corn was the mainstay of the traditional Cherokee diet. Women planted the grain in hills and tilled it with simple hoes. They cooked corn into a popular mush and less frequently into bread. Women beat the kernels in large mortars with pestles made of logs. They shaped the resulting meal into loaves and baked them on hot stones, covered by large earthenware bowls. The women also planted beans, pumpkins, and squashes among the cornstalks, and added to their families' diets by gathering wild fruits, nuts, and other edible plant foods from the forest. Some of the village fields were tended in common by all the inhabitants, while others were the special property of individual clans or kinship groups.

Meat for the village came from game killed primarily by men. Deer, bear, bison, and smaller game were the favorite quarry of Cherokee hunters. The men used bows and arrows and later guns to secure these animals in twice-yearly hunting expeditions. After making the proper sacrifices, they dried or barbecued the meat in the forest before bringing it home to the village. Fish were also important to the Cherokees. Villagers gathered them from mountain waters with spears carved from split canes, hooks fashioned from deer bones, and fish traps woven from reeds, splints, and canes.

The Cherokees' way of life made them keenly aware of the close connection between human life and the natural environment. Rituals and ceremonies helped to remind the tribe of the importance of the delicate relationship between humans and the forests, the animals, and the earth. While the Cherokees held very few formal religious beliefs as such, they were anxious to maintain themselves in a state of ritual purity and continued harmony with the various forces of nature. Conjurers and other magical experts specialized in the ceremonial practices that were intended to preserve these propitious conditions.

The most important festival of the year was the Green Corn Ceremony, held when the first ears of corn became edible. Fasting, purifying drinks, and repeated bathings were followed by sacrifices of the first fruits of corn and meat, and then by a round of feasting and dancing. When the corn became fully ripe, a second, longer round of dancing and thanksgiving began and continued for five days.

Hunting customs also taught the Cherokees to respect the fruitfulness of the earth and the fundamental unity of all living things. Fasting, bathing, and purification preceded and followed all major hunts. The conjurer sacrificed the tongue of the first deer killed to ensure success in the remainder of the hunt. The Cherokees wore masks representing animals and covered themselves with the skins of their prey, not only to approach them undetected, but also to establish a magical affinity with the animal being sought. When bears were the quarry, special precautions were taken, for tribal legends taught that bears had once been men who had forgotten the importance of avenging the deaths of their own kinsmen. Bears had thus become fair game for people, but the Cherokees were careful to ask the bear's permission before taking its life.

Cherokee culture was closely tied to the land and its resources, but the Cherokee way of life was not immune to change. Tribal customs altered significantly as Indian contact with whites increased. Three kinds of houses in Oconaluftee illustrate this evolutionary development. The earliest Cherokee homes were built of sapling logs stuck upright in the earth in the shape of a rectangle. The walls were formed like the sides of a basket, by canes woven around the logs and then plastered inside and out by clay mixed with grass. Slabs of bark laid over light rafters formed the roof. The door was a simple opening, and there were no windows; a fire burned on the packed-earth floor, but no chimney carried away the smoke. Later in the eighteenth century, Cherokees began to make cabins out of notched logs like the white settlers. These buildings had chimneys made of sticks covered with mud. When iron tools became widely available in Cherokee country, hewn square-sided logs and oak shingles went into a third style of Cherokee construction.

The families who lived in these houses puzzled European onlookers, who were used to an overwhelmingly male-dominated society. Cherokee men and women specialized in different tasks, but each participated in the particular activities of the other. Men concentrated, for example, on hunting and fighting, but they aided women with the heavier work in the fields. More surprising to Europeans, certain Cherokee women took part in the hunt, spoke out in war councils, and decided the fate of prisoners of war. There were seven clans among the Cherokees; individuals in the same clan were considered too closely related to marry each other. Most Cherokee men took only one wife at a time, but divorce was distressingly frequent and casual from the point of view of missionaries and other reforming whites. Some reported that a Cherokee might take up with three different spouses in a year, but this was not the usual practice. Children belonged to their mother's clan, and individual houses and fields belonged to women, not men. In the event of a separation, the man returned to the maternal relatives of his own clan, while the woman continued to control her own property and offspring. Preferring the patriarchal customs of his own society, the English trader James Adair found a more equal relationship between the sexes disturbing and claimed that the Cherokees suffered from "petticoat government."

Contrary to Adair's supposition, men held the preponderant influence in Cherokee public affairs. The Council House at Oconaluftee is a replica of the building that stood in every Cherokee town and in which all major public decisions were made. It has seven sides and contains tiers of benches circling the council fire, which stands on an oval mound of earth in the center. The eighteenth-century naturalist William Bartram described the Council House as "a large rotunda, capable of accommodating several hundred people. It stands on the top of an ancient artificial mount of earth about twenty feet perpendicular, and the rotunda on the top of it, being about thirty feet more, gives the whole fabric an elevation of about sixty feet from the common surface of the ground." During meetings and ceremonies, each of the seven clans sat in a body on its own side of the chamber. Presiding over the discussions and the rituals were two chiefs, one who governed in time of peace and another who commanded the town's warriors in battle. Real decisions were made by consensus, and the chiefs' main authority was based on the respect they commanded for their valor or their wisdom.

The most important decisions taken at the Council House were those pertaining to war. The Cherokees were inveterate fighters, and no youth was considered fully grown until he had taken his first captive or claimed his first scalp. When the British asked the Cherokees to seek a truce with neighboring tribesmen, the chiefs refused, saying "we cannot live without war. Should we make peace with the Tuscaroras, with whom we are at war, we must immediately look for some other, with whom we can be engaged in our favorite occupation." In 1814 a band of Cherokees under Chief Junaluska helped Andrew Jackson win the Battle of Horseshoe Bend, in what is now the state of Alabama, ending the Creek War and opening the future cotton states to white settlement. The federal government removed Junaluska, along with many other Cherokees, to the West, in 1838, but he later returned to North Carolina, where the legislature granted him land and legal citizenship for his service in the Creek War. Unlike whites, however, the Cherokees did not make war to gain national advantages or to conquer a permanent empire. Their principal objectives were retaliation and prestige. If a clan had lost a certain number of kinsmen in battle, it was the responsibility of the surviving clan members to avenge the deaths by inflicting an equal number of casualties in return. The occasional captive who escaped death by torture lived on as the slave of the warrior who had taken him.

A striking difference between white and Indian cultures lay in their respective attitudes toward wealth and material possessions. Before the arrival of whites, Cherokees traded with other tribes for needed materials, but they did not expect to gather a larger and larger surplus every year in order to trade for a profit. The tribe gathered food and meat for their yearly needs but no more than that. Indeed, personal property was buried with the dead and household possessions were destroyed annually in a major ceremony marking the beginning of the year. Because there was no incentive to use the labor of others to accumulate surplus property, slaves did not work much harder than their masters. A slave thus increased his master's prestige but not his wealth. In fact, Cherokee men kept few possessions of any kind besides clothing, weapons, and the trophies of battle because fields belonged to women and scratching in the dirt in search of useless riches was beneath the dignity of a warrior. Initially, the white man's love of acquisition invoked only the contempt of the Cherokees. On seeing the ostentatious Tryon Palace, Methodist minister Jeremiah Norman was reminded of the Indian saying: "White men build great & fine Houses as if they were to live allways, but white men must die as well as Red men."

The Indians' resistance to commercial activity began to erode as soon as white soldiers and traders could demonstrate the superior qualities of European technology. Woolen cloth and iron tools had obvious advantages over buckskin and chipped-flint implements, while the power of muskets over bows and arrows could not be denied. In order to purchase the white man's products, Indians began to gather and sell the commodities desired by whites. By 1735 James Adair estimated that the Cherokees were supplying him and other traders with over a million pelts a year, the largest number of which were deerskins. Cherokees also learned to sell their human property. Instead of destroying their prisoners of war in ceremonial tortures, Cherokees dabbled in the slave trade and supplied South Carolina traders with captive enemy tribesmen for resale to the West Indies. Eventually, white colonists became wary of Indian slaves, for bondsmen with aggrieved relatives just beyond the frontier were dangerous investments compared to Africans, who left kith and kin beyond the ocean. Sometimes forced by war and later compelled by debt, Cherokees began selling the last commodity left to them: their land. Between 1777 and 1819 Cherokees ceded a total of 8,927 square miles to whites in North Carolina alone. When the tribe was finally reduced to a tiny fragment of its once-expansive domain, opponents of further cessions finally forced a halt, and the Cherokees sold no more land until they were forcibly ejected from the southern Appalachians in the winter of 1838–39.

Before the grim story of expulsion was completed, however, the Cherokees made a remarkable recovery as a people. More than any other tribe in the United States, they continued the policy of selective borrowing from white culture. They took up the practice of stock-raising and cotton cultivation, began to embrace the Christian religion, and sent their children to mission schools. Tribal leaders intermarried with whites and began to purchase slaves instead of selling them. These Cherokees soon adopted a lifestyle that was virtually indistinguishable from that of the upcountry planter aristocracy. During the same period, the Cherokee Nation adopted a code of written laws, transformed itself into a self-governing republic, and began to publish a tribal newspaper in English and Cherokee, using an alphabet invented by a mixed-blood Cherokee named Sequoyah. Most of these cultural innovations took place in northern Georgia, where commercial agriculture and its accompanying changes were more accessible and more practical. North Carolina Cherokees were more deeply isolated in the remote coves of the Great Smokies, where they clung tenaciously to a traditional way of life. Unfortunately, the Cherokees' success in Georgia aroused their white neighbors' hostility, and, as an ultimate result, the whole body of the Cherokee Nation was forced to relocate beyond the Mississippi. A handful of North Carolina Cherokees evaded the federal soldiers who were sent to escort them to what is now Oklahoma, and it is their descendants who have reconstructed Oconaluftee Indian Village. For generations after the

The famous Cherokee Sequoyah, depicted with his syllabary, which he devised to enable his people to become literate.

removal of most of their fellow tribesmen, the Eastern Band of Cherokee Indians maintained a subsistence economy in the depths of the North Carolina mountains.

One white missionary who lived among the North Carolina Cherokees in the years before removal reported that "their cabins are not much inferior to those of the whites of the neighborhood." Housing was not the only area of resemblance between Cherokee culture and the lifestyle of the pioneer white

Allen House (ca. 1782), Alamance Battleground State Historic Site

family. The large majority of these white settlers were called "yeomen." People of this class were small farmers and livestock producers who owned their own land and tilled it with their own labor. Like the Indians, white yeomen had limited contact with the market economy and depended for subsistence on the yield of the fields and the surrounding forests. A series of small houses in the Piedmont and central Coastal Plain reveals repeatedly the patterns of wilderness adjustment experienced by these men and women and their families. One of the simplest examples now stands on the Alamance Battleground State Historic Site, the home of John Allen (1749–1826) and Rachel Stout Allen (1760–1840). Built in 1782, the house stood for many years on the Allen family farm near Snow Camp before it was moved to its present site and restored in 1967.

When he was about thirteen years old, John Allen came to North Carolina with his widowed mother, Phoebe, and her four other children. The Allens were Pennsylvania Quakers, and they were looking for 600 acres of land that Phoebe's husband had acquired but never settled before his death. Mrs. Allen joined some of her late husband's relatives in the Cane Creek Friends Meeting in Orange County, but she soon remarried and moved to Holly Spring, in nearby Randolph County. When young John came of age, it fell to him to take up his father's land on Cane Creek in Orange County. Returning to Pennsylvania to find a bride, John Allen married Rachel Stout in 1779 and brought her back to North Carolina. Thereafter, his small, temporary house gave way

Main room in the Allen House

to a more substantial log dwelling that came to house five generations of his descendants.

The Allen House is a simple box of hand-hewn timbers. A massive stone chimney dominates one wall, and an enclosed stairway climbs beside it to a loft above. Cracks between the logs are sealed with mud and grass, but window glass was costly and the Allens did without. Two doors, at the front and back of the cabin, are the only sources of light and ventilation in the main room, though a tiny window, shuttered but unglazed, opens from an upstairs gable. The wide eaves of the shingle roof extend over each entrance to form substantial porches at both ends of the house. Planks enclose half of one porch to form a small third room that could variously serve as a storage area, a visitor's room, a post office, and a store. Of John and Rachel's twelve known children, ten grew to adulthood in the little cabin, although the oldest were married and

Loft of the Allen House

gone before the youngest were born. The shape of the house and the character of its furnishings indicate the lifestyle of this fairly typical yeoman family.

Many of the Allens' important household activities undoubtedly took place outdoors or on their cabin's broad porches. Both doors typically stood open to admit air and light, so children, pets, and chores must have flowed over the steps and onto the packed bare earth of the yard. Tidy housekeepers, the Allens carefully prevented the growth of grass or weeds near the house. Grass was a fire hazard and harbored insects; there was no simple way to trim it; and, perhaps most important, it was a symbol of nature that the pioneers were determined to keep at bay. At night or in bad weather, cooking, eating, sleeping, making clothes, mending tools, and learning lessons must have been concentrated in the cabin's one main room. Its furniture, much of which originally belonged to the Allens, reflects this combination of functions. Iron cooking utensils fill the hearth, while shelves and cupboards hold the dishes. Most of these were earthenware of local manufacture, but eighteen pewter spoons and eleven pewter vessels were among the family possessions as well. Other belongings were stored in chests, which must have served for seats as well, for there were never enough chairs to go around. A loom fills one corner, while cards for preparing fibers and spinning wheels for twisting them into thread stand nearby. Opposite sits a bed for father and mother, with a trundle bed beneath for small children and a cradle at hand for the baby. Corn husk mattresses for the older children would have lain on the floor of the loft. Numerous travelers' accounts confirm that pioneer families routinely lived and even put up overnight guests in even more crowded conditions than these. In such close quarters, modern notions of privacy and separate personal space clearly had no chance to develop.

Like the all-purpose nature of their living space, the workaday life of the Allens was varied and had to accommodate a wide assortment of tasks and skills. No single career limited the scope of man's or woman's labor. John Allen was a teacher, for example, and regularly contracted with his neighbors to instruct their children in reading, writing, spelling, and arithmetic. His pupils at Rock Spring School were prohibited from "baring the Master out of school," "pinching or picking at one a nother or lafing," or "Scribing on one a nothers Books," among a long list of rules of deportment. Allen was also a farmer and a merchant, and, because he was blessed with good lands and the labor of eight sons, he had achieved a modest competence by the time of his death at the age of seventy-seven.

The papers relating to John Allen's estate show the range of his diverse work activities. The store held a very limited inventory, but shoppers could find yellow silk, satin, calico, buttons, pins, pencils, shoes, and hardware. The farm was more elaborate. Wheat, oats, and corn were the field crops, but five cattle, fifteen sheep, ten hogs, and two beehives were equally important for the family's well-being. A collection of shovels, hoes, pitchforks, scythes, and sickles formed the tools for cultivating and harvesting these crops, and several hogsheads were the receptacles for storing them. Allen owned a wagon to carry his grain to the mill and to haul any surplus to market, but there were no draft animals to pull it or to draw his three plows and one harrow. By the end of his life, the aging farmer was probably borrowing horses or oxen from his grown sons, each of whom was now established on a farm of his own, carved from the father's original land grant. A stocked chest of carpenter's tools rounded out the family's working gear. These were essential to shape the wood that formed so many items of daily use, but Allen may have done some carpentry work for hire as well.

Candle-making was a regular chore for women who operated households.

The skills and labor of Rachel Allen were as varied and as essential to the family's welfare as those of her husband. She bore twelve children and did the cooking, spinning, sewing, and mending for her burgeoning family. The yard of the Allen House contains a vegetable and herb garden and an ash hopper for making soap, both of which were Rachel's responsibility. One North Carolina woman described how early inhabitants made soap. They "saved wood ashes, put them in the lye hopper, poured water on them and the water dropped down into the ashes into the lye barrel. When it got strong enough to float an egg, it was strong enough to combine with the animal fat that had been saved and to make soap." Apparently, "it was some soap! It would take the skin off of your hands." Such were the tasks of every pioneer housewife.

In addition, Rachel Allen grew very skilled in the uses of roots, herbs, and the traditional folk medicines of her neighborhood. Her services were much in demand in cases of illness, injury, and probably of childbirth as well, and she owned a riding mare to carry her to the homes of her many patients. Her notebook contains home remedies for burns, infected sores, warts, consumption, rheumatism, "bad blood," "yaws or Country distemper," kidney stones, palsy, and "any Inward Weakness," even cancer. Her prescription for a "raging fit of [kidney] stone" was to "Beat Onions into a pulp & apply them as a poultis part to the back and part to Each Groin[.] She claimed that "it gives Speedy Ease in the most Racking pain." For cleaning teeth, she advised rubbing them with ashes of burnt bread. Rachel Allen's role as a healer was closely tied to her traditionally female duties as mother and nurse, but no professional restrictions or taboos prevented her from exercising her gifts to the fullest extent possible in her time and place. As a woman of skill and strength in the growing backcountry, her economic importance to the family was as essential and obvious as it was varied.

Washday was an all-day affair.

The combined efforts of John and Rachel Allen produced a comfortable but very simple standard of living at the end of a long life together. Yeoman farmers back in England often had no choice but to bequeath all their real estate to the oldest son, in order to leave even one child with a farm large enough to support the next generation. The same conditions were coming to exist in some northern states, which may have been a reason why John's father had wanted to leave Pennsylvania. The North Carolina forest was kinder to the pioneer than those older environments. Dividing his lands into scrupulously equivalent legacies, John Allen left each son with an adequate farm and each child with an equal portion of cash. He had also loaned each son considerable amounts of money to get started and had probably been the source of their first tools and livestock as well. Daughters got less, not because they ranked lower in their father's esteem, but because Allen took for granted that all his children would marry and his daughters would benefit from their husbands' inheritances. The North Carolina experience gave John Allen an opportunity to do what might have been denied him elsewhere: a chance to treat his children with what he regarded as equality.

As a result of their father's bequests of land, John Allen's sons lived and raised their own families in a cluster of bordering farms in Orange and Chatham Counties. They took an active role in Cane Creek and Holly Spring Friends Meetings, married women who were members of the same congregations (some of whom were their distant cousins) and generally shared their lives with the circle of friends and relatives who composed their respective communities. Rachel Allen presumably kept practicing her healing arts. She followed a circuit through her children's families, boarding with each son in successive intervals until she died in 1840. The Allen grandchildren grew up surrounded by aunts, uncles, and cousins, and with a grandmother who joined their households frequently. As these children looked out at the world, they saw an ever-widening set of concentric circles made up of immediate family members, close relatives, distant relatives, church members, and neighbors, with no strict distinctions between each group. The intermingling of family and community was surely a central part of how they learned to view the world and other people.

Just as John Allen's grandchildren saw society from a special viewpoint as they peered beyond his cabin, outsiders looking in also saw things from a particular perspective. Eighteenth-century travelers frequently found much to criticize in the lifestyles they observed among North Carolina yeomen. Such observers might have felt that the Allens' mud-chinked cabin was excessively drafty and dark. They might also have found fault with the spelling of John Allen, the self-certified schoolmaster, or questioned the efficacy of Rachel Allen's homemade potions. Those who came to Cane Creek from parts of the world where different conceptions of family were beginning to take hold might have thought to themselves that the Allens lacked a proper sense of privacy and that personal living space was altogether too public for their own good and for the comfort of others. It is quite true that the Allens' standards of writing, medical treatment, and building differed from ours. But, though their house was small and seemingly crude, the Allens' acquisitions represented a solid achievement. John's persistent interest in education testified that his life on the frontier had not lapsed into unlettered barbarism. At the end of his life, three items had special meaning for John Allen as symbols of his material and cultural accomplishments: a grandfather clock, a walnut Chippendale desk, and a collection of twenty books received special mention in his will. These handsome and expensive articles were to be auctioned off within the family and the proceeds divided with the other cash of the estate. The same clock and desk are in the house today. The juxtaposition of these luxuries with the simpler tools and furniture serve as an appropriate expression of the aspirations of one pioneer family as well as the limitations of the backcountry environment.

Because the Allens lived in the Piedmont, the desk and clock they treasured probably had come to them over a long, rough wagon road from a distant market center like Fayetteville or Petersburg, Virginia. The crops they grew in exchange for such comforts were likewise very tedious and expensive to haul away for sale. The cost of traveling back and forth to market ensured that families like the Allens would try their best to "live at home" by raising or making themselves the food, clothing, and other materials they used in daily life. They worked to raise a small surplus for sale only so they could get the necessary cash for taxes and for items like salt, sugar, or a clock that they could not make themselves. The Allens' tiny store kept them more closely tied to the market economy than most of their neighbors, but on the whole theirs was not a highly commercialized lifestyle. The Allens proved that this could be a reasonably comfortable way to live, but it was not the way to bring rapid economic growth to a family, a region, or a state. Growth required specialization on a cash crop or crops and a commitment to the market economy, but neither of these was practical while the Piedmont remained isolated. As long as transportation costs stayed high, John Allen's children and grandchildren would continue to live just as he had, and thoughtful observers would begin to note that Piedmont North Carolina was taking a remarkably long time to progress beyond the frontier stage of development.

Though hardly perfect, transportation in eastern North Carolina bettered that in the Piedmont. Numerous rivers and broad streams made navigable channels across the Coastal Plain. Once their rafts and flatboats arrived at market towns like Edenton, New Bern, and Wilmington, easterners still faced the hazards of getting past the Outer Banks, but at least the inland portions of their journeys were less difficult than the journeys of settlers farther west. Higher soil fertility and a longer length of settlement were further advantages for eastern North Carolina. During the late eighteenth century, eastern farmers took advantage of their opportunities to enjoy a somewhat higher standard of living than was common farther to the west, but these differences should not be exaggerated. As late as 1810 a Duplin County resident noted that, although a few "framed Clapboard Houses with Clay Chimneys" had replaced the inhabitants' original log structures, "the greatest Number of the Citizens yet build in the old Stile." Even when a farmer found the money to build with sawn lumber instead of logs, the results were hardly grandiose. The Duplin County writer emphasized that in spite of recent improvements "there are no Stone or Brick walled Homes, nor any that can be called Edifices in the County." Beneath some superficial details of materials and design, the similarities between yeoman farmers in the east and the west were at least as significant as the differences.

The building that is now called the Pender Museum in Tarboro illustrates the advantages eastern farmers enjoyed as well as the continued limitations that affected them. Silas and Rebecca Everitt built the small frame cottage about 1810 on their farm in the Conetoe community of eastern Edgecombe County. Farmers in that section were well known for their excellent hogs, which thrived on the rich vegetation of surrounding swamps. The drier patches of light, sandy soil made fertile fields for corn, peas, potatoes, cotton, and flax. Careless of their soil's fine quality, landowners cleared new grounds for fields, rapidly exhausted their fertility, abandoned them, and then cleared more.

These wasteful methods were identical to those prevailing in the frontier sections of the west. Naval stores were also still important in Edgecombe County, and they and other products were floated down the Tar River in long flatboats for sale in the town of Washington.

Later in the antebellum period, Edgecombe's natural advantages would make it the leading cotton county in the state and a well-known center for the most advanced agricultural techniques. But in Silas Everitt's time, the days of plantation glory were several decades away. In 1811, when the Everitt's house was still new, an Edgecombe County doctor could say with a fair degree of accuracy that "the inhabitants of the county generally live comfortably; & in proportion to their industry, enjoy the luxuries of life. There are no overgrown 'estates' here; & there are comparatively few oppressed with poverty."

The farmhouse of Silas and Rebecca Everitt reflects this intermediate stage of economic development. Heated by two brick chimneys and resting above the ground on brick foundations, the house was carefully designed for warmth in winter and ventilation in summer. The front door is flanked by two sash windows made of fifteen panes of glass, and every outside board has a handmade beaded edge for shedding rainwater. Finely turned columns support a shed porch projecting over the front door, and finely detailed molding highlights the eaves and cornices of the roof. These aesthetic and practical refinements were significant advantages over the rough simplicity of the Allen House of Orange County.

A close inspection shows, however, that the Allens and the Everitts shared many ideas about how a house should look. The Everitt House is a typical coastal cottage with a hall-and-parlor floor plan. Common throughout eastern North Carolina, this type of house is rectangular, with a long off-center partition dividing it into one large room—the "hall"—and one small room—the "parlor." A lean-to room projects from the rear, adding a third chamber to the downstairs. This old-fashioned design had come from England with the earliest Virginia colonists. The hall was used for most family activities, and the parlor was used for secondary purposes like storage.

Family living was much the same in both the Allen and Everitt Houses. The hall-and-parlor floor plan allowed these households only a slight degree of privacy. In the average-sized family, there were no separate rooms for sleeping and at least one bed probably sat in every room. Family members began to encounter household activity as soon as they approached the porch and plunged into the hubbub of personal life as soon as they crossed the threshold. Visitors faced the same conditions, for no neutral passageways guided a person from one part of the house to another, or screened the casual visitor from intimate family business.

Why did the Everitts and the Allens fail to hide from themselves and from their guests cooking food, drying laundry, crying children, and bedridden invalids? Was it simply because they could not afford to build "proper" houses? If so, why did Silas Everitt squander his means on beaded weatherboarding and similar luxuries? Were these families simply primitive backwoodsmen who did not know any better? John Allen's desk, clock, and books testify to the contrary. It is more likely that the Allens and the Everitts both built their houses in ways that reflected contemporary attitudes toward family living. Like most other eighteenth-century men and women, they made few sharp distinctions between what was public and what was private, between what was suitable to show the outside world and what ought to be kept invisible, even from the family itself.

Not only were there striking similarities in the lifestyles of eighteenth-century yeoman farmers in eastern and western North Carolina, but there was also a common—and a distinctly premodern—concept of family existence. The Allens and the Everitts did not live in specialized spaces, nor did they lead compartmentalized lives. Each family had the skills to perform a variety of tasks, and when possible they performed these tasks themselves. There was no rigid line between the world of the workplace and the world of the family because almost all work was done at home by parents and children. Nor was each household an isolated unit. Each farm stood by itself at some distance from its neighbors, but the individual households of parents and children were relatively open to temporary members like grandmother Rachel Allen. Moreover, the extended family blended imperceptibly outward into a surrounding community of relatives. Property lines were kept distinct, but other boundary lines were blurred in this society, just as they were in the physical space between the cabins. All was not sweetness and light in such communities; there could be overwhelming pressures on individuals to live and to think by a community consensus, or fierce and deadly feuds could erupt out of so much togetherness. But, if the Allens were a representative family, the general effect of this way of life was first to re-create and then to preserve a traditional sense of family and rural community coherence that harked back to the peasant societies of Europe. Unlike their European and New England counterparts, these southern white yeomen did not live in physically compact villages, but a distinctive sense of community was equally central to their world view.

Other small homes of the late eighteenth century show variations of the characteristics apparent in the Allen and Everitt Houses. The Boggan-Hammond House (1783) in Anson County and the John Haley House (1786) in Guilford County are town and country examples of other Piedmont construction. These houses supplied basically the same amount of living space.

Though humbly born but successful men could join the elite in the backcountry, particularly after the Revolution, serious economic obstacles prevented their achieving more than a modest standard of living. One feature of the Haley House design corresponds to that of the Allen House: each house had one room other than the main room that could be entered from the outside. This made them independent of the activities in the main room of each house and presaged the attempt to separate family and work that would become more common in the century that followed.

3

PLANTERS AND SLAVES

Hezekiah Alexander was yet another immigrant from farther north who moved to Piedmont North Carolina in the 1760s. Alexander was a Presbyterian from Scotch-Irish stock, but the other contours of his life were remarkably similar to those of yeomen like John Allen. He was born in 1728 in Cecil County, Maryland, not far from the Pennsylvania border. Like Allen's, his grandfather had come from Ireland to the Delaware River Valley in the seventeenth century. His father became a man of some substance in his neighborhood, but Hezekiah and six other of his father's fifteen children eventually tried their luck in Mecklenburg County, North Carolina. Hezekiah Alexander was a blacksmith who bought land and became a farmer and cattle grower. He died in 1801, survived by his wife and nine of their ten children, having earned an enviable position as an elder in his church and a distinguished Revolutionary patriot.

The most obvious difference between Hezekiah Alexander and his yeoman counterparts was his house. Known as the "Rock House," it stands on its original site in the present city limits of Charlotte and forms a part of the Mint Museum of Art. The Rock House is two-and-a-half stories high, with a dressed stone exterior and two interior stone chimneys. There are three rooms downstairs; each one is heated by its own fireplace. The upstairs and downstairs are well lighted by many large glazed windows; there are even several small windows in the attic. Alexander's estate inventory showed comparable signs of affluence: a silver watch and a series of loans to sons and other borrowers. Unlike his contemporaries John Allen and Silas Everitt, Hezekiah Alexander cut quite a figure in the world.

The probable explanation for Alexander's good fortune appears in the clauses of his will: "I give unto my said wife Mary two negro men viz: Sam & Abram and four Work Horses her choice. . . . I likewise give and bequeath unto my wife Mary her Bed & furniture her mare and Saddle and all the Dresser furniture and one Negro Woman Bet to her and her assigns forever." Similar bequests of human property were made to five of Alexander's nine surviving children; the others had apparently received slaves when they married.

For most ambitious men, labor was the key to riches in eighteenth-century North Carolina. There was plenty of land available at cheap prices; the secret was to find workers who could make it pay. A father lost his children's labor as soon as they reached adulthood, and few white men would work very long for wages when land could be had practically for the asking. For the man who was determined to accumulate more property than he could earn by his own efforts, slaves were the solution. Silas Everitt owned none in 1810, but by 1820 he had acquired a slave family of four: a man, a woman, and two small boys. John Allen owned no slaves. Hezekiah Alexander owned as many as thirteen slaves, a number that placed him in the top 1 percent of slaveholders in late eighteenth-century Mecklenburg County. Alexander's labor force was the simple fact that accounted for the difference of scale between his Rock House and the more modest dwellings of nonslaveholders.

Slavery had been a part of North Carolina society from its beginning. The leading Lords Proprietors had been planters and slave traders in the West

Hezekiah Alexander House (1774), Mint Museum of Art, Charlotte

Indies, and they included the "peculiar institution" in their plans for their mainland colony. In Virginia and South Carolina, slave plantations were central features of society from the early eighteenth century onward. Cultivating tobacco to the north and rice to the south, slave labor in the colonies bordering North Carolina paid for the beautiful homes and elegant lifestyles of the colonial aristocracy. The same geographical handicaps that kept many yeomen out of the planter class kept North Carolina's smaller number of slaveholders from reaching the levels of affluence enjoyed by their counterparts to the north and south. As a result, the plantation system in North Carolina was never as fully developed as it was elsewhere. Nevertheless, slavery was crucial to the character of North Carolina society.

Nonslaveholding white farmers and herdsmen were the most numerous group in the population, but slaveholders were the wealthiest and most powerful citizens, while the slaves themselves were central participants in the emergence of a common southern culture. In some eastern counties, blacks were a majority of the local population by the mid-eighteenth century. Even the Cherokee Indians adopted the practice of slaveholding. The presence of these slaves had a powerful impact, moreover, on the feelings of nonslaveholding whites. Yeoman farmers might aspire to become slaveholders themselves; they might come to resent blacks as symbols of the planter's superior advantages; or they could fear blacks as potential competitors or enemies of all white people. Most likely their attitudes could embrace all of these emotions to one degree or another. Though relatively limited in its extent, slavery touched the lives of all North Carolinians.

Most North Carolina blacks originally came to the province from other British colonies. As Governor George Burrington had reported in 1733, "as none come directly from Affrica, we are under a necessity to buy, the refuse, refractory and distemper'd Negroes, brought from other Governments." Burrington's assumption that most blacks involved in the intercolonial slave trade were sold for some defect of their own was questionable, but it does appear that most imported slaves came singly or in small groups to North Carolina. For example, one correspondent of the prominent Blount brothers—merchants, landowners, and politicians Thomas, John G., and William Blount—paid off his debts with human property. "I have shiped on board the sloop Washington Capt. Kirbey a Negro Boy named David who is a Smart Active fellow," wrote James Aiken of Philadelphia. "Part of his time Imployed as a waiter which he is very expert in," Aiken explained, "& Lukwise [likewise] Understands farming well. . . . please pay the Amt. of what you may sell him for after Expenses Deducted to [Mr. Barr]." Torn away from his family and friends by the caprice of a commercial economy, David brought his diverse talents as a house servant and fieldhand to a still-unpolished society with a great demand for all types of skills.

Not all the slaves who came to North Carolina experienced previous periods of adjustment in another colony. On 10 June 1786 the brig *Camden* docked at Edenton, its hold packed with eighty African men and women brought directly from the Guinea coast. "They talk a most curious lingo," one observer remarked, and "are extremely black, with elegant white teeth." The newcomers were all between twenty and twenty-five years old, had each cost £28 sterling, and, the observer added, were clad only "in a state of nature." These naked and frightened young people were the property of Josiah Collins, an English-born merchant of Edenton who had recently formed a partnership with two other gentlemen to dig a canal from Lake Phelps, in Washington County, to the Scuppernong River. Calling their partnership the Lake Company, the partners intended to sell lumber from the surrounding swampland and to raise rice on the thick alluvial muck that the timbering and draining operations would uncover. The canal would be essential to carry both products to market. Joined by other slaves from the neighborhood, the newly arrived Africans were to be the essential workforce for the Lake Company's ambitious undertaking. Robert Hunter Jr. noted in 1785 that Collins "expects to finish it by Christmas if it ceases raining . . . in keeping 150 slaves daily at work." Hunter further observed that when the project was completed, the slaves "will have cleared 100,000 acres of the finest woodland that almost was ever known (oak, sycamore, popular, cypress, etc.)—which is an amazing object and a very great undertaking."

Collins and his partners built their canal. Still visible today, it stretches for six miles, twenty feet wide and six feet deep, through the otherwise impenetrable fastness of the Great Alligator Dismal Swamp. Water flowing through the canal turned sawmills and gristmills and powered sophisticated corn-shelling and wheat-threshing equipment. A network of ditches and sluices drained the surrounding fields of corn, wheat, and rice, and, when necessary, flooded the latter with water from the lake. The canal and its machinery became the economic focal point for a cluster of plantations on the shores of Lake Phelps, the largest of which was Josiah Collins's Somerset Place.

Now a state historic site, Somerset Place was the property in turn of the original Josiah Collins, his son Josiah Collins II, and his grandson Josiah Collins III. The mansion that stands there today was built for Josiah Collins III around 1830. For the Collins slaves, Somerset Place was home from the late 1780s until the era of the Civil War. Surviving business records and an ongoing program of archeological investigation make it possible to reconstruct the pattern of their work and daily life with some assurance.

The "Guinea Negroes" who arrived in Edenton in 1786 had probably been captured in a tribal war as many as several hundred miles inland from the West African coast. They had survived a grueling march to the ocean and a harrowing three- or four-month voyage across the Atlantic known as the Middle Passage. Many others had no doubt died from these experiences; many more died from the ordeal of digging the canal.

The work was exhausting and dangerous. Joined by an almost equal number of "country-born" slaves who had grown up in the New World, the Africans were forced to clear timber, to remove the earth from the bed of the canal, and to construct a road to run beside it. When Charles William Jansen, an English businessman, visited a similar canal project in adjoining Hyde County, he found a "gang of about sixty negroes, whose daily work was in water, often up to the middle, and constantly knee-deep." This waterway was the venture of the tireless Blount brothers, entrepreneurs in so many different efforts, but conditions at Lake Phelps could not have been much different. Work progressed so slowly there that the task that the Lake Company had hoped to finish by Christmas of 1786 stretched on until 1789.

According to the slaves' overseer, disease, overwork, and exposure took a heavy toll of African lives. By his account, "when they were disabled they would be left by the bank of the canal, and the next morning the returning gang would find them dead." Those who withstood the physical demands of their work sometimes succumbed to the psychological strain of homesickness and wrenching personal disruption. "At night they would begin to sing their native songs," the overseer reported, "and in a short while would become so wrought up that, utterly oblivious to the danger involved, they would grasp their bundles of personal effects, swing them on their shoulder, and setting their faces towards Africa, would march down into the water singing as they marched till recalled to their senses only by the drowning of some of the party." Unwilling to lose his laborers, Collins soon forbade these demonstrations.

Not all of Collins's slaves came directly from Africa. He had imported 80 adults in 1786, but the company apparently intended to put at least 150 laborers to work on the canal project. The remaining slaves seem to have been brought in from the partners' other farms in the Albemarle area or purchased from smaller farmers nearby. Already acclimated to American diseases, the "country-born" slaves probably lived through the first years in greater numbers than the Africans. Few of the Africans seem to have lived until 1839, when the first surviving slave inventory for Somerset Place was prepared.

One who did live that long was Guinea Jack, who had crossed the ocean when he was about eighteen years old. We can reconstruct the main outlines of this Carolinian's life from the information recorded about him in the 1839

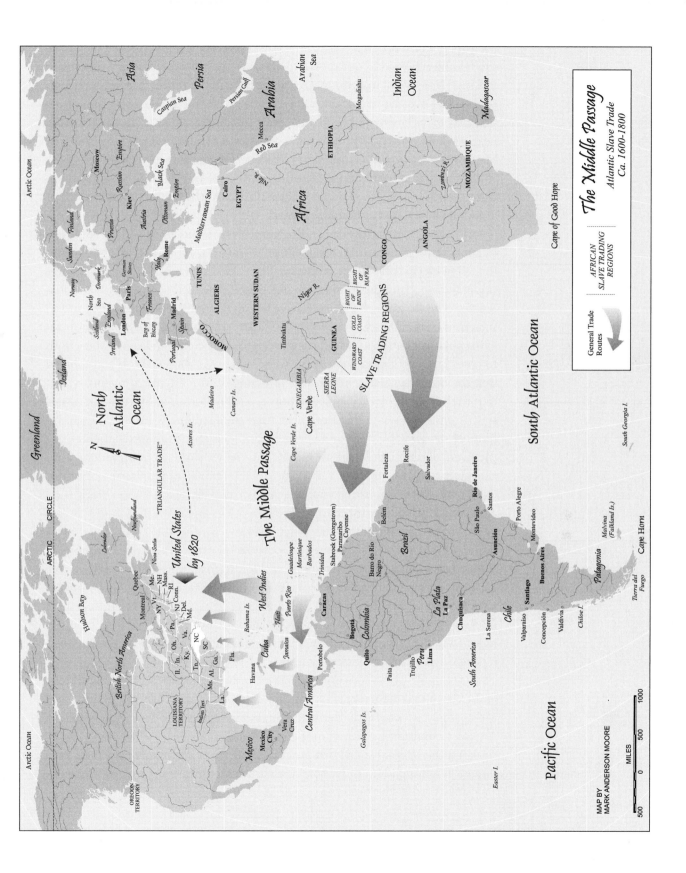

The Middle Passage

Atlantic Slave Trade
Ca. 1600–1800

General Trade Routes

AFRICAN SLAVE TRADING REGIONS

Arctic Ocean

Greenland

Iceland

Asia

Persia

Arabia

Arabian Sea

Indian Ocean

Madagascar

Caspian Sea

Persian Gulf

Mecca
Red Sea
Nile R.
Cairo

Moscow

Russian Empire

Finland

Sweden

Norway

Kiev

Prussia

Austria

Ottoman Empire

Denmark

North Sea

Scotland

Ireland

England

London

Paris

France

Italy

Rome

Mediterranean Sea

Spain

Madrid

Portugal

Bay of Biscay

German States

ETHIOPIA

EGYPT

Africa

MOZAMBIQUE

Zambezi R.

Mogadishu

ANGOLA

CONGO

TUNIS

ALGIERS

MOROCCO

WESTERN SUDAN

Niger R.

Timbuktu

BIGHT OF BENIN
BIGHT OF BIAFRA
GOLD COAST
GUINEA
WINDWARD COAST
SIERRA LEONE
SENEGAMBIA
Cape Verde

SLAVE TRADING REGIONS

Cape Verde Is.

Madeira

Canary Is.

Azores Is.

North Atlantic Ocean

N

"TRIANGULAR TRADE"

United States by 1820

Cape of Good Hope

South Atlantic Ocean

South Georgia I.

Arctic Ocean

ARCTIC CIRCLE

OREGON TERRITORY

British North America

Hudson Bay

Labrador

Newfoundland

Nova Scotia

Quebec

Montreal

Me.
Vt. NH
NY Mass.
Pa. RI Conn.
Oh. NJ Del.
In. Va. Md.
Ill. Ky. NC
Tn. SC
Ms. Al. Ga.
La. Fla.

LOUISIANA TERRITORY

Indian Terr.

Mexico

Mexico City

Vera Cruz

Central America

Portobelo

Havana

Cuba

Jamaica

Haiti

Puerto Rico

Bahama Is.

West Indies

The Middle Passage

Guadeloupe
Martinique
Barbados
Trinidad

Stabroek (Georgetown)
Paramaribo
Cayenne

Belém

Barro do Rio Negro

Caracas

Bogotá

Colombia

Quito

Peru

Lima

Trujillo

Paita

Galapagos Is.

South America

La Serena

Chile

Valparaíso

Concepción

Valdivia

Chiloé I.

Santiago

Chuquisaca
La Paz

La Plata

Asunción

Buenos Aires

Montevideo

Porto Alegre

Santos

São Paulo

Rio de Janeiro

Salvador

Recife

Fortaleza

Brazil

Patagonia

Malvina (Falkland Is.)

Tierra del Fuego

Cape Horn

Pacific Ocean

Easter I.

MAP BY
MARK ANDERSON MOORE

MILES

500   0   500   1000

inventory. Not many years after he arrived at Lake Phelps, Guinea Jack married Fanny, who was about the same age as he or a little older. She gave birth to a son named Will in 1790. As he would have done in his African homeland, Guinea Jack took a second wife, Grace, who became the mother of Sam in 1797. The two wives presented their husband with at least one child each for the next several years. African polygamy was not typical in the slave community, but it was not altogether unheard-of or unconventional either. Guinea Jack's children learned both an African and an African American cultural tradition from their parents and represented the fusion of the slave communities that gradually developed at Somerset Place.

Other signs of cultural blending appeared in the areas of language and religion. After the Civil War, a local physician, Dr. Edward Warren, recalled that the elderly Africans at Somerset Place used to speak "a medley of their original dialect and the English language, and to me [it] was perfectly unintelligible." The Africans of 1786 may have belonged to the same ethnic group and spoken the same language, but the African Americans of the Albemarle region spoke English. As a result, the slaves probably combined elements of both tongues in a pidgin language to use with each other. Dr. Warren also reported that the Somerset slaves adopted Christianity in the nineteenth century, but that the African-born slaves, as he put it, "still had faith in evil genii, charms, spirits, philters, metempsychosis, etc., and they habitually indulged in an infinitude of cabalistic rites and ceremonies in which the gizzards of chickens, the livers of dogs, the heads of snakes and the tails of lizards played a mysterious but very conspicuous part." The doctor's tone was patronizing, but it is clear from his account that traditional African religious practices flourished alongside Christianity for many decades.

A striking example of African culture survived in the "Jonkonnu" ceremony, which the slaves at Somerset performed every Christmas morning. A leading man of the slave community would disguise himself as Jonkonnu in a garb of rags and animal skins. Joined by another slave in American Sunday-style clothing, Jonkonnu would lead a large group of followers to the master's house. Accompanied by drumming, dancing, and chanting, the pair demanded money from the master, mistress, and all white residents of the plantation. Success was followed by a general celebration in the slave quarters. The Jonkonnu ritual appeared on other eastern North Carolina plantations and also among slaves in Jamaica. The drums, the dancing, the chants, and the costume seem clearly derived from African models. When they used an African ceremony to extract money from their masters, the Somerset slaves reversed the normal social order of the plantation and reaffirmed their own dignity as independent human beings. Cultural expressions of black humanity

A modern-day performer re-creates the Jonkonnu ceremony at Somerset Plantation, Washington County.

Reconstructed slave house, Somerset Plantation

were a vital part of the slaves' resistance to the psychological burdens of life in bondage.

From the earliest days of the Lake Company, the Somerset slave community lived in a row of cabins that extended away from the canal along the lakeshore. The remains of these buildings have not yet been found, so we cannot be sure of living conditions at Somerset Place in the eighteenth century. Most contemporary observers who commented on them seemed to think that slaves lived in buildings that were similar to those of poor settlers generally. An anonymous Scottish author thought slaves were quite comfortable. "They have small houses or huts, like peasants, thatched, to which they have little gardens, and live in families, separated from each other," "Scotus Americanus" assured the readers of his "Informations concerning the Province of North Carolina." Writing in 1811, Dr. Jeremiah Battle of Edgecombe County was less sanguine and believed that slave housing was conducive to poor health. According to Dr. Battle, "The negro huts [in Scotland Neck] are generally built of round pine or cypress logs, with dirt floors, & dirt in the interstices between the logs.

They are small, crowded, & smoky; & as might be expected very filthy." Leading medical authorities were aware of the connection between cleanliness and disease, but many eighteenth-century slaveowners were not. Farsighted masters might insist that quarters be kept sanitary and be certain that slaves had ample time for housecleaning, but others viewed the hours spent away from field labor as a waste of valuable time.

Slave food was like slave housing—adequate to sustain life but far from satisfying. According to Charles William Jansen, the weekly allowance of Thomas Blount's slaves in Hyde County "consisted of *salt herrings*, of an inferior quality, and a peck of *Indian corn in the cob*, to each." When Jansen visited their quarters, the Blount slaves had not received salt beef or pork for months, "and Mr. Overseer, with perfect indifference, observed, that he did not expect any fresh supply for some time after what was brought them should be consumed." William Attmore and other eighteenth-century travelers agreed that the typical slave ration in eastern North Carolina included a peck of corn per week, and sometimes an additional portion of salted fish or meat. The food furnished by masters provided slaves with an adequate number of calories for each worker but neither variety nor an adequate supply of vitamins. Nutritional requirements were not well understood in the eighteenth century, and dietary-deficiency diseases were consequently common among lower-income white and black North Carolinians until well into the twentieth century.

Archeological investigation at Somerset Place has provided evidence that the slave diet there was not strictly limited to the rations issued by Josiah Collins. Archeologists have uncovered the foundations of a large kitchen and storehouse complex that seems to have been used as a food preparation area from the earliest days of the plantation. The slaves who dug the canal were probably fed communally from this kitchen or one like it. Bones of butchered cows, pigs, deer, turtles, and other animals appeared in the remains, indicating that slaves were able to supplement their diet with their own hunting and stock-raising efforts. Black bean fragments testify to additional vegetable items on the slave table.

Travelers' accounts confirm that many masters provided a minimum ration to slave families and expected their bondsmen to supplement these supplies from their own gardens. "Scotus Americanus" reported that slaves on the lower Cape Fear were given a daily task that could be finished by the early afternoon. Afterward, they were free to cultivate plots provided by the master, to hunt, to fish, or to otherwise occupy their time independently. Each family received "5 or 6 acres each, for rice, corn, potatoes, tobacco &c. for their own use and profit, of which the industrious among them make a great deal." Scottish traveler and diarist Janet Schaw agreed with this observation and added calabashes

Thomas Blount. Portrait attributed to Charles J. F. St. Memin, owned by heirs of Lida T. Rodman.

and other vegetables to the list of slave produce. Later generations of Collins slaves raised corn in a "Negro patch" behind their quarters, though their work for the master normally kept them in his fields until sundown.

Some slaves raised hogs and poultry that they sold to the master at current prices, and spent their earnings on clothing, pocketknives, and other personal items. "Scotus Americanus" was sure that the slaves worked on their own plots "for amusement, pleasure, and profit," and not for subsistence, but, in view of what others have said about slave rations, his interpretation seems overly generous. Making slaves partly responsible for feeding themselves was too good a disciplinary device for most masters to pass up. It was also in the master's interest to be sure that his slaves were not kept hungry, for if they did not feel well-fed, most slaves did not hesitate to steal what they needed from a tight-fisted owner.

Eighteenth-century slaves were less successful in clothing themselves than they were in finding enough to eat. While traveling through Craven, Carteret, and Onslow Counties, Ebenezer Hazard wrote in his diary on 8 January 1778 that he saw "a Negro Woman with nothing on her but a very ragged Petticoat." William Attmore described the Tar River ferrymen as "ragged" in late December 1787, while one revolutionary officer in 1781 commented in his journal that "their Negros tho' at this Season of the year [late November] are almost Naked in General. Some of them Quite as Naked as they were born have come into our Camp to look for pieces of Old Clothes." Children fared especially poorly in the distribution of apparel. Hazard saw "a Number of negro Children of both Sexes, stark naked today; they have never been clothed yet." Attmore saw a naked child in a tavern yard near Greenville in late December 1787 and five others near Washington who wore nothing but a shirt. The children at Thomas Blount's canal project went entirely bare, including the boy who waited on the white folks' table, and Scottish gentlewoman Janet Schaw was escorted through the streets of Wilmington "by a black wench half naked." Presumably, the slaves who suffered through the winter with no clothing at all were noteworthy for being unusual, but in general slave clothing was very scanty by the standards of eighteenth-century white observers.

Regardless of how well slaves ate, or how they lived, or the difficulty of their tasks, the human relationship between slaves and masters was a difficult one. Slavery was based on compulsion and exploitation, a fact that eighteenth-century slaveowners accepted candidly. "It is the most disagreeable labour in the world," sighed Mrs. Ann Blount Shepard Pettigrew, "that of making others work." No tales of loving black nursemaids or loyal family retainers appear in the letters of Mrs. Pettigrew, who married Ebenezer Pettigrew, the plantation neighbor of Josiah Collins II. Bonds of genuine mutual affection sometimes bridged the gap between master and slave, but nineteenth-century defenders of slavery tended to exaggerate such cases as part of their campaign to defend the South's "peculiar institution." Less sentimental than later generations, Mrs. Pettigrew and her husband realized that the slaves' obedience was never truly voluntary and that a variety of measures was necessary to enforce the master's will.

Perhaps the most efficient methods were rewards for good work and the granting of privileges in recognition of superior talents or performance. Once these concessions had been given, the implicit threat of their removal could be an effective disciplinary measure. Common rewards were cash or prizes for extra work, permission to visit friends or relatives off the plantation, permission for a party or a religious service, or promotion to a position of skill or trust on the plantation. Most of the time, these positive incentives were sufficient, but the system of plantation discipline would have collapsed without the constant threat of punishments as well. When a slave's work was unsatisfactory to the master, he or she could be sold, but this was not always convenient. The slave could not be fired, fined, or put in prison, for slaves were prisoners already. When a master believed that more punishment than the withdrawal of privileges was necessary, the simplest alternative was to inflict physical pain. The commonest tool for this purpose was the whip.

According to Charles William Jansen, "this instrument of punishment is made of the skin of an ox or cow, twisted hard when wet, and tapering off like a riding whip; it is hard and elastic, inflicting dreadful wounds when used with severity." Jansen, an observer hostile to slavery, believed that whippings were common. "Often have I witnessed negroes dragged, without regard to age or sex, to the public whipping post, or tied up to the limb of a tree, at the will of the owner, and flogged with a cow-skin, without pity or remorse, til the ground beneath is dyed with the blood of the miserable sufferer." Other travelers slighted the subject of corporal punishment and focused on more casual forms of mistreatment like overwork, hunger, and cold. Some commentators, "Scotus Americanus" among them, insisted that North Carolina slavery was a benign institution. "Good usage is what alone can make the negroes well attached to their master's interest," he declared. "The inhabitants of Carolina, sensible of this, treat these valuable servants in an indulgent manner, and something like rational beings." The pamphleteer's slighting reference to slave rationality may betray his basic unreliability as an observer of blacks. Nevertheless, there were very few travelers who were in close contact with the most intimate details of plantation life, and a consistent account of slave punishments does not emerge from their writings.

A clearer picture appears in the writings of the slaveholders themselves.

The Reverend Charles Pettigrew. Portrait by W. J. Williams, owned by Allen R. Pettigrew.

One example from the letters of the Pettigrew family provides valuable insight into the human complexity of an institution that the law insisted was merely a property relationship.

The Reverend Charles Pettigrew (ca. 1744–1807) was an Episcopal minister of Edenton and vicinity who owned three plantations in the region of Albemarle Sound. Bonarva, the largest and most lucrative, bordered on the shores of Lake Phelps adjoining Somerset Plantation. Belgrade lay between Bonarva and Albemarle Sound, near the present town of Creswell, while Scotch Hall stood in Bertie County. Despite his extensive landholdings, Pettigrew owned no more than about thirty-five slaves, which put him somewhat closer to the average North Carolina master than the owner of Somerset Place. Pettigrew's son Ebenezer inherited his father's property and expanded it by careful management and by his marriage to Ann Blount Shepard. The papers of father and son are a rich source of information on the daily reality of antebellum slavery in North Carolina.

Charles Pettigrew was not so different from other planters. He was a pious man who desired to be a kind master and a devoted Christian but who also wanted a productive plantation. He had been elected first bishop of the Diocese of North Carolina in the Protestant Episcopal Church but failed twice to obtain proper consecration from another bishop. He finally abandoned the attempt when it became clear that religious duties would interfere with the profitable operation of his farms. He prayed for peace in Europe, but, when an upsurge of warfare sent the prices of his staple exports soaring, he could scarcely disguise his elation. Pettigrew's contradictory desires forced him frequently to acknowledge "the difficulty of serving both God and mamon." The difficulty was nowhere more apparent than in Pettigrew's relations with his slaves.

The minister frequently complained that his slaves refused to work whenever his back was turned, but, as he explained to one correspondent, "we have no overseer, Choosing rather to oversee the negroes [ourselves], than an Overseer & them too." Pettigrew consequently relied on a set of trusted male slaves to supervise the work of the others. Among them were Fortune, who was in charge at Bonarva; Pompey, who normally lived at Belgrade but who shuttled frequently between the plantations; and Anthony, Cambridge, and George, who assisted at Belgrade.

The Pettigrews gave these men extra responsibility and depended on their cooperation, but they also viewed them with continual mistrust. "In regard to your wheat, I am afraid it is to[o] much exposed to the th[i]evishness of the negroes," Charles Pettigrew warned Ebenezer. "It is a very ready article of trade, & Fortune has his mercantile correspondents, who are ready at all times to receive him kindly." Hostility and dependency bred frustration on both sides of the racial chasm, a combination that flared into resistance by the slaves and violent retaliation by Pettigrew. "To manage *negroes* without the exercise of too much passion, is next to an impossibility," the minister remorsefully acknowledged. "After my strongest endeavors to the contrary, I found it so. I would therefore put you on your guard," he urged his son, "lest their provocations should on some occasions transport you beyond the limits of decency and christian morality."

Most of the specific occasions when Pettigrew lost his temper are now lost to view, but one incident involving Pompey was probably typical. One Sunday morning in 1803, the aging minister directed his slave to accompany the family to church. Pompey objected, for this was not his regular job, but Pettigrew insisted because the other slaves were busy at their tasks. Pompey obeyed reluctantly, and Pettigrew did not ruffle the Sabbath calm with further reprimands. Early the next morning, however, Pettigrew "began to chide him for his behaviour on that occasion & he could not bear reproof." Angered, Pompey lashed back in self-defense; in the jargon of racial etiquette, he became "impudent" and suddenly the genteel man of the cloth was threatening his foreman with violence. Pompey stifled his rage a second time but he had evidently heard more than he could bear. During the confusion surrounding breakfast, the trusted foreman bolted for the woods.

No one knows now the pattern of indignities that somehow climaxed for Pompey when Pettigrew ordered him to church. He may have felt that driving the carriage and carrying the prayer books was too menial a job for the foreman, or he may have resented Christian proselytizing. He almost certainly had the customary right to a day off on Sunday. At all events, Pettigrew feared that Pompey's flight was no impetuous display of temper, but the result of a careful plan based on long-standing grievances. "I am afraid he has gone to Edenton," the minister wrote his son, "& perhaps intends trying to get to a Brother whom Cambridge boasts of having a white wife somewhere northward. . . . I am sorry, I had occasion to take him to Town lately, as he had opportunity to hear of so many getting off so easily from there." Knowing how much family ties meant to slaves, the elder Pettigrew warned Ebenezer to have Pompey's father in Edenton watched so that the fugitive might be captured with ease.

Pettigrew's fears were not fulfilled, for Pompey returned the following Sunday. Unwilling as always to violate the Sabbath, Pettigrew postponed Pompey's whipping until Monday, when he "made George give him a civil cheek for his impudence, & the loss of just a week's work." Stripped of his rank, Pompey was exiled to Bonarva to work under Fortune in disgrace.

In this complicated interchange, the whip was a last resort, the final symbol of Pettigrew's authority. The master preferred not to use it, but he did not hesitate when confronted with a challenge to his right of command. The power to inflict pain was essential to the system of slavery, and Pettigrew could not have operated his plantation without it.

In reflective moments, the well-meaning minister acknowledged reality bitterly. "It is a pity that agreeably to the nature of things, Slavory [*sic*] & Tyranny must go together—and that there is no such thing as having an obediant & useful Slave, without the painful exercise of undue & tyrannical authority." Violence was so crucial to eighteenth-century slave discipline that North Carolina's planter-dominated Assembly did not forbid the killing of slaves by masters until 1774. The murder of slaves by masters did not carry the same penalty as other murders until 1791, and even then the law did not apply to slaves who died as the result of "moderate correction."

Conscience-stricken, Charles Pettigrew could suddenly declare, "I sincerely wish that there was not a Slave in the world," but he made no attempt to give up his power or to put his antislavery sentiments into practice. Many masters had none of Pettigrew's squeamishness. Conversing with William Attmore in 1787, Judge John Williams of Williamsboro "wished that there was an immediate addition of One hundred Thousand Slaves to the State . . . for the present ease and affluence," even though he admitted that the result might be a calamity for future generations. Not much given to such philosophizing, most North Carolina slaveowners accepted the world as they found it, enjoyed the material comforts that slaves produced, and dreaded the possibility that their slaves might rise against them in insurrection.

For the most part, North Carolina slaves resisted the power of their masters by individual and collective actions that made their condition more bearable but did not challenge the system of slavery as such. Bondsmen feigned sickness or ignorance, broke tools, stole food, sheltered runaways, and protected each other from the master's abuses. Among slaves, families were a source of personal pride and mutual support for parents, children, and relatives alike. The slave community as a whole supported musicians, preachers, storytellers, healers, and craft workers who created a dynamic African American culture that affirmed the human dignity of even the most persecuted inhabitant of the quarters. Weddings, funerals, religious services, and holiday celebrations gave slaves an opportunity to assert their humanity and their rightful equality with whites. When Jonkonnu gave orders every Christmas and Josiah Collins obeyed, the slave participants in the ritual had slyly claimed a moral right to change places with their owners. Opposition to slavery periodically went beyond foot-dragging on the job and cultural challenges in the quarters, but most acts of slave resistance were individual actions comparable to Pompey's brief flight from Belgrade.

Occasionally slave rebelliousness inspired more than individual resistance. But in North Carolina as a whole, whites outnumbered blacks by two to one, and slaves were kept isolated on remote plantations, without the means of communicating plans or coordinating movements so it is not surprising that slave insurrections were an uncommon occurrence. On at least two occasions, North Carolina slaves may have made an attempt to surmount these obstacles, although the evidence is ambiguous, as in all such cases.

In 1775 the colony was rife with rumors that the British government would arm the slaves and send them against their masters in an attempt to halt the rapidly growing independence movement. The Pitt County Committee of Safety discovered what they called "a deep laid Horrid Tragick Plan laid for destroying the inhabitants of this province without respect of persons, age or sex." Forty slaves were arrested, and at least ten received eighty lashes each. Others had their ears cut off. A large quantity of confiscated ammunition lent credence to the patriots' claim that they had nipped a major conspiracy just in time.

Almost two decades later, eastern North Carolina teemed again with rumors of slave conspiracies. Religious revivals and political controversy had unsettled community tranquility in 1802, and a widely publicized conspiracy planned by Gabriel Prosser had been thwarted in Richmond, Virginia, only two years earlier. Influential whites claimed to have discovered written messages between groups of plotters up and down the Roanoke River Valley, and many planters, including Charles Pettigrew and Thomas Blount, felt sure that their own slave households harbored some of the plotters. Retaliating instantly, courts in Bertie, Martin, Camden, Currituck, Perquimans, Hertford, Washington, Edgecombe, and Halifax Counties hanged a total of twenty-one suspected participants and whipped and deported an unknown number of others. Across the border in Virginia, two dozen slaves lost their lives in the aftermath of the suspected uprising. Exaggerated white fears undoubtedly played a role in this and all other responses to the threat of slave rebellion, but white terror of black revenge was not entirely without foundation.

To Carolina slaveowners, the benefits of slave labor justified the risks that came with it. Historians have traditionally used the ownership of twenty slaves or more as an arbitrary cutoff point between the moderately prosperous farmer and the plantation owner. Whatever the size of their labor force, masters put their slaves to all kinds of labor, from plowing fields and sawing logs to cooking food and tending children. For the most part, slaves did work that would bring their owners the highest financial return, so they were especially active in producing goods for the export market. In the turpentine forests, slaves hacked and scraped the pine trees and chopped "boxes" in the trunks to catch the sap. When the juices stopped flowing in winter, slaves made tar and lumber or ventured into swamps to cut shingles and barrel staves. Some of the largest "plantations" in the colony were actually more like logging camps. According to Janet Schaw, who visited the lower Cape Fear in 1774, Mr. John Rutherfurd had a "vast number of Negroes employed in various works" at his Hunthill plantation on the Northeast Cape Fear River. "He makes a great deal of tar and turpentine," she wrote, "but his grand work is a saw-mill, the finest I ever met with." Skilled slaves made rafts and barrels for the products of Hunthill, and Rutherfurd was able to float 50,000 planks and one or two hundred barrels of naval stores to Wilmington every two weeks. "Everybody agrees," Miss Schaw noted admiringly, "that it [Hunthill] is able to draw from twelve to fifteen hundred [pounds] a year sterling money."

Cape Fear planters also grew rice along the narrow stretches of riverbank where fresh water rose and fell with the tide. They constructed elaborate dams and sluices to flood and drain their fields by tidal action. Rice cultivation was back-breaking work, for slaves were given hoes and sickles to cultivate and harvest the crop instead of more efficient plows and scythes. When they could be spared from the rice fields, slaves of the Cape Fear plantations grew indigo in the upland fields that could not be flooded. Indigo production ceased when the War for Independence put an end to the British subsidy for the crop, but rice and naval stores continued to be Cape Fear River staples until after the Civil War.

Farther inland, North Carolina planters grew the same kinds of crops their yeoman neighbors did, but in greater quantities. Even large planters wanted to be self-sufficient and tried to raise or make almost everything eaten or used on the plantation; but, much more than yeoman farmers, they counted on selling a large surplus every year as well. Backcountry plantations sold corn, wheat, peas, pork, beef, tobacco, flaxseed, and dairy products. Piedmont slaveholders were also likely to expand their operations with a sawmill, a gristmill, a tannery, or a store. The planter used these facilities himself and sought customers from the surrounding community as well.

Whether they owned one slave or dozens, North Carolina's slaveholders clearly had the chance to live more comfortably than the average small farmer. Just how much better they lived was something contemporaries disagreed about. Writing in 1773, an anonymous Scottish pamphleteer painted for prospective immigrants to North Carolina a glowing portrait of the lifestyle of colonial merchants and planters. "Their houses are elegant, their tables always plentifully covered and their entertainment sumptuous," declared "Scotus Americanus." "They are fond of company, living very sociable and neighbourly, visiting one another often. Poverty is almost an entire stranger among them, as the settlers are the most hospitable and charitable people that can be met with." The enthusiastic traveler could not find enough compliments to bestow on the leaders of the rapidly growing province, soon to be a colony no longer. "They are generous, well bred, and dress much; are polite, humane, and hospitable, and never tired of rendering strangers all the service in their power." All in all, the author concluded, Scotsmen dissatisfied with conditions at home could hardly do better than to come to North Carolina, where moderate efforts and slight expense could enable any hard-pressed farmer to share the lifestyle of such gentlemen.

At about the same time that "Scotus Americanus" was composing his glowing account, one of his countrywomen was forming a different opinion. "The people in town live decently," Janet Schaw admitted, "and tho' their houses are not spacious, they are in general very commodious and well-furnished." Once she left the homes of Wilmington merchants, however, Janet Schaw began to miss the elegance and good taste that "Scotus Americanus" had ascribed to plantation living. "There are two plantations on the banks [of the Northeast Cape Fear River]" she recalled, "both of which have the most delightful situations that is possible to imagine." If only the owners had the elementary sense of good taste to keep down the underbrush, she implied, they could perfect a magnificent landscape. "This however is too much for the listless hand of indolence and this beautiful place is overgrown with brambles and prickly pears, which render it entirely useless, tho' a few Negroes with their hoes could clear it in a week." What was worse, she observed, the stately mansion planned by one owner was abandoned half-finished "and he and his wife live in a hovel, while this handsome fabrick is daily falling into decay."

Who was right: "Scotus Americanus" or Janet Schaw? Their two accounts pit one stereotype against another, the myth of Old South gentility against the image of a rawboned provincial society with only the clumsiest sense of the social graces. In a sense, both Scottish travelers were correct. "Scotus Americanus" described the ideal lifestyle of many planters and the reality enjoyed by a few, while Janet Schaw criticized the gap that sometimes appeared between aspiration and performance. In most cases, neither stereotype was completely valid. The lives of two occupants of one of the oldest of the Piedmont plantation houses illustrate the wide variation that existed among planter families and their circumstances.

The House in the Horseshoe sits on a gentle hill in northern Moore County. Below the house, wide, level fields stretch out toward the wooded

House in the
Horseshoe (1772),
Moore County

banks of the Deep River, which reaches in a wide bend around three sides of the property. Now a state historic site, the spot is peaceful, picturesque, and fertile; it is easy to see why Philip Alston (d. 1791) wanted to own it when he came to the district in 1772 and started to purchase land. Tradition says that a Scot named McFadden built the House in the Horseshoe for Alston. It also claims that after McFadden struck a white servant and found himself prosecuted for assault, he became disgusted with American notions of equality and returned to Scotland.

Alston had a stormy career that belied the apparent tranquility of his homestead. He came to Deep River from Halifax County, where his relatives were established and highly respected planters. Like many families in the Albemarle and Roanoke regions, the Alstons had come to North Carolina from Virginia. Alston had married Temperance Smith, heiress to a large tract of land on the Roanoke River, and Alston's father had given him slaves before he moved to the Piedmont. When old Mr. Alston died, he owned 150 slaves and 100,000 acres, but there was no further bequest for his son Philip. The young man had

made unseemly haste to leave the Roanoke section, some whispered, because he sought to avoid a counterfeiting charge.

Philip Alston was not left without resources. Prior to 1777 he bought almost 7,000 acres of land in Cumberland County. He resold much of this land, but in 1780, he still retained 2,500 acres, 20 slaves, 9 horses, 30 heads of cattle, and £2,200 in cash. Alston was not only one of the two largest slaveholders in his district; the cash value of his taxable assets made him one of the wealthiest individuals as well. Alston was able to translate his economic position into political power. He was a justice of the peace, member of the legislature, and colonel of the county militia.

During the American Revolution, Alston put his assertive nature at the service of his country. He commanded a band of soldiers against the actions of Tory (British sympathizer) guerrillas when they became active following the British invasion of North Carolina in 1780. On one occasion, Alston's company captured an accomplice of the Tory officer David Fanning. They beat their prisoner with musket butts in an unsuccessful attempt to obtain information and

Dining room of the House in the Horseshoe

Patriot reenactors defend the House in the Horseshoe from attack by Tories.

then left him to die. Discovering the murder, Fanning swore revenge and ambushed Alston and his men at the House in the Horseshoe on 5 August 1781. After a fierce skirmish, Alston was forced to surrender and to promise not to fight the king's forces any longer. Bullet holes from this fight still scar the walls of Alston's home.

After the Revolution, Moore County was split off from Cumberland and Alston served as its first clerk of court and later as state senator. When it was discovered that Alston stood indicted for the murder of yet another prisoner during the Revolutionary War and that he had denied the existence of God, the Senate expelled him from his seat, and he was later stripped of his post as justice of the peace. Governor Richard Caswell pardoned him for the murder. Soon thereafter, Alston tried to install his son as his successor in the post of Moore County clerk of court. A political rival who objected was soon discovered murdered on a night when the Alstons had been entertaining the neighborhood with a ball. Alston's slave Dave was charged with the crime, but Alston seems to have connived at Dave's escape. Jailed for contempt of court, Alston escaped and fled the state in 1790. He got as far as Georgia, where in 1791 an unknown assailant shot and killed him while he slept in bed.

Philip Alston was a powerful and violent man whose life and death exemplified the brutal aspects of frontier empire-building. The House in the Horseshoe was acquired in 1798 by Colonel Benjamin Williams, a man whose career bore some resemblance to Philip Alston's but whose character was remembered in a very different way by those who knew him.

Benjamin Williams. Portrait by an unknown artist, owned by the University of North Carolina at Chapel Hill.

Williams came from a planter family of Johnston County and married Elizabeth Jones of Halifax County. She was the daughter of a colonial official and half-sister of Willie and Allen Jones, both well-known Revolutionary leaders. Williams was a member of the First and Third Provincial Congresses and served under George Washington in the Continental Army, eventually reaching the rank of colonel. Widely respected and owning land in scattered counties, he was able to represent Craven, Johnston, and Moore Counties in both houses of the General Assembly. His constituents sent him to the Third U.S. Congress (1793–95) but he did not seek reelection. To cap his political career, Williams received four one-year terms as governor of North Carolina in 1799, 1800, 1801, and 1807. He also sat on the board of trustees of the University of North Carolina from 1789 to 1802 and while governor acted as its chairman ex officio.

Benjamin Williams named the House in the Horseshoe "Retreat," and he used it initially as a country home and as an experimental cotton farm. The district was isolated, Williams complained, mail service was poor, and he did not particularly care for his neighbors. Later on, Williams moved to Deep River permanently and spent his last years there, raising cotton and training racehorses. He added wings to Alston's house (now removed), and he also built a granary, stable, weaving house, smokehouse, carriage house, and cotton house. The overseer and his family occupied a separate house, and nearby cabins sheltered the 103 slaves that Williams eventually acquired. When he considered the fertility of the land, the quality of the improvements, and the availability of more good land for purchase nearby, Williams could wax enthusiastic: "I think it may be justly ranked among the most valuable Estates in North Carolina," he announced to one potential purchaser, and declared its worth to be $30,000, a very sizable sum for 1803.

In a letter of 25 July of that year, Williams described his Deep River plantation to his friend John Steele. "The river thro' these Lands," he informed Steele, "forms the shape of an Horseshoe, leaving on the North side in a bend in the River about 1900 Acres, on which is a plantation of 454 Acres cleared . . . all of which except 50 Acres where the Houses are placed is . . . low ground under good fences & cross fences." He referred to the main house as "a tolerable two story House with the frames now ready to put up a Wing 24 by 20, at each end." He also brought to Steele's attention "A Cotton House 60 by 20 feet pitch, long body, frame Roof, two range of floor divided by partitions proper for reception of & ginning of Cotton."

Plantation life agreed with Colonel Benjamin Williams. "I can assure you," he wrote to one friend, "with the little experience which has fallen my lot that in no pursuit have I yet found that enjoyment of contentment which agriculture affords." Nevertheless, planting carried its share of difficulties. Upland cotton had not been a profitable crop until Eli Whitney discovered how to separate the fibers from the seed. Whitney had perfected his cotton gin in 1783, and while planters like Benjamin Williams were eager to try the new staple, they lacked experience in its cultivation. "In addition to my former Enquiries I beg leave to further trouble you on the Subject of the Culture of Cotton," he wrote to General William Henry Harrington. "How many Seed (when you plant in Hills) do you put in? Is it thought most advantageous to top and sucker Cotton & whether high or low should it be toped?" Williams also struggled against slaves and neighboring whites who tried to rob his fields at night, and he searched long and hard for a sober and competent overseer. When he finally secured the services of a certain Mr. Morrow, Williams called him "indeed a treasure, the best behaved man alive," but he worried about how he could continue to pay Morrow competitive wages. As an improving farmer, Williams experimented with mules instead of draft horses or oxen, but he found them hard to obtain. He complained about North Carolina's lack of good rivers or internal improvements, and a bad experience with Fayetteville merchants led him to market his cotton directly in London. Williams was an enterprising country gentleman who obtained great wealth and extensive landholdings in North Carolina and the western states, but he never felt satisfied with the economic or cultural achievements of his native state.

Williams's personal letters show him to have been solicitous of his wife's health and of his son's education. He was fond of gracious living, and the House in the Horseshoe frequently bulged with guests. For several weeks in the summer of 1806, the old place sheltered five visiting relatives and one tutor, plus Colonel and Mrs. Williams and their son, Benjamin William Williams. By the time of his death in 1814, Williams had achieved a reputation as a model planter and ideal southern gentleman, for he was wealthy, hospitable, generous, public-spirited, conscientious, moderately progressive, an effective master, a devout Christian, a loving husband and father. The Raleigh *Minerva* honored his passing with a respectful tribute: "He died as he had lived, much respected and highly esteemed by those who knew him, and from his general demeanour and devout professions as well previous to as during his last illness, he has left his relations and more intimate friends the cheering consolation that he died a believer, resigned and happy in the hope of mercy through the atonement and merits of the Redeemer." Even when due allowances are made for eulogistic license, Benjamin Williams seems to have represented the best sort of man that his social class produced, just as Philip Alston may have represented the worst.

The wives of these two planters were both essential members of the plantation community. Little is known of Temperance Smith Alston except that she brought a large tract of land to her marriage, bore a large number of children, and negotiated the truce between her husband and David Fanning. Like Mrs. Alston, Elizabeth Jones Williams came from a distinguished family and no doubt contributed property to her husband's wealth. As plantation mistress, she probably supervised the work of slaves in the big house, the weaving house, and the kitchen. She had close contact with slave families and, as her will later revealed, developed special fondness for some of them, especially the women. Mrs. Williams's health was poor, however, and she may have lacked the strength for household tasks. She enjoyed the company of an intimate circle of female friends and relatives, but most of these women seem to have lived quite a distance from Deep River, some as far away as New Bern. Elizabeth Williams spent much of her time entertaining her friends and relatives as houseguests and paying extended visits to them in return, but she did not like to leave home without taking young Benjamin with her.

Elizabeth Williams survived her husband by three years and died in 1817 while visiting in New Bern. Her will lays open the web of close female and family relationships that composed her social world. Her son, Benjamin William Williams, inherited most of the property and served as executor along with William Martin, but Martin's wife Florah was entrusted with distributing personal bequests of clothing and other items. Two women witnessed the will, Laura Blake, who signed her name, and Sarah Taylor, who made her mark.

In a provision that Colonel Williams may have approved before his death, Mrs. Williams emancipated Essex, the trusted groom who had trained her husband's racehorses, and his wife Juno, as well as Phebe, the wife of Arnold. Essex and Juno also received "one cow and calf, one sow and pigs and two ewes and lambs." The bulk of Mrs. Williams's "black cloths," which she had undoubtedly worn in mourning for her late husband, went to Juno, Phebe, Silva, and Hanna, with the remainder going to other slave women at Mrs. Martin's discretion. Certain other slaves were not freed but given to special friends, with careful attention to preserving family ties. Mrs. Ana Maria Littlejohn received Evelina and her two children, Lovelace, Evelina's brother, and Nanny and her child. John W. Guion of New Bern received two couples and their children and one of the husbands' brothers. Simon was to be sold to a master of his own choice in Fayetteville, perhaps to reunite him with loved ones there, and Guion was to receive the money from the sale. It is impossible to know how these slaves felt about the arrangements made for them, or to know whether they reciprocated the feelings of affection that no doubt motivated Mrs. Williams. Individual manumissions tended to reinforce the slaveholders' sense of self-regard and were therefore ultimately self-serving, but it is also true that genuine feelings of mutual sympathy and respect could occasionally transcend the barriers between white and black. The other slaves of the Williams plantation remained in bondage.

The differences between the lives of Rachel Allen and Elizabeth Williams were striking. The pioneer's wife labored hard in her community, bore many children, and made an indispensable economic contribution to her household. For outside help, she drew on a dense network of friends and relatives in the immediate neighborhood, while she and her husband were partners in the myriad tasks of family survival. On the plantation, Elizabeth Williams doted on her only child, endured ill health, and spent her days in the restricted and conventional world that was the genteel woman's "place" in the nineteenth century. Her circle of female friends spread all over the state, but she had little to do with her close neighbors. Her husband was a soldier, politician, and man of the world. It was he who supervised the crops, chose an overseer, handled infractions of slave discipline, and made the final decisions about his son's education. Planter and patriarch, Benjamin Williams necessarily exercised his authority with a firm hand, for final responsibility for making the coercive system of slavery work rested on him. As a slaveholder, Elizabeth Williams was a beneficiary of that system, but, as a woman, she was restricted by male-dominated society and thus victimized by it. Her will reflected this ambiguous social position. On the one hand, she did not disinherit her son or outrage public opinion and (perhaps) violate her own convictions by emancipating all her slaves. On the other hand, she had been free as a woman to develop the close emotional ties to slaves that were usually denied to white men. She shared her feelings with a tight circle of female friends, and their web of shared relationships helped to mitigate some of the worst rigors of the system, though they did nothing to change its fundamental characteristics.

Like its two most famous owners, the House in the Horseshoe exemplified the extremes of plantation society. Its architectural details showed a close familiarity with the latest British fashion and its basic design and floor plan foreshadowed the most common house types and family living patterns of the nineteenth century. At the same time, the House in the Horseshoe is no lavish mansion. It is a plain, wooden, four-room house, with only a limited resemblance to the stately residences that contemporary landed magnates owned in tidewater Virginia or lowcountry South Carolina. Planters like Benjamin Williams cherished high hopes for their estates, but their actual achievements were limited by substantial obstacles. Like the House in the Horseshoe, their homes revealed the fundamental simplicity of the world they really lived in.

Even when they were large, English houses of earlier centuries had been like the hall-and-parlor houses of coastal North Carolina. They tended to be asymmetrical; each room led directly into the other without the use of passageways, and they did not provide for much privacy or a specialized use of space. During the intellectual and artistic movement known as the Enlightenment, these features began to change. Ideas of order, balance, and symmetry became important aesthetic values in British culture. "Georgian" architecture, named for the three King Georges of the eighteenth century, reflected the popularity of these values. Built in 1770, Tryon Palace at New Bern was the outstanding example of Georgian architecture in the colony, but the House in the Horseshoe reflects Georgian principles in a domestic setting.

The Georgian style became very popular in America. The basic pattern of the House in the Horseshoe began to appear in many late eighteenth-century houses and was repeated endlessly in North Carolina farmhouses of the next century. Two rectangular rooms above, two beneath, a center hall on each floor, and a stairway in between—this was the simplest and cheapest way to arrange four rooms to make a broad and impressive exterior. The plan gave every moderately prosperous farmer a conspicuous symbol of respectability and status. Termed the "central hallway I-house" by some architectural historians, because of its tall, thin profile, this type of dwelling has been called "perhaps the most common folk house type in the eastern United States." Long after classical Georgian architecture had come to seem outdated, the basic I-house floor plan with different stylistic embellishments persisted as the standard dwelling of the rural middle class.

Its popularity lay in its potential for the fulfillment of new ideals of family life and the separation of family life from work. Unlike in earlier houses, each room in this dwelling had its own special function. The dining room was on the left, the parlor on the right, and visitors waited in the hall until the family was ready to receive them. Cooking took place in the kitchen, a separate building in the rear. Sleeping, dressing, and bathing took place upstairs. There was one bedroom for parents and perhaps a baby; there was a separate room for the older children. The broad upstairs hallway belonged to everybody and was a good place for indoor work like spinning. Unlike the log cabin or the hall-and-parlor house, the spatial arrangement of the I-house seems recognizably modern.

The new house form mirrored and reinforced dramatic changes in the domestic life of the middle classes. In proper middle- and upper-class nineteenth-century households, work was something for servants and slaves, or for men to do away from home. This left the home increasingly a refuge for weary men and for women and children who, depending on one's point of view, were either trapped or sheltered in its confines. Parents relied less on the labor of their offspring, and modest progress against childhood diseases made it more likely that babies would live to maturity. Both of these developments encouraged parents to limit the size of their families. The reduced economic role of women elevated the importance of mutual affection as the basis of marriage. Among the upper and middle classes, home became "home, sweet home," lovingly presided over by wives idealized as mothers and restricted to domestic duties. The outside world impinged less directly on the family, and a corresponding sense of privacy developed. A growing insistence on individual political rights seemed to find an echo in decisions to allocate private space to particular family members and to particular functions of the household. In the century to come, middle-class North Carolinians built fewer one-room cabins and hall-and-parlor houses, while the central hallway I-house spread across the landscape. As she sat with her only child in the tidy parlor of the House in the Horseshoe, Elizabeth Williams presided over a household that was the forerunner of a new kind of family, a changing set of values, and the slow but unmistakable emergence of a different kind of society.

TOWNS IN A RURAL SOCIETY

"Places of wildness and rudeness, intemperance, ferocity, gaming, licentiousness, and malicious litigation!" President Joseph Caldwell of the University of North Carolina, who penned this description, found the county seats of early nineteenth-century North Carolina tumultuous dens of iniquity, but not everyone agreed with him. Some travelers were more bored than shocked by the urban places of North Carolina. "The generality of towns are so inconsiderable," wrote J. F. D. Smyth, "that in England they would scarcely acquire the appellation of villages." Robert Hunter Jr. felt equally unimpressed but spoke more bluntly. "Wilmington without exception is the most disagreeable sandy barren town I have visited on the continent," the young British merchant fumed in 1786. "I am extremely happy to think I shall leave it tomorrow." Even as the impatient traveler complained about North Carolina's second-largest town, he was forced to acknowledge the little port's significance to the state. "Several vessels are now lying in the harbor," Hunter recorded, "bound to the northward and different parts of Europe, laden with tobacco and naval stores." Hunter believed that the merchants of Wilmington exported 3,000 hogsheads of tobacco annually; had he also estimated the traffic in naval stores, he would have found an even larger volume of trade.

Out of a total population of less than 200,000 in 1770, there were fewer than 5,000 North Carolinians who lived in places that might be called urban. Though they were all quite small, towns served North Carolina society as centers for government and trade. Every county courthouse attracted a collection of storekeepers, tavernkeepers, and artisans to serve the rural citizens as they transacted legal business. Moreover, even the most self-reliant pioneer could not make his own salt or iron, and few free families felt they could do without sugar, coffee, tea, or similar imported products. These articles could come only from stores, and a conveniently located store soon attracted enough business to form the basis for a hamlet.

An inland settlement like the twin villages of Campbellton and Cross Creek (later united under the name Fayetteville) was the first stop in a journey that would carry plantation products to consumers around the world. An observer described the process. Storekeepers in Cross Creek bought backcountry products, he explained, and sent them down the Cape Fear River to Wilmington: "These merchants, or the settlers along the river, make large rafts of timber. . . . Upon these they lay their beef, port, and flower, in barrels, also their live stock, Indian corn, raw hides, butter, tallow, and whatever they have for market. . . . The planters dispose of their goods to merchants in town, or to ships at Wilmington, where there are many now from Britain, the West Indies, and the different colonies; to these they sell their goods, and in return, bring back sugar, rum, salt, iron, &c. and the rest in cash." Typical of the shipping merchants who dealt in such trade was Duncan McCleran, who, with shipwright labor, built the Nimocks House (ca. 1804), which is located in Heritage Square in Fayetteville.

A visitor described Fayetteville in 1788: "Not withstanding all which has been said against Fayette I think it by far one of the most agreeable towns in the State. I am sure it abounds more in all the good things of this World than the whole of the others put together. We have plays performed by the most eminent Actors for tragedy comedy etc. on an elegant Theatre. The wonders of the Magic Art are displayed in a most masterly manner by a little crooked leged fellow to the utter amazement of the gaping Yahoos." He further teased his correspondent: "I would earnestly recommend to all the belles in Edenton District who are in want of husbands to come to this place. I will insure them at a very moderate rate that they shall not remain on hand more than three weeks[.] [T]he chance is excellent, there are several Rich old Batchelors who have very much a consumptive appearance. Our Land lady is a good smart little woman but nothing uncommon[.] [S]he speaks Scotch Irish most divinely scolds like the devil is 25 Years of Age has dispatched two husbands already & is ready & looking for a third."

Settlers were unwilling to live in the backcountry without occasional purchases from the outside world. For the planter who planned his whole year's work with the expectation of selling staple crops, market towns were clearly central to every economic activity. Though few in number, North Carolina's townsmen were crucial to the rural way of life.

Commerce called the towns into existence, but the little settlements meant far more to the average country family than sites for buying and selling, or even for carrying out legal business in the courts. Elections were held in towns and so were meetings of the Assembly. Militia members gathered in towns to drill, and the congregations of the established church worshiped there. Taverns abounded in every town from the tiniest hamlet to the busiest seaport and ranged in quality from filthy dramshops to elegant hostelries for gentlemen.

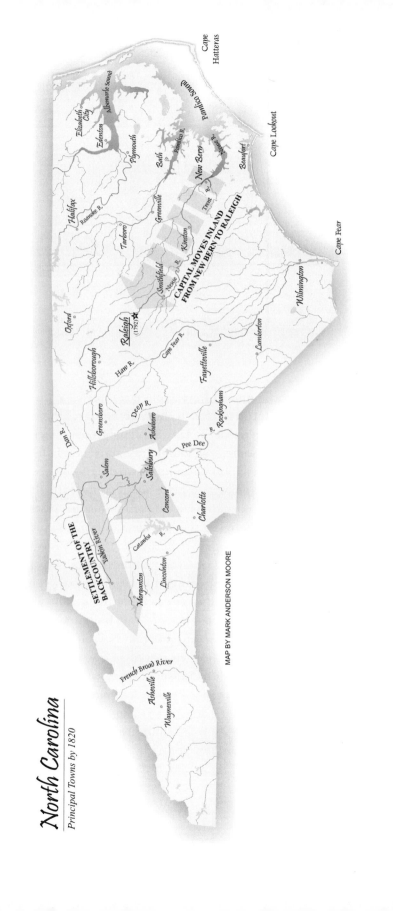

North Carolina

Principal Towns by 1820

Cape Hatteras

Cape Lookout

Cape Fear

Elizabeth City

Albemarle Sound

Edenton

Plymouth

Pamlico Sound

Bath

New Bern

Neuse R.

Beaufort

Halifax

Roanoke R.

Greenville

Trent R.

Tarboro

Kinston

CAPITAL MOVES INLAND
FROM NEW BERN TO RALEIGH

Smithfield

Neuse R.

Oxford

Raleigh
(1792) ★

Wilmington

Hillsborough

Cape Fear R.

Fayetteville

Haw R.

Lumberton

Greensboro

Deep R.

Asheboro

Rockingham

Dan R.

Pee Dee

Salem

Salisbury

SETTLEMENT OF THE
BACKCOUNTRY

Yadkin River

Concord

Charlotte

Catawba R.

Morganton

Lincolnton

French Broad River

Asheville

Waynesville

MAP BY MARK ANDERSON MOORE

Cameron-Nash Law Office (1801), Hillsborough. Photograph by Paulette Mitchell.

Public accommodation was often cramped and dirty, with poor service and worse food. But in a letter to his wife in March 1778, the prominent lawyer and future member of the U.S. Supreme Court James Iredell wrote of his delight in finding something better. "We arrived in Hillsborough about one," he told her, "found a most elegant tavern, dined with great satisfaction, and proceeded in the evening to a place about 10 miles further. Hillsborough rather exceeded my expectations; it is far from being a disagreeable town, as to appearance, and there is a remarkable handsome church in it." County courts set tavern rates. In August 1774 the Chatham County Court set the rate for "A Hott Dinner with beer or Cyder" at one pound four pence and a "Cold Dinner" at eight pence. The court authorized tavernkeepers to charge four pence for "Lodging in a good feather bed per night."

County seats attracted lawyers, who built offices in which to conduct their business. Because these were generally well-built, useful little structures, many have survived. The office (ca. 1800) of lawyer, legislator, and congressman Archibald Henderson in Salisbury, in Rowan County, subsequently became a schoolhouse and then a library. Among others that remain are the office (ca. 1818) in New Bern, in Craven County, of William Gaston, legislator, congressman, and state supreme court justice. Still another is the Cameron-Nash Law Office (1801) in Hillsborough. For some lawyers, attending the county courts and enjoying them were two different things. Henderson, for example, wrote to Gaston on 7 March 1810: "I am tired, seriously tired, of attending these County Superior Courts. Nothing but noise, confusion and ignorance. The profit is trifling, the Honor nothing."

Entertainment in the towns was a welcome relief from the monotony of rural life, and the typical visit to a town became the occasion for cutting loose from the restraints of ordinary existence. In a variety of ways, moreover, the pleasures that North Carolinians sought in towns were reflections of the same concerns, hopes, and fears that arose out of their work and their less dramatic daily lives. Consuming alcoholic beverages was a common practice and drunkenness often a problem in the new state. One visitor, William Attmore, recorded North Carolinians' drinking habits. "It is very much the custom in North Carolina," he wrote in his journal, "to drink Drams of some kind or other before Breakfast; sometimes Gin, Cherry bounce, Egg Nog, etc." On Christmas morning, he recalled, "according to North Carolina custom we had before Breakfast, a drink of egg nog." The *Raleigh Register* of 20 February 1818 reported an incident that proved fatal: "Joseph Steele and Joshua Wody, on the 3d instant, were drowned in Haw River, from crossing John Thompson's Ford, one on horse, in a state of intoxication. Both have left wives and families to lament their premature end." The same issue of the *Register* noted that "the body of Bartlett Dowdy, of Chatham county, was found in the Snow on the 6th instant, after lying six days. It is supposed he was in liquor, and [upon his] lying down, the Snow fell and covered him, and he rose no more!" The chance for a drink, a hand of cards, or even an eye-gouging fight was a source of excitement that few pioneers would pass up. The popularity of these entertainments probably said more about the character of North Carolina society than President Caldwell would have preferred to admit.

The most influential and conspicuous townsmen were merchants. When Robert Hunter Jr. left Edenton in 1786, he thought that "the people are almost all merchants here," but, as a literal statement of fact, that was far from true. Instead, most of the people depended on a relatively small number of merchants for their livelihood, and these merchants dominated the port both economically and politically. The home of Thomas Barker (1713–87), now on Edenton's waterfront, reflected the wealth and standing of this class of eighteenth-century townsmen. Men like Barker owned stores, warehouses, sailing vessels, and often plantations as well. They controlled town politics and, by close association with the governor and the Assembly, won high office in colonial and state government as well. Thomas Barker, for example, served as North Carolina's colonial agent to Great Britain shortly before the Revolution, a post that gave him responsibilities somewhat comparable to those of an ambassador to the mother country. Barker also acted as justice of the peace in Bertie County,

*Barker House
(ca. 1782), Edenton*

assemblyman for Edenton in Bertie County and for Chowan County, colonial treasurer, and collector of customs for Port Roanoke.

Towns were administrative and political centers, and the men who controlled these urban functions were also very important residents. Attorneys, judges, and royal officials maintained their homes and offices in the seaports, while a few other public servants lived in the smaller county seats. English-born James Iredell (1751–99) came to Edenton as deputy collector of the royal customs in the decade prior to the American Revolution. Iredell became a distinguished lawyer who sided with his adopted country in the contest for independence and who later sat on the United States Supreme Court. Iredell married Hannah Johnston (1747–1826), the niece of a former royal governor who brought to her husband a large fortune in land and slaves. In his proposal to Hannah, Iredell declared: "It is not perhaps very becoming in a young man with so scanty an Income as I have to offer his hand and Heart for a young Lady's Acceptance—I rely Madam, upon your Goodness for an excuse of the Impropriety." Begun about 1773 by an earlier owner, the Iredells' house on

Iredell House (1800),
Edenton

Bedroom in the Iredell House

East Church Street in Edenton was a monument to Iredell's personal success as well as a symbol of the close association between leading townsmen and powerful families in the country.

The Iredell-Johnston match was not unusual, for all segments of the colonial elite had the opportunity for similar personal ties. The principal lawyers and government officials were the merchants' close associates, for they protected business property in the courts and often asked businessmen to fill key posts in government. The merchants and lawyers together kept close ties with the largest planters, their principal customers and clients. Throughout the colonial period, merchants, lawyers, and planters held most of the seats in the Assembly, occupied most of the appointive posts in colonial government, and managed the trade of the province. Where the established Anglican Church had gained a foothold, these gentlemen sat on the parish vestry and regulated the religious life of the neighborhood. If there was a school in the vicinity, they served on the board of trustees, and their children composed most of the student body. Their families mingled freely with one another and frequently intermarried. Planters' sons who tired of the country sought training as merchants and lawyers, while wealthy townsmen plowed profits into the purchase of land and slaves in the countryside. In the cases of some gentry families, urban and rural activities were so deeply intertwined that it sometimes became difficult to say where planting ended and commerce or politics began. In the closing

decades of the eighteenth century, the planters and leading townsmen of eastern North Carolina comprised a unified elite that controlled the economy as
well as the government of the province and, to a lesser extent, dominated its
religious and cultural life as well.

Not all urban residents enjoyed the wealth or comforts of Thomas Barker
and James Iredell. The towns contained a middle class of smaller merchants
and of artisans who crafted shoes, clothing, furniture, and houses for the other
inhabitants, as well as barrels, boats, wagons, and wheels for the commercial
traffic. Doctors, teachers, printers, and ministers found employment in the
towns, and so did unskilled laborers. "The poorest set of people whom I saw
there," reported one admiring traveler, "are such as ply as sailers, or watermen
rather on boats and lighters, up and down the rivers." These men led hard
lives, and the pamphleteer thought they tended to ease their troubles with too
much strong drink, but their presence was essential to the smooth operation
of North Carolina's commerce.

Urban merchants had no intention of admitting the laboring classes—
drunk or sober—to equal political rights in North Carolina's towns. In 1772
the leading gentlemen of Campbellton complained of an excess of democracy in town elections. "The men of property are the fewest in Number," they
explained to the royal governor, "which must ever throw the power of determining the Election in the Hands of transient persons, Boatmen, Waggoners
and other Laborers, and to take it from their Employers, who are principally
interested in securing or improving from their right of Representation, the
property of the Town." The merchants petitioned Governor Josiah Martin for
a property limitation on the right to vote, and the king's representative lost no
time in granting their request.

The Andrew Johnson birthplace in Raleigh is one of the few surviving
houses associated with the poorer class of North Carolina townsmen. Measuring eighteen feet long by twelve feet wide, the tiny cottage stood for many
years in the courtyard of Peter Casso's Inn, which opened in 1795 as one of the
first hotels in Raleigh. Its cramped quarters and the overhead loft are reminiscent of the frontier log cabin, though, like most urban structures, the Johnson house was made of sawn lumber. Jacob and Mary McDonough Johnson,
parents of the seventeenth president of the United States, lived in the house
with their two sons while Jacob labored as a hotel porter and Mary worked as a
serving woman indoors at the inn. Lacking the independence of rural yeomen,
the Johnsons were subject to their employer's call night and day.

Jacob Johnson died in 1812, when young Andrew was only three years old.
Mrs. Johnson took up weaving on a hand loom to support herself and her children. She could not send the boys to school, but, when they reached their

Andrew Johnson House (ca. 1795), Raleigh

teens, she bound them to a tailor to learn the trade of making clothes. Unlike most other apprentices, Andrew Johnson escaped from the status of an artisan by a timely flight to Tennessee, where he married, learned to write, became a lawyer, and entered politics. Few North Carolina workingmen could even approximate this urban equivalent of the log-cabin-to-White-House success story.

Many urban residents were slaves who lacked even the minimal rights of the Johnson family. According to the U.S. Census, Edenton in 1790 contained 600 whites, 34 free blacks, and 941 slaves. Edenton's population seems to have been almost two-thirds black, but the statistics may include many plantation slaves whose owners lived in town. Fayetteville's population in the same year was more than one-third slave. Black men and women worked as house servants for white townspeople and as laborers, teamsters, and artisans in the town's commercial economy. Town slaves sometimes lived separately from their masters and could not be supervised as closely as slaves on the plantation. Whites consequently feared them even more than slaves who were confined to the plantation. Ebenezer Pettigrew urged that the Edenton town guard be kept strong, for "the negros are two [sic] numerous there to have uncurbed liberty at night, night is their day" and warned his town-dwelling friends against complacency. White residents shared his worries, and subjected all blacks, both slave and free, to a dense array of special rules and prohibitions that were designed to prevent conspiracy.

The size and functions of towns could vary considerably according to the section of the state. "Towns we have none," wrote an anonymous resident of Moore County in the eastern Piedmont. "Fagensville [now called Carthage] a village at the Court House containing 8 or 10 dwelling Houses is the only place that claims a title to the name." Milton, located in Caswell County some eighty-five miles to the north, was not much larger. "Situated in the fork of Country-line [Creek] and Dan-river, it has 2 stores, a Saddler's shop, a Hatter's Shop, a tavern with about 15 or 20 houses," wrote Bartlett Yancey. These two pithy descriptions summarized much that could apply to the inland villages of the state: they were quite small; they came into existence around a courthouse or a juncture of transportation routes; and the principal inhabitants were store-keepers, tavern operators, and artisans.

One backcountry town that seemed exceptional was nevertheless like the others in the role it played within the region. Salem was the central, or congregation, town of the Moravian settlement at Wachovia. The Moravians, also known as the Unitas Fratrum or Unity of Brethren, were German followers of the early Protestant martyr Jan Hus. They came to America to establish an ideal Christian community in the wilderness. Moving from Georgia to Pennsyl-

Single Brothers'
House (1769–86),
Old Salem

vania to North Carolina, they purchased nearly 100,000 acres of prime Pied-mont land from Lord Granville in 1753 and began to establish the settlement called Wachovia that same year. Their first town was a farming village named Bethabara, and Bethania soon joined it. By 1766 the agricultural operations were fully established, and the Moravians agreed to build a third town, "not designed for farmers," as they put it, "but for those with trades."

The Brethren called the new town "Salem," a Hebrew word that means "peace." They built the community to reflect their conception of the Chris-tian way of life and to express their Central European ideas of orderliness and compact planned development. In the beginning, property in Salem was held in common. Individual families leased house lots on a yearly basis, but most of the town's trades and businesses were controlled by the community, acting through the church. The central town square, surrounded by church, schools, and other public buildings, conveys the sense of communal planning eloquently, as the congregation strove to reproduce the solidarity of a German village. Communal organization touched individual lives as well as the town's economy. Strong traditions of education and congregational music bound the generations to each other and fostered a sense of their collective identity. Moravians grouped themselves into "choirs" according to age, sex, and marital status. Children lived with their parents until the age of twelve, when they were apprenticed to learn a trade. Apprentices usually lived with their masters until they reached eighteen and lived thereafter with members of their choir, in the Single Brothers' House or the Single Sisters' House. The Saal (hall) of the Single Brothers' House was used for daily religious services. Single men and boys lived and worked in the house, each boy apprenticed to an artisan as economic demand dictated. (Today, demonstrations of many trades take place daily in the Single Brothers' House at Old Salem, while the nearby Winkler Bakery gives visitors an opportunity to see, smell, and taste the products of skilled Moravian bakers.)

The skills acquired by Salem youngsters distinguished the town from the rough-and-ready society of the frontier. "Every man follows some occupation," marveled one visitor in 1790. "Every woman is engaged in some feminine work; a tanner, shoemaker, potter, saddler, tinner, brewer, distiller, etc., is here seen at work; from their labors, they not only supply themselves but the country all around them." Eighteenth-century travelers unfailingly praised the display of frugality, neatness, hard work, and skilled workmanship they found among the Salem inhabitants. The Moravians, wrote one traveler, "live in brotherly love and set a laudable example of industry, unfortunately too little observed and followed in this part of the country." Elkanah Watson of Massachusetts agreed. "The moment I touched the boundary of the Moravians, I noted a marked and most favorable change in the appearance of buildings and farms," he wrote. "Even the cattle seemed larger, and in better condition. Here, in combined and well-directed effort, all put shoulders to the wheel, which apparently moves on oily springs."

Moravian craftsmanship attracted a steady stream of customers to Salem. J. F. D. Smyth took particular notice of "a very extensive [manufactory] of earthenware, which they have brought to great perfection, and supply the whole country with it for some hundred miles around." In 1773, the Salem potter Brother Aust had the luck to hire a journeyman potter from the English Wedgewood factory and learned from him the techniques of making queensware, a high-fired, cream-colored earthenware of rococo design. This gave the Moravian pottery an excellence unmatched in the colonies at that time. In Salem itself, the Market-Fire House on the town square was the focal point of

Elkanah Watson

buying and selling of Moravian products, while the Miksch Tobacco Shop is a further example of the Moravians' commercial architecture and lifestyle. Like most of the families in Salem, the Miksch household conducted their business on the ground floor and used the upper story for living space. Many of the customers at the tobacco shop came from several days' journey away and stopped there as part of an extended shopping trip for manufactured products. Hundreds of these Piedmont farmers camped by the roadside as they traveled; others pampered themselves at the well-appointed Salem Tavern, which adjoined the town square.

President George Washington was only one of many distinguished tourists who found an evening's shelter in the tavern's comfortable chambers. About his 1791 visit to Salem, Washington recorded in his diary: "Salem is a small but neat village; and like all the rest of the Moravian settlements, is governed by an excellent police—having within itself all kinds of artisans. The number of souls does not exceed 200." He wrote that on 1 June, he "spent the forenoon

*Salem Tavern (1784),
Old Salem*

in visiting the Shops of the different Tradesmen, the houses of accommodation for the single men and Sisters of the Fraternity, and their place of worship. Invited six of their principal people to dine with me and in the evening went to hear them sing, and perform on a variety of instruments Church music." Then, "At the close of the day the wind instruments were heard sweetly beside the Tavern." An inventory of Salem Tavern taken in 1807 shows 17 double featherbeds, 17 double chaff beds, 10 blankets, 17 woolen counterpanes, 17 cotton counterpanes, 65 bed sheets, 35 towels, 25 tablecloths, rafts of pillows and pillowcases, 17 double bedsteads, and 60 chairs.

Organized, disciplined, and highly trained in specific crafts, the Salem Brethren lived very differently from the more individualistic pioneer farmers and jacks-of-all-trades who surrounded them. The Moravians and the back-countrymen nevertheless needed each other. Salem was a market for all varieties of country produce, and Moravian teamsters made regular trips to Cross Creek and other fall-line towns to dispose of surplus commodities like corn and flour. In return, Salem supplied the backcountry with all varieties of manufactured products and also served as a distribution point for imports like sugar, coffee, tea, and salt. Salem's community organization was unique, as were the high standards of workmanship and the appearance of the town itself, but the position it held in the backcountry was not unlike the role performed by Hillsborough, Salisbury, Charlotte, and the smaller Piedmont villages.

When the Moravian storekeeper measured out English yard goods to a Stokes County customer, he was acting as the last link in a chain of buyers and sellers that relayed foreign manufactures westward across the Atlantic. When the customer paid for his cloth with a load of flour or country ham, he was starting a flow of transactions in the opposite direction that would send American products across the ocean to repay the English manufacturer. The next step in this steady stream of business typically took place in a town farther east, where a sudden drop in elevation put waterfalls and rapids in the way of further upstream navigation. Towns sprang up at the "fall line," where coastal shippers transferred their freight from river craft to covered wagons and countrymen did the reverse.

The Moravians ordinarily hauled their customers' products to Cross Creek, at the head of navigation on the Cape Fear River. Cross Creek grew up beside a gristmill site about a mile from the river itself; Campbellton was the village that actually bordered on the waterfront. As the two towns grew together, they adopted a common government, and in 1783 they assumed the name Fayetteville in honor of the Marquis de Lafayette. The merchants who accepted the Moravians' shipments loaded the pork, flour, butter, hides, tallow, flaxseed, beeswax, and tobacco onto rafts and floated them to Wilmington. Returning homeward, the flatboat crews poled up heavy loads of foreign imports for Moravians and other storekeepers to retail throughout the backcountry. Cross Creek was the largest of these midland North Carolina towns, but it was by no means alone. Halifax and Tarboro served similar functions, as did Kinston and Lumberton on a smaller scale.

Tarboro was the embarkation point for tobacco raised by planters throughout the upper portion of the Coastal Plain. After packing his leaf in a hogshead, the farmer passed an axle through the center, hitched a team to the huge cask, and rolled his crop directly to market on country roads. After visiting the inspector at Tarboro, the planter deposited his tobacco in exchange for a warehouse receipt, which he could then sell for cash or store goods from one of several village merchants. The tobacco business made Tarboro an important place, and the legislature chose to meet there on occasion. "The Town contains about twenty Families, and for the size of it has a considerable Trade," The traveler William Attmore reported in his journal. "It is situated on a high flat piece of Ground, and is a very pleasant place." On stopping at Tarboro on his tour of the South, President Washington noted that the town was "less than Halifax but more lively and thriving." Thomas Blount (1759–1812) took

advantage of Tarboro's location and put one of his family's principal stores and warehouses there. Besides serving Tarboro as town commissioner, Blount was a justice of the peace, assemblyman, trustee of the University of North Carolina, and U.S. congressman. The Blount-Bridgers House in Tarboro is a reminder of his contribution to the town's past.

Of all the eighteenth-century trading centers on North Carolina's inland rivers, Halifax is the best preserved today. J. F. D. Smyth visited the little port in the 1770s and described it very favorably. "Halifax is a pretty town on the south side of the Roanoke," Smyth told his readers. "About eight miles below the first falls, and near fifty miles higher up than the tide flows, but sloops, schooners, and flats, or lighters, of great burden, come up to this town against the stream, which is deep and gentle. Halifax enjoys a tolerable share of commerce in tobacco, pork, butter, flour, and some tar, turpentine, skins, furs, and cotton." Of the town's architecture, he declared, "There are many handsome buildings in Halifax and vicinity, but they are almost all constructed of timber, and painted white."

Founded in 1757 as a commercial venture, Halifax boasted some sixty houses twelve years later. Traveler Hugh Finlay recorded in his journal of 1773–74 that Halifax "contains about 50 houses, stores are kept here to supply the country round with European and West India Commoditys for which Pork, Tobacco, Indian corn, Wheat and Lumber are taken in turn." President Washington thought the population was less than a thousand when he came through in 1791. When the railroad bypassed the town after 1839, Halifax dwindled in size, but during the late eighteenth century, it was the center of trade and government for the entire Roanoke River Valley. The Fourth Provincial Congress assembled there in 1776 and recommended that North Carolina join with the other colonies to declare independence. Nine months later, the Fifth Provincial Congress met in Halifax and adopted North Carolina's first state constitution. The little town was a county seat, the center of a judicial district, and one of the few towns guaranteed a seat in the legislature by the 1776 constitution.

Market Square was the center of activity when Halifax was in its heyday. A three-day market fair was held there annually in the last two decades of the eighteenth century. The square was also the spot for militia drills, election rallies, playing, promenading, and grazing livestock. As in Tarboro, an official state tobacco warehouse and inspection station stood nearby. Legal business could be taken care of at the courthouse or at the law office of one of Halifax's several resident attorneys. Built in the early nineteenth century, the Burgess House served as both the office and residence of local attorney Thomas Burgess. Business completed, planters from the rich plantation district up and down the river gathered to socialize with their peers at the Eagle

Burgess House
(early nineteenth
century), Halifax

Tavern (ca. 1800), which J. F. D. Smyth called "the best house of public entertainment in Halifax." Alternatively, they could try out the facilities of a smaller
ordinary, now called the "Tap Room," which was constructed in the late eighteenth and early nineteenth centuries.

The families who made Halifax their permanent home had come to the
Roanoke Valley from Virginia and from the older settled regions around Albemarle Sound. They brought housing styles from the east with them. The Owens
House in Halifax is a merchant's dwelling that reflects the builder's place of
origin. The gambrel roof was popular all over eastern North Carolina in the
eighteenth century; it may have originated as a device for building a two-story
house that required the tax payments of only a one-story structure. The side-
hall plan of this house originated in the Albemarle area, and clearly separates
the parts of the house according to family function. One downstairs room is
furnished as a family parlor, the other as the merchant's office. Upstairs, two

bedrooms are for the merchant's family, the other for his clerk. The kitchen is in the rear. This late eighteenth-century urban family was able to keep its private life separate from business, and preferred to do so.

Inland traders who carried on the commerce of towns like Halifax, Tarboro, and Cross Creek shipped backcountry staples onward to seaport towns like Edenton, Washington, New Bern, and Wilmington. Throughout the late eighteenth and early nineteenth centuries, these towns were the largest and most imposing in North Carolina. Here lived the largest merchants, the royal officials, and the lawyers and judges who dominated all of colonial and early federal society and government. These gentlemen saw to it that North Carolina's port towns, though small, were more comfortable and attractive than any other settlements in the state. "Edenton was the first town we came to

Owens House (late eighteenth century), Halifax

A table set for a game of cards in the Owens House

in North Carolina," wrote German traveler Johann David Schöpf, "and it is none of the worst, although consisting of not more than 100 framed houses, all standing apart and surrounded with galleries or piazzas." The galleries were tropical innovations, introduced from the West Indies as a means to escape the heat. The Barker family used a two-story piazza running the full length of their house to catch the evening breezes off the sound, and most of their affluent fellow townspeople did likewise.

The same Englishman who detested Wilmington agreed that Edenton was much more agreeable. "They reckon about 1,000 to 1,500 inhabitants in Edenton," Robert Hunter Jr. reported. "The town is laid out in the form of a square, built on the Albemarle Sound, which is to the southward. . . . They have here a tolerable good brick statehouse, a brick church, and a market place from whence they are supplied every day." Many of the stately public buildings that graced Edenton when Hunter arrived in 1786 are still standing. The "good brick statehouse" was the Chowan County Courthouse (1767 [see Part I, Chapter 4]), which has been called "perhaps the finest Georgian courthouse in the South." Like the courthouse, the brick St. Paul's Episcopal Church (1736–74) is still in active use, as are many of the wooden homes of merchants and officials whom Hunter would have been able to visit.

Edenton and Wilmington were important commercial centers, and each had proponents who saw it as the most attractive or wealthiest port in North Carolina. But both were exceeded in size and significance by New Bern. Located in Craven County where the Neuse and Trent Rivers came together in a broad estuary leading toward Pamlico Sound and Ocracoke Inlet, New Bern had been founded in 1710 by Baron Christoph von Graffenried, a Swiss nobleman who sought to create a place of refuge for the Protestant victims of Swiss and German wars. After Bath, New Bern was the second oldest town in the province. The baron's settlement had been virtually wiped out by the Tuscarora Indians in 1711, but the location, halfway between the flourishing settlements in the Albemarle and the Cape Fear regions, was advantageous to commerce. After the defeat of the Tuscaroras, the Neuse River Valley continued to grow and became an important center of population in its own right.

New Bern remained small until after midcentury, but its central location made it increasingly popular as a meeting place for the Colonial Assembly. When William Tryon became royal governor in 1765, he quickly asked the Assembly to make it the permanent capital of North Carolina and to appropriate funds for the construction of a building to contain government offices, Assembly and Council chambers, and a residence for the governor and his family. The result was Tryon's Palace, an architectural gem that was the marvel of foreign visitors, the pride of the little capital, and an object of resentment for backcountry taxpayers. The economic burden of paying for Tryon's Palace contributed to the uprising of Regulators on the Piedmont frontier, but the economic benefits to New Bern were instantaneous. As soon as the town became North Carolina's seat of government, the number of licensed ordinaries or taverns

St. Paul's Episcopal Church (1734–74), Edenton

shot up to twenty-six in anticipation of annual throngs of thirsty legislators. The steady stream of official visitors to courts and offices kept the innkeepers busy year round. Planters and merchants with court business found it convenient to combine commerce with politics and lawsuits, and the little seaport boomed. When Governor Josiah Martin took office in 1771, he reported back to London that New Bern had gathered the trade of Beaufort to itself and was "growing very fast into significance." If only the navigation difficulties that obstructed the channel leading to the open ocean were removed, he speculated, "I do think it would then soon become a City not unworthy [of] notice in the great and flourishing Empire of my Royal Master." Growth accelerated in

Interior of St. Paul's Episcopal Church, Edenton

the decades following American independence, but New Bern never seriously rivaled the eminence of Charleston, South Carolina, or Chesapeake ports like Norfolk, Virginia, and Baltimore, Maryland. New Bern expanded from 150 houses and 1,000 persons in the mid-1770s to 400 houses and 2,000 persons in the 1790s. By 1800 New Bern was the largest town in the state, with 2,567 residents, as compared with 1,689 in Wilmington, 1,565 in Fayetteville, and 1,302 in Edenton.

Throughout the eighteenth century, merchants' wharves clustered along New Bern's Trent River shoreline. The public wharf of Craven County dominated the waterfront at the foot of Craven Street. Lumber and naval stores were the principal articles of commerce, but, as elsewhere in the state, tobacco and provisions were eagerly traded as well. West Indian vessels landed with sugar, salt, molasses, rum, and an occasional consignment of slaves. The number of vessels bound directly from Europe dropped off after the Revolution, but coastal vessels from Philadelphia, New York, and New England took their places. Processing industries sprang up in New Bern to further refine the commodities that traveled through the port. A tanyard prepared leather from the hides of backcountry livestock, and a distillery transformed West Indian molasses into rum. Elsewhere about town, artisans' and tradesmen's shops lined the streets. Coopers supplied the shippers with barrels to carry their products. Shipwrights repaired the sailing vessels and wheelwrights serviced vehicles from the country. Luxury blossomed from the skills of cabinetmakers, tailors, milliners, silversmiths, and even a wigmaker. Slaves, seamen, and flatboat crews jostled planters, lawyers, merchants, and sea captains in the streets, arousing a concern for municipal security. A statute of 1773 imposed the first tax for the purchase of a fire engine and a night watch and banned fast driving in the city streets. The lawmakers also noted that "sundry idle and disorderly Persons, as well as Slaves, and Children under age, do make a Practice of firing Guns and Pistols within the . . . Town" and prudently forbade such activity in the future. Little New Bern was a frontier village no longer.

Visitors to New Bern always noticed the impressive brick public buildings that contrasted with the wooden stores and dwellings of the inhabitants and with the rough-and-ready structures of the backcountry. Besides the palace, other public buildings were noteworthy to visitors. The county courthouse, raised on arches in a public square where the road from the Cape Fear region entered New Bern, housed the offices of local government and shaded a public market twice a week. Country people with fresh produce could vend beneath the arches, but a more common practice was to carry fish and vegetables in canoes to the waterfront and hawk one's wares along the docks. Not far from the courthouse, at the intersection of Broad and New Streets, stood

Drawing of Christ Episcopal Church, New Bern, from Jonathan Price map, ca. 1810. Nothing remains of the eighteenth-century structure except some foundation stones in the corner of the churchyard. The present church dates from 1822–24 and 1871–75.

the old Anglican parish church. Graced with a square cupola, Christ Church for many years was the only building for public worship in New Bern. The graves of leading citizens fill its quiet churchyard, and more can be found in Cedar Grove Cemetery not far away. Francis Asbury, first bishop of American Methodism, who road the circuit throughout North Carolina, described New Bern in 1802 as "a traditional and growing town; there are seven hundred or a thousand houses already built, and the number is yearly increased by less or greater additions, among which are some respectable brick edifices; the new courthouse, truly so; neat and elegant. . . . The population of the town, citizens and transient persons, may amount to three thousand five hundred or four thousand souls."

Urban amusements unknown to frontier North Carolinians competed for patronage in the crowded lanes of the colonial capital. Troupes of visiting players offered theatrical performances such as *Isabella, or the Fatal Marriage* and comic operas like *The Poor Soldier.* A theater was devised in the "still Room" of the molasses distillery that included a gallery for free black patrons. Townsmen enjoyed billiards, cards, music, horse races, and drinking in taverns. Gambling was a pastime that attracted every level of society. Much to his dismay, William Attmore found "white boys and negroes eagerly betting ½ a quart of Rum, a drink of Grog &c., as well as Gentlemen betting high" at one Saturday's horse race. More refined entertainment was available from the first bookseller to locate in North Carolina and from the lessons being offered in drawing, music, dancing, and French by itinerant instructors.

An outstanding community celebration in New Bern graced the 1791 visit of President Washington. The festivities included a parade, a public dinner, and an exclusive ball in the palace. The wedding that year between Daniel Carthy and Sarah Hasler was, if anything, more lavish still. The ceremony was followed by tea, then by dancing and a "very elegant set supper" with two wedding cakes. Parties continued for four days thereafter, concluding with a shipboard "relish" for the gentlemen of the wedding party. Dainty confections for such a fête could be whipped together from the wares of a tropical fruit shop, one of the few places in North Carolina to stock oranges, pineapples, lemons, coconuts, and almonds on a regular basis. On more solemn occasions, affluent New Bernians marked funerals with white linen scarves and hat bands for the minister and the pallbearers. After the funeral, the linen was sufficient to make each man a new shirt. Even in death, a high level of consumption was expected of New Bern's leading families.

John Wright Stanly (1742–89) was a New Bern merchant who typified North Carolina's small urban elite. The topsy-turvy business conditions of the American Revolution and its aftermath lifted Stanly to the height of opulence and more than once dropped him almost as far in the other direction. Through all his vicissitudes, Stanly hung on to the personal connections and the business acumen that were the secret of his success, and in the end he left a promising family whose members reestablished the family fortune and exercised substantial leadership in the independent state of North Carolina.

A lawyer's son from Amelia County, Virginia, Stanly was early thrown on his own resources by the death of his father and his mother's remarriage. After starting work as a merchant's clerk at the age of fourteen, Stanly followed the current of British imperial commerce from Williamsburg to Nova Scotia to Jamaica. An allegation of association with counterfeiters followed Stanly from Williamsburg to Nova Scotia, but the eighteen-year-old youth was never prosecuted, and he later blamed ignorance and inexperience for any involvement he may have had with the misdeeds of others. Quarrels with a Philadelphia partner landed him in the debtors' prison in that city until vindicated by the courts, but Stanly recouped his finances and regained the respect of Philadelphia's merchant community.

When he was thirty, a chance visit to North Carolina introduced John Wright Stanly to Ann Cogdell (1753–89), daughter of one of New Bern's leading families, and the footloose entrepreneur decided to marry her and settle down. After moving his business to New Bern, Stanly became what his eulogist later called "a merchant of the greatest enterprise and most extensive business ever known in this State." Success silenced all questions about the past, and Stanly took a prominent position as one of the state's most admired businessmen. His trade was so extensive that he maintained two homes, one in Philadelphia and one in New Bern, and his frequent visits to the northern metropolis kept him in regular contact with leading revolutionary figures like Thomas Jefferson and Robert Morris, the financier.

A substantial part of John Wright Stanly's fortune derived from the Revolutionary War, during which Stanly outfitted as many as fourteen privateering vessels in New Bern and Philadelphia and deployed his private navy to capture British prizes valued at as much as £70,000. A cannon from HMS *Lady Blessington* stands in the yard of Christ Church as a trophy of Stanly's privateering conquests. Stanly also lent large sums for the prosecution of the war and supplied American armies with weapons and provisions, for most of which he was never repaid.

Stanly's fortunes suffered a reversal when the British captured his privateering fleet in the Caribbean and raiding Tories burned his wharves and warehouses. Struggling to recoup, Stanly held on to his house in New Bern, his large wharf and distillery, his plantation, and his sixty slaves. New Bern's leading merchant staved off bankruptcy, but his finances had not fully recovered when a yellow fever epidemic swept over the town in 1789. John Wright Stanly and his wife were among its victims. Within a month of each other, they were buried side-by-side in the cemetery of Christ Church.

The most stable element of Stanly's fortune was his opulent mansion on the corner of Middle and New Streets. Tradition identifies the architect as John Hawks, designer of Tryon's Palace itself. Like the palace, the Stanly House is in the Georgian style, but it displays many decorative features of country estates in the Hudson and Delaware River Valleys of Stanly's New York and Philadelphia associates. The house has a hipped roof, two interior chimneys, a center hall on each of two floors, and four symmetrically arranged rooms downstairs and up. It is made entirely of wood, with long pine timbers laid flush on the outside for a smooth appearance and carved at the corners to resemble quoins. The woodwork inside and out is richly carved and heavily decorated, "certainly the finest of the period in the state." Once a penniless clerk, John Wright Stanly had accumulated the fortune of a merchant prince, and he spent it in princely style.

A pitcher showing the Tuley, *a privateer owned by John Wright Stanly. North Carolina Museum of History Collection, Raleigh.*

Stanly's failures reflect the instability of mercantile wealth just as his successes show that skill, a fortunate marriage, and the right connections enabled the favored individual to weather temporary reverses. In Stanly's case, success counterbalanced failure and admitted him to the small elite that controlled the economy, society, and government of the new state. The position of the North Carolina elite was less exalted than than that of its counterparts in Virginia and South Carolina. In contrast to the elite in those colonies, North Carolina's leading families had more recent origins, less sizable estates, and less social exclusivity. Stanly was fortunate in his selection of North Carolina as a permanent home, for it is unlikely that such a relatively unknown adventurer could have made a prestigious marriage or won such easy confidence among the elite of Charleston or the Chesapeake. By the same token, North Carolina's plant-

John Wright Stanly
House (1779–83),
New Bern.
Photograph by
Paulette Mitchell.

ers and merchants probably held a more slippery position at the top of their society than their counterparts elsewhere in the late colonial period. Some historians have suggested that the precarious position of the upper class made its members less scrupulous and more openly exploitative than they might otherwise have been, and thus more tolerant of those government abuses that finally provoked the Regulator uprising in the 1760s and early 1770s. The relative openness of North Carolina's elite did not necessarily make the society more democratic or more just.

Recurrent incidents in Stanly's career suggest that his route to success might have involved pushing beyond the limits of what was legal or honorable to exploit a favorable opportunity. There was the counterfeiting charge, the prison sentence, and lingering hints of improper actions. When Stanly first applied for a privateer's license, for example, William Tisdale of the New Bern Committee of Safety testified to Stanly's patriotism in a letter of praise and commendation. Weeks later, however, Tisdale lamented his earlier recommendation: "I am sorry to say that since the writing of the s'd letter, I have been inform'd of several Circumstances in the Conduct of the afores'd gentleman which puts me under the disagreeable necessity of desiring you to look upon that letter as tho' it was never wrote." Nonetheless, Stanly obtained his license to plunder British shipping.

Members of the transatlantic trading community, like Stanly, lived by a code that required rigid punctuality in the fulfillment of contracts and a vigorous pursuit of their own interests within the stipulations of any agreement. In his will, Stanly proudly insisted that "my debts be honestly paid, I mean in such kind of money as I agreed to pay when I contracted them, and not depreciated paper for Gold and Silver." No merchant could long survive without personal independence and a reputation for reliability, but merchants were not the only people who prized these qualities. Lawyers, planters, and other members of the elite guarded their reputations for the same reasons. Lawyers lived in a world of courtroom combat, tempered and regulated by strict rules of proper competition. In a credit economy, planters, too, relied on personal trust and notes of hand for business transactions.

But, in the late eighteenth- and early nineteenth-century South, the commercial virtues of independence and reliability took on an intensely personal and emotional significance. They constituted a man's "honor"—and to question whether a man possessed such virtues involved physical risk. No family came to know those risks better than that of John Wright Stanly.

The honor of a gentleman was his reputation for independence, reliability, and physical courage. The gentleman could not be commanded or insulted by others. He was always in control of his own actions and could therefore be relied on for rigid personal honesty and for meeting every contractual obligation. His power to command himself as well as others set him apart completely from those who allegedly lacked these attributes most: poor whites, slaves, and women, who were known as "the weaker sex." In a system based on personal credit, honor had clear economic value, and it also stood for the privileges of race, class, and sex. Vital to a gentleman's economic and social standing, it had to be defended at all costs. In a competitive society, others were always ready to advance their own positions by deliberately impugning the honor of their rivals. Insults were therefore not uncommon, and the practice of dueling was the bloody result. A canny man, John Wright Stanly avoided the ultimate test of his reputation, but his heirs did not. Three of his five sons and at least one grandson participated in duels; two of those sons died, and the other killed his opponent.

The son who survived was John Stanly (1774–1833), the oldest of nine children and inheritor of his father's stately mansion. John Stanly idealized his father and seemed to justify his own imperious behavior by his father's example. "My father was as much superior to me as I am to common men," he is said to have arrogantly declared. All his life, he expected the obedience from others that a domineering father might have demanded from a submissive son. Trained as a lawyer and having no other source of income, John Stanly followed his father's example and launched his career by a judicious marriage. His bride was Elizabeth Franck, or Frank, whom one old New Bernian described as "a country heiress without cultivation, or opportunity . . . [who] inherited from her father, Martin Franck, large estates in Jones County which laid the foundations of Mr. Stanly's prosperity."

John Stanly, son of John Wright Stanly

At an early age, the younger John Stanly threw himself into politics. He became Craven County's clerk and master in equity at the age of twenty-five, sat in the Seventh (1801–3) and Eleventh (1809–11) U.S. Congresses, represented New Bern for twelve terms in the lower house of North Carolina's General Assembly, and served two terms as the Assembly's speaker. Contemporaries remembered him as a brilliant lawyer and a merciless debater. "In repartee and sarcasm I never saw his equal," one associate recalled. "His efforts in that line were absolutely withering. The composure of no suitor, witness, or rival advocate could survive his pungent criticism. Ever bold and fearless, he at once rose to the breadth of the occasion, always wielding a polished scimitar with the energy of a giant and the skill of an artist." It was artistry in sarcasm that led him to the dueling ground in 1803.

Richard Dobbs Spaight

Stanly won election to Congress in 1801 over a fellow New Bernian and former North Carolina governor, Richard Dobbs Spaight. Republicans like Spaight were often just as aristocratic in private life as Federalists like Stanly, but they won popular approval by branding Federalism as undemocratic and injurious to rural interests. In 1802 Spaight sought election to the state Senate, and Stanly worked against his election. By throwing doubt on Spaight's private adherence to Republican tenets, Stanly offended Spaight's honor as a gentleman, and Spaight instantly called for "that satisfaction which one gentleman has a right to demand from another." Although at first Stanly averted the duel by a timely explanation, an escalating exchange of insults and insinuating handbills finally led to Stanly's challenge to Spaight, and a duel was set for 5:30 P.M. on 5 September 1802, in the rear of the Masonic hall on the outskirts of New Bern. The outraged gentlemen would not let any piddling city ordinance against gunfire stop them; the weapons were pistols at ten paces. An eager crowd of onlookers turned out to gawk at the spectacle.

The demands of honor were technically satisfied by a single exchange of shots, but, when the first pair of balls missed their targets, Spaight and Stanly kept firing. On the fourth round, Spaight fell, wounded in the side, and died the next day. Stanly was then twenty-eight years old. Spaight was fifty-four, roughly the age of Stanly's deceased father. The young man took refuge

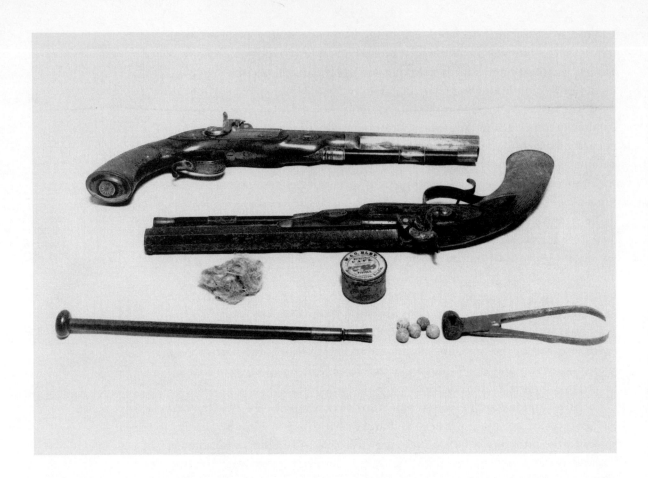

Dueling pistols of
Richard Dobbs
Spaight

from prosecution in Virginia, but, confident that the law would not preclude a gentleman's right to defend his honor, he asked for executive pardon from Governor Benjamin Williams. The request was promptly granted, and Stanly continued his distinguished career without further interruption.

Gentlemen's use of violence to defend themselves against threatened domination by others spread down the social scale to combatants who could not be bothered with the punctilio of dueling. Fighting was common at market days, militia musters, elections, and other places where men gathered and liquor was freely available. William Attmore's visit to Washington, North Carolina, coincided with a militia muster. "Many disorders in town," the Philadelphian noted, "the militia some of them fighting. This is the practice every Muster-day." The same diarist noted brawls among celebrating legislators and hangers-on of the General Assembly, while Johann David Schöpf described a fistfight between two casual traveling companions.

Visitors were particularly horrified by the practice of "gouging." An antagonist in a brutal fight might twist his fingers in his opponent's hair to brace his hands, and then, "when these are fast clinched, the thumbs are extended each way to the nose, and the eyes *gently* turned out of their sockets." Drawing on numerous travelers' accounts, the Reverend Jedidiah Morse wrote in his *American Geography* (1789) that "the victor for his expertness, received shouts of applause from the sportive throng, while his poor, *eyeless* antagonist is laughed at for his misfortune." William Attmore witnessed the preliminaries of a fight in which gouging was proposed in a manner not dissimilar to a challenge to a duel in more polished circles. "They were going to fight out in the Road, when one of the company declared he wou'd massacre the Man who should attempt to Gouge. . . . Womble, one of the disputants declared 'I cannot fight without a Gouge.' One of the company supported his declaration saying 'Ay! A Gouge all weathers, by G—.'" Deterred perhaps by the prospect of blindness, the men called off their quarrel. "The terms were not accepted; their passions cooled by degrees and the gouging man said, 'tho I am but a little Shoemaker, I won't be imposed upon.'"

As an artisan, the shoemaker did not enjoy social or economic equality with gentry members like the Stanlys. He may have been imposed upon by gentlemen every day, but he was powerless to resist his domination by the upper class. Threats of violence against his fellow artisans may have been Womble's way of compensating for his weak position in an unequal society, but the fighting shoemaker was scarcely alone. At every social level, North Carolina men squared off violently against each other in ritual declarations of personal independence.

Several commentators believed that fighting was an integral part of the culture of the slaveholding gentry. New England observers linked violence to gambling, drinking, and the whole gamut of nonpuritanical pastimes. With stern disapproval, Jedidiah Morse reported that "the general topics of conversation among the men, when cards, the bottle, and occurrences of the day do not intervene, are negroes, the prices of indigo, rice, tobacco, &c." Asserting that Carolinians did not work as hard as New Englanders, Morse explained that "the citizens of North Carolina, who are not better employed, spend their time in drinking, or gaming at cards or dice, in cockfighting, or horse racing. Many of the intervals are filled up with a boxing match; and these matches frequently become memorable by feats of *gouging*." New England ministers were not alone in criticizing these activities. Apparently believing that the cause of American liberty demanded superior popular virtue and that there was something inappropriate about Carolina recreation, the Wilmington Committee of Safety endorsed the stricture of the First Continental Congress against "every species of extravagance and dissipation, especially all horse-racing, and all kinds of gaming, cockfighting, exhibitions of shows and plays and other expensive diversions and entertainments." The committee justified itself on the grounds that "nothing will so effectively tend to convince the British Parliament that we are in earnest in our opposition to their measures, as a voluntary relinquishment of our favorite amusements. . . . He only is the determined patriot who willingly sacrifices his pleasures on the altar of freedom."

The pleasures condemned by Morse and the Wilmington committee did not really consume the energies of North Carolina citizens, and it would be unfair to suggest that idleness and dissipation were dominant features of North Carolina culture. Nevertheless, there were clear parallels between the work that North Carolinians did and the games they played. Fighting, whether between gentlemen at the dueling ground or between shoemakers in the inn yard, was part of the process of asserting one's privileges as a free white male. The copious consumption of liquor was another way for men to exhibit their personal prowess, whether at the grogshop, in the drawing room, or on the muster ground. Nonchalant gambling for high stakes displayed the size of a gentleman's estate and established his superiority to lesser mortals who had to worry about losing. Gambling at the racetrack or the card table was thus an extension of the uncertain and competitive business activities that built the House in the Horseshoe and the John Wright Stanly House. The lavish balls, where dancing occurred, were further arenas for gentlemen and their ladies to display their finery and to size up each other's power. Like most people's games, North Carolinians' pastimes were very serious business.

These games grew out of the concerns of rural plantation society, but the reports we have of them originated from North Carolina's towns. In many ways, urban places provided the testing grounds and rewards of North Carolina's rural culture. The climax of commercial farming operations was not plowing, planting, or even harvest, but the sale of the crop in town. The perfect expression of rivalry among competing planters was not found in magnificent rural isolation, but in the lawsuit, the duel, or the contest for political office that frequently took place in an urban setting. The popular amusements that reflected the farmers' fundamental concerns were not only found among the joys of country life but also in the intermittent trips to town, where dancing, gambling, tippling, and the opportunity for display awaited the visiting families of gentlemen and yeomen alike. North Carolina towns were tiny, and their inhabitants were not typical of the state in the eighteenth century, but the state's urban settings satisfied deeply rooted needs of its overwhelmingly rural society. The urban vices deplored by President Joseph Caldwell were less eradicable than the well-meaning educator might have supposed.

THE CULTURE OF THE REPUBLIC

In the early 1770s, James Iredell of Edenton was young, indebted, and struggling. Repeatedly he wrote his parents and his benefactors, outlining for them his current problems and his steady and resourceful efforts to overcome them. Frequently he told his confidants of the goal that constantly lay before him. "I cannot expect every thing at once," he solemnly informed his mother in 1771. "[I] shall be only 20, Saturday, and all I wish for is enough to live upon independently." Addressing his patron and creditor, Henry Eustace McCulloh, the next year, Iredell vowed that "the sole object of my thoughts at present is how to extricate myself out of the Labyrinths I am in, and get into the [marvelous] Road that leads to Happiness and Independence." Months later, Iredell told his father that his prospects were looking up. "In England I must in any way be some years in a dependent and consequently an insecure position," he explained. "Here I have a tolerable certainty of something, tho' a mean one, and a probable expectation, by the fruits of my own Industry (all I depend upon with assurance) of procuring in the course of a few years a genteel Independency."

The independence that Iredell longed for was release from debt and from reliance on the patronage of others. He worked for the opportunity to take his place in the world of men as an autonomous gentleman, who lived well and relied on his own resources. Before he turned thirty, Iredell's hopes were fulfilled. His law practice was successful, he was an admired and trusted leader in North Carolina's government, and he was married to a wealthy and well-connected lady whom he loved very deeply. Of their four children, three would survive infancy and one, James Iredell Jr., would become governor of the state and a United States senator. As a man of affairs, a master, a husband, and a father, James Iredell had achieved his "genteel Independency."

His adopted state had done the same. "Independence" was a word that earlier generations of North Carolinians had shunned. When the Lords Proprietors held sway over the infant colony on the Albemarle, the inhabitants had acknowledged their constant need for help from Britain about as often as they protested the terms upon which that help was offered. "Wee need not Informe

James Iredell Sr. Portrait by unknown artist, owned by John Gilliam.

yoʳ Lordshipps how weak & uncapable wee are of manginge things of so Concerne as yᵉ well layinge a foundation of a ᶜountry by wholsom Law wᵗʰ out advertisement:& Direction from yoʳ Lordship," read one humble and at least partially sincere petition of 1672. For a century thereafter, the mother country remained a place that many colonists called "home," even though they had never seen it. Eventually, however, North Carolinians and other Americans became ready to strike out on their own. As early as 1761, Governor Arthur Dobbs had denounced "a republican spirit of Independency" in the pretensions of the colonial Assembly. Over the succeeding decade, Britain's efforts to tighten control over the colonies aroused furious resistance in North Carolina and the other colonies. By 1774 attorney William Hooper was predicting that all the colonies "are striding fast to independence, and ere long will build an empire on the ruin of Great Britain."

Two years later, the American Revolution had begun. The War for Independence grew out of a clash between the colonists' convictions about liberty and constitutional rights and the needs of the British Empire as determined by

Hannah Johnston Iredell,
wife of James Iredell Sr.

Parliament and the crown. Legalistic theories, however, were not the sole reason for the colonists' willingness to rebel. Free citizens fought for revolutionary ideas because the principles embodied key aspects of their daily social experiences. As James Iredell made clear, "independence" was a personal objective for North Carolinians just as it was a political objective for their state. Men as different from Iredell as John Allen, the pioneer Quaker who lived in a log cabin, and Philip Alston, the unruly planter who lived in a Piedmont mansion, shared Iredell's ambition to be free from coercive authorities. Their goals were shared by thousands of the Revolution's potential supporters throughout the colony. When illegal British taxes were first imposed by the Stamp Act, gentlemen and yeomen joined together readily under the slogan "Liberty, property, and no stamp duty," and their alliance continued until national independence had been won.

The colonists' fondness for liberty flourished in spite of the fact that inequality and a lack of freedom were widespread in their society. White men of the "middling" or "lesser sorts" found themselves restricted by the power and privileges of the "better sort" or gentry. Propertyless freemen had no legal

William Hooper

right to vote. In the colonial Assembly, an established elite of planters, merchants, lawyers, and other leading gentlemen from eastern towns and counties dominated the underrepresented farmers from the backcountry. Colonial women had virtually none of the rights that men had, and married women had no legal identities apart from those of their husbands. The gravest inequality and lack of liberty burdened the lives of the black slaves whose labor supported the privileges of white society. Colonial North Carolina was no egalitarian utopia.

From the beginning, some North Carolinians wanted to turn the traditionalist campaign for the rights of Englishmen to a more universal struggle for the rights of man. To a certain extent, they were successful. The new state constitution put strict limits on the power of government and gave the vote to propertyless male taxpayers. The Revolution itself tended to make men of talent leaders regardless of their social origins. In 1811 Jeremiah Battle of Edgecombe County recalled a Revolutionary hero who rose to the legislature on the basis of native ability. "Altho' he was almost destitute of education he was a considerable orator; & whenever he rose to speak in those public assemblies, the greatest attention was paid to his opinions, as they carried the strongest marks of good sense." In 1783 a Latin American visitor, Don Francisco de Miranda, was likewise struck by the leveling effect of the Revolution on Carolina manners. Witnessing the celebration of American victory at New Bern, Miranda reported that "a barbecue (roast pig) was held at one o'clock, and a barrel of rum was opened. There was promiscuous eating and drinking, the principal officers and citizens mixing freely with the coarsest elements of society, all shaking hands and drinking out of the same glass."

Miranda's remarks are very illuminating. The Revolution had made civic equality the basic principle governing relations among white men, so the laborers, artisans, and tradesmen of New Bern had very good reasons to toast its outcome. But in spite of the ritual familiarity between the elite and the populace, Miranda made clear that the Revolution had hardly swept away class lines, even among whites. The new constitution limited the right to vote for state senators to the owners of fifty acres of land, and higher property requirements restricted access to elected offices. The rights of women and slaves were not improved by a fight for the liberty of white males, and the hierarchical principles of patriarchal and slave-based society continued. The legacy of the Revolution was therefore ambiguous. The outcome gave all citizens something to celebrate, but inequality and enslavement still persisted.

Tories, or Loyalists, were not an insignificant proportion of North Carolina's population during the war. Charles Biddle, a Philadelphian who lived in North Carolina during the Revolution and represented Carteret County in the

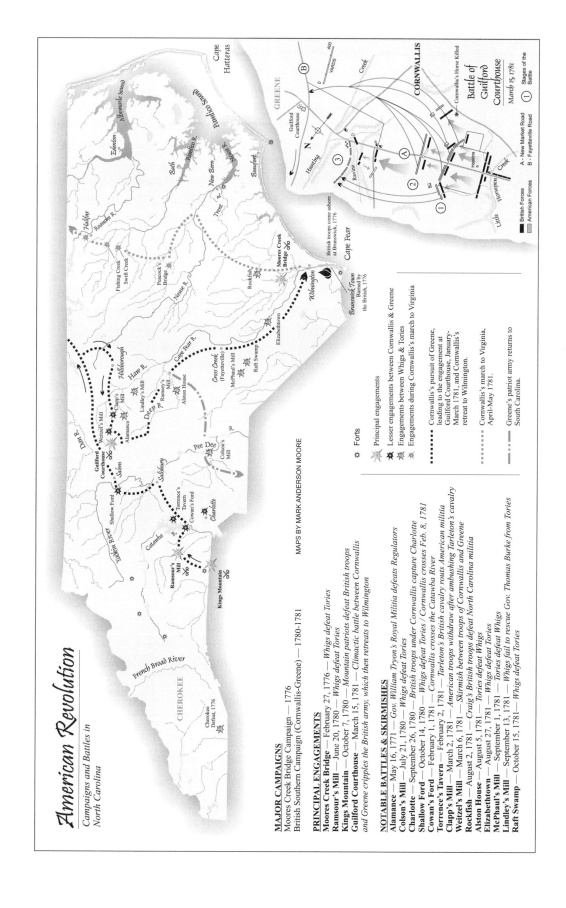

American Revolution

Campaigns and Battles in North Carolina

MAJOR CAMPAIGNS
Moores Creek Bridge Campaign — 1776
British Southern Campaign (Cornwallis-Greene) — 1780-1781

PRINCIPAL ENGAGEMENTS
Moores Creek Bridge — February 27, 1776 — Whigs defeat Tories
Ramsour's Mill — June 20, 1780 — Whigs defeat Tories
Kings Mountain — October 7, 1780 — Mountain patriots defeat British troops
Guilford Courthouse — March 15, 1781 — Climactic battle between Cornwallis and Greene cripples the British army, which then retreats to Wilmington.

NOTABLE BATTLES & SKIRMISHES
Alamance — May 16, 1771 — Gov. William Tryon's Royal Militia defeats Regulators
Colson's Mill — July 21, 1780 — Whigs defeat Tories
Charlotte — September 26, 1780 — British troops under Cornwallis capture Charlotte
Shallow Ford — October 14, 1780 — Whigs defeat Tories / Cornwallis crosses Feb. 8, 1781
Cowan's Ford — February 1, 1781 — Cornwallis crosses the Catawba River
Torrence's Tavern — February 2, 1781 — Tarleton's British cavalry routs American militia
Clapp's Mill — March 2, 1781 — American troops withdraw after ambushing Tarleton's cavalry
Weitzel's Mill — March 6, 1781 — Skirmish between troops of Cornwallis and Greene
Rockfish — August 2, 1781 — Craig's British troops defeat North Carolina militia
Alston House — August 5, 1781 — Tories defeat Whigs
Elizabethtown — August 27, 1781 — Whigs defeat Tories
McPhaul's Mill — September 1, 1781 — Tories defeat Whigs
Lindley's Mill — September 13, 1781 — Whigs fail to rescue Gov. Thomas Burke from Tories
Raft Swamp — October 15, 1781 — Whigs defeat Tories

MAPS BY MARK ANDERSON MOORE

✷ Forts

✸ Principal engagements

✴ Lesser engagements between Cornwallis & Greene

✴ Engagements between Whigs & Tories

✴ Engagements during Cornwallis's march to Virginia

········ Cornwallis's pursuit of Greene, leading to the engagement at Guilford Courthouse, January-March 1781, and Cornwallis's retreat to Wilmington.

········ Cornwallis's march to Virginia, April-May 1781.

———— Greene's patriot army returns to South Carolina.

Battle of Guilford Courthouse
March 15, 1781

① Stages of the Battle

A - New Market Road
B - Fayetteville Road

■ British Forces
■ American Forces

CORNWALLIS

GREENE

Cornwallis's Horse Killed

Guilford Courthouse

N

British troops come ashore at Brunswick, 1776

Brunswick Town Burned by the British, 1776

General Assembly, remembered the Loyalists: "I never felt the least angry with any of these people for their attachment to Great Britain; on political subjects every man has a right to enjoy his opinion and provided he does no mischief, should not be disturbed." The state, however, passed a number of punitive laws against the Tories, authorizing confiscation of their property and banishment. A number of Loyalists fled North Carolina out of fear of reprisals for their loyalty to Great Britain.

Landmarks of the War for Independence survive in every part of North Carolina. Moores Creek National Military Park, in Pender County, commemorates the battle site of a 1776 American victory over Tory Highland Scots. Guilford Courthouse National Military Park, in Guilford County, commemorates Lord Charles Cornwallis's Pyrrhic victory over the Americans under General Nathanael Greene in 1781. But the cultural monuments of independence, though less conspicuous than the battlefields, are even more significant. When the shooting died away, North Carolinians continued to work out the meaning of independence in the fabric of their daily lives and to fulfill the seemingly profound opportunities and obligations that liberty brought them.

As they shaped their new commonwealth, the state's citizens tried to follow the same principles that had led them initially to independence. The Provincial Congress made North Carolina a republic when it declared "that all political power is vested in, and derived from, the people only." Beginning as a political description, "republican" came to be a cultural standard that North Carolinians tried to apply to every institution in their society. When the citizens thought that their families, churches, schools, and economic arrangements were truly republican, they sought to protect that fragile quality from the hostile forces of a changing world. If they thought their institutions failed to measure up to republican standards, the citizens sought appropriate reforms. The struggle to establish and maintain an independent republican society was the pervasive theme in North Carolina's history from 1770 to 1820.

Protecting the world of independent freeholders was the touchstone for North Carolina's republican doctrine. Institutions or public policies that tended to shore up that world were "republican"; those that undermined it were not. Predictably, not everyone agreed about the possible effects of various measures. Proponents of equality among white males insisted that the state be wary of entrenched privileges, concentrated private power, or the rise of aristocracy. More conservative republicans fought restrictions on the rights or the authority of the individual property holder, no matter how much land or how many slaves he had accumulated. Similarly, some republicans feared entanglement in the snares of the commercial economy and cherished self-sufficiency as the secret to continued agrarian independence. The republican friends of economic development replied that no one could be independent who was poor. Debate over the nature of true republicanism therefore characterized North Carolina public life in the first generation of independence.

The stakes of the debate were high. For these North Carolinians, the future of liberty itself hung in the balance. "It will in great measure depend upon ourselves whether by our diligence and integrity we shall be a happy and respectable, or by our neglect or abuse of the greater trust committed to us, a miserable and degenerate People."

More than three decades later, a sense of moral urgency still hovered over public life. Comparing America to God's chosen people, spokesmen warned incessantly that America's blessings were as fragile as those of the children of Israel. "We are indeed a favoured people," thundered Samuel Dickins, a congressional candidate in 1816. "It rests with ourselves whether we shall be so favoured for ages to come. . . . When we fall it shall be by the fatal effects of our own folly and vices." Armed with solemn moral purpose, and with a deep sense of how easy it would be to make a ruinous mistake, free North Carolinians took up the responsibilities of an independent society.

North Carolinians assumed their task with a seriousness that showed in the buildings they constructed as well as in the speeches they made. Architectural motifs from ancient Greece and Rome enjoyed a vogue as Americans tried to inculcate the sense of balance, moderation, and civic virtue thought to have been the hallmarks of those early republics. The Beaufort County Courthouse, though built many decades later, reflects these qualities. A triangular pediment of the roof directly over the entrance suggests the form of a Greek or Roman temple. A pair of delicately fan-shaped windows and an elaborately molded front doorway completed the decoration of this simple monument to republican government. Other early courthouses no longer extant featured comparable details. Similarly, the state's leaders designed the streets of Raleigh, the new capital, in a simple geometric form that reflected the practicality and directness of the new political order, and they also included five public squares as gathering places for an active and enlightened citizenry. The central square would contain the State House and would be called Union Square to indicate the importance of the federal government, and the four surrounding plazas would carry the names of notable North Carolina statesmen to commemorate the example of heroic local founding fathers.

The most outstanding product of the cult of classical antiquity was the larger-than-life-size statue of George Washington that the legislature authorized in 1816. Completed by the great Italian sculptor Antonio Canova, the statue depicted the father of his country in the garb of a Roman general who has turned from the exercise of the sword to the arts of peace. Seated on a

State House (1794, burned 1831), Raleigh

stool, the statesman was shown in the act of composing laws for the good of his countrymen. The figure of Washington touched a deep chord of emotion among North Carolinians; the *Raleigh Register* called it "that proud monument of national gratitude, which was our pride and glory," and most of its viewers seem to have agreed. As a work of political art, the sculpture was heavily didactic, and, according to a later legislative report, its message was plain. "While it refuted the calumny which stigmatizes republics as ungrateful," the solons declared, "it taught that true glory is the meed of virtue, and that, though temporary popularity may be gained by courting public favor, permanent renown, the renown which triumphs over the grave, is awarded to him alone who seeks the public good with pure and devoted disinterestedness." The citizens placed the image of Washington in the rotunda of the State House, where it silently demonstrated to legislators and visitors alike the glory of republican government and the qualities expected from an ideal republican statesman.

Like many republic-minded Americans, however, North Carolinians were suspicious of bestowing too much power on politicians. As early as 1777, Ebe-

Italian sculptor Antonio Canova's statue of George Washington was lost when the State Capitol was destroyed by fire in 1831. The Washington statue in the present State Capitol (1834–40) is a marble copy made in the 1960s.

nezer Hazard described their reluctance to trust power in one person's hands for too long. Joseph Hewes, a signer of the Declaration of Independence for North Carolina, had not been returned to the Continental Congress, "as he has served 3 years, & the People think that a sufficient Length of Time for One Man to be entrusted with so much Power."

Public life was not the only arena in which North Carolinians explored the meaning of their newfound independence. Changes in personal life reflected a new sense of national self-confidence and the lure of new opportunities. Ser-

Daniel Boone

vice in the Continental Army had given some North Carolinians a chance to travel, to meet the inhabitants of other regions, and to prove their abilities under extraordinary conditions. Many "young men of the Revolution" seized the chance to get ahead in careers of public service and personal accomplishment. James Iredell perfected his legal abilities as attorney general of North Carolina and by 1790, at the age of 39, had become the youngest justice on the United States Supreme Court. John Wright Stanly built on his wartime business to become the state's largest importer and exporter.

For less prominent soldiers, the trans-Appalachian West beckoned as the country for a fresh start. North Carolina had promised western lands to Revolutionary War soldiers in lieu of more conventional payment. The Cherokees had been defeated along with the British, and attempts to forbid settlement beyond the Blue Ridge perished with other imperial policies; consequently the way was clear for large-scale white penetration of the North Carolina mountains. Following a trail blazed by North Carolina backwoodsman Daniel Boone,

Dwelling (early nineteenth century) at
James K. Polk Memorial, Mecklenburg County

pioneers streamed across the ridges to the new states of Tennessee and Kentucky, or wound up rocky streams to the fertile coves tucked between the highest peaks of the mountain region. A Piedmont farmstead depicting the period of the early 1800s can be seen today at the James K. Polk Memorial Historic Site in Mecklenburg County.

David Vance was one of the settlers who chose the North Carolina side of the mountains. A veteran of the Continental Army and the Battle of Kings Mountain, Vance came to the Reems Creek area of Buncombe County between 1785 and 1790 to work as a teacher, lawyer, and land surveyor. He purchased a farm from William Dever in 1795 that is now maintained as the birthplace of Zebulon Baird Vance, David Vance's grandson and the Civil War governor of North Carolina. The house on the property was built of logs, but it was larger and more elaborate than the typical settler's cabin, for David Vance was more prosperous than the average settler; he was a slaveholder who became first clerk of court for Buncombe County, colonel in the county militia, and representative in the General Assembly. The remote location of Colonel Vance's farm ensured that his family would continue to rely on traditional handicrafts to produce items for daily use in the home and on the farm. Once common in eastern and Piedmont North Carolina, these skills survived in the more recently settled mountains because the difficulty of access kept machine-made products at a distance until relatively late in the twentieth century.

Another surviving Appalachian log dwelling is the Carson House (1780) at Pleasant Gardens community in McDowell County. The structure served as a tavern and stagecoach stop. It is built of foot-square logs covered with clapboard and has hand-carved and paneled interior woodwork. Also in the west, in the established pattern of early surveyors, General William Lenoir speculated in land and accumulated wealth, which enabled him to build a house known as Fort Defiance (1789), east of Patterson in Caldwell County. He furnished the dwelling handsomely. The site contained the ruins of an obsolete outpost against the once-powerful Cherokees. A builder named Thomas Fields constructed the house according to a contract that specified a dwelling forty by twenty-eight feet with four rooms on each of two floors and two staircases. Fields was paid in land.

Appalachia was not the only section of North Carolina to see new growth at the end of the eighteenth century. The Revolution had stripped Americans of the privileged terms of trade they had enjoyed in the British Empire: a postwar economic slump had been unavoidable. Two events of the early 1790s marked the end of these doldrums and gave North Carolinians and other Americans a renewed sense of economic opportunity. In 1792 a war broke out between revolutionary France and the great powers of Europe. The war lasted intermittently until 1815, and while Napoleon and his British adversaries kept the Old World torn by conflict, Americans reaped the benefits by selling provisions and other raw materials to both sides. In 1793 a Connecticut tutor named Eli Whitney perfected a machine that could separate the seeds from the fibers of short staple cotton—a hardy upland plant that could thrive in the soil of most southeastern states. One slave operating the device could do what it had previously taken twelve slaves to do by hand. Before the invention of the gin, twenty-five slaves, working a hundred days, were needed to pick the seed from the cotton of one slave's produce for one growing season. Whitney's gin removed the last technological bottleneck to full-scale mechanization of British textile manufacturing, and the Industrial Revolution was completely under way. Demand for the versatile fibers skyrocketed, and cotton cultivation spread across the American South from the coast to the Piedmont, and over the mountains into the fertile "Black Belt" soils of frontier Alabama and Mississippi. Conditions for cotton were ideal in the Deep South, but several North Carolina regions could produce the new crop too. The parallel rise of King Cotton and the Em-

Birthplace (ca. 1795) of Zebulon B. Vance, Buncombe County

peror Napoleon gave North Carolina republicans new access to prosperity and another reason to celebrate independence.

War and industrialization fanned demand for North Carolina staples like corn, pork, flour, and naval stores, as well as cotton. The plantation economy thrived as large farms worked by slaves became the most efficient suppliers of North Carolina's popular exports. The old plantation regions of the east felt

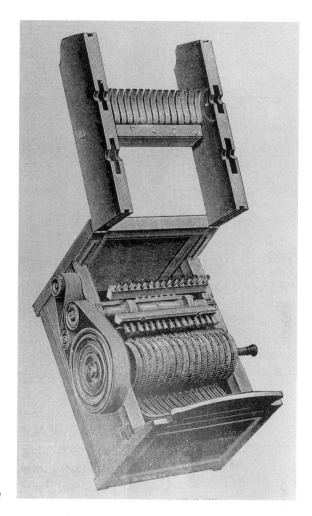

Eli Whitney's cotton gin

the new prosperity first, but the planters' world also moved west as opportunities developed. Josiah Collins and the Reverend Charles Pettigrew grew rich on the shores of Lake Phelps by selling rice and corn to the combatants in Europe. Moore County's House in the Horseshoe witnessed the advantages of cotton culture during the residence there of Governor Benjamin Williams. North of Charlotte in Mecklenburg County, immigrant peddler James Latta rode the cotton boom to planter status and left his mark on a substantial homestead known as Latta Place. Latta adorned his house with mirrors, gilt-framed pictures, and elaborate dressing cases from Philadelphia. To the north, Richard Bennehan made his sturdy farmhouse at Stagville in Orange (now Durham) County the center of a plantation domain that endured for five generations in the same family.

Bennehan House (1787–99), Stagville Plantation, Durham County. Photograph by Paulette Mitchell.

The expansion of commercial agriculture also stimulated the merchant's business, and new stores sprang up to market the planter's crops and supply him with the wares of distant places. The store of Boston-born merchant and shipper William Rea in the new town of Murfreesboro is now the oldest commercial structure in North Carolina. Rea kept a retail shop on the first floor, while the heavy-duty hoist outside transferred bulky cotton bales and tobacco hogsheads to the upstairs warehouse. Rea kept a close eye on his business. "No one was permitted to remain idle about him. When his clerks were not otherwise engaged, he made them empty nail kegs and count nails, or rub hardware in the store and the like." Rea's schooner *Belinda* and his brother's sloop *Phenix* brought to the Murfreesboro wharves West Indian rum, coffee, sugar, and molasses as well as limes, oranges, coconuts, and muslin.

The same sort of business took place on a smaller scale at the tavern, store, and post office of Jethro Brown in Caswell County, where planters gathered to transact their business, enjoy a convivial glass, read the newspapers, and discuss the issues of the day in a neighborhood debating society that met there regularly around 1810. As they exercised their economic, cultural, and political freedoms, the new planters of Caswell County were shaping themselves and their peers into a self-confident and interconnected social class that would dominate North Carolina until the end of the Civil War.

Hope Plantation of Bertie County is a particularly striking example of North Carolina's expanding plantation society. Hope was the home of David

Stone (1770–1818), U.S. senator and governor of North Carolina. He was the son of Zedekiah Stone, a Cashie River merchant and planter who had migrated from Massachusetts in 1766. A promising young man with good looks, impressive talents, and valuable connections, David Stone graduated from Princeton with highest honors and read law under his fellow Princetonian William Richardson Davie of Halifax. Before Stone turned twenty, Bertie County freemen had sent him to the state convention that ratified the U.S. Constitution in 1789. They followed this honor with continuous terms in the North Carolina House of Commons until 1794, when he won election to the bench as a superior court judge. Thereafter, Stone was never absent from public office until he left the U.S. Senate in 1814. Successively he was U.S. congressman, U.S. senator, judge again, governor of the state, member of the legislature, and once more U.S. senator. In spite of this long record of public confidence, Stone resigned from the Senate under fire, when his opposition to the War of 1812 stirred the anger of his North Carolina constituents. When he was only forty-eight, in 1818, Stone died at Rest Dale, his plantation in Wake County.

Hope Plantation, however, was David Stone's original plantation and home. He received the land, 1,051 acres in all, as a wedding present from his

Hope Plantation (1796–1803), Bertie County

father, one month before his marriage to Hannah Turner in 1793. In his farming operations, Stone's estate inventory shows that he continued some of the activities that had succeeded for his father. Like Zedekiah, David Stone raised corn and livestock and traded in lumber products, but instead of tobacco and rice he planted cotton. The change was evidently successful. When David Stone was serving his first term in the House of Commons, his father had owned 25 slaves and 1,078 acres of land. By the time Senator Stone died, he had accumulated some 138 slaves and 5,062 acres in Bertie County alone. Cotton clearly brought some North Carolinians a long way from the rustic lifestyle of the late colonial period.

The house that David Stone erected at Hope Plantation was the monument to his success. The newlywed husband began its construction on the basis of a plan he found in *The British Architect,* a builders' pattern book published by Abram Swann. The results were completed by 1803. Hope has two stories over an elevated basement. Chinese Chippendale balustrades ornament the double portico of the main entrance and the rooftop captain's walk. The two main rooms are on the second story. One was a long drawing room suitable for the balls and receptions so central to the gentry's lifestyle. The other was a magnificent library with built-in shelves for the 1,400 volumes in David Stone's personal collection of books. The senator was both a gentleman and a scholar.

The excitement of independence spread through North Carolina's towns as well as through the countryside. Plantation products traveled through ports like New Bern on their way to American and foreign customers, and merchant communities battened on the growth of business. New Bern's population doubled between 1780 and 1800, and civic pride expanded correspondingly. Following their counterparts in other seaboard ports, New Bern's businessmen fostered a new style of building in their homes and public edifices as a proud expression of their autonomy and newly found prosperity.

The style has been called "Federal" in honor of the new United States, but it shared a great deal with the Georgian architecture that preceded it. Federal architecture was less massive than Georgian, the ornamentation was more delicate and more profuse, and the incorporation of Greek and Roman themes was more widespread and self-conscious. For a brief period, it became the most popular American style, and left its mark everywhere—from the porticos of the U.S. Capitol to the homes of North Carolina merchants.

The John Stevenson House is a good example of Federal domestic architecture in New Bern. It was built for a sea captain whose vessels plied the oceans between New Bern, New England, and the West Indies. The sea captain displayed his success with becoming republican simplicity. Like the typical Federal house in New Bern, the Stevenson House has a "side-hall" plan. A passage runs along the side of the house on all three floors, and two rooms open off each hall. Designed to save space, this plan is ideal for a town house where land is scarce. Also, as in other Federal houses, the interior woodwork is especially fine in the Stevenson House. A wooden archway in the downstairs hall features a molding carved like a ship's cable. There are as many as twenty-four original Federal side-hall houses in New Bern today, each one differing from the others in the elaborateness of its details or in the quality of the details' execution, but all sharing the same basic features.

Three important public buildings remain from New Bern's Federal past: the Masonic Temple and Theater, the New Bern Academy building, and the First Presbyterian Church. As elsewhere in North Carolina, the Masonic order in New Bern was an exclusive fraternity of leading planters and townsmen who joined it to strengthen the personal, political, and economic ties that bound them together as an elite. When it was completed in 1809, the temple contained a theater and a ballroom for public entertainment and a meeting chamber for private ceremonies. Masonic ritual stressed mutual assistance, public service, and rational virtue; the classical lines of the temple and its mixture of public and private functions expressed the organization's principles directly. Like the Masonic Temple, the New Bern Academy catered to the gentry and also served a wider public. Chartered as a private secondary school in 1764, the academy trained the sons of eastern North Carolina's leading families and a selected number of other students as well. One historian has declared that "this school had more influence upon the history of the state in the early years of the Commonwealth than any other save the University." The original building constructed in 1766 was destroyed by fire in the 1790s. The present academy was completed in 1806. The classical lines and elegant symmetry of the two-story brick schoolhouse were Georgian in basic plan and Federal in decorative details, much like the Masonic Temple. When George E. Badger—future jurist, U.S. senator and secretary of the navy—attended the academy in 1807, his school clothing included the following: "2 cambric cravats," "3 pr cotton stockings," "2 summer jackets," "1 summer coat," "4 summer waistcoats & 4 winter ditto," "3 pr summer Panterloons & 3 pr [winter] ditto," "7 linen shirts," "1 winter jacket & 1 winter coat", and "4 Pocket Handkerchiefs." In function and appearance, both the Masonic Temple and the New Bern Academy encouraged an association between the leading classes of eastern North Carolina and the patrician citizens of the Roman Republic.

From an architectural standpoint, the most outstanding Federal building in New Bern was the First Presbyterian Church, which was begun in 1819 and completed in 1822. Like New Bern's other impressive structures, the church is evidence of a dedicated body of civic leaders who wanted the best for them-

*New Bern Academy
(1806–10).
Photograph by
Paulette Mitchell.*

selves and for their small city and who possessed the means to obtain it. The church's finely carved woodwork and the balance of its proportions testify to a group of skilled craftsmen who could borrow designs from published sketches and shape them into a pleasing and original style. The popular motifs of Federal New Bern spread over eastern North Carolina, giving rise to a variety of graceful structures. The Sally-Billy House in Halifax is another good example of the region's unique Federal designs that expressed the values and prosperity of North Carolina's emerging republican leadership.

The self-assurance that stimulated architecture in New Bern and elsewhere and supported the activities of diverse planters like David Stone, Benjamin Williams, James Latta, and Richard Bennehan rested on a growing commercial economy. National independence brought these men closer to the currents of international trade and gave them a personal status that rested on a complex interplay between agricultural production, the demand for staple crops, and world economic conditions.

But what did liberty mean for the independent farmer who tilled the earth with his own hands, lived in a log cabin, and usually avoided stores and merchants as much as possible? According to Thomas Jefferson, these yeomen

First Presbyterian Church (1819–22), New Bern

*Sally-Billy House
(ca. 1810), Halifax*

farmers and their families were the ideal citizens of a republic. "Those who labor in the earth," Jefferson wrote, "are the chosen people of God, if ever he had a chosen people, whose breasts he has made his peculiar deposit for substantial and genuine virtue." For Jefferson and for his North Carolina neighbors as well, public virtue and not wealth or aesthetic expression was the supreme test of a republic. Did pedimented porticos and Chinese Chippendale balustrades have anything to do with the great body of the American people or with the moral conditions of their republic?

As the eighteenth century drew to a close, many North Carolinians were deciding that the dominant culture of the republic was unsatisfactory to them. For one thing, the cultural world that embraced Federal architecture, Masonic ritual, and the cult of classical antiquity was the private preserve of an exclusive elite. Common freemen in North Carolina were closed off from the education, leisure, and powerful social positions that made this culture meaningful to the gentry, and they were often made to feel inferior because they did not share in the gentry's "refinement." These citizens also lacked the economic advantages provided by the expansion of the market economy. Numerous quiet citizens found a public life that was dominated by fighting, gambling, and drunken electioneering morally repugnant. They had reason to be disappointed that the Revolution had failed to complete its promise of liberty, equality, and progress for everyone.

There were also signs of a spiritual and moral crisis in North Carolina and the rest of the nation. The eighteenth-century gentry admired what they regarded as enlightened and rational virtue and often had minimal faith in divine revelation. A philosophy called "Deism" grew popular. It held that God had originally created the universe but had left it alone to operate by scientific laws ever since. Writing to a friend in 1797, Joseph Caldwell, then a young instructor at the University of North Carolina, summed up the situation frankly. "In North Carolina and particularly in the part east of Chapel Hill everyone believes that the way of rising to respectability is to disavow as often, and as publicly as possible the leading doctrines of the Scriptures. They are bug-bears, very well fitted to scare the ignorant and weak into obedience to the law; but the laws of morality and honor are sufficient to regulate the conduct of men of letters and cultivated reasons." The Reverend George Micklejohn, an Anglican clergyman who remained in North Carolina after the Revolution, shocked his more orthodox colleagues with his outspoken Deism. Presbyterian minister and educator Henry Pattillo wrote to the Reverend Charles Pettigrew in 1788 that Micklejohn was "an artist at avoiding Jesus Christ, both in nature and substance" and gave "the first thorough deistical sermon I ever heard." A 1798 letter of John W. Norwood, a lawyer, scientific agriculturist, and legislator, to William Lenoir, a planter and legislator, tells a similar story: "I never understood Deism was preached till lately, a person . . . said to be a man of education, preached in favour of it some time past, at Halifax, Warrenton, and Wmsborough in Granville, his discourses were highly approv'd by most of the Rich, the fashionable and polite, and his performance by them, profusely Rewarded." For wealthy and educated Deists, unaided human reason was enough to guarantee the moral success of the republic, but more pious North Carolinians felt the need of religious guidance too.

The churches of colonial North Carolina had frequently been the national churches of pioneer immigrant groups. The Church of England itself was the most obvious example, and the colonial government had provided it with legal privileges and public subsidies. The colony built several beautiful Anglican churches at public expense in eastern towns and counties but could not make the Church of England a spiritual home for the common people. Nutbush Church, now known as St. John's Church, in Williamsboro, was a balanced and harmonious architectural gem. It was constructed in 1773 by John Lynch, a master carpenter. Tobacco planters flocked to its services from all corners of Granville County, but sincere dissenters objected that the ministers there preached Deism and they would not tender it their support. Other localities complained that the missionary priests sent out from England were immoral and incompetent drunkards. All the Anglican churches in North Carolina fell into disuse after the Revolution cut off their subsidies and supply of ministers. Even when Anglicans reorganized themselves as the Protestant Episcopal Church, they made little headway with the populace.

The churches of the other immigrants were not in a similar state of decline. The Germans had strong religious roots in their Piedmont settlements, and their traditions continued after the Revolution as before. The Moravians constructed Bethabara Church in 1788, and Lutherans and other German worshipers built comparable structures like Zion Lutheran Church (1795) in Rowan County, St. Paul's Lutheran Church (1808) in Catawba County, and Lower Stone Church (1795) in Rowan County. Ethnically based Presbyterian churches remained active among the Scotch-Irish and the Scottish Highlanders, but, many of these congregations, like their German counterparts, worshiped in a foreign language. Except for some Scotch-Irish clergy, the ministers of these ethnic congregations had limited appeal beyond their particular nationalities. The colonial churches of North Carolina could not meet the spiritual aspirations of many thousands of the state's citizens after the Revolution.

Passed over by the economic and political order, isolated from the gentry's republican culture, scandalized by Deism, and unsatisfied by traditional churches, thousands of nonelite Carolinians turned to dissenting Protestant ministers who came from the same social backgrounds as themselves. Joseph Caldwell described these preachers condescendingly. "One reason why religion is as scouted from the most influential part of society," he explained, "is that it is taught only by ranters, with whom it seems to consist only in the powers of their throats and the wildness and madness of their gesticulations and distortions." The fervor of evangelical preaching was indeed unconventional to those more used to academic-style sermons, but most itinerant preachers had little interest in trimming their pulpit styles to suit more sedate tastes.

Radical Protestants often had a low opinion of upper-class culture, regarding it as frivolous and worldly at best, unjust and wicked at worst. In extreme cases, religious social criticisms touched on slavery itself, the institution that laid the foundation of the planters' power over others. North Carolina Quakers began to criticize slavery and to free their slaves in the eighteenth century, but resentment of bondage and the power it gave to the gentry did not stop with the Society of Friends. In an angry letter to the Reverend Charles Pettigrew, the Episcopal planter-priest of Tyrrell and Washington Counties, local Baptist spokesman Amariah Biggs had trouble with his spelling, but he made his message clear. "Sir," he began, "I Labour trewly and honestly to get my one Living In that State of Life which It has pleased god to Call me and am Contented theirwith but you are not so[.] you put the yoke of Iron on the poor Ethiopens and get your riches by their rod of oppression[.]" Evaluating Pettigrew's economic, political, and religious role in the county, Biggs drew a literally damning conclusion. "The Scripture saith tis Easir for a Camel to go through the Eye of an needel then for a rich man to Enter into the Kingdom of heaven[.] I have greater reason to believe that at the last day . . . You will be found at the Left of the throne of the magesty on high Where you will call for a drop of water to Cool your tungue seeing that all ready tis on fiers of hell."

Not all evangelicals were so positive about the gentry's future prospects. More commonly, the dissenting ministers merely shrugged off the planters' culture, unless it could be rededicated to religious purposes. Thus Methodist pioneer Francis Asbury noted in his journal that the town of New Bern contained a "famous house, said to be designed for the masonic and theatrical gentlemen," and then noted dryly, "it might make a most excellent church." Aptly called the "Prophet of the Long Road," Asbury spent almost forty-five years, averaging 6,000 miles a year, traveling and preaching. In 1783 he wrote that "hitherto the Lord has helped me through continual fatigue and rough roads; little rest for man or horse, but souls are perishing—time is flying—and eternity comes nearer every hour." Armed with faith that gave them the necessary confidence to distance themselves from the gentlemen of New Bern, Asbury and his colleagues launched a religious movement that came to dominate North Carolina's popular culture in the century to come.

The crusade was known as the Great Revival. It embraced a variety of churches, individuals, and groups, but the most important denominations involved were the Baptists, Methodists, and Presbyterians. The movement's hallmark was evangelicalism, or an emphasis on personal conversion as the test of Christian salvation. Without an overwhelming personal experience of rebirth, evangelicals held that no amount of good deeds or pious thoughts could justify a person in the sight of God. To the humble individual, the evangelical churches offered a reassurance and a source of personal esteem that did not depend on riches, status, or education. To the collective body of believers, the churches offered a vision of the virtuous republic that did not depend on classical erudition, European nationality, or invidious class distinctions.

The evangelical denominations grew steadily throughout the latter half of the eighteenth century. Methodist bishop Asbury and dozens of local circuit riders crossed and recrossed North Carolina, preaching at farms, inns, and crossroads whenever anyone would listen. Exposed to the rigors of travel and makeshift shelter, any itinerant preacher could have duplicated William Ormond's accommodations one night in 1792: "At bed time three of the Children & myself lodged in an indifferent bed in an open house, & the Man & Woman lay on the dirt floor before the fire."

Baptists received an important boost from the arrival of the Reverend Shubal Stearns from Connecticut, and the rapid emergence of the six churches of the Sandy Creek Baptist Association that soon followed him. The Reverend David Caldwell's "log college" in Guilford County prepared dozens of young men for the Presbyterian ministry and exposed them to the fiery eloquence of northern-trained evangelists. Caldwell's log college was supposed to have been modeled on a similar school Caldwell knew in his native Pennsylvania— a two-story structure of squared-off logs and a central chimney. Log churches appeared in numerous communities, offering an institutional home for new converts after the traveling preachers had moved on.

The evangelicals directed their message to all who felt demeaned or disfranchised by the "world," or in this case, by North Carolina's dominant hierarchical culture. Those who responded were frequently young people, white yeomen and artisans, women of all classes, and slaves. Blacks were not treated the same as whites in the churches, but the evangelical denominations came closer than any other white institutions to recognizing the spiritual equality of all men and women. Some masters opposed slave conversions for exactly this reason, but others encouraged it, supposing that religion would make the slaves more contented with their lot. Slaves seem to have embraced the new religion because it gave them an opportunity to acknowledge the obvious power of Western culture while condemning the sin of their own enslavement. The mass conversion of African Americans from traditional African religions probably dates from this period, although the process undoubtedly continued for many decades. The black freeman and preacher Henry Evans exerted such a good influence on the morals of his slave adherents that their masters welcomed his preaching in Fayetteville, supported his efforts, and attended his services. Like the slaves, ordinary white North Carolinians joined the churches at least in part because they wished to reject the cultural values of those who stood above them in the eyes of the "world."

The piecemeal process of conversion reached explosive proportions in the Great Revival of 1801–5. Beginning in the summer of 1801, word trickled back to Orange County (including what is now Alamance County) of remarkable works of God in the frontier state of Kentucky. Several ministers had moved west from these Piedmont communities, and thousands had gathered to hear their preaching at a place called Cane Creek. Assembled in huge crowds, multitudes of convicted sinners had cried out, wept, and fainted in near despair. When the possibility of salvation began to glimmer hopefully before them, the new converts manifested their joy with extraordinary physical "exercises." They laughed, sang, trembled, jerked uncontrollably, and even barked like animals. Many doubted that such undignified behavior could truly come from God, but others were convinced that the revival was a genuine visitation of the Holy Spirit. In October 1801 the friends of revival held the first five-day camp meeting in North Carolina at Hawfields Presbyterian Church, in Orange (now Alamance) County. They hoped for a repetition of the Kentucky phenomenon, and they were not disappointed. The Reverend Jesse Lee recorded in his memoir that in late 1775 "we had the greatest revival of religion, I have ever seen. I have been at meetings where the whole congregation would be bathed in tears: and sometimes their cries would be so loud that the preacher's voice could not be heard. Some would be seized with a trembling, and in a few moments drop on the floor as if they were dead; while others were embracing each other, with streaming eyes, and all were lost in wonder, love, and praise."

Camp meetings spread throughout the state, and soon the entire upper South was ablaze with the spirit of revival. In October 1808, the banker, editor, and jurist John A. Cameron wrote to his brother, the wealthy planter, jurist, and politician Duncan Cameron, about a camp meeting. "As I passed through Montgomery [County]," John informed Duncan, "I passed by a great Camp Meeting—there were many hundreds collected. A Mr. McIntyre preached in the Gaelic and a Mr. McMillan in the English language; being quite a novelty to me, I stopped, tied my horse and walked into one of the congregations. The greatest decorum presided, the preachers were zealous in the cause and the audience attentive. There was a vast number of Scots from Moore [County] there."

Inevitably, enthusiasm eventually waned and opposition roused itself. The Reverend Charles Pettigrew complained that his parishioners "were warmed, but not instructed" by the revival. "Their religion was placed in their passions, & these are now cooled, & their religion is fled. . . . Their last State is worse than the first," Pettigrew concluded sadly. Not unmindful of this possibility, evangelicals sought to counter it with institutions that would capture and preserve the intense emotions that the revival had evoked. They built new churches first of all, and later they would turn to Sunday schools, prayer meetings, temperance societies, denominational colleges, and annually scheduled camp meetings.

The Mount Pleasant Methodist Church in Forsyth County was among the new congregations formed in the wake of the Great Revival. Located on a hill overlooking the Yadkin River and now on the grounds of Tanglewood Park, Mount Pleasant bears the date 1809 on one of its timbers and was built by a man named Henry Eccles. Moravian documents from nearby Salem record that camp meetings were held there regularly as early as 1810. More prosperous than most early Methodist congregations, the members of Mount Pleasant Church were able to house their meeting in a frame building instead of a log cabin. Inside, a gallery seated slaves, who formed a part of every early Methodist congregation. Downstairs, the room is severely plain. No cushions pad its high-backed pine benches; no carpet covers its bare wooden floors. The worshipers came to praise God and to hear the preached word. They would not be distracted by worldly decoration.

One effect of churches like Mount Pleasant was to rekindle seriousness of purpose in rural North Carolina society. The evangelicals took their converts into a disciplined new world where no vain pastimes or frivolous amusements were permitted to distract believers from their godly missions or to disturb the solemnity of their sanctified lives. Drinking, gambling, dancing, cardplaying, theatergoing, and Sabbath-breaking were strictly forbidden, and violators faced suspension or expulsion from church if they did not mend their ways and repent. Not by coincidence, these forbidden activities were considered the vices of the planter aristocracy, who frequently placed the evangelicals beneath themselves in social dignity.

Writing in 1810 and 1811, scattered observers of North Carolina were unanimous that the revival had a pervasive influence on popular mores. A correspondent from Moore County reported to a Raleigh newspaper that "formerly cock-fighting, Gander-pulling, Horse Racing, and card playing, were the principal Amusements—The present religious impressions of the people has laid aside the two former as cruel and barbarous and contrary to benevolence and humanity." He also believed that gambling and fox hunting were likewise on the decline. From Edgecombe County, Jeremiah Battle observed that gambling was declining and that dancing and family visiting had become the favorite amusements. A Duplin County writer said of cards, racing, and dancing that "these Amusements are now much Neglected where religion Progresses." Having fun did not become extinct in North Carolina, but it certainly became less boisterous and less conspicuous. In place of idle amusements, the churches gave their members a new experience, a new community, and a new measure of themselves as human beings.

The initial impact of churches like Mount Pleasant was strongest among the middle and lower classes of rural society, but the appeal of the evangelical churches eventually spread up the social scale. Hardworking middle-class Christians began to get ahead in life, and pious wives of planters converted their husbands and children. Perhaps most significant, evangelicals decided it was more important to convert slaves than to criticize slaveholders. They exchanged the vision of a morally perfect society in this world for the goal of a converted society fully prepared for the world to come. Planters came to see the advantages of a sober, united, churchgoing population. As Caswell County planter Bartlett Yancey noted in 1810, "The great revival of religion . . . seems to have contributed much to the dissemination of morality, sound principles and good order in society." Acting on Yancey's insight, planters began to give the evangelical movement their support and even opened themselves to hear its message.

By 1819 religion had gained great prestige among the gentry, according to the grandson of a North Carolina signer of the Declaration of Independence. In a sermon of that year preached to the well-heeled founders of the North Carolina Bible Society, the Reverend William Hooper recalled the days "when religion with downcast eye and timid step never ventured to approach the mansions of the opulent and elite, and only found casual entertainment among the cottages of the poor and ignorant." Hooper rejoiced with his audience that the churches "had grown respectable in the eyes of men" and had won the allegiance of "the men occupying the station and possessing the political influence of those who are now the patrons and pillars of our Bible Society." As North Carolina's commitment to evangelical religion deepened, the churches' style and doctrine became fixed features of the people's common culture. Beginning as a spiritual challenge to the established order, the churches in time became a part of it and gave their blessing to North Carolina's stable, agrarian, republican way of life.

The most conspicuous collaborative project of the planters and the evangelicals was the University of North Carolina. Led by General William Richardson Davie, prominent secular politicians believed that a university to train each rising generation of the elite in the principles of science, reason, and virtue would be an incomparable asset for the future of North Carolina. Prominent Presbyterian clergy, inspired by the Reverend Samuel E. McCorkle, hoped that a religiously oriented school would train future ministers in Greek, Latin, and moral philosophy, while preparing other godly youths for honorable service in diverse fields. Both groups urged the legislature to act, and the University of North Carolina was the result.

Chartered in 1789, the college opened in 1795 as the first state university in America. McCorkle devised the first curriculum; it stressed moral education and the classical languages of Latin and New Testament Greek. A little later, the trustees substituted a different course of study proposed by Davie. The new curriculum was more practical, stressing modern languages and mathe-

General William Richardson Davie

matics. A student could, if his parents chose, avoid the "dead" languages altogether and earn an English diploma that was based on the study of science
and mathematics and their practical applications. In Davie's view, there was
more virtue to be found in skills useful for the new country than in the ambiguous speculations of philosophers, theologians, and dead poets. Under the
Reverend Joseph Caldwell, the university's second president, a compromise
was struck that provided for more secular versions of the traditional classical
subjects.

When it opened, the university met in a new building that foreshadowed
Davie's curriculum far more than McCorkle's. Severely practical, the structure
now known as Old East was a barnlike pile of plain brick that housed students,
tutors, and classrooms. Only an ordinary band of decoration at the roofline
accentuated the triangular pediments and suggested the appearance of a classical temple. The University of North Carolina would sponsor no more than a
rough-hewn enlightenment. In June 1796 one of the students described conditions at the Chapel Hill institution: "The number of students has increased
to ninety four, and room for more cannot possibly be had here—I have read
through Geography, the English grammar and have cifered through Arith-

metic on which I expect to be examined in July. . . . The provision furnished by the steward consists chiefly of Bacon, Beef, & Mutton; no luxurious Diet, but strong wholsome Food very fit for laborious Men, but by no means suited to the Organs of sensation."

A simple but forceful lesson in the social and economic differences between North Carolina and the neighboring state of Virginia comes from a glance at their respective state universities. After he left the White House in 1809, Thomas Jefferson designed an "academical village" at the University of Virginia that would rank as a triumph of American Greek Revival architecture. No such extravagance tempted North Carolina. Though the state had fostered a modest plantation economy, great wealth and superlative cultural achievements still eluded her citizens. North Carolina planters' sons would study their lessons in the simplest possible quarters, while the scions of the Old Dominion's aristocracy would learn to love the classics in exquisite surroundings, each one in his own miniature Monticello.

The obvious contrast between Old East in Chapel Hill and the Rotunda

Drawing of the University of North Carolina's first building, Old East, as it originally looked to John Pettigrew, a student in 1797

at Charlottesville was seen by later North Carolinians as a sign of North Carolina's inferiority relative to the rest of the Union. Though foreign war and the cotton boom had stimulated the state's economy, other states had profited too, and most had done better than North Carolina. The tide of immigration that had flooded the Carolina backcountry in the middle of the eighteenth century had veered across the mountains after the Revolution, and North Carolina's relative rank in population dropped from third in 1790 to fifth in 1830. Persistent geographical obstacles barred her citizens from the highest profits of the new commerce, and many state citizens began to contemplate removal to the richer cotton lands of the Southwest. In spite of the significant gains that had appeared since the Revolution, the changes were not enough for North Carolina to keep up. By 1815 the state had come to seem backward.

More than local pride was at stake in the question of North Carolina's development. The emigration movement damaged land values for those who left and those who chose to stay. Departing planters took large numbers of slaves with them, and land and slaves were the principal components of the state's meager tax base. Declining population spelled frustration and political impotence for North Carolinians ambitious for preferment in the U.S. Congress, the courts, or the executive branch. Migration drove families apart, and forced energetic youths to choose between their parents and their futures. Most fundamentally, perhaps, economic decline reflected poorly on the republican experiment, and reminded a younger generation that they had not lived up to the towering achievement of their illustrious founding fathers. As the 1820s approached, North Carolinians were facing a painful dilemma, for the dream of independence was in danger of being lost.

The question was what to do about it. A substantial and respectable body of opinion maintained that the wisest course was to do nothing. Led by Senator Nathaniel Macon, conservatives warned that backwardness was not the only danger that North Carolinians faced. The kind of greatness desired by the reformers would carry North Carolina further and further from the world of self-sufficiency to the networks of international trade. No matter how backward he seemed, the independent freeholder owed nothing to anybody. The bustling entrepreneur depended on a hundred different parties for one essential item or another, and failure on their parts could drag him into ruin. The independent republic could best preserve itself by keeping such operators at a distance.

Macon and his associates went one step further. Observing the pace of social and economic development in other portions of the Union, they noted that rapid change led men to think that anything was humanly possible. Macon scoffed at the miracles of steam technology and at what he called "the fashionable & favorite expression, 'to conquer Space'" and at the notion that "the power of science was omnipotent, it could do everything." What if the quest for a perfect society should lead men to question the institution of slavery? Looking at the emerging moral reform movements of the North, Macon did not like what he saw. Reformers had brought about the abolition of slavery in the states beyond the Mason-Dixon line, and the lesson for white North Carolinians was clear: progress of all kinds was dangerous. "Why depart from the good old way?" Macon pleaded from the floor of the U.S. Senate. "[It] has kept us in quiet, peace, and harmony—every one living under his own vine and fig tree, and none to make him afraid. Why leave the road of experience, which has satisfied all, and made all happy, to take this new way, of which we have no experience. The way leads to universal emancipation." For Macon, independence for white people required that black people remain slaves, and, in order to preserve white supremacy, he was perfectly willing to stop all sorts of progress in its tracks.

Archibald D. Murphey

Some North Carolina politicians thought Nathaniel Macon was unnecessarily alarmist. They were confident that republican government was equal to any task the people gave it. How could anyone be independent who was poor, they inquired, and how could North Carolina prosper when private initiative alone lacked the power or the incentive to restructure the state's economy? Governor William Miller was as much a supporter of independent farmers as Nathaniel Macon was, but he wished to protect them a different way. Repeating republican clichés in his 1816 address to the legislature, Miller praised agrarian life as "the parent of health, plenty, and contentment; the nurse of patriotism and every virtue." However, he added, "agriculture . . . flourishes most where she can, with ease, pour her superabundant stores into the lap of a liberal market. Thus situated, commerce, the mechanic arts, and their fruits, the comforts and elegancies of life, follow in her train." North Carolina should foster economic development by undertaking the "improvement of our roads, cutting canals, and opening the navigation of our rivers," or, in other words, by sponsoring what the nineteenth century called "internal improvements."

The outstanding reformer Archibald D. Murphey had a similar message for the 1815 General Assembly. "The time has come," intoned the senator from Orange County, "when it behooves the legislature of North Carolina to provide efficiently for the improvement of the inland navigation of the state. To delay this provision is to postpone that national wealth, respectability, and importance which only follow in the train of great internal improvements." When transportation costs were made lower by the construction of canals, Murphey argued, prosperity would ensue, and North Carolina could take its rightful place in the world of progressive republican independence.

The visions of Nathaniel Macon and Archibald Murphey were radically different, but both were logical versions of North Carolina's republican ideals. Both stressed the independence of the individual white freeholder and promised to guard his world from external assault and internal corruption. Macon sought to protect the institution of slavery by sealing off the influence of destabilizing social change. Equally devoted to slaveholders' interests, Murphey sought to strengthen the plantation economy by cutting the planter's freight rates and by enabling the isolated yeoman to sell the crops and buy the slaves that would raise him to planter status too. Each in his own way, Macon and Murphy were legitimate heirs of North Carolina's eighteenth-century republican heritage.

Development was uneven, but the path that North Carolina chose was closer to Murphey's than to Macon's. Before the Orange County senator ever filed his famous reports calling for reform, the legislature had chartered the State Bank of North Carolina to provide the credit that would ease the transition to an intensified market economy. The bank's original building stands as a handsome Federal monument to the ideals of republican commerce. As Macon was uttering his direst warnings, the state was chartering navigation companies to speed the shipment of staples along North Carolina's shallow rivers. Perhaps the most successful corporation was the Roanoke Navigation Company, which opened the water route for cotton and tobacco to float down the Roanoke River to Albemarle Sound. The centerpiece of the company's improvements was a short canal around the river's waterfalls at Weldon. The stone locks of this canal are still in place, and the aqueduct that carried the waterway over Chockoyotte Creek on the outskirts of Weldon is an outstanding example of the engineer's genius and the stonemason's skill. Another vital water route, the Dismal Swamp Canal (chartered 1790), connected Albemarle Sound with Chesapeake Bay.

Banks and internal improvements did not remake North Carolina overnight, but the cumulative changes they introduced did reorient the economy of the state to the demands of national and international commerce. They also strengthened the grip of the slave plantation on the life of the state, committed North Carolina politicians to the inflexible defense of slavery itself, and set the stage for a bloody sectional conflict. The social and economic revolution wrought by internal improvements in the nation at large was more profound than any material outcome of the War for Independence itself.

These changes were hardly visible in 1820. The nostalgic world of Na-

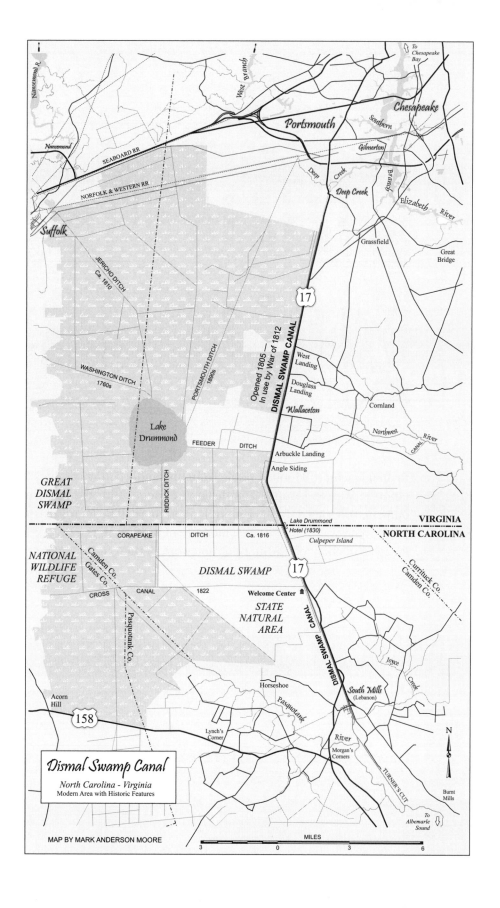

Dismal Swamp Canal

North Carolina - Virginia
Modern Area with Historic Features

MAP BY MARK ANDERSON MOORE

State Bank building (1818), Raleigh

thaniel Macon still looked viable from his simple cottage at Buck Spring Plantation in Warren County. The debate he fought with the advocates of development still raged for a generation or more. The mere existence of the controversy was nevertheless a measure of how much the lives of North Carolinians had changed within the framework of their independent society.

Thomas H. Clayton

Part III

CLOSE TO THE LAND NORTH CAROLINA, 1820-1870

OVERVIEW

1

Victorian America

It was the Victorian Age. Born in 1819, Victoria ascended the throne of England in her teens and in 1870 was still queen. Her reign remained constant in a half-century that was otherwise tumultuous with change. New words suggested the altering dimensions of thought and the material world: technology, industrialist, engineer, journalism, individualism, booster, sodbuster, saloon, and Sunday school. Most life had been lived at a walking pace in the century before. New inventions from this period accelerated the tempo of life and linked remote parts of the country and the globe: the railroad, the telegraph, the steamship, the reaper, the sewing machine, the transatlantic cable.

In the American portion of the Victorian world, the United States was first and foremost a young republic. One of every three persons was under ten years old. Over half the population was under thirty. The population grew so fast—doubling in size every twenty-five years—that if the pace had continued, today we would be a nation of 1 billion.

Young people were not only numerous; they were restless. The restlessness and ambition of youth were fueled by an explosion of opportunities for adventure and advancement. New land provided an enormous boon to this generation. The American portion of the continent had doubled in 1803 with the Louisiana Purchase. Near midcentury it doubled again, and the United States became a continental nation, with the acquisition of Texas, Oregon, and the massive southwestern territory wrested from Mexico in 1848.

Treaties and war made the expansion of the agricultural frontier possible; canals, railroads, steel plows, and the reaper made western settlement and farming profitable. Long before gold was discovered in California in 1848, young men and women were leaving the East behind. As many as one of every four persons born in the seaboard states and New England swarmed inland in search of new opportunities, with the aspiring from the Carolinas journeying to the southwestern lands of Alabama and Mississippi as well as Indiana and Illinois in the Old Northwest.

Settlers migrated to North Carolina seeking new opportunities.

But the energy and optimism of the Republic in this half-century came not only from the westward surge. The era was one of unprecedented growth in towns and cities, industry and commerce. By 1860 New York City had its first million inhabitants. The populations of other coastal and inland cities doubled and redoubled. One day in Chicago in the mid-1830s, lots that sold for $150 in the morning sold for $5,000 by nightfall. Even small towns throbbed with business, as blacksmiths and merchants, artisans and lawyers set up shop and rang up profits. While few factories in the modern sense existed, the hum of cottage industry became a din of manufacturing. With power provided by rivers and then steam-driven machines, with labor supplied first by young New England women and then by immigrant families, textile manufacturing led the way. In 1820 eight of ten Americans had made their living on the farm. By 1870 over half of the nation's employed worked in pursuits outside of agriculture.

The furious expansion of commerce and industry was made possible by breakthroughs in transportation. The creation of an ambitious network of canals followed the dazzling success of the Erie Canal in 1825 and linked coastal cities with the interior. In the 1830s the steamboat made the Mississippi the nation's great inland waterway. Dwarfing and dominating the canal system from the 1840s onward was the railroad. By 1860 the railroads of the nation had laid 30,000 miles of track and had attracted a billion dollars of investment. In 1869 the Golden Spike commemorated the linking of New York and California by a transcontinental railway.

Little wonder, then, that much of the era from 1820 to 1870 was characterized by buoyant optimism. A continent possessed, space conquered by locomotives, productivity multiplied by mechanization: what boundaries had not

Locomotive of the Raleigh and Gaston Railroad

or could not be broken? Leading political figures of the era—Andrew Jackson, Abraham Lincoln, Ulysses Grant—had risen from poverty or obscurity to the presidency. They were stunning symbols of an America in motion, of a society of self-made men.

The creativity of the period was not confined to business or politics or to men alone. It was also an age of remarkable social experiment. The inspiration for much social innovation was anxiety: would the rush of the young to the frontier and the city create a nation of rootless and profiteering vagrants? Thousands turned their energy into the effort to reform and reinforce the moral character of Americans. Public schools forged good character, Sunday schools implanted virtue, YMCAs gave Christian shelter to restless youth. Victorian Americans pioneered in the creation of penitentiaries, insane asylums, and reform schools, each designed to reclaim and reform those driven to crime or insanity by the temptations or insecurities of commercial life. Social innovation extended even to the Victorian family. The family was asked to become a refuge of affection in a world of turbulence and amorality. Women especially, as mothers and teachers, were called on to domesticate the passions and uplift the sensibilities of men competing for place and fortune.

Perhaps it is not surprising that a society immense in its creative energies would also be colossal in its contradictions. A slave society existed and grew amid a free one. The mechanization that enhanced productivity for many, degraded the skills and made hireling laborers of others. The benefits of communications with distant markets were matched by the risks of ties to the national economy, which reliably collapsed every twenty years. Women who joined the movement to free slave families discovered their own bonds, and initiated their own movement, when men sought to silence female speakers at antislavery forums. Indeed, breaking from bondage became a motif for many by mid-century, and the American vocabulary of 1870 reflected the struggles undertaken to resolve Victorian tensions. "Woman's rights" and "free love," strike and socialism, emancipation and Reconstruction—what a different world it was from that of fifty years before!

The Tar Heel State

A traveler visiting North Carolina in 1820 would immediately have noticed that all things visible seemed to be agricultural. The dwellings that dotted the landscape—plantations and slave quarters, frame houses and log dwellings, gristmills and weatherboard churches—all were country places. The pace of people at work was decidedly rural. From sunup to sundown, most worked hard but without great hurry. Play was intermixed with work, rather than reserved until day was done. Frequent drams of liquor lubricated the day's labor; songs accompanied toil in the fields; a barn raising was a mixture of boisterousness and brawn. If the visitor looked closely, he would also have detected a paradox. Few who farmed did farming only. If a small farmer wanted a wagon, he made it. Whiskey? He distilled his own. The same multiplicity of talents was evident in slave communities, where blacks were preachers and trappers, midwives and home-gardeners, as well as tillers in a master's field.

The visitor would eventually have found towns and townspeople too, of course. Carolinians from the countryside and village came to town to trade and sell at the marketplace, to talk politics and do legal battle at the county courthouse. Town residents supported skilled furniture-makers and able schoolmistresses and schoolmasters, who provided cosmopolitan amenities for a cultivated society. Yet even town physicians and lawyers, ministers and bankers doubled, or at least dabbled, in agriculture. For the overwhelming majority of North Carolinians in 1820, agriculture was the main business of life and shaped decisively the way they lived.

If the same traveler had returned to North Carolina in 1860, he might well have recorded contradictory impressions in his letters home. Signs of change abounded. Almost a thousand miles of railroads laced the state, linking east and west. North Carolina's notorious illiteracy, circumscribing the mental horizons of the majority in 1820, was now under attack in the 2,500 common schools that brought a few months' learning each year to 100,000 children. The dozen newspapers of 1820 had become seventy-five in 1860, a handful of hamlets had grown into flourishing small towns, and modest water-powered textile mills had established a factory frontier in the state.

Yet what might have struck the traveler most about the forty years between 1820 and 1860 were not the signs of change but the strength of continuities. The great planters had expanded in number and diversified their crops to include cotton as well as leaf tobacco. But, as a class, this elite remained small, its lands the best, its influence large. In 1860 as in 1820, a third of North Carolinians were black and most were enslaved. Still predominant were the mass of yeomen farmers and their families, cultivating small farms with methods and tools familiar to their grandfathers. If making money and a life of elegance were the ambitions of the planters, and making both possible was the duty of enslaved blacks, to "make do" remained the goal and self-sufficiency the ultimate accomplishment of most small farmers.

The persistence of simple self-sufficiency and tradition in farming and daily life might well have troubled the traveler in 1860. For much of the rest of the nation had taken a different course in the nineteenth century. Outside the South, cities and factory towns, machines and improved transportation had changed the pace of life. On the farm, in villages as well as cities, a spirit of enterprise had taken hold. The market economy had spread everywhere, and both single people and families moved frequently in search of the best opportunities of "Commerce, Commerce, Commerce!" To outsiders who traveled through North Carolina and to many natives as well, the Tar Heel State—by doing most things as it had always done them—had fallen behind.

Yet, for all its traditionalism, North Carolina was not a stagnant society. The Tar Heel of legend, content to live lazily off the fat of the land, a bit of a brawler, proud that his mind was unpolluted by book learning, suspicious of higher culture as effeminate and alien, was more myth than reality. Curiosity, resourcefulness, and invention abounded, but they occurred within the boundaries of a rural world. Those boundaries frequently were narrow, often limited to the locality where a North Carolinian had grown up. Yet that small world was known with matchless intimacy. Footpaths and streams, soil and climate, neighbor and kin—these were the objects of curiosity and passion, loyalty and legend, struggle and mastery. Family was central, and a true map of North Carolina would record not only the roads and streams and farms and churches, but also the connections of kin. It was a countryside of cousins.

Clans of cousins formed family alliances and intricate networks of mutual aid. It was a folk society, personal and passionate, ambitious and enterprising in its own terms.

The terms of life were altered by 1870. Not only did emancipation change the relationship between black and white, planter and freedman. The Civil War expanded horizons and shook old premises. Over 100,000 North Carolinians had left their localities, traveled hundreds of miles from home, and seen a wider part of the world. Women had managed farms and plantations while their men were away. Though most Tar Heels returned to rebuild after the war, deprivation created new opportunities. More and more farmers would plant crops for market. Others were ready to go beyond the plow and the plantation to take their chances with factories and the life of commerce. Ambitions and forces for change—channeled and contained for fifty years within the bounds of plantation life, slave communities, and local enterprise—were unleashed. The next half-century would be dramatically different from the last.

Sydney Nathans

RURAL COMMUNITY

2

Provincial and conservative, the people of the "Rip Van Winkle State" were invariably characterized by outside observers, such as Frederick Law Olmsted, as well deserving their proverbial reputation for "ignorance and torpidity." Overwhelmingly rural, North Carolinians were isolated from the world around them, as well as each other, by geographical barriers, limited means of transportation, and their own independent spirit. However "backward" and "indolent," most Tar Heels had a more discerning, if not more favorable, view of their lifestyle and themselves. Times were hard; there is no doubt. Days were long and rewards were slight. Yet an increasing number of Carolinians had succeeded in purchasing their own farms. And, as the *Fayetteville Observer*, in 1837, proudly pointed out: "The great mass of our population is composed of people who cultivate their own soil, owe no debt, and live within their means. It is true we have no overgrown fortunes, but it is also true that we have few beggars."

Beyond pride in personal accomplishment, nineteenth-century Carolinians, regardless of economic means or social status, were sustained by an unequivocal commitment to family life and a strong sense of local community. Young and old alike met in the hundreds of rural churches that dotted the landscape to share in a common religious experience and the animated conversation that invariably followed the sermon. The essential economic goods and services provided by the country store or nearby mill were complemented by its social function as a public forum for the lively discussion of any and every topic from tomorrow's weather to today's politics. And the growing number of academies and schools served to heighten the community's esteem as well as prepare its younger members to meet the challenges of the outside world.

Yet undoubtedly the most important bond among those who composed the rural community was their common interest in cultivating the land. Agriculture was their way of life, and it informed their every thought and action. The farm, whether 10 acres or 10,000, was the basic unit of economic production and social organization. It was there that the vast majority of Carolinians could be found—working their fields, preparing their meals, rearing their children, and living out their lives.

Plantation Life

In North Carolina the "Old South" of fiction and film did not exist. There were vast plantations and belles, white-columned mansions and "poor white trash." But the Old North State in the antebellum period was a land of yeoman farmers rather than gallant planters, of free blacks as well as slaves, and of corn and livestock in addition to tobacco and cotton. Though there were some 300 plantations of 1,000 acres or more in the state in 1860, there were more than 46,000 farms of less than 100 acres. If the economic, political, and social influence of the larger planters outweighed their numerical proportion, in terms of lifestyle they represented an anomaly. Remodeled in 1826 from a 1785 dwelling of planter Henry Lane, the Mordecai House features the Greek Revival style of many plantation houses. The structure, which is now located in Raleigh's Mordecai Historic Park, once stood north of the city on the plantation of Moses Mordecai. In contrast to the multistory manor house of Greek Revival design, the dwelling on the average farm was a three-room log or frame structure conceived and constructed by the occupants themselves.

For a large number of Carolinians, however, plantation life did represent a norm. Approximately a third of the state's population was enslaved, and of this group over half were held by planters who owned twenty slaves or more. Although most bondspeople had little occasion to participate directly in the affairs of the "big house," it was the slave community around which life on the plantation largely revolved.

Mordecai House (1785, remodeled 1826),
Mordecai Historic Park, Raleigh.
Photograph by Paulette Mitchell.

The Planters

Somerset Place State Historic Site in Washington County offers a provocative glimpse of life among the planter elite in the antebellum South. Begun in the late eighteenth century, the plantation was largely the creation of Josiah Collins of Edenton, who had emigrated from England in 1773 and made a fortune as a merchant during the American Revolution. Along with two partners whom he later forced to sell out, Collins formed the Lake Company to develop the desolate and, at the time, worthless swamplands bordering Lake Phelps. The company arranged for a direct shipment from Africa of eighty slaves, who were put to work digging a canal twenty feet wide from the lake to the Scuppernong River, a distance of six miles. Upon completion of the three-year project, a large estate was drained and cleared, grist- and sawmills were constructed along the canal, and the company began gradually divesting itself of the 100,000 acres it had acquired in the area.

Though Collins and later his son, Josiah II, maintained their residence and mercantile business in Edenton, they retained a meticulous interest in Somerset and its continued development. Thus, when twenty-one-year-old Josiah Collins III assumed control of the plantation in 1830, he inherited not only thousands of acres of arable land and almost 300 slaves with whom to maintain it, but also a brilliantly designed system of waterways and water-powered labor-saving devices that made the agricultural operation one of the most technologically advanced in the South. Originally conceived as a drainage and irrigation system for rice culture, the network of secondary canals served as a versatile means of transport when in the early nineteenth century the Collinses shifted to the large-scale production of corn. Huge barges could be floated alongside the fields during planting and harvest to move bulk quantities of the crop to and from the storage barns and processing plant located on the main canal. Yet it was the ingenuity of the processing mechanism itself that impressed visitors such as Edmund Ruffin, the noted agricultural editor and reformer, who, in 1838, explained the procedure in as follows:

When it is desired to prepare a cargo of corn for the Charleston market, there is no need of commencing until notice has been received of the vessel having arrived in the river below. The shelling of the corn is then commenced, by a shelling machine of immense power, then fanned, next lifted up by elevating machinery, from the first to the fourth story of the house, there measured, and then emptied through a spout into a large flatboat lying in the canal, which, as soon as loaded in bulk, is conveyed along the canal to the vessel. Thus the risk of keeping a large quantity of shelled corn in bulk is avoided, and by the aid of water, all the operations necessary to load a vessel may be completed in a very short time.

Somerset Place (ca. 1838–40), Washington County

Life at Somerset for young Collins and his family was quite profitable in an economic sense, yet the costs of their existence in the region must not be overlooked. Though the environment of Lake Phelps and the surrounding swamps proved to be as abundant as it was hauntingly beautiful, it could be a liability as well. Travel to and from the plantation was difficult, time-consuming, and sometimes dangerous. Overland transport by horse, cart, or carriage meant traversing roads that were often little more than muddy footpaths, in addition to fording the numerous streams that dissected the low-lying area. Water travel required following the circuitous route down the main canal and along the slow-moving river before facing the contrary winds and shifting shoals of Albemarle Sound. Edenton, the nearest town of any consequence, was a full day's journey away—that is, if the weather held.

Frequent storms and even occasional droughts multiplied the problems at the plantation itself. floods washed away dikes along the canals and the lake, high winds flattened the corn and uprooted trees, hail destroyed crops as they stood in the field, and lightning periodically ignited fires in the nearby swamps. On several occasions livestock were drowned and various outbuildings were inundated as a result of severe weather. A hurricane that struck in 1839 reportedly raised the lake level six feet in several hours and left water standing as high as the ridges in the cornfield.

And of course Somerset Place saw its share of illness and death. Malaria, generally known at the time as "ague," was endemic. Since there was no effective cure, the sufferer could merely hope to minimize its recurring symptoms of chills and fever. The threat of smallpox and cholera epidemics repeatedly reached the lake region. And in 1839 what was termed "epidemic influenza" raged in the area, frequently causing its victims to rave for several days before the relief of recovery or death. "Flux" (dysentery), "consumption" (tuberculosis), rheumatism, and skin cancer were also common complaints. But often as dangerous as the diseases that threatened every member of the community were the accidents that occurred during day-to-day plantation activity. Snake bites, serious cuts, crushed or broken limbs—injuries of all types were a constant concern and, as the Collinses were well aware, could result in permanent disability or even death. Edward and Hugh Collins, aged eight and ten, along with two black playmates, drowned in 1843 in the murky water of the main canal. And several years later a third son, William, died in a riding accident on the carriageway leading to the house.

Only slightly less obvious than the physical hazards of their dismal environment was the social and psychological isolation that the Collinses felt at Somerset. Educated in the North, Josiah III thrived on the cosmopolitan atmosphere and cultural amusements available to the wealthy in such cities as Boston and New York. His wife, Mary Riggs Collins, was a native of New Jersey and maintained close ties of family and friendship in northern society. Thus the Collinses felt little affinity with the increasing number of small farmers who moved into the region and were occasionally hired to supplement the labor force at Somerset Place. Surprisingly, a similar coolness characterized the Collinses' relationship with the distinguished Pettigrew family, who owned the adjacent plantation of Bonarva. Ebenezer Pettigrew, who was almost fifty when Josiah III and his bride took up permanent residence at the lake, had devoted his entire life to the careful development of his property in the region. As intractable as he was conscientious, Pettigrew regarded his young neighbor as something of a dilettante planter; Collins for his part imperiously rejected Pettigrew's views on almost every topic from politics to religion. Though the

Josiah Collins III.
Portrait by
William G. Brown,
owned by Mrs.
Frank Williams.

Ebenezer Pettigrew

two families maintained a polite cordiality, their relationship was marred by pettiness, jealousy, and outright competition.

Still, it would seem difficult to be lonely in the midst of what actually constituted a sizable community of more than 300 people living and working on the plantation. Undoubtedly the Collinses did develop a close personal relationship with many of those individuals with whom they were in day-to-day contact. Yet the fact remains that the antebellum slaveholder was bound to a brutal system of perpetual exploitation that could be maintained only by the constant threat of violent force. Consequently the Collinses found themselves surrounded by a people whose labor they could not afford to be without, but whose very presence posed a potential danger to livelihood, lifestyle, and even life itself.

The Collinses responded to the environment confronting them at Somerset in ways that were typical of the planter class throughout the South. Shortly after their arrival in 1830, Josiah III and Mary began an extensive renovation and expansion of the plantation house that stands today on a magnificent site overlooking Lake Phelps. The rear wing and broad porches that now characterize the structure were added a decade later, creating a mansion almost triple the size of the original dwelling. The house was sumptuously decorated with the finest available furniture, imported carpets and fabrics, and costly works of art. An inventory compiled in 1839 listed some 60 chairs, numerous chests and cabinets, and 3 large dining tables. The accessories in the dining room alone included a 151-piece set of fine gold-and-white china, over 100 knives and forks, 10 carving sets, and 16 decanters.

The aura of stability, wealth, and power created by the mansion was complemented by the order imposed upon the surrounding natural landscape. The front of the house was parallel with the main canal and perpendicular to the shore of the lake. A row of stately oaks stood along the broad levee that bounded the canal and doubled as a carriageway leading to the entrance of the estate. A formal English garden was planted next to the house and adjacent to a group of several outbuildings, some of which were reoriented to create a more aesthetically pleasing setting for the expanded mansion. Across the canal, in what had once been a tangled jungle of dense vegetation, was an open lawn of several acres surrounded by large shade trees and an oval race course. Completing the patterned arrangement of the plantation complex was a uniform row of slave cabins that began some distance from the rear of the main house and extended in an uninterrupted line along the lake and down a secondary canal.

Yet for the Collins family not even the opulence of the mansion at Somerset could offset the social, cultural, and physical isolation of life on Lake

*Interior rooms,
Somerset Place*

Phelps. Accordingly, they thrived on the visits of relatives and friends, who
often stayed for weeks and were always lavishly entertained. Even the Pettigrews remarked on the "energy" their neighbors displayed "in catering for the
amusement of their numerous guests." Though they considered the Collinses'
hospitality to be aimed as much at overwhelming as entertaining their visitors,
the Pettigrew family was ordinarily represented at the formal receptions, ele-

gant dinners, and lively quadrilles that the Collinses held in honor of their guests.

The Collinses were also extremely concerned with maintaining an atmosphere of cultural refinement. They not only own an excellent library, but also organized a reading club that met during the winter months for several years. The periodic sessions, which typically consisted of reading aloud, along with interludes of music and singing, included any guests who happened to be in residence at Somerset as well as several of the younger members of the Pettigrew family. Their appreciation of music was such that the Collinses felt they needed two pianos in the humid climate of the region; thus one would always be available for use while the other was in Norfolk being tuned. Yet the most remarkable of the Collinses' cultural endeavors occurred in 1845 when Josiah III hired a French tutor with the intention of adopting French as "the language of the house."

Despite the Collinses' elaborate efforts to compensate for the dangers and deficiencies of their life at Somerset, the only effective way to ease their dilemma was to escape. The family spent several months of every year touring the fashionable summer resorts and springs in Virginia and the North: White Sulphur, Saratoga, and others. Rarely did they pass up additional opportunities to get away on business or pleasure, even during the most critical seasons in the agricultural cycle. In fact Ebenezer Pettigrew came to consider Josiah III's extended absences a dereliction of duty that would ultimately lead to the young planter's ruin. When in 1835 severe weather was causing considerable damage to the crops in the area, Pettigrew mused: "[Mrs. Collins] stays on the Lake scarcely any and Mr. C. not much more. These things must needs be. But, woe unto him. . . ."

The Slaves

Though they too felt the anxieties and suffered the hazards of plantation life, enslaved Carolinians had no viable means of escape. For it was not just their masters who subjected African American slaves to bondage, nor the various overseers, patrollers, and slave catchers who kept the system intact. The crucial factor sustaining slavery in the antebellum South was the acquiescence of the overwhelming majority of southern whites. In spite of the fact that some 70 percent of white families in North Carolina owned no slaves, most nonslaveholders condoned the subjugation of black Americans, whom they considered part of a subordinate race. Thus arrayed against slaves who attempted to question or alter their status was the full weight of a dominant white society, convinced of the salves' inferiority and prepared to use force to keep them in their

Slave quarters

place. That American slaves transcended the physical punishment and psychological abuse that slavery entailed is a tribute to the resilience of the African American community.

The material remains of slave life in North Carolina are all but gone. Yet on a gentle knoll in Durham County, surrounded by the fields and forests known as Horton Grove, several weatherworn structures stand as a reminder of the vital culture that African American slaves developed in the state. Now part of Historic Stagville, Horton Grove in the mid-nineteenth century was a productive component of the vast estate owned by the powerful Bennehan and Cameron families. The four substantial but decaying dwellings, which can be visited at the site, housed a portion of the hundreds of slaves who worked the Bennehan-Cameron properties and formed a cohesive community with roots in the colonial period and descendants in the region to this day.

The Bennehan and Cameron families, who were linked by business partnership as well as marriage, were among the wealthiest in the state. Paul C. Cameron, on whom the management of their combined holdings devolved in the decades prior to the Civil War, was known for his conscientiousness as a planter and his willingness to adopt innovative agricultural techniques. But the primary source of success for any planter, whether a Cameron in the Carolina Piedmont or a Collins on the Coastal Plain, was the industry and labor provided by the plantation workforce. Ebenezer Pettigrew begrudgingly acknowledged this debt: "Negroes are a troublesome property, and unless well managed, an expensive one, but they are indispensable in this unhealthy and laborious country, for these long canals, that are all important in rendering our swamplands valuable, must be dug by them or not at all."

Working from dawn to dusk, six days a week, slave laborers throughout

Slave house (ca. 1851) at Horton Grove, Stagville Plantation, Durham County. This house would have been home to four slave families. Photograph by Paulette Mitchell.

the South accomplished the arduous and irksome tasks associated with the large-scale production of staple crops. What is often overlooked in this day of mechanized agriculture is the skill and effort that was required to cultivate successfully such crops as cotton, tobacco, rice, corn, and wheat. Not only were lowlands like those surrounding Lake Phelps drained, but thousands of acres had to be cleared of massive trees, dense underbrush, and exposed rock. The process, according to one observer, could take as much as thirty man-days per acre, and given the continued demand for the high yields that rich "new soil" afforded, clearing additional acreage was an annual necessity.

Correct plowing, planting, and cultivating were also essential for a bountiful harvest. Each crop required varying levels of care and agricultural techniques. Corn demanded from one to three replantings to ensure a good stand against the ravages of cutworms, deer, and severe weather. The sprouting crop had to be thinned and hoed at least twice and finally "hilled" by pulling loose dirt around each stalk to provide additional support. Tobacco was started in carefully prepared seedbeds, then transferred plant by plant into the fields. In addition to normal cultivation, each plant required "priming" by stripping away several leaves at its base, "topping" by pinching off the top of the stalk when a sufficient number of leaves had developed, and "suckering" by removing the extraneous shoots that grew at the base of the leaves. The procedure not only depended on the experience and judgment of the slave workforce but required numerous trips over the same fields throughout the growing season.

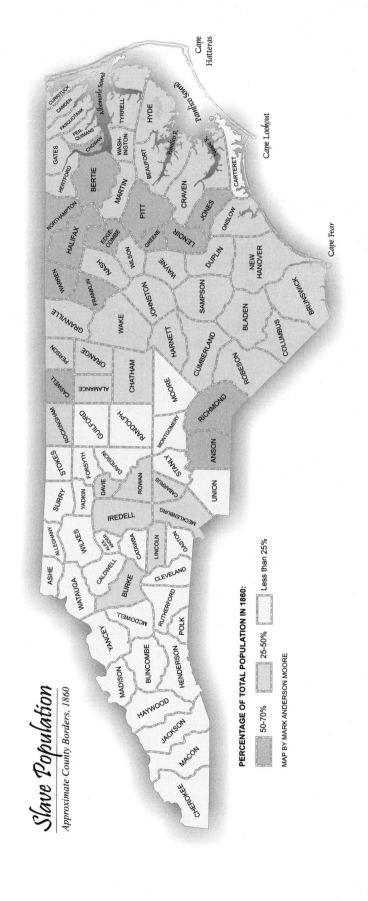

Slave Population
Approximate County Borders, 1860

PERCENTAGE OF TOTAL POPULATION IN 1860:

50-70%	
25-50%	
Less than 25%	

MAP BY MARK ANDERSON MOORE

Cape Hatteras

Cape Lookout

Cape Fear

Pamlico Sound

Albemarle Sound

Pamlico R.

N. usan R.

CURRITUCK
CAMDEN
PASQUOTANK
PER-QUIMANS
GATES
HERTFORD
CHOWAN
WASH-INGTON
TYRRELL
HYDE
BEAUFORT
BERTIE
MARTIN
NORTHAMPTON
PITT
CRAVEN
CARTERET
JONES
HALIFAX
EDGE-COMBE
GREENE
LENOIR
ONSLOW
NASH
WILSON
WAYNE
DUPLIN
NEW HANOVER
WARREN
FRANKLIN
JOHNSTON
SAMPSON
BLADEN
BRUNSWICK
GRANVILLE
WAKE
HARNETT
CUMBERLAND
COLUMBUS
PERSON
ORANGE
CHATHAM
MOORE
ROBESON
CASWELL
ALAMANCE
RICHMOND
ROCKINGHAM
GUILFORD
RANDOLPH
MONTGOMERY
ANSON
STOKES
FORSYTH
DAVIDSON
STANLY
SURRY
YADKIN
DAVIE
ROWAN
CABARRUS
UNION
ALLEGHANY
WILKES
ALEX-ANDER
IREDELL
MECKLENBURG
CATAWBA
LINCOLN
GASTON
ASHE
WATAUGA
CALDWELL
BURKE
CLEVELAND
RUTHERFORD
POLK
MCDOWELL
YANCEY
HENDERSON
MADISON
BUNCOMBE
HAYWOOD
JACKSON
MACON
CHEROKEE

Slaves planting rice

Harvest was the most difficult and taxing period in the agricultural cycle. The entire plantation community contributed to the concentrated effort, and work invariably continued for sixteen to twenty hours a day until the job was completed. Only those crops brought in at the peak of their development could command the highest prices. Bad weather was the primary concern, for not only did it slow the harvest; it endangered the crop as well. A storm could flatten a field of wheat, and even if it could be reaped, the wetness made threshing almost impossible. Grain allowed to lie cut on damp ground was likely to be ruined by sprouting.

Although planting more than one staple crop multiplied the labor and the problems associated with agricultural production, a versatile workforce allowed the planter to spread his economic risk through diversification. The field hands on the Bennehan-Cameron properties in the 1850s were respon-

Slaves planting cotton

sible for producing vast quantities of tobacco, corn, and wheat for the market in addition to growing cotton, oats, rye, and flax largely for plantation use. At the same time, Bennehan-Cameron slaves were charged with the care of several hundred swine, sheep, and beef cattle, as well as numerous horses, mules, and other livestock essential to the estate's operation.

From curing tobacco to butchering hogs, the processing of agricultural products was also handled almost entirely by skilled slave labor. Bondsmen ran the intricate processing plant at Somerset, just as a slave mechanic named Ben Sears managed the threshing machine owned by Paul Cameron. A slave miller known as Cyrus operated the Cameron's gristmill in Person County, while Matthew, who was owned by the Bennehans, directed their mill in Orange County.

Yet the competence and proficiency of the enslaved labor force went beyond the production of agricultural products. By providing the basic goods and services necessary for day-to-day operation, slave artisans made many larger plantations virtually self-sufficient. Slave blacksmiths designed and repaired tools and essential iron implements, while coopers constructed the vari-

Slaves loading cotton for shipment

ous wooden containers, from buckets to hogsheads, required for storage and shipment. Carpenters and masons built and repaired plantation buildings with materials furnished by sawyers and brickmakers. Enslaved spinners, weavers, tailors, and seamstresses provided the community with clothing, and tanners, cobblers, and harnessmakers supplied shoes and other essential leather goods. A mulatto bondsman named Virgil Bennehan served as a doctor for his fellow slaves on the Bennehan-Cameron estate, while a Pettigrew servant known as Airy acted as a nurse and a midwife for black and white alike.

Many bondsmen even took part in plantation management. The employment of black foremen known as "drivers" was a common practice throughout the South. Responsible for work gangs of from ten to thirty hands, the foremen directed agricultural operations in the field. Although placed in an ambiguous position between the labor force and his overseer or owner, the driver had the opportunity to intercede on behalf of his own people as well as the obligation to carry out the instructions of those above him. On several plantations

Slaves working in turpentine forest

a slave actually served as the overseer. A bondsman named Jim Ray managed one of the Bennehan-Cameron properties in Person County, while at Lake Phelps, William S. Pettigrew entrusted the operation of the plantations he had inherited from his father, Ebenezer, to two slave overseers, Moses at Belgrade and Henry at Magnolia.

The material quality of life for slaves in antebellum North Carolina was directly related to their owner's wealth, humanity, and economic self-interest. Theories as to what constituted adequate housing, clothing, and diet for slave labor were almost as numerous as planters themselves. The dwellings that remain today at Horton Grove represent the best in a broad spectrum that ranged from shabby hovels with dirt floors and leaky roofs to the sweltering attics and musty basements of the "big house." Paul Cameron's major concern in regard to slave housing was that it provide a disease-free environment for his workforce, thereby reducing the expense of slave illness. The quarters at Horton Grove, which were constructed by slave craftsmen in the early 1850s,

Great Barn (1860) at Horton Grove, Stagville Plantation. Slave carpenters helped erect the barn, which housed mules and eventually horses and cattle. Photograph by Paulette Mitchell.

were the culmination of decades of gradual improvements aimed primarily at increasing labor efficiency.

Similar to housing projects of a more modern age, the four buildings at Horton Grove are of identical design and construction and stand in a single row behind an earlier house that likely served as an overseer's residence. The two-story frame structures are built on pilings, and their thick exterior walls are filled with brick nogging covered by board-and-batten siding. On each floor are two rooms divided by a passageway that contains a narrow flight of stairs. Each of the four chambers is approximately seventeen feet square and has two windows and one large fireplace.

Each of the rooms in the dwellings at Horton Grove housed an entire slave family. Furnishings were sparse and consisted primarily of those items that family members could make or obtain for themselves. A crude table served as the center of domestic activity, a discarded chair provided an honored seat for an elderly relative, and a woven mat or shuck mattress offered a convenient if uncomfortable place to rest. The whitewashed walls were functionally ornamented with hanging pans and baskets, strings of drying herbs or fruit, and maybe even a conjurer's mark or talisman meant to ward off unwelcome visitors as well as evil spirits. Ebenezer Pettigrew allowed his slaves to exchange products grown or crafted in their limited free time for household and personal goods in his plantation store. In addition to such essentials as cooking utensils, plates, and bowls, slave purchases included small pieces of furniture, mirrors,

Some enslaved African Americans, such as carpenter Haywood Dixon, pictured here, were skilled craftsmen. Tintype courtesy of Bill Murphy.

and colorful curtain material, all of which helped to transform a dreary room into a warm if Spartan home.

Food and clothing were generally allocated to enslaved Carolinians in family units. Josiah Collins III, who like Cameron was comparatively generous in providing for his slaves, directed that they be clothed as follows: "They are to have Two good Suits of Clothes—one for Summer, and one of good woolen cloth for Winter—two pair of good double-soled shoes and one pair of woolen Stockings, one good wool hat [and] a Blanket not less than six feet long. A woman having one child is to have a Blanket for such child; when a woman has more than one child a Blanket is to be supplied for every two children; where the number of children in any one family is an odd number, then a Blanket is to be supplied for such child also."

As with their dwellings, any embellishment or addition to the coarse uniform that bondspeople were issued was the result of their own enterprise. Ebenezer Pettigrew's account book indicated that demand for such items as buttons, handkerchiefs, stockings, shoes, and cloth such as calico and gingham was quite high. A slave named Will, for example, worked to buy some cotton stockings for his wife, while Pompey saved enough to purchase a shawl and a pair of shoes for his.

Whenever possible, slaves attempted to supplement their meager food allotment as well. Corn and pork were the dietary staples for most of the slave population in North Carolina. Normally, at the beginning of each week, every family was provided with several pounds of hog meat and a peck of cornmeal for each of its members. Periodically those planters who considered it essential to the maintenance of their slaves' strength substituted beef for pork and included a measure of molasses along with any available vegetables. Though such a regimen supplied sufficient calories to meet the demands of a strenuous workday, it was woefully lacking in the vitamins and protein necessary for proper development and good health. Most enslaved families augmented their ration in some way, whether by hunting, gathering, fishing, or theft. Many were allowed to cultivate their own gardens and maintain livestock in what little spare time they had. But despite their efforts, bondsmen and -women were rarely in adequate physical shape to resist common respiratory and intestinal ailments. And they were regularly afflicted with a variety of complaints, from skin irritations and visual impairment to rickets and pellagra, now associated with dietary deficiency.

Yet slavery in the antebellum South involved more than toil, disease, and death. It meant the sexual exploitation of black women, the brutal punishment of black men, and the arbitrary rending of black families as well. The resilience that enabled African Americans to withstand the persecution that enslavement entailed stemmed from their development of a distinctive culture that served to mitigate the physical abuse and offset the psychological degradation. It was in the "quarter," not the "big house," that bondspeople found their social and moral frame of reference. Drawing on both African heritage and American experience, the slave community evolved its own system of values and ideals and created the vital cultural forms that fostered and sustained them. Religion, music, and folklore all helped promote solidarity, build self-esteem, and perpetuate hope. But the foundation of slave culture was the family.

The overwhelming majority of enslaved Carolinians chose to live in family units centered by the monogamous relationship of husband and wife. Although slave marriages were not legally recognized anywhere in the South, most masters accepted the practice as a settling influence on their servants as well as a means of expanding their workforce through natural increase. The slave's family surrounded him with the love and support necessary to endure the oppression of plantation life and passed on the traditions and skills required to survive with his identity intact. It was the bondsman's wife who massaged his tired muscles with her own aching fingers after a long day's work, just as it was the assurance of a knowing grandparent that restored the courage of the frightened child whose mother was being whipped.

The significance that slaves attached to familial ties was evident in their names. Despite the fact that it was customary to adopt the surname of one's current owner, many slaves tenaciously clung to a former name, whether of African or American derivation, which identified them with their own lineage. Given names, too, indicated a desire to reinforce the sustaining bond of kinship. Approximately 40 percent of the children in the Bennehan-Cameron slave community bore the first name of a beloved aunt, uncle, or other member of their extended family.

The old man who spun allegorical tales in the quarter on warm summer nights was also an agent of African American culture. The misadventures of a "Br'er Rabbit," who depended on guile and valor to outwit, if only temporarily, his powerful antagonists, brought more than smiles to a perceptive slave audience. Patterned after the folklore of their African past, the stories dealt creatively with the realities of their American present. Though intended to entertain, the imaginative tales provided a source of encouragement as well as a means of covertly expressing hostility. Often the strategies utilized by characters such as "Trickster John," who cleverly manipulated his adversaries by pretending to be ignorant and humble, could be directly applied to a slave's own situation. Although state law prohibited teaching slaves to read and write, a number of slaves secretly learned these skills and passed them on to others.

George Moses Horton, a Chatham County slave, wrote poetry and sold his services to University of North Carolina students, who saw no irony in paying a black man to do their literary wooing for them. For himself, Horton wrote:

Some slaves were literate, like this one reading to his daughter.

How Long have I in bondage lain,
And languished to be free!
Alas! and I still complain—
Deprived of liberty.

Music was another creative outlet that often had profound implications. The countless songs, both secular and religious, composed by American slaves offered a psychological if not a physical release through which slaves could vent their emotion and verbalize their aggression. Thus it was employed to satirize subtly an evil master or condemn blatantly the inequity of plantation life.

Spirituals as well were regularly used to communicate such subversive concepts as equality and freedom. In the classic "Go Down, Moses," which recounts in some twenty verses the biblical story of the Israelites' deliverance from Egypt, there was little doubt as to whose "people" African American slaves were actually referring to:

When Israel was in Egypt's land,
O let my people go!
Oppressed so hard they could not stand,

O let my people go!
CHORUS—O go down Moses
Away down to Egypt's land,
And tell King Pharaoh
To let my people go!

An anonymous slave song also depicted the despair and resentment of black North Carolinians forced to serve whites:

We raise de wheat,
Dey gib us de corn;
We bake de bread,
Dey gib us de crust;
We sif de meal,
Dey gib us de huss;
We peel de meat,
Dey gib us de skin;
And dat's de way
Dey take us in;
We skim de pot,
Dey gib us de liquor
And say dat's good
Enough for nigger—

Religion in itself was central to slave culture. Some plantation owners, such as the Collinses and Camerons, built chapels for their bondsmen and -women and brought in white missionaries to preach. The slaveholders' concern for the spiritual well-being of their black "family," however, tended to manifest itself in an emphasis on the authoritarian and paternalistic aspects of Christianity. Lunsford Lane, a black North Carolinian who was fortunate enough to purchase his freedom in the 1830s, described the sermons he had heard as a slave: "So great was the similarity of the texts that they were always fresh in my memory: 'Servants, be obedient to your masters'. . . . 'He that knoweth his master's will and doeth it not, shall be beaten with many stripes;' and some others of this class. Similar passages, with but few exceptions, formed the basis of most of these public instructions. The first commandment was to obey our masters, and the second like unto it: labor as faithfully when they or the overseers were not watching, as when they were."

Infused by a vibrant spiritual heritage and vitalized by more radical Christian tenets, such as the brotherhood of man, African American slaves developed their own brand of religion. In the intimacy of secret "hushharbors" deep in the woods, with wet blankets hung from branches to muffle the sound, bondspeople sang and shouted to the glory of an all-powerful though benevolent God who would succor them in slavery and deliver them to freedom, in this world as well as the next.

Their distinctive culture not only instilled in black Carolinians the will to endure slavery but also the resolution to resist. The most powerful weapon the slave community possessed was its potential to disrupt agricultural production. The economic success of any plantation was dependent on its smooth and efficient operation. Yet there were any number of actions that slaves could take, either individually or collectively, to sabotage its function. It was easy "inadvertently" to break a hoe on an unnoticed rock, "unknowingly" to chop down the young plants along with the weeds, or "accidentally" to drop a hammer into the mechanism of a mechanical thresher. An individual slave could feign illness or pretend to misunderstand the simplest instructions, while the community, as a whole or in part, could hold up production with a work slowdown.

Obviously laborers who subverted plantation operations risked punishment that might range from whipping, to the assignment of more onerous tasks, to a reduction in rations. Ebenezer Pettigrew charged the cost of breakage and other damage done by his slaves to their accounts in his plantation store. Bondspeople did have the advantage of knowing that, except in the most extreme cases, their owners could not afford to inflict permanent physical harm. Besides, not even the most conscientious of masters or overseers could possibly keep tabs on their every action.

Theft, too, was rampant. Slaves stole from the plantation storehouses on their own and other plantations to supply personal needs as well as to participate in the clandestine "black market" that flourished in most parts of the South.

Yet the most valuable property that slaves could steal was themselves. For a successful escape not only resulted in the master's loss of a considerable capital investment, it also renewed the hope of freedom in the entire slave community. The odds against a runaway slave in the antebellum South were overwhelming, but undoubtedly the most important deterrent to flight was the fact that escape meant leaving behind friends, relatives, and often even one's spouse and children. Numerous runaways never attempted to leave the region in which their families were located, while others chose to join the large "maroon" communities that inhabited desolate areas such as the Dismal Swamp. A Pettigrew bondsman named Dave hid for over two years in remote parts of Jones and Craven Counties. Some slaves did reach the relative security of the northern states, where they were free from bondage but rarely from racial prejudice. Mary Walker, who was owned by Paul Cameron's sister, escaped to Philadelphia and was soon followed by her eldest son, Frank. Her mother and two children remained enslaved in North Carolina, and some time later she prevailed on a friend to write a poignant inquiry about their purchase: "I have come to know one Mary Walker formerly in your family, and I have seen how sick at heart she is about her mother [Siller] and expecially her two children [Agnes and Briant]. . . . Her motherheart yearns unspeakably after them and her eyes fail with looking towards the South, over the dreary interval which separates them from her. She has saved a considerable sum of money to buy them, can command more from friends, and will sacrifice anything to see them once again and have their young lives renew the freshness of her own weary spirit." Apparently the Camerons were unmoved, for Agnes and Briant continued in bondage until the Civil War.

Slaveholders in North Carolina often punished chronic runaways and troublemakers by sale, not into the freedom of the North but into the brutality of the expanding "Cotton Kingdom" in the lower South. Aside from further attempts at escape, the bondsperson's options for countering such action were few. Suicide was not uncommon, nor was physical retaliation, though both were likely to lead to the same end. Slaves could threaten the lives of their masters if they were willing to die themselves. Fire and poison were also available to avenging bondspeople, thus precluding the necessity of an overt assault. Cameron's grandfather was the target of a poisoning attempt, and his in-laws' house was set on fire by a house servant while his wife was there for a visit. But the greatest fear of planters throughout the South was large-scale slave revolt. Though never successful in an absolute sense, "conspiracies" and "uprisings" occurred just often enough to incite terror in the white population of North Carolina and to inspire courage in the black.

Nevertheless it was life, not death, toward which the resistance of slaves was generally directed. Their willingness to resist mitigated the suffering to which they were subjected. Enslaved Carolinians utilized the threat of sabotage and violence not only to secure the social space necessary for their culture to flourish but also to force practical improvements in their living and working conditions. The Pettigrew slaves, for example, went on a rampage in 1836 when overseer Doctrine Davenport, in their master's absence, altered some of the more lenient plantation policies that Pettigrew had worked out with his labor force. Thefts multiplied, runaways increased, and even the slave foremen refused to obey direct orders. By the end of the year, Davenport reported: "The negrose has bothered me near to death . . . after keeping celebrating Christmas a week before I could get them to work I had to give them one thousand lashes." Even though Pettigrew upon his return quickly restored normal plantation routine, his slaves made certain that he never forgot the potential danger represented by their presence. In fact only weeks before he died, perhaps sensing the hollowness of his control, Pettigrew wrote: "I of late never go from here without being made sick. . . . My negroes have within the last twelve months given me more trouble than in all the time I have been here before, & I see no end to it but with my life."

Farm Life

The majority of nineteenth-century North Carolinians knew neither the ostentatious gentility of the white-columned veranda nor the vivid counterculture of the "quarters" stoop. The population of the state was comprised largely of ordinary farmers, not planters and slaves. Whether white yeoman or free black, landowner or agricultural laborer, most Tar Heels lived on small farms, over two-thirds of which in 1860 were composed of a hundred acres or less. Despite the pervading influence of the plantation, rural society was built around this broad middle class.

Typical of that class were Benjamin and Serena Aycock, who established a

Children were an important part of the rural workforce.

prosperous farm near the town of Fremont in Wayne County. In the 1840s, the couple moved into the then-new farmhouse that still stands on the property. In that dwelling, in 1859, the future governor Charles B. Aycock (known as the education governor) was born, the youngest of ten children. By 1870, with more than 1,000 acres, Benjamin Aycock was the seventh-wealthiest householder in the township.

Farms like the Pioneer Farmstead, on the Oconaluftee River, in Swain County, in the Great Smoky Mountains National Park, encompassed virtually everything that independent and isolated mountain farmers needed to survive. Beyond the family dwelling, many outbuildings—among them barn, crib, pigpen, chicken house, springhouse, and blacksmith shop—were vital for self-sufficient farmers "to make do or do without" in the wilderness.

Although awareness of social gradations permeated the antebellum South, the economic hierarchy, at least for white Carolinians, was only loosely fixed. Examples of "rags to riches" success were rare, but it was not uncommon for a family, over several generations, to improve its standard of living and thereby its social status. If prosperity often seemed less a function of skill and energy than of opportunity, inclination, and luck, the possibility of achievement stimulated personal aspirations and industry. A day laborer could strive toward renting a plot of land to work for himself, while a tenant farmer and his wife might dream of purchasing a small farm of their own.

James and Nancy Bennett were one such couple whose determination and effort were rewarded. In their early forties, after years of toil, the Bennetts succeeded in purchasing a modest farm in what is now Durham County with some $400 of borrowed capital. Though in a real sense a monument to the perseverance and good fortune of this enterprising rural family, the Bennett Place State Historic Site stands today as a memorial to a momentous event over which the Bennetts ironically had no control. Because of its convenient location on the old road between Raleigh and Hillsborough, which linked the final position of the Confederate army under Joseph E. Johnston to that of the Union army led by William T. Sherman at the close of the Civil War, the farm was chosen as the site at which to negotiate the terms for Johnston's surrender.

The reconstructed Bennett House and its outbuildings provide more than a glimpse of the surroundings in which these two war-weary generals met in the days following Appomattox. For the lifestyle of the Bennetts, and of the many Carolinians like them, is reflected in the simple but sturdy structures. Nancy Bennett spent her mornings in the log kitchen contemplating next spring's garden or the afternoon's chores while she prepared her family's midday meal. James Bennett spent his evenings in the main room of the paneled frame (originally log) dwelling looking over the latest issue of the *Hillsborough Recorder* or

*Bennett Place
(ca. 1836), Durham*

smiling with his wife as they listened to one of their children recite a favorite Bible verse.

Though rural life in nineteenth-century North Carolina may, by today's standards, have been less hurried and complicated, it could also be quite rough. Nancy Bennett had already lost one husband when she married James in 1831. As the young farmer and his wife attempted to build a new life together, the state was engulfed in a serious agricultural depression. One of nearly 40 percent of nonslaveholding farm families in the South who did not own the land they tilled, the Bennetts were particularly hard hit by the drop in agricultural prices. Forced to produce cash crops such as cotton or tobacco in order to pay their rent, tenant farmers were dependent on an unpredictable market over which they had absolutely no control. In a good year—one with heavy demand and a bumper crop—they might make a profit; but when the market was depressed, it was almost impossible to avoid a loss. During the 1830s Bennett lost some twenty suits for debts totaling almost $300, and on at least two occasions the court ordered his personal property seized in order to settle judgments against him.

In the following decade, as a result of their persistent efforts and a more favorable economic climate, the Bennetts fared somewhat better. The court appearances for debts ceased, and, though they still did not break even in every year, the family accounts for the 1840s showed a profit of $30.74. More important, in 1846 the Bennetts purchased their farm. Though landownership entailed the burden of a considerable long-term debt, by providing security and independence, it transformed their lives.

Unlike the larger planters and even most tenants, antebellum yeomen were typically more concerned with self-sufficiency than with surplus profits. If a farm family could subsist on the goods produced on its own land by its own labor, the only costs incurred were taxes and mortgage payments. Thus most rural landowners concentrated both their acreage and energy on the production of the food crops necessary to feed themselves and their livestock and allotted only a portion of their arable land to products intended primarily for the market. After buying their farm, the Bennetts made the logical choice of growing foodstuffs such as corn or wheat as a cash crop and were thereby able to pay their debts with the same commodities that provided their nourishment.

Corn, because of its hardiness and versatility, was the most important crop on the Bennett farm. Inasmuch as it could be consumed on the cob, creamed, or roasted, could be cooked as bread, hoecakes, grits, hominy, mush, or succotash, could be distilled into whiskey or could be fed to hogs, the grain served as the basis of the diet for the farm family and its livestock. Stalks and shucks also provided fodder for the livestock. Although maize could be planted in Carolina as early as March so as to avoid the annual summer drought, the Bennetts normally sowed their crop in April or May for an early fall harvest. Despite the general shift to row planting in the mid-nineteenth century, they persisted in planting their corn "Indian style" in hills. Thus, though Bennett prepared his fields with a horse-drawn plow, most of the cultivating was done by hand, using heavy grub hoes to form the soil into mounds. This back-breaking labor, however, usually paid off. For example, in 1847, in addition to supplying their needs for home consumption, the Bennetts sold eight bushels of corn for $3.67½, one-third bushel of cornmeal for $.20, 198½ pounds of fodder for $1.51¼, and $.05 worth of shucks.

But corn was only one of a number of agricultural products that the Bennetts produced. For diversification not only added a degree of variety to their diet; it helped protect them from the instability of the market as well. The Bennetts regularly grew oats and wheat, sweet and Irish potatoes, peas, and even watermelons for both home use and sale. And occasionally their garden yielded sufficient cucumbers, onions, squash, and turnips to be marketed along with the fruit of the apple and cherry trees that grew in the yard.

Livestock was also an integral part of the family's livelihood. As on many other southern farms, hogs provided the Bennetts with a primary source of both protein and profit. Because swine were generally branded and turned loose in the woods to forage on their own for two or three years, they were easy and inexpensive to raise. If penned and fattened before slaughter, they generally brought a reasonable market price. The Bennetts owned as many as seventeen hogs at one time, and during the decade of the 1840s their sales of pork, bacon, and lard totaled $77.45, which represented approximately 10 percent of their income.

Other domestic animals served the Bennetts in a variety of ways. The chickens that scratched for food in the barnyard were sold periodically at a dime a head and thus offered a source of supplemental earnings as well as of eggs and meat. On the other hand, the products furnished by their small herd of cattle—milk, butter, cheese, and beef—were almost entirely consumed by the family itself. At least one horse provided the power necessary to plow the fields and transport surplus crops to market. Even family pets gave more to their masters than loyalty and love. A nimble cat was as essential to keeping the smokehouse and kitchen free of rodents as an alert dog was to a successful hunt.

The Bennetts largely succeeded in producing their own food supply, but they had to clothe themselves as well. Before buying their farm they had grown cotton and even experimented with raising some sheep. Yet because they chose to concentrate their principal agricultural endeavors on foodstuffs, it was necessary to develop an alternative means of offsetting the expense of clothing. Though both ready-made garments and shoes were available at most country stores, the Bennetts began purchasing their own tailoring supplies and shoe leather as early as 1833. Working intensively during the winter months, when the demands of their farming operation were least, the family was not only able to dress itself but to manufacture additional coats, vests, pants, and shoes for sale. Though their clothing business seldom showed a profit, in terms of covering the costs of their own apparel the Bennetts did very well.

In a similar attempt to turn expense into income, in 1845, after years of renting wagons from various neighbors for 25 cents a day, James Bennett resolved to build one of his own. Though the vehicle cost almost $43.00 in parts and labor and took some six months to complete, it soon began to generate a substantial return. In addition to saving several dollars a year in rental fees, by the end of the decade the practical farmer had earned over $19.00 with his wagon through lending and hauling, including $1.95 for transporting 775 pounds of meal to Raleigh and $5.50 for conveying students and their luggage to and from the academies in Hillsborough.

Carrying passengers and freight was only one of many ways in which the Bennetts attempted to supplement their income. Taking advantage of their strategic location, they regularly sold horse feed and tobacco plugs to travelers and occasionally took in paying guests for a meal or even a night's lodging. A Mr. Cox, for example, paid $.40 for breakfast in January 1848, while the next month a pair of visitors were charged $1.00 each for lodging and two meals. At times the family marketed liquor by the quart as well. After making almost $1.00 profit on a $5.00 keg of brandy during 1847, the Bennetts repeated the venture using whiskey the following year.

Despite their best efforts, both agricultural and entrepreneurial, nineteenth-century farmers were rarely able to attain total self-sufficiency or to neutralize all costs. The Bennetts and their fellow yeomen were becoming increasingly active participants in the expanding market economy of the state as consumers as well as producers. They were dependent on the nearby country store for staple goods such as salt, sugar, and coffee, just as they required the services of the local miller to grind their corn and the neighboring blacksmith to repair their tools. And often during peak periods in the agricultural cycle the Bennetts had to employ day laborers to assist them on the farm itself.

Frequently the Bennetts were tempted by the broad spectrum of nonessential and even luxury items available to them as well. Their accounts included a wide variety of purchases, from exotic foodstuffs like coconut and lemonade to such popular products as shaving soap and Dr. Brandreth's Pills. The family seemed particularly partial to seafood as a means of diversifying their diet and often feasted on saltwater delicacies like oysters, herring, and shad. Books too were a special interest. Besides an annual almanac and several spelling and arithmetic texts for the children, their acquisitions included such works as *The Young Brides*, *The Lady at Home*, and a two-volume *Bible History*. On occasion the Bennetts were even known to splurge on a very special gift, like the bottle of cologne that James found for Nancy the year after their marriage or the parasol that the couple bought to surprise their fifteen-year-old daughter, Eliza. In one of his carefully kept account books, James Bennett (or Bennitt) wrote: "James Bennitt his Pocket Book Bought at Hillsborough July the 30th 1823." He later added: "Don't steel this Book for fear of shame for just above stands the owners name this the 18th day of March 1827."

As a result, in spite of their high degree of self-sufficiency and the diversity of their sources of income, the Bennetts were seldom totally out of debt.

Although from the 1840s on they were generally able to repay what they owed with goods, services, or cash, their annual accounts for four of the ten years in the decade showed a loss. Still, the Bennetts seemed satisfied with their lot.

They might well have fared better economically had they attempted to maximize their profits by concentrating entirely on the production of marketable staples, but such a course of action involved inherent risks. As landowners, the Bennetts were not forced to place themselves at the mercy of the market merely to pay their rent. And unlike larger planters, they simply did not have the capital to invest in more fertile land, technologically advanced implements and machinery, or improved agricultural techniques that could increase efficiency and thereby lower production costs. The substantial debt incurred by the purchase of a deeper plow or the stronger mule necessary to pull it would have jeopardized their hold on the farm itself. Thus the Bennetts, and thousands of Carolina yeoman farmers like them, made do with what they had—employing the methods of their parents before them, basking in the warmth and love of their family and friends, and reveling in the independence and security afforded by working their own land.

Community Life

Conservative and self-sufficient as they may have been, nineteenth-century farm families like the Bennetts did not live their lives in isolation. Few weeks passed without the distraction of a trip to the local store, the stimulation of an enthusiastic religious gathering, or the conviviality of a neighborhood quilting bee. A strong sense of community pervaded rural life, buttressed by a tradition of social responsibility and communal interdependence. The expanding market economy and increasing political democracy of the Jacksonian era (named for President Andrew Jackson, who served from 1828 to 1836) also encouraged active involvement in community affairs.

Commercial centers such as the country store and nearby gristmill offered antebellum farmers more than essential goods and services. They provided a nucleus for community life. There rural Carolinians, whether planter or tenant, free black or white, converged to purchase supplies, grind their corn, or simply visit with neighbors and friends. The men seldom passed up the opportunity to discuss the prospects for their crops or exchange the latest political gossip, while their wives compared prices of newly available merchandise or laid plans for a forthcoming social event. If not playing near the millpond, the children could be found marveling at the whir of the mill machinery or gazing at the mouthwatering confectionery prominently displayed on the storekeeper's shelf.

The social and economic attraction of mills and stores made them the center of rural civic and political activity as well. While there, one could pick up mail or read the numerous broadsides announcing estate sales, runaway slaves, camp meetings, horse races, or other matters of community interest. At the larger commercial centers, the county sheriff came at appointed times to collect taxes, and the local militia met at least twice a year to train all morning and carouse all afternoon. Holidays and election days were celebrated there as well, with many a politician plying his constituents with powerful oratory and potent drink.

The backcountry merchants who operated the stores and the rural industrialists who owned the mills were often one and the same. Such was the case at West Point on the Eno River in Durham County, where Herbert Sims and later his stepson John McCown controlled a multifaceted complex that in the mid-nineteenth century included a general store, grist- and sawmills, a blacksmith shop, a cotton gin, a distillery, and a post office. The West Point gristmill, which once served a thriving community of some 300 farm families, has been reconstructed on its original foundation and stands today in a Durham city park along with McCown's house and a working blacksmith shop.

Carolina yeomen and -women, who worked so hard to earn their livelihood, were not only cautious about how they spent their money, but where. Consequently the business of supplying their commercial needs was quite competitive, and the more services an entrepreneur could offer the greater his chances of success. As with modern shopping centers, a convenient location was even more important than the range of products and services offered. It generally took hours, not minutes, to travel the miles to the nearest store or mill, even in the densely settled Piedmont. Thus, trading in a readily accessible location could save a farmer as much as half a day. Sims's West Point complex, for example, was built next to the north-south thoroughfare that crossed the Eno at Shoemaker's Ford and therefore had a substantial advantage over competitors that could be approached from only one side of the river.

The fact that its various owners had the political power necessary to ensure West Point adequate access and governmental patronage was also a major factor in the mill's successful operation for over a century and a half. Only a few years after it opened, the county government ordered a new road built to link the mill with Hillsborough. Sims, who was a colonel in the militia and a representative in the General Assembly as well as a large landowner, saw to it that a post office was established at the site. And its future seemed assured in 1851 when McCown and the community were able to exert sufficient pressure on the county court to authorize a bridge over the river at West Point.

With prices high and money scarce, it was necessary for storekeepers to offer antebellum farmers more than a good location in order to move their merchandise. The bulk of their goods, from farm implements to foodstuffs, had to be sold on credit or not at all. Accounts were secured by forthcoming crops and were normally settled once a year in the winter, when both harvesting and marketing were largely complete. It was not unusual for two-thirds or more of the proceeds from a farmer's marketable crops to go to the merchant. Many families, particularly those who were farm tenants, often had little or nothing left. Because they could pay their rent and other overdue accounts only by farming yet another year, they were forced deeper and deeper into debt.

The risk of extending liberal credit and the cost of overland transport occasioned markups in rural stores as high as 100 percent. Since buying on credit was the norm, no interest charges were added to the purchase price except on overdue accounts. Customers received a discount if they actually paid for their purchases at the time of sale. Despite the merchant's substantial costs and considerable risks, returns were large, normally averaging around 70 percent. An item that sold for $1.00 had likely been purchased for 50¢. Because only about 15¢ from the proceeds covered the storekeeper's operating costs, he was left with a profit of 35¢. The overhead invested in stocking a store, however, could be quite high, and the volume of sales was often very low. Thus, while numerous Tar Heels, like Paul Cameron's grandfather, Richard Bennehan, found storekeeping to be the way to wealth, not every owner became rich.

The amount of currency in circulation during the antebellum period was insufficient to function as the sole means of exchange. Consequently rural storekeepers were forced to accept agricultural products as payment for their merchandise. Typically the merchant turned the situation to his advantage. Because most Carolina yeoman farm families lacked the time and money to travel to large markets, such as Fayetteville or Petersburg, they were dependent on the nearby store as the principal outlet for their cash crops. By concentrating the output of a large number of small producers and carefully selecting the market in which to trade, country storekeepers were generally able to obtain more for agricultural staples than they had allowed their customers, and thus they could realize an additional profit.

Although attracted by the convenience of a local market and the availability of easy credit, Carolinians came to the country store primarily for the merchandise. Whether a crude cabin along a mountain road or a two-story brick edifice in the more prosperous east, stores lured farm families by their curious blend of sights and smells, both familiar and unknown, and the pleasing array of a multitude of items from the essential to the extravagant. A broad range of foodstuffs tempted the palate: bags of fresh flour, barrels of salted meat, strings of dried fruit, tubs of homemade preserves, and jars of imported spices. Dry goods included bone buttons and metal needles, adjustable suspenders and felt hats, as well as bolts of material both gaily colored and drab. Washtubs, churns, oil lamps and all the latest appliances were available for the overworked housewife, along with an entire line of farm implements, from wooden pitchforks to iron plows, for the farmer himself. Harness, rope, paint, nails, powder, and shot could be found at the store, too, as well as dictionaries, wedding rings, and often perfume. Some stores even carried spectacles to improve weak vision in addition to castor oil and epsom salts for ailing stomachs and one or more patent medicines guaranteed to cure everything from common colds to "female complaints."

Generally customers were more interested in having access to a wide variety of articles than in having a broad choice of quality and price, and storekeepers did their best to oblige. The merchandise carried reflected not only the rural character of the community served, but also its desire to sample what the outside world had to offer. A typical inventory might include Belgian lace, West Indian rum, Italian macaroni, or English novels, along with butter, bacon, homespun, and whiskey that were locally produced. Because brand names were few, farm families were dependent on the character and competence of the merchant, as well as their own good judgment, to ensure the quality of their purchases.

In its dual capacity as a local market and community center, the country store was open from early in the morning till late at night. The storekeeper and his family often lived on the premises, so that regardless of the hour someone could always be found stocking the shelves, working on the books, sweeping the yard, or feeding the chickens in the nearby coop. And likely as not a customer or two would be there as well, trying on a starched collar, sampling a piece of cheese, or sharing a story over a pint of ale. Kemp Plummer Battle, who became president of the state university after the Civil War, remembered a visit to Richard Mendenhall's store (1824) at Jamestown, in Guilford County. "Near Greensborough," Battle recalled, "we met an old acquaintance of my father, a refined and educated Quaker named Richard Mendenhall. On parting he said courteously, 'Come and see me Kemp and I will entertain thee for thy father's sake until I know thee and can entertain thee for thy own.'" Warren's store (ca. 1850), at Prospect Hill in Caswell County, was a typical general store of the antebellum period, providing a post office and the clerk's lodgings in addition to the store itself.

Gristmills also provided an essential economic service for the rural community. Milling was necessary not only to transform corn into meal and wheat into flour for human consumption, but also to reduce the cost of transport-

Laurel Mill (mid-nineteenth century), near Louisburg, Franklin County

ing these bulky agricultural commodities to market. The yield of an entire acre of corn could be reduced to around five barrels of meal, while a barrel of flour contained approximately five bushels of threshed wheat. In addition to decreasing the problems of transport, processed farm products generally brought a higher market price. It often paid southern planters or merchants who handled large quantities of staple crops to construct a gristmill, a cotton gin, or even a tobacco factory for their own use and that of the neighboring community.

Sims's mill at West Point incorporated numerous technological improvements that had been developed over centuries of milling. Built on a rock foundation, the three-story frame structure housed two runs of millstones, each of which could grind either corn or wheat. The power generated by the overshot waterwheel was transferred by a carefully devised series of pulleys and leather belts to the heavy cylindrical stones, which could be adjusted to control the texture of the product. The unground kernels and the ground flour as well moved between floors of the building through the entire process of grinding, sifting, and bagging along an ingenious system of gravity-dependent chutes and belt conveyors, also powered by the waterwheel. The intricate operation is still a pleasure to behold.

By the antebellum period, most mills were run by skilled artisans rather than the owners themselves. The job was both difficult and dangerous. It not only entailed a thorough knowledge of the mill's mechanics and the constant lifting of heavy bags of meal and flour, but it also required working constantly in a noisy, dust-filled environment and in close proximity to the heavy mill machinery, much of which was unprotected. Many millers were maimed or killed while attempting to free a frozen gear or to replace a worn millstone, each of which weighed approximately a ton. Respiratory disease was simply accepted as an occupational hazard. Despite all the hazards, the miller's pay was relatively low, from $150 to $200 per year, and because many prosperous owners, like the Bennehans and the Camerons, depended on slaves to operate their mills, their labor costs were even less.

Rather than charging a fee for the service to local farmers who brought their wheat and corn to be ground, the miller assessed a toll of from one-twelfth to one-eighth of the resultant meal or flour. As in the rural store, returns in the milling business were high. When operating at full capacity, an efficient mill like that at West Point could grind up to six bushels of both corn and wheat in an hour. That translated into an income of approximately $60.00 in a ten-hour working day and, after subtracting costs, could result in a profit of as much as S2,000 per year.

But there were also risks involved in operating a mill. The investment required was quite large. The West Point mill, for example, was valued at $6,500 in 1860. In addition to the problem of fluctuating demand because of heavy local competition or poor crop yield, there was the constant threat of breakdowns or floods. A freshet could wash out the milldam or the waterwheel, and severe flooding could sweep away the building itself. As a result, the services of good millwrights were always at a premium. For, while the dam might be at least temporarily patched or a drive belt repaired within a few days, rebuilding an entire mill could take months.

Rural communities attracted numerous skilled artisans in addition to millers and millwrights. The services of a blacksmith, who had both the faculties and the facilities to repair farm tools and produce household implements more efficiently than the average yeoman, were becoming increasingly important to the successful operation of a nineteenth-century farm. James Bennett depended on nearby smiths not only to construct the more intricate parts of his wagon but also to sharpen a grub hoe, mend a lock, or shoe a horse. Sawyers, threshers, ginners, and distillers, too, came to operate the expanding enterprises of rural entrepreneurs, as did storekeepers and clerks to run the country stores and teamsters and wagoners to transport agricultural products and commercial goods to and from distant markets.

Ministers and teachers were an integral part of rural society as well, for on an even more fundamental level than the local commercial center, churches and schools provided a focus for community life. Beyond the family, religious and educational institutions were most responsible for shaping antebellum Carolinians' consciousness and culture. The congregation and the classroom often encompassed the entire sphere of one's day-to-day acquaintances, and

A blacksmith shop

it was within this context that young and old alike were exposed to many of the ideas and much of the information on which their worldview depended. Here too, while learning and laughing together on wintry mornings in a rustic schoolroom or worshiping and talking with one another in a shady church-yard in the sweltering summer heat, Tar Heels were likely to develop their most viable and intimate personal relationships.

Debate over the establishment of a system of public education in North Carolina raged throughout the antebellum period. The issue involved more than determining whether the family, the church, or the state should assume the primary responsibility for educating society's youth. It was inevitably linked to larger questions concerning the necessity of formal education and the proper role of government itself. Finally, in 1839, the legislature passed a bill calling for the development of a statewide school system supported by county taxes and appropriations from the "Literary Fund," which had been created for that purpose over a decade earlier. But, because of public apathy and inadequate direction, public education was not firmly established in North Carolina until the 1850s, and even then not in every county and only for whites.

Consequently the majority of rural schools in the state through the mid-nineteenth century were funded by private subscription and were the result of

A shoemaker

Ebenezer Academy (ca. 1823), a subscription school in Bethany, Iredell County

local initiative rather than statewide mandate. At times a number of concerned parents joined together to secure an instructor for their children, yet just as often subscription, or "old-field schools," were established through the efforts of the teachers themselves. For example, Mary Gash circulated the following proposal in the western North Carolina community of Burn's Creek:

Mary A. Gash proposes to teach a school at Burn's Creek schoolhouse for the term of 3 months or 12 weeks commencing May 1857.

Spelling Reading Writing and Arithmetic	$2.40
Geography English Grammar Philosophy & Composition	3.60
Astronomy Chemistry and Rhetoric	4.20

She obligates herself to preserve good order so far as is within her power, and those who are not willing to be governed by the rules of the school may expect to be expelled.

Twenty scholars are desired though she will commence with sixteen.

The subscribers are expected to pay their tuition at the close of the school.

Though most rural communities supported a subscription school at one time or another, these schools' tenuous existence depended on continued demand as well as the availability of a satisfactory teacher.

Capable and qualified instructors were rare. With the exception of a few well-educated ministers who supplemented their income by teaching and various university graduates who began their careers in the rural classroom, most primary school teachers were themselves only marginally proficient in the three R's. Pay was extremely low and in subscription schools often difficult to collect. More important, since the annual term was normally limited to only three or four months during the winter lull in the agricultural cycle, it was impossible to subsist solely by teaching. As a result, Calvin H. Wiley, state superintendent of public instruction, in 1853 offered the county school boards the following pragmatic advice: "I would suggest to you to encourage good teachers to locate permanently in the neighborhoods, as they can thus be more useful in creating and fostering a spirit of education, can have their salaries, in time increased by private subscriptions, and can also, in other respects make their vocation more profitable by cultivating farms or carrying on, or having carried on, other industrial or commercial occupations. Encourage as much as possible the very poor, and especially poor females to become teachers."

Recruitment and retention of competent teachers was inhibited not only by low salaries but also by the heavy demands of the job itself. The school day extended from early morning till nearly dark, undoubtedly stretching both the children's attention span and the instructor's patience to the breaking point. The difficulty of dealing efficiently and effectively with a myriad of age and ability levels compounded the problem. Professor C. W. Smythe, at a meeting of the State Education Association in 1860, aptly described the educator's plight: "There is no greater purgatory to which teachers can be sent than many of our common schools. . . . Children of every age, from lisping ABC darians, and those who are sent to get them out of their Mother's way, up to those bold youths who are exploring the mysteries of the Rule of Three or Cube Root, are huddled promiscuously together, each confounding the other and adding to the teacher's distraction who flutters from one to another like a bewildered bird."

Setzer School (at Rowan County's Supplemental Education Center, in Salisbury) was a "common school" in 1842 and may have earlier been an "old-field school." Behavior was strictly supervised and lashes given for infractions of rules: ten for playing cards at school, "seven for telling lyes," seven for making swings and swinging on them, two for not saying "No Sir and Yes Sir or Yes Marm or No Marm."

AT SCHOOL.

For most children, schooling was short and primitive.

The curriculum of most antebellum elementary schools offered little more than the rudiments of an "English Education": spelling, reading, writing, and arithmetic, and occasionally a smattering of grammar and geography. The books that Superintendent Wiley authorized for use in the public schools included *Webster's Elementary Spelling Book,* known popularly as "Old Blue Back," *Davies' Primary Arithmetic, Bullion's English Grammar,* and *McNally's School Geography,* as well as his own *North Carolina Reader.* An interesting blend of grammar, literature, geography, and history, Wiley's book, much like promotional literature of more recent vintage, extolled the quality of life in the state and the character of its inhabitants. Like all readers of the period, it was intended to stimulate young scholars to read "with propriety and effect, to improve their language and sentiments, and to inculcate some of the most important principles of piety and virtue."

Few of North Carolina's rural schools had blackboards, much less the globes, diagrams, charts, and other apparatus commonly associated with primary education. The children generally sat on crude benches and worked in practice ledgers or on rough slates. The building, where one existed, was often no more than a converted barn or abandoned cabin with dirt floor, leaky roof, smoking chimney, and few windows for ventilation or light. Critics in both the legislature and the press were particularly distressed at the deplorable condition of many of the state's public schools, which they likened to everything from "Calcutta holes" to "a bear trap" and characterized as "utterly unfit for workshops" or "for civilized persons to inhabit."

Despite deficiencies in both facilities and instruction, schools were increasingly accepted as a necessary part of the nineteenth-century socialization process. Most Americans believed the very existence of the Republic to be dependent on the continuous development of a virtuous, orderly, and knowledgeable citizenry. Thus, in addition to its educational role, the school was expected to train the nation's youth in political participation, law-abiding behavior, and responsible community membership. Whether or not institutionalized education ever had such a modulating effect, its impact was undeniably great. As editor William W. Holden suggested in 1857: "We can never forget . . . The rude cabins in which we studied our lessons . . . The long and weary walks to school; The books we thumbed . . . The rivalry in spelling . . . The Master's looks . . . The rustic playground, and the mossy spring, by which, in the thick shade, we took our meals at noon; the ghosts we thought we saw, returning home late in the biting or the mellow eve."

Religion too was a vital part of nineteenth-century American life. Though only about half of the free adults in North Carolina were members of an organized church, religious ideology, custom, and practice shaped the state's culture; and the local congregation, regardless of its denominational affiliation, formed the very core of the rural community. Although in a minority, Episcopal and Catholic churches operated in antebellum North Carolina. They included St. Joseph's Church, near McAdenville, in Gaston County, which is one of the earliest Catholic churches in the state. It was built for Italian and Irish immigrants who worked in the nearby gold mines. Among the Episcopal churches representative of the period are Zion Episcopal Church, near Washington, in Beaufort County; St. Andrews's Episcopal Church, near Woodleaf, in Rowan County; and Christ Episcopal Church in Raleigh.

Many Carolinians of Scottish and Scotch-Irish descent clung staunchly to their Presbyterian heritage. At Brown Marsh Presbyterian Church near Clarkton, in Bladen County, the free black builder, Thomas Sheridan, chalked his name on the ceiling.

Approximately 80 percent of the church congregations in the state in 1860 were either Baptist or Methodist. Rehoboth Methodist Church, east of Pleasant Grove, in Washington County, had a total membership of 160 blacks and whites in 1861. Skewarkey Primitive Baptist Church near Wiliamston, in Martin County, shows the simplicity typical of the sect and contrasts with Bethel Baptist Church, in Perquimans County, built by the prominent Skinner family. Evangelical in their orientation and revivalistic in their approach, the predominant denominations directed their message toward the yeoman farmer and won an increasing number of Tar Heel converts, from Cape Hatteras to the Blue Ridge. While the Baptists confined their efforts largely to proselytizing within the white rural community, the Methodists' commitment to social reform attracted a considerable number of black Carolinians and "respectable" urban whites. The Episcopal Church was strong in urban areas and, because of the wealth and power of many of its adherents, was more influential throughout the state than its limited membership would suggest. The Society of Friends, or Quakers, was quite active in the central Piedmont, particularly in Guilford County, as were three major German denominations—Lutheran, Moravian, and Reformed Evangelical—centered primarily in Rowan and Forsyth Counties. Disciples of Christ, Roman Catholics, Jews, and various other isolated groups completed an intricate religious mosaic, diverse at its fringes but cemented by the similarity of its European origins and the compatibility of its central tenets.

In addition to dictating both the form and content of religious practice, the nineteenth-century church demanded that its members adhere to a high standard of social and moral conduct. Thus, while yielding to civil authorities in matters of criminal justice, each denomination established and enforced its own rules of behavior. Offenses such as drunkenness, "disputing with a member," "neglecting Church service," or sexual immorality brought penalties ranging from censure to excommunication. Beyond "breaking the Sabbath," many churches disapproved of dancing, "fiddling," theatergoing, and "sports of pleasure" such as horse racing and tavern hopping. The Society of Friends forbade its members to swear oaths, bear arms, and, most important in antebellum society, to own or hire slaves.

Church buildings in the rural South were generally constructed by congregations themselves. One member of a congregation donated a small tract of land and others the building materials and furnishings. All shared in the labor and took pride in the structure that they created. A simple cabin served many a congregation until they could enlarge or replace it with a frame meetinghouse. Some were eventually able to erect a more substantial structure of stone or brick. The buildings of five of the churches that composed the Orange Presbytery in 1829, for example, were log, whereas twenty-four were frame and five were brick. Although the building costs of the four structures located in cities totaled $19,000, the average value of the thirty country churches was approximately $63.00 apiece.

Most denominations were plagued by a severe shortage of ministers. Like teachers, clergymen received salaries that were generally inadequate, rarely more than several hundred dollars per year. If they devoted their entire time to their pastorates, rural preachers were seldom able to support their families or fully pay their bills. Consequently many farmed or taught school to supplement their income. It was commonly said of Methodist circuit riders that they "preached by day and plowed by night," and in numerous cases it was true. How else could they be expected to deliver sermons at two to three different churches in a single day?

Neither Baptists nor Methodists required any formal education for the ministry; they placed more emphasis upon "the call" and a candidate's "public gift" than his knowledge of grammar or rhetoric. Presbyterians and Episcopalians, along with the three German denominations, however, maintained strict educational requirements. Though frequently the most learned and respected member of the community, many an antebellum clergyman was not above chewing, smoking, or drinking as hard as the staunchest members of the congregation. Occasionally a church even found it necessary to discipline the minister himself.

Because of the scarcity of qualified clergy and the time-consuming distances that ministers as well as their congregations were required to travel, country churches normally held services only once or twice a month. It was customary for entire families, from suckling infants to graying patriarchs, to attend. When the preacher had arrived and the congregation had filed in, a deacon or elder known as the "precentor" rose to lead the singing. Hymnals as well as organs were rare, and it was the precentor's task not only to carry the tune but also to "line out" every new or difficult hymn as it was being sung.

When the mood had been set, the sermon began. Given the rural clergyman's limited contact with his pastorate, he considered "teaching the scriptures" an essential part of every service. Utilizing a particularly weighty biblical passage, he expounded upon such basic Christian themes as the "terrors of hell" or the "benevolence of God." Animated and compelling in his presentation, a particularly enthusiastic preacher often spoke for a couple of hours and characteristically elicited a vocal response of emphatic "amens" and exuberant "hallelujahs" from the inspired in the congregation.

Church services were more than an occasion to renew religious commitment; they were also a social event. Rural Carolinians gathered on the church grounds well before the meeting was to begin and lingered there long after the minister had departed. Many visited the graveyard, where one or more loved ones were buried, while others earnestly discussed the day's sermon. Yet invariably the topic of conversation turned to more temporal matters, such as the outcome of a forthcoming horse race or the current price of tobacco. Everyone, regardless of age or gender, enjoyed the opportunity to meet with friends, share a laugh over a clever anecdote, and catch up on local gossip. While the more staid chatted quietly among themselves, the young at heart could be found carefully plotting a practical joke or preoccupied with the uncertain initial steps of courtship. Children wiled away the time playing tag in a nearby meadow or searching for salamanders in an adjacent creek. When at last the crowd broke up, it was common for "over half the congregation to go home with the others to eat late Sunday dinner."

Social Life

The lives of antebellum North Carolinians were not rigidly segmented into periods of work and play as are ours today. There were no timeclocks or two weeks of annual vacation. For the farmer, home and workplace were one and the same. Whether winter or summer, day or night, there was always something to be done. Many tasks, such as weeding the fields or boiling lye soap, could be onerous, while others, like tracking a deer or picking wild blackberries, involved less labor than fun. As for birthing a colt, building a chair, or baking fresh bread, the skilled effort required was amply rewarded by the pleasure of the accomplishment. Consequently it was within the context of their agricultural lifestyle, rather than outside of it, that most Tar Heels looked for their leisure as well as their livelihood.

This merging of occupation and avocation was clearly reflected in rural social life. Purely recreational events were few, but any gathering of a more practical nature, whether political or economic, and even though ostensibly a serious occasion, could be transformed into a time of fun and frolic. Crowds gathered early at the store or mill, which served as the local polling place, to be wooed by the rival candidates and to join in the merrymaking. Liquor flowed freely, and the political oration that marked the day was periodically interrupted by a horse race, a wrestling match, or a turkey shoot for which one of the politicians put up the prize. Inevitably, according to the *Raleigh Register*, "if some staid sober citizen was observed making his way to any spot where votes were to be taken," he was immediately surrounded by electioneers, "employing their talents, energies, and lungs . . . in order to gain his attention to their various claims, until the four points of the compass became . . . a matter of doubt and uncertainty." Though there might be some question as to whether the best man was elected, a good time was had by all.

The cooperative work and mutual assistance that characterized rural life also stimulated social interchange. A house raising was customary when a local couple married or a new family moved into the community. Yet it was difficult to determine who enjoyed it more, the thankful recipients or their generous friends. When sufficient timber had been cut and all the necessary materials collected at the site, the entire neighborhood turned out on the specified day. While the men, both young and old, worked on framing the house, the women prepared a huge midday meal. Not even the sound of the pounding hammers could compete with the hearty laughter and boisterous chatter than emanated from the scene. When at last the smells wafting from the open cooking fire overcame the hungry company and they stopped to eat, their eyes as well as their stomachs were treated to a veritable feast: smoked ham, fried chicken, roasted sweet potatoes, and buttered hominy—not to mention garden vegetables, biscuits and gravy, thick molasses, and black coffee, strong and hot. And of course there were always sufficient freshly baked pies and cakes to allow everyone three or four slices apiece. After dinner the troupe labored to finish the roof before dark, leaving only the interior and siding for the new owners to complete. But the celebrating had only begun, for, as the last nail was driven, the fiddle was tuned. And the music and dancing, along with the drinking, lasted well into the night.

A similar combination of collective work and play could turn the most difficult or tedious task into a social occasion. Whether clearing new fields, building fences, or butchering beef, it was simpler and more enjoyable if a few neighbors could be mustered to help. Thus, while polite urban society might entertain with an afternoon tea, it was more common in rural Carolina to hold a quilting bee. The hostess provided the necessary material as well as the refreshments; her guests brought their needles and nimble fingers. And after several hours of lively conversation and deft needlework the group produced a durable quilt of attractive design and warm color.

Corn shuckings also served as an efficient means of preparing the crop to be milled and a good excuse to meet for some fellowship and fun. People came from miles around to partake of the lavish "shucking supper" as well as to join in the sport of the event. When almost everyone had arrived, the entire assemblage divided into rival teams. After situating themselves around a vast pile of the host's corn, the competition to determine which group could remove the leafy shucks from the most ears began. Before long someone struck up a familiar "corn song" and everybody chimed in on the chorus. A jug or two

Music was an important part of home entertainment. These performers lived in Rockingham County.

of brandy or whiskey circulated among the adults, as the tempo of both the shucking and the singing increased. To add spice, whoever came upon an ear with red kernels was allowed to kiss the person of his or her choice. Needless to say, many a clever young man ensured his success by arriving at the party with a red ear hidden in his pocket. The contest might continue until well past dark. Often it was followed by a spirited square dance, after which the crowd, with loud huzzahs for the victors, finally departed for home.

Weddings and funerals also occasioned large gatherings of family and friends. Marriage celebrations were eagerly awaited, and the festivities sometimes lasted several days or as long as the relatives could stay. Picnics and parties, hunts and hoedowns, suppers and sings, were climaxed by a day-long wedding feast. Even a wake, though fundamentally a solemn affair, could be transformed into a buoyant occasion, as the old men dealt with their grief by swapping the favorite yarns of the deceased or a graying woman contemplated aloud the potential represented by a new grandchild's life.

For many North Carolinians, however, the most exciting and important annual social occasion was principally a religious event. Since the Great Revival at the beginning of the nineteenth century, churchgoers gathered during the late summer in the rural South and Midwest for several days of services and celebration known as "camp meetings." Intended to renew the zeal of believers and to gain new converts, many such convocations attracted several hundred to several thousand participants. They offered an inviting opportunity to interact with old friends and fellow Christians as well as a welcome respite from normal routine.

By 1830 the Methodist churches that composed the Lincoln Circuit in the western Piedmont had designated a wooded tract near Rock Spring in Lincoln County as the permanent site of their yearly camp meeting. Though the families who gathered there each August held their services in the open air, within a few years a large rectangular "arbor" was built to protect the assembly from the blazing midday sun and the frequent summer showers. Constructed of handhewn timbers, the open shelter remains on its original site shaded by a grove of sturdy oaks. A pine pulpit on the low platform at the west end of the historic structure stands silent watch over the rows of empty wooden pews. Ordinarily, with the exception of the shrill calls of the resident bird population or the gentle rustling of the trees in the wind, all is quiet.

A series of crude single-story row houses, known as "tents," surrounds the central structure, forming a broad square. As their name suggests, these shed-like dwellings, built as temporary quarters for individual families during the annual meetings, gradually replaced the less permanent shelters employed by the earlier participants. Each consists of one or two rooms and a loft, the walls are unfinished and unadorned, and the floors are hard clay covered with sawdust or straw. Nineteenth-century worshipers, caught up in the fervor and the fellowship of a vital religious experience were little concerned with material comfort. And the same is true today when Rock Springs Campground once again springs to life in late summer. For Methodist congregations from the surrounding region continue to gather at the rustic site in annual renewal of a tradition that has sustained them for over a century and a half. A similar campground is Tucker's Grove, also in Lincoln County.

Antebellum Carolinians came from far and wide to attend camp meetings, and some participated in as many as two or three in one season. On the day services were to begin, all roads leading to the grounds were crowded with wag-

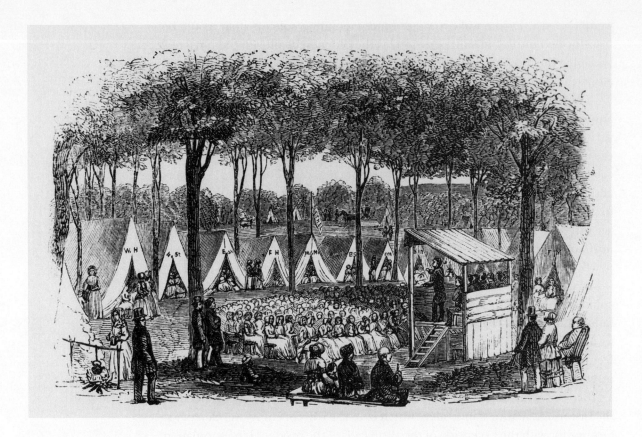

A midcentury camp meeting. Frame structures subsequently replaced cloth tents.

ons and carts, groups on horseback, and entire families on foot. Everyone was there: young and old, rich and poor, black and white. The site bustled with animated activity, cheerful sounds, and colorful sights. Women chatted amicably as they set up housekeeping in adjacent dwellings and their children played together out front. A young girl sweeping the porch of her family's tent in her best dress returned the smile of the strapping lad who kept strolling proudly by in a pair of new, yet ill-fitting boots. An old-timer remembered that "the camp meetings at Rock Springs . . . had been the 'mating grounds' for the state for fifty years." And various church officers scurried about to confer with their counterparts among the numerous congregations and to inform the heads of each household of the scheduled order of events.

The meetings typically continued from three to five days depending on the weather, the tenor of the assemblage, and the determination of the evangelists. Formal services could be held in the morning, the afternoon, or at night, yet there was always plenty of time in between for personal reflection, group Bible study, and casual socializing. Each day began with early morning prayer meetings and was punctuated with family-style meals and impromptu musical performances. In fact, according to one knowledgeable observer, the site of an effectual camp meeting "ought to be almost continually vocal with psalms and hymns and spiritual songs, even the prayers should alternate with singings."

The principal services normally began with a hymn as the crowd gathered at the central arbor. Women and children filled most of the available seats while the overflow of men crouched at the end of a pew or stood under the surrounding eaves. Neither the wail of a discontented infant nor the whir of handheld fans distracted the congregation as one after another of the several preachers who occupied the rostrum rose to speak. They might talk of God, of eternity, or of the judgment to come, alternately agitating and calming their listeners with the perils and promise of Christianity. At last, with the tension among the audience visibly apparent, the final orator brought his sermon to a powerful climax: "Aye! Ye are come as to a holiday pageant, bedecked in tinsel and costly raiment. I see before me the pride of beauty and youth; the middle-aged . . . the hoary hairs and decrepit limbs of age;—hustling each other in your haste—on one beated road—the way to death and judgment! Oh! Fools and Blind! Slow-worms, battening upon the damps and filth of this vile earth! Hugging your muck rakes while the glorious one proffers you the Crown of Life!" Many of the congregation were in tears. An old man exclaimed, "That Preaching!" Another blurted out a loud "Amen!" Several female voices broke into a familiar spiritual as the evangelist issued a call for the destitute to "come home" and be "washed in the blood of the Lamb!" And, as the "convicted" amid shouts of thanksgiving and cries of despair made their way to kneel at the "seeker's bench" in front of the pulpit, the ministers came down from the platform and moved through the crowd praying and shaking hands.

Emotional outbursts at such services were often accompanied by peculiar physical actions known collectively as "exercises": trembling, jerking, dancing, laughing, barking, and, probably the most common, "falling down." Overcome by the passion of the moment, a victim would fall to the ground where "he might either become unconscious at once or he might lie where he fell groaning and praying until he was exhausted." At times only a few persons were seized by such an "exercise" while at others it might strike the entire congregation.

One attendee at a camp meeting described the event: "The whole area before the pulpit, and in the distant aisles of the forest, became one vast, surging sea of sound, as negroes and whites, slaves and freemen, saints and sinners, slave-holders, slave-hunters, slave-traders, ministers, elders, and laymen alike joined in the pulses of that mighty song. A flood of electrical excitement

seemed to rise with it, as, with a voice of many waters, the rude chant went on."
At age ninety-one, former slave Catherine Beale recalled an African American
camp meeting:

Every August they would have a Big Meetin' and all the [slaves] that had died durin' the
year, they would preach them a funeral that day. They would build a big Bush Arbor an'
Old Miss would give us this and that and we would cook it up and everybody would take
dinner an' they would come for miles, all around in wagons and car's an' spread a big dinner.... I had my brogan shoes over my shoulder and had my dresses an' my pantalettes tied
up with a string to keep 'em from getting dirty in the dust. I let my dress an' pantalettes
down and put on my shoes when I got in sight of the meetin'.

Because of the emotional excitement produced, many ministers actually
opposed camp meetings, and the southern gentry remained somewhat reti-
cent in their support. "Scoffers" were often present at revivals "to heckle the
preacher or to steal among the fallen, feeling their pulse, or, in some cases, if
there were any Negroes among the fallen, applying coals of fire to their feet."
Drunkenness was always a problem, and in many cases enterprising entrepreneurs took advantage of the presence of the large crowds to sell liquor and
produce from wagons or stands right on the campgrounds. Even organizers,
such as James Jenkins, were concerned about the vulgar attitude that many
participants assumed: "I am grieved to see so much labour and parade about
eatables, and such extravagance in dress, I think we might do without pound-
cake, preserves, and many other notions. . . . Many, I have no doubt, live much
better, and dress much finer at camp meetings than they do at home; and this
is one great reason why more good is not done; for while they come to serve
tables, to eat, drink, and dress, the poor soul is little regarded, whereas it ought
to be the all-engrossing care."

Although camp meetings were a popular recreational outlet for rural and
urban Carolinians alike, for the most part, they retained their basic religious
character. And, when it came time to return to the problems and prospects of
everyday life, laymen and clergy alike did so with the vivid memory of their involvement in a moving communal experience, a deeper commitment to their
Christian beliefs, and a renewed awareness of their own self-worth.

TOWN LIFE AND ENTERPRISE

Throughout the nineteenth-century, North Carolina was economically, socially, and politically a rural state. At midcentury no more than 2.5 percent of the population could be considered urban, and only the port city of Wilmington claimed as many as 5,000 inhabitants. Yet, while "progressive" Carolinians bemoaned the state's lack of business centers to compare with Richmond or Charleston, the process of urbanization, so apparent today, was clearly if gradually under way. The population of Raleigh doubled during the decade following the completion of the Raleigh and Gaston Railroad in 1840. The location and layout of Raleigh, established as the state capital in 1792, were carefully deliberated and planned. The present Capitol (1840) stands on the central of the original five squares delineated as open spaces in the city grid. And some twenty-five commercial and judicial centers throughout the state, such as Hendersonville, Salisbury, Warrenton, and Washington, were considered important enough in the federal census of 1860 to merit the appellation of "town."

The primary factor stimulating the growth of towns was trade. Consequently most were located at points convenient to water or overland transport. New Bern, the state's second-largest city, was situated near the mouth of the Neuse and served as a principal market for the region drained by the river and its tributaries. Fayetteville, on the other hand, was located near the fall line of the Cape Fear River and gained its prominence as a mercantile link between the coast and the Piedmont.

In most cases, important market centers became the seat of local government. But in the developing western region, because of the convenience of trading where legal matters could be handled as well, designation as the county seat was in itself often sufficient to create a town. Thus, many an urban settlement grew up around a rude backcountry courthouse on a site selected not as a result of its relationship to established trade routes but its proximity to the geographic center of a newly formed county.

Although a few cities in the state, like Raleigh, were built according to a

*Wilmington,
ca. 1853*

carefully devised plan, the majority developed haphazardly. Patterns of growth were shaped by a variety of natural and man-made features. The availability of water was critical to the siting of urban dwellings, as was proximity to the courthouse or the town market for commercial buildings. The orientation of a particularly pleasing ridgeline or stream had an impact on the direction and timing of expansion, as did the desire of local entrepreneurs and speculators who owned the majority of the town lots.

The courthouse occupied a prominent site in almost every county seat: on the main square or at the head of the one street that comprised the commercial district. Shops of local craftsmen were interspersed with stores of various sizes and shapes. Lawyers' offices, and the offices of a doctor or two, might well be found near the courthouse or scattered among the substantial residences that stood along the opposite end of the main street. In larger communities a bank was certain to dominate at least one corner of the busiest intersection, while a hotel, which was filled to overflowing during every "court week," stood on another.

When court was in session in Dallas, in Gaston County, lawyers enjoyed the amenities of the Hoffman Hotel (1852), fronting the courthouse square. (The building is now a private home and may be viewed from the street.) In Wentworth, the county seat of Rockingham County, Wright's Tavern, near the courthouse square, did a large business on court days. Below are the tavern's rates in 1821:

Orange County Courthouse (1845), Hillsborough

Breakfast	.25
Dinner	.37½
Supper	.25
Lodging per night	.10
Whiskey & Brandy per ½ pt.	.10
West India Rum per ½ pt.	.20
New England Rum per ½ pt.	.12½
Holland Gin per ½ pt	.15
Country Gin per ½ pt	.15
Corn per gallon	.10
Fodder per bundle	.03
Oats per gallon	.10
Hay per hundred	$1.00

Though largely economic and political in their origin and orientation, antebellum towns were important social and cultural centers as well. Urban churches were likely to be as architecturally impressive as the county court-house and clearly reflected the interests as well as the affluence of their membership. Many towns could boast of the quality education offered by one or more private academies in addition to the civic awareness and moral uplift fostered by local chapters of various fraternal orders and benevolent societies. In a less formal vein, what could surpass the good food and fellowship of a midday meal at a popular tavern or the lively fun and frolic of a Saturday night at a backstreet saloon?

County Government

Ordinarily centerpieces of antebellum towns, courthouses in North Carolina ranged from dilapidated wooden structures with decaying walls and crumbling chimneys to impressive monumental edifices of stone or brick. In the newly formed counties of the mountain region, a convenient tavern or converted barn might well serve to house the quarterly sessions of the county court until a suitable structure could be erected at the county seat. Farther east one was likely to find larger, more substantial court buildings, often with an adjacent clerk's office and jail, which embodied the aura of permanence and stability that local authorities wished to project.

The Old Orange County Courthouse, Hillsborough, is one of the most attractive of the antebellum period. The members of Eagle Lodge laid the cornerstone in 1844. The clerk's office (1831) in the county seat and market town of Jackson, in Northampton County, housed all the court documents. A similar office (1833), also in brick for fire prevention, with brick flooring and a zinc roof, stands in Halifax, in Halifax County. At the Old Wilkes County Jail in Wilkesboro, the legendary murderer Tom Dula was imprisoned before his lawyer, former Civil War governor Zebulon B. Vance, had his trial moved to Iredell County. The notorious Dula is remembered today in the anonymous ballad "Tom Dooley." Law offices of the period also abound. They were usually one-room frame structures like the one belonging to Governor Charles Manly in Pittsboro, in Chatham County.

The magnificent Caswell County Courthouse in Yanceyville mirrored the growing wealth of the northern Piedmont that stemmed from the mid-nineteenth-century development of bright leaf tobacco. The imposing two-story structure, completed in 1861, was constructed of stuccoed brick on an elevated foundation of granite blocks. Heavy pilasters embellish the exterior facade of the building, and an octagonal cupola crowns the low hip roof. From the ornate Corinthian capitals above the main entrance, carved to depict tobacco leaves and ears of corn, to the coffered plaster ceiling of the elegant courtroom itself, the edifice is rich in architectural detail.

Prior to the Reconstruction era, the county court in Caswell, and its counterparts throughout the state, served as the administrative as well as judicial branch of local government. In addition to levying county taxes, the court filled the majority of lucrative and influential county offices, including register of deeds, surveyor, treasurer, solicitor, coroner, overseer of roads, and superintendent of schools. It was the county court that licensed peddlers and retailers of "spiritous liquor," authorized the erection of public mills and toll bridges, bound out apprentices, and appointed guardians for orphans and the insane. Consequently the men who composed this multifunctional governing body exercised considerable control over the economic development of the county and the daily lives of its citizens.

Presiding over the county court were three to five justices of the peace. Commissioned by the governor on the recommendation of the local delegation to the state Assembly, the justices of the peace were invariably selected from the county's economic and political elite. Customarily addressed as "Squire," the justices served for life or as long as they maintained their local

Old Wilkes County Jail (1858–59), Wilkesboro

residence. Each had the power to convene his own magistrate's court whenever necessary to "maintain, keep, and preserve the peace." As a magistrate, the justice had the right to settle civil disputes involving an amount not exceeding $100 and to collect various fines and forfeitures established by state law. The magistrate's criminal jurisdiction included the summary trial and punishment, up to thirty-nine lashes, of slaves charged with minor offenses, as well as the arrest and interrogation of all suspected felons.

Four times a year the local justices gathered in Yanceyville to convene the county court. With power to summon grand and petit juries, the court had the authority to decide major civil actions and all criminal cases not punishable by death or dismemberment. However, because it was a common practice for the county court to deal exclusively with administrative matters during two of its quarterly sessions, it often took months for even the simplest case to come to trial.

Fortunately, North Carolina's system of justice was not totally dependent on the county court and the discretion of local magistrates. The state's superior courts had joint jurisdiction with the county courts in most civil and criminal matters as well as original jurisdiction in all felonies. Inasmuch as a superior court convened twice a year in every county, litigants had some choice as to where their cases would be heard. Judges for the superior court were elected by the combined vote of both houses of the state Assembly, and each rode a circuit of approximately twelve counties. Theoretically at least, they were less subject to local prejudices and pressures than the county justices of the peace. The same could be said of the three judges who composed the state supreme court and offered the confounded and the condemned a final avenue of appeal.

Punishment during the antebellum period was often discriminatory and generally quite severe. English common law, from which the American legal system was largely derived, prescribed a sentence of death for almost every significant crime. Even after 1855, when the state's criminal code was thoroughly revised and the number of capital offenses dramatically reduced, death by hanging remained the statutory penalty for seventeen major crimes. Obstructing railways and stealing slaves or aiding in their escape, as well as murder, rape, sodomy, burglary, arson, and insurrection, all carried the death penalty. Branding or dismemberment was still prescribed for certain felonies; perjury, for example, was punished by the removal of an ear. Conviction for a misdemeanor might bring a number of lashes or an hour in the pillory, along with a substantial fine and possibly even imprisonment.

Through most of the nineteenth century, justice was an overtly public affair. An execution invariably attracted a large audience, which not only transformed the event into a lurid spectacle but seemed to lend the direct sanction of the community to the act of punishment itself. Yet even the most impervious of spectators gave a start when the trapdoor of the gallows dropped open and the victim's body writhed in final agony before falling limp in death. The example of what was to become of those who failed to conform to the dictates of society, as interpreted by the courts, was not lost on the crowd.

Communal scorn and public ridicule played a large part in other, less extreme penalties as well. Typically the county's stocks and whipping post were a prominent feature of the courthouse square. Not until midcentury did protests against the inhumane and offensive nature of such punishments become widespread. A report carried by the *Raleigh Register* in 1846 was characteristic of this carefully delimited, yet growing concern: "We have, this day, witnessed the most humiliating scene that has ever been exhibited before us. Two white men were, by order of the court, led to the public whipping post, there stripped and fastened, and lashed with nine and thirty, until their skin was rough with whelks and red with blood. We have never beheld a scene more degrading to the noble sentiments that should be nurtured and cultivated in the breast of every freeman. It makes us almost hate ourselves, to think that we are of their kind—yea, their fellow-citizens." But, in a statewide referendum later that year, North Carolinians overwhelmingly rejected the proposed state penitentiary that reformers were certain would prove the ideal form of social retribution.

For the litigants involved in the cases on the docket, "court week" could be a grueling experience. Yet for the community as a whole the periodic sessions of the county and superior courts were a lively time of camaraderie and commerce. Judges, lawyers, witnesses, jurors, and spectators all converged on the county seat. The courtroom was always packed and, whether winter or summer, "reeked of tobacco juice, whiskey, and sweating bodies." According to one young lawyer, there was "a continual fuss, a continual talking, so that the Court, the Council nor the jury cannot hear the testimony." The proceedings were repeatedly interrupted by distractions in the gallery or outside in the street.

Although the court itself was the primary attraction, agricultural societies chose this period to hold their fairs and political parties their district meetings. Enterprising merchants made the most of the occasion by offering special sales or hawking merchandise in the street. Roving musicians, jugglers, sleight-of-hand artists, and even tightrope walkers entertained the milling crowds by day while bands of traveling players filled the town hall every night. As long as it was not oneself, a close relative, or a good friend awaiting trial in the dank and dismal county jail, court week could be great fun.

Commercial Activity

Although a town's role as the seat of county government preoccupied its citizens during the periodic sessions of the county and superior courts, it was the municipality's function as a commercial center for the surrounding rural area that largely dictated the pattern of antebellum urban life. In North Carolina, coastal metropolis and backcountry village, regardless of size or sophistication, were still part of an agrarian society. Their development, in terms of both physical growth and available services, reflected the economic needs and aspirations of the entire region, for the fortunes of town dwellers and country folk were intrinsically intertwined. A good crop year meant increased sales, steady wages, prosperity, and possible expansion, whereas a poor yield raised the specter of high overhead, unemployment, growing debts, and impending decline.

This interdependent economic relationship was epitomized in the town market. There, whether daily, weekly, or just once or twice a month, in an open portion of the village square or within the boisterous confines of a municipal hall erected specifically for the purpose, the basic exchange of marketable goods took place. The wholesaler and the housewife dickered with agricultural producers who offered everything from tobacco by the hogshead to flour by the sack, from turpentine by the barrel to tallow by the tub. Planter and peddler alike selected from a variety of manufactured or imported products like Brazilian coffee and Cuban sugar, tenpenny nails and osnaburg cloth, which had been transported by the wagonload across the limited network of plank roadways and rutted cow paths that linked remote hamlets in the western Piedmont to the expansive market towns of the east.

Nowhere was the importance of the market and its attendant commerce more clearly evident than in Fayetteville. Well before the city's incorporation in the late eighteenth century, enterprising Scottish merchants had made it a prominent center of inland trade. Here the antebellum farmer or country storekeeper had no need to halt his overloaded wagon in order to ask for directions when he arrived. The Market House, constructed in 1838 at the intersection of the four major thoroughfares leading into Fayetteville, was the focal point of the town, in which the buildings of its Liberty Row reflect two centuries of change. The Market House site was also the location for the sale of slaves. One slave, Sarah Louise Augustus, remembered the slave auction block at the market. "I was born on a plantation near Fayetteville, North Carolina," she recalled, "and I belonged to J. B. Smith. . . . He owned about thirty slaves. When a slave was no good he was put on the auction block in Fayetteville and

sold. The slave block stood in the center of the street, Fayetteville Street, where Ramsey and Gilliespie Street came in."

Market House (1832), Fayetteville

The splendid two-story Market House is a brick structure of Georgian design and a classic blend of form and function. The ground level is an open arcade that served as the center of daily market activity. Stalls were set up in and around the building, while wagons filled with produce jammed the broad intersection. Yet Fayetteville's Market House was more than the nucleus of local commerce. The town hall on the second floor provided a seat for municipal government and a focus for community life and culture. On a given afternoon or evening, though the market might be quiet, the building was still likely to be crowded with people attracted by a meeting of the town commission or a lyceum lecture. Even those who seldom had business there could not easily escape the impressive structure's subtle influence. The hourly chimes of the four-sided clock in the base of the cupola could be heard throughout the city, along with the mellow tone of the mighty bell that was rung four times each day: at breakfast (7:30 A.M.), dinner (1:00 P.M.), sundown, and the curfew hour (9:00 P.M.) imposed on slaves by the city fathers.

In addition to mandating the curfew, the town commission was responsible for the formulation of all local ordinances and had the power to levy taxes on real estate, the sale of liquor, shows or exhibitions, and livestock that ran loose in the street. More democratic than the county court, the city government in the mid-nineteenth century was normally vested in a mayor and three to seven commissioners elected annually by the vote of all white male citizens. The commission was charged with maintaining public health, keeping the streets in repair, and establishing a night watch. In many larger cities, it was also responsible for recruiting a standing fire brigade and developing a municipal waterworks. Fayetteville by the 1850s could boast of two engine companies and a hook and ladder brigade composed entirely of slaves. Yet perhaps the most important prerogative that the town commission possessed was its power to establish and regulate the public market. Scales were erected and an official weigher appointed who augmented the municipal coffers by charging a fee for the service.

A Yankee schoolteacher, George Hood, described conditions in Fayetteville in 1834:

The market too, you seldom see anything of consequence in it save Tobacco, Cotton and Slaves—the provision market is supplied from the country settlements. Some mornings they go to market and can get nothing—When I first came here Venison and wild Turkies was in the market—the season for those has passed and now we have fish. I board at a good boarding house—but still there is very little diversity—our breakfast is coffee, Corn & flour bread, Cold Ham—Fresh or Salt Shad and occasionally eggs—Dinner, Bacon & greens, Shad, line of venison or Veal occasionally, Corn bread and Apple pie. Supper, Shad, Corn bread, hot biscuits, crisp, and coffee.

Antebellum Carolinians often traveled several days to bring their produce to market. Almost every night, particularly in the fall, the roadsides leading into Fayetteville and other substantial commercial centers were dotted with the campfires of those eager to be on hand when the trading started early the next morning. At sunrise the market came alive as teamsters jockeyed to get their wagons into the best positions and farm boys vied with merchants' apprentices setting up their inviting displays. The air was filled with the sounds of crowing roosters, barking canines, and shrill human voices already beginning to hawk their wares. And the pleasing sight of snow-white cotton, bright red apples, and golden ears of corn joined the rich smell of hay and manure as morning melded into day.

In eastern cities the faces one saw at the marketplace were as likely to be of dark complexion as they were of light. Many planters and merchants depended on trusted slaves to transport goods to market, conduct their sale, and make any purchase required. Black traders, both slave and free, were also there to offer a wide range of merchandise obtained legitimately through their own labor or surreptitiously on the flourishing "black market." And the public market, where all other commodities were so readily exchanged, was normally the site at which those considered human chattel were auctioned as well. Few issues of the *Fayetteville Observer* were without such an announcement:

TRUSTEE'S SALE

On Tuesday of September Court next, at the Market House, in Fayetteville, in Pursuance of a Trust to me executed by James Sundy, dec'd, I shall sell at Auction.

EIGHT LIKELY YOUNG NEGROES

Consisting of one Woman and the remainder Boys and Girls. These are remarkably likely, and of excellent character.

William Cade, Trustee

The town market, however, was by no means the sole location of commercial activity in antebellum cities. Stores and shops lined the principal streets near the market hall and around the courthouse square. Typically such retail outlets offered a broader selection of merchandise in terms of quality and sold items in smaller quantities than could be purchased wholesale at the central market. While country storekeepers attempted to carry a complete range of products, their urban counterparts were becoming increasingly specialized, with dry goods shops, groceries, apothecaries, and hardware stores all competing for the business of town dweller and rural visitor alike.

Urban areas were a magnet for craftsmen as well. In addition to the blacksmiths and millers found in the countryside, almost every town could count carpenters, coopers, harness makers, cobblers, and tailors among the ranks of its mercantile community. Usually the services of at least one butcher, baker, printer, gunsmith, jeweler, milliner, and barber were available too. In fact, artisans and shopkeepers, along with their families and associates, were the very backbone of urban society. Living above their shops or in the unpretentious dwellings along the side streets of every Carolina town, these men and women, both black and white, provided the essential goods and services that attracted trade, stimulated cultural development, and brought the fledgling hamlet as well as the busy metropolis to life.

One of the state's best known and most competent craftsmen was a free black cabinetmaker named Thomas Day. Born in Virginia, he moved during the 1820s to Milton in Caswell County, which was rapidly becoming the center

Union Tavern (1818), Milton, Caswell County, was converted by Thomas Day into a workshop and residence. A private home now, the shop may be seen from the street.

of the northern Piedmont's prosperous tobacco economy. Though he began his furniture-making business in a modest way, most likely on his parents' farm outside of town, within a few years he had established a thriving shop on Milton's main street. By midcentury, Day had purchased the Union Tavern, once the largest and finest in the area, and converted the handsome two-story brick structure into a commodious residence, convenient showroom, and functional workshop.

Despite their substantial contribution, free blacks in antebellum North Carolina and elsewhere in the South were generally considered by whites to be an absolutely subordinate, though potentially dangerous, caste. In a society in which black skin was synonymous with servitude, the presence of free blacks, particularly those who even by white standards had to be judged a success, created a considerable dilemma. Their enterprise and ability contradicted the very assumption of inferiority upon which the entire system was based. As a result, they were denied full citizenship and restricted by various state and local regulations intended both to control and to intimidate. In many larger cities,

such as Fayetteville and Raleigh, where in 1860 free blacks comprised almost 10 percent of the population, municipal ordinances required registration with the town clerk, the posting of a bond for good behavior, and even the display of a cloth arm badge marked "Free." The legislature in 1826 prohibited further immigration of free blacks into North Carolina, and the revised state constitution of 1835 deprived them of the vote. Although they retained the right of trial by jury throughout the antebellum period, free African Americans were never allowed to testify against whites.

This stifling atmosphere notwithstanding, Day and his family persevered. The quality of his work could not be overlooked. Many of the wealthy planters in the area as well as the citizens of Milton recognized his presence, regardless of his race, as a valuable asset. Day's services were in great demand. Working in solid walnut or mahogany veneer over local poplar and pine, his shop turned out elegant settees, ingenious extension tables, and elaborate marble-topped bureaus of unique design. Plantation owners depended on him to craft distinc-

Chairs crafted by Thomas Day

THOMAS DAY.

CABINET-MAKER,

RETURNS his thanks to his friends and the public for the patronage he has received, and wishes to inform them that he intends continuing his business at his old stand, and is well prepared to manufacture all kinds of

Mahogany. Walnut, and Stained Furniture.

He has on hand a small stock of Mahogany Furniture, made of the best St. Domingo mahogany, in the newest fashion, and executed in the most faithful manner;—and also some Walnut and Stained Furniture, and high and low post Bedsteads, turned according to the latest patterns; all which he will sell at reduced prices and on the most accommodating terms

Feb. 22.   62—6w

Alexander Harrison & Co.

on Queen Street,

OFFER FOR SALE

Saddles, Bridles, Carriage and Gig

Notice from the Milton Chronicle advertising Thomas Day's furniture

tive stairways, mantelpieces, and interior woodwork for their houses as well as rude coffins for their slaves. Townsmen contracted with him to custom build well-proportioned sideboards and graceful secretaries or simply purchased his practical wardrobes and sturdy bedsteads ready-made. As a result, Day prospered, and, with the assistance of the young craftsmen, both slave and free, whom he trained to work in his shop, he became one of the most prolific furniture manufacturers in the state.

Thomas Day was exceptional, but not simply because he was able to develop his extraordinary skill and achieve a measure of success. The degree to which he and his family were accepted by the dominant white society was even more unusual than the esteem he was granted for his work. As early as 1830, when Day went back to Virginia to marry free black Aquilla Wilson, the white citizens of Milton successfully petitioned the state legislature for a special exemption from the law prohibiting her immigration. The Days were active members of the predominantly white Milton Presbyterian Church—for which his shop built the pews. Day was very likely one of the church's ruling elders, because at least two of their session meetings were held in his home. In his business, Day could count among his regular customers the governor, David S. Reid, and several of the most prominent families in the state. And he was personally selected by the president of the university at Chapel Hill to execute the interior work for the splendid debating halls of the fashionable Philanthropic and Dialectic Societies in the historic buildings known today as New East and New West.

But even a free black of Day's stature, who commanded wide acclaim and personal respect, could not escape the daily reality of prejudice and oppression. His entire family was acutely aware of the perverse character of southern society and sensitive to the anomalous nature of their position in it. Though Day and his wife remained in Milton, their three children were sent north for their education, and Thomas and Aquilla longed for the time and place they might ultimately find both acceptance and contentment. Day's touching correspondence with his beloved daughter, Mary Ann, at Wilbraham Academy in Massachusetts in the early 1850s revealed his strong sense of isolation as well as the persistent hope that sustained him:

You inquire how long before I leave & also observe you cant—se[e] how I have lived so long in Milton—I can tell you it will not be a verry great while before I hope to leave Milton—and I can also tell you I have long since learned to Enjoy my life in a higher circle than depending on human society for my comfort or happiness. . . . No doubt my great concern at this time & will be is to get some sootable place for you and your Brothers—us all—to settle down—I want you to be in some place whare your turn of feelings & manners can be well met with associates—& I fully Expect to affect my purpose if I live long enough.

Unfortunately for Day, and countless other Carolinians, his dream was unattainable.

Society and Culture

Although not everyone shared equally in the pleasures or the problems of urban life, Carolinians of every station were attracted by the economic opportunity, the energetic spirit, and the cosmopolitan atmosphere of the antebellum town. Beaufort was no Boston, nor could Charlotte be compared with Charleston, the preeminent cultural center in the South. Even so, the budding urban character of such Tar Heel towns as Elizabeth City and Kinston, Tarboro and Henderson, not only stimulated more intensive commercial activity

Joseph Bonner House (ca. 1835), Bath

but also increased social interaction and the liberating exchange of attitudes and ideas.

The elegant town houses of planter and merchant alike reflected their desire to be as much a part of the flourishing social life of the urban community as of its economic enterprise. Among antebellum urban buildings reflecting the life and enterprise of the merchant-planter class that can still be seen today are the Joseph Bonner House (Bath, Beaufort County), the Zebulon Latimer House (Wilmington, New Hanover County), the Maxwell Chambers House (Salisbury, Rowan County), the Roberts-Vaughn House (Murfreesboro, Hertford County), the John Vogler House (Winston-Salem, Forsyth County), Liberty Hall (Kenansville, Duplin County), and the Oval Ballroom (Heritage Square historic buildings, Fayetteville, Cumberland County). Churches also displayed the prosperity of antebellum Tar Heel towns. Among significant structures still standing are Christ Episcopal Church in Raleigh, Purvis Chapel in Beaufort (built by the Methodist Church in 1820 and now an AME Zion church), and the First Presbyterian Church in Fayetteville. Fraternal Lodges—such as the Columbus Lodge (1838) in Pittsboro, in Chatham County, and the Eagle Lodge (1828) in Hillsborough, in Orange County—were also a part of the urban architectural milieu.

Craftsmen, too, found more in the state's developing towns than a heightened demand for their various services. Not only did they enjoy more extensive

Christ Episcopal Church (1848–61), Raleigh. Photograph by Paulette Mitchell.

contact with colleagues and peers than did their counterparts in the surrounding rural area, but they also had a greater voice in government and communal affairs. Even enslaved Tar Heels were likely to welcome the chance to dwell in the heady climate of a bustling port city or a vigorous inland town. Though it could mean separation from family and friends, and did not bring an end to demeaning and demanding toil, an urban environment afforded the slave a freedom of movement and association unknown within the restrictive bounds of the tidewater plantation or the upland farm. Here too, as a result of an expanding market economy and an increasingly sophisticated and active press, one might learn more of a world beyond Carolina, where, if African Americans were unlikely to escape prejudice and oppression, at least they could be free.

Despite towns' multiple attractions, many of the very institutions that made them important social and cultural centers served to reinforce the hierarchical precepts that split antebellum society apart. The urban church, like its rural equivalent, was a vital force uniting the diverse elements of the local community. Believers of all classes and colors gathered to worship simultaneously the same God under the same roof. But, regardless of their religious affinity, most congregations remained spatially segregated by race, sex, and wealth. In fact, church members often paid graduated prices according to location in order to "purchase" the right to occupy a particular pew. The composition of the numerous fraternal orders, mutual benefit societies, mechanics' associations, and other social organizations that sponsored the majority of the varied cultural and recreational activities associated with town life reflected similar socioeconomic distinctions. Though there were women's societies in New Bern, Fayetteville, Raleigh, and elsewhere, for the most part women and blacks, as well as propertyless or non-Christian whites, were excluded from membership.

To a great extent the enhanced educational opportunities available in an urban setting were also shaped by social and economic considerations. The principal means of progressing beyond parsing sentences and memorizing multiplication tables was the private academy, one or more of which were located in almost every town. There students refined their basic academic skills and were introduced to the classics of literature and philosophy. The most promising scholars, whose families could afford the expense, looked forward to continuing their education at one of the growing number of colleges in the state, while the remainder prepared themselves for more enlightened, if not more successful, careers in agriculture or commerce. Yet access to secondary education was not merely predicated on social status, ability to pay, or even race. Beyond the elementary level, female pupils found their educational prospects, like their vocational possibilities, circumscribed by their sex.

In essence, the only role available to women in nineteenth-century society was that of housewife and mother. As James B. Shepherd, a prominent state legislator and advocate of education, explained to the young ladies of Wake Forest Female Seminary in 1840, "To be economical as the head of a family—diligent in the employment of time—tasteful in the recreations of leisure hours—devoted wives—kind daughters—to render yourselves pleasant friends, benevolent in all relations of life are clearly the true interest and should be the sole object of your sex." Women did exercise considerable authority in certain additional areas in which their direct involvement was considered appropriate, such as church and charity work. But in general their participation in matters beyond the domestic sphere was limited to exerting influence on the decision-making process of men. Not only were they without a vote in political affairs; apart from their husbands they had virtually no legal rights.

The rigid dichotomy of sexual roles was both reflected in and augmented

by the educational process. Only a limited number of private academies accepted female students, and, even in those institutions established exclusively for women, instruction was more likely to be oriented toward developing "skill and grace in the home" than toward stimulating intellectual achievement. Elementary academic skills and practical household arts were supplemented by studies in novel reading, needlework, music, dancing, drawing, and painting. Yet, in spite of the popular conception of the woman's place in society, a few schools went beyond preparing young ladies to be "serviceable and pleasant companions" for their future husbands. In some instances, the rigorous curriculum that was offered compared favorably with that available in the better male academies in the state.

One of the best and most widely known female academies in antebellum North Carolina was the Burwell School, located in the thriving court town of Hillsborough, in Orange County. The quality of the school's direction, along with its commitment "to cultivate in the highest degree [the] *moral* and intellectual powers" of its students, attracted scholars from as far away as Florida and Alabama, and secured the patronage of some of the most prominent families within North Carolina. In accordance with accepted legal practice and social custom, the owner as well as the titular head of this remarkable institution was a male, the Reverend Robert A. Burwell; but, in fact, the school was originally conceived, painstakingly organized, and meticulously managed by his energetic and capable wife, Margaret Anna.

The Burwells first came to Hillsborough from Virginia in 1835, when Robert assumed the pastorate of the Presbyterian church. To help support their growing family on a minister's modest income, Mrs. Burwell began tutoring several local girls on an individual basis. As a result of what she perceived to be a compelling need, as well as her own interest in teaching, she gradually expanded the scope of her efforts. Within several years she was accepting boarding students in her home at the Presbyterian manse and had financed the construction of a frame classroom and refectory on the grounds.

Anna Burwell's school proved such a success that by 1848 her husband was able to purchase the property from his congregation and give up his pastorate to assist in its operation. An addition to the main building more than doubled its size and altered its orientation to overlook a beautiful sloping yard shaded by hardwood trees. And like the Burwells' own family, which eventually numbered twelve children, the school continued to grow and prosper. At its height the academy's enrollment was approximately thirty pupils per session, six or eight of whom lived with the Burwells at the school, while the remainder boarded "with some of the most respectable families in town."

The school year consisted of two terms of twenty weeks each with a break of six weeks at Christmas. Normally the annual schedule was coordinated with the schedules of the various male academies in the Hillsborough area that brothers and cousins of the Burwell girls were likely to attend. Though not every girl expected to complete the four-year course of study offered at the school, the curriculum as a whole was comprehensive and difficult. In addition to standard subjects like grammar, geography, and history, the Burwells and their various assistants directed courses in mathematics, stressing both algebra and geometry; the sciences, including botany, astronomy, and chemistry; and such provocative disciplines as moral and intellectual philosophy, "evidences of christianity," and rhetoric. No wonder young Jane Bell's father, who recognized "that females and brains were not biologically incompatible," sent her to the school.

Mrs. Burwell placed great emphasis on writing and speaking English well. Her forte was literature, and she was particularly fond of requiring her scholars to parse the lengthy sentences of Milton's *Paradise Lost*. The girls were also expected to put their grammatical skills to practical use, for as student Mary Pearce explained to a friend: "We have to write compositions every week, and

I know you would feel sorry for me, if you knew how difficult it is for me, especially as we have to write something imaginative, and I am nearly exhausted of *subject, substance* and everything else."

The daily routine at the school began early, with prayers and scripture recitations. Normally breakfast was a simple meal of bread, butter, and milk. "Divisions," or classes, followed at 9:00 A.M. and extended until 2:00 P.M., when the girls ate their main meal, prepared daily by the family's slave cook. Afternoons were devoted to the "ornamentals": piano, guitar, drawing, painting, and needlework, as well as languages such as Latin, French, Spanish, and Italian. In the evening, after a light supper, the Reverend Mr. Burwell led the girls in devotions, and Mrs. Burwell made sure she kissed each of them before going to bed for the night.

Saturdays were free. After writing a letter home, the girls, properly chaperoned, could go "downstreet" to patronize Mrs. Vasseur's confectionery or the other shops in Hillsborough. "Authenticated callers" were also welcome, though the Reverend Mr. Burwell strictly prohibited casual visits of beaus from the neighboring academies. On Sunday mornings every girl went to church, and they were all required to attend catechism classes in the afternoon.

The last week of every session was devoted to review, and each year at the close of the spring term the school held its annual public examinations. The girls' copybooks, compositions, and varied works of fine and domestic art were put on display. Local luminaries were invited to question the girls concerning their studies, both individually and as a group, in order to evaluate their progress. Musical interludes punctuated the day, and the evening was entirely devoted to a gala "Soirée Musicale" at which the girls performed selections ranging from Strauss's "Tambour Polka" to arias from Donizetti's *Don Pasquale*.

If Anna Burwell accepted the precept of the woman's place in nineteenth-century society, she refused to be inhibited by it. According to Burwell graduate Lavinia Cole, she "neglected no duty, kept the house beautifully, had the personal supervision of the thirty boarders, attended to their manners and morals, saw that their beds were properly made—was particular about their health—kept house, made her own bread, washed the dishes, with our assistance—taught six hours a day—was the mother of twelve beautifully clean, healthy, and attractive children, dressed well always and entertained as much company as any other lady in the village."

It was not her intentions to alter social attitudes toward women, but to encourage her girls to make the most of what latitude they were allowed. By her example, as a successful administrator and mother, teacher and friend, she inspired a generation of young women to develop their own ability and intellect and to strive for excellence and achievement in their daily lives.

City Hall, Wilmington, N. C.

J.A.L.
10/21/1907

Thalian Hall (1855–58), Wilmington

The formative influence of Burwell School and other private academies was significantly enhanced by the urban cultural milieu. Literary clubs and debating societies were in vogue. Though such organizations were largely social in orientation, their implicit purpose was to educate as well as entertain. In most sizable towns, a library association offered its subscribers access to a wide variety of reading material gathered in its private "reading room." The collection of the Raleigh Library Company, for example, included books, documents, maps, magazines, and a selection of sixty-seven newspapers, "one from every State in the Union and three printed in foreign languages." The local lyceum society annually sponsored a series of public lectures for the edification of its membership and the moral and intellectual "enlightenment" of the community as a whole. The periodic concerts and plays presented by amateur musical and theatrical groups offered merchant and mechanic alike a taste of the "fine arts."

The dramatic productions of the Thalian Association in Wilmington compared favorably with "professional legitimate drama" in Richmond, Charleston, and New Orleans. The annual repertoire of the association, which was founded in 1788, ranged from Shakespearean tragedy to contemporary com-

Cockfighting drew spectators and gamblers.

edy. The all-male company included such luminaries as Governor Edward B. Dudley and James S. Green, the treasurer of the Wilmington and Weldon Railroad, who was a star comedian. Often the Thalians engaged well-respected, professional actresses to take the female lead, though various members of the association appeared in female roles as well. William M. Green, who later became bishop of Mississippi, was known for his "somewhat feminine" beauty and regularly won accolades for his performances as a heroine.

So popular were the Thalians that Wilmington's city fathers prevailed on the state legislature to authorize $50,000 in municipal bonds to build a combined city hall and theater. The magnificent neoclassical structure (1855–58) was designed by New York architect John M. Trimble and executed by the finest local craftsmen, both slave and free. Constructed of stuccoed brick, the imposing two-story building is still in use: the front portion houses the city administration while, the rear contains the beautifully renovated Thalian Hall.

JACKSON JOCKEY CLUB
SPRING RACES, 1833.

Mr Edmund Wilkins pay to John White,
proprietor, *Ten* DOLLARS.

M. Calvert Sec'y.

*Horse racing was popular with
North Carolinians.*

A former slave, John H. Jackson, remembered the building of City Hall–Thalian Hall:

I was born in 1851, in the yard where my owner lived next door to the City Hall. I remember when they was finishin' up the City Hall. I also remember the foreman, Mr. James Walker, he was general manager. The overseer was Mr. Keen. I remember all the bricklayers; they all was colored. The man that plastered the City Hall was named George Price, he plastered it inside. The men that plastered the City Hall outside and put those colum's up in the front, their names was Robert Finey and William Finey, they both was colored. Jim Artis now was a contractor an' builder. He done a lot of work 'round Wilmington. Yes'm, they was slaves, mos' all the fine work 'round Wilmington was done by slaves. They called 'em artisans. None of 'em could read, but give 'em any plan an' they could foller it to the las' line.

On opening night in October 1858, the ornate auditorium was alive with the sights and sounds of actors and audience. Wilmington's social elite, elegantly garbed in velvet and silk, filled the orchestra level and lower balcony, while their servants crowded the gallery above. All eagerly awaited the initial performance of "The Honeymoon" by the professional company of G. F. Marchant, brought in for the occasion from Charleston. The glow of 188 gas burners highlighted the rococo proscenium arch that enclosed the stage and played on the fanciful vines and grapes that decorated the slender columns supporting the balcony floor. At last the drop curtain, which was painted with an idealized Greek scene, quivered and began to rise. And then as now, the hushed crowd was transported by the dramatist's insight and the players' craft to a different place and time.

Theater was only one of a variety of amusements that punctuated the daily routine in nineteenth-century towns. Gala subscription balls, formal suppers, and afternoon teas were held year-round, but it was at more rustic pursuits that average townspeople were most likely to be found. Hoedowns were as suited to urban stables as to rural barns, particularly on a cool summer night. Cockfights were common in the spring and fall. And no Tar Heel town was complete without a racetrack, for horse racing was every Carolinian's favorite sport. Holidays such as the Fourth of July were typically celebrated with speeches, parades, games, and barbecues. And every few years a traveling circus, with its acrobats, animals, and exhibits of "natural curiosities," visited the larger communities in the state.

Despite the varied social and economic activities that added color and excitement to the urban tableau, the lives of antebellum townspeople differed little from those of their rural relatives and friends. Their days were spent in honest effort, whether at work or at play, and their nights in contemplation of the promise of tomorrow.

4

FORCES FOR CHANGE

Although antebellum North Carolina lagged behind the nation as a whole in terms of social and economic development, by the middle of the nineteenth century there were unmistakable signs of an awakening in the "Rip Van Winkle State." An expanding network of iron railways and wooden roadways linked the coast to the interior. The budding Tar Heel textile industry had grown as large as any in the South. State asylums for the deaf, dumb, and blind as well as for the insane demonstrated Carolinians' broadening commitment to humanitarian reform. Not even the debilitating impact of the Civil War could bring the progressive impulse to a halt. For out of the devastation and dislocation wrought by four years of conflict came increased economic diversity and positive social change.

Amid the rising expectations and buoyant optimism of the Jacksonian era, emigration was the most critical problem facing the state. Every year thousands of energetic and capable Carolinians left their friends and farms to seek better opportunities in the West. A correspondent from Buncombe County reported to the *Western Carolinian* in 1827: "During the last four months the flow of emigration through Ashville has surpassed any thing of the kind the writer has ever witnessed. It was not uncommon to see eight, ten, or fifteen waggons, and carts, passing in a single day." Soil exhaustion, limited availability of new land, inadequate transport facilities to cross rivers and difficult terrain, and a lack of political and economic democracy plagued North Carolina during he 1830s, when the flow of emigrants reached its peak.

Legislators, planters, educators, and reformers all sought to reverse the trend by expanding opportunity within the state, though by and large the measures they proposed served only those Tar Heels who were free and white. The long-awaited North Carolina Convention in 1835 resulted in the ratification of a series of amendments aimed at liberalizing the state constitution. Henceforth, seats in the House of Commons would be apportioned solely on the basis of county population, and every white male taxpayer would be eligible to vote in statewide elections for both the lower house and the governorship. For the first time, however, free blacks were explicitly excluded from the electorate.

Ferry on the French Broad River

Ironically, North Carolinians within the government and without overwhelmingly approved of the forced emigration of a certain segment of the population on the grounds that it could not, or would not, fully assimilate. Thus the proud remnant of the Cherokee Nation was "removed" from the southwest corner of the state by federal troops in 1838. Although the tribe had been guaranteed "inviolable" rights to its homeland in treaty after treaty with the United States, the Indians' legitimate claims were superseded by what President Andrew Jackson considered to be the demands of "civilization." Approximately one-fifth of the 18,000 Cherokees driven from their towns and farms in Georgia, North Carolina, Alabama, and Tennessee died in military detention camps while awaiting departure or along the "Trail of Tears" on their way to Oklahoma. A number of North Carolina Cherokees, however, escaped removal to the West. They and their descendants subsequently occupied the 63,000 acres of the Qualla Reservation in Swain, Jackson, and Haywood Counties. But as a result of the removal of most of the Cherokees to the West, white

Sterling silver medal created for the first North Carolina state fair.

Carolina gained over 1,000 square miles of territory for new settlement. The funds garnered from the sale of these Cherokee lands enabled the state to embark on an aggressive program of "internal improvements."

The appearance of numerous journals devoted to improving farm methods and the quality of rural life, such as the *Farmer's Advocate*, *North Carolina Farmer*, and *Carolina Cultivator*, testified to an increasing interest in agricultural reform. Crop rotation, deep plowing, hillside terracing, better seed, improved implements, and the use of fertilizer were all promoted as means of increasing productivity and reducing soil exhaustion. A distinguished group of progressive planters organized the North Carolina Agricultural Society in 1852 with the goal of encouraging and coordinating local reform efforts throughout the state. The following year, the society held the first of its annual state fairs, offering cash prizes to attract a broad range of exhibitors. "Let it no longer be said," wrote the editor of the *Farmer's Journal*, "that the farmers of North Carolina are blind to their interests, and that they have no spirit of pride as regards the advancement of farming among them."

The work of agricultural reformers notwithstanding, the welcome prosperity of the 1850s in Carolina and the nation as a whole was primarily the result of greater demand for agricultural products, higher market prices, and improved transportation. The total value of the state's crops mushroomed during the decade from $22,900,000 to $33,400,000, and land values rose by over 100 percent. Tobacco production almost tripled; that of cotton doubled; and,

Handmade plow

though the rate of increased output of corn during the ten-year period was less spectacular, the practical yellow grain remained North Carolina's leading crop in 1860 with a yield of over 300 million bushels. It seemed to planters and politicians alike that their optimistic visions of collective progress coupled with personal wealth were on the verge of becoming a reality.

Despite North Carolina's considerable prewar economic growth, other states north and south were experiencing equal or greater development. Consequently, in a relative sense, most Tar Heels could be considered both backward and poor. Few yeomen fully accepted the concepts of "scientific" farming; crude methods and outmoded implements endured. Money was scarce and commerce was limited. Average income and the standard of living were comparatively low. Markets and manufacturing in North Carolina were as yet underdeveloped. Travel and transport through most of the state remained prohibitively expensive and frustratingly slow.

Transportation and Communication

From the colonial period onward, geographical barriers inhibited commercial development and intrastate cohesion. Although several major rivers dissect North Carolina's broad Coastal Plain, only the Cape Fear empties directly into the Atlantic. The southerly flow of the mighty Yadkin and Catawba Rivers in the Piedmont, coupled with the attraction of superior ports at Charleston and Norfolk, directed agricultural producers to markets outside the state. In the west, the mountains obstructed overland transport as well as social interchange with the east. As a consequence, most North Carolinians felt little more affinity with fellow Tar Heels beyond their own region than with their counterparts in neighboring states.

During the antebellum era, waterways served as the primary means of transport, and the advent of steam-powered vessels magnified their importance. Various schemes were advanced to increase access and improve navigability by building canals, dredging principal rivers, and cutting additional inlets through the Outer Banks. The National Republicans, and later the Whigs, projected a new entrance to Albemarle Sound as part of their nationwide plan for internal improvements, but the proposed passage was never opened.

The only viable entry for ocean shipping to North Carolina's extensive coastal sounds and the important rivers that flowed into them was Ocracoke Inlet. Even there deep-draft vessels had to contend with strong currents and dangerous shallows. A light marking the inlet was erected before the end of the eighteenth century, but it was rendered useless by a major shift in the channel. The federal government authorized the construction of a new lighthouse on Ocracoke Island in 1823.

Fashioned of brick and covered with mortar, the sixty-nine-foot conical tower is the oldest operating lighthouse in the state. (Bald Head Island Lighthouse, "Old Baldy," built in 1818, is the oldest still standing.) The walls of the Ocracoke Lighthouse are five feet thick at the base, and a spiral staircase circles the interior to the top. Twelve trapezoidal lens panes are encased in the cast-iron dome. A valve lamp with reflectors originally served as the light source, though in 1860 it was replaced by a more powerful Franklin lamp. Towering above the low dunes and the gnarled island vegetation, the structure was visible some fourteen miles at sea. Its height made it quite an attraction for the well-to-do planters who summered at Ocracoke. Prominent jurist and politician Asa Biggs recorded the thrill of climbing to the top to take in the view, for "from this may be seen all the Island and looking toward the sea the eye may spot any immensity." Islanders also congregated on the high ground of the keeper's quarters to wait out the worst of the frequent coastal storms.

During the antebellum period, the federal government began building a new series of lighthouses on the North Carolina coast in response to the nation's growing maritime commerce. The first and prototype of the new lighthouses was the Cape Lookout Lighthouse, built in 1859. The Civil War interrupted lighthouse construction, but following the war, three more lighthouses

*Ocracoke
Lighthouse (1823)*

were built in relatively quick succession at Cape Hatteras (1870), Bodie Island (1872), and Currituck Beach (1875). Each of the four had its own distinctive paint markings to distinguish it for mariners. To assist shipwreck victims, the U.S. Life-Saving Service (later called the Coast Guard) began building its stations along the North Carolina coast in the 1870s.

Overland transportation was time-consuming and difficult. The state's roadways were for the most part ill marked and poorly maintained cart paths that became impassable in wet weather. The result, according to Governor John M. Morehead, in 1842, was that it cost half the value of a farmer's crop "to transport the other [half] to market." Whether driving hogs or cattle on foot or traveling in heavily loaded wagons, it was almost impossible for rural producers to cover more than ten to twenty miles per day. Passenger travel was largely by stagecoach, and travelers often had to stay overnight at taverns and hotels. Among such facilities was Walker's Inn, in Cherokee County, which was famed for its hospitality. "At William Walker's at Old Valleytown, was one of the very best houses in Western North Carolina, the bill for man and horse was fifty cents," one lawyer reported. The famous landscape architect Frederick Law Olmsted found the house "unusually comfortable" but the food greasy. He declared that "what we call simple dishes, such as boiled rice and toast, were served soaking in a sauce of melted fat." At another Mountain overnight stop,

Lighthouses & Lifesaving Stations of the North Carolina Coast

Lifesaving Stations:

☀ **BUILT 1874**
1. Jones Hill (Whale Head/Currituck Beach)
2. Caffeys Inlet
3. Kitty Hawk
4. Nags Head
5. Bodie Island (Oregon Inlet)
6. Chicamacomico
7. Little Kinnakeet

✦ **BUILT 1878**
8. Deals Island (Wash Woods)
9. Old Currituck Inlet (Pennys Hill)
10. Poyners Hill
11. Paul Gamiels Hill
12. Kill Devil Hills
13. Tommys Hummock (Bodie Island)
14. Pea Island
15. Cedar Hummock (Gull Shoal)
16. Big Kinnakeet
17. Creeds Hill
18. Hatteras (Durants)

✳ **BUILT 1880-1888**
19. Cape Hatteras - 1880
20. New Inlet - 1882
21. Ocracoke - 1883 (Hatteras Inlet)
22. Cape Fear - 1883
23. Oak Island - 1886
24. Cape Lookout - 1888

❋ **BUILT 1894-1905**
25. Portsmouth - 1894
26. Core Banks - 1896 (Atlantic)
27. Ocracoke - 1904
28. Fort Macon - 1904
29. Bogue Inlet - 1905

🗼 **Lighthouse** - Date Constructed

Currituck - 1875

Bodie Island - 1872

Roanoke I.

Cape Hatteras - 1870

Diamond Shoals - 1966

Cape Hatteras

Ocracoke - 1823

N

Albemarle Sound

Elizabeth City

Edenton

Lake Phelps

Lake Mattamuskeet

Pamlico Sound

Bath

Pamlico R.

New Bern

Neuse R.

Beaufort

Cape Lookout - 1859

Cape Lookout

Atlantic Ocean

By 1905, along the Outer Banks, North Carolina's lifesaving stations stood within five to seven miles of each other.

Roanoke Rapids

Roanoke R.

Tar R.

Greenville

Rocky Mount

Tarboro

Goldsboro

Neuse R.

Kinston

Trent R.

Jacksonville

Cape Fear

Bald Head Island - 1818

Frying Pan Shoals - 1817

Wilmington

Price's Creek - 1848

Oak Island - 1958

Cape Fear River

Kemp P. Battle remembered: "On our way back to Lenoir we spent the night in the only habitation in Blowing Rock, Mr. Sherrill being the owner. There were several gentlemen in the waiting-room. Our bedroom adjoined the waiting-room, with a bedquilt hung over the opening instead of a door. However, the food was good."

Cape Lookout Lighthouse (1859)

Many believed the solution to North Carolina's transportation problem lay in an exciting new invention: the steam locomotive. The state government stimulated railway construction by purchasing substantial portions of stock in various private railroad companies chartered by the legislature, thereby underwriting much of the cost and assuming a large share of the risk. By 1840 the first two lines were complete. The Wilmington and Weldon Railroad, which

Cape Hatteras Lighthouse (1870)

stretched 161 miles from Wilmington to the Roanoke River, was at the time the longest railway in the world. The Raleigh and Gaston line linked the capital city with the Roanoke as well, and with the existing rail connections from the river to Virginia's attractive markets.

Rail construction continued unabated until the outbreak of the Civil War, by which time approximately 900 miles of track had been laid in the state. Most

*Bodie Island
Lighthouse (1872)*

*Currituck Beach
Lighthouse (1875)*

Chicamacomico Lifesaving Station (1911), Hatteras Island. This structure replaced the first station, built in 1874.

important was the North Carolina Railroad, completed from Goldsboro via Raleigh to Charlotte in 1856. Although it followed a somewhat circuitous route through Hillsborough, Greensboro, and Salisbury—the respective homes of Governors William A. Graham, John M. Morehead, and John W. Ellis—it provided a functional link between east and west. Morehead, influenced by his teachers David Caldwell and Archibald D. Murphey, urged or actually effected many of the internal improvements that took place at the end of the antebellum period. He supported railroad building, turnpikes, industry, and the establishment of an asylum for the deaf, to which the blind were subsequently admitted. After serving as governor in the 1840s, he became president of the North Carolina Railroad and a promoter of the Atlantic and North Carolina Railroad and the Western North Carolina Railroad. Blandwood (1845), his home in Greensboro, still stands and reflects the wealth that he acquired.

Speeding along at fifteen to twenty miles per hour, trains cut the cost of transporting freight in half. Lower transportation costs meant higher agricultural profits, and an increasing number of farmers were encouraged to produce a marketable surplus. Both intra- and interstate communication improved with faster travel and more frequent mail service. Railroads opened an entire range of new employment for both slave and free labor. Yet, as is often true with technological innovation, rail service proved most beneficial to those who were in the best position economically and politically to take advantage

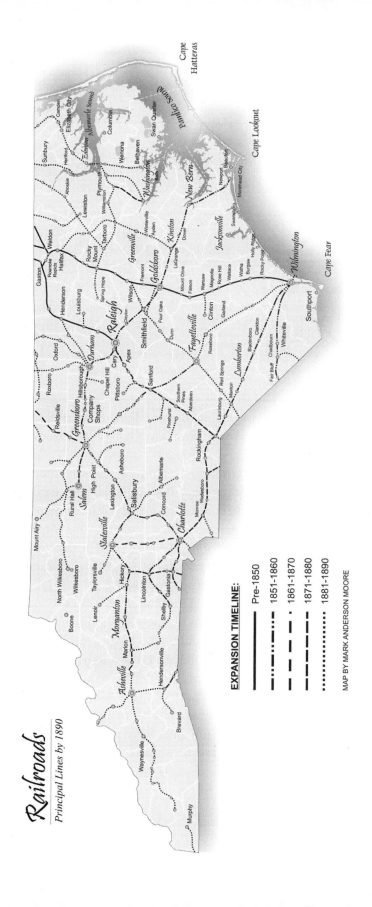

Railroads
Principal Lines by 1890

EXPANSION TIMELINE:

Pre-1850
1851–1860
1861–1870
1871–1880
1881–1890

MAP BY MARK ANDERSON MOORE

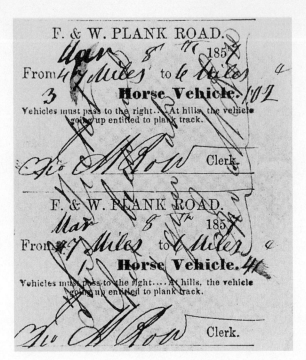

Vehicle ticket for the Fayetteville and Western Plank Road

of it. At midcentury, though the state had incurred a debt of some $9 million to finance railway construction, over half of its citizens were still wholly dependent on the horse and wagon.

During the 1850s farmers and merchants agitated for the construction of a system of all-weather roads that would reduce the difficulty of transporting their goods to market or the nearest rail connection. The legislature chartered numerous private companies to construct "plank roads" with the modest financial backing of the state. Because most of the stock in these ventures was purchased by individual farmers living along the proposed route, plank roads came to be known as "farmers' railroads."

Although such roads were built in almost every part of the state, Fayetteville served as a focal point for their development. Six plank roads converged at this thriving market center, the longest being the Fayetteville and Western, which ran 129 miles northwest through Salem to the Moravian town of Bethania, in Forsyth County. A letter from one W. N. Tillinghast to his brother John, on 9 April 1850, reported: "The Plank Road is now finished to the Factory and Toll is now charged, the Country people do not seem to like it as much as they did before the toll gates were built. . . . The land near town . . . has increased in value four or five fold."

Over 500 miles of these wooden turnpikes were constructed in North Carolina, representing an investment of approximately a million dollars. Roadbeds eight to ten feet wide were surveyed and graded, then allowed to settle. Parallel rows of heavy timbers were laid lengthwise along the entire roadway and planks of heart pine, three to four inches thick, were placed across them. The structure was then covered with sand and the road was opened to traffic. According to a contemporary observer: "All classes profited, but the farmer gained most directly. Their peculiar merit was the diminution of friction, by which a horse was able to draw two or three times as great a load as he could on an ordinary road."

Travelers were charged a toll of .5¢ to 4¢ per mile depending on the number of horses in their team. In comparison to the railroads, most plank road companies realized only moderate profits during their initial years. But, because of the rapid deterioration of the wooden planks, maintenance costs soon became prohibitive. Thus many roads closed as rapidly as they had appeared.

As improvements in transportation began breaking down the geographic isolation of North Carolinians, the concurrent expansion of journalism put them in closer touch with one another and the world beyond. Seventy-four newspapers, including eight dailies, were published in the state in 1860—over three times the number published forty years earlier. Because many were primarily intended to voice the concerns of political parties, they emphasized state, national, and foreign affairs rather than local news. After the telegraph was introduced in the state in 1848—the initial line running from Virginia through Raleigh and Fayetteville—items received "by telegraph" soon began to dot the front page. One source estimated that by midcentury one in every three white males read a newspaper. The state's newspapers were supplemented by a broad range of almanacs, journals, and pamphlets dealing with every conceivable topic from religion to agriculture.

The steamboat, the locomotive, the telegraph—"internal improvements" and technological advances were everywhere apparent. The changes they wrought were cause for both wonder and concern. The editor of the *Raleigh Register* in 1850 voiced grave misgivings: "This is the age of high pressure. . . . Men eat faster, drink faster, and talk faster, than they did in our younger days, and, in order to be consistent on all points, they die faster. . . . It is to be feared that the invention of the lightning telegraph will give an additional go-ahead impulse to humanity, equal to that imparted by the rush of steam. If so, Progress only knows where we shall land." But, in reality, "Progress" was yet to have an appreciable impact on the lifestyle of most North Carolinians. Despite the exciting advances in transportation and communication, few had

Commercial fishing with a seine net

more than limited contact with the outside world. Over a third of the state's population remained illiterate, and many Tar Heels still lived and died without leaving the county of their birth.

Industry

Industry in antebellum North Carolina developed as an adjunct to agriculture. From mining to commercial fishing, turpentine distilling to textile manufacturing, industrial enterprise was related to, and coordinated with, basic agrarian pursuits. Local planters not only provided the necessary capital, labor, and raw materials for nascent industries; they also formed the principal market for the goods produced.

Although nineteenth-century Tar Heels mined limited quantities of iron and coal, it was gold that captivated the state's fancy. Begun on a part-time basis by Cabarrus and Mecklenburg County farmers, the gold-mining industry in North Carolina employed some 30,000 laborers and ranked second only to agriculture in economic importance at its height.

Gold was first discovered in the state in 1799 on John Reed's farm southeast of Concord, in Cabarrus County. While fishing in the shallow waters of Little Meadow Creek, John's young son, Conrad, was attracted by a large yellow rock. Unaware of its value, the Reeds used the seventeen-pound stone as a doorstop. When Reed carried the rock with him on a marketing trip to Fayetteville some three years later, he encountered a jeweler who promptly recognized the metal and purchased the nugget, worth several thousand dollars, for $3.50.

Reed soon discovered that he had been duped and came to realize the potential bonanza that he possessed. Along with three partners who supplied slave labor and tools, he scoured the creek bed each year in late summer after the crops had been put in and the stream had all but dried up. A growing number of nearby farmers began digging along their own creeks, and such seasonal placer mining continued throughout the region for over twenty years with considerable success. By 1824 the haphazard excavation on the Reed property alone had yielded an estimated $100,000 worth of gold. In that same year, gold was discovered at Gold Hill in south Rowan County, and a large mine began operating at that site.

During the late 1820s the budding industry boomed. Rich underground veins of gold were discovered in Mecklenburg County, and the corporations that controlled them brought in experienced European miners who employed the latest and most sophisticated mining techniques. John Reed, preferring to maintain a close-knit family operation, resisted the expensive transition to vein mining and the importation of outside workers, values, technology, and capital it entailed. But within a decade the younger members of the family had sunk several shafts of up to ninety feet at Reed Mine. After John Reed's death, the property changed hands several times until purchased in 1853 by the New York–based Reed Gold and Cooper Mining Company. The firm installed the most advanced processing equipment and sank fifteen separate shafts that were connected by a series of tunnels over 500 feet in length. Despite its impressive effort, the company went bankrupt, and, though the mine continued to lure a succession of new investors, it was never successfully operated again. It is now a state historic site.

The decline of the Reed mine mirrored the fate of the industry as a whole in North Carolina. When the first branch of the United States Mint opened at Charlotte in 1837, there were over fifty active gold mines in the state. But, with the discovery of rich and relatively accessible ore in California, few Tar

Riding an ore bucket, miners ascend a shaft at the Gold Hill Mine in Rowan County.

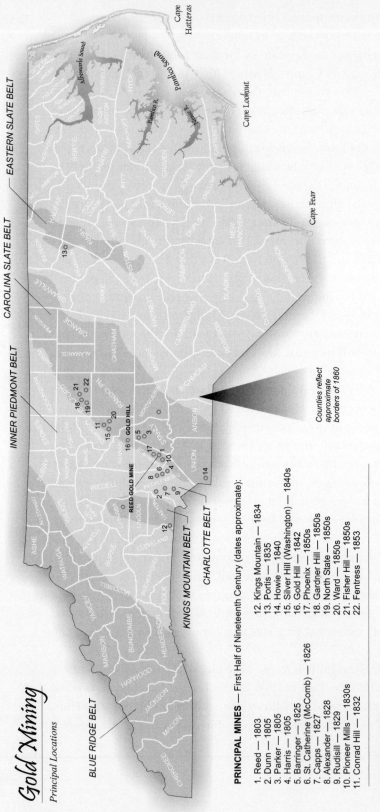

Gold Mining
Principal Locations

BLUE RIDGE BELT

KINGS MOUNTAIN BELT

CHARLOTTE BELT

INNER PIEDMONT BELT

CAROLINA SLATE BELT

EASTERN SLATE BELT

Counties reflect approximate borders of 1860

PRINCIPAL MINES — First Half of Nineteenth Century (dates approximate):

1. Reed — 1803
2. Dunn — 1805
3. Parker — 1805
4. Harris — 1805
5. Barringer — 1825
6. St. Catherine (McComb) — 1826
7. Capps — 1827
8. Alexander — 1828
9. Rudisill — 1829
10. Pioneer Mills — 1830s
11. Conrad Hill — 1832

12. Kings Mountain — 1834
13. Portis — 1835
14. Howie — 1840
15. Silver Hill (Washington) — 1840s
16. Gold Hill — 1842
17. Phoenix — 1850s
18. Gardner Hill — 1850s
19. North State — 1850s
20. Ward — 1850s
21. Fisher Hill — 1850s
22. Fentress — 1853

REED GOLD MINE

First documented discovery of gold in the United States — Conrad Reed, 1799

MAP BY MARK ANDERSON MOORE

Heel mines could continue to compete profitably. Although estimates of North Carolina's total gold production prior to the Civil War range from $55 million to $65 million, in 1860 there were only six operative mines in the state.

Manufacturing, even more than mining, reflected the economic dominance of agriculture in antebellum North Carolina. The overwhelming majority of factories and mills were merely a subsidiary of their owners' principal agricultural interests. Based on the value of its product, distillation of turpentine was North Carolina's leading industry in 1860. Concentrated primarily in New Hanover, Bladen, and Cumberland Counties, the turpentine industry yielded the state's only product with a substantial export market. Two-thirds of the turpentine produced in the United States came from North Carolina. Milling grain—largely corn and wheat—ranked as the second most important industry, followed in order by processing tobacco and sawing lumber. Though no other southern state could match the thirty-nine cotton textile factories operating in North Carolina, the value of the factories' combined output placed that industry no better than fifth.

The Schenck-Warlick spinning mill, in Lincoln County, the first textile factory opened in the state, was established in 1815. Shortly thereafter, Joel Battle drew on the expertise of Scotsman Henry Donaldson to set up a similar mill on the Tar River near Rocky Mount. Although the original stone structure was destroyed during the Civil War, Rocky Mount Mill operated well into the twentieth century on the same site. By the mid-1850s Edwin Holt was producing his famous "Alamance Plaids" on steam-powered looms at his mill on Great Ala-

Near North Carolina's gold mines, a branch of the U.S. Mint was established in Mecklenburg County in 1837. The building, now within the city of Charlotte, houses the Mint Museum of Art.

Rocky Mount Mill (ca. 1860s), the second-oldest cotton mill in the state. The pre–Civil War buildings had been destroyed when this photograph was taken.

mance Creek, yet North Carolina's textile industry as a whole had progressed only slightly beyond the system of domestic manufactureing that it replaced.

Like most of the state's manufacturers, antebellum textile producers could not successfully compete in the national market. In fact, North Carolina was becoming less self-sufficient in terms of manufactured goods and more dependent on exchanging agricultural staples for items produced in the North. Ironically, improvements in the state's transportation facilities tended to inhibit rather than stimulate North Carolina's industrial development. For expanded waterways and railroads merely opened the state's isolated markets to increasing competition from the more efficient mills of New England.

Education and Reform

Nineteenth-century Americans trusted in the promise of social reform. To many, the expansive, individualistic attitude of the Jacksonian era signified a dangerous erosion of traditional values. The acquisitive forces unleashed by the growing market economy seemed to threaten the cohesion of the family, the community, and the young Republic itself. Continued social stability under such circumstances required the highest moral and ethical standards of every citizen. A growing segment of the population came to believe that the community at large should take direct action toward shaping individual character. Public schools were promoted as a means of instilling in every youngster a sense of morality and social order along with a knowledge of grammar and arithmetic. Benevolent societies were organized to combat vice and corruption, as well as to alleviate the plight of the "worthy poor." Asylums and prisons were called for to "rehabilitate" social deviants by isolating them in a well-ordered environment until they were capable of coping with the pressures of a changing world. The crusade of Dorothea L. Dix, of Massachusetts, for state care of the insane resulted in the establishment of mental hospitals in a number of states. Construction of the State Hospital for the Insane in North Carolina was begun in 1849 on a tree-covered hill in Raleigh that came to be called "Dix Hill." In her appeal to the North Carolina legislature, Dorothea Dix gave a graphic example of the state's care of its insane. "In Granville County poor house," she reported, "is an unfortunate man, who for years has been chained to the floor of a wretched room; miserable and neglected, his now deformed and palsied limbs attest the severity of his sufferings through these cruel restraints; flesh and bone are crushed out of shape by unyielding irons."

The expanding interest in higher education both reflected and reinforced the impetus toward social reform. The University of North Carolina, chartered by the state legislature in 1789, had been damned by some as a "school for the rich." Yet during the nineteenth century, "enlightened" administrators broadened its classical curriculum to include history, law, literature, modern languages, and natural sciences with such practical application as agricultural chemistry. David L. Swain, who became the president of the university in 1835 upon completing his term as state governor, "popularized" the institution by multiplying its enrollment and emphasizing the importance of training the state's brightest young men for careers in public service. During the same period, the principal religious denominations in North Carolina became actively involved in providing advanced study for "the humble student who would go out among the people and breathe into them the Soul of Education." The Baptist, Methodist, Presbyterian, German Reformed, and Lutheran Churches all established colleges for men. And, following the lead of the Moravians and the Quakers, most denominations sponsored similar schools for women. By 1860 "progressive" Tar Heels could boast of sixteen colleges, with a combined enrollment of over 1,500, enhancing the knowledge and virtue of the citizenry in every section of the state.

Eumenian Hall (1849), Davidson College, Mecklenburg County

The worthy social objectives behind the creation of such institutions did not necessarily ensure their success. Davidson College, in Mecklenburg County, for example, was founded in 1837 on the basis of a noble, yet abortive, experiment. Seeking a means by which "the cost of a Collegiate education . . . might be brought within the reach of many in our land, who could not otherwise obtain it," the churchmen of Concord Presbytery organized Davidson as a "Manual Labor School." In exchange for a reduction in boarding fees, every student was required to perform three hours per day of "manual labor, either agricultural or mechanical." Those who had mastered a trade worked in the college blacksmith and carpenter shops, while the remainder toiled on the school's farm. The faculty included a "steward" charged with supervising both the students' labor and the dining hall, which utilized most of the foodstuffs produced.

Although Davidson's founders were convinced that compulsory labor promised "the most happy results in training youth to virtuous and industrious habits," it soon proved as unprofitable for the administration as it was unpopular with the students. The majority of the young men studying at Davidson had grown up working on family farms, and many considered their time misspent on similar endeavors at school. Procrastination and pranks abounded, for as one observer of student behavior suggested, "To cheat the overseer out of their labor, if practicable, was almost as much an instinct on the College farm, as it was on the cotton and rice plantations of the South, with the added zest that there was infinite fun in the thing, and it called for the exercise of superior adroitness." Wheels were mysteriously removed from the farm's wagons; tools were thrown under the chapel or buried in the woods; plows were purposely dulled and even broken. Within several years, despite the best efforts of the steward, the relative cost of the farming operation had become prohibitive, and enrollment had significantly declined. The trustees of the college were left with little alternative. In 1841 the democratic ideal of manual labor was abandoned for the standard classical curriculum suited to the sons of the "better" class.

The "Manual Labor System" was not the only aspect of campus life influenced by the provocative vision of social improvement. Formal literary and debating societies provided a focus for educational as well as social activity at Davidson and other colleges throughout the state. At Davidson intellectual debates and oratory were nurtured in the college's elegant Eumenian Hall (1849), one of two debating halls. The University of North Carolina at Chapel Hill had equally elegant quarters for the Dialectic (Di) and Philanthropic (Phi) Societies, organized in 1795. (Today, the Di Chamber, New West Building, is shown as part of the campus tour.) Like their counterparts beyond the academic sphere, such organizations offered a forum for the lively discussion of topical issues—philosophical, political, social, or economic. The arguments, orations, and compositions presented not only gave members an opportunity to hone their polemical skills, but also stimulated careful thought and continued concern about such controversial topics as social reform. Following the lead of more militant humanitarian movements like that for temperance, many collegiate groups went so far as to impose a rigid code of moral behavior on their membership. Both the Eumenian and Philanthropic Societies at Davidson established fines for fighting, swearing, intoxication, and "lying to the faculty." They even maintained "vigilance committees" specifically charged with reporting any such offense.

It was not uncommon for benevolent societies outside the collegiate environment to mix educational and social motives as well. Such was the case in Spring Hill, near Wagram in what is now Scotland County, where a group of upper- and middle-class farmers gathered to form the Richmond Temperance and Literary Society in 1855. Their goals were forthright and their concerns real, as their constitution vividly suggests:

We a portion of the citizens of this community being convinced of the deadly influence that intemperance is now exerting over the morality of our country, and plainly seeing the ravages that it is daily making in our midst, burying the brightest talents in an untimely grave, levelling man the noblest work of God's creation with the beasts of the field, staying the hand of everything that has for its object the advancement of virtue and religion; do ordain and establish . . . this Society . . . its objects being uncompromising hostility to intemperance and an untiring zeal for the advancement of literature.

The temperance movement arrived in North Carolina in the 1820s in conjunction with demands for a wide range of humanitarian reforms. James F. Cain, a student at the University of North Carolina, wrote his sister, Mrs. Tod Caldwell, in 1849 that the Hillsborough Presbyterians "are exulting, proclaiming aloud, with their hands raised to Heaven, for the 'success of the Temperance cause' and the downfall of all the grogeries in H[illsborough]—every institution of the kind in the place has been refused license to retail spirituous liquors—." At midcentury some 12,000 Tar Heels had taken the temperance pledge to "neither make, sell, buy, nor use as a beverage any intoxicating drink whatever." The Richmond Society was more active than most, meeting every other Saturday—2:00 P.M. in winter, 3:00 P.M. in summer. The bylaws were strictly adhered to, including the 25¢ fine for absence. Meetings were alternately devoted to the presentation of a member's literary composition and to open debate. After singing a rousing stanza or two of "Round the Temperance Standard Rally" or "The Teetotalers are Coming," the twenty or so members and guests might begin a thoughtful discussion of an esoteric topic such as "Which is most sought after, Wealth or Honor?" or a more volatile debate over a timely question such as "Has the Insurrection at Harper's Ferry been a Benefit to the Union?" Though it might never match the garish excitement of a barroom bash, a temperance meeting, by all accounts, could be a truly edifying experience.

War and Reconstruction

The Civil War ravaged North Carolina—both its families and its farms. Forty thousand men, more than from any other southern state, were lost in their prime. Thousands more were scarred and damaged, left with only their courage and their pride. Millions of dollars in local, state, and Confederate revenue were spent for naught as well. Investments, savings, loans, and currency were all rendered worthless with no hope of reparation. Countless banks,

Dead Confederate soldier

mills, stores, and schools were closed forever. Blighted crops, empty barnyards, fallen fences, and broken dreams all had to be dealt with in the midst of defeat.

More threatening still to conservative whites was the specter of social revolution. More than 331,000 enslaved black North Carolinians and 30,000 free African Americans, together more than a third of the state's population, experienced the joy of "Jubilee." Now the enslaved would be free—to rejoin their scattered families, to take up vacant farm lands, to compete for available jobs, and to demand their civil rights. Indeed, North Carolina would never be the same.

While 125,000 Tar Heels marched off to battle in service of the Confederate States of America, almost eight times that number remained at home. Faced with scarcities, exorbitant prices, and depreciating currency, farm wives and plantation mistresses, old men and small children, free blacks and domestic servants strove to make ends meet. Houses were stripped of draperies and carpets to provide clothing and shelter for North Carolina's troops. Parched corn was substituted for coffee, and spinning wheels once more competed with power looms. Yet opportunistic merchants and unscrupulous blockade-runners continued to sell their goods at the highest prices the market would bear. Bacon jumped from $.33 to $7.50 per pound, wheat went from $3 to $50 a bushel, and coffee was selling at $100 per pound.

North Carolinians also experienced the direct and violent impact of the

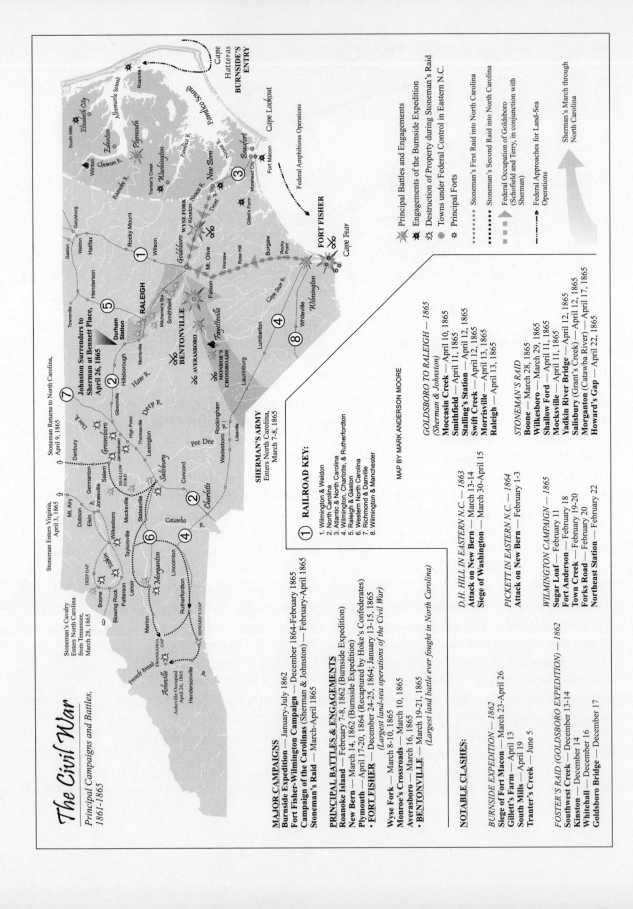

The Civil War
Principal Campaigns and Battles, 1861–1865

MAP BY MARK ANDERSON MOORE

MAJOR CAMPAIGNS
Burnside Expedition — January-July 1862
Fort Fisher-Wilmington Campaign — December 1864-February 1865
Campaign of the Carolinas (Sherman & Johnston) — February-April 1865
Stoneman's Raid — March-April 1865

PRINCIPAL BATTLES & ENGAGEMENTS
Roanoke Island — February 7-8, 1862 (Burnside Expedition)
New Bern — March 14, 1862 (Burnside Expedition)
Plymouth — April 17-20, 1864 (Recaptured by Hoke's Confederates)
• FORT FISHER — December 24-25, 1864; January 13-15, 1865
    (Largest land-sea operations of the Civil War)

Wyse Fork — March 8-10, 1865
Monroe's Crossroads — March 10, 1865
Averasboro — March 16, 1865
• BENTONVILLE — March 19-21, 1865
    (Largest land battle ever fought in North Carolina)

NOTABLE CLASHES:

BURNSIDE EXPEDITION — 1862
Siege of Fort Macon — March 23-April 26
Gillett's Farm — April 13
South Mills — April 19
Tranter's Creek — June 5

FOSTER'S RAID (GOLDSBORO EXPEDITION) — 1862
Southwest Creek — December 13-14
Kinston — December 14
Whitehall — December 16
Goldsboro Bridge — December 17

D.H. HILL IN EASTERN N.C. — 1863
Attack on New Bern — March 13-14
Siege of Washington — March 30-April 15

PICKETT IN EASTERN N.C. — 1864
Attack on New Bern — February 1-3

WILMINGTON CAMPAIGN — 1865
Sugar Loaf — February 11
Fort Anderson — February 18
Town Creek — February 19-20
Forks Road — February 20
Northeast Station — February 22

GOLDSBORO TO RALEIGH — 1865
(Sherman & Johnston)
Moccasin Creek — April 10, 1865
Smithfield — April 11, 1865
Stalling's Station — April 12, 1865
Swift Creek — April 12, 1865
Morrisville — April 13, 1865
Raleigh — April 13, 1865

STONEMAN'S RAID
Boone — March 28, 1865
Wilkesboro — March 29, 1865
Shallow Ford — April 11, 1865
Mocksville — April 11, 1865
Yadkin River Bridge — April 12, 1865
Salisbury (Grant's Creek) — April 12, 1865
Morganton (Catawba River) — April 17, 1865
Howard's Gap — April 22, 1865

RAILROAD KEY:
1. Wilmington & Weldon
2. North Carolina
3. Atlantic & North Carolina
4. Wilmington, Charlotte, & Rutherfordton
5. Raleigh & Gaston
6. Western North Carolina
7. Richmond & Danville
8. Wilmington & Manchester

Legend
★ Principal Battles and Engagements
✸ Engagements of the Burnside Expedition
✸ Destruction of Property during Stoneman's Raid
◉ Towns under Federal Control in Eastern N.C.
✴ Principal Forts
······· Stoneman's First Raid into North Carolina
——— Stoneman's Second Raid into North Carolina
➤ Federal Occupation of Goldsboro (Schofield and Terry, in conjunction with Sherman)
---- Federal Approaches for Land-Sea Operations
——— Sherman's March through North Carolina

SHERMAN'S ARMY
Enters North Carolina,
March 7-8, 1865

Johnston Surrenders to
Sherman at Bennett Place,
April 26, 1865

Stoneman Returns to North Carolina,
April 9, 1865

Stoneman Enters Virginia,
April 3, 1865

Stoneman's Cavalry
Enters North Carolina
from Tennessee,
March 28, 1865

Asheville Occupied
April 26, 1865

war. Early in the conflict, Federal troops captured and occupied much of the coastal region, including all of the important ports with the exception of Wilmington, guarded by the formidable Fort Fisher. From coastal bases such as New Bern, Union troops raided the interior of eastern North Carolina. Plantation mistress Catherine Edmondston of Halifax County described her feelings about a nearby Federal raid in 1863: "Heard distinctly the report of two heavy guns in the direction of Weldon. The boom was unmistakable. . . . What a sad solemn sound it is! The deep toned roar! This note of horrid war which comes booming over the peaceful fields & through the still quiet swamps & woods, awakening echoes which until now have slept to all save peaceful sounds. It makes the blood tingle through ones veins and brings the war home to our very thresholds." Toward the end of the war, General George Stoneman and his Union cavalry troops raided the western part of the state. In the outer Coastal Plain, the Mountains, and the Piedmont's "Quaker Belt," North Carolina Unionists who opposed the war struggled and sometimes fought with those who supported the Confederate war effort.

Among the military facilities secured by the Federal army was Fort Macon, located at Beaufort Inlet in Carteret County. Before the war, the fort (completed in 1834) was a United States fortification, constructed to defend the inlet. At the outbreak of the conflict, North Carolina troops seized the fort. But in April 1862 a Union expedition easily recaptured and held the stronghold. Today, Fort Macon is a state park.

Far more difficult to capture was Fort Fisher, bolstered by its much smaller auxiliary, Fort Anderson, located at Brunswick Town. Protected by Fort Fisher, which had the largest earthworks of any Confederate fort, Wilmington remained until the last months of the war a vital supply line for the Confederacy and an active blockade-running port. A Federal attempt to conquer the fort failed in December 1864. But then in January 1865, the Union army and navy finally overwhelmed the garrison and seized the fort after a ferocious battle. Fort Anderson was quickly overrun, and the fall of Wilmington, the last of the Confederate ports, soon followed. Fort Fisher is now North Carolina's most-visited historic site.

In addition to its coastal forts, the Confederate government attempted to defend the sounds and rivers of North Carolina with with a number of ironclad gunboats. Among these vessels was the CSS *Neuse*. Workers began constructing the *Neuse* in the fall of 1862 at White Hall (Seven Springs) on the Neuse River in Wayne County. Local carpenters built the vessel of lumber from nearby pine forests. Not yet complete, the gunboat was floated down river in 1863 to the town of Kinston to be fitted with armor, weapons, and machinery. The *Neuse* departed Kinston in April 1864 to take part in a Confederate attempt to re-

Fortifications at Fort Fisher (1865), near Wilmington

capture New Bern. But the vessel ran aground in the Neuse River; and with a rise in the river, it returned to Kinston, where it remained for the next ten months. As Federal troops threatened in March 1865, the crew of the *Neuse* set fire to her, which resulted in an explosion that sank the ironclad. The remaining hull of the vessel was raised in 1963 and presently is on display at the CSS *Neuse* and Governor Caswell Memorial in Kinston.

The Civil War was in its final weeks when a large Union army under the command of General William T. Sherman invaded North Carolina from the south. As Sherman's army moved toward Goldsboro to unite with U.S troops driving inland from the coast, John and Amy Harper of Bentonville in Johnston County experienced firsthand the horrors of war. For in March 1865, the Battle of Bentonville, the largest land battle ever fought in North Carolina, took place before their doorstep. Located behind the Union line, the Harper home was commandeered for a field hospital. Colonel William Hamilton of

the Ohio cavalry described the bloody sight: "A dozen surgeons and attendants in their shirt sleeves stood at the rude benches cutting off arms and legs and throwing them out of the window where they lay scattered on the grass. The legs of the infantrymen could be distinguished from those of the cavalry by the size of their calves, as the march of 1000 miles had increased the size of one and diminished the size of the other." With the brutal horror of warfare thrust unexpectedly upon them, the Harpers did what they could to relieve the suffering, acting as "nurses, surgeons, commissaries, chaplins and undertakers" for the dead and dying. The Harper House still stands at Bentonville Battleground.

For all practical purposes, the Civil War ended at the farm of James Bennett in Durham County on April 26, 1865. On that date, General Sherman and Confederate general Joseph E. Johnston met at Bennett Place and signed final terms of surrender.

Although the Civil War resulted in hardship for white North Carolinians, it brought the opportunity for a new life—one free of the bonds of slavery—for

Union naval bombardment of Fort Fisher, January 15, 1865

*Recovered hull of
the sunken ironclad
the* CSS *Neuse*

the state's African American population. As they heard news of the arrival of
the Federal army in eastern North Carolina, thousands of them seized the opportunity to flee to freedom and security within the Union lines. The numbers
of these so-called "contrabands" became such a logistical problem that camps
were established to house the new "freedmen" at various locations in the occupied eastern portion of the state. Volunteers and missionaries from the northern states assisted in setting up schools, clinics, and other necessary services,
while the freedmen themselves were assigned small tracts of land on which
they could eke out an existence. Many of them found employment with the liberating army as laborers, cooks, teamsters, stevedores, scouts, and spies. Their
status as free people became official when President Abraham Lincoln issued
his Emancipation Proclamation in its final form in January 1863. In April of
that year, a large number of the former slaves began joining the famed African
Brigade of the U.S. Army, serving with distinction in North Carolina, South
Carolina, Florida, and Virginia. Ratified shortly after the end of the war, the

Thirteenth Amendment to the U.S. Constitution ensured that the prohibition of slavery throughout the nation had a permanent basis in federal law.

    The wartime experience gained in the freedmen camps led in March 1865 to the establishment of a federally funded Freedmen's Bureau, charged with easing the transition from former slave to free citizen. The bureau operated throughout the South, with regional offices in every state. The headquarters for North Carolina were located in the impressive Greek Revival main building of what is now Peace College. Despite the bureau's efforts to assist freedmen in finding employment, negotiating fair contracts, and settling legal disputes, black Carolinians remained at a distinct political, economic, and social disadvantage. The state's conservative leadership marshaled the entrenched racism and staunch solidarity of the white population in order to thwart black achievement and to maintain control.

Harper House (1855–59), Bentonville Battleground, Johnston County

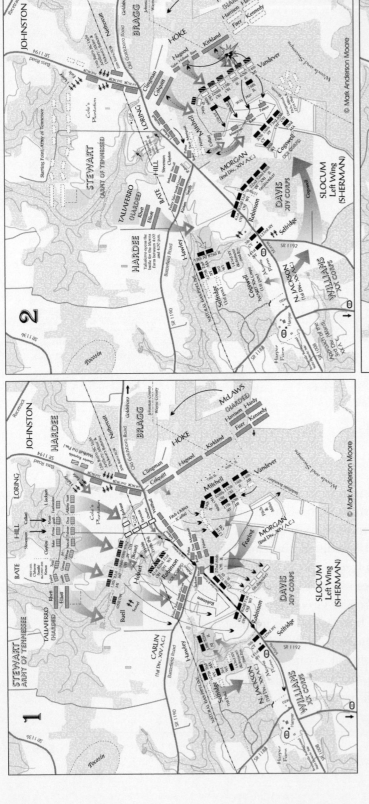

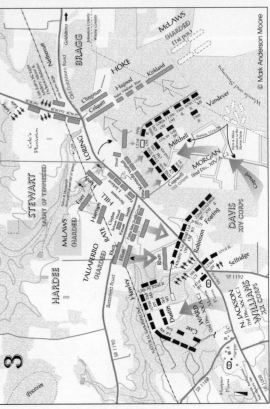

Battle of Bentonville, N.C.

March 19, 1865
The First Day . . . .

Map 1 — 2:45 - 3:45 P.M.
Last Grand Charge of the Army of Tennessee:
• Rout of Carlin's Division (Cole's Plantation)
• Fearing's Counterattack

Map 2 — 3:45 - 4:30 P.M.
Fighting below the Goldsboro Road:
• Attack of Hoke's Division
• Hill's Attack in Rear of Morgan
• Cogswell's Advance

Map 3 — 4:30 P.M. - Dark
The Final Attacks:
• Cogswell's Battle below the Road
• Attacks of Taliaferro and Bate (Morris Farm)

PRINCIPAL MOVEMENTS:

⟹ CONFEDERATE

⟹ FEDERAL

▬ FEDERAL TROOPS

◣ FEDERAL CAVALRY

▬ CONFEDERATE TROOPS

▥ Positions of Buell, Briant, and Robinson when routed by the Army of Tennessee

▥ First positions, Army of Tennessee

☐ Loring's Confederates when flanking Briant's position

† Artillery

Ⓗ Federal field hospital locations

© Mark Anderson Moore

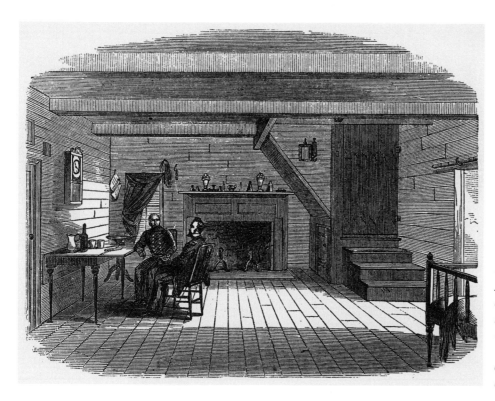

Confederate general Joseph E. Johnston discusses terms of surrender with Union general William T. Sherman at Bennett Place, Durham County.

The first two years of postwar Reconstruction, known as Presidential Reconstruction, did little to further the rights and protection of the newly liberated African Americans in the South. But in March 1867, Congress, dominated by the Republican Party, seized control of Reconstruction from President Andrew Johnson, who was not sympathetic to former slaves. Under the congressional plan of Reconstruction, freedmen in North Carolina and throughout the South received political and basic civil rights when Congress passed, and the states ratified, the Fourteenth Amendment (known as the Civil Rights Amendment) and the Fifteenth Amendment (known as the Voting Rights Amendment) to the U.S. Constitution.

With the advent of Congressional Reconstruction, the Republican Party, supported by the newly enfranchised freedmen, gained control of politics in the Tar Heel State. Influenced by African American delegates and white fellow Republicans, a state convention prepared a new North Carolina constitution that was the most democratic the state had ever had. Among other reforms, the Constitution of 1868 created the new county commissioner system, which broke up the old, often-corrupt "courthouse rings," in which justices of the peace, elected by political cronies in the state legislature, controlled the

*Union soldiers
surround Bennett
Place during the
annual reenactment
of Johnston's
surrender to
Sherman.*

*An African American scout for
the Federal army*

TRENT RIVER SETTLEMENT, OPPOSITE NEWBERN, NORTH CAROLINA.—[SKETCHED BY THEODORE R. DAVIS.]

SCHOOL-HOUSE AND CHAPEL AT TRENT RIVER SETTLEMENT.—[SKETCHED BY THEO. R. DAVIS.]

NEGRO HUTS AT TRENT RIVER SETTLEMENT.

GENERALS STEEDMAN AND FULLERTON CONFERRING WITH THE FREEDMEN IN THEIR CHURCH AT TRENT RIVER SETTLEMENT.—SKETCHED BY T. R. DAVIS.—[SEE PAGE 56.]

Scenes from Trent River Settlement, a freedmen's camp near New Bern

Built as a school for young women, Peace Institute (ca. 1860) in Raleigh served as a Confederate hospital in the Civil War and then became headquarters for the Freedmen's Bureau during Reconstruction before being rededicated to its original purpose as Peace College for women.

administrative functions of county government. Under the new county commissioner system, commissioners elected by the people for specific terms became responsible for the operation of the counties. (North Carolina counties still operate under the commissioner system.) The new constitution also established universal male suffrage and eliminated high property qualifications for holding state offices. It further mandated a system of tax-supported public schools, which meant that for the first time African Americans in North Carolina would be allowed access to public education.

Outraged at such reforms and determined to invalidate the new political power of African Americans, the Conservatives, as whites who opposed Congressional Reconstruction were called, launched a campaign of intimidation to keep blacks and their white Republican allies from voting. To achieve that end, the Ku Klux Klan arose as a violent arm of the Conservative Party and began a crusade of terror and lawlessness. The Klan assaulted, tortured, and even murdered blacks who attempted to vote. In the Caswell County Courthouse in 1870, the Klan killed in cold blood John W. Stephens, a white Republican state senator and supporter of Congressional Reconstruction.

Although the federal government took measures to combat the Klan and protect the rights of African Americans in the South, its support and enthusiasm for Reconstruction eventually waned. By the time Reconstruction came to an end in all the southern states in 1877, white Democrats (formerly called Conservatives) had been in control of state government in North Carolina for a number of years. They persisted in their efforts to undo as much as possible the reforms of Congressional Reconstruction. With the withdrawal of federal protection, African Americans in North Carolina and the rest of the South faced an uncertain future in a largely hostile environment.

Following Reconstruction, the majority of former slaves found themselves bound to the land as farm tenants, sharecroppers, and laborers. They would be fixed in those economic strata for many years to come. For the majority of whites, "rural" and "self-sufficient" remained the appropriate description. But signs of a new era were beginning to appear on the horizon. In tobacco and textiles, new technology, ready capital, and cheap labor were soon to have revolutionary effects.

Sydney Nathans

Part IV

THE QUEST FOR PROGRESS
NORTH CAROLINA, 1870–1920

OVERVIEW

1

The Industrial Age

Americans by 1870 had grown accustomed to the notion that boundaries were made to be broken. In the previous half-century, the United States had become a continental nation, begun its ascent as the manufacturing titan of the globe, overcome the distances between its cities and its shores with 50,000 miles of railroad tracks, and emancipated the enslaved members of its society after a four-year civil war.

Yet, even for those who took for granted that change was an American way of life, the transformations of the next fifty years came on a scale and with a completeness that proved startling. New inventions hastened the pace of life and work for millions. Electric power and the electric trolley, the telephone and the typewriter, the automobile and the airplane, made acceleration synonymous with American society. When Outer Banks resident William J. Tate answered Orville and Wilbur Wright's inquiry about Kitty Hawk as a site for their glider experiments, he won for North Carolina a role in the Wrights' historic victory of powered airplane flight. "If you decide to try your machine & come," wrote Tate, "I will take pleasure in doing all I can for your convenience & success & pleasure, & I assure you you will find a hospitable people when you come among us." The Wright Brothers National Memorial at Kitty Hawk, in Dare County, chronicles the history of the Wrights' struggle to fly and the moment on 17 December 1903 when their heavier-than-air, power-driven machine rose in the face of a twenty-seven-mile-per-hour wind and changed the course of human events.

The physical scale of virtually everything exploded in the industrial age. In business, Standard Oil, the American Tobacco Company, and United States Steel were but a few of the giant industries that emerged by the turn of the century—their work forces in the thousands, their capital in the hundreds of millions, their power and influence unparalleled. In the half-century after 1870, the nation's population doubled from 50 million to 100 million. Americans from the countryside and immigrants from abroad swarmed to the nation's cities and gave the United States an urban majority by 1920. One of every ten Americans lived in a city of more than a million inhabitants. the surging growth of cities and the expansion of the nation's railway network to 200,000 miles set the stage for mass production, mass advertising, and accumulation of vast fortunes. If Andrew Jackson and Abraham Lincoln stood as symbols of the self-made men of the nineteenth century, Andrew Carnegie and Henry Ford—the one a corporate empire-builder, the other the master of assembly-line production—embodied values of the twentieth.

During the late nineteenth century, a number of foreign immigrants arrived in North Carolina seeking the new opportunities offered by a changing state. For example, the Waldensians, a French-speaking Prostestant sect from northern Italy, bought a 3,000-acre tract in Burke County in 1893. At first cooperatively owned and agricultural in economy, the community soon set up textile mills and other industry in a free enterprise system. The architecture of the Waldensians and their own town name, Valdese, reflect their cultural heritage.

The new possibilities of American life created new pressures. Cities with skyscrapers and clanging trolleys and diverse inhabitants, though exhilarating to many, proved unsettling to others. Many people placed a new premium on privacy and sought refuge from the raucousness of life in enlarged homes or suburban neighborhoods, in exclusive clubs or remote resorts. The growing intensity of work led to a new emphasis on the need for relaxation. Baseball became a national pastime, bicycling became a craze, and Coney Island and other amusement parks flourished as places of release and revelry away from the cares of the job.

In the half-century after the Civil War, a new industrial society emerged in the United States and renewed the country's historic promise as a land of opportunity. Yet, though the nation was one of new invention, new wealth, and new diversions, a gnawing question loomed large. Who would reap the gains of the immensely productive and powerful society that emerged by the end of the nineteenth century? Farmers wondered as they saw their bumper crops turn into harvests of debt and dependency in the 1880s and 1890s. Factory workers wondered as they found themselves forced to subordinate their ingenuity and work habits to the demands of machinery and intensified supervision. Enterprising businessmen wondered as they confronted corporations of enormous size and power. Black Americans and ambitious women, their hopes stirred by the expansive energies of the nation, wondered whether or not the country's new opportunities included them. The answer for all was clear by the turn of the century. Gains would not come without struggle. The age of unprecedented riches produced a generation of rebels.

The Tar Heel State

Princeville,
Edgecombe County

Though North Carolina had been spared the worst ravages of the Civil War, few would have predicted in 1870 that the "Rip van Winkle State" would within fifty years become the most industrialized state in the South. Communities that were still barely hamlets five years after the war's end, such as Durham and Winston, and towns that served as commercial centers for the surrounding countryside, such as Greensboro and Charlotte, would in the decades ahead become centers of industry. But factories did not burgeon in cities alone. A rushing stream and a willing workforce opened the way for the creation of mill villages in the countryside wherever the capital could be collected. The value of goods manufactured in North Carolina was less than $10 million in 1870. It was almost $1 billion by 1920.

Though the folkways of country life persisted into the twentieth century, rural North Carolina was also transformed. Emancipation set the stage for the emergence of tenancy and sharecropping as the predominant labor system for the black farmers of the state. The coming of the railroads and the growth of commercial centers opened the way for thousands of white and black farmers to shift from subsistence agriculture to a concentration on the growth of cash crops. Greatest was the expansion of the tobacco crop of the state, which by the turn of the century surpassed 100 million pounds. By 1920 North Carolina tobacco filled many of the nation's cigarettes and pipes.

For black North Carolinians, the half-century after 1870 was a time of new freedom, new striving, and new setbacks. Enfranchised through federal law by the 1870s and politically active for three decades thereafter, they saw their voting and civil rights systematically revoked by state legislation after 1900. Widely employed as skilled artisans in North Carolina towns through the 1890s, they found their opportunities increasingly restricted and confined after the turn of the century. Throughout the uncertain years between legal emancipation and legal segregation and amidst the adversity intensified by disfranchisement and formal passage of Jim Crow laws, blacks built communities, churches, colleges, and business enterprises. In Edgecombe County, just across the Tar River from Tarboro, freed slaves started the community of Freedom Hill in 1865. After the community grew and was incorporated in 1885, its name was changed to Princeville to honor a resident, Turner Prince. The black institutions fashioned between 1870 and 1920 nurtured the spiritual strength and commitment to racial betterment that ultimately provided powerful resources for a renewed struggle to reclaim the rights of North Carolina's African American population.

Finally, between 1870 and 1920, the rustic beauty of North Carolina, long familiar to inhabitants, was discovered by other Americans. The western part of the state, with its fresh air and relaxed pace, became a haven of health for the ill. By the 1890s travelers seeking recuperation and relaxation away from the congested Northeast found in the breathtaking mountains of the west and the sandhills of the Coastal Plain an ideal place to play. North Carolina became the site of a boom for recreation of all sorts.

THE RURAL WORLD

In 1920, for the first time in American history, the United States census revealed that a majority of Americans lived in urban areas. Not so in North Carolina. Despite the steady growth of towns and cities and the dramatic expansion of industry in the state, in the fifty years after 1870 the lives of most North Carolinians remained rooted in agriculture and centered on the farm. Day-to-day life as it would have been on a late-nineteenth, early twentieth-century middle-class family farm can be seen today at Horne Creek Living Historical Farm in Surry County. On the farm, in 1900, Thomas Hauser and his family and hired hands raised typical regional crops of fruit, corn, wheat, oats, rye, hay, and vegetables.

As the old century ended and the new one began, the contrasts between city and countryside intensified in North Carolina. Machinery and a ceaseless flood of inventions accelerated the pace and expanded the scale of city life: electric power, the telephone, the typewriter, steel for skyscrapers, the automobile, moving pictures, the wireless radio. The latest wonders of technology found their way to some Tar Heel farms, to be sure. Yet the predominant rhythm of life remained rural; the hoe and the plow persisted as the essential tools for work, and the power supply of the farm continued to be men and mules—"machines with meat." Above all, between metropolis and hinterland there emerged a growing contrast in wealth. Despite appalling urban poverty, the cities' upper class grew rich as never before, and all city folk seemed devoted to making money. Until the beginning of the twentieth century, notwithstanding moments and scattered examples of prosperity, most North Carolina farmers were locked in a struggle to subsist. For many it remained an achievement to "make do."

Making Do

Day by day, season by season, agricultural life in the state after 1870 seemed to perpetuate much that was unchanged from the past. The major

Barning tobacco in Nash County

crops were those that had predominated before the Civil War—tobacco, cotton, corn—and the methods of work were little altered. Tobacco had to be tended constantly by hand. When the tobacco was ready for harvest, women and children brought the ripe leaves to the tobacco shed, and men hung them to age and cure. Young and old alike knew and executed the mysteries of curing—tending the fire that slowly drew the excess moisture from the leaves, telling tales through the aromatic nights, and, when the tobacco was ready, taking the crop to market for its sale. Cotton made similar demands on the hand labor of the entire family. After plowing and planting, the primary task was "chopping"—not the cotton plant but the hungry weeds that competed relentlessly for the nutrients of the soil.

As in the past, so in the late nineteenth century, the calendar of the crops dictated the activities of the year: plowing, planting, harvesting; corn shucking, tobacco curing, cotton ginning. Such were the rhythmic demarcations of life. There were special times for relaxation and fun: long country nights filled with stories spun before the fireplace; summer circuses on Saturday afternoons; weekend "frolics" at "different houses the country round," when hosts would clear out a room and invite neighbors to "kick up and dance" to the music of accordions and fiddles, banjos, and washboards. But often recreation dovetailed with work. Improvised field "hollers," sung at a high-pitched shout, relieved the solitude of a man working alone in the field. Hot suppers followed community work-gatherings such as a barn raising or a corn shucking. The county fair mixed whiskey and whimsy with the pageant of products from the farm.

Familiar ways of farming, year-round family labor, and seasonal celebrations persisted in North Carolina well into the twentieth century. That way of life is visible today in the Great Smoky Mountains of Appalachia at the Pioneer Farmstead of Swain County. Until the early decades of this century, the same way of life could have been observed flourishing in neighborhoods of the Blue Ridge or far to the east in the tenant houses and sharecropper cabins of black freedmen, first-generation pioneers in the enterprise of small-scale agriculture and family self-sufficiency. Rosser C. Taylor observes that the "frontier customs, based on neighborliness, charity, and necessity, survived in log rollings, house raisings, corn shuckings, hog killings, and quilting." Pioneer self-sufficiency was evident in the home-remedy medicine practiced by rural families. "Almanacs, distributed by makers of patent medicines," declares Taylor, "were suspended from a nail just underneath the fireplace mantel for consultation concerning the weather, phases of the moon, and factual information which was interspersed with testimonials of miraculous cures of this-or-that ailment through the faithful use of the advertised product." When home remedies failed, a physician, if available, was consulted. Two doctors' offices, of 1857 and 1890, are combined and restored in the Country Doctor Museum at Bailey, in Nash County.

Of course, there were important differences between the white settlers of the west, the landowning yeomen throughout the state who had farmed independently for generations, and the postwar black and white tenants of the

Spring planting on a mountain farm

Piedmont and Coastal Plain. Most newly emancipated blacks began their lives as freedpeople in cramped "slavery-time cabins." Made of logs, with one room down and one room up, the typical home had a few small window openings, wooden shutters to close off the cabin from the elements, and an earthen floor that was "hard as cement." Most had log chimneys plastered with mud and stone. A barrel of water rested nearby to douse a fire if it got out of control, and a ladder stood handy to topple an inflamed chimney away from the cabin. Only over time, as some tenants became landowners and others became long-term sharecroppers for the same owner, did the physical appearance of the homestead become less rudimentary. Gradually, the sharecropper's house might change with the addition of larger windows paned with glass, board-and-batten siding to cover the log exterior, and perhaps even a small shed porch to keep the rain from beating through the front door.

Far outweighing differences between rural tenants and landowners, however, was a common necessity that bound thousands of North Carolina farm

Drying apples by a
mountain fireplace

families into a shared pattern of life. All had to be resourceful to survive. Visitors to the Pioneer Farmstead can see rural resourcefulness on display and in practice in the farm cabin, sorghum mill, blacksmith shed, and bee-gum stand. Demonstrators—both male and female—show the skills and folk knowledge that passed from one generation to the next. The ingenuity, the patience, and the pride of those who "made do"—and did without—surprise and delight the guest.

Local mills for the grinding of corn persisted as an important component of rural communities. Still surviving are Mingus Mill at the Pioneer Farmstead; Jessup's Mill (1903), north of Francisco, in Stokes County; and Laurel Mill, Gupton vicinity, northeast of Louisburg, in Franklin County, which may incorporate an antebellum mill.

At the root of dozens of shared customs was shared scarcity. East and west in rural North Carolina, those who "come up poor" were the majority. Rural ingenuity enabled thousands of farming families to live on their own resources with little cash income. "Making do" involved the women of a household in the production of their own soap by boiling lye and animal fat. It meant plucking geese or chickens to make downy feather beds for the grown-ups, stuffing corn

A log footbridge in rural North Carolina

shucks or straw into bed-ticks for the young. "Getting by" meant a large garden and as much cropland as could be spared given over to raising one's own food: corn, wheat, sweet potatoes, orchards, milk cows, hogs, goats. And it meant knowing how to salt the meat and preserve the fruit and vegetables. "Making do" meant feed-sack blankets to keep in the warmth on snowy nights, quilts crafted from colorful scraps of cloth, rugs woven of bright yarn. It meant clothing sewn at home—and then patching and more patching, so "it got to where we couldn't tell where the clothes left off and the patches began." It meant a knowledge of folk medicine: how to use snake oil to lubricate childbirth and how large a dose of calomel to give the grandchildren each spring "to cleanse them out," as well as how much was healthy and how much would "take your teeth out." It meant relying on community midwives or "granny women" to deliver babies.

Whether they owned their land or worked someone else's, North Carolina farm families rarely relied on their own resources alone. Sharing was a vital

A rural family

feature of country living. While the crops were growing, a family "caught up" on its work might help neighbors and relatives with theirs. In times of need— illness, death, accident, debt—family members contributed food and support to each other. Many of the young continued to choose their mates among close neighbors and to reside in home communities that abounded with cousins and kin. Family ties and well-worn footpaths known to those in the community provided links and grassy highways from home to home. Sundays would see the members of each community gather at a neighborhood church in their Sabbath best. Churches that survive from the period include the Chapel of the Good Shepherd (1871), in Warren County; Piney Creek Primitive Baptist Church (1875) in Alleghany County; Grassy Creek Methodist Church (1904) in Ashe County; and Lystra Baptist Church (1852) in Chatham County. What-ever the denomination, whatever the race, most rural religion was communal and fervid. Sunday brought the sharing of fellowship, release, and spiritual renewal.

The Perils of Productivity

Continuities of custom notwithstanding, in dramatic and paradoxical ways rural life in North Carolina was transformed by 1890.

To begin with, the plantation system was gone, ended by the Civil War and emancipation. Had the former masters had their way, black freedmen and -women would have stayed on the old homeplace and continued to work under strict supervision in exchange for food, housing, and a nominal wage. Most blacks rejected such terms, so similar to slavery. But, because emancipation brought freedpeople neither land nor mules, seed nor credit, most settled for the halfway houses of tenancy or sharecropping and farmed a portion of a white owner's land as renters or for a third- to a half-share of the crop. For former planters, the new system at least provided laborers for their land, though profits fell. For the black sharecroppers or tenants, the new order afforded a limited but vital measure of freedom—the freedom to live away from the "Big House," to decide whether the wife and the children of the family would work and at what pace they would labor, to choose what goods they would buy with their livelihood, and perhaps above all the right to serve the Lord in their own church and to seek an education for themselves and their children.

Yet by the 1880s it was clear that a second change—as momentous as emancipation—was under way in rural North Carolina. Thousands of the state's farmers began growing the bulk of their crops for market. The shift seemed eminently sensible. The reconstruction of the state's railroads, the growth of towns and industries, and the multiplication of cotton gins and tobacco warehouses, where crops could be hauled in a day and sold for cash on the spot, made it entirely practical to farm for profit. With a little credit for mules and tools, with a small advance that would cover the cost of food and goods no longer produced at home, cultivators had every reason to hope that the days of postwar poverty were behind them and that they could get ahead at last.

In case Piedmont farmers had their doubts about concentrating on a cash crop, the brash boosters of rapidly multiplying tobacco warehouses labored to allay their fears. In Goldsboro and Rocky Mount, in Winston and Durham, in Kinston and Oxford, and in dozens of other towns the warehouses still come to life in mid-August and brim with bright leaf tobacco until October. Warehouse transactions are businesslike and routine now, but in the 1870s and for decades thereafter they were sights and sounds to behold. Pepper's Warehouse (ca. 1919) in Winston-Salem (Forsyth County), and Fenner's Warehouse in Rocky Mount (Edgecombe County), are typical specimens of the period surviving today.

Feverish competition for the farmer's tobacco crop began in the countryside with the midsummer appearance everywhere of auctioneers' broadsides promising high profits and a "down-home" welcome. Posters and boldly painted signs, the billboards of their day, brightened the exteriors of hundreds of barns and signaled that market time was near. Once the farmer loaded his sturdy Nissen wagon—canvas-covered to protect the crop, ruggedly designed to navigate the crudest roads—he journeyed to town and unloaded his leaves and himself in the warehouse, where both often spent the night. One North Carolinian, Clyde Singleton, recalled the trip to the Durham market: "We'd leave one morning, spend the night on the road, and get into Durham the next afternoon. We'd take our tobacco to Cap'n Parrish's place; he had a warehouse on what's now Parrish Street. . . . When we'd get close to town he'd have a pair of big mules waiting to hitch on and haul us in to the warehouse. The mud in the streets sometimes would be knee-deep to a mule. He [Parrish] had stalls for the horses and mules and quarters for farmers, some would sleep in their

Horne Creek Farmhouse, built 1875, Surry County

Birthday party, 1913, at Horne Creek Farm

wagons." The next morning, in a cavernous building festooned with flags on the outside and full of bustle and shouting within, the farmer loosely piled up his leaves for the buyers to eye and appraise. Then the auctioneer went to it, "crying the bids like lightning and never a drop of sweat in his collar." Jovial and exuberant, he rarely missed a telltale wink or nod, salute or out-stuck tongue, among the herd of bidders. In 1870 an auctioneer could dispatch a pile of leaves a minute; by 1920 he closed a sale every nine seconds. The farmer had his cash in hand ten minutes after the final bid. Then came time for him to relax, to enjoy the medicine show and banjo-picking outside the warehouse, to wend his way through the peddlers hawking their wares, and perhaps to wander uptown to stores that gladly received him. Throngs came to watch the show, which gave profit and pleasure to all.

No less than the city warehouse, the country store seemed a godsend to the

farmer eager for a chance to make money and to acquire store-bought goods. The merchant furnished plow-points, fertilizer, and seed, all essential for farming. He sold cornmeal and molasses, basic staples for many, and carried as well an abundant supply of link sausages and pepper-seasoned sardines. Corsets, fine calicoes, and nursing nipples, copper-toed shoes and shaving razors—all could be found on the merchant's shelves. And, like the tobacco warehouse, the country store provided more than goods. It offered a congenial setting for country people to gather, swap stories, and play checkers. One rarely had to travel far to find this cornucopia. A country merchant was usually no more than ten or twelve miles from most of his customers. Among the surviving country stores one can visit are Mast General Store at Valle Crucis, in Watauga County, and Pierce and Company, at Hallsboro, in Columbus County.

Pierce and Company was founded in the late nineteenth century by members of the Wyche, Pierce, and Thompson families. Ray Wyche of Hallsboro recalled that

Pierce & Co. carried practically everything needed by its rural customers. Upstairs were furniture and ready-made clothing as well as the company offices; the east side downstairs had shelves of piece goods, hats, shoes, and clothing for men, women, and children. There were patent medicines for man and beast, leather and nails for shoe soles, and sewing supplies. The line of groceries was considered ample (no fresh meats), and in the early days, staples such as salt, sugar, meal, and lard were sold weighed out from bulk containers. . . . There were several wooden warehouses surrounding the store in which were stored feeds, fertilizer, wire fencing, wagons, plows, and other items necessary for the farmer whose trips to larger shopping areas such as Whiteville were limited to a few per year.

Pierce and Company also dealt in lumber and cypress shingles and in the 1920s added a planing mill and a cotton gin.

But the most important commodity provided to farmers by the "furnishing merchant" was not found on his shelves, but in his ledger books. That commodity was credit. With so few banks and so little money in the postwar South — there was but one bank for every 58,000 southerners in 1895, compared with one for every 16,000 inhabitants outside the region — the merchant who advanced supplies without cash was a makeshift banker and a welcome one.

Access to railroads and warehouses, merchants and credit — to many these developments heralded the birth of a New South in agriculture. Writing in 1881, Atlanta journalist and promoter Henry Grady celebrated the emergence of a "prosperous self-respecting race of small farmers, cultivating their own lands, living upon their own resources, controlling their crops until they are sold, and independent alike of usurers and provision brokers." The view of the South as an emerging patchwork of "small farmers" found support in the official returns of the United States census from 1860 to 1900. In those four decades, the number of small farms in North Carolina tripled from 75,000 to 225,000, while the average size of landholdings fell by two-thirds, from an average of 316 acres to 101. The patterns revealed for North Carolina were repeated throughout the South.

Unfortunately, the agricultural statistics of the census were utterly misleading, as perhaps any observant traveler through the state would have detected. The census categorized tenants and sharecroppers as "small farmers," and hence its numbers masked the steady rise of economic dependency among whites and blacks. Even landowning farmers who were self-sufficient found themselves in jeopardy. Far from being an agrarian paradise of independent yeomen, the North Carolina that emerged in the 1880s found itself gradually entrapped in new forms of servitude. Lured and then addicted to the production of cash crops, the state's farmers married their fortunes to the marketplace at a time when prices for farm products were about to collapse all over the globe.

The living conditions of small farmers, tenants, and sharecroppers reflected the poverty resulting from their marketplace entrapment. The poor's unending struggle just to exist, usually in cold, cheerless, bug-ridden substandard housing, took its toll. According to one member of a farm family, "everybody in the country had chinches [bed bugs]. I'd just hate that so bad—'bout twice a year we had to carry everything out of the house, and Mother would fill our big old wash pot full of water and get it so hot and then she'd go in there and throw it all over the walls and scald all the walls down good. And it wasn't just us that did that; it was everybody." Under such conditions, the life of the farm wife was a difficult one. In 1913, the agricultural newspaper *Progressive Farmer* employed a full-time women's editor, who crusaded in her columns for rural clubs for the lonely, overburdened farm wives. She discussed health, food preparation, and home improvements, reinforcing the paper's view that woman's place was in the home.

Rural education remained sporadic and primitive. Subscription schools continued even after the establishment of public schools since the latter were poorly funded. Minnie Lee Spencer remembered hers:

We used to go to subscription schools, and my pappy would pay for me. Seems like it was sometimes a dollar a month. . . . I remember it was just a little bit of a log cabin, and you could stick your fingers down through the cracks in the floor.

There was one single row of windows by the workbench. That was all the light we had, don't you know. But they were all broken out and it was open through there. The bottom of the door was worn away too. . . .

We went just three months during the cold winter-time. We had a big old fire-place, and the teacher and children would go out to the woods and bring in brush to make a fire. Then there was a spring right near there. If we wanted a drink of water, we went to the spring. . . .

We had six lessons a day: Blue Back spelling, arithmetic, reading. . . . Then we had history and geography, and . . . I can't remember what the other one was called. . . . Grammar? I guess that's what it was—grammar.

The former Philadelphus Community Schoolhouse can be seen at the Robeson County Educational Resource Center, northwest of Lumberton. Another one-room schoolhouse has been rescued, restored, and moved to the Charles B. Aycock Birthplace, in Wayne County.

Farmers went into debt to prepare and fertilize their crops and to provision their families during the year. Devoting most of their land and time to cash crops, they purchased food they had once raised for themselves and ready-made merchandise they had once fashioned on the farm. At the year's end, time and again, they discovered that the very abundance of the harvest had depressed agricultural prices. The cost of credit and warehousing and transport

A mountain school

became crucial in making the difference between profit and loss—yet these costs were high and seemingly beyond farmers' control. Nor was there any easy escape back to subsistence. Under the crop-lien system, when the farmer did not "pay out" his debt to the landlord or furnishing merchant, he was legally bound to give the creditor a mortgage on his next year's crop. So he labored to produce still more tobacco and more cotton. Yet greater production seemed to bring only lower prices and profits. By 1890 one of three white farmers and three of four black farmers in the state found themselves tenants or sharecroppers—and the rest were fearful. The unintended harvest of the plunge into commercial agriculture was an annual bonanza crop of debt and dependency.

Reform and Revolt

By the mid-1880s it was becoming evident to many a farming family that the production of crops for market was not the road to independence. Farm

owners and tenants alike knew by the eighties that something needed to be done, but what? As it turned out, three courses of action opened up to rural North Carolinians.

One possibility was simply to leave the countryside altogether. Departure depended in part on opportunity. As the towns of the Piedmont grew and became places where the ambitious might hope to get ahead and where the curious might hope to sample the life of the larger world, young people left in search of urban advantages. But most of those who deserted the farm did so because they had no choice. Young, single individuals streamed to such burgeoning towns as Durham, Charlotte, and Greensboro. Blacks took on day labor, domestic work, or jobs in the stemmeries of tobacco factories, while whites found jobs tending textile and tobacco machinery. As agricultural depression intensified in the 1890s, the ranks of migrants swelled and became dominated by entire families, who packed up possessions on mule-drawn wagons and said farewell to the land.

One-room schoolhouse (1893) at Charles B. Aycock Birthplace, Wayne County

Leonidas L. Polk

But, while thousands of North Carolinians left the land, even more remained. Both the number of farms and farmers continued to grow through the 1930s. First for a handful, then for an ever-increasing number of the rural majority, a second path emerged as the means of deliverance from the tangle of debt and dependency. Eventually called "scientific agriculture," and today magnified in the agribusiness mega-farms that fertilize the soil with chemicals and reap crops and profits with machines, the technological highway to salvation had its bedrock base in the 1880s. "Improvement" and better management would make the progressive farmer free.

The campus of North Carolina State University today is a sprawling monument to the message of better farms through better management and to the ultimate surrender of mules and tradition to machines and technical know-how. The university would bring delight to the eyes of those who in the 1880s had crusaded for its birth. Initially a handful of journalists and legislative leaders, they were mostly men born on small farms who had come to know a wider world when they traveled away to college or war or moved to town in the wake of the Confederacy's defeat. In the decade of the eighties, their target was modernizing the agriculture (and the industry) of their native state—with a land-grant college as the trailblazer of reform.

The undisputed voice of the crusaders was Leonidas L. Polk, founder in 1886 of the *Progressive Farmer.* A man of considerable curiosity and enterprise, Polk had a vitality that found its way into dozens of undertakings. Born to an Anson County small planter in 1837, Polk during the next half-century was a farmer, state legislator (at the age of twenty-three), Confederate soldier, town developer, storekeeper, patent-medicine inventor, and (in 1877) the state's first commissioner of agriculture. But he saw the newspaper that he began in the mid-1880s as "my chosen lifework" and viewed his mission as persuading North Carolinians to fight rural impoverishment by substituting "solid, demonstrated *facts*" for hidebound farming habits. Whether explaining a "remedy for the staggers in hogs" or "why daughters should be taught housework," the Raleigh editor urged farmers to seek and exchange information and to try new ideas. With nearly 11,000 subscribers in 1890, the *Progressive Farmer* had the largest circulation of any newspaper in the state. When politicians dragged their feet over the creation of an agricultural college, Polk mounted a yearlong editorial campaign that was relentless, blistering, and—in 1887—triumphant.

Polk and the other advocates of progressive farm management had high hopes for the work to go on in the agricultural college's first building, Holladay Hall. Today housing the administration that presides over thousands of students and dozens of buildings, the Richardsonian Romanesque structure was erected in 1888 and later named after the school's first president. The reformers of the eighties watched with satisfaction as the first young men came from their farms to learn from agricultural experts and laboratories the latest techniques that research had revealed. Young women followed in the 1890s. They discovered in the classrooms that homemaking and nutrition were also matters for rational management and learned that the savings from home canning could purchase the comforts of an indoor commode. But the college did not simply wait passively for learners to come to Raleigh for baptism in the ways of progress. After 1900 a second generation of reformers took their message to the field through the state Agricultural Extension Service, founded in 1906, and through the county agent program. The progressives' campaign to improve soil and homes, to eradicate insects and ignorance, to encourage "Two-Armed Farming"—a balance of crops and livestock—was in full swing by 1910.

But by no means did all North Carolina farmers deal with the problem of agricultural depression through the remedies of migration or improved management. For those who joined the Farmers' Alliance in the 1880s and who met for over a decade at Alliance halls throughout the state, the best way for farmers to defend themselves was to band together—and fight. Such cooperation was not always easily enlisted. In the 1870s, an industrialist in Gaston County saw the farmer's individualism as his obstacle to prosperity. He proclaimed that "the farmers unfounded dread and hostility to coopiration [*sic*] and acting togather [*sic*] for their common good stands more in his way to wealth and usefulness than the want of capital and all other causes besides."

Those who conducted meetings in Alliance halls, who questioned speakers and debated choices, were angry. They were among 100,000 North Carolinians and 3 million Americans overall who joined a massive farmers' movement to combat the stranglehold of sinking prices and rising costs. Whatever the crop, the story was everywhere the same in the bleak eighties: "five-cent cotton, ten-cent meat." Credit charges on advances of food and supplies from furnishing merchants ran from 40 to 60 percent. Interest on bank loans, freight charges by railroads, fees for warehousemen—each expense seemed increasingly exorbitant and unaffordable, and the sum of the debts murderous. Thousands of tenants, obliged by liens on their crops to plant all their acreage in a money crop and to buy the bulk of their needs at the creditors' stores, were in virtual peonage. Thousands of landowners feared the loss of their farms and descent into "tenantry and peasantry." They were in desperate straits.

The Farmers' Alliance movement that swept out of Texas in the late 1880s offered a powerful democratic answer to despair: cooperation. Consumer and producer cooperatives, organized and run by farmers themselves, would drastically cut the cost of the middleman, would reduce credit charges from a crushing 60 percent to 2, and would allow farmers to hold crops at their own cooperative warehouses until the market price was right. Here was a chance for battered men and women who had come to look on themselves as destined only for annual economic defeat to regain control of their futures. As one Allianceman wrote, "we are going to get out of debt and be free and independent people once more."

When Alliance speakers brought the call for economic cooperation to North Carolina in 1887, the results were spectacular. The state Alliance leader reported that twenty-one North Carolina organizers were not enough. He needed a hundred. In one county there was not "an interval of five miles" that did not have an Alliance chapter. "The farmers seem like unto ripe fruit. You can gather them by the gentle shake of a bush." At the year's end he reported that there were 1,100 suballiances and 40,000 members. By 1890 membership stood at 90,000, and cooperatives were flourishing. Members could take their tobacco to Alliance warehouses in Oxford and Durham. They could buy a wide array of goods from the Alliance "State Business Agency" at Hillsborough, each item offered "at wholesale prices." Seeds, fertilizers, buggies, cookstoves, corn shellers, pianos, washing machines, guns, "Loaded Shells, etc. etc."—all were sold with the "middle man's profit" going to the farmer. As a means to family self-sufficiency, the Alliance's state agency particularly recommended the "Improved High Arm Alliance Sewing Machine"—"Our Price, $18.50, Agents Ask for $45.00"—which had "gone into all classes of homes, rich and poor" and which fearlessly "withstood the unskilled use of those formerly unaccustomed to Sewing Machines." By the early 1890s North Carolinians had Alliance tanneries, sawmills, even shoe factories. Cooperation extended to charity as well as to consumer goods, as in the case of the Alliance chapter that raised $180 to replace the horse of a "poor man with an invalid wife and six small children."

Yet something more fundamental was to occur in the Alliance halls of North Carolina and of the South than the creation of charity associations and Alliance discount stores. Members soon found themselves clashing head-on with bankers and merchants, railroads and warehousemen, none eager to sacrifice their profits to the cooperative competitors. When cooperatives and farmers' exchanges sought credit, they found it scarce and costly. But the problem was more than local or even statewide. Credit and the currency supply of the entire nation, it became evident, were in the viselike grip of the country's largest private bankers, who in the name of "sound currency" had dictated two decades of deflation and tight money. By 1890 the Farmers' Alliance was well on its way toward becoming an insurgent political party, compelled and prepared to take on the vast private interests—bankers, railroads—that held farmers in thrall and to challenge the two major parties, which seemed indifferent to their plight.

Scientific agriculture and agricultural protest were not exclusive but complementary strategies for reform. No life better illustrates their connection—and the forces that drove reformers into insurgency—than the career of Leonidas L. Polk. In 1887 the editor of the *Progressive Farmer* became head of the North Carolina Alliance. He proved as magnetic in the meeting hall as he had been persuasive with the pen. "My own father was one of thousands," a North Carolinian recalled, "who thought of Col. Polk almost as if he had been a God-given Moses to lead them out of the wilderness." Elected president of the National Alliance in 1889, he crisscrossed the country for the next three years, urging farmers from Michigan to Georgia, Kansas to the Carolinas, to trample "sectionalism under our feet" and build a great coalition for the "coming struggle."

By 1892 Polk was a transformed man. The state agricultural reformer had become the national leader of a mass democratic rebellion. In February of that year, speaking in St. Louis, he called for "the great West, the great South, and the great Northwest, to link their hands and hearts together and march to the ballot box and take possession of the government and run it in the interest of the people." He pressed for a revolution at the ballot box and was the certain presidential nominee in 1892 of the rebellious new Populist (or People's) Party. The Populist demands of 1892 were no less than extraordinary: government control of the nation's banking system and currency, national ownership of the country's railroads, publicly owned warehouses to hold the crops of farmers, and government loans and credit at an interest rate of 1 percent a year. Only Polk's sudden death at the age of fifty-five three weeks before the convention denied him the Populist nomination. But by then the Alliance movement had evolved radically from the cooperative crusade. As farm wives and daughters dispensed lemonade outside of Alliance halls throughout North Carolina and the nation, speakers held forth under a banner reading "Down with monopoly for Labor is King."

Notwithstanding the death of their leader and division in Alliance ranks over participation in politics, the Populists of North Carolina did "march to the ballot box." Throughout the decade of the 1890s they constituted an immense force for innovation in the state. The Populist entry into politics shattered the complacent indifference of the state's Democratic Party, brought the election of Populist-supported candidates for governor and United States senator, and radically transformed the legislature and the laws of the state. In the governor's race of 1892, the candidates of the state's Populist and Republican Parties won a majority of the votes cast but failed to unite. In 1894 and 1896 the Populists fused their fortunes and electoral ticket with the Republicans', and the result was a resounding victory for an unprecedented alliance that crossed party and racial lines.

Despite mutual misgivings, Populists and Republicans, white farmers and black, subordinated their suspicions to goals that they shared. The "Fusion" movement stood committed to elections open to all male voters and to balloting free of fraud — "a free vote and a fair count." The coalition stood for longer and better schooling for all the state's children, for the firm regulation of the state's railroads, for a legal interest rate of 6 percent, and for an end to the subservience of state government to business interests.

Triumph nonetheless set the stage for tragedy: a campaign of terror in 1898 that routed the coalition in the name of "White Supremacy." The hope proclaimed by the banner that bedecked the Alliance halls of 1892, "Down with Monopoly for Labor is King," was extinguished by force. The white robes used by Ku Klux Klan night riders in the 1860s gave way to the Red Shirts of new vigilantes in 1898, worn openly in the light of day. Despite the fact that whites never for a moment relinquished control of the Fusion alliance — only 8 of the Republican governor's 800 appointees were black — the incessant cry of "Negro Domination" leaped from every Democratic newspaper and stump speech. Though over half the eligible black electorate risked their safety to vote, thousands who had voted in earlier elections stayed home. Populists defected in droves to the standard of racial self-preservation. Democrats won a smashing victory, and their triumph set the stage for Populist extinction, black disfranchisement, and the reign of Jim Crow. In 1899, North Carolina began enacting segregation laws that called for the legal separation of African Americans and whites in railroad cars, neighborhoods, streetcars, theaters, restaurants, and other public facilities. In the election of 1900, white voters, by violence and intimidation of blacks, dominated the polls and passed a suffrage amendment that disfranchised most of the state's African American citizens, who would not vote again in significant numbers for several decades.

Rising farm prices in the early twentieth century, and particularly during World War I, removed much of the urgency and desperation that had fueled the farmers' movement. Even in times of greater well-being, however, some farmers experimented with cooperatives and farmers' unions to control prices and credit. A more socially responsive Democratic Party took up the Populist call for universal public education and railroad regulation, though Democratic educational expenditures in fact favored the school districts of the white and well-to-do, and though the regulatory commission worked compliantly with the railroads. Tranquility and a moment of prosperity had returned to the farms of the state by 1919, but the good times were brief. The plummeting of farm prices in 1920 set the stage for another prolonged agricultural depression, for the descent into tenancy and poverty of still more thousands of North Carolinians, and for renewed migration to the cities.

3

INDUSTRY COMES OF AGE

Seed of a Tobacco Empire

Industrialization in North Carolina was not born in the factory but on the farm. It did not begin with clanking machines and a vast hired work force but with laborious hand production by members of the family and a few helpers. A visitor to the homestead of Washington Duke in 1871 caught a glimpse of one of the great industries of the state in its infancy. Taking refuge in the Duke household from a bitter winter storm, the visitor was "hospitably taken into a room with a large open fireplace." While he thawed, he watched Duke's young daughter Mary as she sat at a table and worked. Using the light of a lamp on a day darkened by rain, she filled "little cotton bags from a pile of finely-shredded tobacco before her." When each bag was "stuffed to bursting," she drew it closed "with a sturdy string run through the top and tied it with a bow knot. From time to time she took a pen and wrote in ink 'Pro Bono Publico' on an oblong yellow label which she pasted on the filled bag of tobacco." Totally absorbed by the work, Mary Duke hardly spoke to the visitor.

Within twenty years all would be different. By then, Washington Duke and his daughter and three sons had long since moved to the nearby city of Durham, a hamlet of 250 souls in 1870 that grew to a town of thousands by the 1890s. The Dukes and their helpers, once awakened by the crow of the rooster and the glint of the rising sun, were awakened at five in the morning by the factory whistle. Machines had replaced hand manufacture, and advertising had made the Duke name known throughout the world. For thousands of North Carolinians—industrialists, workers, townspeople, farmers—the shift from home industry to mass production reshaped the way they lived.

Washington Duke might have been the last to predict in the late 1850s that he and his sons would preside over a national tobacco empire by the end of the century. A yeoman farmer with 300 acres, he scratched out a living in cotton and corn, adding a few acres of bright leaf tobacco in the 1850s. The Civil War changed Duke's life. Drafted in 1864 by the faltering Confederate army, the forty-four-year-old Duke served only a few months before capture

Washington Duke

and spent the remainder of the conflict in a federal prison. Duke was released and shipped to New Bern in 1865. After walking the 135 miles from the coast to home and arriving with 50¢ in his pocket, he discovered that some farmers in the neighborhood were buying tobacco from their neighbors at 6¢ a pound, processing it, and selling it at 60¢. He decided he had nothing to lose by trying his hand at the manufacture of tobacco.

Duke did not convert his farm to manufacturing overnight, but gradually the family homestead became an industrial plantation. Visible at the Duke Homestead and Tobacco Museum today is a small log structure comparable to that which served as the family's first "factory." In such a shed, Duke and his two young sons hand-processed 400 pounds of tobacco a day. Able in 1866 to manufacture and market 15,000 pounds of his brand, Duke converted a nearby stable into a second makeshift factory in which he produced 125,000 pounds of smoking tobacco. Wagonloads of cured and dried tobacco were brought in through its wide doors, hung from tier poles held by the rafters, and kept moist by the opening and closing of small ventilating doors in the

Washington Duke beside his early tobacco factory

attic. The factory's equipment was suited to hand production: flails, sieves, work tables, weights and scales, barrels. By the 1870s young black workers had replaced Duke's teenaged sons at hand labor. Workers flailed the leaves into granules with wooden sticks and then sifted the crumbled leaf through rapidly shaken screens. Duke's helpers and his daughter Mary packed the granulated smoking tobacco into homemade bags, and Pro Bono Publico—"For the Public Good"—was ready for sale.

Though Duke's production and sales of smoking tobacco expanded dramatically after 1866, it was clear by the early 1870s that even more remarkable growth was possible for men ambitious enough to gamble high. In 1865 nearby Durham's Station was little more than a railroad depot. By 1874 the town was not only a postwar manufacturing center—with factories, warehouses, and a railroad—but it was on the verge of challenging Richmond for tobacco supremacy. Coincidence had helped. In April 1865, while waiting near Durham for the last surrender of the Civil War, troops from both armies had foraged through the area's farms and warehouses, discovered the bright leaf smoking

tobacco, and relished it. They wrote back for more after the war. But the real secret of North Carolina's triumph in the tobacco industry was the brash aggressiveness of its new men. Julian Carr, son of a Chapel Hill merchant and co-owner of the W. T. Blackwell firm, which made Bull Durham tobacco, spent an unprecedented $300,000 a year to distribute posters and paint signs of a bulgingly virile bull from San Francisco to the Pyramids. Simultaneously, Carr

Duke Homestead, home of Washington Duke, Durham County

Label for Bull
Durham smoking
tobacco

offered and paid rewards for new mechanical inventions to increase production and cut labor costs. Triumph came in 1883 to Durham's wizard of advertising when Bull Durham's sales of 5 million pounds of smoking tobacco became
the largest in the nation. The brazenness that built Bull Durham was in the
company motto: "Let buffalo gore buffalo, and the pasture go to the strongest."

In 1874 Washington Duke made his decision. He would go for the higher
stakes and compete directly with the Bull. Duke moved to Durham and built
a new steam-powered factory near the railroad. Though the locale and the
factory were new, Duke's method of production remained traditional. A predominantly black workforce of forty adults and twenty children did the bulk
of manufacturing by hand. Constructing his personal residence directly across
from his factory, Duke essentially transferred the industrial plantation from
his homestead to the city.

Competition drove the Dukes to innovate. Despite the expanded sales of
the family's smoking tobacco, purchases were far from enough to please Washington Duke's youngest son, James Buchanan Duke. By 1880 the rugged and

Duke tobacco
factory in Durham

James B. Duke

ambitious "Buck" Duke had had enough of chasing the tail of Bull Durham. In the rivalry for the smoking tobacco market, the Duke company was "up against a stone wall." The younger Duke decided to gamble on a product that had yet to achieve widespread popularity: "I am going into the cigarette business."

Long popular in Europe, cigarettes began to catch on in the United States toward the end of the Civil War, particularly in larger cities. An alternative to chewing tobacco, cigars, and pipes, the cigarette offered a smoking stimulant suited to a fast-paced urban setting: clean, quick, potent. The manufacture of cigarettes, however, required that each cigarette be hand-rolled. Workers with rolling skills were plentiful in Europe, rare in America. So in 1881 the Dukes brought to Durham more than a hundred skilled Jewish immigrants, recent arrivals in New York, to practice and teach their trade.

Ironically, the genius of the Dukes and other manufacturers in advertising and promoting their new product soon created a demand for cigarettes that outstripped the capacity of the skilled hand-rollers. In Atlanta an enterprising Duke salesman achieved a coup when he obtained from Madame Rhea, a dazzling French actress, permission to copy a lithograph of her and to show a package of Duke cigarettes in her hand. Sales soared. Coupons for gifts and colorful trading cards soon became standard features of Duke cigarettes: purchasers

Colorful trading cards contained in Duke's cigarette packages

bought again and again to acquire their prizes and to complete their collections of scantily dressed women, presidents and monarchs, birds and beasts, flowers and fruits. The promotions paid off. Cigarette orders rose to 400,000 daily in May 1884. On "the glorious 4th" of July 1884, Duke sales reached almost 2 million.

Cigarette orders were massive, but Duke's skilled craftsmen could produce only four cigarettes a minute by hand. It was time to mechanize, and Duke gambled again. He leased two machines invented by an eighteen-year-old Virginian named James Bonsack. Plagued by imperfections, the complex machine had been tried and discarded by a leading Richmond firm in 1880. Duke and William T. O'Brien, a mechanic sent to Durham by the Bonsack Company, labored for months in 1884 to get the machine to work. They succeeded. By the end of 1884 the Bonsack machine could make 200 cigarettes a minute at less than half the cost of hand production. James B. Duke moved to New York, set up a second factory there, and relentlessly pursued his ultimate goal. "If John D. Rockefeller can do what he is doing for oil, why should I not do it in tobacco?" Able to control the leasing of the machine through his contract with Bonsack, Duke used all his power to create a monopoly in tobacco. Duke outproduced, outadvertised, and undersold his competitors. Of 253 tobacco factories in North Carolina in 1894, only 33 were left ten years later. The survivors had all become part of the American Tobacco Company, headed by James B. Duke.

Mechanization revolutionized work and the workplace. The skill and judgment of the cigarette hand-rollers were no longer needed; displaced and embittered, the immigrant craftsmen returned to New York City. The craftsmen were replaced by the Bonsack machines, each of which did the work of forty-eight skilled laborers. The sophistication of the equipment, which can be viewed today in modernized form at tours of major Piedmont factories, was a marvel to behold. Without human intervention it automatically fed the tobacco into the machine, made cigarettes faster than the eye could see, loaded the finished cigarettes onto a tray, packed them into boxes, pasted labels on the packs, and placed the packs into cartons.

So automated was the equipment by 1900 that one worker recalled, "When the work went well, we didn't do a thing!" Only a handful of skilled and highly paid mechanics was needed to repair and maintain the equipment. Others on the cigarette assembly line watched over the machine and corrected its mistakes. When a machine broke down, the worker called a mechanic to mend it. When flawed cigarettes or damaged packages were made, they were removed, taken apart, and reused.

After 1885 demand surged for operatives who could be trained quickly and employed cheaply to tend the machines. Young white men and women from the Piedmont were recruited for the task and seized the chance. Their work opportunities diminished and their marriage prospects blighted by the economic hardships of the countryside, they found in the city the chance for a fresh start and in the factory job the attraction of "making something for myself." Notwithstanding low wages for sixty-five hours a week of work, the "pay seemed like right much" to youths who were not "used to making any money, working on a farm."

Despite the cash wage, some workers were bothered by the loss of independence in the mechanized factory: the "bossing" of the foreman, the endless monotony of the work, the incessant demand to keep pace with the machine, the requirement to stand in place all day. "It aged us before our time," observed a workingwoman. Yet others thought that, despite the machines and the supervision, the tobacco factory floor remained a place of much liberty. They recalled that well into the twentieth century the company's rules were few, the rhythm of work was relaxed, and workers were free to get a drink of water or go to the toilet without first seeking permission. Of course, if you did not like it, as one worker observed, "you could always quit and go to work somewhere else." But for most, quitting was not a genuine option, partly because the wages of other workers—textile operatives and dime-store clerks—were usually lower than those of tobacco factory employees.

Many found that the companionship of fellow employees compensated for the limitations of work and wages. "It was just like a family," one woman recalled. Workers talked to each other above the noise of the machines, exchanged gripes about the foremen, sometimes even sang on the job. In one factory the workers from the entire floor brought their families together on weekends for potluck picnics. "We enjoyed it, had a good time." For other employees, company benefits made the job worthwhile. "We had a hospital, a trained nurse, and a doctor who came once a day and prescribed medicine. It was free." For the most faithful employees there were promotions to higher jobs on the factory floor and even desk jobs for those injured at work. But for many the real joy of the job was living in town. There were churches and revivals, department stores and parks, and soon streetcars and electric lights.

For black workers in the tobacco industry of the Piedmont, factory jobs had also brought a vital measure of independence. City labor provided a foothold off the farm, an escape from the grip of tenantry, release from the prospect of lifelong labor behind the south side of a northbound mule.

Mass production in the tobacco factory meant more jobs for blacks, but not better ones. Much of the work once done by black hands became mechanized, and the running of machines was reserved for whites. Left to the black employees was the arduous physical labor of preparing the tobacco leaves for the machines. The factory's leaf department was usually on a separate floor or in its own building. To prevent the drying out of the leaves, windows were often kept closed. In the hot and humid rooms, where the air was sometimes "so heavily laden with fumes and dust" that workers tied handkerchiefs over their nostrils, black women and men sorted and graded the tobacco and removed stems from the leaves. Most blacks recalled their work as hot and "sticky" labor, which bred short tempers. For "doing all the nasty dirty work," black workers were paid little. Black women received half the wages of white women "on the cigarette side" who were able to wear white uniforms on the job. Black men, who made up the gangs that hauled hogsheads of tobacco weighing 500 pounds to the machine floors, received less than half the pay of white men.

Despite the pay and privation of their labor in the tobacco factories, black workers—like white—found ways to fashion a world they could endure and enjoy. To ease the monotony and enhance the "comradeship" of work, black employees "sang all day long." A man or a woman with a gifted voice would "raise a song"—"it was always spirituals"—and the "whole floor would take up the chant." White passersby and fellow workers found the cadenced chanting "the prettiest thing you ever heard," and even the bosses "used to come out and listen" while hundreds of blacks sang as they worked. Even the insecurity of the job—many blacks were laid off when they completed the preparation of the tobacco leaves—did not diminish the attachment of blacks to their family of fellow workers. "Folks that had laid out would miss it so much until they would be up there at lunchtime." "Nobody had enough to turn anybody's head," one worker summarized. "You enjoyed folks' company more than other assets."

Even in the highly mechanized factory of the early twentieth century, many black and white workers recalled their labor as an "easy-going sort of thing." Ironically, it was the enormous success of the Dukes in tobacco—a field that they dominated by 1899—that set the stage for a pioneering venture that would hasten the end of a genial pace of work in factories throughout the state. The tobacco family took the leadership in the development of hydroelectric power in the region. With increasing wealth at their command by the 1890s, the Dukes began to diversify their investments. They first expanded into the ownership and operation of textile mills and after the turn of the century began to investigate the possibility of tapping the region's cascading rivers—her "white coal"—for industrial use. When James B. Duke asked a brilliant young engineer (and future leader of the power company Duke would form) just what a comprehensive plan of development would cost, William S. Lee answered "about $8,000,000. It was the biggest amount I had ever heard of. It seemed to attract him." Incorporated in 1905, the Southern Power Company within the next twenty years built a chain of dams and ten hydroelectric stations from Bridgewater, North Carolina, to Camden, South Carolina. The dams harnessed the entire Catawba-Wateree river system to supply energy for 300 cotton mills, as well as the cities and other factories of the Piedmont. By 1930 Duke Power—as Southern Power was rechristened—would be among the largest utility companies in the South.

With the triumph of electricity came the certainty that in a matter of time there would be further mechanization of the factory and acceleration of the pace of work.

The Mill Village

Though small-scale industries existed in North Carolina before the Civil War, not until the last quarter of the nineteenth century did manufacturing expanded dramatically. The number of cotton textile mills multiplied at a hundred per decade after 1880. By early in the twentieth century, 200,000 North Carolinians had moved off farms they had tilled for generations to seek employment in towns or factory villages. For the first time they took jobs for wages, known universally as "public work."

For many, the first public work was in a textile factory, and the first place they moved to was a mill village. Most of the early factories were located in the Piedmont, where a plenitude of rivers supplied waterpower to drive the machinery of the mills. Factory owners built entire communities in the countryside for their employees and hoped that the rural setting, "comfortable habitations," and neighborliness of village life would ease the transition from farm to factory.

Glencoe, nestled in the heart of the Piedmont, typifies these self-enclosed mill villages. Located three miles north of Burlington, it hugs a gentle stretch of the Haw River, where the original factory still stands. Though the mill ceased operations in the 1950s and though most of the homes and company buildings are no longer in use, Glencoe remains much as it was in the 1880s, when it was constructed by James and William Holt, descendants of Alamance County's antebellum textile pioneer, Edwin M. Holt. The mill produced bright and multicolored "Glencoe Plaids" and durable "Deckedout Denim." The mill building, the mill office and company stores, the two-story workers' homes, the village barbershop, and the lodge hall have survived for a century. Some of the land is now overgrown and most of the people are gone, but physically Glencoe remains a classic mill village. Other abandoned mill villages in the state are Coleridge (1882) in Randolph County and Henry River (1902) in Burke County.

The Holt family, founders of Glencoe and other mills in Alamance County, looked upon their enterprises as more than a means to make a profit. Earnings were not negligible, to be sure. By the 1890s net profits regularly exceeded 40 percent each year and made millionaires of the Holts. But the entrepreneurs who created mill villages in the New South often proclaimed their ventures to be social philanthropy. Factories would redeem the region from the blight of rural poverty and provide deliverance for white youth who might otherwise sink into the "vice of idleness." The cotton mill, they believed, would rescue whole communities from decay, spare the poorest whites from lifelong tenancy, and prevent the plunge of thousands of whites into direct competition

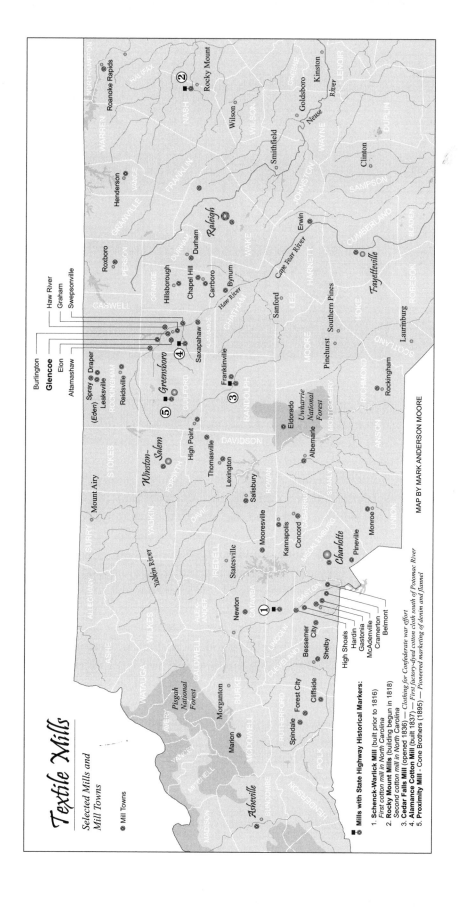

Textile Mills

Selected Mills and Mill Towns

⊛ Mill Towns

Burlington
Glencoe
Elon
Altamashaw
Haw River
Graham
Swepsonville

■ **Mills with State Highway Historical Markers:**

1. **Schenck-Warlick Mill** (built prior to 1816) —
   First cotton mill in North Carolina
2. **Rocky Mount Mills** (building begun in 1818) —
   Second cotton mill in North Carolina
3. **Cedar Falls Mill** (opened 1836) — *Clothing for Confederate war effort*
4. **Alamance Cotton Mill** (built 1837) — *First factory-dyed cotton cloth south of Potomac River*
5. **Proximity Mill** - Cone Brothers (1895) — *Pioneered marketing of denim and flannel*

MAP BY MARK ANDERSON MOORE

Workers' houses (1880s) at Glencoe mill village, Alamance County

with black tenant farmers. All-white mills offered "an escape from competition with blacks" and the means for the moral and material reclamation of the state. It was no wonder that at a revival meeting in Salisbury a preacher holding forth on the plight of the poor declared that the "establishment of a cotton mill would be the most Christian act his hearers could perform." It was in the same spirit that another minister, presiding over the dedication of a new mill in Concord in 1882, celebrated the "roar of the machinery" as "work's anthem to the Lord" and blessed the "smoke from the chimney" as "daily incense to God."

But work alone would not redeem the state or save its indigent from "savagery." Factory owners with a sense of mission sought to create good neighborhoods and well-regulated Christian communities. They attempted to do so, at other mill villages, through paternalism. Paternalism involved in part the physical facilities of the village. At Glencoe the company provided the Union Church, which served Methodists on Sunday mornings and Baptists in the afternoons. The church building survived until 1976, when it collapsed in a winter storm. A school and a village baseball field were added later at Glencoe; in larger mill villages company libraries, company-sponsored flower gardens, and company auditoriums for entertainment were built to enhance the wholesomeness of the community.

More important to the moral management of the village was the direct interest of the owner in his family of employees. At Glencoe, Robert Holt, son

Women found work in the new textile mills.

of the founder, lived in the village. He know all the employees and their children by name. Despite Holt's wealth and authority, he seemed "just like one of us," a resident recalled. In other mill villages, owners dispensed paternal gifts. One saw to it that all his female workers received a parasol at Christmas—which he delivered personally from house to house—and chartered a private train for picnic outings on the Fourth of July. Others shared wood or coal with employees in the event of a harsh winter.

But paternalism involved more than gestures of generosity. It also meant control and intrusion. In several villages the patriarch roamed the village at night to make certain that lights were out by 10:00 P.M. He evicted people who misbehaved and brooked no challenge from "his" people in "his" village. In return for benevolence, the owner expected and often received the loyalty of his employees: a faith that the company would take care of its family of workers and do right by them. Loyalty often diminished the demand for wage increases, as did the custom of renting workers' homes for a dollar a week and providing many village services "free." Few factory owners saw themselves as padding their profits through paternalism. In their view the hard work they required and the moral supervision they provided built character. Employees who labored like the devil were on the road to heaven.

For those who came to Glencoe and to the hundreds of other mill hills that mushroomed in the Carolina Piedmont, the village provided a place of transition to factory life. For many, the change proved relatively easy. Some moved only a short distance from their rural homes. They came with their family or migrated to a community where an older sister or brother was already employed and had recruited them for factory work. To farm people who had worked from sunup to sundown, a dozen hours of factory work a day, six days a week, did not necessarily seem novel or outrageous. Glencoe children—like farm children—began part-time work by age ten. At twelve they went full-time and left school forever. Until the first part of the twentieth century, the factory day—like the country day—offered slack time for breaks or sociability. Children who got "caught up" in their work might play outside for twenty minutes in a kind of factory recess; adults could talk while tending the less noisy machines. Unlike the steel factories of Pittsburgh or Birmingham, the Piedmont textile mill and its village remained physically a part of the country. Many companies provided enough land for families to have a garden plot of their own and grass for a cow. Nearby forests remained a hunter's haven for workingmen and their hound dogs.

Yet the transition from farm to mill village was by no means easy for all. For some—especially children—the adjustment to factory work could be sudden and startling. The whirring and deafening din of the machinery frightened many a novice. One woman recalled that she "fled from the room" with her superintendent in hot pursuit. For children the shock came at the end of the first week's work, with the payment of wages that amounted to 12½¢ a day. "I came home to my momma and I cried," remembered a retired workingman. Nothing on the farm prepared mill workers for the cotton dust of the spinning room, which a Glencoe worker described as "just like a fog." Nor was it easy to adjust to the intense, humid heat of the factory, where moisture was needed to keep cotton fibers from breaking. "You just sweated it out, that's the whole thing there was to it."

Ultimately, many at Glencoe and other textile mills overcame the fear of machinery and factory noise and endured the discomfort of humidity and heat. But did they also accept other circumstances that had become characteristic of mill village life by 1900—low pay, repetitive work, unchallenged owner control—as conditions that had to be borne with resignation and "just sweated out"? A retired worker remembered that in his Glencoe Mill days people thought themselves lucky to be working and to have "food on the table, clothes on their back, and a roof over their head." Were such workers, as textile employers frequently claimed, not only the "cheapest labor market in the United States," but "tractable, harmonious, and satisfied with little," workers who gladly permitted their paternalistic employers "to take care of them" like "children"?

There was much evidence of "adjustment." Having come from a countryside where farms were failing and where women especially were becoming surplus labor, many were simply "glad to be working." Once in the factory, workers took immense pride in their work and in their ability to manage the tasks they were assigned. In the early days of factories, an individual tended the same machines every day. It was not unusual for a worker to talk to the machinery, to cajole it, to give it a whack on bad days and praise it on good. For those who tired of the sameness of the work, there was the chance to move around among different jobs at the plant, from doffer to slubber to spinner. Some rose to the supervisory post of foreman, though the distastefulness of pressuring friends and family to speed their work discouraged many from seeking to manage others. An union organizer said of his years in factory work: "I like the farm better than the factory any day but on a farm you just work yourself to a frazzle and don't get a thing for it."

For most who chose to stay at Glencoe and other mill villages, however, it was not so much the rewards of work as it was the familial and neighborly nature of the village that rooted them in place for a lifetime. Many who lived in the community were kin by blood or marriage, and kinship proved important in getting jobs for the young or in taking care of family members when trouble came. One did not have to be blood kin to share the bounty of plenty and the burdens of want. The rule in Glencoe, one workingwoman recalled, was that in good times, "if one's got anything, they divide it," and in hard times, "your trouble's my trouble." Zelma Murray, another Glencoe worker, recalled that "it used to be that everybody that lived here were kin people. . . . The superintendent, he was my uncle, he married my father's sister. . . . They were all related some way or another. It might not be close, but most of them were, you know, some kind of an uncle or aunt or some kind of a cousin or something along that line."

Mill owners found it in their interest to reinforce the bonds of family in the village. Women with young children who wanted to look after their infants might be given piecework that they could do at home, either by hand or with a small machine lent by the company. Because most women had to work full-time—a husband's income was rarely enough to support his family—the company accommodated mothers by permitting them to walk home at midday to feed their family lunch and by allowing them to leave work an hour early in the afternoon to prepare supper. Ethel Faucette looked back happily to her first factory job. "I made eighty-five cents a day," she boasted. But Zelma Murray described the spinning room where she worked as "awful linty." Mill owners used their power as well as their flexibility to give paternal support to the workers' families. They sponsored Sunday schools for the young, penalized severely men who were found drunk, evicted the families of girls who went astray morally, and encouraged foremen to take a "heartfelt interest" in the home lives of employees. More than a few workers recalled such paternal owners with gratitude and affection. "He was our Daddy." "We loved him."

But the familial closeness of the factory employees did not always work to the advantage of the owners or incline the operatives to be "tractable and harmonious." Factory managers anxious to experiment with new methods to spur production complained of the obstructive clannishness of their workers. Employees preferred to "make do" and stick together rather than speed up and compete for higher output and pay. More inclined to "act under clannish impulses" than to submit to the "common sense" of the mill manager, workers "kicked" and "grumbled" and "agitated" when supervisors sought to get strict and impose tighter controls on the job. Complaining of a "great lack of gratitude," managers "reluctantly came to the conclusion that the less employees are interfered with the more content they are." Leaving "employees strictly alone, giving advice only when they ask for it"—"which is very seldom"—management permitted the workers to impose a relaxed pace and neighborly atmosphere on the shop floor.

Eleven or twelve hours of work a day went differently when workers set their own pace. "It was just like a family operation," recalled one woman. "You had time to fraternize with your fellow workers. You could get up when you had to, sit down when you wanted to." Textile factories required long hours, reflected another worker, "but it was no pressure. When you're working under pressure, it's killing you all the time. We were more like just one big happy family."

Yet for all its expediency—as a racial and economic stopgap for destitute rural whites, as a setting that eased the transition form farm to factory, as a place where family-oriented North Carolinians could resettle in neighborhoods of kin and their own kind—the services of the mill and mill village came at a high price. From the very first, mill owners pledged to prospective investors that "long hours of labor and moderate wages will continue to be the rule for many years to come." From the first, they paid wages so low—20¢ a day for bobbin boys, 50¢ a day for spinners, 75¢ a day for weavers—that the entire family was obliged to work in the mills so that they might eat. In 1910 North Carolina textile workers labored ten hours longer each week for 40 percent less than their counterparts in the cotton mills of New England. Under the "family wage" system, the labor of children for the full seventy-hour work week was virtually mandatory. Child labor and low wages took their toll: in illiteracy, in diet and disease, in bodies made "haggard" by prolonged toil from an early age. The separate identity of the mill village was a matter of pride to some. "They provided for us. We had the best ball fields, the best-dressed ball team. We were the envy" of everyone around. But for others the bleakness and insularity of the village set its residents apart as a distinct caste—"cotton mill folk" and "lintheads"—who were increasingly isolated and socially shunned.

Despite the attempts of the company to create a secure world in the mill village—secure workers, secure families, secure profits—and despite its promise to investors that the "hardy native Anglo-Saxon stock" had "no disposition to strike," there were in fact recurrent symptoms of unrest. Uncertain employment was a chronic difficulty in the 1880s, when a mid-decade depression forced mills to cut production and wages. In response, numbers of Piedmont mill hands affiliated for the first time with a union, the Knights of Labor. They demanded restoration of their wages, reduction of the workweek to sixty-six hours, curbs on child labor, safety inspections, and the creation of a state bureau of labor. They nominated their own candidates for state and local offices. The labor ticket almost won in Alamance County against a slate that included several members of the Holt family and briefly succeeded in Durham and Wake Counties with the election of the Knights' Master Workman to the state Assembly. Alamance mill owner Thomas Holt, who was speaker of the house in 1885 and an aspirant to higher office, responded to the labor groundswell by advocating a state law to limit work to sixty-six hours a week. When the bill failed, he voluntarily cut hours in his own factories—and in 1888 he was elected lieutenant governor as the "workers' friend."

Other mill owners, however, dismissed complaints about work conditions and even claimed that their workers did not want to be harassed by labor reformers. A bill to stop night work prompted J. G. Ragsdale of Oakdale Cotton Mills, in Jamestown, to write in 1895 to Thomas Settle Jr., his representative in Congress. "I have hands," he proclaimed, "from the Reidsville Cotton Mills and from the Greensboro Cotton Mills (both broke and stopped) who came and asked for night work—I went to the expense of Several Thousand Dollars to build houses for them to live in and started a night force who are doing well and well satisfied—work 5 nights a week. My hands unanimously ask that we be not interfered with."

Despite extraordinary success in mobilizing three-quarters of a million workers in the nation and thousands throughout the South in the mid-1880s, the Knights of Labor lost its gains by the end of the decade. But the aspirations expressed in the union's very name—*Knights of Labor*—found new ways to flourish in the 1890s. At a time when mechanized factory work and public contempt threatened to degrade manual labor, the Knights had reaffirmed the dignity and "nobility" of human toil. "God was not less because He worked; neither are men." At a time when massive combinations of capital and chronic economic uncertainty rendered individual self-reliance pitifully inadequate as a means of self-protection, the Knights advocated cooperation among workers. Like other organizations that won millions of adherents in the 1880s and 1890s, such as the Farmers' Alliance and black mutual benefit societies, the Knights crusaded for collective action and mutual aid as indispensable means for working people to achieve self-help and reclaim self-respect.

Partly as a result of Knights of Labor agitation, mill owners of the 1890s were ever alert to stirrings of independence by their workers. As they feared, even in small and paternalistic villages such as Glencoe, there were omens of employee autonomy. In 1896, seeking to make their wages go further, Glencoe's inhabitants deserted the community's company store in favor of merchants miles away who charged a third less for flour, meat, and coal. The mill owner responded with a masterful appeal to company loyalty. Flyers posted all over the village read: "I cannot live without you, or some others like you, and you cannot live without me, or someone like me. Our interests are therefore mutual and the more I make, the better wage I can pay you. You should do what you can to help me."

Notwithstanding such appeals to loyalty, textile unions reemerged in the state in 1900. The failure of owners to share with wage earners the immense textile profits of 60 percent during the previous year had made the "hardy Anglo-Saxons" of Alamance and other counties receptive to union membership, and hundreds joined. When continued high production glutted the textile market in September 1900 and prompted the Southern Cotton Spinners Association to announce that it would hold the line on prices by curtailing production 40 percent, mistrust of the mill owners and anxiety over impending layoffs reigned in the mills. And yet, in their appeals for membership, union organizers did not press for higher wages or fewer hours. Instead, like the Knights of Labor before them, they urged workers to unionize so as to break their dependency on company goodwill. To "organize themselves for mutual benefit," to "help one another," would be the first step toward regaining their independence as "free men and free women."

It was fitting—and prophetic of the decades ahead—that when protest flared in the fall of 1900, its focus was worker independence. When an unpopular foreman of the Haw River Mill challenged a woman weaver for too many trips away from her machine, she defiantly responded that she "would go when she pleased and where she pleased." He fired her on the spot and instructed another woman, described by co-workers as a "powerless orphan," to take her place. Workers in the factory swarmed around the machine, insisted that the foreman had been "rude and unjust," and pressed the young girl to refuse the command. Unable to choose between her job and her fellow workers, she wept. That night the union met, agreed to defy the foreman the next day, and "threw up the machines" when the foreman reissued the order in the morning. Within an hour, the owners shut down the other mills in town.

Workers, mill owners, and editorial writers all recognized the textile industry and the state had reached a historic crossroad. The mill owners, conveniently overstocked with surplus goods, refused to confer with a committee of the labor union. To "yield to such demands" would "be to give up entire control of the management of the mill on the part of the owners." They posted armed guards around the mills of the county, declared they would operate only with nonunion labor, and ordered all union workers to vacate their company houses. Union membership promptly soared into the thousands, and the scope of the dispute broadened beyond the issue of employee "liberty" on the shop floor. Did workers and owners, both "citizens of a common country," have an equal right to organize on their own behalf? Could textile workers continued to endure child labor, which mortgaged the futures of the young and eroded the security of the adult?

The union lost, and the workers' reaction to defeat set a pattern for decades to come. Hundreds of "union mill operatives" left the state for South Carolina and Georgia. "Among them," reported the *Alamance Gleaner*, "are a great many excellent people who prefer to go elsewhere rather than surrender rights and privileges which they as citizens deem they should own and enjoy." For the next generation, departure became the textile worker's alternative to acquiescence or protest. Employer complaints of worker "restlessness" grew increasingly shrill; plant managers wrote in despair that their hands were working only four days a week and left on the slightest pretext. Unwittingly the owners themselves had created the conditions that spawned the most nomadic workforce in the nation. They chose to invest their profits in the construction of new mills, and the building boom created a labor shortage. Dissatisfied workers, though unable to organize to improve their lot, "didn't have any trouble in getting a job." "If they'd see something they didn't like, all they'd do was haul off and quit, move to the next town, and have a job and a company house, too." As one worker recalled of the early twentieth century, "there was a lot of people moving around in those days." Whatever it expressed—ambition, discontent, "a desire to wander"—the turbulent army of floaters reached almost 40 percent of the textile workforce by 1910. The Cone brothers' Proximity Mill (built 1898) offered these incentives to textile workers in 1915:

Mill Runs 60 Hours Per Week
Stops At Noon Saturday
Pays Off 8th and 23rd Of Each Month
Deep Well Drinking Water Pumped Through Mill
Have Modern Village: Streets And Houses Are Lighted With Electricity;
15-Minute Street Car Service To Any Part Of the City Of Greensboro;
Good Graded Schools Nine Months Of Each Year, Best of Teachers Are Employed.
The Health of The People Is Our First Consideration.

The outbreak of world war in 1914 made more acute than ever the need for a productive and stable textile workforce. The war brought a surge in demand for factory goods and—because of a standstill in immigration from Europe—a nationwide shortage of labor. To increase productivity, some North Carolina employers experimented with new methods of "scientific" management, hiring northern superintendents and establishing personnel and cost departments. But many workers resented the "non-productive departments" that siphoned off dollars from their wages, and employers discovered that Yankees had "no idea how to manage Southern workmen." The alternative approach through 1920 was a redoubled employer campaign for "family" loyalty and worker pride. Mill villages were remodeled and modernized. Superintendents and foremen were "picked from the ranks," chosen because they had a "happy way of getting on with people." Often they had "grown up with the people" they oversaw. Revealingly, in the World War I era, workers often referred to their supervisor as "my Uncle." The "Uncle" understood his men, shared their sense of play and fair play, let them out for circuses and fairs, managed their baseball team with enthusiasm and a common love of the sport, and might also be the best fiddler in the factory. His success came not because he was and "order giver" but "because he knows the people and the work; he is part of the family."

The boom in wartime production of textiles brought an increase in wages and a surge in the aspirations of the state's textile workers. A Greensboro reporter witnessed a scene that seemed to capture the mood of 1920. A mill village couple and their three children stood in front of a Greensboro store window, looking in at a display of silks cascading to the floor. As the woman gazed through the plate glass, "inspecting rich brocades woven for mistresses of empire and broad seas," the reporter detected the "gleam in her eyes." A gleam was all there would be, however. The postwar downturn in demand brought a cut in wages of almost 50 percent, a wave of unsuccessful strikes against the cut, and a return to the patterns of the previous half-century. The year 1929 would bring a decade of renewed struggle to change the status quo, but until and even well after that year the mill and mill village remained largely a place where working people labored for family security that could no longer be found on the farm, compelled to leave the brocades of the New South for others. "I'll never walk no streets of gold here," one woman textile worker concluded, but her consolation was faith. "The Lord is preparing me a place. If I don't get no mansion, I'll get me a place. I can walk the streets of gold up there."

A Railroad Fan's Dream

From its opening in 1896 until the middle of the twentieth century, Spencer Shops—in the words of one of its admirers—was a "railroad fan's

Interior Machine Building.   SPENCER, N. C.

dream come true." Located in the Piedmont just two and a half miles northeast of Salisbury—and now operated as the North Carolina Transportation Museum—Spencer Shops was the massive central repair facility of the Southern Railway Company. The excitement and importance of the site has even been preserved in a popular folksong describing the wreck of *Old '97*, near Danville, Virginia, in 1908:

> They handed him his orders at Monroe, Virginia,
> Sayin': 'Pete, you're way behind time.
> This is not Thirty-eight, but it's old Ninety-seven;
> You must put 'er in Spencer on time!'

Southern Railway's thousands of cars and hundreds of locomotives rumbled over 8,500 miles of track that spanned the region from Washington to Atlanta, Charleston to Knoxville, and westward to Birmingham and the banks of the Mississippi River. Crowded into Spencer's 168 acres were locomotives

Unidentified railroad accident

by the scores bustling over miles of yard tracks, an immense roundhouse and turntable, and a five-story Back Shop filled with huge cranes and winches.

The small army of laborers who built Spencer Shops in six months turned open forest and farmland into a clanging workshop that knew no rest. The sights and sounds were those of energies that had brought world supremacy to the heavy industry of America by 1900. Oil, steam, and electricity, the welding of metal and the clanging of hammer. So the shops throbbed as workmen took tired equipment, slicked it up, and returned it renewed to the rails. A panorama of raw energy and engineering efficiency, Spencer was a sooty spectacle of the New South.

From the sheer power concentrated at Spencer one could understand why the railroad fired the imagination of Carolinians and other Americans throughout the nineteenth century and into the next. Few saw the locomotive as a smoke-belching monster that disrupted the calm of the countryside. On

the contrary, the speed and energy of the railroad held out to every hamlet the
promise of growth—outlets to markets, links to centers of credit, conduits to
supplies, and news from everywhere in the nation. Towns saw in tracks avenues
to greatness, entrepreneurs envisioned iron highways to fortune, and children
heard in steam whistles the call of travel and excitement. Especially in a state
struggling in the 1870s and 1880s for its rightful share of the wealth of industrializing America, railroads meant progress, profit, and the promise of a
better day.

By the time Spencer Shops opened in the late 1890s, railroads in North
Carolina and in the South had come of age. The expansion had not been easy.
A half-century before, North Carolina had struggled to complete even a few
hundred miles of track to connect Wilmington and Weldon on the east coast
and to link the Piedmont towns of Goldsboro, Raleigh, Greensboro, and Charlotte from east to west. In the fifteen years following the Civil War, despite the
sale of the state-owned North Carolina Railroad to the larger Richmond and
Danville line, little of the private capital needed for expansion could be found

Aberdeen and
Rockfish Railroad,
a short line that
ran through the
Sandhills of North
Carolina, 1898

in the state or lured from outside. But between 1880 and 1890 investment poured into North Carolina, and railroad mileage more than doubled.

As railroads crisscrossed the state, pounded into reality by "gangs of sweating blacks and whites who cut and graded and bridged their way" across the Piedmont and the Appalachians, the hopes of many Carolina towns and individuals were realized. Not the least of those fantasies was that of John Steele Henderson, who received advance word in 1895 of the plans of the Southern Railway to build a repair facility near Salisbury and persuaded the rail trust to locate the shops on land he owned or promptly bought up from black farmers. As his wife wrote their daughter, "Mr. H—— is selling a small amount of his land for the shops proper and that at a mere nominal price, but the great advantage is that his land surrounds all this spot." A "town of several thousand inhabitants is obliged to spring up right there." When the secret got out, the people of Salisbury shared in the landowner's excitement. There was "great talk of electric lights or of extending Main Street out to the Shops or having electric cars." The delight of one citizen kept him "drunk for two days." Townspeople had "very little money," Mrs. Henderson reported, but "great expectations."

In full operation by the turn of the century, Spencer Shops was a victory for

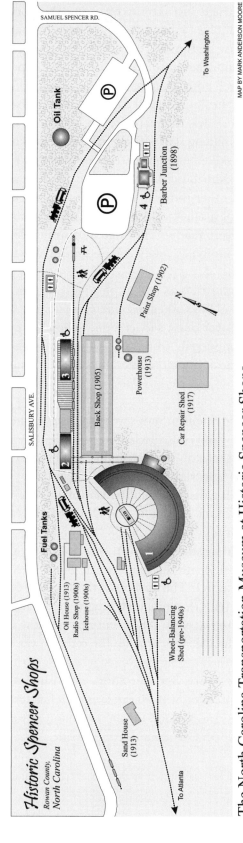

Historic Spencer Shops
Rowan County,
North Carolina

SAMUEL SPENCER RD.

SALISBURY AVE.

Oil Tank

Barber Junction
(1898)

Paint Shop (1902)

Back Shop (1905)

Powerhouse
(1913)

Car Repair Shed
(1917)

Wheel-Balancing
Shed (pre-1940s)

Oil House (1913)
Radio Shop (1900s)
Icehouse (1900s)

Fuel Tanks

Sand House
(1913)

To Washington

To Atlanta

N

MAP BY MARK ANDERSON MOORE

🚂 Train Ride Route

🚻 Public Rest Rooms

Ⓟ Parking

♿ Handicapped Accessibility

🎑 Picnic Area

- - - - Visitor Walking Paths

– · · – Visitor Shuttle Service

The North Carolina Transportation Museum at Historic Spencer Shops

▦ Facilities Open to the Public:

1. **Robert Julian Roundhouse (1924)**
   Railroading exhibits and rolling stock displays.

2. **Flue Shop (1924)**
   Bumper to Bumper Exhibit — A century of automobiles.

3. **Master Mechanic's Office (1911)**
   Wagons, Wheels, and Wings Exhibit — A history of North Carolina transportation
   from Indian canoes to airplanes.
   Slide program, gift station, administrative offices.

4. **Barber Junction (1898)**
   Information and train ride boarding.

the values of the industrialized age. Just as trains ran round the clock, so the repair shops operated day and night. Light and energy came continuously from the nearby electric powerhouse. In the still competitive railway industry of the early twentieth century, reliability and promptness remained imperative, and the Spencer workforce supplied both. Despite the large amount of equipment sent for repair—by the 1930s the figure reached seventy locomotives and forty freight and passenger cars per day—the mechanics of the shops developed a national reputation for the unfailing skill and speed of their workmanship. To minimize the turnover of its skilled employees, the company sold homes and house lots at a low profit and contributed annually toward the operation of the town's churches and YMCA. Luther Burch, a retired railroad worker, remembered that one of the duties of his first job was to wake up the train crews and engineers when their trains were ready. "They had a boarding house over in East Spencer called the Red Onion . . . they had about thirty to forty rooms I'd imagine," declared Burch.

But railroad tracks brought trials as well as blessings. As ever larger corporations bought local railroad lines and consolidated them, the state and its citizens surrendered control over rates, services, and schedules to outsiders. Customers might benefit temporarily from rate-cutting wars and from the competitive duplication of tracks, but more often they found themselves without recourse when railway firms resorted to rate fixing and mergers to curtail "cutthroat" competition.

The Southern Railway and Spencer Shops were themselves the result of a successful effort to consolidate and control a bankrupt earlier line. The predecessor line had overbuilt and nakedly plundered its stockholders during the railroad boom of the 1880s. Incorporated in 1894, the Southern was ruled by a Georgia-born engineer, with a degree from the University of Virginia, who in the eighties was president of the Baltimore and Ohio (B&O) Railroad. But the Georgian—Samuel Spencer—had left the B&O in 1889 to join the New York banking house of J. P. Morgan. It was from New York that Morgan and Spencer made the decision to locate the line's repair shops in North Carolina—and all other decisions as well. The farmers of the Tar Heel State, first to feel the squeeze of rates they felt discriminatory, fought successfully for a railroad regulatory commission in the early 1880s. But not until the first decade of the next century, when urban leaders took up the reform, was an effective commission created.

Well into the twentieth century, Spencer Shops flourished as a double-edged emblem of power. It pulsated with the new energies that the railroad had released within the state. And it stood for the profound power of corporations to shape the fate of North Carolinians from outside.

THE URBAN MAGNET

The late nineteenth century was the age of the metropolis in the United States. Great cities emerged in the Northeast, along the Great Lakes, and in the Far West. The population of cities exploded, enlarged in part by the natural increase of large urban families and swollen enormously by massive migrations from rural America and from Europe. Ethnic enclaves emerged and class disparities widened as the metropolis spawned both dense slums and astonishing fortunes. For better and for worse, the urban centers of the nation became meccas for millions.

But no North Carolina city joined in the mushrooming of the nation's metropolises. There were only six towns with populations over 10,000 at the turn of the century, and the state's largest city in 1920 had just over 30,000 souls. Yet, during the fifty years after 1920, a steady evolution and cumulative change was evident. Towns and small cities became magnets for the ambitious and the restless, as well as havens of hope for those forced off the land by rural poverty. Decade by decade, more North Carolinians made town their home: one in twenty-five in 1870, one in ten in 1900, one in four by 1930.

Of course, there were small towns in North Carolina before 1870, but not all were to expand after the Civil War. Absolutely essential for growth was a railroad line. Then a town might add tobacco factories, as did Durham and Winston, or become a center of the textile industry, as did Greensboro and Charlotte. With a railroad connection, Tarboro, in Edgecombe County, could expand as a marketing center for cotton and tobacco, and Hamlet, in Richmond County, could become a flourishing junction for passengers of the Seaboard Railroad Line. A variety of railroad stations or depots from the period remain. They include those at Tarboro (1908); Hamlet (1900); Thomasville (1870), in Davidson County; and Washington (1904), in Beaufort County.

Yet, while the luck of location and a railroad line were factors in deciding whether or not a town got ahead, so were pluck and energy. At least so thought a native North Carolinian who traveled the state in 1884. Walter Hines Page, who would later go on to become the editor of the *Atlantic Monthly* and American ambassador to Britain during World War I, thought that there were two types of Tar Heel towns in the 1880s. Some remained in the grip of the past, their sleepy tone and leisurely habits set by former planters. In such languishing villages, there was "little animation in man or beast. The very dogs look lazy." Other towns were hubs of enterprise, with reputations for business and energy. They sported "no professional talkers and habitual loafers." It was in these go-ahead towns, which were smaller in scale but identical in ambition to the dynamic cities of the North and the Midwest, that money was pursued without shame, that idleness was scorned, and that the ideology of progress took root.

The Call of the City

The career of George Black illustrates the difference a town could make in the life of a young man. The mud-daubed timber of a log cabin in Randolph County and the sun-dried bricks of the sidewalks of restored Old Salem appear to have nothing in common. But they share something vital: the skills and drive of a family that moved from country to city.

George Black's grandmother and his father were slaves. After emancipation his father acquired five acres of land on his former master's plantation, built his own cabin, and began a free life for his growing family. As a home for two parents, a grandmother, and four boys who shared the same rope bed, it was crowded. Everyone in the household worked. Black's pipe-smoking grandmother, who would live to the age of 117, did laundry for white families. His father raised wheat and cut cords of timber that he sold for firewood. Typically, the Black family could not spare its children for education. Enrolled in the cramped African American school for what seemed like only a few months—long enough to learn his alphabet—George Black was called back to labor in the fields. What life would have held for him had George Black and his family stayed on the farm is uncertain.

But chance brought George Black and his family to Winston and fused their fates with the bricks that built the city. His father walked to Winston in 1889 to bring back George Black's half brother, who had moved earlier to the town and started to "run wild." A brickmaker offered work to the father and his two sons, and he accepted. But he did not return to Winston until winter, and then discovered that brickmaking was a seasonal trade and that the kiln was closed until spring. City blacks mocked the farmer's ignorance, but he stayed and brought his family to town. In 1890 George Black's father died, but the family remained. Eleven people lived in their one-room rented tenement, and all who could worked. George and his brother Will took jobs hauling bricks at 25¢ a thousand. Their daily journeys began at the mud-mill, where the bricks were made in molds, and dozens of times a day they carried the molds to pallets to dry.

One day George Black told his brother: "They can pay us pretty good money, we do the work, and they make more money than we make. How come we can't make brick and get it all?" His brother doubted that white people would buy brick from African Americans. Undaunted, George Black "slipped out and built a brickyard to myself. When I got off work, I'd go work in my brickyard." Customers bought all he could make, and, after selling 100,000, he went into business for himself full time. George Black's own children helped him as soon as they grew old enough, just as he had helped his father on their Randolph County farm. The quality of Black's work was first-rate. All the bricks in the sidewalks in Old Salem, as well as those of its market firehouse, are his. His energy became legendary: he regularly made 7,000 bricks a day.

Town life had unleashed the energy of George Black. In Winston he acquired a marketable skill, started a business, prospered, and won admiration. Said this son of a slave to his brother: "I told you if we made men out of ourselves people would call us Mr. Black."

Main Street

A vigorous middle class prospered in North Carolina's towns and created and supported a diverse array of stores and services. Carolinians who once had bartered for their goods at the antebellum gristmill or who had traded for necessities at the postwar country store, now had new options. At the Briggs Hardware Store in downtown Raleigh, for example, the customer found everything in the hardware line. A large sign and tantalizing wares at the entrance drew the shopper into T. H. Briggs's four-story red-brick store, which in 1874 was "the tallest building in East Carolina and Raleigh's first skyscraper." Buyers might gossip for a few minutes and warm themselves by the stove, but there was rarely the marathon of talking that characterized the country store. The order was placed, service was prompt, the purchase was made. Part of the pleasure in the high-ceilinged store, with its skylight letting in shafts of sunshine from above, was watching the clerk roll the wooden ladder to just the right place, climb high, and pluck down the merchandise in the quantity desired. Even though it was a store of staples, Briggs—like most enterprising merchants— always stocked the new and the novel and invited his customers to try "the latest." A Briggs advertisement in 1877 listed, among it wares, builders' supplies, house furnishing goods, stoves, ranges, sporting goods, guns, paints, oils, varnishes, and wagon and buggy materials.

Just as Briggs offered his Raleigh buyers both the novel and the basic, so

*Briggs Hardware Store (1874),
Raleigh*

the town drugstore offered an array of the essential and the newfangled. Often the drugstore was an elegant little emporium, such as Fordham's of Greensboro. With its marble counters, gilded mirrors, and elaborate iron grillwork, Fordham's doubled as an ice-cream parlor. Frequently, it attracted ladies who dressed fashionably for the occasion of an afternoon chocolate sundae. Fordham's main business was medical nostrums, some to cope with timeless maladies, others to alleviate ailments accentuated by life in the town. "Hall's Hair Renewer" promised to thicken "The Growth of the Hair" and to retard baldness. Lydia Pinkham's Vegetable Compound—21 percent alcohol—offered the "ultimate remedy for female complaints." Remedies for dyspepsia abounded.

Drugstore proprietors frequently were more than passive dispensers of prebottled elixirs. Some invented stimulants and cures of their own. In 1896 New Bern pharmacist Caleb Bradham devised the formula for a revitalizing soft drink and gave the world Pepsi-Cola. In turn-of-the-century Durham, where young blades felled by hangovers staggered to the drugstore of Germain Bernard, they obtained relief that "worked in minutes." When Commodore Thomas Council put up the capital to market Bernard's remedy nationwide, customers everywhere could buy BC Powder. Salisbury druggist Tom Stanback invented his patent medicine in 1911, and sufferers have since been able to "Snap Back with Stanback." The Vick Chemical Company of Greensboro was the creation of Lunsford Richardson, a Davidson College graduate, who began as a self-taught pharmacist. In 1912, he developed Vick's Vaporub, a product that the 1918 influenza epidemic made a household word.

Even in smaller hamlets, where there was no great gusto for becoming the next Chicago, one could find a lively passion for growth. Towns such as Henderson and Tarboro became meeting points between the local rural world and a wider urban one. The ambitious young man who wanted to live in a community with a courthouse square, a newspaper, at least one drugstore, two doctors, and several banks could find himself a delightful town without difficulty and flourish there. He might come to Oxford and enter business on College Street—still a perfectly charming townscape of turn-of-the-century America. Or he might, as did A. C. Zollicoffer in 1882, go to Henderson.

A. C. Zollicoffer moved from Halifax County to Henderson at the age of twenty-eight to open up a law practice and soon hung his shingle on the small Main Street office that has remained in the family for three generations. Much of his practice focused on the usual staple of the law—deeds and defaults, battery and bankruptcy—and he spent as many hours with red, leather-bound, oversized mortgage books as he did palavering in his office with clients. Zollicoffer's comfortable and habitable office, and his reputation as an attorney who could skillfully litigate a suit but who preferred to negotiate a settlement, won him loyal clients over the years. It was a measure of the lawyer's standing and the community's enterprise that he also represented the town's largest corporations: its textile mill, bagging company, and biggest bank.

Many middle-class residents of modest towns were like Zollicoffer. Not out to make a fortune, they practiced their professions or trades and led a full life in a small place. The most successful families enjoyed ownership of "beautiful residences," with "houses set back in tremendous yards, some of them full

*Zollicoffer's Law Office (1887),
Henderson*

of great magnolias and evergreen trees." For ladies there were afternoon teas and Wednesday meetings of the literary society. The pleasures of daily sociability, the barbs of local gossip, sheltered innocence and Gothic intrigue— small-town life looked uneventful only to the outsider. The high point of the week usually came each Friday night and Saturday, when a full tide of humanity swept in from the surrounding area and filled Main Street with customers and peddlers, carriages and wagons.

Town growth made possible a burst of civic enterprise. The new courthouse at Statesville, built in 1889 after the old one had burned, was massive and solid and mirrored the pride of the town. Courthouses at Monroe, in Union County (1886), and Hayesville, in Clay County (1888), are similarly indicative of the late Victorian era. More than a monument, the new courthouse provided an organic center of town life. Before and after transacting civic business, people met and chatted on the courthouse lawn and sat and gossiped on the hallway benches. The town hall of Apex, in Wake County, built in 1912, marked the growth to 500 residents of a locale that got its name in 1873 for being reputedly the highest point on the railroad run between Norfolk and Sanford. The town government made the most of its new municipal building. The first floor served as a farmers' market, with two rooms given over to fruit and vegetable bins and four designated as butcher shops. A first-floor room measuring sixteen feet square was set aside as the jail, divided into one cell for each race. (Members of the Baldwin Gang, notorious bootleggers who operated out of Apex after state prohibition passed in 1907, spent little time in the jail.) The mayor's office on the upper story stood alone in the front corner of the building, while the remainder of the second floor housed the town theater, with an ample stage, side dressing rooms, and "opera seats" for the audience.

Town growth meant hazards as well as amenities. Polluted water, offensive smells, and the danger of epidemics were among the new risks that townspeople had to face and overcome. Communities slowly moved from haphazard provisions made by volunteers or private companies to systematic municipal services. To keep a fire from becoming a conflagration—which nonetheless happened frequently—volunteer bucket brigades were replaced with professional firemen. Towns such as Henderson bought new equipment and housed it in new brick firehouses with high bell towers. Often a disaster—such as the failure of a privately operated water system during a fire or an epidemic linked to open pigpens and the lack of a health department—created a demand for a professional manager to assume control over city affairs. "The day of the specialist, the expert, and system has come," said one exasperated alderman. The time of "the old slipshod jack of all trades method has passed."

Not all the hazards of North Carolina's emerging towns and cities were physical. Moral perils lurked as well, at least in the view of those individuals who belonged to the powerful genteel culture of the late nineteenth century. Many of the communities that became cities at the turn of the century began as industrial frontier towns and attracted large numbers of single young people. When available, work was heavy, demanding more than sixty hours a week from most laborers. But employment was also erratic and seasonal. For those with or without work, emotional release was imperative. It was no surprise that Charlotte had fifteen saloons in the 1880s and that Durham, Winston, and Greensboro were not far behind. Saloons soon created problems. Ladies were annoyed by loiterers. Brawls in bars spilled out into the streets. Clergy began to condemn the saloons as the "spring traps of hell, the devil's octopus, reaching out to grasp the young men of the community."

Prostitution flourished along with the liquor trade. On occasion a respect-

able woman admitted fascination with the afternoon "promenade down Main Street" of a famous town prostitute. Gorgeous, tall, eyes glittering, her superb figure outfitted fashionably, the voluptuous lady seemed haughty with the knowledge that she could blackmail half the men in town. But those who were fascinated were outnumbered by those who were repelled or resentful. By the turn of the century, many women and impressive numbers of men joined in crusades to close the bars and brothels. In town after town they sent the rowdies packing and cleansed the city—at least to the extent of eradicating the prominent buildings that were once palaces of forbidden pleasure.

Once the turn-of-the-century town was domesticated, it became a special haven for women of leisure. As shoppers, they could stroll down Main Street, their long skirts swishing up the dust, and enjoy the courtesies of men doff-

Henderson Fire Station (1908)

ing their fedoras and offering a courtly "good afternoon." They could stop at their favorite dry goods store, exchange juicy bits of news with saleswomen, and choose from bolts of cloth their favorite material to be made into a garment at home or by a dressmaker. One of the great treats was a visit to the millinery shop. None remains today, but what exotic sights they were in their time. Perched high on pedestals, hats were festooned with colorful feathers, flowers, or fur, with ribbons, ruches, or ruffles. To walk through the store was like "strolling through a flower garden." For a youngster, the trip to town might climax with a visit to the candy store, often run by immigrants. There one could savor a chocolate nougat and be enraptured by the sight and smell of sweet syrup boiling in great copper kettles and by the strenuous wonders of the taffy-pulling machine.

Victorian Homes

The widening network of railroads, the dramatic expansion of industry, and the gradual growth of towns and cities brought a new measure of well-being to middle- and upper-class North Carolinians. Reflected in proud new civic and commercial buildings, that wealth also found expression in private residences and suburban development. Though quite different from each other, the Propst House of Hickory and "Körner's Folly" of Kernersville, the suburban homes of Dilworth in Charlotte and the R. J. Reynolds country estate in Winston-Salem, all illustrate shared principles of design that became common after 1880 in homes of the prosperous. Each offered a more spacious enclave for family privacy, and each presented a vivid architectural display of newfound wealth.

The Propst House in Hickory is the stuff of which nostalgia is made. There is a lightness, an airiness, a genteel whimsy about the late-Victorian dwelling. It is more than fantasy, more than a languid longing for a simpler age gone by that endows this home with its aura of charm. The house was designed by its owner, J. Summie Propst, a skilled builder and woodcarver, who erected it between 1881 and 1885.

Propst followed the latest in Victorian fashion in constructing the house. Abundant windows, each framed and set off with elaborate gingerbread fretwork, gave the home almost two dozen eyes to the world. The windows in turn opened the interior of the house to light and shifting shadows at all times of the day. Distinctive about the Propst House is its French mansard roof and tower, stylish signs of elegance and cosmopolitanism. Though the style suggests quality and refinement, the overall effect of Propst's house design is not pompous but playful. The eye dances up the tower, lingers on its hand-carved woodwork, and then easily imagines itself inside the cupola, secretly espying the world from behind lace curtains. The detailed exterior decoration is emblematic of the late-Victorian house itself—full of crannies and nooks, carved curls and crevices, the very opposite of spare and symmetrical. The furniture, the objets d'art, even the wallpaper and carpeting, reinforce the motif of whimsy and embellishment in space and design.

It was no accident that such a stylish and spacious house, done in the fashionable Second Empire motif, had been erected in the tiny hamlet of Hickory in 1880. The coming of the railroad in the previous decade had brought new prosperity to the town and put the community's home builders and buyers directly in touch with the latest trends of the era. On the railroad came the newest pattern books for homes. At sawmills nearby or far away, orders could be placed for elaborate manufactured moldings, factory-produced woodwork

and doors, even for entire stairways. Carolina's traditional house—box-shaped, two-story—gave way to homes more modish and decorative. The sovereignty of skilled local builders like Propst, who could carve elegant ornamental work by hand, yielded to builders whose task was largely one of assemblage. For the rising middle class of the state's small towns, the easy access and ready assembly of manufactured building materials brought the latest in fashion within their reach. Though the Propst House has been relocated to a city park, its original setting was both apt and typical. The house was built so that its front faced the railroad tracks.

A plenitude of space was as much a hallmark of the Propst House as fashionable good taste. Though the Hickory dwelling did not have the endless maze of rooms that distinguished the mansions of the rich—separate rooms for billiards, smoking, sewing, piano, library, servants, greenhouse—it had more rooms and roominess than the typical antebellum home. Working and

Propst House (1881–85), Shuford Memorial Gardens, Hickory

*Körner's Folly (1880),
Kernersville*

eating, sleeping and sewing, no longer had to take place in the same multi-functional chambers. Each person and most activities had discrete quarters of their own. The spaciousness of the home was thought to be an important aid to domestic affection. Family members could gather comfortably on the porch, in the parlor, around the piano, near the fireplace, and warmly share each other's company. Yet there was also privacy to be had in the house; each had a room of his or her own.

At first glance, the home of Jules Körner of Kernersville, about ten miles east of Winston-Salem, seems to deserve the name given to it by contemporaries: Körner's Folly. Built in 1880, the three-story, twenty-two-room residence spreads every which way. A multiplicity of heights and levels and a myriad of building materials give it the appearance of a miniature castle, misbegotten in stone, wood, and eight different sizes of handmade brick. Its sharply pitched roof swarms with spirelike chimneys; recessed arches and narrow windows endlessly ornament the facade.

The interior of Körner's singular dwelling is even more eclectic. There are seven levels in the house, connected by a maze of halls and winding stairways. No two doors are of the same dimensions. The master bedroom features twelve-foot ceilings and the children's playroom six, while other rooms soar to heights

Living room of Körner's Folly

of nineteen to twenty-five feet. First-floor rooms have walls paneled with silk, floors of marble and handmade tile, and lavishly carved woodwork. An elegant reception room is crowded with statuary and overstuffed chairs, its walls decorated by hand-painted murals and frescoes. The Körners' bedroom, forty-two feet long, once held thirty-one paintings and a heaven of velvet carpets. Its walls were bordered with Greek designs of love and marriage, and its three chandeliers were suspended by brass cupids. A soaring room on the third floor, first used for billiards, became a family music room and then a little theater — called "Cupid's Park" — for the performance of plays written by Mrs. Körner. Even the home's adjacent pigpen was built of brick and frescoed inside.

The home seems the perfect expression of Körner himself. A richly successful commercial artist, he "traveled widely, painted everywhere" — "even on the Rock of Gibraltar" — and his most renowned and lucrative portraits were those of the Durham Bull, world-famous symbol of the state's leading tobacco manufacturer in the 1880s. The eccentric Körner relished his reputation for oddity. One oft-repeated tale had it that he periodically donned the clothes of a handyman, stood at the foot of his "Folly," and invited comment about the structure. "Vulgar" and "deranged" were some of the ready replies.

Körner's Folly was idiosyncratic, yet in many ways it was also the extreme culmination of widespread aspirations and possibilities in residential designs of late nineteenth-century America and Europe. Beginning in the 1830s, and with increasing audacity and velocity after 1860, Victorian home builders spurned the rules of beauty of the classical style. Order and harmony, symmetry and proportion, had governed the design and decoration of classical dwellings and were characteristic of antebellum plantation homes and their furnishings. But in a world galvanized by manufacturing, crisscrossed by railroads, and connected by steamers and telegraphs, a deep restlessness prevailed. A hunger for novelty brought in impatience with the "monotony" of the older beauty and a quest for styles more suited to the exuberance and power of an imperial age.

No single new style emerged to displace the classical. Instead, diverse architectural forms came to have equal prominence. Buoyant variety, ever more elaborate ornamentation, and a striving for surprise became the hallmarks of external design in the late nineteenth century. By the time Körner built his house, complete irregularity was the "rule." Residential facades had different elevations; roofs had ridges and turrets. The same dwelling was finished in wildly diverse materials, such as brick, stone, shingle, timber, and slate. Homes had porches and balconies, overhangs and towers, transparent bay windows and resplendent stained glass.

In part, the architectural asymmetry of Körner's home and others' was the result of a new principle of house design. Those who could afford it built from the inside out, not from the outside in. No longer need the owner subordinate a wish for comfort and convenience or a fancy for specialized rooms to the confining dictates of external symmetry. If separate rooms were wanted for smoking, for billiards, for a library, for music, as well as for sleeping and entertaining and dining, so be it. Let the exterior shape of the house be improvised around the expansive demands for varied rooms.

Clearly at work as well was a relentless desire for display and conspicuous consumption. The new rich had wealth beyond the dreams of their forebears, fortunes built on the enterprises and national markets of the industrial age. With no income taxes to tithe away their profits, with minimal government services to support, they could afford splendid monuments to their new wealth. Home and possessions announced social arrival and set the pace in fashionable taste. Raleigh's Oakwood neighborhood is a kaleidoscope of residential styles from the 1870s to the first decades of the twentieth century. Piazzas, turrets, gables, cupolas, bay windows, and French doors produce an exuberant mix. Bordering on Oakwood is the elegant Executive Mansion, which houses the governor and his family. Built by convict labor between 1885 and 1891, it is a triumphant example of the Queen Anne style with Eastlake decoration. The historic district of Tarboro, with houses mostly from 1880 to 1920, supplies another townscape of the period.

Yet the elaborateness of home and furnishings involved more than a battle for social position among the monied few. Landscaped grounds, picturesque dwellings, boldly patterned wallpaper, flowered carpets, looping drapery, and curvaceously carved and tufted furniture doubtless provided an oasis of enchantment to counteract much of the drabness of the industrial scene. The very mechanization that was the taproot for new fortunes served to reduce the cost of art and adornment and to bring scaled-down Victorian elegance and embellishments within reach of a growing middle class. Mechanized printing presses turned out pattern books for the construction of Victorian residences (and stables and even jails). Machines produced shutters and railings, roofing slates and floor tiles, and prefabricated gingerbread trim in endless variety and profusion. From machines came an outpouring of statuary, pictures, vases, flower bowls, carpets, and upholstered furniture. The less costly the adornments, the more they flourished—and propelled the wealthy to more dramatic display.

One man's fantasy? Körner's Folly was surely that. But his defiantly individualistic and whimsical dwelling also captured the aspirations of an entire new class of entrepreneurs determined to break past old boundaries of wealth and taste alike.

Suburban Sanctuary

The United States census of 1890 officially designated as a "city" any community that had over 2,500 persons within its boundaries. North Carolina had a handful of such cities as the decade of the nineties opened, none of them populated by more than 10,000 souls. Yet in 1891 an aggressive forty-one-year-old entrepreneur from Charlotte, Edward Dilworth Latta, announced that his newly formed Charlotte Consolidated Construction Company (the 4Cs) planned to develop a suburban community at the southern outskirts of the city on a rural site that had formerly been the city fairgrounds.

Latta and his 4Cs company would also build the Latta Arcade (1914) to house the company's offices and a few shops. The exterior of the arcade is today

House (private residence) on
East Boulevard Street, Dilworth
neighborhood, Charlotte

badly altered, but the interior, with its marble walls and floors, carved wood-work, and leaded glass, retains its original elegance and simplicity. The concept of shops opening on an inner hall is the ancestor of the shopping mall plan.

Latta's suburb of Dilworth was to be a "city of Avenues." A three-mile boulevard 100 feet wide would encircle the suburb, and avenues 60 feet wide were to crisscross the development. There would be 1,635 lots in all, each "beautifully laid off." The centerpiece of the suburb was to be a picturesque park, also named after the developer. In Latta Park fountains would be every-where, flinging "their spray in an atmosphere laden with the fragrance from thousands of rare flowers and costly roses." The park would have a lily pond, terraced gardens, serpentine paths for promenades, and meandering drives for carriage rides. It would have a lake for boating and a spacious pavilion for light entertainment.

How would visitors get to the park, and, more important, how would residents make the daily four-mile round trip to town? With ease. All would travel on the new marvel of urban transport, the electric trolley. "Clanking, pounding, groaning on curves, audible for blocks," popping blue sparks at the switches and providing hazardous mirth for youths who jerked the trolley pole away from the overhead cable, the electric streetcar first proved its success in Richmond in 1888. It sparked emulation and spurred suburban development nationwide for the next three decades. The Charlotte trolley line and its parent electric company, like Dilworth and its glistening park, were constructed, owned, and operated by the Latta corporation.

But did a North Carolina city of 10,000 need a suburb that could house 10,000? A Charlotte journalist would later wonder whether the laying of trolley tracks, creation of suburbs, and erection of skyscrapers were a megalomaniac fantasy for which a small Carolina city had "little more use" "than a hog has for a morning coat." Latta and his partners in the 4Cs company anticipated and brusquely dismissed such doubts. The only way Charlotte and the state could break decisively from a past of poverty was to emulate the dynamic urban society of the North. "We must go forward or retrograde," Latta declared. "There is no resting point with progress." Suburban development would inaugurate the "march of improvement."

And so the laying out of Charlotte's first suburban paradise for the middle class got under way. Free picnics in the park, boisterous baseball games, and colorful balloon ascensions lured curious citizens out to the treeless countryside for Dilworth's first land sales. Boys with red flags marked the boundaries of the lots, and a bellowing auctioneer took buyers' bids. From 1891 to 1893 sales went slowly, perhaps because prospective buyers did not yet share the vision of the promoters, perhaps because they lacked the ready cash to plunk down for a lot and the construction of a home. But with the trolley in place, the park in use, and the decision of the developers in 1893 to offer low-interest home loans, purchases accelerated.

More fundamental forces also favored Dilworth's ultimate success. The promise of tree-lined streets, away from the tensions of the city and close to the country, had long since demonstrated a deep appeal to Americans. The suburban home represented a retreat from the world of commerce, and nearby nature was a reinforcement for domesticity. The slogan of Dilworth and hundreds of other budding suburbs — "Why Rent When You Can Own Your Own Home?" — had immense power with the growing middle class, eager to become men and women of property. The promise of space and privacy, the security of a neighborhood made up of one's own kind — those who had the time and the money to trolley to work — seemed more credible in the suburb than in the city,

William B. Blades
House (private
residence), built in
1903, Middle Street,
New Bern.
Photograph by
Paulette Mitchell.

with its crowding and clamor of classes. And Dilworth offered its residents the most modern conveniences: running water, electricity, a new sewerage system, incandescent street lamps, and a spanking new school.

The isolation of Dilworth from the industrial city was not complete, however, as it would be for most later suburban developments. Dilworth was adjacent to a small, suburban industrial community. The industrial park was built by Daniel Tompkins, Charlotte textile manufacturer and publisher of the *Charlotte Observer*, who was widely regarded as a leading spokesman for the New South. The industrial suburb housed the Atherton Mill, a machine shop and foundry owned by Tompkins, and the Park Elevator factory. Around the factories was a neighborhood of modest dwellings for the families of workers.

By 1901, ten years after its founding, Dilworth flourished, with thousands of residents, and it continued to grow through 1915. Almost 200 homes built before World War I still stand today along leafy avenues, and their architectural styles reflect the aspirations of the prewar suburban middle class. The Queen Anne fashion popular in Dilworth was ornate and full of gaiety, with gables and steep roofs, curving bay windows and wooden balconies, turreted

cupolas and sunburst motifs. "Effete prettiness" to critics, it was "Sweetness and Light" to its admirers. Part of the "sweetness" of the Queen Anne home came from its unembarrassed delight in delicate beauty; part came from the commodious space it provided for a rich family life. A sense of enlightenment characterized both the interiors of such dwellings and their inhabitants. The furnishings were crafts and objects from all periods of history and all portions of

Electric streetcars on Fayetteville Street, Raleigh, ca. 1915

the globe, and the residents regarded themselves as easygoing and inquisitive, a generation beyond the brash single-mindedness of those who had forged a New South. The Queen Anne style can be seen in neighborhoods throughout North Carolina. An excellent ornate example is the house (1903) of lumber magnate William B. Blades in New Bern.

The southern suburb of Dilworth in the early twentieth century, then, was spacious and comfortable, affordable to the middle class, and as communal or private as its residents wished it to be. A financial bonanza for developers, it became a residential sanctuary for rising social classes, a world promoted and designed to screen out the hubbub of the city and to recreate—in idyllic parks and grassy lawns—the wholesomeness of the countryside.

In a similar fashion, other suburbs developed. In 1912, Myers Park, also a Charlotte suburb, was planned as another trolley-line community. Wide boulevards and tree-lined winding streets, with low-lying areas reserved as parkland, made it aesthetically pleasing. Telephone and electric wires were confined to rear lot lines, and commercial services were unobtrusively provided. Elizabeth (now Queens) College was its centerpiece. Trinity Park, in Durham, was a college-centered development too. Begun in the 1890s, it was laid out in a grid pattern with its utility lines run in back alleys between the streets. Formed from the estate of Brodie Duke, son of Washington Duke, it provided a housing area adjacent to Trinity College (now Duke University). The late nineteenth and early twentieth centuries saw a decided improvement in the quality of city life. Frame Buildings gave way to brick or stone, sewerage and telephone systems were introduced, electric streetcars replaced horsecars, and electric lights replaced gaslights along the streets.

Manor with a Mission

In its heyday, the country estate of R. J. Reynolds and his wife, Katherine Smith Reynolds, had everything that whim could wish for and money could buy. Reynolda House, open to the public since 1964 as a showcase of American paintings and a learning center for the arts, was in 1917 the centerpiece of a domain of a thousand acres. Nestled in farmland a long, winding two miles from downtown Winston-Salem, the country place had polo fields, a nine-hole golf course, a pure-water swimming pool, a formal English garden, a cutting garden and greenhouse, a life-sized doll house for the two Reynolds girls, and a log cabin for the two boys. The main dwelling itself had sixty rooms, furnished with sumptuous elegance then and now. In the 1930s the family would add a bowling alley, game room, shooting gallery, enclosed swimming pool, and

eight-room guest wing. For almost a half-century, Reynolda served its owners and their guests as an oasis of splendor and a recreational paradise.

Yet the design of the manor house and the work carried on at the estate revealed that Reynolda was meant to be more than a palatial retreat for Winston's richest family. The Reynolds home avoided the dramatic asymmetry, endless adornment, and fortresslike immensity of other country mansions of its day. Long, lean, and low, devoid of exterior ornamentation, constructed with "thousands of loads of rock" gathered from nearby fields rather than imported from afar, Reynolda House was built in a deliberately subdued architectural fashion known as the "Bungalow" style. As one contemporary described it, this type of house "looks as if it had been built for less money than it actually cost." The design of the numerous dependency buildings mirrored the restraint of the manor, though there was no masking the reality that it took a

Reynolda House (1917), on the estate of tobacco baron R. J. Reynolds in Winston-Salem

small village of people to run the estate. Reynolda Village was a world within itself, housing living quarters for twenty families, black and white schools for their children, a church and post office, as well as barns and stables, an ice-house and smokehouse, a laundry and blacksmith shop, a power plant and telephone system. But the village was designed to serve more than the pleasure of its patrons. Reynolda was planned as a working "model farm," which would demonstrate to neighbors and those throughout the region the latest methods of scientific agriculture, particularly in the raising of livestock and dairy cattle.

Reynolda's gardens were the result of three influences. L. L. Miller, the initial landscape gardener, contributed the formal parterres along with the total plan of the estate. Thomas W. Sears added the plain garden structures of indigenous building materials in an English setting. But the dominant plantings were Mrs. Reynolds's choice: Japanese cedars, weeping cherries, and London planes.

Reynolda in 1917, then, was a manor with a mission. But why build such a manor and why endow it with a mission?

Like other tobacco magnates and men of wealth who made their fortunes through the industrialization of the New South, R. J. Reynolds lived in town during the nineteenth century. His home was not far removed from his factory and from the employees who labored on his behalf. Of course, no one would have confused Reynolds's sprawling stone residence, with its seven-stall stable that housed the horses he regularly raced about town, for the four-room wooden dwelling of a tobacco worker. Nonetheless, as the astute Charlotte journalist Wilbur J. Cash observed, the very proximity of Reynolds and others of wealth to fellow townsmen of the working and middle classes lent an easy-going sense of familiarity to southern communities.

In the first two decades of the twentieth century, however, not only Reynolds but also upper-class southerners generally began to abandon the center of the city. As Cash saw it, their departure marked a widening social gulf among distant classes. Some moved to exclusive suburbs, such as Myers Park in Charlotte, where winding roads, carefully designed landscapes, and an elegant club set the rich off from the rest of society. Others opted for the more solitary splendor of a country estate. No immigrant "invasion" or massive urban congestion spurred the flight of southern elites to exclusive enclaves, as had happened earlier in the North. Nor was it clear that the rich felt crowded by the ambitious and successful among the middle classes, as had the abrasive New York financier J. P. Morgan, who in discussing his yacht club declared that "one could do business with anyone, but only sail with a gentleman." But the northern nouveaux riches had established the fashion of the day, and the coming of automobiles had made residences far from town accessible. All it took was the wealth to afford both—and New South fortunes were redoubling by the turn of the century.

Reynolds in particular had struck it rich, once in the nineteenth century and again in the twentieth. He had never exactly been poor, of course. Though legend had it that Dick Reynolds was an unlettered lad from Critz, Virginia, who had arrived in Winston on the back of a wagon, barefoot and dead broke, he was never a poor country boy. His father was a well-to-do planter and to-bacco manufacturer with a homestead just over the Carolina-Virginia border. Reynolds had trained at college, gone to business school in Baltimore, and then acquired shrewdness and experience as a "drummer," scrambling from store to country store to sell his father's tobacco. It was not empty-handed but with $7,500 in his pocket that he struck out in 1874 for Winston, a town of 400 with a new railroad line. Over the next four decades, his first small downtown building multiplied to over 100, his workforce grew to 10,000, and his $7,500 became millions. Reynolds built his nineteenth-century fortune through sales-manship and saccharin. His salesmen swarmed everywhere with their posters and calendars, "as thick as bees in a clover field." And Reynolds made his plug tobacco the "sad man's cordial" by treating it secretly with saccharin, while informing his customers that the bright leaf that grew around Winston was uniquely and "naturally sweet."

Reynolds redoubled his wealth between 1907 and 1914. Even though le-gally subservient from 1899 to 1911 to the American Tobacco Trust, which he had been forced to join, Reynolds refused to play lackey to James B. Duke, head of the trust. Anticipating an increase in the demand for smoking to-bacco, Reynolds in 1907 introduced "Prince Albert" and hired the nation's leading advertising agency to promote the "New pipe-Joy" that "can't bite your tongue." Much to the aggravation of the trust (which at one point considered legal action), Prince Albert production soared in four years from 250,000 pounds to 14 million. After the U.S. Supreme Court declared the American Tobacco monopoly illegal in 1911, Reynolds sought supremacy in the ciga-rette business and won it with a rich-tasting blend of burley, bright, and Turk-ish leaves called Camel. Reynolds's advertising agency, with a quarter-million-dollar budget in 1914 to introduce the new cigarette, saturated the country with ads: "The Camels are Coming!" The Camels conquered. The company sold 425 million cigarettes the first year and 15 billion by 1920—more than half the cigarettes smoked in the United States.

It was perhaps no surprise that, as Reynolds and other entrepreneurs saw their fortunes grow in the early twentieth century, they came to view a sub-urban residence as a chance to live with more grandeur and seclusion than they could in the city. Yet, though the building of a country mansion was all but assured by Reynolds's social position, the initiative and design for the estate belonged to his wife, Mary Katherine Smith Reynolds. It was Katherine Smith Reynolds who initially purchased the farmland west of downtown Winston in 1909, who commissioned the landscape and architectural plans in 1914, and who hand-initialed her final approval of the blueprints of the buildings completed in 1917. It was "K. S. Reynolds, Owner," whose name was listed formally on the business stationery of the estate. Above all, it was Reynolds's wife who decided from the outset that "Reynolda"—the Latin feminine of Reynolds—would be a "working farm," run both as a business and as a model of modern agricultural methods for the education of farmers of the Piedmont.

A country estate that attempted to blend beauty, business enterprise, and educational uplift—it was a fascinating and ambitious vision. But then Katherine Smith Reynolds, like many of her generation, was a fascinating and ambitious woman. Katherine Smith was twenty-five years old in 1905 when she wed R. J. Reynolds. He was fifty-four. They were distant cousins, and the millionaire bachelor had known her since her childhood. She had come to work for Reynolds in 1904 as his executive secretary, despite the fact that he usually relied on male secretaries. She proved trustworthy, attractive, and astute—a woman he could marry without fear that she simply wanted his wealth, a woman whose progressive social conscience soon influenced the policies of the company and ultimately shaped the purpose of the Reynolda country estate.

Born in 1880, Katherine Smith came of age at a time when the aspirations of young middle-class women were widening dramatically. Only a handful of women born in 1850, R. J. Reynolds's own generation, had dared go to college. Higher education and ambition were thought to be ruinous to the health of the gentler sex and incompatible with the self-submergence required by family life. Katherine Smith was among the increasing minority of young girls who elected to go to North Carolina's only state-run college for women—the State Normal and Industrial School at Greensboro—and finished at Sullins College, in Virginia. At Greensboro she was exposed to women faculty who were graduates of Bryn Mawr, Wellesley, and the women's medical colleges of Philadelphia and New York. The *College Yearbook* of 1902 reported that, while many girls began school "undeveloped in brain and soul," they gradually learned that "nothing was impossible." Greensboro students left college "with a new and hitherto unknown responsibility for the world in general" and for the "care of the lower classes" in particular.

But women's colleges taught more than paternalism. At Greensboro and elsewhere they taught skills—teaching, stenography, accounting, nutrition—and conveyed an underlying message that women should "know something and be something." At Greensboro "business ability" was especially exalted. As graduates put it in 1902, they realized at college the "necessity of becoming efficient in some line of work." A "busy woman is generally useful and those who lead 'strenuous' lives are usually happy." The legislature had established the State Normal and Industrial School in 1891 and made Charles D. McIver, a staunch believer in higher education for women, its first president. This college (now the coeducational University of North Carolina at Greensboro) and others like it became incubators for leaders of the women's suffrage movement in the first two decades of the twentieth century.

A product of college and the broadened views of her age, Katherine Smith Reynolds—as her husband's business adviser and as Reynolda's director—worked on the assumption that what was humanitarian was also good business. She concerned herself especially with the welfare of those whose lives had been uprooted and dislocated by the economic transformation of the South. For the workers in her husband's factories, she persuaded her husband to open a cafeteria that offered nutritious food at low cost and a nursery for the care and early education of workers' children. A founder of the Junior League of Winston-Salem, she took a leading role in mobilizing wealthy women and the community at large behind the creation of a YWCA, a halfway house to ease the transition of country girls to urban life. When her attention turned to her country estate, she discovered that many local builders did not know how to read blueprints. She set up a school on the spot, where they learned. Once the farm was in operation, she invited neighboring farmers to view demonstrations of the latest agricultural techniques and employed students from the state agricultural college as apprentices. Riding through Reynolda Village on her horse, Kentucky Belle—she always rode astride, never sidesaddle—she gave "prizes for the best flower garden and the best-kept yard." Firmly committed to the education of the children on the estate, she attended regularly the closing programs of black and white schools.

Contemporaries of Katherine Smith Reynolds in North Carolina and elsewhere would not always find it possible to combine beauty and business, welfare and wealth. The concern of other women for the well-being of workers and the fate of farmers more than once led them on a collision course with the state's business leaders over issues of child labor, factory hours, and rural poverty. But, for the wife of R. J. Reynolds and the founder of the Reynolda farm, no such conflict emerged between what was progressive and what was profitable. The Reynolda estate—millionaire's rural retreat, model farm—married the best of both worlds.

5

FROM JUBILEE TO JIM CROW

The Color Line

During the Great Depression of the 1930s a farsighted employment pro-gram—the Federal Writers' Project—produced an extraordinary set of docu-ments. Dozens of writers in North Carolina and hundreds throughout the South and the nation were hired to interview ex-slaves and gather their recol-lections of life in slavery and freedom. Many aged blacks from North Carolina, looking back on six decades as free men and women, felt that emancipation had proved to be a cruel hoax. After slavery there was no more master's lash, conceded one woman, but there was also "nothin' to live on." Slavery and free-dom were like two snakes, each full of poison: "Both bit de nigger and dey wus both bad." Hard work was the rule in slavery, recalled another ex-slave, and unrelieved toil remained the rule after 1865. "It's not what I has done, but what I ain't. Plowed, dug stumps, chopped, broke steers, ginned cotton, cooked for white folks." One Johnston County man admitted to being an ambitious "high-minded young nigger"—but something always undercut him. Cheated on his crop by a warehouseman, he "went crazy," hit him, got "twelve months on the road," and learned his lesson: "no use for me to try to ever make anything but just a living."

Were these recollections from the depths of the depression too pessimis-tic? Possibly. Yet it was beyond question that hard-won freedoms gained in the first three decades after emancipation had come under savage assault at the end of the 1890s and stood gutted by 1920. State constitutional amendments and the all-white party primary had eliminated the right to vote for all but a few blacks after 1900—a far cry from 1896, when 87 percent of eligible black voters cast their ballots. Black jurymen, officeholders, and constables, numer-ous in the eighties and nineties, vanished from public life. Only three in ten black farmers in 1920 owned their own land, and their soil was often the most marginal, the "back bone and the spare ribs." The overwhelming majority of rural black families remained sharecroppers or tenants, and for many "settling

Stripes but no Stars.
Asheville, N. C.

Prison laborers released to the Western North Carolina Railroad, 1915

up" time was reminiscent of slavery: "Naught is naught and figger is a figger, all for de white man and none for de nigger."

Many former slaves had left the plantations and migrated to towns and cities "to find out if I wuz really free." And until 1900 the state's urban centers had indeed proved to be "Black Meccas." Though most black city dwellers were unskilled laborers and domestics, fully half the skilled workers of North Carolina's cities in 1900 were black. They were stevedores and printers in Wilmington, barbers and brickmakers in Durham, masons and carpenters in Greensboro and Winston. Those gains, too, were destroyed by law and custom after 1900, as white employers, lawmakers, and working people segregated the city's skilled jobs and restricted them to whites only.

A Durham woman recalled vividly the imposition of segregation early in the twentieth century and its endless humiliations. Pauli Murray grew up in the "bottoms" of Durham. The marshy lowland was typical of the portion of North Carolina towns reserved for most blacks: a hollow full of "washed-out gullies," "shacks for factory workers," "trash piles, garbage dumps, cow-stalls, pigpens, and crowded humanity." In the 1890s her grandfather had built his two-story wooden house toward the base of a steep hill with a wheat field on it, but by 1900 "the town had moved in upon us" and the sprawling town cemetery "had swallowed the wheatfield."

But it was not her grandfather's loss of his land to the all-white cemetery

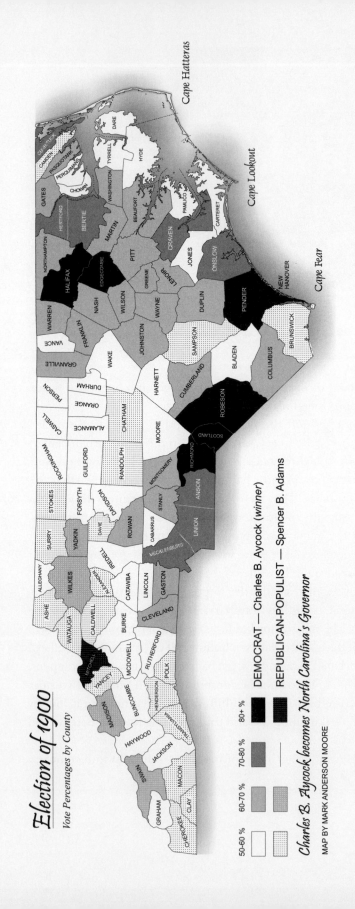

Election of 1900
Vote Percentages by County

50-60 % 60-70 % 70-80 % 80+ %

DEMOCRAT — Charles B. Aycock (winner)

REPUBLICAN-POPULIST — Spencer B. Adams

Charles B. Aycock becomes North Carolina's Governor

MAP BY MARK ANDERSON MOORE

Cape Hatteras

Cape Lookout

Cape Fear

African American steamboat crew, ca. 1900

that festered in Pauli Murray's memory. In her moving autobiography, *Proud Shoes*, she tells of "the signs which literally screamed at me from every side—on streetcars, over drinking fountains, on doorways: FOR WHITE ONLY, FOR COLORED ONLY, WHITE LADIES, COLORED WOMEN, WHITE, COLORED. If I missed the signs I had only to follow my nose to the dirtiest, smelliest, most neglected accommodations." Each morning on her way to school, she "passed white children as poor as I going in the opposite direction. . . . We never had fights; I don't recall their ever having called me a single insulting name. It was worse than that. They passed me as if I weren't there!" The whites' school was a "beautiful red-and-white brick building," its "lawn was large and green and watered every day," their "playground was a wonderland of iron swings, sand slides, seesaws"—always "barred from us by a strong eight-foot-high fence topped by barbed wire." Her own school was dilapidated and rickety, a two-story wooden building that "creaked and swayed in the wind as if it might collapse." Inside, the "floors were bare and splintery, the plumbing was leaky, and the toilets in the basement smelly and constantly out of order."

For Pauli Murray the hurt of segregation was "never the hardship so much as the *contrast* between what we had and what the white children had. We got the greasy, torn, dog-eared books; they got the new ones. They got wide mention in the newspaper; we got a paragraph at the bottom." In Durham, as in every other town in the region, blacks "were bottled up and labeled and set aside—

African American
potter

sent to the Jim Crow car, the back of the bus, the side door of the theater, the side window of a restaurant." Black children soon "came to understand that no matter how neat and clean, how law-abiding, submissive and polite, how studious at school, how churchgoing and moral, how scrupulous in paying our bills and taxes we were, it made no essential difference in our place." It seemed as if "there were only two kinds of people in the world—*They* and *We—White* and *Colored*."

Like many black North Carolinians thwarted and wearied by segregation, Pauli Murray left the Tar Heel State for the North. Her attainments in exile were remarkable. She became a civil rights fieldworker and spokesperson, a distinguished lawyer, a poet and writer, and, in 1977, the first African American woman to be ordained a priest in the Protestant Episcopal Church.

Clearly, Pauli Murray flourished in response to opportunities away from home. Yet she also built upon a long North Carolina heritage of black accomplishment and striving. She built on the achievements of those who opened the first schools for black youths and adults after 1865 and who "taught not merely to impart knowledge but to build character and shape the future." She built on the philosophy of uplift and black self-help—of "dogged work and manly striving"—that had taken root in nearly a dozen black colleges founded in the state after the war. She built on the special heritage of Durham, where the values of self-help and racial solidarity were funneled into business enterprise. The "grit and greenback" of Durham's blacks had produced "the Negro Wall Street of America," a downtown block of Parrish Street dotted with black businesses and dominated after 1921 by the six-story skyscraper of the North Carolina Mutual Life Insurance Company. Above all, Pauli Murray built her life of commitment to racial liberation upon a southern black heritage of spiritual strength and political struggle. That striving for independence surged to the surface in the Year of Jubilee and found expression in all-black churches and all-black conventions that the new freedpeople organized after 1865.

Independence Halls

The Emancipation Proclamation of 1863 and the Thirteenth Amendment to the Constitution in 1865 forever ended slavery in the United States. But the legal actions simply set the stage for a more fundamental struggle. What did freedom mean?

Many of the historic places where that battle was contested in North Carolina are gone. Gone is the Union army campsite of occupied New Bern in 1864, where the sight of "hundreds of colored soldiers armed" and ready to fight for their own emancipation overwhelmed a black sergeant: "I can only say, the fetters have fallen—our bondage is over." Gone is the Front Street Methodist Church of Wilmington, where for the better part of 1865 black members of the congregation struggled for control of the sanctuary. A mood of jubilation and independence among hundreds of black church members was evident at the first sunrise prayer meeting after the occupation of the city in January 1865. "The whole congregation was wild with excitement," recalled the white minister; the meeting was "extravagant beyond all precedent with shouts, groans, amens." After hymns and prayers, the black class leader chose the Ninth Psalm for the day of jubilee and "read as only Charles could read." As he said: "I will sing praise to thy name, O thou most High. When mine enemies are turned back, they shall fall and perish at thy presence. . . . For the needy shall not always be forgotten: the expectation of the poor shall *not* perish for ever. Arise, O LORD." Then a black army chaplain, who a few years before had "left North Carolina a slave," strode to the pulpit. "One week ago you were all slaves; now you are all free. (Uproarious screamings!) Thank God the armies of the Lord and of Gideon has triumphed. . . . (Amen! Hallelujah!)."

Black members fought for nine months to affiliate the congregation with the African Methodist Episcopal (AME) Church—and in the meantime repeatedly came down from the balcony to sit in the body of the church. They finally withdrew and helped form the St. Stephen AME Church, whose present sanctuary, built in 1880, stands on Fifth Street in Wilmington.

From its birth in a brush arbor in Durham in 1869, St. Joseph's AME Church has become one of the leading congregations of that denomination in North Carolina. Its first minister, the Reverend Edian Markham, had been born a slave in 1824 and had escaped bondage by the Underground Railroad. He educated himself in New York and then chose Durham as his first missionary field. The congregation that he formed was first called Union Bethel.

Were it still standing today, the two-story wooden building of the AME Church in Raleigh might be regarded as the Independence Hall of black North Carolinians. In this modest structure, located on a back street just a few blocks from the old State Capitol, black delegates from all over the state declared themselves a "Convention of Freedmen" on 29 September 1865. The 115 men, most slaves just months before, met to find ways to eradicate the legal inequities of the past. They timed their convention to coincide with the assembly of whites who convened blocks away in the state legislative chamber to form a new civil government. For four days they deliberated in the sparsely furnished church, its floor and gallery filled to capacity by 400 delegates, spectators, and reporters. Ever on view behind the pulpit was a lifelike bust of Abraham Lincoln, shrouded in mourning, with the inscription overhead: "With malice toward none, with charity for all, with firmness in the right."

Appointed to draw up a set of resolves to address the white Constitutional Convention, the delegates debated heatedly the issue of charity and firmness. What rights should they seek? Should they request or demand those rights? Alexander Galloway, a former North Carolina slave who had escaped to Ohio in 1857 and become an abolitionist, favored immediate and universal suffrage. In "six months," he contended, white leaders "would be putting their arms around our necks and begging" for black votes. But James Harris, another North Carolinian, advocated reliance on the goodwill of the "intelligent white class of the South." Freed from slavery in 1850, Harris had traveled to Africa and the West Indies—"40,000 miles in search of a better country"—and concluded that the freedman's place was on his home soil. Though he believed unequivocally in the right of blacks to testify in court, to serve on juries, and to vote, he advocated for the moment a "patient and respectful demeanor" to win white confidence. Proving themselves worthy, blacks would "receive what they had a right to claim."

Ironically, it was a northern-born, free black minister, an indomitable leader who spent the rest of his life building the AME Zion church in North Carolina and the South, who presided over the convention and successfully urged it to strike a tone of moderation. James Hood, born in Pennsylvania and formerly a minister in Connecticut, exhorted the delegates to refrain from "harsh language." "We and the white people have to live here together." The best way was "to treat all men respectfully. Respectability will always gain respect." The final address avoided mention of juries and suffrage and appealed to the "moral consciences" of whites. In return for black "industry, sobriety, and moral demeanor," the conciliatory address requested that whites pay blacks properly for their labor, educate their children, and repeal "oppressive laws." "Is this asking too much?"

Bishop James W. Hood

It was. Meeting less than a year later in the same Raleigh AME Church, black delegates denounced the "killing, shooting, and robbing" of "unprotected people" that had characterized the intervening months. They no longer looked to the state legislature for a redress of grievances but to the North and the national Congress. By 1867, under federal edict, black North Carolinians were voting and serving on juries. In January 1868, when a second convention met in the capitol to draft a new constitution and government, fifteen blacks — including Galloway, Harris, and Hood from the first freedmen's assembly — took their seats alongside whites as duly elected delegates.

While churches were often sources of political initiative, they served more fundamentally as vibrant centers of spiritual vitality and communal life. Whether they worshiped in brush arbors built out of branches and leaves or in handsome brick structures such as St. Stephen, black North Carolinians felt most free in sanctuaries they built themselves. The release from bondage offered the chance to serve the Lord without white surveillance or opposition, to plumb the meaning of the Scriptures without outside guidance or rebuke, to express the love of Jesus without the encumbrance of white notions of restraint.

Colleges for Uplift

The difficulties encountered by black North Carolinians in their political struggle highlighted the reality that their path to independence was to be different from the paths more familiar to white Americans. There was no bounteous Promised Land for them to flee to, where they could escape oppression and start afresh. There was no immortal declaration of their right to life, liberty, and the pursuit of happiness—indeed, most whites in 1865 questioned whether the inalienable rights of man belonged to blacks. Nor was it clear that the nineteenth-century road to freedom—ascent through hard work and the assimilation of middle-class cultural traits—would be available to blacks. Even after freedpeople made "earnest efforts by education, virtue, industry, and economy to qualify ourselves for the highest stations in life"—as New Bern ex-slaves pledged themselves to do in 1865—there was no guarantee that whites would open higher stations to worthy blacks. Charles N. Hunter, black Raleigh educator and journalist, maintained that African Americans would have to win their place in society. "We don't seem to realize the fact," he proclaimed, "that to occupy a respectable position among other nations of the world, we must make corresponding advances in literature, the sciences, arts, and everything else having a tendency to elevate and enoble us. That we must sustain colored papers, Doctors and Lawyers; that we must produce historians and men,—and women, too—for be it known that your correspondent is an humble advocate of the rights of women,—of every honorable calling."

The philosophy of uplift and a commitment to black self-help took firm root in nearly a dozen black colleges founded in North Carolina after the war. Handsome buildings named for out-of-state benefactors still grace the campuses of Shaw University in Raleigh, Johnson C. Smith University in Charlotte, and Livingstone College in Salisbury. Each of the schools started in small frame or log buildings, and each began with the mission of training young people to become "Christian workers" and educated ministers who could combat the "spirit preachers" of the day.

Two of the schools received their only early support from northern churches and the Freedmen's Bureau and faced serious opposition from native whites. The Reverend Henry Martin Tupper, the Massachusetts Baptist minister who founded Shaw in Raleigh, was threatened by the Ku Klux Klan in the 1860s. Continuing tension and ostracism in the mid-1870s produced teachers who were, in the eyes of one outside observer, the "most forbidding New England type—with whom duty—in all matters—is always a business and never a pleasure." Yet, "the truth is that a less cold & determined set of people would be badgered almost to death & driven away." The first years of the "Freedman's College" in Charlotte—which would become the Biddle Memorial Institute and finally Johnson C. Smith University—were no less trying for the native white ministers who founded the Presbyterian school in 1867. Fellow churchmen forced the ministers to disaffiliate themselves and the school from the southern church. By the time the African Methodist Episcopal Church established Livingstone College in Salisbury in the 1880s, however, white North

Estey Hall (1874), Shaw University, Raleigh

Carolinians saw the merit of colleges designed to educate black clergy and instruct black youths in both the liberal arts and industrial skills.

Each of the colleges established early a close relationship with northern patrons who nurtured and sustained the schools well into the twentieth century. Estey Hall at Shaw, a handsome dormitory for girls that made possible the "Christian education" of women at the Baptist college, was funded in 1870 by a family from Vermont. The striking administration building at Johnson C. Smith University, as well as the school's dormitories, Science Hall, and Carnegie Library (1911), were the products of northern benefactions and set the stage for the bequest in 1924 from James B. Duke of a 4 percent annual increment from the $40 million Duke Endowment. The national Episcopal Church, which helped found Raleigh's Saint Augustine College as a normal school during Reconstruction, increased its support in 1907. By 1919, the school was operating as a junior college, and today it is a four-year institution. Contributions from British donors helped to establish Livingstone College, in Rowan County. Named after the famous British missionary David Livingstone, the college pledged itself to support Livingstone's work by training "intelligent, moral, and well prepared men, to preach the gospel of Christ" and "elevate their brethren in Africa." The names of buildings on the Livingstone campus—Dodge Hall, Stanford Seminary, Carnegie Library—testify to the continuing interest of philanthropists from the North and West.

James Edward Shepard, a native of Raleigh and graduate of Shaw University, started the National Training School and Chautauqua in Durham in 1910.

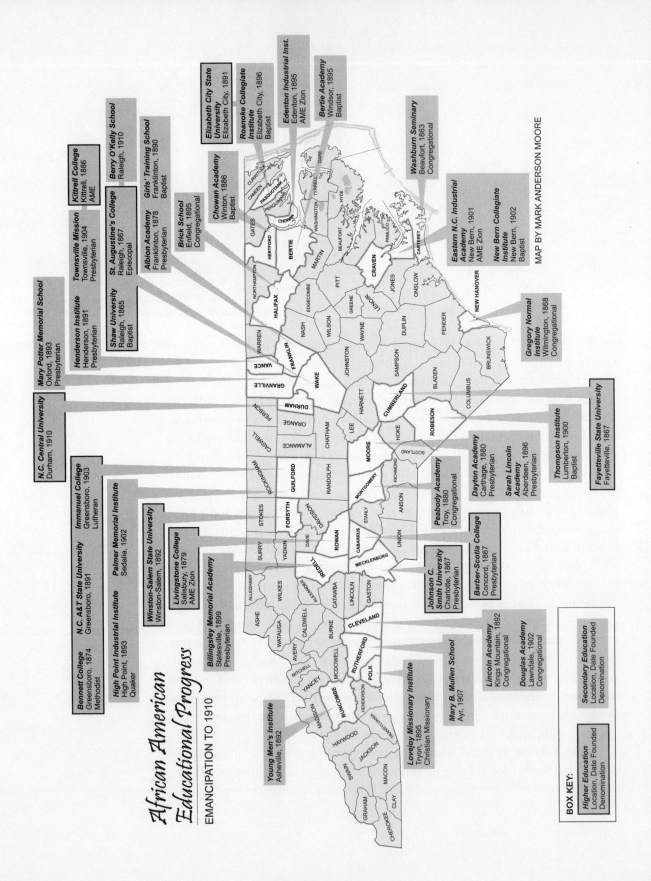

African American Educational Progress

EMANCIPATION TO 1910

MAP BY MARK ANDERSON MOORE

BOX KEY:

Higher Education
Location, Date Founded
Denomination

Secondary Education
Location, Date Founded
Denomination

N.C. Central University
Durham, 1910

Mary Potter Memorial School
Oxford, 1893
Presbyterian

Henderson Institute
Henderson, 1891
Presbyterian

Townsville Mission
Townsville, 1904
Presbyterian

Kittrell College
Kittrell, 1886
AME

Berry O'Kelly School
Raleigh, 1910

Shaw University
Raleigh, 1865
Baptist

St. Augustine's College
Raleigh, 1867
Episcopal

Albion Academy
Franklinton, 1878
Presbyterian

Girls' Training School
Franklinton, 1890
Baptist

Brick School
Enfield, 1895
Congregational

Chowan Academy
Winton, 1886
Baptist

Elizabeth City State University
Elizabeth City, 1891

Roanoke Collegiate Institute
Elizabeth City, 1896
Baptist

Edenton Industrial Inst.
Edenton, 1895
AME Zion

Bertie Academy
Windsor, 1895
Baptist

Washburn Seminary
Beaufort, 1863
Congregational

Eastern N.C. Industrial Academy
New Bern, 1901
AME Zion

New Bern Collegiate Institute
New Bern, 1902
Baptist

Gregory Normal Institute
Wilmington, 1868
Congregational

Bennett College
Greensboro, 1874
Methodist

N.C. A&T State University
Greensboro, 1891

Immanuel College
Greensboro, 1903
Lutheran

High Point Industrial Institute
High Point, 1893
Quaker

Palmer Memorial Institute
Sedalia, 1902

Winston-Salem State University
Winston-Salem, 1892

Livingstone College
Salisbury, 1879
AME Zion

Billingsley Memorial Academy
Statesville, 1899
Presbyterian

Young Men's Institute
Asheville, 1892

Lovejoy Missionary Institute
Tryon, 1895
Christian Missionary

Mary B. Mullen School
Ayr, 1907

Lincoln Academy
Kings Mountain, 1892
Congregational

Douglas Academy
Lawndale, 1902
Congregational

Johnson C. Smith University
Charlotte, 1867
Presbyterian

Barber-Scotia College
Concord, 1867
Presbyterian

Peabody Academy
Troy, 1880
Congregational

Dayton Academy
Carthage, 1880
Presbyterian

Sarah Lincoln Academy
Aberdeen, 1896
Presbyterian

Thompson Institute
Lumberton, 1900
Baptist

Fayetteville State University
Fayetteville, 1867

That school subsequently became North Carolina College, now North Carolina Central University, the first state-supported liberal arts college for African Americans in the United States.

From the 1890s onward, the black colleges and their first generation of graduates faced a time of testing. Black faculty and administrators replaced the predominantly white staffs of the colleges in Raleigh and Charlotte—and performed ably despite the anxieties of some white trustees that blacks were not yet ready for command. Industrial education, favored by some blacks and many whites as the most practical curriculum for black youths, challenged but did not displace the teaching of the liberal arts and the preparation of increasing numbers of students for the professions. But for those students whom the colleges did train for "higher stations" there was frustration. Some graduates went on to become lawyers and physicians, teachers and ministers, but others made their living as porters and chauffeurs and waiters. Many were resented for their achievements, condemned for their aspirations, and commanded to remain second-class citizens in an era that saw the triumph of segregation.

After no small struggle in the 1890s, black graduates found themselves obliged to "make the best of segregation" as the twentieth century began. The choice by 1920 was "between taking segregation standing up and taking it lying down." Until the day when the struggle for an integrated society could be resumed, a commencement speaker advised graduates to concentrate on building black "institutions so that they are as good as anyone else's institutions" and in the meantime repel "spiritual defeat." Their credo should be: "I will not allow one prejudiced person or one million or one hundred million to blight my life. My inner life is mine, and I shall defend and maintain its integrity against all the powers of Hell." In the protracted era of Jim Crow, the mission of the black college was to provide each student with a "solid belief in his own race, a zeal to serve his own people, a spirit of dignity, and a courageous style of life."

Redemption would come in the 1960s. North Carolina's black college students, seating themselves at segregated lunch counters first in Greensboro and then throughout the state, spearheaded the successful struggle against segregation in public accommodations throughout the South. Within weeks of the first sit-in, hundreds met at Shaw University to form the Student Non-Violent Coordinating Committee, which soon funneled the energies of thousands of educated young men and women into the swelling crusade for civil rights. What happened in Greensboro and what happened at Shaw surely would have pleased those who had dedicated a century of effort to educational uplift, racial self-help, and a "courageous style of life."

Black Business and White Supremacy

The North Carolina Mutual Life Insurance Company Building (see Part V, Chapter 4), which dominates the south side of Parrish Street in downtown Durham, and its gleaming twelve-story successor (See Part V, Chapter 5)—a daring architectural pillar of glass and concrete built on the hill that once accommodated the estate of the son of Washington Duke—stand as testimony to black achievement amid adversity. A thousand guests attended the dedication of the Parrish Street office structure in 1921 and celebrated the opening of the building as a monument to "Negro progress." To the keynote speaker, the new Mutual home—with its neoclassical design, marble trim, and solid metallic doors—symbolized the "industrial prowess of our group [and] our potentialities as a race." The speaker saw the edifice as a clear message to North Carolina blacks about how to make the most of forced segregation. "Let us put our money in Negro banks, read Negro newspapers, trade in Negro stores, patronize Negro doctors, employ Negro lawyers, carry life insurance with Negro companies." "The white man builds businesses for the employment of white boys and girls; we must build businesses for the employment of black boys and girls." Whites, too, applauded the "architectural gem . . . of white brick rising above all other buildings on Parrish Street"—the height had been carefully chosen so as not to exceed the tallest white-owned skyscraper in Durham. The Mutual building, editorialized the *Durham Morning Herald*, was "an example of what can be done by the negro if he goes about it in the right way."

To a black Durham tobacco worker, the Mutual Building and the black Mechanics and Farmers Bank housed on its first floor were more than symbols. A Mutual insurance policy provided a measure of family protection, and the black bank offered the enterprising man a way to get ahead. "Back in those times, a Negro was frowned on in a bank when you're talking about a loan unless you had some powerful white man to sanction it. You couldn't get nothing on your merit." With a black-operated bank, "you could underwrite a whole lot of stuff." "They set up the bank right downtown—not in the black community—but in the heart of town. That gave Negroes a push-off."

In the broadest sense, the Mutual was descended from a century-old tradition of black fraternal and burial societies, built around the ideas of self-help and moral improvement and organized to provide sickness and burial insurance. With the end of Reconstruction and the waning of the quest for black advancement through civil rights and integration, black self-help and benefit societies mushroomed. Many, like the Grand United Order of the True Reformers, provided ritual and regalia, recreation and recognition, in addition to the promise of "happiness, peace, plenty, thrift, and protection" through insurance. But few black benefit societies of the 1860s made hard-nosed appraisals of the mortality prospects of their members. Those companies founded in the 1890s, like the Mutual, were the first to offer health and life policies on a businesslike basis. Yet the Mutual was always more than a company dedicated to making insurance pay, a black imitation of the "triumphant commercialism" of the "conquering Anglo-Saxons." It also remained committed to the uplift of the unfortunate and the good of the black community, a company—as its slogan stated—"with A Soul and a Service."

The founding of the Mutual was a by-product as well of the special circumstances of Durham, a booming industrial city of the New South that boasted that it had "no aristocracy but the aristocracy of labor." Within limits, Durham's white businessmen encouraged black enterprise, provided occasional capital to black entrepreneurs, and sanctioned the aspirations of Durham's blacks to be successful men. Washington Duke spoke for many when he told the city's black leaders in 1890 that "a proper ambition is God's call to a higher life." Zeal for Durham as a special seedbed for black capitalism was shared by the town's first Negro newspaper: "Everything here is push, everything is on the move, every citizen is looking out for everything that will make Durham great. The Negro in the midst of such life has caught the disease and . . . has awakened to action. Durham! The very name has become a synonymous term for energy, pluck, and business ability." White contributions to black philanthropies and churches furthered the reputation of the city as an oasis of racial harmony. The interior of St. Joseph's AME Church in Durham, a spacious and beautiful brick sanctuary built in 1892, testifies to the unusual relationship of Durham's black and white elites. Across from the oval stained glass window of Jesus Christ is a window of equal size portraying Washington Duke.

Yet, in a fundamental way, the Mutual was founded in response to the reign of terror visited upon North Carolina's blacks during the successful white supremacy campaign of the 1890s. It was in October of 1898, the first year of the terror, that John Merrick of Durham—a black entrepreneur who owned three white and three black barbershops and who served as the personal barber to Washington Duke—gathered together six other men in skilled trades and professions to lay the basis for the company. In the red-shirted vigilantes who broke up black political rallies and threatened violence to blacks who came to the polls, in the gruesome lynching of a black man between Durham and Chapel Hill, they had seen the handwriting on the wall. Though five of the Mutual's founders had been active in the Republican Party, they concluded that October evening that they must abandon politics and the assertion of their rights. Blacks must instead turn to "education, business and industrial progress," "keep quiet and saw wood," and turn their "attention to making money." In "commercial opportunity" they would "hammer away. The almighty dollar is the magic wand that knocks the bottom out of race prejudice and all the humbugs that fatten on it."

If the Mutual's seven founders needed reinforcement for their decision to withdraw from politics in favor of white-approved business pursuits, it came within a month. Two days after the November 1898 elections, which saw the triumph of a brutal campaign to restore white supremacy to the state, the white leaders of Wilmington authorized and led an attack on the blacks of that city. They unleashed a rampage of white retaliation for years of black striving and political success.

Regarded by its African American majority as a "Black Mecca," Wilmington since the 1880s had pulsated with energetic black stevedores and skilled artisans, black-run cafes and confectionery shops, black lawyers and pharmacists. It had two black newspapers in the 1890s and a core of black political leaders without peer in the state. They had pressed for and received the appointment of modest numbers of blacks to civil service posts in the community. Wilmington had black policemen and firemen, as well as a black coroner and assistant register of deeds; and a black held the important post of collector of customs in the port city.

The white elite of Wilmington decided in the autumn of 1898 to use the election campaign to put the town's blacks—and especially its educated and politically active leadership—back in their place. Throughout the fall, they charged that the black aldermen and white Republicans who constituted a majority on the city council represented "NEGRO DOMINATION!" Repeatedly, they held up to the white workingmen of the city the image of black townsmen living in luxury, with servants in their houses and pianos in their living rooms. Incessantly they reprinted and denounced the editorial of a Wilmington black newspaper that firmly denied that Negroes were rapist fiends, denounced whites as "carping hypocrites" who "cry aloud for the virtue of your women, when you seek to destroy the morality of ours," and boldly asserted that it was "well known" that many blacks "were sufficiently attractive for white girls of culture and refinement to fall in love with them."

On the morning of 10 November 1898, promising an immediate end "to these intolerable conditions" even "if we have to choke the current of the Cape Fear River with carcasses," white leaders struck. They forced the black and white Republican aldermen to resign, smashed the press of the city's black newspaper, and set fire to the building that housed the beleaguered journal. The building had been the mutual society meeting place of Wilmington's black women and was ironically named the Love and Charity Hall. After sacking the hall, white vigilantes proudly posed for a photograph in front of the building, rifles and pistols in hand. The attack triggered a forty-eight-hour invasion of the black community that left numbers of blacks dead and that forced hundreds to flee the city for their lives. After days in the woods and the swamps, afraid to light fires to warm themselves against the steady, bone-chilling rain, the women and children and workingmen cautiously came back to their homes. The most skilled among them would soon see their jobs taken by whites. Dozens among Wilmington's educated leaders, "banished" as "objectionable persons," never returned.

The lesson of the vendetta of 1898 was not lost on Wilmington's ministers or on Durham's black businessmen. The pastor of Wilmington's Central Baptist Church counseled "the Negro race" to "be considerate in all that they do. Conduct themselves as gentlemen and ladies, and try by all means to keep the peace that is necessary in this country." The minister of St. Luke's AME Zion Church, whose sanctuary stood next to the destroyed Love and Charity Hall, had a stern message in his sermon the Sunday after the riot: "If the Negro trusted in God and minded his own business, all would be well." For his part, John Merrick of North Carolina Mutual concluded, "The Negroes have had lots of offices in this state and they have benefitted themselves but very little. . . . Had the Negroes of Wilmington owned half of the city . . . there wouldn't anything happened to them [to] compare with what did. Let us think more of our employment and what it takes to keep peace and to build us a little house."

Out of the ashes of disaster came a rededication to self-help, racial solidarity, and to the magic wand of the "almighty dollar" that would "knock the bottom out of race prejudice."

6

THE NEW LEISURE

The Birth of Recreation

In 1870, few North Carolinians who lived in the countryside thought of formal places or formal times for "recreation." Their pleasures were rural and often linked naturally with the outdoors and with work. Carolinians of all ages loved to fish and to hunt and savored nothing more than the aroma and satisfaction of a fire crackling under a good day's catch. Labor and leisure, music and work, flowed together easily at a typical corn shucking or quilting bee. According to Lucy Spencer of Stokes County, when corn shuckings were held, "every man for miles around came. And about four or five women would come and help cook. And, oh boy, those big old pots of chicken and dumplings! Oh yes, they'd start in the morning. And it'd be in the wintertime when the days weren't so long. Just as soon as the sun got up a little bit, they'd get out there and start shucking. And they'd just shuck all day long. But it was fun."

When the rural workday ended and when the Sabbath came, visiting was the Carolinian's customary way to relax, and the family porch was the customary place. Not all good times, of course, were homebred. Much fun was brewed up in outlaw outposts of leisure—gambling huts, whiskey stills, makeshift cockfight arenas—that were buried in the woods and known only to a privileged few (and sometimes to the sheriff as well).

But, with the passing of time, the improvement of roads, and the growth of towns and cities, new kinds of recreational activities and settings emerged. At the county fair, farmers came and showed their animals, while women arrived with pies and breads. A mix of agricultural display and carnival, the county fair was a place where one could see and smell the livestock, ride the rides, perhaps visit sideshows of freaks and voluptuous shady ladies. The largest of the fairs was the state fair, which took place in Raleigh. William Tillinghast attended the 1875 state fair at a newly purchased fifty-five acre tract on Hillsborough Street, in Raleigh, today opposite the North Carolina State University campus. "The day was beautiful & the fair quite a success," he recalled. "Goods from the stores fill up very much, but on the whole the display except of cookery was

Parade in Forest City, ca. 1915

good. The cookery (bread & cakes) was about 4 or 5 ft. on one shelf. There were many interesting machines which I did not have time to investigate—I saw a one horse cultivator which I thought would suit my garden & vines exactly— The flowers were very pretty. . . . The display of vegetables was excellent. . . . The Grand Stand is an *immense* building & affords room for *all* to see the races easily."

The traveling circus was another attraction. Town and country folk alike enjoyed its opening parade of costumed travelers and the dazzling array of exotic animals and acrobatic feats. The physical sites themselves were as eva-nescent as the big top: pitched today, gone tomorrow.

PASTIME

THIS WAY
TO BOATS

*Rustic Bridge
Bloomsbury Park
Raleigh N.C.*

*Bridge at Raleigh's
Bloomsbury Park*

In towns and cities particularly, recreational opportunities enlarged. Once the civic elite of a community felt itself secure and monied enough to take stock of its amenities, conservatories of music, opera houses for theatrical performances, and lyceum halls for lectures took their places on or near Main Street. Sometimes, as in the town of Apex, the city hall housed both the governmental offices of the community and the town's performance hall. In the first two decades of the twentieth century, the great popular medium of the movies came to town. In gala movie houses with elegant names—the Majestic, the Royal, the Orpheum—Carolina townspeople laughed and wept at the antics and passions of the wider world on film.

Particularly in commercial and factory cities the stress of work created the need for places of repose and release. As Carolina cities grew, there was usually a moment of recognition that the countryside that people had once taken for granted was no longer readily accessible—and that refuges for rest and diversion were more important than ever. Especially if the urban young were not to be left to places of base abandonment—saloons, brothels, gambling dens, dance halls—more civilized arenas of amusement had to be created.

As towns became cities and citizens longed for the open spaces and trees

Carousel at Pullen Park, Raleigh

of preindustrial communities, recreational parks became a part of the urban landscape. Pullen Park, a gift of eighty acres from businessman Richard Stanhope Pullen in 1887, became a site where Raleighites could picnic, boat, skate, and enjoy nature. Bloomsbury, also at the end of a trolley line and built in 1912 by Carolina Power and Light Company, was advertised as the Electric Park Amusement Company and provided diversions associated with amusement parks today, such as roller coasters, penny arcades, and merry-go-rounds. A carousel, built by the Dentzel Carousel Company of Philadelphia (1903–9) and featuring the handcarved animals of Salvatore Cernigliaro, was among the most popular features of Bloomsbury Park. The carved animals, whose glass eyes were produced in Czechoslovakia, are older than those in the Smithsonian Institution. The carousel was moved to Pullen Park in 1921, and, now restored, it remains the park's central attraction.

Bloomsbury Park no longer exists. But in the late nineteenth and early twentieth centuries, it typified the new urban recreational parks. There one could ride on a carved wooden horse of bedazzling color, a knightly steed that rhythmically rose and dipped to the popular music of the day. Nearby was a dance pavilion, a penny arcade, and a roller coaster as well as landscaped grounds with picnic tables and bicycle paths. In its fascinating mix of traditional rusticity and machine-made toys, Bloomsbury restored the energy depleted by work and provided healthy diversion and controlled delights for young and old.

Resorts for the Well-to-Do

Almost since the first human habitation of North Carolina, visitors have been attracted by the majesty and bounty of its unspoiled outdoors. Many came to look, lingered to visit, and stayed to settle. The pattern of discovery was repeated in the late nineteenth century, when northern city dwellers in search of healthful surroundings came to Carolina for its unpolluted air, tarried, and returned to savor its natural beauty. The visitors of the late nineteenth century were the energetic new rich of the Gilded Age. Their patronage not only launched the state's resort industry; by the 1890s some were using their fortunes to purchase vast tracts of land, upon which they would impose their own visions for the region's development. Three such enclaves of the new leisure class—Pinehurst, the Grove Park Inn, and Biltmore, with its adjacent Cradle of Forestry—were fascinating offspring of the Carolina soil and outside wealth.

Health and pleasure first drew urban outsiders to the Sandhills and Appalachian Mountains of North Carolina after the Civil War. A postwar surge in tuberculosis and lung disorders led physicians and their patients to Asheville, where the high altitude, pure air, and pure water were ideal for the founding of America's first sanatorium in the 1870s. Nestled amid glorious scenery were large wooden buildings, girdled by spacious porches and abounding with rocking chairs. The setting guaranteed vast daily doses of curative fresh air. In the mid-1880s promoters from the Sandhills joined the competition for northern pleasure-seekers and invalids and sought to lure them to Southern Pines. For those who simply wanted a southern vacation it was "Only 22 Hours' Ride from New York." For persons with "Weak Lungs or Throats," it was the best resort "for regaining health." Not mountain air but the "health-giving and delicious odor" of the "noble pines" would restore the lungs to vigor.

Tuberculosis had prompted the choice of Asheville and Southern Pines as health resorts for the ailing. By the end of the nineteenth century, important changes in northern values galvanized their growth as vacation havens for the well. That vacations were desirable was by no means obvious to the urban middle class at midcentury. In industrializing America, debate raged over whether or not any play was fitting in a world devoted to work. For aristocrats in the North and South, of course, the cultivation of leisure and resort life had always been part of civilized life. But northerners new to wealth had to be exhorted to take a rest by a new "gospel of relaxation." Neurologists of the 1870s warned that the compulsion to "overwork" led to chronic nervousness or "neurasthenia" and to its symptomatic headaches, melancholy, dyspepsia, insomnia, and spinal pains. By 1900 *Success Magazine* insisted that "Fun Is a Necessity," and the *Saturday Evening Post* dismissed an opponent of paid vacations as "an awful example of . . . industry gone mad."

Enterprising North Carolinians perceived and responded to the heightened demand for middle- and upper-class playgrounds, far away from hyperactive urban centers. But it fell to the richest of their clients, vacationers from outside who had acquired vast fortunes in the Gilded Age, to envision and create North Carolina's most monumental enclaves of leisure.

It was James Tufts of Boston, for example, who founded Pinehurst. His fortune had come through his invention of modern soda fountain equipment that made carbonated water. The head of the American Soda Fountain Company, Tufts was sensitive to the importance of rest and healthful climes because of his own physical frailness. He also loved golf. He heard about the healthful climate of the Sandhills of North Carolina from New Englanders who had wintered there in the 1880s and early 1890s.

In 1895 Tufts decided to build a resort that would bring relaxation and good health to men and women of moderate means. He bought 5,000 acres of cutover timberland, built cottages and stores, graded streets and constructed a trolley line to nearby Southern Pines, built Pinehurst's first golf course in 1898, and opened the Holly Inn and the grand Carolina Hotel for the accommodation of hundreds of guests. With a New Englander's penchant for planning, he hired the nation's leading landscaping firm to lay out winding roads and supervise the planting of a quarter million plants, a fifth of them imported from France. Besides golf, tennis, and polo, Pinehurst offered its guests hunting and target practice. In 1915 the management hired Annie Oakley, who had retired from the vaudeville and circus circuits because of ill health, to teach target-shooting at Pinehurst, where her "wild West" fame added glamour to the new resort. But North Carolina resorts had so successfully exploited the health angle, particularly attracting tuberculosis sufferers, that Tufts feared its effect on general vacationers. In his advertising brochure, he wrote: "No case of consumption nor malaria has been known to originate in the locality *and Pinehurst is the only village* in the country where consumptives are absolutely excluded."

Two years after the beginning of Pinehurst in 1895, North Carolina's climate lured a second millionaire to the state in search of relief from ill health. E. W. Grove was delighted at the disappearance of his bronchial disorder weeks after his arrival in Asheville. But he was even more taken with the grandeur of the mountains and with the unrealized possibility of making Asheville into a resort city on a scale more colossal than any native had contemplated. Thinking on a grand scale had become second nature to Grove. A Tennessee native with a third-grade education who was a self-taught pharmacist, he had accidentally discovered a method for suspending quinine in water and had gone on to found the Bromo-Quinine elixir empire with headquarters in St. Louis. To transform Asheville into a resort for the finest clients, the "Chill Tonic King" decided he had to end that town's career as a sanctuary for the tubercular. So he bought and burned every sanatorium in town. Simultaneously, the multi-

Grove Park Inn (1913), Asheville

millionaire purchased thousands of acres of farmland on Asheville's northern fringe. The stage was set for the fulfillment of his vision: constructing the Grove Park Inn, "the finest resort hotel in the world."

And what a resort it was! Designed by Grove's son-in-law, Freed Seely Jr., who had received three months' architectural training at Princeton, it was built in 1913 by 400 African American laborers working round the clock for eleven months, and it was immense and lavish. To construct the hotel, huge boulders quarried from nearby mountains were brought down by train and slid into place "just as they are," moss and lichens untouched. Some weighed five tons. Masons from Italy laid every floor with handsome porcelain tile. In the hotel's Great Hall, 120 feet long and 80 feet wide, stood two herculean fireplaces. Built with 120 tons of boulders and provided with andirons of half a ton each, they burned a small forest of twelve-foot logs each year to keep patrons warm. Constructed on the side of Sunset Mountain, the inn overlooked the valley and the city and had a 100-acre golf course as a front lawn. The inn was dedicated by the famous orator William Jennings Bryan, who undoubtedly approved of the literary quotations—drawn from writers from Ovid to Emerson—inscribed on the huge boulders over the fireplace.

Big Room, Grove Park Inn, Asheville, N.C.

Like Grove himself, much of the inn's clientele flourished on newly won wealth. Most of the nation's older gentry had already chosen their favorite resorts: the Berkshires, Bar Harbor, Nahant. There they and their families fled the urban melting pot, its discomfort and diversity, for the rustic simplicity of unspoiled villages, quaint natives, and the comforts of caste affinity. Many who came to the Grove Park Inn were more like Grove—individuals whose inventiveness and talent had taken them to the top in a single lifetime. Thomas Edison, Henry Ford, Harry Firestone, Herbert Hoover, and Woodrow Wilson were among the inn's most prominent guests. The inn was an equally popular resort for guests from southern metropolises, the wealthiest of whom fled the summer's heat for months at a time. From Atlanta and Charleston, from New Orleans and Birmingham, they sent their saddle horses by train, brought their own maids and chauffeurs, shipped their automobiles by railroad, and moved in.

Daytime was for sport and socializing. At billiards and bowling, golf and tennis, hiking or bridge, the "best people" appreciated good fun and each other, leaving cares and less congenial social classes behind. Evenings were more regimented occasions. Indeed, the solemn formality of the inn's regulations suggests that Grove harbored some doubt that all his patrons would mind

Lobby of the Grove Park Inn

their manners spontaneously. A 1914 advertisement for the inn warned that the resort was "minus the bizarre, the tawdry, the flashily foolish." Dinner garb was white ties for men and evening dresses for ladies. (The seven-course dinner took two hours to eat.) Men might smoke after dinner but ladies could not, except in the solitude of their own parlors. A good night's sleep was supremely important to Grove, as he made clear in an inn brochure: "A few people who prefer to retire late will thoughtlessly disturb hundreds who desire rest, by loud talking, slamming of doors, throwing shoes on the floor, and a dozen other annoyances. . . . We have the courage to enforce a discipline that makes rest possible." Three decisive steps maximized nocturnal repose at the Grove Park Inn. The flushing system for the toilets was turned off at 10:30 P.M. The gates to the driveway were closed at the same hour. And there was "not a double bed in the inn."

The largest religious denominations in the state developed their own resorts to provide their members recreation with congenial company in an atmosphere of spiritual uplift. The Methodists established Lake Junaluska in Haywood County. The Baptists and Presbyterians founded Ridgecrest and Montreat respectively, both in Buncombe County. These resorts were descendants of the antebellum campgrounds first developed in the North, such as Ocean Grove, New Jersey, and Lake Chautauqua, New York.

A Mountain Refuge

By far the richest man attracted to the mountains of western North Carolina was George Vanderbilt. Son and grandson of railroad tycoons from New York, the bookish but shrewd twenty-six-year-old bachelor found the air and climate of Asheville invigorating and the scenery enchanting. In 1888 he purchased 2,000 acres of land with the notion of building a summer house upon it for himself and his mother. Fortunately, the young millionaire's ideas about what to do with his estate were only half-formed, and he called upon an old family friend to advise him.

The involvement of Frederick Law Olmsted in the shaping of what would become the Biltmore Estate and surrounding forests was momentous, for Olmsted was the designer of Central Park in New York and the nation's leading landscape architect. Olmsted immediately encouraged Vanderbilt to go beyond his initial thought of creating a manor and a private deer park: "The soil is poor, the woods are miserable. It's no place for a park." Olmsted urged Vanderbilt instead to embrace a purpose that was far more ambitious. He should transform the woods he had purchased—runts, ruins, and saplings, depleted by rapacious lumbering, ravaged by the practice of burning or girdling trees to

Biltmore House (1895–1900), Asheville

clear land for pasturage—into a scenic and profitable forest. The key to success was the scientific management of the land and the trees on it. Vanderbilt had the unique opportunity to demonstrate to the nation the value of scientific forestry and to profit from it.

The multimillionaire built both his manor and a model estate. Designed by the aristocratic architect Richard M. Hunt of New York, Biltmore House was a country home without parallel in America. The monumental French chateau was built of Indiana limestone, hauled 600 miles to North Carolina and transported three miles from the main rail line to the house site on a $77,000 private spur. With the terrace and stables, the audacious mansion was 1,000 feet in length and encompassed 250 rooms, all furnished with art treasures from around the world. Its setting was superb and the view from it breathtaking. A critic had only one question: What was it doing "among the one-room cabins of Appalachian mountaineers?"

Yet, following Olmsted's counsel, Vanderbilt expanded his estate beyond a grandiose retreat in the wilderness. He bought over 100,000 more acres by the turn of the century, including a prominent peak in western North Carolina, Mount Pisgah. He built a model village for the employees of the estate; constructed road, water, and drainage systems; and erected a schoolhouse and a hospital—in a countryside not accustomed to such amenities. For better or worse, Biltmore employees "were subjected to almost military discipline—compelled to be prompt, methodical, and continuous" in their labors.

The most enduring legacy of the Biltmore Estate came in the domain of forest conservation. At Olmsted's suggestion, Vanderbilt hired Gifford Pinchot—a young Yale graduate and the first American to choose forestry as a profession—to manage his lands. He gave Pinchot the opportunity to demonstrate his belief that controlled timber cutting and reforestation, done in cooperation with enlightened commercial lumber companies, was the best way to conserve American forests from ignorant plunder. When Pinchot left—eventually to become the first forester in the United States Department of Agriculture—Vanderbilt placed Carl Schenck of Germany in charge of his lands. In 1898 Schenck founded the Biltmore Forest School, the first such school in America, and used the Vanderbilt forest for a campus.

From 1898 to 1910, when Schenck abandoned it, the school attempted to teach practical forestry to the "sons of every lumberman and of every lumber owner in the country." In an age of awakening conservation movements to curb the ruthless exploitation of natural resources, Schenck's efforts eventually suffered from competition by the many institutions that started their own forestry courses and degree programs. The historic role of Schenck and his 300 young trainees on behalf of national conservation was acknowledged in 1961 with the designation of his school and its buildings as the "Cradle of Forestry" in America. Visitors today can take the "campus tour," view exhibits, and walk trails that splendidly illustrate the history of that pioneering enterprise.

The joint creation of Vanderbilt and Olmsted, the millionaire and the landscape planner, became the property of the nation after Vanderbilt's death in 1914. For a modest sum, his widow sold almost 100,000 acres of the Biltmore Estate to the National Forest Reservation Commission, specifying that it become a national preserve. The reforested domain of a single aristocrat became the recreational refuge of millions in 1917 and forms the bulk of North Carolina's modern Pisgah National Forest.

THE PRICE OF PROGRESS

7

North Carolina's participation in the world of industry and urbanization, commercial agriculture and tourism, began slowly in the 1870s, grew steadily through 1900, and exploded in the first two decades of the twentieth century. By the 1920s the state took pride in its reputation as the South's most progressive state—a land of factories and business enterprise as well as farms, good roads and improving schools, urban vitality and civic achievement. In urban centers especially, an exuberant vision of progress had triumphed. Town tried to outpromote town and the state to outdo other states in heralding North Carolina and her communities as magnets of growth and commerce. In 1870 most North Carolinians relied on the skills of self-sufficiency to "make do." By 1920 thousands of Tar Heels were making money and thousands more aspired, with a little luck and capital and business cunning, to join the ranks of those who were getting ahead.

The physical world that North Carolinians saw around them by 1920 ranged from log houses, flimsy shanties, and false storefronts to skyscrapers and the elegance of the latest churches. Architects were largely responsible for the expensive end of this gamut, and in North Carolina Frank P. Milburn's hand is seen everywhere. The courthouse with the top-story jail was his innovation. He built the Buncombe, Durham, Forsyth (now demolished), Mecklenburg, and Vance County Courthouses, as well as a host of railroad stations, college buildings, and banks.

Most North Carolinians, like most Americans of the early twentieth century, celebrated the "go-ahead" spirit and driving economic ambition of the new era. When eight-story skyscrapers went up, they cheered and vied for space. When tourists flooded in, they expanded their businesses. When real estate values soared, they bought and sold. Every new automobile and macadamized street, every new power plant and telephone, brought the Tar Heel State and its people further out of historic isolation and poverty and closer to the mainstream of national prosperity.

457

Thomas Wolfe
Memorial, "Old
Kentucky Home"
(1883–89), Asheville

The Lost Home of Thomas Wolfe

Yet not all Americans joined in praise of the new era, and not all North Carolinians applauded the triumph of a New South. North Carolina's most famous author, Thomas Wolfe, born in Asheville in 1900 and reared in that community—which he would portray in fiction as "Altamont"—as it crossed the threshold from mountain hamlet to resort boom town, saw in the ambition unleashed by growth peril as well as profit, loss as well as liberation.

Emblematic of the loss of "beauty and spirit" that Wolfe found at the core of the New South triumphant was the boardinghouse that his mother bought in 1906 and that she named "Old Kentucky Home." The dwelling is preserved today as the Thomas Wolfe Memorial. On the surface, the house with the nostalgic name strikes the visitor as a rambling turn-of-the-century home built on a large scale. A wide porch and scattered balconies, high-ceilinged rooms and a

Bedroom at the Thomas Wolfe Memorial

sizable kitchen, made the house fit either for a large Victorian family or for a small company of boarders. The piano and overstuffed chairs that crowded the living room suggest the possibility of music and warmth, while the spare furnishings of the bedrooms present a contrast of cold austerity.

There was no ambivalence about the boardinghouse in the memory of Thomas Wolfe. "Old Kentucky Home" stood for the disruption of his family. His mother, Julia Westall Wolfe, mother of eight children who lived past infancy, bought the dwelling at the age of forty-five. In towns with high numbers of tourists or new residents, many married or widowed middle-class women found security and a respectable career in the operation of boardinghouses. Julia Wolfe left the family home to oversee her business venture and took her seven-year-old son, Tom, to live with her. Her husband, W. O. Wolfe, remained home with the older children, a few hundred yards away. From that point on, the youngest son—"with two roofs and no home"—felt that he was a vagabond and a stranger and burned inwardly with the need to understand his loss.

In his novel *Look Homeward, Angel*, Thomas Wolfe portrayed the Old Kentucky Home as the "Dixieland" boardinghouse:

It was situated five minutes from the public square, on a pleasant sloping middleclass street of small homes and boarding houses. Dixieland was a big cheaply constructed frame house of eighteen or twenty drafty high-ceilinged rooms: it had a rambling, unplanned,

Dining room at the Thomas Wolfe Memorial

gabular appearance, and was painted a dirty yellow. It had a pleasant green front yard, not deep but wide, bordered by a row of young deep-bodied maples: there was a sloping depth of one hundred and ninety feet, a frontage of one hundred twenty. . . .

In winter, the wind blew howling blasts under the skirts of Dixieland: its back end was built high off the ground on wet columns of rotting brick. Its big rooms were heated by a small furnace which sent up, when charged with fire, a hot dry enervation to the rooms of the first floor, and a gaseous but chill radiation to those upstairs.

When Thomas Wolfe emerged as a writer in late adolescence, his divided family and the boardinghouse became the focus of his fiction, and both came to stand for the darker possibilities of "progress" in the South and the nation. It was undoubtedly because Thomas Wolfe saw his family's boardinghouse as a symbol of the South that he gave it the fictional name of "Dixieland." In two highly autobiographical novels, *Look Homeward, Angel* and *Of Time and the River*, and in dozens of short stories, Wolfe chronicled the turbulent epic of a family and a region divided and transformed by "money-hunger." The father's sense of tragedy and the vicissitudes of life bred in him a fatalistic "terror and hatred of property." It was "a curse and a care, and the tax collector gets all you have in the end."

But, for the mother and for thousands of others in the New South, "property and freedom" were one and the same. Eliza Gant, the fictional female character based on Julia Wolfe, epitomizes the new disciples of "progress" and money-making. "Eliza," wrote Wolfe in *Look Homeward, Angel*, "saw Altamont not as so many hills, buildings, people: she saw it in the pattern of a gigantic blueprint. She knew the history of every piece of valuable property—who bought it, who sold it, who owned it in 1893, and what it was now worth. She was sensitive to every growing-pain of the young town. Gauging from year to year its growth in any direction, and deducing the probable direction of its future expansion." But the "mounting lust for ownership" that characterized the mother and the era inevitably became a mania for acquisition and brought not comfort but chaos in its wake.

The "mountainous verbal splendor" of Wolfe's prose and his lyrical portrait of "life, life, life" where he grew up—"savage, cruel, kind, noble, passionate, selfish, generous, stupid, ugly, beautiful, painful, joyous"—established him as one of the great American novelists of the century. Few writers ever matched Wolfe in his evocation of small-town society in the first decades of the twentieth century. Wolfe brought vibrantly to life the candy shop with its luscious temptations and the drugstore limeade so cold it made the head ache, the Jewish grocery with its sour pickles, the saloon, and the bawdy house. His fiction abounded with all the extraordinary characters who gave the community its magic and its mystery.

But the "naked intensity" of the young author made him enemies at home. He did not disguise his raw scorn for "Cheap Boosters" who believed that "we are . . . four times as civilized as our grandfathers because we go four times as fast in automobiles, because our buildings are four times as tall." He did not retreat from a rebellious determination to "say what I think of those people" who "shout 'Progress, Progress, Progress.'" The response to Wolfe's work by some in his native state was bitterness. Wrote on editor: "North Carolina and the South are spat upon."

Wolfe found his family more sympathetic to his claim that his book was "not written about people in Asheville—it is written about people everywhere." Their understanding of the family's "young Shakespeare" was fortunate, for it was through the passionately candid story of strife in a family strikingly like his own—the father a volatile stonecutter, the wife a woman who left her husband's home to open a boardinghouse—that Wolfe explored the consequences of the fevered pursuit of property and profit.

Wolfe contrasted life in the boardinghouse and his existence there with the turbulent vitality of the nearby home he grew up in. To the novelist, the two dwellings symbolized the gulf between the "guarded and sufficient strength" of the Victorian household and the unstable and rootless modern world. The home of his first six years no longer stands, but the writer recalled it as a solid and spacious house, designed like many middle-class dwellings to be a bastion of family privacy and a retreat from the stress of work and commerce. Life within the household was both warm and explosive. At the center was a father, the fictional character W. O. Gant, who was an extraordinary Victorian individualist. Wolfe wrote in *Look Homeward, Angel* that "he built his house close to the quiet hilly street; he bedded the loamy soil with flowers; he laid the short walk to the high veranda steps with great square sheets of colored marble; he put a fence of spiked iron between his house and the world." Theatrical and lavish, given to comic tirades and periodic alcoholic binges, he was the very opposite of his prudent and parsimonious wife. The family "came to look forward eagerly to his entrance" after a day's work, "for he brought with him the great gusto of living, of ritual. They would watch him in the evening as he turned to the corner below with eager strides, follow carefully the processional of his movements from the time he flung his provisions upon the kitchen table to the re-kindling of his fire, with which he was always at odds when he entered, and onto which he poured wood, coal and kerosene lavishly."

It was no wonder that the move with his mother to the boardinghouse left the boy vanquished, certain that he had "lost forever the . . . warm centre of his home." Gone was privacy, for in the boardinghouse he had to share food and shelter with strangers. Gone was space and bounty. "As the house filled, they went from room to little room, going successively down the shabby scale of their lives." There was no bed, not even a "quilt to call our own that might not be taken from us to warm the mob that rocks upon the porch and grumbles." Gone even was physical warmth. To save money, the mother scrimped on coal in the winter, walked around the house in an old sweater and a castoff man's coat, and left "Dixieland" a "chill tomb."

Had Wolfe chosen his family as a subject of a history rather than as the springboard of his fiction, he might have produced a far different interpretation of his parents' struggles. The history might have placed his parents' turmoil and his mother's boardinghouse at the very center of crosscurrents of change in family life that were beginning to emerge in North Carolina and the nation by the turn of the century. The son might have questioned why his mother married W. O. Wolfe in 1880. He was a dashing man with a business of his own, to be sure; but he was nonetheless a man she hardly knew. Thomas Wolfe might have answered that for any young woman of twenty-five

*Carrie Nation
addressing a
Salisbury crowd*

in 1880—even one like Julia, independent enough to have gone to college, taught school, sold books, and purchased real estate—independence without marriage was no virtue. "Marriage—even to a gatepost—was the only estate to which a woman should aspire."

But, twenty-five years after her marriage, Julia Wolfe certainly knew that new ideas about the independence of women were emerging. A quasi-separation from her family and entry into business would no longer make her an outcast. Many other women were, directly or indirectly, "getting out of the house," transforming themselves and society in the process. Some from the middle and upper classes joined the Woman's Christian Temperance Union and sought through the WCTU to end the reign of the saloons that so undermined family tranquility. (Before her marriage, Julia Westall Wolfe was an active temperance reformer.) The famous temperance leader Carrie Nation brought her anti-alcohol zeal to North Carolina. Six feet tall, fearless, and a drunkard's wife, she attack saloons with word and hatchet and helped create a mood favorable to the national prohibition of alcoholic drink.

Many women were joining women's clubs—North Carolina's first was founded in Charlotte in 1902—that sought first the physical beautification and then the moral uplift of their communities. On the achievements of women's clubs the Tarboro *Southerner* proclaimed in 1912: "The improvement of health, the betterment of morals, the modernizing of education and the humanizing of penology are perhaps the most vital matters of government in which North Carolina women have interested themselves. Any one who can deny either that all these things need improvement or that the activity of the Federated [Women's] Clubs has improved them betrays a startling ignorance of the facts in this state." Still other women joined the Social Purity Movement, which fought to close down brothels, rehabilitate prostitutes, and convert men from the sexual double standard to a more civilized code of self-control and abstinence.

Julia Wolfe left her home at a time of intensified public debate over "woman's place." With urgency and unprecedented forthrightness, social critics were asking whether it was woman's sole task to provide "touches of beauty and oases of calm for men harried by their work, ambition, and insecurity." Was it woman's highest fulfillment to rear a family and sacrifice her own needs to those of others? Still, the traditional view of woman's sphere that a growing number of women were beginning to combat frequently was shared by women themselves, among them Helen Campbell, who declared in *Household Economics* (1896) that "cleaning can never pass from a woman's hands . . . for to keep the world clean, this is the one great task for woman." But there were abundant indications that women were becoming an "unquiet sex": the widely noted restlessness of women confined to the home, the 100 percent rise in divorces from 1900 to 1920, the rush of young women to colleges and the refusal of many to settle down with husband and family, the small but increasing number of women who were seeking work or careers. With magazines publicly challenging the family household as a "prison and a burden and a tyrant," with feminists calling on women not only to demand the right to vote but to take up paying work outside the home, it was no surprise that one writer called the seething feminine discontent a "volcano."

But almost certainly Thomas Wolfe would have rejected women's restlessness as the reason for the family break and his mother's boardinghouse. He would have insisted on the centrality of his own vision: that the turbulence in his family's life, and of the life of the community and region around him, was connected with the disruptive triumph of the "New South." Everywhere that "progress" prevailed it brought new wealth, but everywhere it also exacted a price. Beauty became ugliness; commerce triumphed over humanity. Asheville had once been a small mountain town, Wolfe's "centre of the earth." Flashy enough for young men to stride downtown wearing peg-top yellow shoes, flaring striped trousers, and broad-brimmed hats with colored bands, the town before its conquest by an ethos of progress was nonetheless a place where "life buzzed slowly like a fly." Even the "thick plume of the fountain" near city hall rose "in slow pulses," fell upon itself, and slapped the pool in lazy rhythms. In Wolfe's vision, Asheville's "beauty and spirit" were lost when the city capitulated to tourists, the real estate boom, and "cheap Board of Trade boosters."

In the mountain countryside, the pattern was the same: economic profit, spiritual loss, beauty disfigured. Slopes and forests "had been ruinously de-timbered; the farm soil on hill sides had eroded and washed down"; deserted mines scarred the landscape. "It was evident that a huge compulsive greed had been at work: the region had been sucked and gutted, milked dry, denuded of its rich primeval treasures: something blind and ruthless had been here, grasped, and gone." The New South had lured away the young of the country-side, swept them off to the town, leaving behind kinfolk "withdrawn from the world." Those who stayed remained in the great Blue Ridge for their love of its immense wild grandeur and rocky streams, holding on to their patch of earth. But, in Wolfe's view, "their inheritance was bare."

Of progress and its perils in his region, of the richness and rending of his family, and later of his tempestuous life in the North, Thomas Wolfe was to write more than a million words. As he traveled beyond the South, he observed everywhere what he had first seen in North Carolina and the boardinghouse of his youth: an obsession with money, an equation of life with the latest goods and styles. Unable to celebrate the triumph of a consumer society in his native state or the nation, Wolfe worried that "we are lost here in America." "We've become like a nation of advertising men, all hiding behind catch phrases like 'prosperity' and 'rugged individualism' and 'the American way.' And the real things like freedom, and equal opportunity, and the integrity and worth of the individual—things that belonged to the American dream since the begin-ning—they have become just words too." Yet ultimately the novelist from Ashe-ville was not despondent. The "true fulfillment of our spirit, of our people, of our mighty and immortal land, is yet to come. I think that the true discovery of our own democracy is still before us." For Thomas Wolfe and for other North Carolinians, the American dream was yet to be accomplished, but its achieve-ment was as "certain as the morning, as inevitable as noon." Whether Wolfe the critic or Wolfe the optimist was correct, the decades ahead would determine.

Thomas C. Parramore

Part V

EXPRESS LANES AND COUNTRY ROADS
NORTH CAROLINA, 1920-2001

OVERVIEW

Although the frontier disappeared in North Carolina before the Revolutionary War, the frontier spirit lived on in the Tar Heel State well into the twentieth century. The ingredients of that spirit included a hardy frontier individualism that made each man the master of his own fortunes and the cause of his own shortcomings. In early times, this spirit had its most striking form in the *code duello* of the well-to-do and the gouging match of the common citizen. In recent times, it has manifested itself in a marked suspicion of any scheme designed to cast people together in organizational patterns or cooperative enterprises. Early and late, it has included a tendency to view government at all levels as a potential menace to the freedom and pocketbooks of individual citizens.

The period covered by this chapter witnessed a considerable erosion of this spirit, though not its disappearance. Along with certain traits of the frontier character—exclusive concern for one's own locality, mistrust of the alien in idea as well as in person—rugged individualism accounts for other of the distinguishing features of native Tar Heel thought and behavior. In time past, it meant that North Carolina was the next to last state to adopt the federal Constitution and the last to join the Confederacy. In the twentieth century, it has meant the repeated rejection of the Equal Rights Amendment and a general skepticism toward national initiatives in the realms of civil rights and social reforms.

Between 1920 and the end of the twentieth century North Carolina's frontier spirit was assailed by powerful forces from elsewhere in the nation and beyond its borders. North Carolinians remained throughout the past eighty years generally leery of "isms," of panaceas, of mere good intentions, of moral calls-to-arms. But Tar Heels still managed to find within themselves the flexibility to avoid outright confrontation with what appeared to be the undeniable will of the American people.

From a distance, the fact that a handful of articulate liberal spokesmen were tolerated and even admired in North Carolina helped give the state a reputation for progressivism beyond its neighbors. Other Americans were likely to identify North Carolina with the ideas of prominent sons such as playwright Paul Green, university president Frank Porter Graham, or editors Gerald W. Johnson and Josephus Daniels. Within the state, the views of such people were as likely to be suspect.

By the end of World War II, North Carolinians were startled to find themselves the beneficiaries of a good deal of praise and publicity from other quarters. Political analyst V. O. Key in 1949 described "progressive plutocracy" as the prevailing strength of the state in the first half of the century. In his view, a comfortable understanding between business and government leaders worked to the advantage of the state and its citizens. In comparison with other southern states, Key found North Carolinians more "energetic and ambitious" and possessing "a closer approximation to national norms, or national expectations of performance." No major scandals tainted the seats of state power, no demagogues disgraced its public deliberations. The state's economy was "virile and balanced"; its people enjoyed a reputation "for fair dealings with its Negro citizens. . . . Nowhere has cooperation between white and Negro leadership been more effective."

Even historian Arnold J. Toynbee found reasons to celebrate North Carolina's more impressive national image in the twentieth century than those of Virginia or South Carolina, which historians had once favored. Toynbee adopted Key's explanation that North Carolina, having less to lose in the way of plantations, slaves, and grandeur, had suffered less profoundly from the Civil War than her neighbors. He claimed to find "up-to-date industries, mushroom universities and a breath of the hustling, 'boosting' spirit which [one] has learnt to associate with the 'Yankees' of the North." *National Geographic* magazine gave the image the stamp of official endorsement in 1962. In an article entitled "Dixie Dynamo," it represented North Carolina as having "something inspiring" about it, "something exciting, dynamic, and somehow youthful." North Carolina, it seemed, had finally arrived.

Perhaps all this was a bit too much. Though the cause of social justice moved forward in North Carolina, organized labor made little headway in these years. Industrial gains were impressive; nonetheless, per capita income remained tragically low. A code of civility cushioned relations between the races, but it also made the rising challenge to segregation seem a matter of bad manners. Still, the enthusiasm of outsiders was not misplaced. As in much of the rest of the nation, the average citizen's standard of living expanded to embrace the automobile, electric utilities, and a busy regimen of recreation and cultural enlightenment.

The period 1920 to the present saw the construction here of the nation's longest state-maintained system of roads, the establishment of great national

forests and state parks, the emergence of a vast panoply of tourist accommodations. It was an age that saw the beginnings of a vital movement in historic preservation from the Outer Banks to the Great Smoky Mountains. Education and health care, literature and art, were far superior at the end of the period to what they had been at the outset.

As the twentieth century came to a close, Tar Heels could look back on the past eight decades with no little satisfaction at what they had accomplished and with greater confidence in their ability to resolve other problems. In terms of their willingness and capacity to respond to challenges, Tar Heels found that they had lost none of their old frontier spirit. They anticipated that the next century would be still better than the last.

The urge of growing numbers of Tar Heels to identify themselves with, and participate more fully in, the national experience mirrored the resurgence of American strength and prosperity. For the nation, the sobering disillusions of a decade of economic malaise after 1929 were all but forgotten

Rural poverty persisted into the twentieth century.

in the 1940s. Never had the virtues of capitalism and democracy appeared more unassailable, whatever the momentary success of the Soviet Union might mean. When the communist-led Soviet Union began to dissolve in the last two decades of the twentieth century, North Carolinians' faith in democracy swelled even more.

It was not just material abundance and vindicated democracy that the nation claimed for itself but a higher moral vision: a vision of a world without racial antagonisms, religious discord, or ethnocentric squabbles. The employment of the states' rights doctrine as a shield against that vision made the doctrine's proponents seem mean-spirited and vicious. Never had the ethical ideals of the nation as a whole seemed more demonstrably just and high-minded. The nation that defeated fascism and communism undertook the construction of a more humane social order abroad and at home.

Perhaps the Red Scare of the 1920s and the McCarthy purges of the 1950s should have suggested more forcefully than they did an element of delusion in the nation's ambitious image of itself. But the shock waves of the 1960s went far toward weakening faith, at home and abroad, in the permanence and benevolence of the national creed. By 1970 the assassinations of prominent leaders, the aroused protests of minorities, and the quagmire of foreign war had brought Americans to a period of uncommon introspection and self-examination. This phenomenon increased with the rise of international terrorism and attacks on Americans and their institutions at home and abroad.

No longer was it quite so certain that the world only hungered to share our vision, to be guided by our inspiration and secured by our might. It had taken the experience of half a century to drive home this lesson, to cast the shadow of realism over the glittering vista of idealism. Perhaps in the long run the nation would be better for it, but the immediate effect was a reassessment of the headlong drive of various states and sections to make a seat for themselves on the national bandwagon. By 1970 one heard talk of a "New Federalism" that emphasized self-help and localism in attacking social problems and other concerns.

Since that time, North Carolinians have been drawing different conclusions from the past decades of change and turmoil. For some, the lesson was that society should abandon altogether collective efforts to remake itself in any image and leave it to individuals once more to strive as best they could for themselves. For others, the state seemed infinitely richer in spirit and talent as a consequence of the barriers broken and programs created through social struggle. Perhaps all North Carolinians might begin to look to their own peculiar heritage for guidance and inspiration. For there were values in that heritage that had nothing to do with oppression of the weak or exploitation of the underprivileged. States' rights and localism did not necessarily mean the reign of bigotry but could as readily mean a fuller participation of the individual in the life of the community, a closer bond between leaders and led. Or so it appeared as the state and nation came to assess a third century of their experience and to prepare for the challenges of a fourth.

2

THE SOD-BUSTERS

"Hog and Hominy" Days

Between 1920 and 1950, for better or worse, the life of the farmer was transformed. Once crowded, the country came to seem empty. "The people are gone!" reported those who remained. Machinery replaced mules and men. Tenants and sharecroppers, once a majority of those who tilled the soil, had virtually disappeared. Less visibly, giant corporations and government agencies gradually replaced many family farms. Agriculture had become a large-scale business.

Farming received a severe blow when the Great Depression struck in 1929 and persisted until relieved by President Franklin D. Roosevelt's New Deal programs and the onset of World War II. Many rural North Carolinians who lived through the hardships of the depression recalled the period as the "Hoover time," after President Herbert Hoover. "In Hoover time," remembered Mollie Alderman of Duplin County, "my sister-in-law's husband gave us a squirrel an' we cooked that squirrel three times. The first time we cooked it we put dumplins in 'im. Next meal comes along we put pastry on 'im, an' the next time we put rice in there. An' that was the last of that squirrel. That Hoover almost perished us to death."

A social historian of the 1930s claimed for the typical North Carolinian five characteristic attitudes: conservatism, individualism, provincialism, sectionalism, and superstition. In these traits Tar Heels of the early twentieth century preserved their continuity and identity with the pioneers of the eighteenth century. And, though none of these attitudes disappeared in the twentieth century, none escaped the assault of the new forces that stirred the hemisphere and swept the nation.

Among the eddies and currents that affected farmers in North Carolina, the most obvious to many Americans were those that exerted themselves from the outside. The coming of the tractor in the 1920s and 1930s, the widespread introduction of electric power in the 1940s and 1950s, the growth of schools and transport facilities, and the vigorous economic interventionism of the

Mules remained a part of farming for decades in the twentieth century.

New Deal were among the most significant of these. Slowly, often reluctantly, farmers bowed to the necessity of becoming agricultural technicians, mechanics, electricians. They acknowledged the need to surrender a measure of their independence to the dictates of distant bureaucrats. But they were equally aware of internal changes in the way farmers related to one another and to the nonfarming society. These included novel forms of cooperative enterprise, new arrangements for ownership, and new marketing techniques. Inevitably, such agents of change sooner or later profoundly affected family relationships and transformed the quality of daily living—not always in agreeable ways.

Only Texas had more farms than North Carolina in 1920. Across the nation the number of farms had peaked, but this would not happen in North Carolina for another thirty years. Cotton, artificially spurred on by wartime and post-war demand, briefly overtook tobacco as the state's leading cash crop. Corn, sweet potatoes, peanuts, and soybeans were other major crops, placing North Carolina among the top seven states in the annual value of farm produce.

Half a century later, nostalgia had transformed the hardships and deprivation of the depressed years between the two world wars into "hog and hominy days," when sturdy yeoman families lived contentedly on the simple abundance of nature. Old-timers in an urban and industrial age remember with special fondness the farm barns of their adolescence, the big cornfields, the vast cribs where the corn was stored, and aromatic smokehouses in which corn-fed pork was cured. During the depression years, as in earlier times, cattle and hogs foraged for themselves in woods and fields and returned in the evening to the high-pitched summons of the cattle call and "coor pig" that resounded across bucolic distances. In the fall, hogs were penned and fattened on "slops" from the kitchen, sweet potatoes, and such corn as was unfit for either people or cattle.

Hog-killing, like corn-shucking or wood-cutting time, was a social occasion during which neighbors gathered to divide the hundred separate chores that had to be performed. Hog killing began soon after the first heavy frosts in December or January, the men going down to the pens in early morning to shoot and bleed the selected hogs. The carcasses were dumped into a vat of hot water that loosened the hair so it could be scraped from the hide. The hog was then hung on a makeshift gallows for butchering, a process that wasted very little of the animal's flesh.

The liver was saved for stew, the intestines for "chitlins" and sausage casing, the ears and snout for souse, the feet for pickling, and the fat meat for lard, crackling bread, and seasoning. The skull, severed from the trunk on the cutting table, was cracked open for the brains, a choice delicacy; the backs and other chunks became pork chops and sausage. Finally the hams, shoulders, and side meat were packed in salt, where they remained for a couple of months before being cleaned and wired for hanging in the smokehouse.

The farmer's palate would not be satisfied until the best of the corn crop had been turned into hominy grits. This was accomplished by boiling the husks loose from the pulp with ashes or lye in an iron pot, then washing off the husks and cooking the pulp for hours to leave it tender. "And then, later on," in the words of a farm woman, "you cook your ham. And take out your hominy and heat that. Nothing better. Hominy and ham. Has a wonderful flavor. Hog and hominy."

The careworn sentinels of "hog and hominy" days still dot the countryside of rural North Carolina: old and decayed tobacco barns, the crumbling remains of livestock barns, hogpens, privies, the shells of abandoned dwelling houses. "It's amazing how many tobacco barns you see when you drive through the Carolinas," reported one visitor. "There's several sitting around every house. Looks like everybody there must be a tobacco farmer." The livestock barn usually included a central passageway that separated cow stalls on one side from mule or horse stalls on the other. But the gambrel roof also covered storage space for feed, tools, and machinery. Here cows were milked, horses shod, equipment repaired, sick animals treated. But it was also the place where one might "pull up a bale of hay," as one farm lad recalled it, "just inside the door during a rainstorm and listen to the rain on the roof while you communicated with your soul." It was where children played hide-and-seek or performed rafter acrobatics with the hay as a cushion against any mishap, where dignity was recovered after a personal setback, and, like as not, where love was made.

The "Cottontots"

Such reverie was likely to be a heritage of the lifestyle associated in the interwar years with farm ownership. But a third of North Carolina's white farmers and two-thirds of the black were tenants, mostly sharecroppers. Tenantry, in fact, was still expanding, and the average size of a North Carolina farm was still declining. As late as 1954, tenants comprised well over a third of all the state's farm families, and the average size of a Tar Heel farm—sixty-eight acres—was the smallest in the United States. Socially, tenantry was a system that may have saved the lives of the former slaves and impoverished whites who had sprung from the ruin of the Civil War. Economically, however, the system was a disaster, fostering a gulf between occupancy and ownership—between labor and its rewards—that wasted some of the country's best farmland.

Not for the typical tenant did the future hold romantic memories of "hog and hominy days." Tenant farmers owned little or no livestock and thus had no need for barns or other outbuildings. Most of them occupied farms too small for anything but total concentration on one or two cash crops. Most tenants were doomed by the long agricultural depression of those years to flee eventually to cities in search of employment. Only a few of them would achieve farm ownership. Tenants, sharecroppers especially, made up a class of itinerant poor who were buffeted from one meager farm to the next, living only for the day or the season. "It's a rare thing to find a sharecropper that's thrifty and saving," declared a Northampton County landlord. "The white ones as a rule ain't no better than the [blacks]. They're usually the slums of the world. . . . If 'twasn't for we landlords, what in God's world would become of this shiftless crowd?"

Mrs. Jim Jeffcoat summed up the tenants' view of their situation. "We have never owned a horse or a mule or a cow or any tools or anything to ride in," she proclaimed. "Of course, we ain't never owned a house, and we never will. The house we've lived in ain't worth owning. They ain't worth nothing to nobody except to furnish pore croppers like us who can't do no better." Another tenant farm woman elaborated on the despair of tenancy. "Tenants ain't got no chance," she lamented. "I don't know who gets the money, but it ain't the poor. It gets worse every year—the land gets more wore out, the prices for tobacco gets lower, and everything you got to buy gets higher. . . . I'm trying to 'be content' like the Bible says and not to worry, but I don't see no hope."

A study of 351 black and white families in northeastern Chatham County in 1923 showed rural life, tenant farming in particular, to be bleak to the point of despair. Almost half the families studied were tenants. Average daily income for a member of a sharecropping family was 9¢; for a member of the relatively comfortable farm-owning family, 33¢. Most tenants lived in unpainted frame houses at least thirty years old. None had running water, and only eight enjoyed the luxury of an outdoor privy. "The bushes and barn lot buildings," the report noted, "are the screens of family privacy for thirty houses." The study enumerated 203 missing windowpanes in various tenant homes, in many of which "it is possible to study astronomy through the holes in the roof and geology through the cracks in the floor."

Most tenant wives worked alongside their husbands in the fields eight to ten hours a day for up to seven months a year. At age seven or eight, boys and girls joined the farm labor force for all but six months of the school year. Doctors were visited or called only when all else failed. Nearly one infant in four was stillborn or died before age six. None of the tenant children had ever been vaccinated for typhoid or smallpox.

Apart from one two-year high school, the northeastern corner of Chatham County offered education in the form of six old, weather-stained, one-teacher schools. The teachers were mostly teen-aged girls and women, none of them a college graduate. Illiteracy among tenants ran close to 10 percent, and most children were finished with formal education by the end of the fifth or sixth grade. One tenant family in four subscribed to a newspaper; books and periodicals were rare. In describing her childhood schooling, Frances Carson noted that "Papa was a farmer and he made us work so hard that we didn't go to school half the time. We had to stay at home in the fall and grade 'backer and pick cotton, and in the spring we had to stay out to plant it. That's why I never got out of the fifth grade."

The unrivaled community focus in rural North Carolina was the church. All the church buildings had been painted at least "once upon a time" and were kept clean and in good repair. Most of the preachers were nonresidents who visited their flocks one Sunday a month; thus, most churchgoers alternated Sundays among several churches and denominations. The signal event of the year was the revival or "protracted meeting," which followed the autumn harvest. During such meetings "even the bootleggers fringed the outskirts of

Picking cotton

the crowds and . . . plied their trades." But sharecroppers often belonged to no church, owing to their inability to read the hymns or contribute to the collection boxes. Though built before 1920, the following churches that can still be seen today are typical of those used in the two decades following that year: Shiloh Church (no longer used), in Penny Hill, at the Edgecombe-Pitt County line; the Chapel of the Good Shepherd, in the Ridgeway vicinity, in Warren County; and Pleasant Green Church, near Cole Mill Road, in Orange County.

The country store, like the church, was destined to retain well into the jet age its role as an important institution. When bad weather prohibited work in the fields, the tenant and landlord alike rode or walked to the general store. Here, swatting flies in summer or huddled around a potbellied stove in winter, the men of rural North Carolina learned from one another and shared the little they knew of the world beyond. Often they brought in some eggs or chicken or beeswax to swap for supplies, and the storekeeper was obliged to keep a little of everything on hand. On leaving, they would carry away as much salt, sugar, snuff, chewing tobacco, coffee, and whiskey as their produce would bring in trade and whatever combs, shoes, paregoric, nails, axheads, or ready-made clothes their feeble credit would allow. Typical of such stores of the period is Patterson's Mill Country Store on Farrington Road in Durham.

Cotton and tobacco were the principal crops, accounting for over half of North Carolina's farm income. These crops were a boon to small farmers because nearly all the work involved in production was done by hand and did not suffer from competition with mechanized neighbors. In fact, little real progress was made in mechanizing either crop before the decade of the 1950s.

Tobacco and cotton were grown throughout much of the state, and by the 1920s North Carolina had the largest tobacco and second largest textile indus-

Grading tobacco

try in the nation. But heavy concentration on nonfood crops lay at the root of the central paradox of the time: North Carolina, despite its devotion to agriculture, was a heavy importer of food. Much of what might have been profit was absorbed in the purchase of food and feed that could have been produced cheaply and in abundance at home. Dependence on nonfood crops also meant that farmers had ready money only for a while after a harvest and lived on credit the rest of the year.

Harvesting cotton involved the brutal labor of stooping and bending for every fluff of the fiber. No genius had done for picking cotton what Eli Whitney did for removing the seeds over a century before. Ginned cotton that had brought 35¢ a pound in 1919 commanded less than 6¢ in 1931. Global overproduction brought a sharp decline in cotton acreage after the mid-1920s, and "King Cotton" abdicated in favor of Duke Tobacco.

Flue-cured tobacco was produced in several sections of the state, while burley was confined to the Mountain region. Farmers who had been unable to keep up with wartime demand, however, found that they had grossly overproduced tobacco in 1920. As with cotton, prices fell until, in 1932, the leaf brought only about a sixth of what it had fetched in 1919. Federally imposed allotments helped to achieve a gradual recovery for cotton and tobacco after 1934, but it was a long time before farmers felt adequately rewarded for the work involved in producing these crops.

The work of cultivating, harvesting, and curing tobacco was an eighteen-hour-a-day ordeal. Seeds planted in a cloth- or mulch-covered bed for about two months were transplanted into rows that had to be repeatedly cultivated to loosen the soil and keep out weeds. When the plant bloomed, the bloom was cut off to allow the upper leaves to develop. This "topping," like "suckering" (removing lateral shoots) and "priming" (picking the leaves as they ripen), was

Tobacco barn

also hand labor. The leaves, often up to 150,000 to an acre, were then sledded to the barn, strung in bunches on sticks, and hung on rocks for curing.

Tobacco barns had to be tight enough to seal in the high curing temperatures achieved by the furnace in the wall or under the floor. Pipes (or flues) circulated hot air that yellowed the leaves, killed the stems to prevent juice from running out, and, finally, dried the leaves. It all required round-the-clock vigilance for several days to keep the heat at proper levels and prevent an accident that could destroy in a few minutes the income of a season. Only after the dried leaves were graded (sorted by quality), tied in bundles, and packed, were they ready for market. Grading was a sociable task; women enjoyed the work. One explained: "Men ain't no good in 'bacca. They can't set still and work steady. They's always got to be goin' outdoors to see about somp'n—even if they ain't got no excuse better'n the dog." A guided tour of Duke Homestead, in Durham, includes a grading bench and an explanation of all the steps in tobacco production from seedbed to market.

A dismayed observer emerged from his sojourn in Chatham with misgivings over the role and fate of the sharecroppers, whose lives were bound so closely to this unremitting regimen. "They lack abiding citizenship," was his somber estimate, "and a sense of proprietary interest in schools and churches and neighborhood enterprises. They lack a sense of responsibility for community morals [and] . . . are widely tempted into the business of making and vending illicit liquors."

Indeed, Prohibition, which became law in North Carolina in 1909 and nationally in 1920, sometimes seemed specifically designed to help the rural poor survive the travails of prolonged depression. Unlike the raising of livestock or poultry, moonshining required little capital—at least when under-

Early tractor and planter

taken on a modest scale as a community service. "I've seen fathers take little kids five and six years old with 'em to the still," claimed a Prohibition era sheriff. "And they just growed up in it; they didn't think there was anything wrong with it. That was their family business." The manufacture of illicit whiskey was the mainstay of many a North Carolina farm family.

Corn mash fermented with sugar, steamed in a boiler, and condensed through copper tubing could produce an agreeable whiskey. Apples, peaches, rye, wheat, barley, potatoes, and many other crops likewise yielded valuable alcoholic potions. A bushel of mash and a hundred pounds of sugar made eleven gallons of high-proof, tax-free whiskey that could mean the difference between failure for a season and breaking even—or perhaps even a small profit. A Duplin County bootlegger related how "I more or less kept my work a secret, I'd go to bed early 'n crawl out the window, work, makin' likker all night, an' then I'd slip back in 'fore the chickens crowed for day. . . . Kept a drunk around so's he could test it. If it didn't kill 'm, why, I could put it on the market. Didn't never kill one tester, not outright."

There were hazards in moonshine liquor. The heads and tails of the brew contained poisonous aldehydes and fusel oil. Any liquor distilled through lead coils instead of copper could cause lead poisoning. And then there was the sheriff or federal revenue agent. Implication in the death of one such officer at a still caused David Marshall ("Carbine") Williams, the most gifted Tar Heel inventor of the epoch, to spend much of his life in prison.

Prohibition's end in 1933 reduced but by no means curtailed moonshining and bootlegging. Huge road-building programs and the popularity of the automobile after World War II laced the state with innumerable Thunder Roads, along which prospective Junior Johnsons pitted their rum-running

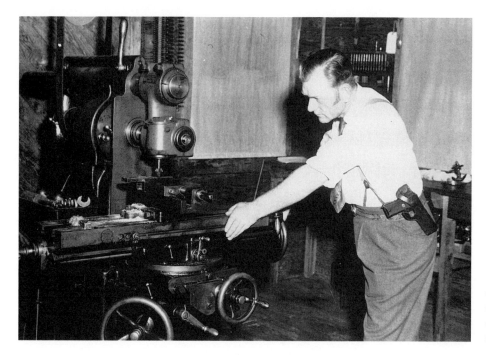

*David M.
("Carbine") Williams
in his gun shop,
Godwin*

skills against the minions of the law. Progress often brought two headaches for every aspirin tablet.

The Case for Interdependence

Some analysts simply wrote off the small farmer as a doomed species. Clarence Poe, a Chatham County native and product of a one-room school there, followed the drift of the times in this regard. After becoming editor of the *Progressive Farmer*, an agricultural newspaper in Raleigh, in 1899, he built it into one of the great mass-circulation farm journals in the world. But Poe's editorials, perhaps reflecting his experience with small-farm America while coming of age in Chatham County, evolved in favor of the large farmer, the most cost-efficient unit. It seemed useless, after all, to preach of tractors and combines to those for whom a good mule was still a status symbol, fruitless to sing the praises of indoor plumbing to those not able to own backyard privies.

Other authorities felt they saw a possible salvation for the small farmer but were puzzled as to how it might be achieved. Farmers, one sociologist observed, "can not or will not act together in group production, group processing, group credit, and self-defensive group action in farm policies. . . . In the lonely life of isolated farms, there is developed an economic and social inertia that is stubbornly resistant to change of any sort." Another sociologist felt that

Clarence Poe

"farmers are bred to think privately and locally in terms of the family and the neighborhood. They do not easily think in terms of the community and the commonwealth. The private-local mind of the farmer in the South is the ultimate obstacle to country community life and cooperative enterprise."

Experience demonstrated the persistence of the provincialism and individualism that lay at the core of the problem. The severe crash in farm prices in 1920 spawned marketing co-ops among cotton, tobacco, and peanut farmers, but only the cotton co-op survived beyond 1925. The Farmers' Union, chartered in North Carolina in 1905, was moribund by the late 1920s. But these were statewide and interstate experiments, and some strictly local co-ops survived, publicizing improved techniques and enabling their members to buy cheaper supplies. The modest success of these small enterprises in turn helped some farmers to overcome their suspicions of cooperative efforts.

A more effective mode of interdependence in the 1920s, however, was that facilitated by what is now the Agricultural Extension Service. This service was jointly created in 1909 by the State Agricultural and Mechanical College at Raleigh (now North Carolina State University) and the U.S. Department of Agriculture. By 1923 the extension service had "county agents" in three-quarters of the state's 100 counties. Most counties also had female demonstration agents who promoted rural home improvement. Boys' Corn Clubs and

Girls' Canning Clubs (later known as 4-H Clubs) were extension groups that paralleled the adult programs.

Extension agents popularized better ways of preparing, cultivating, and fertilizing crops. They encouraged wiser seed selection and drainage, improved livestock production, crop rotation, the organization of cooperative credit unions, and modern ideas of hygiene, diet, and sanitation. The agents also kept farmers abreast of the findings of the Agricultural Experiment Stations operated by State College.

Assistant Director of Agricultural Extension Jane S. McKimmon (the first woman to graduate from North Carolina State College) established home demonstration clubs in every county of the state. These clubs taught women—white and black—how to provide food year-round for their households and earn additional income with the surplus, how to grade and package eggs and vegetables, how to bake bread, and how to beautify their homes through sewing and handicrafts. McKimmon earned a master's degree in 1929 and received an honorary doctor of laws degree from the University of North Carolina at Chapel Hill in 1934. She served as vice chairman of the state Rural Electrification Authority and on a number state boards and committees. Farmers' markets were an outgrowth of McKimmon's program. The curb market on North Church Street in Hendersonville, in Henderson County, began on the sidewalk in 1924, but since 1954 it has had its own building in which to sell flowers, crafts, and food.

The depression of 1929 generated a sense of catastrophe against which the trials of preceding years paled to insignificance. The market collapse cut farm income by 60 percent, and farmers reared to detect Old World tyranny in any formal organization found themselves listening attentively to the firebrands of regimentation. The Grange, defunct in North Carolina since the late nineteenth century, fluttered back to life in 1929 under the inspiration of Clarence Poe. Behind the leadership of Alamance County dairy farmer Kerr Scott, it tried to channel the frustration of farmers. By 1933 it had 12,500 members and claimed success in procuring such legislative relief as tax cuts and steps toward rural electrification. But farmers soon began deserting the Grange, perhaps impatient with its penchant for long-range remedies in the face of imminent disaster.

Increasingly, farmers looked to quicker solutions, and cooperation often seemed to be the answer. The statewide Farmers' Cooperative Exchange and the Central Carolina Cooperative Exchange in the upper Piedmont were two among many such groups formed in the early 1930s. They offered facilities for the cooperative purchase of fertilizers, feeds, seeds, and other supplies; promoted cooperative marketing; and stimulated interest in grading and other marketing fundamentals. The success of these efforts pointed up the growing acceptance among some farmers of the philosophy of common effort and foretold a time when scores of co-ops would serve the interests of farmers in hundreds of ways. "During the 1933–1936 period," one publication rhapsodized, "North Carolina farmers have learned more about cooperation than they had in the entire history of the State."

But co-ops by themselves were no cure-all for the problems of farming. Tobacco farmers, for example, experimented in the early 1920s with the Tri-State Growers' Cooperative. Members turned their tobacco over to the co-op, which graded, redried, and stored it until the best time for marketing. But farmers proved wary of the scheme, and the Tri-State never gained enough control of the crop to create the monopoly it needed. Tri-State folded by 1926. A similar fate met efforts of the Federal Farm Board to organize a tobacco cooperative between 1929 and 1931.

Reacting in time-honored fashion to the emergency of the Great Depression, farmers increased production of their cash crops. This had the effect of driving prices down still further. The agony of these years forced many of them out of business for good. It was an era that was to leave bitter memories of "the sweat of an entire crop," as a Tar Heel recalled it, "with nothing in hand at the end to show for their labors; walking everywhere . . . because there was either no gas or no car; swapping eggs for absolute necessities at a penny apiece; working (when any work was available) at five cents an hour and getting paid in anything but money."

The deprived condition of North Carolina's depression poor remained pervasive and painfully obvious to all who cared to look. As a child, Diana Morgan, who was considerably better off than many of her poorer neighbors, visited her family's laundress, Caroline. "She was always gracious and would invite me in," remembered Morgan. "She never apologized for the way anything looked. I thought to myself at the time: How odd that Caroline uses newspapers to paper walls. I didn't have any brains at eleven or twelve or whatever to think: what kind of country is this that lets people live in houses like this and necessitates their using the Sunday paper for wallpaper."

Roosevelt's New Deal provided many rural North Carolinians with a cushion against the fall that could not be prevented. In tobacco, the result was little short of startling. When the Agricultural Adjustment Administration (AAA) signaled its receptivity to the ideas of farmers in 1933, tobacco men responded with scores of local and mass meetings. They proposed that the AAA find some means of limiting production so as to raise prices. This was accomplished through a contract system that pushed prices from 11.6¢ a pound in 1932 to

15.3¢ in 1933 and added over $50 million in that year to the income of tobacco growers.

Given the political realities of the epoch, it was perhaps inevitable that this and similar programs aided the well-to-do farmer far more than the poor one. "The government farm program hasn't helped me much," declared a Northampton County landlord in 1939. "Some big farmers profited by it. . . . All I drew last year for co-opin' with the government was $25, and half of that went to the sharecroppers." Tenants who made the acreage and crop reductions encouraged by the government often received nothing for their trouble, the landlord simply pocketing the federal checks without sharing them. On the whole, however, the system worked, and complaints never reached serious proportions.

Other federal programs, such as the Rural Electrification Authority, would ultimately play key roles in raising rural living standards. But farmers and other North Carolinians remained on the whole suspicious of the bureaucrat bearing gifts and yielded to federal initiatives with misgivings. Tar Heel congressmen who warmly endorsed the federal tobacco program raised the cry of socialism against parallel ventures in behalf of the cash crops of other sections of the country or for the relief of distressed elements such as the urban poor. "The economic emergency of the 1930s," concludes a recent study of the tobacco program, "failed to shift traditions of individualism and business hostility to federal intervention."

The Guns of Deliverance

No measure of relief or cooperation could replace the stimulus of a resurgent economy and demand for farm produce, and this was the roundabout achievement of Adolf Hitler more than Roosevelt and the New Dealers. An agricultural boom was touched off by World War II, bringing economic blessings destined to rescue North Carolina farms from the blight of preceding decades. Wartime military and industrial demands drew off hordes of young men, including hundreds of farmers. Scarce agricultural labor forced many farmers to acquire tractors and other machines they might otherwise have resisted buying. Returning veterans were offered educational opportunities that would soon be translated into improved farms and higher living standards.

The war's end, however, found North Carolina still agriculturally backward in comparison with many other parts of the country. One farm in seven had running water; telephones were rare, mules abundant. Much corn and other grain was still imported, but the state was in the midst of enormous changes.

Farms began increasing in size during the 1950s, making feasible the use of heavy machinery. Corn pickers, hay bailers, grain combines, trucks, and tractors, often shared among a number of neighbors, came into general use. So did pesticides, herbicides, hybrid seeds, and much else. By the end of the 1950s, three farm families in four had automobiles, every other one had a freezer, and every third one a telephone.

Tenantry declined rapidly in the postwar era, spurred on by a black exodus after 1950. Cotton fell rapidly in importance, but North Carolina produced two-thirds of the nation's flue-cured tobacco. The first transplanters and harvesters appeared in the tobacco fields, emancipating thousands from traditional drudgery. Farmers diversified production, turning to sweet potatoes, soybeans, beef, milk, turkeys, chickens, and eggs. By 1960 poultry that formerly went north for processing could be handled at the rate of 3 million birds a week in the state's processing plants. A diversified farm was one on which tractors and other equipment could be used year-round, rather than merely from time to time. The most successful farmers were those who understood the new relationship between farming and the world of commerce and could transform themselves into agribusinessmen.

The encroachment of urban boundaries into the countryside and the rapid growth of transport facilities meant that many members of farm families could now take full-time or part-time work off the farm. Farm income tended to improve with the availability of outside work, and the gulf that historically separated urban from rural life narrowed. Many who abandoned commercial farming were able to continue as part-time farmers who lived mainly on nonfarm incomes.

Food production so far outstripped population growth that farmers did not often enjoy the full reward of their new methods and technology. The standard of living on North Carolina's farms, for all its progress, lagged well behind that in cities. Many farm homes of the 1960s lacked plumbing, complete kitchen facilities, and other conveniences. Farm income was much lower than urban income, and rural areas usually lagged behind cities in availability of health care, educational quality, and other indexes of social advance. Offsetting such considerations was the reflection that rural America still enjoyed a relative freedom—from crime, pollution, and traffic—for which many urbanites might gladly surrender some of their own benefits. In the flight to suburbia lay an admission that, for many Americans, country living had not lost its charm.

New patterns of ownership and operation emerged as farms became larger and more mechanized. Some farmers pooled their resources in corporate arrangements. Specialized operations, notably in dairying and poultry, became

Mattamuskeet Lodge when it was the pumping station for the New Holland Farm experiment

more common. And, in the 1960s and 1970s, North Carolina witnessed the advent of the "superfarm," perhaps the most exciting development of all.

The vast areas of swampland in eastern North Carolina had for more than a century tempted the imagination of agriculturalists. Beneath much of the wasteland lay some of the blackest, richest soil in the world, soil that could not fail to yield immense farming wealth if it could be cleared and drained. Moreover, such areas raised the possibility of eastern superfarms to rival those already pioneered in the Midwest. But a Tar Heel superfarm, much closer to northeastern population centers and European markets, seemed likely to surpass any profits dreamed of by remote midwesterners.

After several false starts in the vicinity of Lake Mattamuskeet in Hyde County, the 1920s saw the emergence of New Holland Farm, the state's initial superfarm. August Hecksher, a wealthy New Yorker, poured money into canals, ditches, and pumping plants to drain the lake, and brought in Dutch immigrants to do the work and a midwestern superfarmer to head the operation. A landscape architect laid out a town called New Holland. By 1933 the farm had fifty-one tractors, 1,000 acres of rice, the world's largest soybean acreage, and land devoted to the cultivation of buckwheat, lespedeza, barley, celery, asparagus, rye, oats, flax, potatoes, and popcorn.

Neighboring small farms grumbled that the enterprise would not work and perhaps experienced some satisfaction over what happened in 1933. Failing pumps and attacks by regiments of armyworms, grasshoppers, and corn borers so devastated New Holland that Hecksher gave up. The multimillion-dollar investment was written off, and North Carolina's first superfarm ended in disaster. Another Dutch enterprise began in 1925 at Terra Ceia, in Beaufort County. A New York investment company tried to develop its holdings as farmland. That project also failed, but the manager began to use the land for tulips and built a thriving business. A tulip festival with street dancing and big bands became an annual event in Washington, North Carolina, beginning in 1937 and continuing until World War II.

But such experiments were more nearly the beginning of the superfarm concept than the end. Several similar operations were opened in the northeastern section of the state during the 1960s and 1970s. First Colony Farms, the brainchild of former Winston-Salem trucking executive Malcolm McLean, was the most ambitious of these. When First Colony began operating in 1973, it encompassed over 350,000 acres in four counties in eastern North Carolina. McLean envisioned an enterprise that within a few years would produce 1 million hogs and 100,000 head of cattle a year. First Colony Farms became the largest privately owned, single-unit farm in the United States. Although First Colony was the extreme example of large commercial agriculture, there nevertheless has been in the past few decades a growing trend toward larger, more commercial farming in the Tar Heel State. The number of small, family-owned farms has been declining since World War II. The number of farmers continued to decrease, as labor saving machinery reduced the need for labor and large agribusinesses purchased thousands of acres to farm commercially. The average North Carolina farm in 1940 had 68 acres. In 1980 it had 142 acres. In 1947, 40 of every 100 jobs in the state were in agriculture. By 1987, the number of farm jobs had declined to only 3 of every 100.

The age of agribusiness leaves little room for the independent farmer. The corporation's access to credit, influence with government, and links with national foodstore chains give it enormous power. Small or large, farmers increasingly have little choice but to contract or sell out to corporations. Farming is now seen in large measure as a link in the chain of production that runs from factory and laboratory directly to the consumer's refrigerator and linen closet.

Epilogue

In many ways, Chatham County epitomizes rural life and change in present-day North Carolina. By 1973 Highways 64 and 15-501 sped traffic through Chatham County past towering silos and long rows of poultry houses. Here is vivid evidence of the changes that have brought higher standards of living to nearly every farm family. But the driver who turns off the main routes, who pauses for a fill-up or a Coke at Bynum or Farrington, still finds stretches of country whose appearance has changed but little since 1920.

The log structure and the two-room shanty are still to be seen here and there along the back ways, though rapidly giving way to the brick cottage or mobile home. The country church and crossroads general store survive, though there are fewer of the latter than in earlier times. Abandoned houses, boarded-up businesses, and fields gone to weeds testify to the migration that has taken so many away from farming. Yet, the county is still rural and in some respects still geared to the rhythms of earlier times.

Chatham is a large livestock and poultry county. But residents of the wooded back roads are often industrial workers in Durham or clerks in the university town, Chapel Hill. If they farm at all, it is likely to be in some form of subsistence gardening. Recreational opportunities have expanded mightily for them. An immense reservoir known as Jordan Lake has been built by the U.S. Army Corps of Engineers, bringing boaters and others seeking outdoor recreation to Chatham County in droves. Television cables and satellite dishes mark the county's houses and yards, water and sewer pipes stretched beneath its floors, automobiles wait in its driveways. New subdivisions have appeared to serve as bedroom communities for the nearby cities and Research Triangle Park. Health care is readily accessible, and educational opportunity has expanded powerfully. If the county's inhabitants crave heartier cultural fare than TV or movies, the arts and sciences beckoned from Duke University in Durham and the University of North Carolina at Chapel Hill.

3

THE ELECTRIC CORNUCOPIA

The Big Three

Although North Carolina in 1920 might with ample justice have been called an agricultural state, by far the larger part of its wealth at this time came from manufacturing. The leading industries, each thriving on cheap labor and the local availability of raw materials, were tobacco, cotton textiles, and furniture. In the preceding twenty years, North Carolina had advanced from twenty-seventh to fifteenth among all the states in the value of manufactured articles. During the 1920s, it would become the leading industrial state in the Southeast. In this rapid advance lay the source of both the pride and the heartbreak of the Old North State.

The three major industries were largely concentrated in an area roughly the shape of a reaping hook. The tip of this configuration lay in Raleigh, the blade curving west and then southwest along the route of the Southern Railway through Durham, Greensboro, and Winston-Salem to Charlotte. The handle stretched westward from Charlotte, paralleling the South Carolina border to Rutherford County. In this Piedmont region were concentrated most of the main population centers of North Carolina.

Manufacturing was by 1920 a billion-dollar-a-year activity in North Carolina, which ranked second only to Texas in the South. Drawing heavily on tenants leaving or being driven from farms, the state's industrial enterprises employed more than 160,000 people in some 600 plants from the mountains to the sea. Other than the Big Three, the chief Tar Heel industries were pulp and paper, lumber, fertilizer, flour and meal, cottonseed oil, leather, railway car construction and repair, food processing, and publishing and printing. But all the lesser industries combined produced only a third of the wealth of the larger three.

The dominant power source for the major manufacturers was the Southern (later Duke) Power Company, established in 1904 by tobacco magnate James B. ("Buck") Duke. Other producers of electric power (Carolina Power and Light in the east, Tallassee in the west) served the state, but Southern

controlled the industrial Piedmont, supplying energy from its hydroelectric stations on the Catawba River.

The tobacco industry was almost wholly contained within three cities in the same small area of the northern Piedmont: R. J. Reynolds at Winston-Salem, Liggett and Myers at Durham, and the American Tobacco Company at Durham and Reidsville. The great growth of this industry in North Carolina had occurred largely since 1913 and was the result of the burgeoning popularity of the cigarette. An urban society that recoiled from snuff and chewing tobacco and was often too fastidious for pipes and cigars found in the cigarette the ideal form of smoking. Even women and girls of the flapper generation felt comfortable with the cigarette, which was handy to carry, less messy than rival articles, inexpensive, and, to the taste not accustomed to stronger fare, satisfying. Each of the three most popular brands introduced after 1913 — Camels, Chesterfields, and Lucky Strikes — was made in North Carolina, Camels exclusively so.

Reynolds was producing 30 billion Camels a year before the end of the

Women working in a cannery near Rocky Mount in the 1930s

1920s and easily outpaced every other brand in the world. American began to counterattack strongly in 1923 with an advertising campaign that featured the skywriting of "Lucky Strikes" over 122 cities. Soon, diet-conscious consumers were being advised to "Reach for a *Lucky* instead of a sweet," and in 1929 Lucky Strike soared past Camel as the most popular cigarette. Four years later, the Liggett and Myers entry, Chesterfield, also passed Camels. Reynolds in 1934 put over 80 percent of its net revenue into advertising in an effort to regain Camel's priority. Famous personalities like Bill Tilden and Carl Hubbell were hired for testimonials, and a 3,000-square-foot electric "Camel" sign was raised over Times Square and 42nd Street. As a result, Camels were back on top in 1935 and would stay there until after World War II.

Sophisticated equipment in North Carolina factories shot out cigarettes at machine-gun rates to keep pace with international demand. The state's thirty-odd tobacco factories used a quarter of all the leaf in the United States, and the proportion would soon reach and then surpass half. Primarily because of booming cigarette sales, North Carolina paid the federal government more in taxes than all but four other states. Moreover, the cigarette business would continue to expand through the bleakest days of the depression as American consumption more than doubled between 1927 and 1939. Cigars, chewing tobacco, and snuff declined in use during the interwar years, though cigars would make a rally during the 1930s.

So thoroughly was the cigarette industry automated that relatively few laborers were employed in it. Most of the workforce was employed in stemmeries and redrying plants where the workers were mostly unskilled, black, and poorly paid. Though there were many indirect benefits of so large an industry in North Carolina, tobacco manufacture was of little direct help to the state's employment problems.

Employing only a tenth of the state's industrial labor force in 1929, the three main tobacco firms produced more than a third of the value of North Carolina's manufactures.

A swelling national population that demanded huge amounts of housing and furnishings provided the impetus for the surging growth of North Carolina's furniture industry. What was needed to meet the demand was a vast pool of unskilled labor and virtually inexhaustible supplies of various hardwoods, both of which western North Carolina could readily furnish. In addition, the heritage of the western region included a tradition of skilled cabinetmaking brought over in earlier times by Western European craftsmen. But it was the post–World War I housing boom that fueled the great new phase of the furniture industry's expansion after 1920.

This postwar development was experienced mainly in the opening of new shops and plants. Technology in the furniture business improved only slowly, perhaps because of the strong craft roots of the industry. Gradually, however, manufacturing techniques were improved, factory layout was made more efficient, and scientific methods of control were introduced into the wood-drying process, the key production bottleneck. The wider use of waterproof resins and improved finishing processes, along with the adoption of conveyor systems, stepped up production dramatically during the late 1930s and 1940s. By 1939 North Carolina was manufacturing more wooden household furniture than any other state and ranked first in dining room and bedroom furniture, fifth in kitchen furniture, eighth in living room and library furniture. Much of the industry's progress was the consequence of the role of the Southern Furniture Exposition Building, erected at High Point in 1921 as a stimulus to design and sales. The annual market at the building was soon the largest in the South. In 1947 the building could display six acres of furniture on its fourteen floors. Buyers from all forty-eight states and many foreign countries—five thousand of them in that year—swarmed through the building to examine the new lines and place their orders. No other economic event was so important to North Carolina.

Furniture-making also fostered the growth of related industries. Every new chair or bedstead sold was cash in the pockets of loggers and lumbermen. It meant profit for the makers of boxes and containers, veneers, and finishing materials. Upholsterers used quantities of cotton batting and materials from Tar Heel textile plants. The furniture industry gave incentive to the producers of paints, hardware, springs, glue, and resins. On furniture's steady currents were carried flotillas of business enterprise. Many North Carolina furniture companies were family owned, such as the Broyhills' Lenoir Furniture Company, the Finches' Thomasville Chair Company, the Tates' and Holdens' Continental Furniture Company at High Point, and the Whites' furniture company at Mebane.

Furniture-making, like the other major industries of North Carolina, was not simply supplying a recognized need. Consumerism by the 1920s was already a flourishing psychological science complete with laboratories and instructional manuals. Some of the nation's best brains were occupied in the study of how to stimulate consumption, how to give life's furbelows the appearance of necessities. Throughout the state and nation, values and tastes were being gradually nationalized and urbanized. The movies and media advertising helped to create a sense of inadequacy among those who had not yet tied into electric and sewer lines. Interior decor took on the dimensions of an important art form.

Rags and Riches

J. Spencer Love

Textiles ranked first among the leading industries of North Carolina. There were 700 mills within a radius of 100 miles of Charlotte, and others scattered across the state.

By 1920 North Carolina boasted the world's largest mills for the manufacture of hosiery (Durham), towels (Kannapolis), denim (Greensboro), damask (Roanoke Rapids), and underwear (Winston-Salem). Eighty-five percent of the nation's combed yarn—used primarily in the more expensive types of women's wear—was made in Gaston County's 100 mills. But much of this productivity was a response to inflated wartime demands, and the decade of the 1920s brought a gradual decline in the per capita consumption of textiles. Intense competition among thousands of small firms scattered all across the state also had adverse effects on the industry, which, like farming, entered the Great Depression in poor condition to cope with it. For a time in the 1920s, tobacco replaced textiles as North Carolina's industrial leader.

But the textile industry had its entrepreneurial geniuses who not only coped but also prospered even in the darkest interwar years. Probably the outstanding textile manufacturer in North Carolina was J. Spencer Love of Burlington. The son of a Harvard mathematics professor, Love was graduated from Harvard in 1917, saw brief service in World War I, and afterward went to work as paymaster for a small textile firm in Gastonia. During the postwar recession, he was able to purchase the plant with his modest savings, only to be forced to auction off all but the machinery in 1923. With a business acumen seasoned by a keen interest in experimental fabrics and new technology, Love became a pioneer in the production of rayon, which gave Burlington its first big boost. In 1934 Burlington was the country's largest weaver of rayon fabrics. By the time of his death in 1962, Love had built Burlington Industries into the colossus of textile manufacturing; the company then operated 130 plants located in sixteen states and seven foreign countries. Shrewd innovation, sound management, and an ability to parry the thrusts of organized labor enabled Burlington to prosper in an arena where thousands of rivals had failed.

More than any other North Carolina industry, textiles fostered the concept of the mill village: a compact aggregation of houses located in the vicinity of a mill, owned by the company, and rented to the workers. Like the feudal manor and antebellum plantation, the mill village fostered a suffocating paternalism that frustrated the efforts of labor organizers long after the owners surrendered control of the villages themselves. Although reformers not infrequently missed the point in decrying the manifest evils of these communities, these small frame dwellings usually represented a step up in life for those who resided in them. A family coming in from a leaky shanty in rural Chatham County, for example, might encounter in a mill village its first experience with electric lights and indoor plumbing. On the other hand, mill villagers sometimes took little interest in the appearance of their rented quarters. The result was that the mill village could become a squalid place, the resort of bootleggers and prostitutes.

Not every mill village could be described this way. Some mill owners practiced an enlightened form of paternalism that expressed itself in a day-to-day concern for the welfare of the mill people. At Cramerton, in Gaston County, owner Stuart W. Cramer provided attractive houses set off by lawns, hedges, and flowers. He maintained a community center and golf course as well as a farm that furnished villagers with fresh eggs, milk, chickens, and vegetables. Pay scales and productivity were said to be higher at Cramerton than at most textile mills. There were also mill towns in which the residents took a keen interest in the appearance of their houses and the moral atmosphere of the community.

Mill worker Lacy Wright described conditions in the Cone Mills village: "Cone Mills was always a little bit better to their help, and paid a little better wages. . . . When we were living in the village there was lots of things that they did for us that saved us money. . . . They had good company stores . . . and if you got in bad circumstances they would see that you had something to eat. . . . They gave us all our electric current. . . . And they sold us coal for six dollars a ton when it was eight and ten dollars . . . and they put men out with plows and plowed your garden in the spring of the year." Mill owner Moses Cone pointed out, however, that such paternalism "is not prompted altogether from philanthropic motives. We regard as a good business investment such amounts as we can spend in securing the comfort and good will of our people. Most of them show their appreciation by giving us their best efforts."

Most of the mill villages were sold to their occupants after the early 1930s as textile owners found them expensive to maintain and a burden to operate. An exception was Kannapolis, where owner Charles A. Cannon clung doggedly to the village as it expanded into a town and small city. In 1970 Kannapolis was the largest unincorporated municipality in the United States, its inhabitants still without political influence in the governing of the town. Cannon's mild but eccentric paternalism embraced a program, launched in the 1930s, of rebuilding downtown Kannapolis in pseudo-Williamsburg style. At his death in 1971, Cannon owned only about a fifth of the housing, but he had built one of the world's great textile empires, with 24,000 employees in North and South Carolina.

When mill houses were sold to individual owners, the village lost its homogeneity and the mill workers the stereotype that had dogged them. Mill worker Julius Fry explained that "the people that didn't work in the plant and who didn't live exactly on the village thought they were better than we were . . . they weren't cotton millworkers, they weren't lint dodgers. . . . And there's just such a feeling of second class citizenship, because the people uptown were 'better' than we were."

Even if most mill villages had company-owned schools, churches, and recreational facilities, the house rent of 50¢ a week per room could cut deeply into workers' wages, which were often as low as $9.00 a week or less. Mill town ministers identified their own fortunes, as well as those of their flocks, with the fortunes of mill owners and preached a gospel attuned almost exclusively to the Life Beyond. It was, in fact, the same gospel preached from many of the pulpits of rural North Carolina.

Fruit of the Loom

Organized labor could expect little encouragement in this setting. A spate of unsuccessful strikes in North Carolina at the turn of the century was apparently one reason why unionism languished in the state after World War I. But there were other reasons as well. Among these were the strong opposition of mill owners and the responsiveness of state government to the sentiments of the owners. There may also have been a residue of rural provincialism, individualism, and conservatism among the workers that militated against all forms of regimentation. This, at least, has long been suggested as part of the reason for the disorganization of labor in North Carolina. On the other hand, worker acceptance of factory labor was in itself a notable concession to regimentation.

A series of wage cuts at the onset of the recession of 1920–21 brought a brief round of strikes, but Governor Cameron Morrison sent the National Guard to the strike centers, and the ardor of the unionizers quickly cooled. For most of the the 1920s, the Tar Heel textile industry remained sluggish, and unionism in this and other industries remained minimal.

Textile men struggled to counter the business slump by layoffs, pay cuts, and economies of operation. Such measures sometimes gave relief for the firms but tended also to aggravate the poor working conditions in the mills. Mill hands, a third of whom were women and children over the age of fourteen, typically worked ten or eleven hours a day, fifty-five hours a week. The mills were thick with dust, cotton fibers, and an oppressive humidity that caused a high incidence of respiratory ills. "I had seen women," said a mill worker, "going all day in that unbearable heat with their clothes stuck to their bodies like they had been dipped in a pail of water. Going up and down the alleys weeping, working, all day long." Zelma Murray, an Alamance County textile worker, reported, "We worked ten hours a day and five on Saturday. I worked fifty-five hours a week, and I drawed $11.55." The workers existed on grits, beans, bread, field peas, cornmeal, and fatback, which approximated the diet of the antebellum slave. Fruits and vegetables were rare; mortality rates were relatively high.

Mounting distress among workers found expression in a new rash of textile strikes in early 1929 in North Carolina, South Carolina, and Tennessee. Most were spontaneous, with no unions involved, but three of the four in North Carolina were organized by the National Textile Workers' Union (NTWU), a Communist-led group. Far and away the most serious strike was that at the Loray Mill in Gastonia, reputedly the largest factory in the world under one roof.

Gastonia was described in 1929 as "a pretty little Southern town" of some 20,000 people. Most Loray workers were former mountaineers and sharecroppers who occupied the mill village just outside the town limits. The plant produced fabric for automobile tires and was struggling frantically against competition from manufacturers of balloon tires.

Loray's owners in 1927 hired an efficiency expert who raised production despite reducing the workforce by almost half. Pay scales were cut to an average of about $13.00 a week and even lower for most women and the blacks who made up the custodial staff. But much of the expert's success lay in the introduction of the so-called "stretch-out" system, under which weavers were assigned additional looms to operate. This system was already in use in the Cone textile mills in Greensboro and in other North Carolina plants.

The stretch-out was the source of prolonged and bitter complaints. "It used to be," as a Loray worker put it, "that you could git five, ten minutes rest now and then, so's you could bear the mill. But now you got to keep a-runnin' all the time. Never a minute to git your breath all day. I used to run six drawing frames and now I look after ten. You just kaint do it. A man's dead beat at night." "Hundreds of people," said another, "go to jail every year and spend the best part of their lives there for doing things not half as harmful to their fellow man as the stretch out."

The efficiency expert was replaced late in 1928, but by that time it was too late to prevent the NTWU from obtaining a toehold at Loray. The workforce walked off the job in March 1929. They demanded $20.00 for a five-day, forty-four-hour week, an end to the stretch-out system, equal pay for women, lower rent for mill housing, improved sanitary conditions, and recognition of the union. The arrival of radical agitators from New York and elsewhere alarmed most of the workers and caused them to return to work in a few days. But several hundred stayed on strike.

A history of sour relations between townspeople and mill people, coupled with the presence of several Communists, created a volatile situation in Gastonia. A police raid on union headquarters in June resulted in the killing of Gastonia's police chief, which in turn led to the demolition of the union headquarters and its adjacent tent village by an angry mob. During the ensuing weeks, a union sympathizer was kidnapped and beaten, an English journalist was assaulted, two graduate students were run out of town, and fires broke out mysteriously in many places. In September a truckload of strikers was attacked outside Gastonia, and a passenger and labor organizer, Ella May Wiggins, was killed. Several strikers were convicted in the death of the police chief, but no one in that of Wiggins. She had composed a number of ballads on the plight of women mill workers, among them one that was sung at her funeral:

> We leave our Children in the morning,
> We kiss our Children good-bye,
> While we slave for the bosses,
> Our children scream and cry.
>
> .   .   .   .   .
>
> Now listen to me, Workers,
> Both women and men,
> We are sure to win our union
> If all would enter in.

Organized labor in North Carolina was dealt a setback of incalculable dimensions by the events of 1929 in Gastonia. The mutual antipathy of townspeople and workers there was not uncommon in industrial centers, and the memory of the strife is still a sore one in Gaston County. The National Guard, which was sent to Gastonia by Governor O. Max Gardner (himself a mill owner), appeared to some to be there to protect the mill and other property. Thereafter, the specter of Communism was raised against every serious strike in North Carolina. Lacy Wright told what happened when the workers at Cone Mills tried to form a union: "And the company got on them people so bad about trying to organize . . . that they fired I don't know how many of them, take their furniture and set it out in the streets, out of the mill houses and out in the streets. Wouldn't even let the people have time to find them another house and move into it."

Sporadic strikes have marked the history of North Carolina's textile industry since 1929. Wage cuts and poor working conditions brought cotton mill

NORTH CAROLINA!

Jewish Daily Forward

A textile strike at Loray Mill, in Gastonia, resulted in violence, including the shooting death of labor leader Ella May Wiggins, depicted in this drawing from Labor Age, October 1929.

strikes at High Point, Rockingham, and elsewhere in 1932. Nearly a hundred North Carolina mills joined the general strike of 1934. Burlington's J. Spencer Love was not speaking for himself alone when he told *Forbes* magazine that unions were "fundamentally unsound." This was because "to live they must promote strife, distrust, and discontent and set employee against employee, class against class, and group against group."

Unionism received a boost when the right of collective bargaining was recognized in the National Industrial Recovery Act (1933), and in 1937 state laws further restricted the employment of children. Working hours for females in industry were limited to forty-eight a week and nine a day, while male hours were reduced to fifty-five weekly and ten daily. But North Carolina, which ranked forty-seventh in 1939 in the percentage of its nonagricultural workers who were unionized, slipped later to last among the states, where it has remained ever since. "Folks can talk all they want about their right to join a union," as a disillusioned mill hand put it, "but right don't count much when money is against you."

While unions enjoyed some local victories during these years, some groups of workers continued to experience discrimination and hardship. Notably, the 10,000 or so migrant laborers who worked each year in North Carolina suffered from poor working conditions and lack of adequate legal protection. Women, in 1970 as in 1920, continued to receive the low wages that helped bring on the violence of 1929.

Affluence and Effluents

Ignited by the unprecedented demands of World War II, North Carolina industry in the 1940s entered upon an epoch of rapid expansion. A student of the subject ranked the state as the South's industrial leader in 1954, one of the twelve foremost industrial states in the nation. The primary industries were still textiles, tobacco, and furniture, but the share of the first two in the state's overall industry was beginning to slip. Along with sawmills and related industries, the Big Three in 1954 accounted for almost half of North Carolina's manufacturing concerns. Already, as reported in the *North Carolina Almanac and Industrial Guide*, the state had two and one-half times more manufacturing concerns than it had had on the eve of the war. Substantial growth had occurred since 1939 in rubber, chemicals, electrical machinery, and other industries.

In textiles, the multiplication of spindles was replaced as the focus of development by the employment of more sophisticated machinery, by research aimed at the production of better yarns and fabrics, and by improved dyeing and finishing techniques. More North Carolinians were employed in textiles than in all other industries combined, but at wages still well below the national average. In its concern to keep textile prices and costs down by minimizing wages, the industry was beginning to move away from large urban areas and into the countryside, where competition for labor was less severe. The pressure of foreign competition was also taking a toll of anxiety among textile people.

North Carolina by the 1950s produced 40 percent of all the hosiery manufactured in the nation and led the South in woolens and worsteds. But the major new trend in textiles was the shift of the northeastern apparel industry to North Carolina. Truck and highway facilities that brought Tar Heel mills within overnight proximity to the New York garment district were key factors in the shift. So was the availability in North Carolina of a large labor force of employable women, who ultimately comprised 85 percent of the apparel workers in North Carolina. But, even as they helped to perpetuate North Carolina's notoriety as a cheap-labor state, apparel plants sprouted in previously unindustrialized parts of the Mountain and Coastal Plain regions. Other industry followed apparel's lead, dispersing North Carolina industry from its traditional base in the Piedmont.

In the postwar era, as before, North Carolina remained the nation's leading tobacco manufacturing state, producing more than half the country's smoking tobacco, snuff, and chewing tobacco. P. Lorillard of Greensboro, maker of Old Gold cigarettes, took its position in the 1950s beside Reynolds, Liggett and Myers, and American Tobacco as a tobacco giant. Pipe tobacco remained chiefly the province of the older three, while Brown and Williamson of Winston-Salem was the chief manufacturer of snuff. Greensboro's El Moro was the only leading brand of cigar produced in North Carolina.

Furniture's boom not only continued but accelerated, with output more than tripling between 1939 and 1957. Though the business was still centered largely in the Piedmont counties of Guilford, Davidson, Catawba, Burke, and Caldwell, plants were emerging as far east as Goldsboro and as far west as Waynesville. Two-thirds of all the furniture manufactured in the South was made within a 150-mile radius of High Point; this area contained the greatest concentration of furniture factories in the world. Like textiles, furniture remained a labor-intensive, low-wage industry.

State government played an important role in the growth and dispersal of North Carolina industry, especially after Luther Hodges became governor in 1954. Hodges, a former textile manufacturer, rejuvenated the State Department of Conservation and Development and initiated the Building and Development Corporation to provide long-term capital for new and expanding industries. Hodges also sponsored tax concessions and an ambitious program of industry hunting, including missions to six nations of Western Europe. In the six years of his administration, the state gained over 1,000 new plants and the expansion of more than 1,400 others.

Hodges would be best remembered for his work in launching the Research Triangle. The basic idea had been bandied about for several years, chiefly through the interest of social scientist Howard W. Odum at the University of North Carolina at Chapel Hill and Romeo H. Guest, head of a Greensboro contracting firm. Hodges became interested in the possibility of using the research capabilities of the three major universities at Raleigh, Chapel Hill, and Durham as a lure to bring corporate laboratories and research centers to North Carolina. Through private contributions, the Research Triangle Institute acquired funds with which to purchase a tract of 4,000 acres of rural land lying within a "triangle" formed by the three schools. By 1959 the Research Triangle was a reality, its parks soon to be dotted with facilities representing Chemstrand, the U.S. Forest Service, IBM, Burroughs-Wellcome (now GlaxoSmith-

Kline), the U.S. Environmental Protection Agency, and many more. Even more dramatically than the adjacent urban complexes, the Triangle Park sprouted glacial monoliths of steel and glass to soar above the embracing glades and pastures. Piedmont farming communities within the Triangle found themselves abruptly cheek-by-jowl with enclaves of Ph.D.'s and aerospace engineers. The twentieth century seemed almost to have been bypassed in a headlong plunge from the nineteenth century into the twenty-first.

The scope of industry's problems grew apace with the scale of manufacturing enterprise during the 1950s and 1960s. The mining industry avoided a recurrence of the Coal Glen disaster of 1925, during which sixty men died in an explosion near Sanford, but North Carolina still had major mining interests as the nation's leading producer of feldspar and mica as well as large quantities of talc and other minerals. Caldwell County had the largest known deposit of ilmenite in the world, Surry County the largest open-faced granite quarry, and Vance County the nation's largest tungsten mine. In the 1950s North Carolina produced 100 percent of the nation's kaolin, 70 percent of its ground and scrap mica, and 35 percent of its feldspar.

Continuing tension between industry and labor was underscored by troubles at the Harriet-Henderson Cotton Mills at Henderson in the 1950s, the Roanoke Rapids plant of the J. P. Stevens textile firm, and elsewhere. Although the textile union eventually did organize J. P. Stevens employees, the success of the union movement in North Carolina was small compared to its success in the rest of the country. Only about 10 percent of the workers in the state are now union members. The national average is about 25 percent.

With industrial growth came industrial waste. The valuable commercial fishing industry began to feel the effects of chemical pollutants, which damaged the wetlands and rich shellfish grounds along the coast. Areas of scenic beauty and archeological significance were not always defended against the consequences of urban and industrial sprawl, nor the state's population protected from the daily hazards of air and water pollution, which brought on respiratory and other health problems.

At the close of the 1960s, North Carolina's industry represented over 14 percent of industry in the South as a whole and almost 4 percent of industry in the United States. By the 1980s, North Carolina had become the nation's most industrialized state, with 78 percent of its workers employed in manufacturing. The leading industries were textiles, furniture, clothing, electronic and electrical equipment and appliances, food processing, machinery, chemicals, lumber and wood, and tobacco. But within a decade, a changed in employment occurred, as the service sector of the economy began growing faster than manufacturing and agriculture. In 1990, two-thirds of all Tar Heel work-

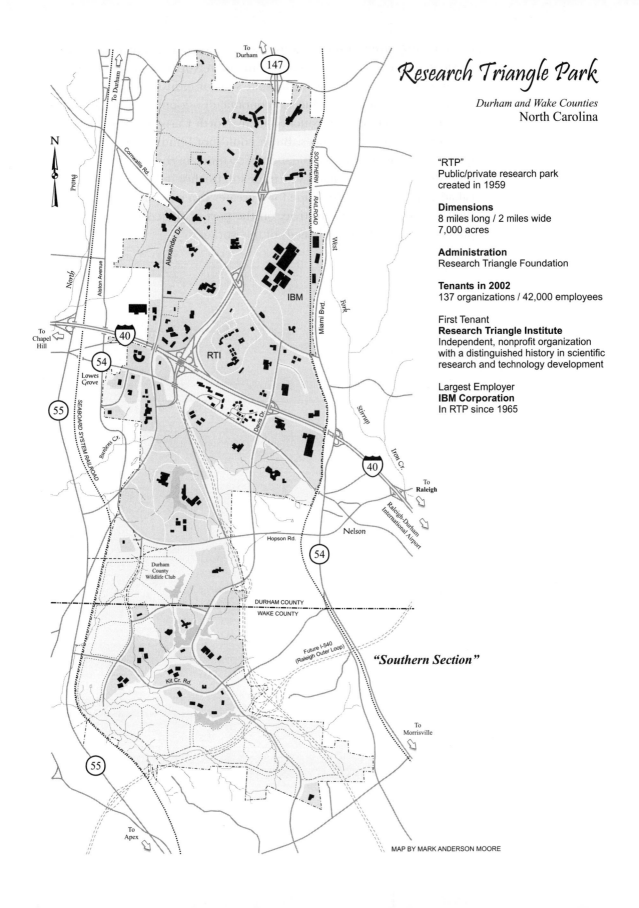

Research Triangle Park

Durham and Wake Counties
North Carolina

"RTP"
Public/private research park
created in 1959

Dimensions
8 miles long / 2 miles wide
7,000 acres

Administration
Research Triangle Foundation

Tenants in 2002
137 organizations / 42,000 employees

First Tenant
Research Triangle Institute
Independent, nonprofit organization
with a distinguished history in scientific
research and technology development

Largest Employer
IBM Corporation
In RTP since 1965

"Southern Section"

MAP BY MARK ANDERSON MOORE

ers were employed in service jobs, such as food service, medical care, repair services, teaching, and retail sales. Tourism in North Carolina has boomed in recent years and is now one of the state's major industries.

The unquestionable value of economic development and change for the creation of a better life reconciled many North Carolinians to attendant dislocations and inconveniences. But it could not blind them to the sweatshop quality that was the early foundation of so much of the state's economic progress. Most North Carolinians yearn for still further industrial and technological advance, but they also hope for a greater diversity of employment opportunities and a growing sensitivity on the part of the corporation toward the physical and psychological needs of the worker.

VENDORS AND LENDERS

4

Patient and Physician

The stock market crash of 1929 foreshadowed a halt to a long period of commercial growth in North Carolina. Since the beginning of the century, urban development had generated a proliferation of wholesale enterprises as well as retail shops and stores. Banks, savings and loan associations, insurance companies, and other financial institutions multiplied in North Carolina as they did across the nation. The state's publicists pointed out that its $500 million in bank resources in 1927 represented a 200 percent increase in just one decade. Banking grew in North Carolina at a rate double the national average, and the per capita income of Tar Heels in the 1920s increased at a rate more than triple that of the country as a whole.

But figures expressed as rates of growth from very small beginnings masked North Carolina's relatively weak financial and commercial position on the eve of the crash. For example, the state's total bank resources in 1929 were barely a third of the average nationally. When farm income plummeted by two-thirds between 1929 and 1933, it was not only business but the very life of the state that was threatened.

The first big bank in North Carolina to go under was Asheville's Central Bank and Trust Company, which held millions in bond-borrowed city and county money. A last-ditch attempt to stave off collapse with city funds sent the bank's president to prison, and, as hometown boy Thomas Wolfe described it in *You Can't Go Home Again,* led to the suicide of the former mayor. The eighteen Asheville bank failures of 1929 were multiplied statewide several times in the next three years and stood at 215 in March 1933. The drop in retail sales cut drastically into tax receipts and in turn into public salaries and other expenditures. Bank resources fell by a quarter and unemployment skyrocketed.

After a national bank holiday was declared in early 1933, Roosevelt's first Congress passed the Emergency Banking Act, which fostered the reopening of sound institutions. Aided by loans from the Reconstruction Finance Corporation, the creation of the Federal Deposit Insurance Corporation, and additional federal programs, most of North Carolina's financial institutions were soon stabilized. Such measures salvaged the fiscal integrity of the state, but massive injections of relief were also needed simply to ward off widespread starvation.

Two of the most important New Deal relief programs were the Civilian Conservation Corps (ccc) and the Works Progress Administration (wpa). By late 1935 there were more than three score ccc camps in North Carolina. They provided work, wages, and board for thousands of young men engaged in flood-control and reforestation projects, road building, and the like. Reforestation of what had been worn-out cotton and tobacco land near Raleigh revived a large area that was subsequently included within Umstead State Park. ccc workers built a migratory bird refuge at Swan Quarter, complete with ponds, seawalls, fire towers, and truck and foot trails. Other workers quartered in the western mountains supplied labor used in completing Mount Mitchell State Park, on the highest peak east of the Mississippi. Others worked on portions of the Blue Ridge Parkway and the Great Smoky Mountains National Park.

Although the ccc's main work was reforestation, soil conservation, and flood control, its tasks expanded to include disaster relief and the construction of facilities in state and national parks. North Carolina's legacy from the ccc's many camps may be seen in such structures as the stone lodge in Morrow Mountain State Park, in Stanly County; the heartpine buildings used as campsites at Singletary Lake, in Bladen County; the migratory bird refuge at Swan Quarter, in Hyde County; and the stone bridges and walls along the 469 miles of the Blue Ridge Parkway.

The wpa, broader in scope and enrollment, found work for the unemployed on roads, bridges, buildings, airports, and other construction projects. But programs were also provided by the wpa for unemployed artists, writers, scholars, musicians, and actors. One group was paid to locate and record the personal narratives of former slaves, another to compile a state guidebook, still others to undertake historical research. By the time it was phased out in 1943, the wpa had spent $172,000 on projects employing some 225,000 Tar Heels.

Another federal relief endeavor was the planned community of Penderlea, launched in Pender County in 1934. To provide farmers living on marginal land with a fresh start (as well as to restore the land), the government bought a 4,000-acre woodland tract and built 142 houses on 20-acre homesteads. Each had a four- to six-room dwelling, barn, poultry house, hog house, smokehouse, washhouse, hot and cold running water, and electricity. A lake, school, and community center were provided, each family being allowed to buy its homestead on favorable terms. When the first phase was completed in 1936, a new

The Blue Ridge Parkway in North Carolina

The Parkway Covers 469 Miles of Scenic Highway along the Crests of the Southern Appalachian Mountains, Linking Shenandoah National Park in Virginia with Great Smoky Mountains National Park in North Carolina

SECTIONS OPENED TO THE PUBLIC:

1930s

Between . . .
- Cumberland Knob and Deep Gap
- McKinney Gap and Gooch Gap

1940s

Between . . .
- Beacon Heights and McKinney Gap
- Gooch Gap and Balsam Gap
- Soco Gap and Big Witch Gap

1950s

1960s

Between . . .
- U.S. Hwy. 321 and Holloway Mtn. Rd.
- Balsam Gap and Swannanoa River
- Flat Laurel Gap and Reinhart Gap
- Big Witch Gap and Oconaluftee

1980s

Between . . .
- Holloway Mtn. Rd. and Beacon Heights

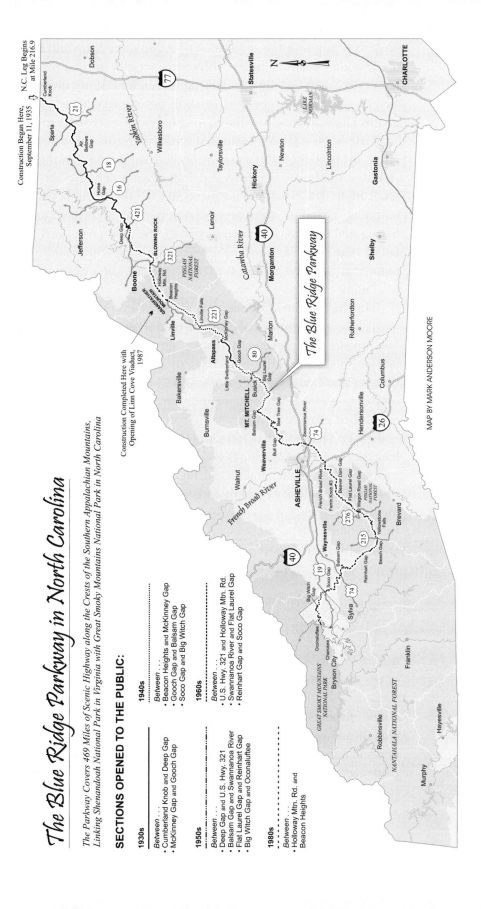

MAP BY MARK ANDERSON MOORE

one was begun with the acquisition of 6,000 more acres and the construction of 158 additional homesteads. (Penderlea was not the first planned rural community in North Carolina. St. Helena, in Pender County, and Castle Hayne, in New Hanover County, were successfully developed early in the twentieth century by Hugh MacRae of Wilmington as agricultural colonies for Wilmington.)

Federal New Deal measures stopped the economic tailspin of the early 1930s and brought about a slow recovery in the years following. By 1937 nearly all indexes of business activity—including bank deposits, life insurance sales, retail trade, construction contracts, and freight revenues—showed substantial gains. "Grinning storekeepers," reported the *Greensboro Daily News*, "told of having sold out their Christmas stock for the first time in seven years." By the fall of 1939, with the war in Europe hampering cotton and tobacco exports but otherwise boosting the Tar Heel economy, the trauma of the depression was fading.

The United States' support of its allies and eventual entry into World War II in 1941 increased production and further boosted North Carolina and the nation out of the depression. Activity at the state's many U.S. military bases significantly aided recovery. Fort Bragg (originally established as Camp Bragg in Cumberland County during World War I) swelled to tremendous size, housing over 100,000 soldiers. Seymour Johnson Air Force Base in Wayne County was established in 1941 as an Army Air Force technical training school. The federal government constructed Camp Lejeune in Onslow County in 1942 as a base for the Second Marine Division and a place to train troops in amphibious assault. Other smaller military facilities appeared throughout the state. The shipbuilding industry employed many North Carolinians to meet the demand for war vessels. Shipyards in Wilmington, as well as in New Bern and Elizabeth City, built submarine chasers, minesweepers, and cargo and troop ships. Federal contracts brought over $10 billion to North Carolina as its citizens labored to provide textiles, lumber, ammunition, metals, and food for the war effort.

Sweethearts and Rivals

Heavy involvement of government in business—and vice versa—began before the depression, was quickened by it, and became a permanent feature of the economic landscape in the New Deal and war years. But many entrepreneurs were convinced that theirs was a lonely struggle against the economic elements, in which they prospered or perished solely according to their wits. Business journals expended much ink on the evils of government regulation and the ennoblement of unfettered competition. Burlington textile baron J. Spencer Love told the Antitrust Subcommittee of the United States Senate

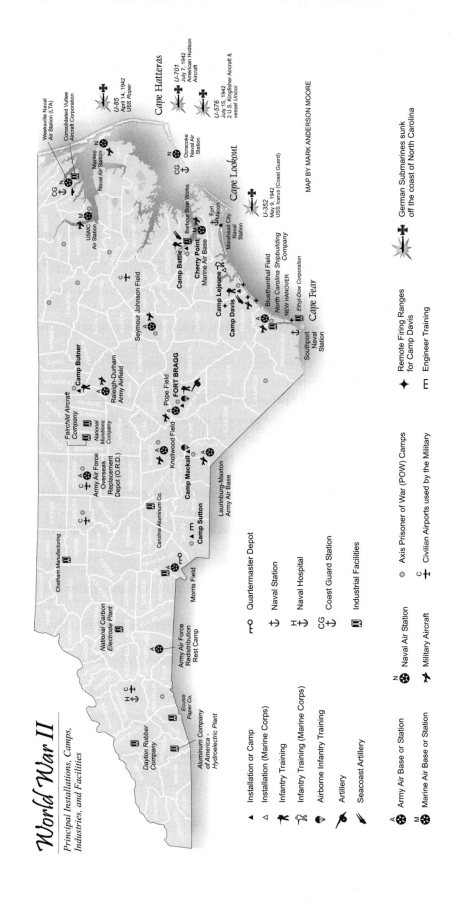

World War II

Principal Installations, Camps, Industries, and Facilities

MAP BY MARK ANDERSON MOORE

Cape Hatteras

U-85
April 14, 1942
USS *Roper*

U-701
July 7, 1942
American Hudson
Aircraft

U-576
July 15, 1942
2 U.S. Kingfisher Aircraft &
vessel *Unicoi*

Cape Lookout

U-352
May 9, 1942
USS *Icarus* (Coast Guard)

Cape Fear

Weeksville Naval
Air Station (LTA)

Consolidated Vultee
Aircraft Corporation

Manteo
Naval Air Station

Ocracoke
Naval Air
Station

Barbour Boat Works

Fort
Macon

Morehead City
Naval
Station

Cherry Point
Marine Air Base

USMC
Air Station

Bluethenthal Field

North Carolina *Shipbuilding*
Company

Ethyl-Dow Corporation

Camp Battle

Camp Lejeune

Camp Davis

NEW HANOVER

Southport
Naval
Station

Seymour Johnson Field

Camp Butner

Raleigh-Durham
Army Airfield

Pope Field

FORT BRAGG

Fairchild Aircraft
Company

National
Munitions
Company

Army Air Force
Overseas
Replacement
Depot (O.R.D.)

Knollwood Field

Camp Mackall

Laurinburg-Maxton
Army Air Base

Camp Sutton

Carolina Aluminum Co.

Chatham Manufacturing

National Carbon
Electrode Plant

Army Air Force
Redistribution
Rest Camp

Morris Field

Ecusta Paper Co.

Dayton Rubber
Company

Aluminum Company
of America -
Hydroelectric Plant

Legend

◄ Installation or Camp

△ Installation (Marine Corps)

Infantry Training

Infantry Training (Marine Corps)

Airborne Infantry Training

Artillery

Seacoast Artillery

N Army Air Base or Station

M Marine Air Base or Station

┌○ Quartermaster Depot

⊹ Naval Station

H⊹ Naval Hospital

CG⊹ Coast Guard Station

Industrial Facilities

○ Axis Prisoner of War (POW) Camps

C⊹ Civilian Airports used by the Military

N Naval Air Station

✈ Military Aircraft

Remote Firing Ranges
for Camp Davis

⊓ Engineer Training

✠ German Submarines sunk
off the coast of North Carolina

as much in a 1955 hearing. Government, he assured the Senate, could not regulate the law of supply and demand. Then business, interposed a Wyoming senator, did not need antitrust laws. Love agreed. Neither did business need price controls, the senator continued. Love agreed again. Then, observed the legislator, business did not need government regulation in general. Love answered that business would be much better off without it. "Then you don't need a great deal of tariff protection," the senator stated. "Well, you sort of have me there," was Love's reply.

But the business ambience of the mid-twentieth century owed little to the spirit of the frontier. Like farmers, businessmen functioned within a complex network of integrated and mutually dependent private and public associations. A strong element of competition remained, adding spice and zest to the working day, but it operated within carefully coordinated matrices, such as that which linked the service station manager with an international brotherhood of oil riggers, refiners, common carriers, auto assembly workers, licensees, insurers, and the like. The character of modern business was in some respect incompatible with the traits that traditionally defined what it was to be a Tar Heel.

Business ventures blossomed or fizzled daily for all that. When Malcolm McLean of Red Springs went into the trucking business in 1934, he had one truck, which he drove himself. But a great new day was just dawning for trucking with the introduction of balloon tires, which minimized truck damage to highways, and new engine and drive systems for power on the road. Thirty years later, McLean's firm, the fifth largest in the country, owned 5,000 trucks and trailers and 65 terminals in 20 states. McLean's Winston-Salem facility had the largest individually owned truck terminal in the world in 1954, and the rise of trucking was doing much to offset the relative weakness of North Carolina's port facilities.

A key factor in the post-depression business surge in North Carolina was the role of large urban banks. The outstanding example for many years was First Union National Bank in Charlotte. Founded in 1908, First Union made a number of important mergers in the 1950s and 1960s, notably with Cameron-Brown of Raleigh, a bond and mortgage company. First Union was the state's third largest bank in 1966, with 140 offices in 67 North Carolina communities and Nassau in the Bahamas.

Still more important to North Carolina's business was Wachovia Bank and Trust Company of Winston-Salem. Both founder-president Francis H. Fries and, following his death in 1931, his successor, Robert M. Hanes, were scions of great textile families. By an ambitious series of mergers, including that with black-owned-and-operated Forsyth Saving and Trust Company in 1930,

Wachovia developed into the largest bank between Washington, D.C., and Atlanta. Its $1.5 billion dollars in resources ranked it in 1969 as one of the major banking firms in the nation. Recently, Wachovia and First Union Bank combined to form an even larger financial institution. North Carolina National Bank (NCNB), third largest in the region from the day it was chartered, was formed in 1960 by the merger of large banks in Charlotte and Greensboro in a calculated challenge to Wachovia's southeastern leadership. NCNB subsequently became NationsBank, which in 1998 merged with Bank of America.

The architecture of corporate finance and commerce became as much the symbol as the substance of North Carolina's incipient economic maturity. Downtown shops and retail outlets retreated toward the urban periphery as soaring professional and commercial buildings transformed city skylines. Space for horizontal expansion and construction was ample in North Carolina, but lateral growth alone could not fulfill the sense of pride or the vaulting aspiration of the new corporate age. For this it would take skyscrapers, and North Carolina now boasted the financial resources to convert the new business attitudes into significant architectural statements. Major banks were leaders in setting the trend.

A symbol of another kind was the modern department store. In a sense, department store layout and architecture represented the extent to which women, in particular, were experiencing emancipation from the fetters of tradition. The elevator and escalator that carried shoppers effortlessly through capitalism's cornucopia of wares belied the slow and difficult transition of women from ancient roles, but the plenty and convenience of the department store was perhaps as much an inspiration as a reflection of social change. The stores played an important part in generating a "revolution of rising expectations" among those who were lured from one tempting display to another in fairylands of material abundance.

Perhaps the prince of Tar Heel tradesmen of the era was William Henry Belk of Charlotte. Belk opened his first dry goods store at Monroe in 1888. As a merchandising innovator in North Carolina, Belk borrowed many ideas from John Wanamaker of Philadelphia, who, like Belk, was a Presbyterian philanthropist. Fixed prices, cash sales, and returnable merchandise make Belk stores different and instantly successful. By the time of his death in 1952, Belk had built a sprawling system of department stores. But the more than 400 Belk stores in eighteen states and Puerto Rico in 1970 were not organized as a chain. Instead, Belk and his successors associated in partnership arrangements under which each store was operated as an independent unit, though each was supplied from Belk's warehouses in Charlotte and elsewhere. More conventionally managed but similarly successful was the Rose's Stores network

*North Carolina Mutual Life Insurance
Company Building (1921), Durham*

of over 200 units in nine states. Founder Paul H. Rose of Northampton County had launched his "five and dime" operation at Henderson in 1915.

It is due these titans of commerce to acknowledge that some of them became lavish philanthropists, patrons of the arts and letters, and community leaders. None could match the largesse of James B. Duke's Duke Endowment, but Belk, for example, established the John M. Belk Memorial Fund, through which millions in donations were made to churches, orphanages, and educational institutions, chiefly Presbyterian. Davidson College was a principal recipient of Belk gifts.

Minority-owned enterprises, laboring under added burdens, rarely attained the stature of regional significance; and the wonder is that a few did. A remarkable saga of black free enterprise is the North Carolina Mutual Life Insurance Company of Durham. The Mutual was begun in 1899 by ex-slave John

Merrick, salesman C. C. Spaulding, and Dr. Aaron McD. Moore. Merrick and Moore had died by the end of 1923, but Spaulding then presided over a business that covered eleven states and the District of Columbia. At Spaulding's own death in 1952, North Carolina Mutual was a nationwide concern with almost $180 million of insurance in force, a figure that would be quadrupled by 1970. It was, in fact, the largest black-owned business in the United States.

Board of directors of North Carolina Mutual Life Insurance Company, 1911. Left to right: Dr. Aaron McD. Moore, John M. Avery, John Merrick, Edward Merrick, and C. C. Spaulding.

Siren Song

The business of tourism, destined to become a major industry in North Carolina, developed haltingly in the years before World War II. Many travelers passed through the state en route to and from winter playgrounds in sunny Florida, but few were tempted, or even invited, to tarry. From the window of a speeding train or automobile the North Carolina scene was one of "rutted roads winding aimlessly off through piney woods," in the eyes of one traveler, ". . . a slab shanty, unpainted, forlorn, dismal, lop-sided; a dooryard as shaggy as a barber's Saturday night; an untended field runnelled with gulleys and grown up in sassafras sprouts; a scrub-cow, a razor-back hog, a swarm of lank dogs; a tumble-down rail fence; and everywhere the multiplying signs of slackness and untidiness and indifference."

In 1924, humorist Irvin S. Cobb felt constrained to come to North Carolina's defense. "What North Carolina should provide," he wrote, "is a beneficent hold-up man . . . who'd halt every train and . . . tell all the travelers what they were missing. His work would be in the nature of a liberal education to numbers . . . who apparently think of North Carolina only in terms of Asheville, a health resort, and Pinehurst . . . where one may break the long jump to the Florida Peninsula and . . . shoot a mess of quail or lay by a few holes of golf."

But it was still not precisely clear what there was to see or do beyond the limits of Asheville and Pinehurst. Spokesmen for the storied coast or picturesque mountains must also concede that they were accessible only to the heartiest adventurers, that tourist accommodations were uncertain at the journey's end. Some North Carolinians, however, did not welcome an influx of outsiders. "I resented, and still do resent," declared one native, "being quaint, stimulating and strange. It's like being background music for somebody else's Technicolor daydreams."

Deliberate attempts to attract tourists were infrequent before the late 1940s, by which time paved roads and hotels were fairly common. A commemoration of the three hundred and fiftieth anniversary of the birth of Virginia Dare, first English child born in America, at the site of her birth on Roanoke Island, in Dare County, was a prewar event that presaged the future drawing power of North Carolina for visitors from other sections of the country. The 1937 event featured an outdoor drama written by Pulitzer Prize–winner Paul Green of Chapel Hill entitled *The Lost Colony*. President and Mrs. Roosevelt and critic Brooks Atkinson gave the play high marks in its first summer. Scheduled to be performed only one season, *The Lost Colony* was repeated annually until it was interrupted by the war, and since the war has become a permanent summer entertainment. In 1950, Fort Raleigh was excavated and reconstructed on Roanoke Island. The fort is a re-creation of a 1585 earthworks constructed by an English colony led by Ralph Lane. The colony, the predecessor to the famed Lost Colony of 1587, was the first English settlement on the North American continent. Also drawing tourists on Roanoke Island today are the *Elizabeth II*, a working model of a sixteenth-century English sailing vessel; Roanoke Island Festival Park; and the Outer Banks History Center. Other major sites along the Outer Banks that attract thousands of tourists every year include the Pea Island Wildlife Refuge and the National Park

Service's Wright Brothers Memorial and Cape Hatteras and Cape Lookout National Seashores.

The success of *The Lost Colony* inspired similar historical dramas in later years. The most popular of these included Kermit Hunter's two mountain epics, *Unto These Hills*, which opened in 1949 at Cherokee, and *Horn in the West*, begun two years later at Boone. The rise of tourism at these extreme ends of the state helped generate funds for the restoration of Fort Raleigh at Roanoke and the inauguration of mountain attractions such as "The Land of Oz" on Beech Mountain at Banner Elk and Tweetsie Railroad near Blowing Rock. Every year visitors flock to the Great Smoky Mountains National Park, the Blue Ridge Parkway, the Oconaluftee Indian Village at Cherokee, the Biltmore Estate at Asheville, and sundry other mountain sites. The lure of mountain ski slopes and rhododendron-bowered trails and coastal deep-sea fishing and beaches add to the tourist influx in the state.

Public and private campaigns were launched to advertise such attractions across the nation and abroad. The State Department of Conservation and Development's Travel and Promotion Division took a leading role in these activities, as did the Travel Council established during the Hodges administration. Private enterprise created the Innkeepers' Association in 1945, the Restaurant Association in 1947, and the Motel Association in 1954, all with the promotion of tourism as part of their rationale.

The rebuilding of Tryon Palace at New Bern in the 1950s was a milestone in the growth of interest in historic restoration and preservation that also aided tourism. Local initiative often played the key role in such projects, which restored the eighteenth-century Moravian village of Salem and whole clusters of early buildings at Edenton, Halifax, Murfreesboro, Wilmington, and other towns. The battleship USS *North Carolina* at Wilmington, Maggie Valley Ghost Town, and numerous other ventures, often frankly commercial in conception, contributed toward North Carolina's advancing reputation as a tourist mecca. So did a plethora of parks, museums, battlegrounds, sports events, and scenic attractions.

Travelers in 1969 spent over $750 million in North Carolina. Nearly half a million tourists were received that year at the state's first two "welcome centers" along interstate highways. They came for the Highland Games, the Fiddler's Convention, the Hollering Contest, the Herring Festival, the Ramp-Eating Festival, and the Man-Will-Never-Fly Memorial Society's annual meeting at Nags Head. They looked for the Brown Mountain Lights, puzzled over the Devil's Tramping Ground, waited for the Maco Ghost—and searched in vain for a cocktail. (The quaint Tar Heel approach to mealtime alcohol, in which diners brought it with them, was called "brown-bagging," and it remained a puzzle and nuisance to visitors until mixed drinks were legalized in most counties in the late 1970s.)

Irvin S. Cobb could rest in peace: the rush to get through North Carolina had ended.

Selling Point

By the 1950s a booming North Carolina wholesale and retail trade led the South Atlantic Region. The state had become the hub of the eastern seaboard's trucking industry, with the home offices of more long-time interstate trucking firms than any other state in the union. The wholesale trade of Charlotte exceeded that of Richmond by 55 percent and was gaining rapidly on Atlanta's. There were 41,000 retail and nearly 6,000 wholesale establishments between Murphy and Manteo.

In port facilities and seagoing business, North Carolina's ports ranked well behind Savannah and Norfolk but had overtaken the ports of South Carolina in business volume. With the aid of the State Ports Authority, established in 1945, Wilmington's maritime business rose steadily. By 1968 it was handling the cargoes of more than 500 ships, 23,000 trucks, and 8,000 railroad cars per year. Morehead City, with its shallower harbor, handled less than half of Wilmington's commerce but hoped for greater progress following completion in 1968 of a bulk facility with a half-mile-long conveyor belt and 600,000 square feet of warehouse space.

The most notable phenomenon in retail trade was a vast shift from smaller to larger places and stores. In 1980, *The State* magazine described the bygone era of the small community grocery store: "A grocery store of the early twenties was a proud specialty store, aloof from general merchandise. Gathering groceries in a cart would have been seen as the first step in shoplifting. And besides, merchandise was stacked to the ceiling in uncertain pyramids, and the practiced hand of the clerk, holding a long, hooked wand, was necessary to bring down some Gold Dust or White Horse coffee or Mother's Cocoa, without bringing it all down." Supermarkets evolved in California and Texas in the post–World War I era but became widespread only after World War II created shortages of time and labor and an abundance of cars and good roads. Supermarkets, with the conveyance of everything under one roof, unlimited free parking, and self-service, provided efficient and cheap marketing. They applied the department store concept to the sale of food and household products.

Small towns, bypassed by interstate highways and airlines, often withered as the major cities grew in size in the decades following World War II. The 1950s witnessed the advent of the shopping center in the Tar Heel State. When it opened, Raleigh's Cameron Village, the largest shopping center in the Southeast, had forty stores, all on street level, underground wiring, covered sidewalks, and carefully regulated lighting and building codes. Nearby apartments helped provide a village atmosphere in which people could live and shop.

As the twentieth century drew toward a close, shopping centers and massive shopping malls dotted the landscape. They appeared when growing urban populations began settling in the surburbs to live. Simultaneously, trade tended to shift from the downtown areas of cities and towns to the new surburban retail centers. Faced with a serious decline, large numbers of downtown businesses closed or "moved to the malls," thereby contributing to inner-city blight. Robert Simpson, a resident of the town of Rose Hill, observed the changing scene: "Back in the late fifties an' early sixties the U.S. economy was boomin' an' there were jobs available everywhere. . . . But the town has changed a lot now. They're movin' stores out to the highway an' puttin' up these big shoppin' centers, an' the trains don't run through like they used to. . . . We're still a small town . . . but things are definitely less personal, y'know? Even in little ol' Rose Hill, North Carolina, nothin' is ever goin' to be the same."

The growing populations of cities and the changing character of urban life and trade also made possible many kinds of specialty shops and enterprises, from high-fashion stores to specialized medical services, that less populous areas could not hope to support. From a business perspective, as from others, the process of urbanization was the really dramatic development of the twentieth century.

5

GOING TO TOWN

Tobacco Towns

A statistical analyst, confronted with figures showing the importance of industry in North Carolina in 1970, would have assumed that, as in all other leading industrial states, most of its people lived in cities. Surprisingly, however, this was not the case; alone among such states North Carolina remained more rural and small-town than urban, though nearly two-thirds of all Americans lived in cities in 1970.

The reasons are well enough known. Early North Carolina, burdened by shallow harbors and ports, its terrain laced with rivers and swamps that deterred road building, came late to the process of urbanization. Only when the center of population shifted in the nineteenth century to the Piedmont was the rise of cities possible, and other factors made for slow growth even then. One such factor was the nature of the state's leading industry: textiles. Because small textile plants were as efficient as large ones, textile manufacturers were not tempted to cling to the largest urban centers. Rather, textile and apparel firms found it desirable to remain in small-town or rural settings, where wage scales were lowest. Thus North Carolina's small towns held on more tenaciously—and its cities grew more slowly—than did small towns in most of the country.

It was not until the 1880s that as much as 5 percent of the Tar Heel population lived in urban areas; and not until 1940 could North Carolina claim its first city of more than 100,000 people: Charlotte. There were six such metropolitan areas in North Carolina in 1970, but none was comparable to major cities outside the state in its degree of urban concentration. No city dominated the life of the state, but five of the leading six in 1970 lay in an arc along the route of the Southern Railway, developed in the mid-nineteenth century to link Raleigh, Durham, Greensboro, and Winston-Salem to Charlotte.

The Coastal Plain, its broken topography still not knitted by compensatory highways and railroads, developed no sizable urban area even by North Carolina standards. Wilmington, with less than 50,000 inhabitants, was the largest place east of Raleigh but still somewhat isolated from the rest of the state. More representative of the very gradual urbanizing process in the east was a cluster of towns in the central Coastal Plain: Rocky Mount, Wilson, Greenville, Goldsboro, and Kinston.

The five towns ranged in population from Kinston (22,000) to Rocky Mount (34,000), with only Greenville undergoing any significant increase in the 1960s. Kinston and Goldsboro actually declined during the decade. In 1860 all but Rocky Mount had been among the ten largest towns in the state; in 1970 none was. Such prosperity as they enjoyed could be attributed largely to the fact that they were the five largest bright leaf tobacco markets in the world, with Wilson the world leader.

"Marketing," as newspaper editor and author Jonathan Daniels wrote of these towns in 1941,

is the farmer's fate but the towns' frenzy. . . . It is a competition for the tobacco between the towns which exceeds even the wildest moments in the Coastal Plain baseball league. On all highways are huge billboards advising the farmer to sell his tobacco in the Suchandsuch tobacco market which always gives a fair deal and high prices. . . . Whole communities [are] united in the will to make the farmer happy within their gates. It was not accident that Kinston . . . kept for so many years . . . the gay and good-looking girls in its gaudy Sugar Hill. . . . Loving the farmer is the chief industry from Raleigh to the sea.

Kinston labored forlornly through the depression, when every industry but the Hines Brothers Lumber Company closed down. No Prince Charming came to kiss it into prosperity. The meatpacking plant built in 1945 and later taken over by Frosty Morn helped—but not enough. In 1953 a prince seemed actually to appear in the form of DuPont's (and the world's) first Dacron plant. DuPont was the developer of Dacron, a polyester staple used in durable and wrinkle-free fabrics. An industrial grade was made for fire hoses, tires, and other products where strength is vital. DuPont was "a dream come true," in the ecstatic view of the Kinston *Free Press*, "the beginnings of a new industrial era."

Perhaps so, but not for Kinston. DuPont put 2,000 people to work and by 1962 had pumped $14 million into the local economy and lent impetus to the opening of an industrial education center (which later evolved into Lenoir Community College). Nevertheless, the population of Kinston, after expanding for a time, decreased by 10 percent during the 1960s, tarnishing the luster of the "new industrial era." Real growth was not even foreseeable; what Kinston could realistically count on was mere survival on the strength of its tobacco, Dacron, and shirt factories, its lumber mills and its food processors.

It was much the same in Rocky Mount, which, though it was not faced with imminent decline, was not growing much either. What visitors remembered

*June German dance,
Rocky Mount*

most about Rocky Mount was not its scattering of cotton-yarn and lumber mills, its producers of cottonseed oil, cordage, overalls, and the like, or even the spring fling known as the Gallopade—but rather the June German. This was a ball held annually since the 1880s and always in a gaily decorated tobacco warehouse. A Methodist pastor in 1923 worked himself into a froth over "women under the influence of liquor . . . bottles dropped on the ballroom floor" and other enormities of the revelers. But this was in the years when the punch was sometimes spiked with as much as forty gallons of "bootleg," and the illicit hooch was half the fun. Jonathan Daniels, who witnessed a more sedate affair in 1941, thought it still "the biggest dance in the State, maybe in America— probably the world." German weekend meant thousands of dancers and onlookers and a ball that began at 9:00 P.M. and ended at dawn when "everyone would pile into cars and head for the beach." It was always a big-band affair, too, with the likes of Jimmy Dorsey or hometown boy Kay Kyser. But interest dwindled in the 1960s when other recreational opportunities crowded it out, and the German slid quietly into oblivion.

The tobacco towns that fared best were those that had something extra going for them besides the leaf and some small industrial concerns. The ability of Goldsboro, for example, to maintain a faltering pace owed much to the federal government. The establishment of Seymour Johnson Air Base there during World War II gave the area a major military installation and a vital injection to local payrolls. Goldsboro's retail trade held up well because the town had commercial primacy over large portions of several surrounding counties; and there were also locally made leather products, electronic components, machinery—there was even an easternmost outpost of the furniture industry. But not even the Strategic Air Command could safeguard Goldsboro against the uncertainties of the postwar epoch, and the town could not keep pace with similar communities to the west.

The slight, relative advantage at Wilson was mainly Atlantic Christian College (now named Barton College), Hackney Body Works, and 2 million square feet of tobacco warehouse space (including Smith's, the world's largest tobacco auction market). Wilson's annual tobacco festival and exposition paid due homage to the "folk dance attended by chanting," as Daniels termed it, which marked every market day between mid-August and Thanksgiving and poured green bills into the local economy. Processions of buyers during these days moved quickly between rows piled high with tobacco, while clusters of farmers trailed along to hear the bids and reject or register those made on their own baskets. What astonished the neophyte was the ability of all those people to make sense of the auctioneer's jet-propelled "bafflegab" of numbers and exhortations, but somehow the procession rolled on and the leaf was sold. The Wilson and Greenville markets each handled over seventy million pounds a year.

Greenville faced much the same economic strains of fluctuating markets and black and white exodus as the other towns but weathered them better because of the expansion of its college. East Carolina Teachers College ("Eeseeteesee," as it was known down east), originally a girls' school, was long an ugly duckling in North Carolina's extensive system of higher education. A period of aggressive leadership after World War II carried it rapidly to higher status as East Carolina College and, ultimately, East Carolina University, complete with a medical school and big-time athletics. Greenville was also blessed with a respectable mixture of business and industry, including plastics, concrete products, cotton yarn, lumber, fertilizer, bricks, metalworks, and meatpacking. By 1970 the town could claim educational and cultural leadership over a large section of eastern North Carolina.

But nowhere in eastern North Carolina was the future particularly promising. "Once a year," as Jonathan Daniels concluded, "while the auctioneer chants and sways and the buyers march to his chanting, the intoxication of riches spreads through the towns and overflows the land. That exaltation is emphasized by the sadder years when the chant is a wail and merchants and bankers and farmers walk together in sorrow."

East Hargett

Berry O'Kelly

The passage of Jim Crow laws and the practice of racial discrimination after about 1890 created in most North Carolina towns and cities clear patterns of racial separation. Black houses and businesses that had emerged in earlier years within white-majority districts were pushed out, often leaving blacks as the sole occupants of designated fringes or islands within the urban area. Placement in such areas of segregated schools and other public and private facilities that served only black patrons minimized contact between the races and suspended for generations the attainment of the economic and social aspirations of the black communities.

This pattern was clear enough in Raleigh, the state capital, though perhaps less rigidly imposed than in most urban areas of the South. Various factors, not always discriminatory, combined in the first decades of the twentieth century to concentrate black business along a stretch of Raleigh's East Hargett Street, which became, in effect, the city's "Negro Main Street." Pominent black commission merchant Berry O'Kelly acquired the real estate for the district. O'Kelly began as a small merchant in the community of Method, now part of Raleigh. His efforts on behalf of better agriculture, education, and industry for African Americans led to a variety of positions: chairman of a local school committee that consolidated three rural black schools into the Berry O'Kelly Training School, founder of the National Negro Business League, president of realty and shoe companies, chairman of a life insurance company, and vice president of the Raleigh branch of the Mechanics and Farmers Bank of Durham. O'Berry's leadership and the erection in 1915 of the Lightner Building for professional offices helped make East Hargett Street attractive to black businesses. By 1923 blacks outnumbered whites there, and, though the black influx leveled off with the coming of the depression, East Hargett remained predominantly black through the 1960s.

East Hargett Street early gained a good reputation in the city. Distinctly middle-class, it drew black doctors, lawyers, tailors, beauticians, dentists, and barbers, as well as black insurance companies and undertakers, a black theater, hotel, and bank, and a wide assortment of retail stores. But the street was at least as important socially as it was economically. The annual black Debutante Ball originated there, and the hotel dining room, in the recollection of an old-timer, "used to be on the front and everybody ate in there. That was the place to go to eat. You could go in and get a soft drink or coffee or the like and a piece of pie and sit and talk half the day if you wanted to." Many people, according to another, "just came and stood outside and looked in; they could see all the important people there."

The poolroom on East Hargett was the gathering place for a clientele less elite than that at the hotel dining room. "Fellows who had hot stuff to sell," said a denizen, "would show up at the poolroom because that's where the folks were. Since the poolroom has been off the street, got burned in '56, there's no place to hang out." The American Legion clubroom over the Royal Theater was another popular East Hargett social resort.

East Hargett flourished because it was convenient to the heavily black southeastern section of Raleigh and to other scattered black neighborhoods. Also it lay hard by the city's central downtown business streets and had a share of white patronage. Black clients knew that their accounts were welcome there and that the street's restrooms and drinking fountains carried no "white only" signs. But the popularity of the street owed something in the 1920s and 1930s to the convivial informality that pervaded it. "Anyone who wanted to pass the time away and just generally 'shoot the breeze' made his way to Hargett St.," said one veteran. "There was no YMCA then . . . the churches had no activities to interest young men, and the city had none. . . . It was the only place Negroes could go for ice cream even. . . . One group hung out on the south side of the street and another group on the north side. The north side group was made up of professional men who had offices on the street. . . . The younger group hung around on the south side of the street. If you were looking for fun, hilarity, talking about girls, whistling at girls, etc., then you joined the young group on the south side."

The Raleigh black community's most charismatic personalities were to be found on the street, as were its most talented professional men and entrepreneurs. Roger Demosthenes O'Kelly, America's only deaf-mute lawyer, a graduate of Shaw University and Yale University Law School, established an office there in 1921. He was a widely respected expert on real estate transactions, domestic relations, and corporate law, and he served white clients as well as black. O'Kelly explained how he managed as a deaf-mute:

My almost sole dependence now, when not conversing with deaf-mutes, is pencil and pad: they carried me through Shaw and Yale and they carried me through many important business deals. One can write with much more care and deliberation than he can speak. Did you ever think of it? a pencil puts one on his guard. Spoken words are easily forgotten, written words stay and are remembered.

East Hargett was where the rural poor came in wagons on Saturdays to sell their eggs and butter and visit the rummage sales (or, when these were banned, the secondhand clothing and furniture stores). It was where the African American newspaper was published, where the professional and social clubs met and had their chief functions. The Raleigh Safety Club, a cooperative funeral society,

Young Men's
Institute (now
closed), Asheville

met there for years on the upper floor of the Odd Fellows Building. It paid
$1.00 per member to the family of any member at the time of his death. A
ladies' auxiliary also provided food and other assistance to the bereaved.

The 1940s brought changes in the character of East Hargett, but the street
continued to be the focus of black business in the Raleigh area. Traffic and
parking congestion drove some of the doctors, undertakers, and other professionals elsewhere in quest of more space. Many businesses previously owned by
one individual became partnerships or corporations, while a general improvement in the civil position of blacks made them less dependent upon black-
owned businesses. Gradually, East Hargett Street became more impersonal in
its business style, less important in its social dimension. But the street in its heyday provided the black community with services and opportunities that were
available through no other channel. In Asheville, a similar successful black
business venture was the Young Men's Institute.

Dukedom

A godchild of the Piedmont's Victorian era industrial surge, the city of
Durham struggled indignantly in the middle decades of the twentieth century

against its reputation as an overgrown factory town, ill at ease with the university brought in for cultural uplift by the city's new rich. It was more than Durham's humble beginnings and hard-driving growth that inspired a mixture of derision and envy in others. Durham was the raw embodiment of the persisting gulfs in the industrial New South between rich and poor, slum and suburb, squalor and gentility.

It was no wonder that novelist Thomas Wolfe, scarred already by the crassness that commerce had brought to his childhood home and hamlet of Asheville, would find Durham a "dreary tobacco town" with "a thinning squalor of cheap houses." To Wolfe and fellow undergraduates at Chapel Hill, Durham existed to serve one need only. Portrayed as the town of "Exeter" in *Look Homeward, Angel*, the town was seen as a "sordid little road, unpaved, littered on both sides with negro shacks and the dwellings of poor whites" that led to a much-frequented brothel.

Pauli Murray, black attorney and one of the first women ordained as an

*Drugstore in the
Young Men's
Institute*

Episcopal priest, grew up in Durham in the 1920s and afterward recalled its poorest sections in images entirely compatible with those of Wolfe. It was a collection, she wrote, of shanty-hamlets called "Bottoms" that clung precariously

to the banks of streams or sat crazily on washed-out gullies and were held together by cowpaths or rutted wagon tracks. . . . It was as if the town had swallowed more than it could hold and had regurgitated, for the Bottom was an odious conglomeration of trash piles, garbage dumps, cow-stalls, pigpens, and crowded humanity. You could tell it at night by the straggling lights from oil lamps glimmering along the hollows and the smell of putrefaction, pig swill, cow dung, and frying food. Even if you lived on a hill just above the Bottoms, it seemed lower and danker than the meanest hut on a graded street.

Another observer gave the following description of a black laborer's house in Durham:

One enters a bare room lit by an open electric bulb. The chief piece of furniture is the white enamel iron double bed covered by a neat counterpane. On the left is a golden oak bureau . . . covered with an assortment of old medicine bottles. On the other side is an old fashioned board trunk. In the center of the room, gathered around the cast iron stove, are grouped the family . . . seated on straight chairs. . . . On the mantel with the alarm clock is a vase with crepe paper roses. Brightly colored calendars are on the walls. . . . There are no rugs, and not even curtains at the windows.

Of graded streets there were but few in the 1920s, especially in the Durham neighborhood of Hayti (pronounced *Hay-tie*). Hayti flourished in the years of Prohibition with bootleg whiskey. Illicit liquor stores—known and notorious as "blind tigers"—abounded and asked patrons neither color nor creed. A den of iniquity to its detractors, Hayti was a homeplace for thousands. Small black groceries and businesses served customers by day, and some of the South's legendary blues and jazz musicians—including "Sonny" Terry and "Blind Boy" Fuller—brought their magic to the nights.

Elsewhere in town, for whites, there were two silent-movie houses and a burlesque theater. For highbrow entertainment, the Academy of Music offered concerts and road shows. Nonetheless, to Jonathan Daniels—ancient Raleigh antagonist of the Duke family—Durham in 1941 was still mainly muck and dilapidation. "Ragged children played in the dirt before the dirty houses," and "unpaved streets" ran "up and down hilly, muddy lanes to slums."

Needless to say, perhaps, there were more Durhams than those described by Thomas Wolfe, Pauli Murray, and Jonathan Daniels. Quite apart from attractive residential areas, an imposing tower by this time rose impressively above the Gothic and Georgian buildings of "Buck" Duke's "instant univer-

Washington Duke Hotel (1925; now demolished), Durham

sity" of the 1920s. By an enormous outlay of cash, buttressed by a $40 million endowment, Duke had transformed a small Methodist school called Trinity College into a leading educational institution. By the time the foundations of its huge English chapel were laid in 1930, Duke University was a complex of stone structures surrounding a large court. Besides its sprawling medical complex, its law school, comprehensive library, and formal gardens, Duke by the mid-1930s could even boast a powerhouse of a football team. The "Blue Devils" hosted the 1942 Rose Bowl, relocated from California because of the war, losing 16–20 to Oregon State.

But Durham, in the 1920s, was more than its university. North Carolina

*New North Carolina Mutual Life Insurance
Company Building (1966), Durham*

College (later North Carolina Central University) had outlived its critics and
was emerging as one of the South's foremost institutions of higher learning
for blacks. Durham's downtown, with its twenty-odd restaurants packed into a
five-block area, lacked aesthetic appeal, but the gleaming Washington Duke
Hotel and the new Union Bus Terminal might well divert the eyes of the itinerant from much that was not pleasing. Every fifth American cigarette was made
in the aromatic factory district, and Durham was at the time North Carolina's
second largest city.

Efforts by owners and workers alike improved Durham's working class.
West Durham, under the enlightened paternalism of mill magnate William A.
Erwin, was a mill village of advanced design. Even before 1920 Erwin introduced lights and plumbing, a day-care center and playgrounds. In 1922 he
built a three-story auditorium with a bowling alley, library, and classrooms for
instruction in the "domestic sciences." Erwin Mills also sponsored contests and

awarded prizes to those workers with the best-kept yards, or to those who were best in cooking and canning foods.

By the 1970s promoters could declare with only a hint of hyperbole that Main Street "meanders between sentinels of trees and potted plantings from the new County Judicial Building to the Muirhead Plaza Fountains at Five Points." Gone were most of the eateries of yesteryear; in their place was a complex of government and institutional edifices. A nationally recognized black bourgeoisie, its center of gravity located in the stunning twelve-story headquarters of the North Carolina Mutual Life Insurance Company, testified to the achievement of Durham blacks despite the "Bottoms" and other barriers to racial achievement. A symphony orchestra gave tone to the city's cultural life, and a street arts celebration annually drew 50,000 people and more to the city's center for sociability and good cheer. A healthy rivalry pitted Durham against Raleigh and Chapel Hill for the right to house and trade with the gilded salariat of the Research Triangle.

"Altamont"

If it was ever really true that "you can't go home again," Thomas Wolfe was as good a living example of that aphorism as anyone. Ashevillians read his *Look Homeward, Angel* in 1929 and saw it as a mean little hatchet job, a needless reminder of the town's old grudges and past sins and grubby secrets that every town has but tries to hide. The mill hands at Durham might not flinch at Wolfe's strictures against them, but the residents of Asheville were accustomed to the image of their town as presented in travel brochures that alluringly portrayed the beauties of the "Land of the Sky." The public library would not put the book on its shelves, and the local papers gave it bad reviews. Wolfe paid his hometown one more brief visit in 1937 when his fame lent an air of glamour even to his taunts, but he probably never came back in spirit.

And, anyway, Tom had his way of needling what he loved best. He had a soft spot in his heart for the "Old Kentucky Home" ("Dixieland" in the book), his family's boardinghouse at 48 Spruce Street, but he wrote of it as a "big, cheaply constructed frame house of rambling, unplanned, gabular appearance." He spent many happy hours around Pack Square, the business center where his father's monument shop stood, but the book called the locale a "treeless brick jungle of business—cheap, ragged and ugly, and beyond all this, in indefinite patches, the houses where all the people lived, with little bright raw ulcers of suburbs further off, and the healing and concealing grace of tall massed trees." Such was "Altamont," as Asheville was called in Wolfe's novel.

Asheville during Wolfe's adolescence—the World War I era—was a place

Thomas Wolfe and his mother, Julia Wolfe, 1937

of horses and wagons and trolley cars, a saucerlike depression on the French Broad and Swannanoa Rivers, overshadowed by Summit and Beaucatcher Mountains. It was essentially a resort town that blossomed with color and activity from June to September and then shriveled to half its summertime size in fall and winter. Some native Ashevillians distrusted seasonal visitors. According to one authority, "it took quite a bit of education to cause the local

people to accept tourists. This was one of the most provincial areas that you can imagine. They resented these Northerners coming in here: they were strange people, they didn't speak like they spoke, and they didn't dress like they dressed."

For a brief period in the mid-1920s, Asheville went through a wild spell of land speculation when con men fresh from the Florida boom (and bust) moved

Pack Square, Asheville, 1930s

Asheville High School (1927)

in and pushed prices for prime lots to several thousand dollars and more a front foot. The opening of the Battery Park and George Vanderbilt Hotels in 1924 signaled a dizzy spree of building schools, parks and golf courses, a city hall and library, a tunnel through Beaucatcher Mountain, and a subdivision platted from surrounding farms. The Battery Park Hotel and Asheville's New Arcade (1926) were constructed by E. W. Grove, builder of the Grove Park Inn. Asheville's arcade was similar to Charlotte's Latta Arcade and Greensboro's Irvin Arcade (1930).

The bubble burst, of course, and in the spring of 1926 ultimately shut down six local banks. Like a terrible omen, Wolfe's novel presaged the coming of even worse: the Great Depression, during which construction dwindled, factories closed, and even the tourist business dried up. The Edisons and Firestones and Fords still came sometimes to the Grove Park Inn during the 1930s (President Roosevelt overnighted there in 1936), but lesser mortals stayed home and the town suffered. Jonathan Daniels in 1941 found Asheville "circled with such magnificent mountains and . . . so steeply tawdry within," with a "driving, hungry, resort-town frenzy which stripped all the prettiness, all the dignity, off the town."

But Daniels was cursing the town and, indirectly, himself for not having appreciated Wolfe's genius or respected his viewpoint in the beginning. Asheville had, perhaps, a rather shabby and unkempt appearance after a decade of depression, but it nevertheless offered many advantages that the casual visitor might not notice. It was the marketing center for burley tobacco, livestock, fruits, and other farm products of western North Carolina. There was Biltmore, the striking two-hundred-fifty-room mansion of George W. Vanderbilt; a spectacular June rhododendron festival; a July mountain folk music and dance festival; and various golf and tennis tournaments.

In spite of its potential, Asheville languished through the 1940s and 1950s. The quaint but unfrequented town suffered from a relative inaccessibility and the failure of local businesses leaders to anticipate fully the burgeoning post-war tourist boom. Emigration reduced Buncombe County's population by 10,000 during the dreary decade before 1960. But the trend was reversed in the 1960s after urban renewal projects had freshened up the town's appearance and attracted new tourist accommodations. Moreover, new highways were opened through the town's mountain environs, and modern hotels replaced some of the antiquated inns and boardinghouses of the predepression boomlet.

By 1970 Asheville was alive and well again, the seventh largest city in the state, with 58,000 inhabitants. Nearly encircled by a million acres of national forest and serving as the gateway to the Great Smoky Mountains National Park, Asheville gained a year-round clientele as ski slopes opened in the adjacent hills. Year-round occupancy was also enhanced by the evolution of little Asheville Normal and Teachers College into the University of North Carolina at Asheville. By 1970 prosperity had banished the old resentment of Thomas Wolfe, and the town had learned to bestow due homage upon its prodigal son.

Colossalopolis

Demographers and urban planners looking toward the twenty-first century foresaw huge supercities stretching north and south from Los Angeles on the Pacific Coast and from Boston southward to the Potomac in the East. From the perspective of 1970, North Carolina seemed unlikely in the foreseeable future to become engulfed in any such urban sprawl, but the state's leading population centers were, indeed, beginning discernibly to merge. This raised the prospect of a vast, uninterrupted urban complex, a "Charleigh" or "Ralotte"

Jefferson Standard Building (1923), Greensboro

that would pave the tobacco fields of the Piedmont and make parks of its rolling forests.

The term "Triangle" was already frequently heard for the Raleigh–Durham–Chapel Hill area, though distinct rural expanses still largely separated the three. "Triad" would soon be coined to designate the Greensboro–Winston-Salem–High Point area, and a contest in the Charlotte vicinity in 1968 had brought forth the term "Metrolina" as the label for the urbanized region of which Charlotte was the hub. Moreover, all three of these incipient supercities formed points along a 300-mile strip reaching from Lynchburg, Virginia, to Anderson, South Carolina, that seemed likely to become a southern version of megalopolis by the year 2000. At the end of the twentieth century, North Carolina's population exceeded 8 million, and 5.4 million (68 percent) of the state's inhabitants were living in urban areas.

Metrolina embraced everything within a fifty-mile radius of Charlotte. It included Rock Hill, South Carolina and the North Carolina towns of Hickory, Salisbury, Shelby, Monroe, and others regarded as being in some degree related—by proximity to Charlotte or to one another. Planners deemed it useful to think in terms of such urban systems as a means of coordinating various services and activities. The time had come, they declared, when municipalities could no longer "work in a vacuum of narrow local interests."

Megalopolis, then, was the urban counterpart of the central theme of the epoch. It embodied the same sort of thinking that impressed itself in these years on the farmer who joined a co-op, the industrialist and businessman who learned the lessons of commercial and industrial integration. Planning, for the urbanologist, was needed not only to ensure a better quality of city life but also to prevent the horrendous consequences that dogged the tracks of city growth. The Soviet Union pursued its program of development through forced "five-year plans" and the like, but in the West it still seemed possible to realize humanity's hopes through cooperation and voluntary means. The phantom of prospective force haunted the planner's work, but the need for cooperative effort seemed ever more inescapable as the century progressed.

Metrolina in the 1960s had an aggregate population of over a million, fourth in the Southeast behind the Miami, Atlanta, and Tampa–St. Petersburg urban complexes. Its growth during the decade far outstripped that of the state (although an unequal pattern of distribution left Metrolina's southeastern corner, Union County, still heavily rural). A quarter of Metrolina's inhabitants were engaged in manufacturing—mostly in textiles and apparel, but also in furniture, nonelectrical machinery, chemicals, and other products. But their manufacturing wages were lower than the state's as a whole, pulled down by the textile and apparel factories that dotted the area.

Metrolinians tended to be slightly better educated than the typical Tar Heel (ninth-grade average), though well below the national norm. They were still mostly Democratic, but Republican candidates made big gains in the region during the 1950s and 1960s. A graduate of the area's high schools could choose from among four technical institutions, seven two-year colleges, and thirteen senior colleges without leaving Metrolina. Cultural uplift was available through the Mint Museum of Art, the Mint Museum Dance Guild, the Charlotte Symphony Orchestra, the Charlotte Opera Association, and a wide variety of satellite programs and institutions. Carowinds amusement park had lately brought popular entertainment to Metrolina on a grand scale.

The growth of urban areas also resulted in the proliferation of hospitals and improvements in medical care. Nevertheless, certain epidemic diseases remained threats to both urban and rural inhabitants. North Carolinians, like all Americans, endured a nightmare in the form of summer polio epidemics

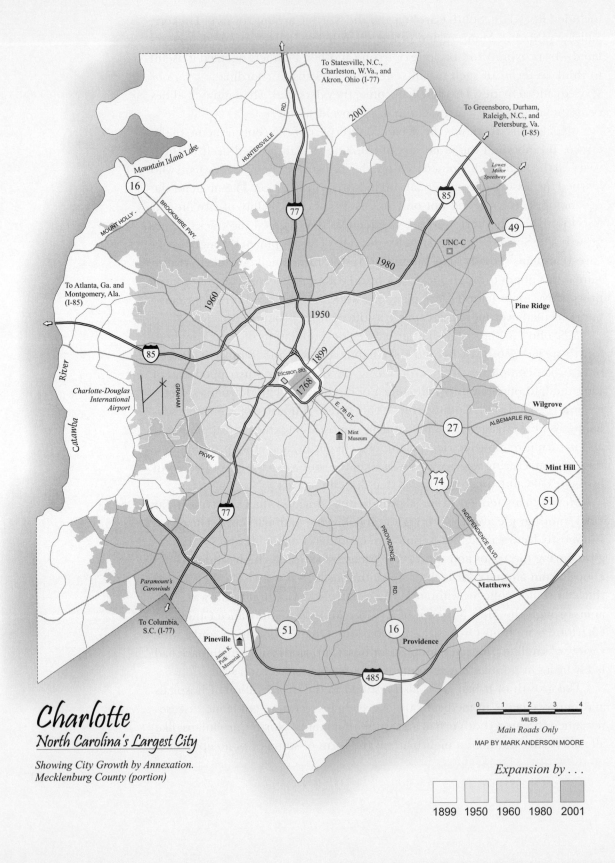

Charlotte
North Carolina's Largest City

Showing City Growth by Annexation.
Mecklenburg County (portion)

To Statesville, N.C.,
Charleston, W.Va., and
Akron, Ohio (I-77)

To Greensboro, Durham,
Raleigh, N.C., and
Petersburg, Va.
(I-85)

Mountain Island Lake

16

Lowes
Motor
Speedway

85

49

HUNTERSVILLE RD.

2001

77

UNC-C

1980

Pine Ridge

MOUNT HOLLY

BROOKSHIRE FWY.

To Atlanta, Ga. and
Montgomery, Ala.
(I-85)

1960

1950

85

River

Catawba

GRAHAM

Charlotte-Douglas
International
Airport

1899

Ericsson Sta.

1768

E. 7th ST.

Wilgrove

ALBEMARLE RD.

27

Mint Museum

Mint Hill

74

51

PKWY.

INDEPENDENCE BLVD.

77

PROVIDENCE RD.

Paramount's
Carowinds

Matthews

To Columbia,
S.C. (I-77)

51

16

Pineville

James K.
Polk
Memorial

Providence

485

0   1   2   3   4
MILES

Main Roads Only

MAP BY MARK ANDERSON MOORE

Expansion by . . .

1899 1950 1960 1980 2001

that terrorized the state from 1929 to 1948. No section was spared these seasonal visitations. In 1948 North Carolina had the worst epidemic in the country with over 2,500 cases and 100 deaths from the disease. Apart from the toll in human suffering, the epidemics frequently meant disruption of school schedules, recreational activities, and other normal patterns of living. In 1944 Hickory, in Catawba County, and Greensboro, in Guilford County, were forced to provide special polio hospitals to handle the numbers of cases. Only with the introduction of the Salk vaccine in the late 1950s was the disease finally brought under control.

As the twentieth century drew to a close, urban planners puzzled over the contradiction inherent in the evolution of Metrolina and similar supercities. Vast numbers of people identified the good life with easy access to the amenities of big-city living, but most also felt that the good life meant abundant space between oneself and one's neighbors. The effort to reconcile these ideals underlay the city's evolution into an urban region and the fostering of regional, as opposed to local, attitudes and allegiances. Hence, Metrolina was already the object of a regional coordinating committee, an environmental concern association, an air quality control program, a soil and water conservation effort, an area development association, and other regional planning groups. Would Charlotte, Winston-Salem, Raleigh, and Greensboro eventually be boroughs within a megalopolis? In some respects, by the end of the twentieth century, they had become exactly that.

6

EXPRESS LANES

Getting There

The provincialism that was said to be a primary trait of the quintessential Tar Heel reflected North Carolina's geography and early pattern of growth. A want of good harbors reduced North Carolina's contact with the outside world, and a superfluity of rivers and streams inhibited rather than facilitated contact among settlers. Tar Heels were slow to be drawn into either the federal Union or the Confederacy in part because it was difficult for propagandists to reach and influence them.

The sectionalism of the Carolinian arose from the peculiarity of eighteenth-century immigration into the Piedmont and Mountain sections. The settlers there did not, in the main, come from the older English and Scottish settlements in the east but rather from Germany and Ireland by the way of the northern colonies. This heightened the differences between easterner and westerner and made for political ramifications that lasted well into the twentieth century.

To the extent that geographical isolation was the root of provincialism and sectionalism in North Carolina, good roads, railways, bridges, and airports were important modifiers of the traditional character traits. But facilities of modern transport and communication sufficient to alter the Tar Heel personality did not come until the twentieth century was well advanced and did not have a remarkably rapid or pronounced effect even then. An important step toward ending North Carolina's relative isolation was taken in 1921 when the state legislature approved a $50 million bond issue—the state's largest to that date. The object of the new program, financed by automobile and gasoline taxes, was to complete and maintain a 5,500-mile system of primary roads. When finished, it would connect all of North Carolina's 100 county seats, its principal towns and cities, its state parks and state institutions, and link these with the highway systems of neighboring states. A key part of the program was a central route—now Highway 70—reaching from Beaufort on the coast through Raleigh, Greensboro, and Asheville to the Tennessee line.

Besides realizing the aims of the state's new highway program, the 1920s witnessed the commitment of another $50 million to the enlargement of the primary road system. The 1921 Highway Act was in large part the achievement of Harriet Berry through the North Carolina Good Roads Association. Berry campaigned in every county, organized petitions, wrote letters and circulars, and obtained money and members for the organization. Politically astute, she led the association to the accomplishment of its aims: ambitious road legislation and a strong highway commission.

Good roads made possible the consolidation of rural schools and the use of school buses. Thomas Built Buses, Inc., of High Point, in Guilford County, the largest manufacturer of school buses in the world, supplied the buses. Thomas made the New Orleans trolleys, still in use. A Thomas trolley may be seen in the High Point Museum.

But money was scarce and progress for highways slow during most of the 1930s and 1940s. By 1948 the state had responsibility for a total of 64,000

Early twentieth-century roads were frequently impassable.

Early road grader

miles of roads and highways, but many secondary routes were impassable in bad weather. World War II traffic had been hard on the primary roads, and municipalities, unaided by the state, were struggling to cope with the onrushing increase in automobile traffic and the flight to suburbia. Only 7,000 miles of North Carolina's roads had any sort of hard surface.

Kerr Scott made roads a central campaign issue when he ran for governor in 1948. He promised to improve the routes used by the state's 6,000 public school buses and to "get the farmer out of the mud." After winning election, Scott startled many by gaining legislative and referendum approval for a whopping $200 million road bond issue. In addition to building 14,000 miles of roads, his administration oversaw the passage of the "Powell bill," which provided funds for municipal streets. This bill also helped soften the resentment of city folks over the cost to them of Scott's rural road bonds.

With the federal government's entry into interstate road building in the 1950s and Governor Dan Moore's successful 1965 campaign to obtain approval of a $300 million bond issue, North Carolina emerged from its isolation and began shaking off its provincialism. In the Coastal Plain, the $10 million Wilmington Memorial Bridge was completed across the Cape Fear River in 1969. Meanwhile, the picturesque Herbert Bonner Bridge had been built over Oregon Inlet on the Outer Banks and the big Lindsay C. Warren Bridge across the Alligator River in Tyrrell County. In the west, the most impressive new span was

that over the Green River Gorge in Polk County, opened in 1968. Altogether, there were some 15,000 bridges in the state system.

Raleigh-to-Greensboro bus

In places where bridges had not been built, as between Ocracoke and Cedar Island, across Currituck Sound, and over Hatteras Inlet, the state established ferry service. The state's fleet of sixteen ferryboats included the big *Silver Lake* and *Pamlico*, built at a cost of over $500,000 each; these vessels served the Ocracoke–Cedar Island route. In a single summer month in 1968, the Bogue Sound ferries carried 31,000 cars and 85,000 passengers between the mainland and Emerald Isle. Within a decade, however, a modern, high bridge crossed Bogue Inlet, and the number of vacationers flowing across it to the beaches was increasing every year.

By 1970 the interstate highway system in North Carolina covered 450 miles. A spectacular 22-mile-long section, opened in 1968, stretched from Cove Creek in Haywood County to the Tennessee line on Highway I-40. This section, which wound through the Pigeon River Valley, with the river on one

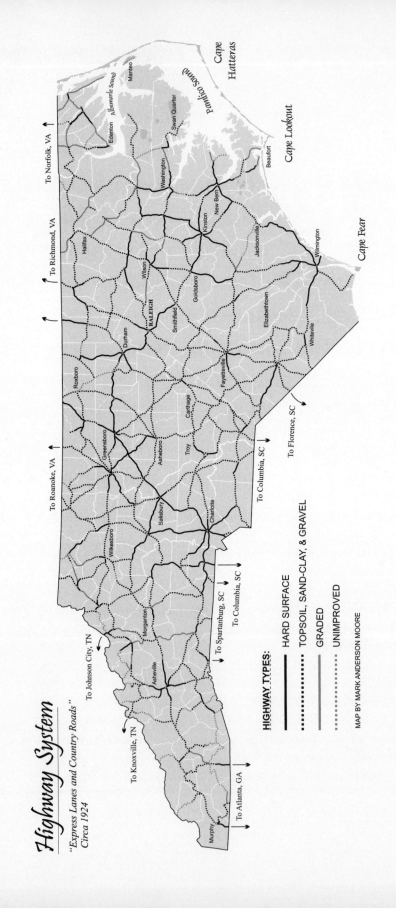

Highway System

"Express Lanes and Country Roads"
Circa 1924

HIGHWAY TYPES:

HARD SURFACE

TOPSOIL, SAND-CLAY, & GRAVEL

GRADED

UNIMPROVED

MAP BY MARK ANDERSON MOORE

To Norfolk, VA

To Richmond, VA

To Roanoke, VA

To Johnson City, TN

To Knoxville, TN

To Atlanta, GA

To Spartanburg, SC

To Columbia, SC

To Columbia, SC

To Florence, SC

Edenton

Albemarle Sound

Manteo

Pamlico Sound

Cape Hatteras

Cape Lookout

Cape Fear

Swan Quarter

Beaufort

Washington

New Bern

Kinston

Wilmington

Jacksonville

Goldsboro

Elizabethtown

Whiteville

Halifax

Wilson

RALEIGH

Smithfield

Fayetteville

Durham

Roxboro

Carthage

Greensboro

Asheboro

Troy

Charlotte

Salisbury

Wilkesboro

Morganton

Asheville

Murphy

Highway Patrol car and trooper, 1935

side and jagged mountain slopes rising sharply on the other, was a cut blasted out with 125 train carloads of explosives. Other interstate routes connected Virginia and South Carolina across the Coastal Plain (I-95) and Piedmont (I-77), while I-85 swept across the Piedmont through Durham, Greensboro, and Charlotte.

The policing of so large a system of highways, the most extensive state-maintained one in the United States, required the expansion of the State Highway Patrol from the 37 "road sheriffs" who served in 1929 to a force of nearly 900 troopers in 1970. By the latter year the state had 73,000 miles of roads and 2.5 million licensed drivers. Yet Morehead City and Wilmington remained the only two major American ports not served by the interstate highway system, and Wilmington still had no four-lane route to promote its development. Nor had North Carolina responded promptly to the opening of the Chesapeake Bay Bridge-Tunnel, which might have directed huge fleets of traffic into the state's tidelands if a suitable North Carolina connection had been provided. Nor for another several decades could North Carolina expect to see its key highway problems solved.

In 1977, however, the state legislature approved a referendum on a $300 million highway bond package, and the voters of the state approved it by a two to one margin. In July 1989, the legislature passed a bill establishing the North Carolina Highway Trust Fund and approved $8.8 million for the thirteen-year construction of interstate highways. In 1995, the North Carolina Department of Transportation announced that it had spent $2.6 billion on construction in the past three years and planned to spend $7.4 billion on needed construction in the next seven years. Between 1993 and 1995, the department spent $64 million on road and bridge maintenance. In May 1995, Governor James B. Hunt Jr. signed an executive order to create the Transit 2001 Commission to develop and implement a master transit plan. But for the most part, a mass transit system remains largely undeveloped in the state.

For many years, the want of modern access to Wilmington and Morehead City could be seen as a lingering taint of regressive sectionalism. In earlier times, Coastal Plain legislators had gleefully denied advantages to the Piedmont and west; in the twentieth century the Piedmont-dominated General Assembly took its revenge. Bold arteries crisscrossed the Piedmont and snaked with federal aid across the Appalachians—but the main roads stopped well short of the coast. In the panoply of Tar Heel characteristics, sectionalism had outlived provincialism. But by the end of century, that too had changed, as I-40 was completed to Wilmington. That highway now runs all the way from Wilmington to Barstow, California. As traffic congestion increased, travel along I-40 was made easier with the completion of the Winston-Salem bypass, additional lanes near Burlington, and the I-440 beltline at Raleigh. In 1996, the North Carolina Department of Transportation won the National Quality Initiative Award for Raleigh's I-440 beltline.

The Press Gang

Invigorated by rural free delivery and improved means of transportation, North Carolina's newspapers between 1920 and 1970 improved steadily in quality and increased considerably in size. Newspaper circulation, which passed 2 million in 1926, was led by the city dailies such as the *Charlotte Observer*, Raleigh *News and Observer*, and *Greensboro Daily News*. The number of papers fell as metropolitan dailies encroached on the territory of small-town and rural weeklies. In 1939, for example, the state had 227 papers; by 1960 the figure was down to 194, including 47 dailies. The *Charlotte Observer* captured and held the lead in circulation over its competitors, raising its pressruns to almost a quarter of a million per issue by 1960.

For its relatively poor condition in some respects, North Carolina enjoyed a high reputation for the quality and dynamism of its newspaper press. Josephus Daniels, secretary of the navy and ambassador to Mexico, earned renown for the influence he exercised as editor of the *News and Observer*. His fearlessness extended to attacks on the powerful tobacco and textile interests, which controlled so much of his newspaper's advertising. The chief voice of liberalism in the state in the 1920s was that of Gerald W. Johnson of the *Greensboro Daily News*, an eloquent firebrand who was not infrequently instrumental in directing the drift of popular opinion and the impetus of public policy through his editorials.

Josephus Daniels

Frequently, however, journalistic interest focused not so much on the pow-

William Oscar Saunders

erful-but-staid city papers as on the gifted eccentrics who sometimes emerged in the provinces. The most controversial newspaperman in the state during the interwar years was W. O. Saunders, owner and editor of the little Elizabeth City *Independent*, in the far northeastern corner of the state. Saunders was famous for such escapades as parading along New York's Broadway and Fifth Avenue in his pajamas to protest the discomfort of men's summer attire. His blast at a New Deal privy-building program in 1934 was reprinted from coast to coast, and he was an advocate of birth control and abolition of the death penalty when only the lost and despised could be so. Ordered by the courts to retract a headline calling a Pasquotank County man "An Ass," Saunders gleefully heralded in yet bolder type the revelation that the man was "Not an Ass." In a moment of high editorial drama in 1924, Saunders attacked Mordecai Ham, an anti-Semitic revivalist who held a revival in Elizabeth City. Ham reviled philanthropist Julius Rosenwald of Sears, Roebuck and Company and accused Jews of plotting the destruction of gentile civilization. Saunders called Ham "a charlatan, a four-flusher and a liar." Saunders declared that "The Prophet Ham came to Elizabeth City to dynamite Hell out of Elizabeth City. In the course of events it became necessary for me to dynamite a little hell out of Ham." That attack brought down the wrath of the community on Saunders's head. Still, he survived to record his opinions not only in his own paper but also in *Collier's, American Magazine,* and other national publications.

Less provocative but equally interesting was Louis Graves's *Chapel Hill Weekly.* Graves, an Orange County native formerly employed by the *New York Times,* inaugurated his Chapel Hill paper in 1923. His ability to write engagingly about the foibles of day-to-day existence enabled him to give the *Weekly* a folksy, chatty style that caught on with the egghead community and flourished amid the competition of the Durham and Raleigh dailies. A cat rescued from a tree, the burning question of whether dogs should be allowed to roam freely on the University of North Carolina campus, a raid by chickens on a backyard garden—such was the stuff of an essayist's delight in Graves's skilled hands. By 1949 a panegyrist could declare that the paper was "as much of a State institution as the University of North Carolina."

Among the rising number of women journalists was Nell Battle Lewis, who made a name in journalism writing for the Raleigh *News and Observer* and other publications. She championed progressive stands on public welfare, politics, education, and women's rights while attacking institutions and traditional values that trammeled individual freedom and the inquiring mind.

Many Tar Heel journalists went on to national prominence in both the newspaper and television fields: Wilmington's David Brinkley with NBC, Greensboro's Edward R. Murrow with CBS, Raleigh's Vermont Royster with the *Wall Street Journal,* Hamlet's Tom Wicker and Zebulon's Clifton Daniel with the *New York Times.* Some who stayed behind also achieved national recognition, as when W. Horace Carter of the *Tabor City Tribune* won a Pulitzer Prize in 1952 for his editorials against the Ku Klux Klan. It was the first time the award had ever gone to a weekly paper; then the semiweekly Whiteville *News Reporter* took a Pulitzer in 1953. Charles Kuralt and Charlie Rose became noted television journalists.

North Carolina's magazines, however, fared ill in the century's middle decades. The *North Carolina University Magazine* was discontinued in 1920 after three-quarters of a century of publication and was soon followed into eclipse by the *North Carolina Booklet,* which was directed at state history buffs. Subsidized journals such as Duke University's *South Atlantic Quarterly* and the state-published *North Carolina Historical Review* (founded in 1924) weathered depression and popular indifference, but unsubsidized ventures nearly always ended in failure.

An exception to the rule of the failure of periodicals was Clarence Poe's *Progressive Farmer.* Poe took over what was then a small farm newspaper in 1899 when he was an eighteen-year-old with no college background. His blend of practical, down-to-earth matter directed at farmers and their families touched a popular chord and built the *Progressive Farmer* into one of the world's great mass-circulation farm journals. *Golf World* was a Southern Pines publication with a national following, and the *North Carolina Folklore Journal* a Raleigh periodical of more limited appeal. The *State* magazine managed to appeal to a broad popular audience and withstand the tides of adversity by incorporating a mixture of personality profiles, down-home lore, and sketches of this and that sort of North Caroliniana. The *State* survives today as *Our State* magazine, which employs full color and enjoys a wide readership. The magazine *Business North Carolina* keeps North Carolinians abreast of the major events and people in the state's businesses and corporations.

Airways

The integration of North Carolina's once-fragmented provinces and sections was not due entirely to better highways and the periodical press. It also owed something to the expansion of telephone and radio service, the introduction and development of television and the airplane, and the role of railroads.

In 1920 the railroad was still, as it had been for three-quarters of a century, the workhorse of the state's public transportation. But railroads were soon to feel injury from the competition of more flexible trucks and buses and speedier airplanes. The spread of automobile ownership did further harm to railroads. Moreover, North Carolina travelers found the main north-south routes awkward because the schedules served the convenience of passengers

Club car of the New York–to–New Orleans Crescent Queen, 1949

boarding in the metropolitan Northeast or the Deep South. East-west rail routes, never well developed in North Carolina, generated only sporadic traffic, even to the port towns of Morehead City and Wilmington.

What the railroads did well—the rapid transit of overland bulk cargoes—they were unrivaled in. The three routes by which the Norfolk & Western fed coal to the industrial Piedmont carried nearly 6.5 million tons—or 91,000 carloads—in 1970. Also brought into the state by the Norfolk & Western were some 200,000 cars and trucks, many of which were unloaded and stored temporarily at the company's 5,600-vehicle lot at Walkertown. Carried along the same routes were nearly 3,000 carloads of furniture, as well as grain, beer, paper and printed material, food products, and much else. The three largest railroads that served North Carolina in 1970—the Southern Railway, the Norfolk & Southern, and the Seaboard Coast Line—were important to the state's economic well-being, but not in proportion to their importance half a century before. In recent years, the Amtrak Corporation, the federal passenger rail operator, has supplied rail passenger service in cooperation with the State of North Carolina. In 1985, a shortage of revenue led Amtrak to end the Carolinian, an experimental one-year passenger service between Charlotte and Richmond, Virginia, via Rocky Mount. Five years later, however, the Governor's Rail Passenger Task Force and a state subsidy of $2 million resurrected the Carolinian. The new Carolinian made its first run on May 11, 1990. During 1994, the Carolinian carried 189,000 passengers, "making it the country's best-performing passenger train supported jointly by any state and Amtrak." On May 25, 1995, another jointly supported passenger train, the Piedmont, began daily round-trip service from Raleigh to Charlotte, stopping at a number of cities and towns en route. North Carolina assumed responsibility for 75 percent of the Piedmont's costs, while Amtrak paid the remainder and provided maintenance.

Commercial air service was not a significant factor in North Carolina until World War II. As late as 1960 the state in which aviation began had only six airports with scheduled air carrier service. Legislative foot-dragging on the subject of airport construction meant that between 1962 and 1966 North Carolina received less than 3 percent of the federal funds allocated for that purpose among seven southern states. A tardy but vigorous response to the mounting need was bringing improvement as the decade of the 1960s ended.

In 1970 North Carolina had thirteen airports with scheduled service. The busiest of these was Douglas Airport at Charlotte, which was served by five airlines; Greensboro–High Point, Raleigh-Durham, and Asheville were each served by three lines. A total of twelve airports in the state were served by the largest of the intrastate carriers, Piedmont Airlines (subsequently absorbed by

Piedmont Airlines DC-3 Pacemaker, 1950s

U.S. Airways) of Winston-Salem. In 1967 Douglas and Raleigh-Durham each handled well over half a million passengers and 400 daily operations. But airport managers and others close to the situation foresaw trouble unless greatly increased funds were soon made available for the vast physical requirements of the dawning big-jet era. With direct flights from North Carolina cities to other parts of the country limited in number, the route to Heaven itself, many Tar Heels joked, involved changing in Atlanta. But in the past three decades, the state's three major airports—Raleigh-Durham, Charlotte, and Greensboro—have grown significantly in size and services, and further expansion is continuing. Raleigh-Durham International Airport and Charlotte-Douglas International Airport began offering direct flights to London and Paris respectively in the 1990s.

Since the beginning of the twentieth century, urban public transportation has evolved from the horsecar to the trolley car to the city bus, but the popularity of the automobile made buses generally a losing proposition for city taxpayers. More successful financially were the interstate and intercity lines such as Greyhound and Carolina Trailways. The latter was a Raleigh-based firm that began in 1925 with routes between Raleigh and towns within a radius of about seventy-five miles. Later, Carolina Trailways was a charter member of the national organization known as Nationwide Trailways. By 1966 Carolina Trailways, through the development of new routes and the purchase of rights to existing ones, had terminals in five states and a fleet of 240 buses. In that year the line logged 23 million miles and carried 5.7 million passengers. In the intervening years, it had evolved a wide range of one-stop or nonstop routes to as far away as New York City, and its buses had been equipped with air conditioning, lavatories, and other modern conveniences.

Telephones were a nineteenth-century invention, but their widespread use came slowly to North Carolina. There were only 179,000 in use in the state in 1939 and not yet twice that many in 1947. During the next few years, however, telephone lines were extended into many rural areas previously without them; by 1960 there were well over 1 million telephones in the state—and the number was increasing rapidly. By 1969 Southern Bell (now BellSouth) alone, largest of the state's twenty-four companies, had more than 1 million telephones in operation, though there were many rural families who still lacked the service.

No device has revolutionized work and communication among North Carolinians more than the computer. That electronic marvel—with its capacity to store and retrieve data, to conduct research online, to correspond using e-mail, to perform word processing and desktop publishing—has become an indispensable part of every business and government office. And the number of households possessing computers grows at a remarkable rate.

Linked ear-to-ear by telephone, connected town-to-town by road and rail, attuned to the pulse of the nation and the world through newspapers, interstate highways, jet planes, network and cable broadcasting, and the internet, their views and activities rehearsed and analyzed hour-by-hour on radio and television, North Carolinians enter the twenty-first century far more aware than they have ever been of the world within as well as the world beyond. By the end of the twentieth century, a new, more cosmopolitan Tar Heel personality had emerged. For good or ill, the North Carolinian of the year 2001 probably would be a stranger to his 1920 predecessor.

7

THE DESERT BLOOMS

"Evilution"

The year 1920 saw North Carolina reeling dolefully toward a dreaded show-down between conflicting factions of its cultural and intellectual leadership. A small but earnest and vocal element was concerned about the threat to tradi-tional values posed by the whirlwind of new ideas and gadgets of the past gen-eration or so. Another group, similarly articulate and committed, conceived of itself as precursors of a bright new world that would be safe for novel gad-gets and ideas. By 1920 it was becoming clear that the two groups had settled upon evolutionary science as the central issue over which they would first test their relative strength. Evolutionary theory was based on the conclusions of nineteenth-century English naturalist Charles Darwin. According to Darwin, the origin and development of human beings, animals, and plants could be explained according to the concept of natural selection. To many religious fun-damentalists, such an idea denied the biblical interpretation that man was cre-ated by God.

Evolution was wonderfully designed to crystallize a thousand differences on other matters. Bewitchingly inviting to the rationalist mentality, it seemed from the perspective of the biblical literalists a thing of sin and sacrilege. Those who favored the Darwinian theory also were perceived by their critics as toler-ant of socialism and unionism, permissive toward sexual behavior, sympathetic to the rights of women and minorities, and so on. Those arrayed against Dar-winism tended to oppose these and related views. The first group was called "liberal," the second "conservative." Most Tar Heels were not strictly identifi-able with either group, but the tug of centuries of sentiment drew them more toward the latter.

In North Carolina the issue between the two groups reached a crisis in the mid-1920s. Focal points in the ensuing struggle included W. O. Saunders's furi-ous combat against evangelist Mordecai Ham in Elizabeth City in the fall of 1924 and an effort by fundamentalists to oust from office Dr. William L. Poteat,

Mordecai Ham

proevolutionist president of Wake Forest College, the state's leading Baptist school. (Governor Cameron Morrison personally banned two textbooks from the public schools because they taught evolution.)

In early 1925 a bill to prohibit the teaching of evolution in the public schools was introduced in the state legislature. The so-called "Poole bill" failed by one vote to win the endorsement of the Education Committee and went on to defeat on the floor of the House. By this margin was North Carolina spared the humiliation of another Scopes trial. That trial occurred in Tennessee when antievolutionists objected to the teaching of Darwin's theory in the public schools.

The fate of the Poole bill, coupled with a successful defense of Dr. Poteat, beguiled the liberal faction into unwarranted self-confidence. Politically, North Carolina remained safely under moderately conservative government throughout the interwar years and for some time thereafter. The overwhelming majority of public-school teachers shunned the subject of evolution in the classroom. Sexual emancipation, unionism, theological liberalism, and other tenets of the modernists found little acceptance among Tar Heels. In 1934 Mordecai Ham, at a tent meeting outside Charlotte, took his revenge on the evolutionists by planting the spark of spiritual rebirth into the bosom of a farm lad named Billy Graham.

The fragility of the liberal position was made manifest in 1950 with the defeat of Frank Porter Graham, moderately liberal president of the University of North Carolina, in his bid for nomination by the Democratic Party as its candidate for the United States Senate. Scion of an old and respected family, well-known across the state and nation, strongly backed by a popular governor, Graham was beaten by Raleigh attorney Willis Smith, a solid conservative. The campaign was marked by vicious calumnies that portrayed Graham as a supporter of racial equality who was soft on Communism. More than any election in many years, the senatorial primary of 1950 pitted liberal and conservative viewpoints in stark confrontation.

Still another round in the running dispute occurred in 1963 over the "Speaker-Ban Law." Alarmed by noisy student civil rights demonstrations in Greensboro, Chapel Hill, and elsewhere, conservative legislators drafted a bill to impose restrictions on visiting speakers who made use of state property. Passage of the act raised a pained outcry from the academic community, then far more populous than in the 1920s. Anxious to find a peaceful resolution, Governor Dan Moore appointed a study commission, which recommended certain modifications of the law. Authority over visiting speakers was ultimately returned to the state campuses, but it required an order of a federal district court to abrogate the Speaker-Ban Law as unconstitutional.

Again, the Tar Heel liberal element had won a victory that smacked more of symbol than substance. Skeptics had only to observe the state's grudging response to court-ordered public school desegregation to understand that North Carolinians remained largely committed to conservative values.

Lunch at Woolworth's

In contrast with more militant states of the Deep South, North Carolina in the mid-twentieth century found itself with an unwonted reputation for moderation. No fire-eating Tar Heel senator raged against New Deal policies, no spokesmen for the state made himself conspicuous as a racist or patriotic witch-hunter. As in the 1850s, some saw North Carolina as a potentially valuable happy medium between the extremes of North and South—a reconciler and healer of divisions, capable of helping to bind the sections of the Union more closely together. That the state was unprepared to shoulder such a burden was soon to become as evident in regard to the issues of the twentieth century as it had been concerning those of the nineteenth.

Following the Supreme Court's desegregation decision in the *Brown v. Board of Education of Topeka* case in 1954, Governor William B. Umstead appointed the Advisory Committee on Education to deal with the problems the decision posed for the state's long-segregated public school system. Umstead shortly thereafter died in office, but the committee's proposals were adopted by his successor, former lieutenant governor Luther Hodges. What the committee recommended was that desegregation be approached by means of a locally controlled pupil assignment plan. By an act of the General Assembly of 1955, parents wishing their children reassigned to a segregated school of the other race had to go through an almost prohibitively complicated application

*Governor Luther Hodges's Pearsall Plan, 1955,
attempted to thwart meaningful school
desegregation. Cartoon by Hugh Haynie,
Greensboro Daily News.*

procedure. Theoretically, this so-called "Pearsall Plan" might have thwarted
any desegregation at all, but this, according to its sponsors, was not its purpose.

North Carolina's white leaders sought no "massive resistance" to the federal government. The Pearsall Plan would permit a handful of black children
to attend previously all-white schools, resulting in the desegregation of perhaps 1 percent or less of the school system. Token compliance with the federal
government was supposed to accomplish two things: it would keep the hounds
of integration effectively at bay and would prevent a white backlash that might
well destroy the public schools. Evidence that such a rebellion might actually
occur was lacking, but the possibility seemed enough to legitimize the Pearsall Plan. To some sympathetic onlookers, the Pearsall scheme contributed to
North Carolina's image as a moderate state with relatively wholesome racial relations. But the United States Supreme Court saw such schemes as the Pearsall
Plan as merely further attempts to evade integration. In May 1955, the court
ordered North Carolina and other southern states to proceed with integration "with all deliberate speed." Federal district courts would ensure that the
Supreme Court's decision was carried out. A year later, North Carolina began
making token efforts toward integrating its public schools, when a few African

American students were admitted to white schools in Charlotte, Greensboro, and Winston-Salem.

In the spring of 1955, three black graduates of Hillside High School in Durham applied for admission to the University of North Carolina at Chapel Hill as undergraduates. (A limited number of blacks had been admitted to its law, medical, and graduate schools since 1951.) The university denied the three students admission, and the National Association for the Advancement of Colored People (NAACP) took their case before a federal court. The court ordered the university to admit the students. Thus John L. Brandon and brothers Ralph and Leroy Frazier became the first African American undergraduates to attend the University of North Carolina. As a result, the University of North Carolina became the first state college or university in the South to accept black undergraduates. In 1956, the Supreme Court prohibited segregation in all tax-supported colleges and universities, and eventually private colleges and universities also began to admit African Americans—including Davidson College and Duke University in 1961.

Black frustration over the state's foot-dragging on desegregation was one of the factors behind the protest movement that began in Greensboro on 1 February 1960. On that day, four students from all-black North Carolina Agricultural and Technical (A&T) College sat down at a lunch counter in the Woolworth's department store and asked for service. Refused on the ground that local custom forbade it, the students occupied their seats until closing time and returned the next day with reinforcements. In subsequent days they were joined by others, including a few white students. When the Woolworth counter was fully occupied by protesters, others moved on the S. H. Kress store down the street.

Sit-ins had occurred at other places throughout the country in earlier years, but those in Greensboro became the impetus for social revolution. A week later they had spread to Winston-Salem and Durham, the seats of other black colleges. Within two weeks they were occurring in other states and touching off sympathetic demonstrations in the North. When the Woolworth, Kress, and Myers stores in Greensboro relented in July and allowed blacks to eat at their lunch counters, it seemed that the seas had parted at last for the black community. The commotion had called forth another resurgence of the Ku Klux Klan (as well as leading to the Speaker Ban), but it had also produced a dynamic and charismatic new black leader, A&T College football star Jesse Jackson. Sit-ins were an important component of the civil rights movement, which began in the late 1950s, most notably under the leadership of the Southern Christian Leadership Conference's Dr. Martin Luther King Jr., and employed, beyond sit-ins, tactics such as freedom rides, boycotts, voter registration drives,

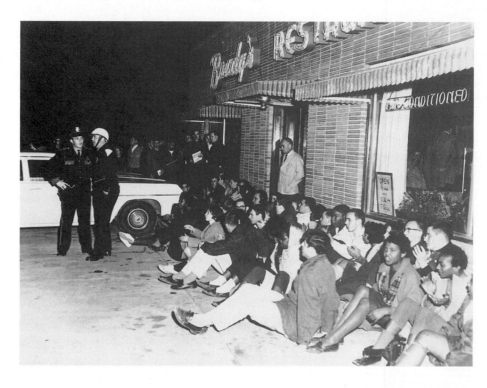

Students protest segregation at a sit-in at Brady's Restaurant in Chapel Hill, 1964.

and nonviolent demonstrations, with the participation of such African American organizations as the NAACP, the Congress of Racial Equality, and the Student Nonviolent Coordinating Committee.

And yet, the sit-in victory was in some respects a hollow one. The right to eat lunch in a department store was not, after all, the American dream. It carried with it no political power, no economic clout, no access to better housing or better jobs. It did nothing to improve educational opportunity for blacks still victimized by the Pearsall Plan. Greensboro's white leaders, like many elsewhere in the state and region, for the most part submitted reluctantly to the Civil Rights Act of 1964, the Voting Rights Act of 1965, and other federal initiatives. The sit-ins had raised expectations among blacks that were not to be fulfilled immediately. Nevertheless, they were a start, and this first small step was crucial.

Federal laws and the enforcement of those laws ensured that further steps continued to be made. A large number of North Carolina's public schools had been integrated by 1965, but integration was neither uniform nor complete. In an effort still to avoid full integration, the state enacted a freedom-of-choice plan in 1965. The plan, which allowed parents to choose a specific school for their children, was declared unconstitutional by a federal court in 1968. A federal court also ruled that the Pearsall Plan was unconstitutional in 1969. A year

Sit-ins occurred at the lunch counter of S. H. Kress Company, Greensboro, in 1960.

later, a federal district court ordered busing to accomplish desegregation in the public schools, and the U.S. Supreme Court upheld the decision. Public school desegregation was achieved in the 1970s in large part because of the activities of the federal Office of Civil Rights, which the Civil Rights Act of 1964 had established.

The Voting Rights Act of 1965 empowered the federal government to bring legal action against local election boards that attempted to prevent African Americans from legally registering and voting. That act restored the right to vote that had been denied to the majority of African Americans in North Carolina from the time they were disfranchised in the white supremacy election of 1900. The state's African Americans immediately exercised their newly won political power. In 1968, they elected Henry E. Frye of Guilford County to the General Assembly. He was the first African American to serve in the

The Ku Klux Klan used terror and violence to resist integration in North Carolina.

legislature in more than seven decades. In 1974, Frederick Douglas Alexander of Mecklenburg County and John W. Winters of Wake County were elected to the state Senate and House respectively. From 1970 to 1997, 506 black North Carolinians served in political offices. Among them were members of Congress: Eva Clayton of the First District and Mel Watt of the Twelfth District. In that same period, more than sixty African Americans served in the General Assembly, and 354 served in city and county governments. In 1983, Governor James B. Hunt Jr. appointed Henry Frye to the state supreme court. Frye won statewide election as an associate justice in 1984 and 1992, and he became chief justice in 1999. Dan Blue of Wake County presided as Speaker of the North Carolina House of Representatives from 1991 to 1994, and Ralph Campbell Jr. served as state auditor in 1992 and 1996. During the 1980s and 1990s, a number of black North Carolinians served in state positions under both Democratic and Republican administrations.

Rebel Rib

The decade of the 1920s opened with the Nineteenth Amendment on the verge of adoption and North Carolina in a position to be the state that guaranteed the enfranchisement of women. The North Carolina Federation of Women's Clubs became an active leader in the effort to secure the vote for women. But, amid warnings that "politics are bad for women and women for politics," the state legislature rejected the amendment, and it remained for Tennessee on the next day to provide the last vote needed for ratification, thereby bestowing the franchise on American women.

Equality of status, nevertheless, continued to elude the Tar Heel woman throughout the next fifty years; only after World War II would she gain the right to sue and recover for personal injuries, to keep her earnings and property separate from her husband's, and to dispose of her real property without her husband's consent. Even then, there remained numerous realms in which women were accorded inferior legal status.

Some continued to defend the legal double standard as providing as much in protection for women as in limitation. It was the husband, after all, and not the wife, who was required by law to support a couple's children. A husband must pay for his wife's funeral expenses but not vice versa. Criminal conduct was found in a man who peeped through a bedroom window at a disrobing woman, but not when a woman peeped at a man.

Such distinctions had their origin and rationale in an age in which women rarely held jobs outside the home. And this pattern held true in North Carolina until the era of World War II, when large numbers of women took jobs formerly held by men. Many returned home with the coming of peace, but the demonstrated ability of women to perform well many jobs previously reserved for men helped to kindle a spark of ambition in the younger generation of North Carolina womanhood.

Changes in education facilitated the fulfillment of these ambitions. The University of North Carolina opened its first housing for women students in 1921. Despite opposition from the male students ("Women Not Wanted Here" thundered the *Daily Tar Heel*), the university opened a women's dormitory in 1925, a year after awarding its first doctoral degrees to women. Even so, women students at UNC in the 1920s were all graduate and professional students; undergraduate admission for women came only many years later. The state's "Woman's College" remained sexually segregated until 1965, when it was renamed the University of North Carolina at Greensboro. By 1972 women made up almost 40 percent of the student body at Chapel Hill and were rapidly overtaking the men. For many years before this, Tar Heel men had trailed women by about a year in average formal education.

Role models for the emancipated generation of women were provided by a small number of female doctors, lawyers, nurses, suffragettes, and others.

Charlotte Hawkins Brown

A notable standard of achievement in this era was the career of Charlotte Hawkins Brown, a Vance County native. The daughter of former slaves, Brown was educated at Wellesley College, in Massachusetts, and returned to North Carolina in 1902 with a missionary zeal to devote her life to the improvement of the lives of black people. At Sedalia, in Guilford County, she founded Palmer Memorial Institute, which gradually gained strength and recognition as a private elementary and high school for black children.

The school was, however, only one of the many contributions of its founder. Brown published a novel of black life in 1919 (the first of her several books) and helped to organize the North Carolina Federation of Colored Women's Clubs and the Colored Orphanage at Oxford. The Home Ownership Association, which she helped to launch at Sedalia is credited with increasing home ownership there from 2 percent to 95 percent by 1930. Before her death in 1961, she had been awarded four honorary doctorates and many other awards and distinctions. Her life and achievements are presently commemo-

rated at the Charlotte Hawkins Brown Museum (the campus of the former Palmer Memorial Institute), North Carolina's first historic site honoring the contributions of its African American citizens.

A beacon to those interested in a larger role for women in public affairs was the career of Ellen Black Winston. Born in Bryson City, she earned a doctorate at the University of Chicago in 1930. After teaching at Meredith College in Raleigh in the early 1940s, in 1944 she became the state's commissioner of public welfare, a post she held for nineteen years. Winston also served terms in the 1950s and 1960s as president of the American Welfare Association and National Conference for Social Service. The capstone of her career was her appointment in 1963 as commissioner of public welfare for the U.S. Department of Health, Education, and Welfare. Winston was also a United States representative to the United Nations International Conference of Ministers of Social Welfare.

Susie Marshall Sharp, a Reidsville lawyer, enjoyed the distinction of serving as a justice on the North Carolina Supreme Court at a time when few women obtained law degrees. A graduate of the University of North Carolina law school and editor there of its law review, she became the first woman appointed judge of the Superior Court. In 1974 she was elected chief justice of the state supreme court by the largest majority on the Democratic ticket, the first woman in the state's history to attain so high a judicial position.

Other North Carolina women who achieved success in the field of public service include Juanita Kreps, who was vice president of Duke University when President Jimmy Carter appointed her the nation's secretary of commerce in 1977. In 1983, President Ronald Reagan appointed Elizabeth Dole, a native of Salisbury, as secretary of transportation, making her the first female to hold that national office. President George Bush appointed Dole secretary of labor in 1989, and from 1991 to 1998, she served as head of the American Red Cross. Former state senator Elaine Marshall, from Harnett County, became the first woman elected to the North Carolina Council of State when she won election as secretary of state in 1996. In 2001, former Democratic state representative and senator, Beverly Perdue, of Craven County, became

the first female lieutenant governor of North Carolina. As the twentieth century came to a close, the number of women holding political office and professional positions as lawyers, physicians, scientists, university presidents and chancellors, government administrators, and corporate executives had grown significantly. Many North Carolina women also had discovered a new activism in such national feminist organizations as the National Organization for Women and the National Women's Political Caucus. These groups called on Congress for further reforms for women and to pass the Equal Rights Amendment. Between 1973 and 1982, women activists lobbied the state legislature to ratify the amendment, which would be the twenty-seventh to the U.S. Constitution and would remove gender as a classification in law. By a narrow margin, however, the assembly voted against ratification. The nation has yet to ratify the amendment.

Susie Marshall Sharp became the first woman to serve on the North Carolina Supreme Court, pictured here in 1962. In 1974 she was elected chief justice.

Fields of Glory

As Rome was hellenized by its conquest of Greece, so the twentieth-century city fell cultural captive to its rural vassals. The first generation or two of migrants from the "branch-heads" might experience misgivings about city life, but three centuries of rural Tar Heel culture proved highly resistant to asphalt and acetylene. Gradually, country people learned to soften the geometrical contours of the city and tame it into livability. The chamber music guild survived, but it learned a new respect for bluegrass and country.

An intriguing example of the vitality of rural culture was the half-century's religious experience. North Carolina in colonial times had been widely considered lost and perhaps unredeemable. But the Great Revival at the opening of the nineteenth century welded the people of the state firmly into the Bible Belt. Church membership outstripped population growth. By 1926 the state's sixty-seven religious denominations enrolled half of all North Carolinians. The huge majority of church members were Protestant, and the greatest proportion of these were Baptists, with Methodists and Presbyterians trailing well behind. Overwhelmingly, the churches of the 1920s were small rural affairs averaging about a hundred members each.

On rare occasions, as in the struggle over Darwinism in the mid-1920s, the country churches could be marshaled into strong coordinated activity. This was also true of the 1928 presidential campaign, when the Democrats sponsored an anti-Prohibitionist Roman Catholic. Many southern Protestant clergy campaigned actively against Al Smith in the most widespread social agitation since the Populist revolt. But these were exceptional instances, and the country church normally exerted its influence on a local and personal level rather than a state or regional one. For this reason, the profound social impact of the rural church was often unnoticed by the urban-centered social analyst.

A survey of North Carolina's churches in 1929 noted with dismay the number of rural institutions found to be discontinued or abandoned. "Enthusiasm in many of the country churches," a commentator observed, "is gone, hope is waning, members are leaving, and the churches are dying." Observers sometimes jumped from such a discovery to the conclusion that religion itself was threatened. But the waning of the small, rural edifice did not portend a decline of religious interest or activity. In this transitional epoch, the ruralist-turned-urbanite was feeling his way toward an accommodation of his religious ideas to his city life.

In the contest of rural and urban religious values, it was not infrequently the former that emerged victorious. One result was the rise of big new churches near or within the fringes of urban centers. These institutions, directed by ar-

William ("Billy") Graham

dently evangelistic leaders, combined the modern facilities and bus fleets of the sophisticated municipal churches with the forcefully biblical impulses of the inspired rural congregations. The new churches, urban in appearance but rural in character, were often strong enough to enable their members to resist the intense forces of social reform after World War II. Church-operated day-care centers, schools, and Sunday schools preserved the rural heritage amid the clamor of social upheaval.

The wedding of rural evangelicalism with urban electronic media produced spectacular results. Instead of being tamed into urbane blandness, the evangelicals found vast new audiences for their appeals. The obstacles of poor roads and isolated congregations overcome by technology, the best evangelistic preachers became extraordinarily effective radio and TV sermonizers. A prodigy of the new mass-appeal approach was Charlotte's William Franklin ("Billy") Graham.

Two experiences seem to have been profoundly important in Billy Graham's early development. One was his own "decision for Christ" at a 1934 evangelistic tent meeting. The other was a highly successful stint as a summer Fuller Brush salesman following his graduation from high school. After taking his college degree at Wheaton, Graham for a time was only a moderately successful "sawdust trail Bible-thumper." But a "Crusade for Christ" he led in Los Angeles in 1949 transformed him into a national figure and a personality of magnetic self-confidence.

Graham's career was propelled forward by a number of conversions of well-known people at his Los Angeles crusade. In the next five years, he perfected his publicity techniques and toned down the fierce emotional rant of his earlier days. By the time his crusade hit New York in 1957, Graham was a smooth and polished media celebrity. In less than four months in New York, he spoke before well over 2 million people and claimed more than 60,000 conversions. By then he regularly preached on his "Hour of Decision" radio program and wrote a syndicated newspaper column. He would later add a monthly magazine to his international media campaign, along with recordings, leaflets, and thirteen books written by himself. In the meantime, his crusades were further moderated in tone, becoming, in the words of one critic, "less like . . . a circus and more like . . . a cathedral."

Once as conservative and superpatriotic as others in his theological mold, Graham racially integrated his crusade audiences in the early 1950s. Strongly emphasizing the need for individual regeneration, he did not scorn social reform. From his wide travels around the world and his contacts with the world's movers and shakers, he seemed to acquire increasing tolerance and breadth of vision. Scores of others adopted his techniques in the 1950s and 1960s, but none so effectively as their originator.

Evangelicals became involved in politics in the 1970s and 1980s, when they formed an organization called the Moral Majority. Television boosted the careers of such evangelists as Jim and Tammy Bakker in Charlotte. But television evangelism lost much of its impact when Jim Bakker was convicted of mail fraud and sentenced to federal prison.

If the new evangelicals made a marked impression on personal morality among Tar Heels, they did not retard the exuberant flowering of popular recreation and entertainment. The filling of leisure time with suitable activities and spectacles became the basis of a number of major industries in North Carolina. Easily the most successful of these in the middle decades of the century were spectator sports.

Big-time football was the earliest of the era's athletic spectacles. By the 1920s the larger colleges had developed keen rivalries in various sports, but the people's choice was clearly the fast and rugged action of the gridiron. A contest between the universities of North Carolina and Virginia was, besides, a chance to even the score against generations of Old Dominion "witlings," as the state song phrased it, who had "defamed" and "sneered at" their less fortunate neighbors. But it was the Wallace Wade powerhouses at Duke in the 1930s and 1940s that brought national attention to North Carolina and gave football firm claim to center stage. Other post–World War II coaches who developed football powerhouses and brought gridiron glory to their institutions included Carl Snavely, Jim Hickey, and Bill Dooley at UNC; Earl Edwards, Lou Holtz, and Dick Sheridan at North Carolina State; and Douglas Clyde (Peahead) Walker of Wake Forest. They all coached their teams in winning seasons that propelled them into major bowl games.

The participation of two Wade teams in Rose Bowls, the marvel of his unscored-on 1939 team, and the renown of stars such as "Ace" Parker and George McAfee made Duke a catalyst for rival schools in the state. The University of North Carolina recovered its dignity in the late 1940s behind the all-around prowess of Charlie ("Choo-Choo") Justice, but the teams of the state and region were not generally competitive with those of other parts of the country after Wade's glory years. Then too, football lost some measure of its prominence after World War II when North Carolina State College (now North Carolina State University) hired for its new basketball coach a high school coach from Indiana named Everett Case.

Case brought down several outstanding Indiana players with him and proceeded to convert North Carolina into "basketball country." The major teams in the state in 1949 put together a tournament known as the "Dixie Classic," which was for years the outstanding spectator attraction in North Carolina. (It was abolished in the 1960s because of the discovery of criminal involvement in it.) Wake Forest responded to Case's challenge with excellent teams of its own, coached by Pamlico County's "Bones" McKinney and featuring such local talent as All-American center Dickie Hemric of Jonesville. Duke guard Dick Groat brought luster to the program at that school, while coach Frank McGuire's undefeated 1957 national champions ignited a long era of basketball fanaticism at the University of North Carolina at Chapel Hill.

The coaching success of Case, McKinney, and McGuire was followed by that of Dean Smith at Chapel Hill, Vic Bubas and Mike Krzyzewski of Duke, and Norm Sloan and Jim Valvano at North Carolina State University, all of whom won major tournaments with their teams. At the predominately black colleges and universities, basketball also flourished. Al Attles of A&T and Earl Monroe of Winston-Salem State were among the splendid products of the black schools. Unlike in football, the state's basketball teams after the 1940s were competitive with the best of those in any region of the country. Major regional and national playoffs—such as the Atlantic Coast Conference (ACC), Central Intercollegiate Athletic Association, and National Collegiate Athletic Association tournaments—consistently featured North Carolina teams and drew large numbers of the state's basketball aficionados. In recent years, collegiate basketball for women, has risen in popularity, under the leadership of women coaches like North Carolina State University's Kay Yow, who has also coached an Olympic team.

Baseball, which enjoyed a popularity independent of the college rivalries, nevertheless (or therefore) failed to maintain its reputation as the "national pastime." Numerous Tar Heels went on to celebrity in the major leagues, notably brothers Rick and Wes Ferrell of Durham (Rick as a catcher and Wes as a pitcher), infielder Billy Goodman of Concord, pitchers Johnny Allen of Lenoir, Jim and Gaylord Perry of Williamston, and Jim ("Catfish") Hunter of Hertford, and outfielder Enos ("Country") Slaughter of Roxboro. In the Negro National League, outfielder Buck Leonard of Rocky Mount was a premier player, and he was elected to baseball's Hall of Fame in 1972. But baseball was a way to while away an hour or two rather than a focus of popular enthusiasm.

Track and field also had a following among sports enthusiasts. Outstanding in coaching track was North Carolina Central University's head coach, Leroy Walker. He coached a number of Olympic medalists and college stars and was head coach of the successful United States men's Olympic team in 1976. In 1962, track star Jim Beatty, a native of Charlotte and a graduate of the University of North Carolina at Chapel Hill, became the first runner in the world to break the four-minute mile in indoor competition. Ten years later, in the Munich Olympics, Vince Matthews of Johnson C. Smith University won the 400 meters. Among the state's many women track stars were Kathy McMillan of Raeford, who won a silver medal in the 1976 Olympics in the long jump, and North Carolina State University's cross-country runners Julie Shea, Mary Shea, Betty Springs, Suzie Tuffey, and Joan Benoit.

Other sports ranked generally well behind these in popularity. Maxine Allen of Seaboard became the leading women's duck-pin bowler in the nation in 1952 and, later, a top ten-pin bowler. Similar in popular appeal was collegiate lacrosse and pocket billiards (in which Elizabeth City's Luther Lassiter was three times world champion in the 1960s). But soccer has grown in public appeal in the late twentieth century. Virtually every city and town now has youth leagues, and high schools and colleges include it among their organized competitive sports. North Carolina also has a professional women's soccer team, the Carolina Courage.

At such places as Pinehurst, country clubs, tennis clubs, and city courts,

Maxine Allen

tennis gradually grew as a relatively popular sport between the two world wars. During that period the North Carolina Championships were held in Asheville and the Middle Atlantic Tournament in Charlotte. The North Carolina State Closed Championships were begun in Raleigh. African American tennis players had to play in the segregated American Tennis Association. Brothers Nathaniel and Franklin Jackson of Wilmington dominated the association's national championships in the 1930s.

Recreational golf and the number of courses available for its play have steadily increased since the beginning of the twentieth century. Spectators increasingly turn out for major tournaments such as those held at Pinehurst, the state's mecca for golf, and at the Greater Greensboro Open, held every year. The state has also produced a number of outstanding amateur and professional golfers. During the 1930s and 1940s, female golfer Estelle Lawson Page became one of the best amateur golfers in the world and won many championships. After World War II, Charlotte's Clayton Heafner, Morganton's Billy Joe Patton, and Tarboro's Harvie Ward became nationally known professional golfers. Duke University's Mike Souchak and Art Wall had illustrious college careers before becoming major players in the Professional Golfers' Association (PGA). In 1954, Wake Forest University's Arnold Palmer became ACC champion and then joined the PGA, where he became one the most successful and popular players. Probably the best professional golfer that North Carolina ever produced is Raymond Floyd of Fayetteville. Floyd has won more than twenty professional tournaments, including the PGA tournament in 1969 and 1982, the Masters in 1976, and the United States Open in 1986.

Outside the college area, the sports phenomenon of the post–World War II epoch in North Carolina is unquestionably stock-car racing. The sport originated in the 1930s among groups of bootleg-runners and shade-tree mechanics and developed rapidly after the war. By 1949, when Grand National racing with late-model cars began at the Charlotte Motor Speedway, stock cars were a regional addition. The thrill of high speeds and flaming crashes led to such institutionalized tireburners as the Charlotte 600 and National 500, both of which began in 1960. Within a few years, the North Carolina Motor Speedway at Rockingham added the Carolina 500 and the American 500 to the Grand National tour. But there were many smaller tracks all over the state. Big prize money and the opiate of mortal danger brought forth numbers of drivers eager to test their machinery and engineering skill against one another.

Stock cars made living legends of boys like Junior Johnson of Ronda. Johnson was a bootleg-runner who, before joining the stock-car circuit in 1954, had done a stint in prison after being arrested for manufacturing illicit whiskey. "Instead of going into the curves and just sliding and holding on for dear life like the other drivers," says writer Tom Wolfe, "Junior developed the technique of throwing himself into a slide about seventy-five feet before the curve by cocking the wheel to the left slightly and gunning it, using the slide, not the brake, to slow down, so that he could pick up speed again halfway through the curve and come out of it like a shot. This was known as the 'power slide,' and — yes! of course! — every good old boy in North Carolina started saying Junior Johnson learned that stunt doing those goddamned *about-faces* running away from the Alcohol Tax agents."

Johnson retired in 1966, but Richard Petty of Level Cross, NASCAR's "Rookie of the Year" in 1964, was already emerging as the new nonpareil "king of the road." Following in the steps of his father, stock-car pioneer Lee Petty, Richard in 1972 won his fourth Grand National championship, becoming the first driver in the history of the business to win over $1 million. Like Johnson, Petty was a folk hero before his thirtieth birthday.

Individual sports such as golf and tennis, once the preserve of the country-club set, grew as municipalities provided public links and courts. The Southern Pines and Pinehurst areas had long provided outstanding golf facilities for tourists and wealthy visitors from out of state, but it was only after World War II that golfing became a weekly recreation for numbers of professional people. Skiing, often on artificial snow, gained a following at Beech Mountain and other Blue Ridge slopes. And sport fishing, from mountain stream to continental shelf, became a major activity among all types and classes of Tar Heels.

In recent years, the popularity of professional major-league sports has grown with the surge in business and industrial growth, the burgeoning urban population, and a large influx of people relocating from other parts of the United States. Charlotte now boasts of a professional football team, the Carolina Panthers. Even major-league hockey, longtime a northern sport, has found a home with Raleigh's National Hockey League team, the Carolina Hurricanes. New grandiose sports arenas, such as the RBC Center in Raleigh and the Dean Smith Center on the campus of the University of North Carolina at Chapel Hill provide the latest in accommodation for fans of both professional and college sports. Professional minor-league baseball, which declined with the advent of television in the 1950s, has recently undergone a resurgence in popularity with teams such as the Durham Bulls and the Carolina Mudcats, whose stadium is located near the town of Zebulon, playing before enthusiastic crowds.

In addition to sports, entertainment and recreation for North Carolinians throughout the twentieth century have included dances and other social events, as well as gambling, radio, television, and motion pictures. Dancing of all types, from square dancing to the shag, has remained a popular activity. One North Carolinian described the pleasure of dance in the 1940s and 1950s. "When I was in high school," he recalled, "what was the thing was bobby socks an' slicked-back hairdos an' bebop music, all this kinda stuff. Doin' the shag. Even the music was real simple, a straight direct beat. You could dance fast an' then you'd do the slow ones, and it wasn't supercool, it was romantic."

In 1997 legalized gambling became a popular pastime for North Carolinians and out-of-state visitors. On November 13 of that year, Harrah's Cherokee Casino opened on the Qualla reservation of the Eastern Band of Cherokee Indians in western North Carolina. According to historian Christopher Arris Oakley, "In the small town of Cherokee, traffic was backed up for miles as thousands of gamblers waited in line in the cold rain for a chance to try their luck at one of the hundreds of new video gaming machines." Presently a debate rages in the halls of the legislature and in the news media about whether or not to introduce a state-sponsored lottery into North Carolina.

Commercial radio broadcasting began in North Carolina in 1922, when a license was issued to station WBT in Charlotte. Earle Cluck, one of the organizers of the station, had earlier operated an experimental station from a private

home in Charlotte, transmitting from an abandoned chicken house. The chief innovator among the stations, however, was the next one established—WPTF in Raleigh. WPTF won renown for its "firsts" in Tar Heel broadcasting, including football and basketball games, live broadcasts from the state fair, and a regularly scheduled farm program. By 1971 there were 231 commercial and noncommercial radio stations operating in the state, an increase of about 25 percent over the previous decade.

The era of commercial television in North Carolina was inaugurated in July 1949 by WBTV in Charlotte, followed within weeks by WFMY in Greensboro. Within three decades, more than 90 percent of the homes in the state had TV sets, and there were fifteen commercial and three educational stations. The North Carolina Association of Broadcasters was the fifth largest such organization in the country, and the influence of the television medium was attested to in 1972 when the Tar Heel TV commentator Jesse Helms won election to the United States Senate.

Motion pictures captured the imagination of North Carolinians and all Americans in the 1920s. Films became even more alluring with the advent of sound and color in the twenties and thirties. The Carolina Theatre in Durham was constructed in 1926 as the Durham Auditorium and adapted to show motion pictures in 1929. It was designed by the architectural firm of Milburn and Heister of Washington, D.C., and continues to show films today. The popularity of movies steadily grew in the decades after World War II, although recently many of the old, ornate movie palaces, such as the Carolina, have been replaced by large multitheater complexes. North Carolina also became a part of the motion picture industry as Hollywood sought out the state as a site for making films. During the 1990s, the Tar Heel State became the third largest moviemaking state in terms of revenue spent, surpassed only by California and New York. Today film companies have facilities in North Carolina from Wilmington to Asheville.

Laurels at Last

A unique institution in North Carolina was the annual late-fall Culture Week, when various statewide organizations devoted to history, literature, and the arts held meetings in Raleigh. It was during Culture Week that those groups sponsoring awards for meritorious Tar Heel work in cultural endeavors announced their winners. The Mayflower Cup, for example, was presented for the best work of nonfiction, the Sir Walter Award for the finest work of fiction, the Roanoke-Chowan Poetry Award for the outstanding book of poetry. Whether Culture week added incentive or inspiration to cultural achievement in North Carolina was open to question, but it did symbolize the desire of many Tar Heels to recognize those of special talent or distinction.

Although it lacked a long tradition of important contribution to arts and letters, North Carolina in the 1920s experienced a significant cultural awakening. Polkville's Hatcher Hughes won the Pulitzer Prize in 1924 for his folk drama *Hell-Bent for Heaven,* and Lillington native Paul Green won it in 1927 for his play *In Abraham's Bosom.* A series of novels by James Boyd of Southern Pines won critical and popular success in the 1920s and 1930s. Lamar Stringfield of Raleigh won the Pulitzer Prize in music with his suite *From the Southern Mountains,* and Hunter Johnson earned the *Prix de Rome* in 1938 for his musical compositions. Meanwhile, Thomas Wolfe's novels and Howard Odum's studies in the sociology of the South had been gaining a worldwide audience. In 1945 the Pulitzer Prize winner Carl Sandburg, poet and biographer of Abraham Lincoln, moved to Flat Rock in western North Carolina. His house there can be seem today at the Carl Sandburg Home National Historic Site.

The state had no such institution as a genuine art museum until 1936, when Charlotte's Mint Museum of Art was established. Hickory's museum of art was organized eight years later, but these were the only two such institutions in North Carolina at the close of World War II. The North Carolina Art Society, recipient after 1929 of limited public funds, established a small museum in a room at the State Agricultural Building—but painting was the exotic interest of the few as the decade of the 1950s began. As president of the North

Katherine Clark Pendleton Arrington

Carolina Art Society, Katherine Clark Pendleton Arrington was an important force in the establishment and operation of the Mint Museum of Art and the North Carolina Museum of Art.

An improbable proposal to inaugurate a state art gallery emerged in the General Assembly during World War II and for a number of years lurked in the shadows of indifference and derision. In 1951 an offer by New York mercantile tycoon S. H. Kress to donate $1 million worth of art to the state on a matching basis galvanized interest in the project. New efforts in the legislature produced money with which to acquire the Kress Collection and convert the old Highway Building in Raleigh into an art gallery. In 1956 the North Carolina Museum of Art opened its doors and ultimately evolved into one of the nation's major museums. A new building for the museum opened in 1983. But the private sector was also astir with new energies in behalf of art. Asheville, Statesville, and Chapel Hill acquired museums between 1948 and 1958, lending artistic credibility to one of the states comprising a region that had formerly been, in H. L. Mencken's harsh indictment, the "Sahara of the Bozart."

The North Carolina Symphony in concert

State funds also gave impetus to the North Carolina Symphony, which was founded in 1933 as the first state symphony in the nation. Several energetic local groups such as the Friends of the College at North Carolina State University promoted ambitious programs by visiting performers, and the North Carolina School of the Performing Arts at Winston-Salem became an important training center for young musicians and other artists. An inventory in the late 1960s enumerated seventeen symphony orchestras and concert groups across the state, as well as seventeen community arts councils, sixty-four display centers for art, sixty-five theater groups, and seventy-four concert series. The appropriation for the arts of $1.8 million by the legislature for 1966 alone denoted a strong public commitment to the state's cultural life.

Private support for the arts likewise expanded impressively. A group of banks in 1967 sponsored a tour of the schools in the state by a Shakespearean company. Corporate contributions figured heavily in the founding of the

Raleigh Little Theatre in 1964, the Grass Roots Opera Company (later the National Opera Company) in Raleigh in 1948, and other cultural ventures. Meanwhile, the burgeoning growth of outdoor drama had brought cultural enrichment to thousands in the hinterlands.

African Americans made significant contributions to the cultural life of the state. Prominent among black literary figures is writer, poet, playwright, actress, and theatrical director and producer Maya Angelou. Born Marguerite Johnson in St. Louis, Missouri, in 1928, Angelou became Reynolds Professor of American Studies at Wake Forest University in 1981. The poetry of African American Gerald W. Barrax, a professor of creative writing at North Carolina State University in Raleigh, speaks eloquently of the experience of black Americans. In the late twentieth century, blues and jazz, with increasing improvisation, remained a vital part of the black musical repertoire. Black North Carolinians who were masters in that genre included musicians and composers Thelonius Monk of Rocky Mount and John Coltrane of Hamlet. Billy Taylor of Wilmington, a jazz pianist, composer, conductor, and educator, earned a prominent reputation for his performances and lectures, including regular appearance of CBS television's *Sunday Morning* and hosting a series on jazz for National Public Radio. Artistic dance showed traditional African influence. Chuck Davis, artistic director and founding director of Dance Africa, is one of the foremost teachers and choreographers of traditional African dance in the nation. He founded the Chuck Davis Dance Company in New York in 1968 and the African American Dance Ensemble in Durham in 1983. Davis received the North Carolina Dance Alliance Award, the North Carolina Artist Award, the North Carolina Order of the Longleaf Pine, and the North Carolina Award in Fine Arts, the state's highest artistic award.

Black North Carolinians also excelled in painting and sculpture. John Biggers, born in Gastonia in 1924, is especially remembered for his murals and use of African symbolic imagery. A former head of the Art Department at Texas Southern University, Biggers displayed his art at many museums in the United States, including the North Carolina Museum of Art, prior to his death in 2001. Minnie Evans was another black North Carolina artist who achieved fame. Born near Wilmington, she worked many years as a domestic before she became a recognized painter. Her surreal-style paintings depict mystical fantastic creatures and lush foliage. They too have been exhibited in various museums, including the North Carolina Museum of Art.

Following World War II, North Carolinians witnessed a tremendous growth in educational opportunities. Local governments combined small schools into large, consolidated schools in order to improve instruction and facilities for rural students. During his term as governor (1961–65), Terry Sanford increased the state sales tax to improve education. He created the summer Governor's School at Winston-Salem to encourage bright students to attend college. He established kindergartens for poor children throughout North Carolina, and he founded the School of the Arts in Winston-Salem for the study of fine arts. Sanford and the legislature also created the Department of Community Colleges. The two-year institutions offered both technical training and beginning-level college courses. The number of such schools increased from twenty in 1963 to fifty-eight in 1990. In the latter year, the largest of the community colleges, Central Piedmont Community College in Charlotte, enrolled about 17,000 students.

With the support of federal funds in the 1960s, North Carolina launched its Head Start program to provide disadvantaged children with preschool classes. This early childhood education initiative was continued under the state's Smart Start program begun during the third term of Governor James B. Hunt Jr. In an earlier term, Hunt established the North Carolina School of Science and Mathematics in Durham, a free school for gifted high school students, with an emphasis on science and mathematics.

North Carolina's colleges and universities gained in quality and reputation. The University of North Carolina at Chapel Hill and Duke University rank among the top twenty-five universities in the United States. North Carolina State University in Raleigh, Wake Forest University, and Davidson College also earned national respect.

The Social Organism

Implicit in the transformation of cultural life in North Carolina was a recognition that it was not enough for Tar Heels to come to terms with the rest of the region, the nation, the world. They must also come to terms with each other. No age demanded this recognition more insistently.

The pressure for minority rights for blacks, women, children, gays and lesbians, the aged, and the poor were so many reminders of an ancient but evidently doomed social and sexual hierarchy. Conceivably, some new hierarchy was emerging to replace it. But hierarchy itself was in ill-repute. The American Indian rejected ascriptions of inferiority. The many Latinos migrating into the state from Mexico seeking work in agriculture and industry added their labor and elements of their culture and language to everyday life in the Tar Heel State. By the year 2000, Hispanics comprised 5 percent of the state's population. Advocates of migrant laborers appeared in North Carolina courtrooms and social programs. The handicapped won recognition of their right to ramps and other special facilities in public places. North Carolina discovered that it had not one or two minority groups but scores, that all of us belonged to one such group or another.

Self-recognition and sometimes strident self-assertion by subgroups appeared to be a new and permanent component of social and cultural relations. From every quarter arose the demand that respect be accorded on equal terms to all groups and, ultimately, to every individual. There might remain ways of circumventing the demand; there seemed to be no prospect of squelching it. To be a Tar Heel was no longer to be white, male, adult, and middle-class only; the term now had wider meaning and content, a new promise for all North Carolinians of the spiritual and material benefits of the good life.

STATE HISTORIC SITES

Unless otherwise indicated, information regarding the sites listed below
is available on the Internet at <www.ah.dcr.state.nc.us/sections/hs>.

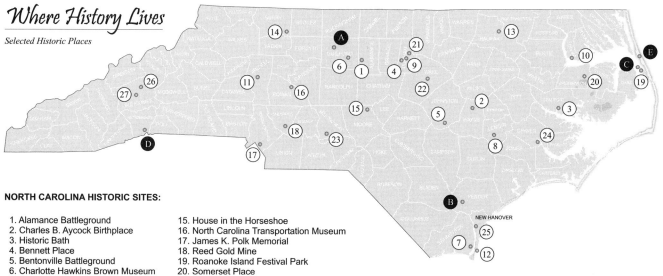

Where History Lives

Selected Historic Places

NORTH CAROLINA HISTORIC SITES:

1. Alamance Battleground
2. Charles B. Aycock Birthplace
3. Historic Bath
4. Bennett Place
5. Bentonville Battleground
6. Charlotte Hawkins Brown Museum
7. Brunswick Town / Fort Anderson
8. CSS *Neuse*
9. Duke Homestead
10. Historic Edenton
11. Fort Dobbs
12. Fort Fisher
13. Historic Halifax
14. Horne Creek Living Historical Farm

15. House in the Horseshoe
16. North Carolina Transportation Museum
17. James K. Polk Memorial
18. Reed Gold Mine
19. Roanoke Island Festival Park
20. Somerset Place
21. Historic Stagville
22. State Capitol
23. Town Creek Indian Mound
24. Tryon Palace Historic Sites & Gardens
25. USS *North Carolina* Battleship Memorial
26. Zebulon B. Vance Birthplace
27. Thomas Wolfe Memorial

NATIONAL PARK SERVICE:

A. Guilford Courthouse National Military Park
B. Moores Creek Bridge National Battlefield
C. Fort Raleigh National Historic Site
D. Carl Sandburg Home National Historic Site
E. Wright Brothers National Memorial

MAP BY MARK ANDERSON MOORE

Alamance Battleground
5803 South N.C. 62
Burlington, NC 27215
336-227-4785

Charles B. Aycock Birthplace
P.O. Box 207
Fremont, NC 27830
919-242-5581

Historic Bath
P.O. Box 148
Bath, NC 27808
252-923-3971

Bennett Place
4409 Bennett Memorial Road
Durham, NC 27705
919-383-4345

Bentonville Battleground
5466 Harper House Road
Four Oaks, NC 27524
910-594-0789

Charlotte Hawkins Brown Museum
P.O. Box B
Sedalia, NC 27342
336-449-4846

Brunswick Town / Fort Anderson
8884 St. Philip's Road S.E.
Winnabow, NC 28479
910-371-6613

CSS *Neuse*
2612 W. Vernon Avenue (U.S. 70
Business)
Kinston, NC 28502
252-522-2091

Duke Homestead
2828 Duke Homestead Road
Durham, NC 27705
919-477-5498

Historic Edenton
108 North Broad Street
P.O. Box 474
Edenton, NC 27932
252-482-2637

Fort Dobbs
438 Fort Dobbs Road
Statesville, NC 28677
704-873-5866

Fort Fisher
P.O. Box 169
Kure Beach, NC 28449
910-458-5538

Historic Halifax
P.O. Box 406
Halifax, NC 27839
252-583-7191

Horne Creek Living Historical
Farm
320 Hauser Road
Pinnacle, NC 27043
336-325-2298

House in the Horseshoe
324 Alston House Road
Sanford, NC 27330
910-947-2051

North Carolina Transportation
Museum
P.O. Box 165
Spencer, NC 28159
704-636-2889

James K. Polk Memorial
P.O. Box 475
Pineville, NC 28134
704-889-7145

Reed Gold Mine
9621 Reed Mine Road
Stanfield, NC 28163
704-721-4653

Roanoke Island Festival Park
1 Festival Park
Manteo, NC 27954
252-475-1500
www.roanokeisland.com

Somerset Place
2572 Lake Shore Road
Creswell, NC 27928
252-797-4560

Historic Stagville
5825 Old Oxford Highway
Bahama, NC 27503
P.O. Box 71217
Durham, NC 27722
919-620-0120

State Capitol
1 East Edenton Street
Raleigh, NC 27604
919-733-4994

Town Creek Indian Mound
509 Town Creek Mound Road
Mt. Gilead, NC 27306
910-439-6802

Tryon Palace Historic Sites and
Gardens
610 Pollock Street
P.O. Box 1007
New Bern, NC 28563
800-767-1560 / 252-514-4900

USS *North Carolina* Battleship
Memorial
Eagles Island
P.O. Box 480
Wilmington, NC 28402
910-251-5797
www.battleshipnc.com

Zebulon B. Vance Birthplace
911 Reems Creek Road
Weaverville, NC 28787
828-645-6706

Thomas Wolfe Memorial
52 North Market Street
Asheville, NC 28801
828-253-8304

NATIONAL PARK SERVICE SITES

Information regarding National Park Service sites is available on the Internet at <www.nationalparks.com>.

Guilford Courthouse National
Military Park
2332 New Garden Road
Greensboro, NC 27410
336-288-1776

Moores Creek Bridge National
Battlefield
40 Patriots Hall Drive
Currie, NC 28435
910-283-5591

Fort Raleigh National Historic Site
Roanoke Island
1401 National Park Drive
Manteo, NC 27954
252-473-5772

Carl Sandburg Home National
Historic Site
1928 Little River Road
Flat Rock, NC 28731
828-693-4178

Wright Brothers National
Memorial
Kill Devil Hills
1401 National Park Drive
Manteo, NC 27594
252-441-7430

BIBLIOGRAPHY

PART I. NATIVES AND NEWCOMERS

Alvord, Clarence W., and Lee Bidgood. "The Discoveries of John Lederer." In *The First Explorations of the Trans-Allegheny Region by the Virginians, 1650–1674.* Cleveland, 1912.

Angley, Wilson. "A History of St. Thomas Episcopal Church, Bath, North Carolina." Report, North Carolina Division of Archives and History, 1981.

Bishir, Catherine W., and Michael T. Southern. *A Guide to the Historic Architecture of Eastern North Carolina.* Chapel Hill, 1996.

Blethen, H. Tyler, and Curtis W. Wood Jr. *From Ulster to Carolina: The Migration of the Scotch-Irish to Southwestern North Carolina.* Raleigh, 1999.

Boyd, William K., ed. *Some Eighteenth Century Tracts concerning North Carolina.* Raleigh, 1927.

Brickell, John. *The Natural History of North Carolina.* Dublin, 1737. Reprint. Raleigh, 1911.

Byrd, William. *Wililam Byrd's Histories of the Dividing Line betwixt Virginia and North Carolina.* Edited by William K. Boyd. Raleigh, 1929.

Caruthers, Eli W. *Interesting Revolutionary Incidents and Sketches of Character.* Philadelphia, 1856.

Clifton, James M. "Golden Grains of White: Rice Planting on the Lower Cape Fear." *North Carolina Historical Review* 50 (1973): 365–93.

Coe, Joffre L. "The Cultural Sequence of the Carolina Piedmont." In *Archeology of the Eastern United States,* edited by James B. Griffin. Chicago, 1952.

———. "The Formative Cultures of the Carolina Piedmont." *Transactions of the American Philosophical Society* 54 (1964).

Corbitt, David Leroy, ed., *Explorations, Descriptions, and Attempted Settlements of Carolina, 1584–1590.* Raleigh, 1953.

Crosby, Alfred W., Jr. *The Columbian Exchange.* Westport, Conn., 1972.

Cross, Jerry L. "Historical Research Report for the Palmer-Marsh House, Bath, North Carolina." Report, North Carolina Division of Archives and History, 1976.

Crow, Jeffrey J. *The Black Experience in Revolutionary North Carolina.* Raleigh, 1977.

Cruickshank, Helen G., ed. *John and William Bartram's America.* New York, 1957.

Cumming, William P., et al. *The Discovery of North America.* London, 1971.

———. *The Exploration of North America, 1630–1776.* New York, 1974.

Durant, David N. *Raleigh's Lost Colony.* New York, 1981.

Ekirch, Roger A. *"Poor Carolina": Politics and Society in Colonial North Carolina.* Chapel Hill, 1981.

Few, William, Jr. "Autobiography of Col. William Few of Georgia." *The Magazine of American History* 8 (1881): 343–49.

Foote, William Henry. *Sketches of North Carolina, Historical and Biographical.* New York, 1846.

Fries, Adelaide L., et al., eds. *Records of the Moravians in North Carolina.* 12 vols. Raleigh, 1922–2000.

Garrow, Patrick H. *The Mattamuskeet Documents: A Study in Social History.* Raleigh, 1975.

Goodwin, Gary C. *Cherokees in Transition: A Study of Changing Culture and Environment Prior to 1775.* Chicago, 1977.

Gray, Lewis Cecil. *History of Agriculture in the Southern United States to 1860.* 2 vols. Gloucester, Mass., 1958.

Hazard, Ebenezer. "The Journal of Ebenezer Hazard in North Carolina, 1777 and 1778." Edited by Hugh B. Johnston. *North Carolina Historical Review* 36 (1959): 358–81.

Hudson, Charles. *The Southeastern Indians.* Knoxville, 1976.

Janson, Charles W. *The Stranger in America, 1793–1806.* London, 1807. Reprint, edited by Carl S. Driver. New York, 1935.

Johnson, Frank Roy. *The Tuscaroras.* 2 vols. Murfreesboro, N.C., 1968.

Kars, Marjoleine. *Breaking Loose Together: The Regulator Rebellion in Pre-Revolutionary North Carolina.* Chapel Hill, 2002.

Kay, Marvin L. Michael. "The North Carolina Regulation, 1766–1776: A Class Conflict." In *The American Revolution: Explorations in the History of*

American Radicalism, edited by Alfred F. Young. DeKalb, Ill., 1976.

Kay, Marvin L. Michael, and Lorin Lee Cary. "Class, Mobility, and Conflict in North Carolina on the Eve of the Revolution." In *The Southern Experience in the American Revolution*, edited by Jeffrey J. Crow and Larry E. Tise. Chapel Hill, 1978.

Lawson, John. *A New Voyage to Carolina*. Edited by Hugh T. Lefler. Chapel Hill, 1967.

Lee, E. Lawrence. *Indian Wars in North Carolina, 1663–1763*. Raleigh, 1963.

———. *The Lower Cape Fear in Colonial Days*. Chapel Hill, 1965.

Lee, Robert E. *Blackbeard the Pirate: A Reappraisal of His Life and Times*. Winston-Salem, 1974.

Lefler, Hugh T., and William S. Powell *Colonial North Carolina: A History*. New York, 1973.

Lewis, T. M. N., and Madeline Kneberg. "Oconaluftee Indian Village: An Interpretation of a Cherokee Community of 1750." Report, Cherokee Historical Association, 1954.

Mathis, Mark A., and Jeffrey J. Crow. *The Prehistory of North Carolina: An Archaeological Symposium*. Raleigh, 2000.

McPherson, Elizabeth G. "Nathaniel Batts, Landholder on Pasquotank River, 1660." *North Carolina Historical Review* 43 (1966): 66–81.

Merrens, Harry Roy. *Colonial North Carolina in the Eighteenth Century: A Study in Historical Geography*. Chapel Hill, 1964.

Meyer, Duane. *The Highland Scots of North Carolina*. Raleigh, 1968.

Milling, Chapman J. *Red Carolinians*. Columbia, S.C., 1940.

Mooney, James. *Myths of the Cherokee*. Washington, D.C.: Government Printing Office, 1900. Reprint. New York, 1970.

Morgan, Edmund S. *American Slavery, American Freedom: The Ordeal of Colonial Virginia*. New York, 1975.

Morison, Samuel Eliot. *The European Discovery of America: The Northern Voyages, A.D. 500–1600*. New York, 1971.

Murray, James. *The Letters of James Murray, Loyalist*. Edited by Nina M. Tiffany and Susan I. Lesley. Boston, 1901.

Nash, Francis. *Hillsboro: Colonial and Revolutionary*. Raleigh, 1903.

Paul, Charles L. "Colonial Beaufort." *North Carolina Historical Review* 42 (1965): 139–52.

———. "Factors in the Economy of Colonial Beaufort." *North Carolina Historical Review* 44 (1967): 111–34.

Perdue, Theda. *Native Carolinians: The Indians of North Carolina*. Raleigh, 1995.

"A Petition from the Inhabitants of Craven Precinct, N.C." *North Carolina Genealogical Society Journal* 6 (1980): 107–9. Transcribed by Kathleen B. Wyche from microfilm of the British Record Office document, in C.O. 5/308, part 2.

Powell, William S. *John Pory, 1572–1636: The Life and Letters of a Man of Many Parts*. Chapel Hill, 1977.

———. *North Carolina through Four Centuries*. Chapel Hill, 1989.

———. *The Proprietors of North Carolina*. Raleigh, 1968.

———, ed. *Ye Countie of Albemarle in Carolina: A Collection of Documents, 1664–1675*. Raleigh, 1958.

———, *Dictionary of North Carolina Biography*. 6 vols. Chapel Hill, 1979–96.

———, et al. *The Regulators in North Carolina: A Documentary History*. Raleigh, 1971.

Quinn, David Beers. *England and the Discovery of America, 1481–1620*. New York, 1974.

———. *The Lost Colonists: Their Fortune and Probable Fate*. Raleigh, 1999.

———. *New American World: A Documentary History of North America to 1612*. 5 vols. New York, 1979.

Ramsey, Robert W. *Carolina Cradle: Settlement of the Northwest Carolina Frontier, 1747–1762*. Chapel Hill, 1964.

Rankin, Hugh F. *The Pirates of North Carolina*. Raleigh, 1976.

Rights, Douglas L. *The American Indian in North Carolina*. Winston-Salem, 1957.

Salley, Alexander S., Jr., ed. *Narratives of Early Carolina, 1650–1708*. New York, 1967.

Saunders, William L., ed. *The Colonial Records of North Carolina*. 10 vols. Raleigh, 1886–95.

Sprunt, James. *Chronicles of the Cape Fear River*. Raleigh, 1914.

———. *The Story of Orton Plantation*. Wilmington, 1958.

Todd, Vincent H., ed. *Christoph von Graffenried's Account of the Founding of New Bern*. Raleigh, 1920.

Ward, H. Trawick. "A Review of Archeology in the North Carolina Piedmont: A Study of Change." Paper presented at the North Carolina Prehistory Symposium, North Carolina Division of Archives and History, Raleigh, 1980.

Watson, Alan D. *Society in Colonial North Carolina*. Raleigh, 1996.

————, ed. *Society in Early North Carolina: A Documentary History*. Raleigh, 2000.

Whittenburg, James P. "Planters, Merchants, and Lawyers: Social Change and the Origins of the North Carolina Regulation." *William and Mary Quarterly* 34 (1977): 215–38.

"William Logan's Journal of a Journey to Georgia, 1745." *Pennsylvania Magazine of History and Biography* 36 (1912): 1–16, 162–86.

Williams, Justin. "English Mercantilism and Carolina Naval Stores." *Journal of Southern History* 1 (1935): 169–85.

Williams, Samuel Cole, ed. *Adair's History of the American Indians*. Johnson City, Tenn., 1930.

Wood, Peter H. *Black Majority Negroes in Colonial South Carolina from 1670 through the Stono Rebellion*. New York, 1975.

PART II. AN INDEPENDENT PEOPLE

PRINTED SOURCES

Allen, Beulah Oyama, comp. *Allen House and Some of Its Allens*. Nashville, Tenn., 1980.

Anderson, Jean B. "A Preliminary Report on Stagville Plantation: The Land and the People." Report, North Carolina Division of Archives and History, 1977.

Asbury, Francis. *Francis Asbury in North Carolina: The North Carolina Portions of The Journal of Francis Asbury*. Edited by Grady L. Carroll. Nashville, Tenn., 1964.

Ashe, Samuel A. *A Biographical History of North Carolina, from Colonial Times to the Present*. 8 vols. Greensboro, 1905–17.

Attmore, William. "Journal of a Tour to North Carolina." In *James Sprunt Historical Publications*, vol. 17, no. 2. Chapel Hill, 1920.

Bartram, William. *The Travels of William Bartram*. Edited by Mark Van Doren. New York, 1940.

Bassett, John Spencer. *Slavery in the State of North Carolina*. Baltimore, 1899.

Battle, Kemp Plummer. *History of the University of North Carolina: From Its Beginning to the Death of President Swain, 1789–1868*. Vol. 1. Raleigh, 1907.

————. "Letters of Nathaniel Macon, John Steele, and William Barry Grove." In *James Sprunt Historical Publications*, vol. 3. Chapel Hill, 1902.

Bernard, John. *Retrospections of America, 1797–1811*. New York, 1887.

Bernheim, G. D. *History of the German Settlements and of the Lutheran Church in North and South Carolina*. Philadelphia, 1872.

Bernheim, G. D., and George H. Cox. *The History of the Evangelical Lutheran Synod and Ministerium of North Carolina*. Philadelphia, 1902.

Biddle, Charles. *The Autobiography of Charles Biddle*. Philadelphia, 1883.

Boles, John B. *The Great Revival, 1787–1805: The Origins of the Southern Evangelical Mind*. Lexington, Ky., 1972.

Bonath, Shawn. "Buck Springs: Archeology of an Old South Plantation." Report, North Carolina Division of Archives and History, 1978.

Boyd, William K. *Some Eighteenth Century Tracts concerning North Carolina*. Raleigh, 1927.

Boyd, William K., and Charles A. Krummel. "German Tracts concerning the Lutheran Church in North America during the Eighteenth Century." *North Carolina Historical Review* 7 (1930): 79–147, 225–82.

Brawley, James S. *Rowan County: A Brief History*. Raleigh, 1974.

Brooks, E. M. *History of Rocky River Baptist Church*. N.p., 1928.

Brown, Alexander C. *The Dismal Swamp Canal*. Chesapeake, Va., 1967.

Brown, Nelson. *Life of Henry Evans Sought Out by Nelson Brown*. Fayetteville, 1893.

Calhoon, Robert M. "An Agrarian and Evangelical Culture, 1780–1840." Draft in author's possession.

Carraway, Gertrude S. *The Stanly (Stanley) Family and the Historic John Wright Stanly House*. High Point, N.C., 1969.

Cashion, Jerry Clyde. "Cherokee Indian Removal from

North Carolina." Report, North Carolina Division of Archives and History, 1966.

Clark, Walter, ed. *The State Records of North Carolina.* Vol. 22, *Laws, 1715–1776.* Goldsboro, 1904.

Clifton, James M. "Golden Grains of White: Rice Planting on the Lower Cape Fear." *North Carolina Historical Review* 50 (1973): 365–93.

Connor, R. D. W. *Canova's Statue of Washington.* Raleigh, 1920.

———. *Race Elements in the White Population of North Carolina.* Raleigh, 1920.

Crittenden, Charles C. *The Commerce of North Carolina, 1763–1789.* New Haven, 1936.

Crow, Jeffrey J. *The Black Experience in Revolutionary North Carolina.* Raleigh, 1977.

———. *A Chronicle of North Carolina in the American Revolution.* Raleigh, 1997.

Cruickshank, Helen G., ed. *John and William Bartram's America.* New York, 1957.

Daniels, Jonathan. "North Carolina." *Holiday,* October 1947.

Davis, Edward Hill. *Historical Sketches of Franklin County.* Raleigh, 1948.

Dickins, Samuel. "To the Electors of the District Composed of the Counties of Wake, Orange, and Person" [broadside]. Raleigh, 1816.

Dill, Alonzo T., Jr. "Eighteenth Century New Bern, A History of the Town and Craven County, 1700–1800." *North Carolina Historical Review* 22 (1945): 1–21, 152–75, 293–319, 460–89; 23 (1946): 47–78, 142–71, 325–59, 495–535.

Dunn, Charles W. "A North Carolina Gaelic Bard." *North Carolina Historical Review* 36 (1959): 473–75.

Durrill, Wayne K. "Origins of a Kinship Structure in a Slave Community: The Blacks of Somerset Place, 1786–1862." Report, North Carolina Division of Archives and History, 1980.

Finlay, Hugh. *Journal Kept by Hugh Finlay, 1773–74.* Brooklyn, 1867.

Foote, William Henry. *Sketches of North Carolina, Historical and Biographical.* New York, 1846.

Fries, Adelaide L., et al., eds. *Records of the Moravians in North Carolina.* 12 vols. Raleigh, 1922–2000.

Gadski, Mary Ellen. "The History of the New Bern Academy." Report, New Bern Academy Historical Commission, 1977.

Gehrke, William H. "The Transition from the German to the English Language in North Carolina." *North Carolina Historical Review* 12 (1935): 1–19.

Genovese, Eugene D. *Roll, Jordan, Roll: The World the Slaves Made.* New York, 1974.

Gowans, Alan. *Images of American Living: Four Centuries of Architecture and Furniture as Cultural Expression.* Philadelphia, 1964.

Griffin, Frances, ed. *The Three Forks of Muddy Creek.* Winston-Salem, 1974.

Grissom, W. L. *History of Methodism in North Carolina.* Nashville, Tenn., and Dallas, Tex., 1905.

Hammer, Carl, Jr. *Rhinelanders on the Yadkin.* Salisbury, N.C., 1965.

Harper, Margaret E. *Fort Defiance and the General.* Hickory, N.C., 1976.

Haworth, Blair. *Museum of Old Domestic Life: Springfield Friends Meeting.* High Point, N.C., 1976.

Hazard, Ebenezer. "The Journal of Ebenezer Hazard in North Carolina, 1977 and 1978." Edited by Hugh B. Johnston. *North Carolina Historical Review* 36 (1959): 358–81.

Henderson, Archibald. "The Creative Forces in Westward Expansion." *North Carolina Booklet* 14, no. 3 (1915): 111–33.

Higginbotham, Don, ed. *The Papers of James Iredell.* 2 vols. Raleigh, 1976.

High Point Historical Society. *John Haley Family History.* High Point, N.C., 1973.

Hill, Michael R. "Historical Research Report: The Person Place of Louisburg, North Carolina." Report, North Carolina Division of Archives and History, 1980.

"Historic and Architectural Resources of the Tar-Neuse River Basin." Report, North Carolina Division of Archives and History, 1977.

Holder, Edward M. "Social Life of the Early Moravians in North Carolina." *North Carolina Historical Review* 11 (1934): 167–84.

Hooper, William. "An Address Delivered before the North-Carolina Bible Society, December 1819. . . ." Fayetteville, 1820.

Hoyt, William Henry, ed. *The Papers of Archibald D. Murphey.* 2 vols. Raleigh, 1914.

Hudson, Charles. *The Southeastern Indians.* Knoxville, 1976.

Hunter, Robert, Jr. *Quebec to Carolina in 1785–1786, Being the Travel Diary and Observations of Robert Hunter, Jr., A Young Merchant of London.* Edited by Louis B. Wright and Marion Tinling. San Marino, Calif., 1943.

Iobst, Richard. "A Personal History of David Stone." Report, North Carolina Division of Archives and History, n.d.

Janson, Charles W. *The Stranger in America, 1793–1806.* London, 1807. Reprint, edited by Carl S. Driver. New York, 1935.

Jefferson, Thomas. *Notes on the State of Virginia.* Edited by William Peden. Chapel Hill, 1954.

Johnson, Guion Griffis. *Ante-Bellum North Carolina: A Social History.* Chapel Hill, 1937.

Johnston, Francis B., and Thomas T. Waterman. *The Early Architecture of North Carolina: A Pictorial Survey.* Chapel Hill, 1941.

Kay, Marvin L. Michael, and Lorin Lee Cary. "A Demographic Analysis of Colonial North Carolina with Special Emphasis on Slave and Black Populations." Paper presented at History of Blacks in North Carolina and the South Symposium, North Carolina Division of Archives and History, Raleigh, February 1981.

Keith, Alice Barnwell, and William H. Masterson, eds. *The John Gray Blount Papers.* 3 vols. Raleigh, 1952–65.

Lee, Jesse. *Memoir of the Reverend Jesse Lee with Extracts from His Journal.* Edited by Minton Thrift. New York, 1823.

Lefler, Hugh T., and Albert R. Newsome. *North Carolina: The History of a Southern State.* 3d ed. Chapel Hill, 1973.

Lefler, Hugh T., and William S. Powell. *Colonial North Carolina: A History.* New York, 1973.

Lemmon, Sarah McCulloh, ed. *The Pettigrew Papers.* Vol. 1, *1685–1818.* Raleigh, 1971.

Lewis, T. M. N., and Madeline Kneberg. "Oconaluftee Indian Village: An Interpretation of a Cherokee Community of 1750." Report, Cherokee Historical Association, 1954.

Massengill, Stephen E. "The House in the Horseshoe." Report, North Carolina Division of Archives and History, 1973.

Mathews, Alice E. *Society in Revolutionary North Carolina.* Raleigh, 1976.

Mathews, Donald G. *Religion in the Old South.* Chicago, 1977.

McDonald, Forrest, and Ellen Shapiro McDonald. "The Ethnic Origins of the American People." *William and Mary Quarterly* (April 1980): 179–99.

McMurray, Helen Johnson. "Historic Mount Pleasant Methodist Episcopal Church in Tanglewood Park." 1974. Methodist Church Papers, Historical Sketches, Duke University Manuscript Department, Durham.

McRee, Griffith J., ed. *The Life and Correspondence of James Iredell.* 2 vols. New York, 1857.

Medley, Mary L. *History of Anson County, North Carolina, 1750–1976.* Wadesboro, N.C., 1976.

Merrens, Harry R. *Colonial North Carolina in the Eighteenth Century: A Study in Historical Geography.* Chapel Hill, 1964.

Meyer, Duane. *The Highland Scots in North Carolina, 1732–1776.* Chapel Hill, 1957.

Miller, Stephen F. *Recollections of New-bern Fifty Years Ago.* Raleigh, 1874.

Miller, William. "Governor's Annual Message, 1816." In *Journal of the North Carolina House of Commons, 1816,* 3–5.

Morris, Francis G., and Phyllis M. Morris. "Economic Conditions in North Carolina About 1780." *North Carolina Historical Review* 16 (1939): 107–33, 296–327.

Morse, Jedidiah. *The American Geography,* 1789. Reprint. New York, 1970.

Newsome, Albert R., ed. "Twelve North Carolina Counties in 1810–1811." *North Carolina Historical Review* 5 (1928): 413–46; 6 (1929): 67–99, 171–89, 281–309.

Parramore, Thomas C. *Cradle of the Colony: The History of Chowan County and Edenton, North Carolina.* Edenton, 1967.

———. "A Year in Hertford County with Elkanah Watson." *North Carolina Historical Review* 41 (1964): 448–63.

Paths toward Freedom: A Biographical History of Blacks and Indians in North Carolina by Blacks and Indians. Raleigh, 1976.

Perdue, Theda. *Slavery and the Evolution of Cherokee Society, 1540–1866.* Knoxville, 1979.

Powell, William S. *When the Past Refused to Die: A History of Caswell County, North Carolina, 1777–1977.* Durham, 1977.

———, ed. *Ye Countie of Albemarle in Carolina: A Collection of Documents, 1664–1675.* Raleigh, 1958.

Price, William S., Jr. "Nathaniel Macon, Planter." *North Carolina Historical Review* 78 (2001): 187–214.

Rankin, Hugh F. *North Carolina in the American Revolution.* Raleigh, 1996.

Rippy, J. Fred, ed. "A View of the Carolinas in 1783" [extracts from Francisco de Miranda's diary]. *North Carolina Historical Review* 6 (1929): 362–70.

Robinson, Blackwell P. *A History of Moore County, North Carolina, 1747–1847.* Southern Pines, N.C., 1956.

Saunders, William L., ed. *The Colonial Records of North Carolina.* Vols. 9 (*1771–75*) and 10 (*1775–76*). Raleigh, 1890.

Schaw, Janet. *Journal of a Lady of Quality.* Edited by Evangeline W. and Charles McLean Andrews. New Haven, 1921.

Schöpf, Johann David. *Travels in the Confederation.* 2 vols. Translated and edited by Alfred J. Morrison. New York, 1968.

Smith, Daniel Blake. *Inside the Great House: Planter Family Life in Eighteenth-Century Chesapeake Society.* Ithaca, N.Y., 1980.

Smyth, John F. D. *A Tour in the United States of America.* 2 vols. Dublin, 1784.

Stokes, Durward T. "North Carolina and the Great Revival of 1800." *North Carolina Historical Review* 43 (1966): 401–12.

Swaim, Doug, ed. *Carolina Dwelling.* Raleigh, 1978.

Tarlton, William S. "Somerset Place and Its Restoration." Report, North Carolina Division of State Parks, 1954.

Taylor, Melanie Johnson. "David Stone: A Political Biography." Master's thesis, East Carolina University, 1968.

Turner, Herbert S. *Church in the Old Fields: Hawfields Presbyterian Church and Community in North Carolina.* Chapel Hill, 1962.

Wall, Bennet H. "Ebenezer Pettigrew: An Economic Study of an Antebellum Planter." Ph.D. dissertation, University of North Carolina at Chapel Hill, 1947.

———. "The Founding of the Pettigrew Plantations." *North Carolina Historical Review* 27 (1950): 395–418.

Walton, Gary M., and James F. Shepherd. *The Economic Rise of Early America.* New York, 1979.

Washington, George. *The Diaries of George Washington, 1748–1799.* 5 vols. Edited by John C. Fitzpatrick. Boston and New York, 1846.

Watson, Elkanah. *Men and Times of the Revolution, or Memoirs of Elkanah Watson.* New York, 1856.

Waugh, Elizabeth Culbertson. *North Carolina's Capital, Raleigh.* Raleigh, 1967.

Weeks, Stephen B. *Southern Quakers and Slavery.* Baltimore, 1896.

Western Piedmont Council of Governments. *Historic Sites Inventory: A Survey of Alexander, Burke, Caldwell, and Catawba Counties.* N.p., 1975.

Wheeler, John Hill. *Historical Sketches of North Carolina.* Philadelphia, 1851.

Wilborn, Elizabeth W., Boyd Cathey, and Jerry L. Cross. "The Roanoke Valley: A Report on the Historic Halifax State Historic Site." Report, North Carolina Division of Archives and History, 1974.

Wilson, Edwin M. "The Congressional Career of Nathaniel Macon." In *James Sprunt Historical Publications*, vol. 2. Chapel Hill, 1900.

Winborne, Benjamin B. *Colonial and State History, Hertford County, North Carolina.* Murfreesboro, N.C., 1906.

Winston, Robert W. *Andrew Johnson, Plebeian and Patriot.* New York, 1928.

Woodward, Grace Steele. *The Cherokees.* Norman, Okla., 1963.

Wrenn, Tony P., and Ruth Little-Stokes. *An Inventory of Historic Architecture, Caswell County, North Carolina.* Raleigh, 1979.

MANUSCRIPT SOURCES
Manuscript Department, William R. Perkins Library, Duke University, Durham
    George F. Davidson Papers
    James Iredell Papers
    Thomas Lenoir Papers
    Methodist Church Papers, Historical Sketches
    Journals of William Ormond Jr.

North Carolina State Archives, Raleigh
  Bertie County Records, Minutes of the Court of
    Pleas and Quarter Sessions
  Chatham County Records, Minutes of the Court
    of Pleas and Quarter Sessions
  Josiah Collins Papers
  Mecklenburg County Records, Wills
  United States Census Manuscript Returns: 1790,
    1800, 1810, 1820
  Governor Benjamin Williams Papers
Southern Historical Collection, Louis R. Wilson
  Library, University of North Carolina, Chapel Hill
    Edmund Ruffin Beckwith Papers
    Cameron Family Papers
    William Gaston Papers
    Ernest Haywood Collection
    Major John A. Lillington's Diary
    Jeremiah Norman's Diary, Stephen B. Weeks
      Papers
    John Steele Papers

PART III. CLOSE TO THE LAND

PRINTED SOURCES

Anderson, Jean B. "A Community of Men and Mills."
  Eno Journal, March 1980.
———. "Piedmont Plantation." Report, North
  Carolina Division of Archives and History, 1977.
Angley, Wilson, Jerry L. Cross, and Michael Hill.
  Sherman's March through North Carolina: A Chronology.
  Raleigh, 1996.
Atherton, Lewis E. *The Southern Country Store,
  1800–1860.* Baton Rouge, 1949.
Barfield, Rodney. *Thomas Day, Cabinetmaker.* Raleigh,
  1975.
Barrett, John G. *The Civil War in North Carolina.* Chapel
  Hill, 1963.
Battle, Kemp P. *Memories of an Old-Time Tar Heel.*
  Chapel Hill, 1945.
Blassingame, John W. *The Slave Community: Plantation
  Life in the Antebellum South.* New York, 1972.
Brooks, Jerome E. *Green Leaf and Gold: Tobacco in North
  Carolina.* Raleigh, 1997.
Bruce, Dickson D., Jr. *And They All Sang Hallelujah.*
  Knoxville, 1946.

Butler, Lindley S. *A Courthouse Inn and Its Proprietors.*
  Wentworth, N.C., 1973.
Campbell, Wanda S. *Brown Marsh Presbyterian Church,
  Bladen County, North Carolina, Historical Records.*
  Elizabethtown, N.C., 1970.
Carter, Samuel, III. *Cherokee Sunset: A Nation Betrayed.*
  Garden City, N.Y., 1976.
Cashion, Jerry. "Fort Butler and the Cherokee Indian
  Removal from North Carolina." Report, North
  Carolina Department of Archives and History, 1970.
Cathey, Cornelius O. *Agricultural Developments in North
  Carolina, 1783–1860.* James Sprunt Studies in
  History and Political Science. Chapel Hill, 1956.
Coon, Charles L. *North Carolina Schools and Academies,
  1790–1840.* Raleigh, 1915.
Cross, Jerry L. "Historical Research Report for the
  Harper House, Bentonville, North Carolina."
  Report, North Carolina Division of Archives and
  History, 1975.
Edmondston, Catherine Ann Devereux. *"Journal of a
  Secesh Lady": The Diary of Catherine Ann Devereux,
  1860–1866.* Edited by Beth G. Crabtree and
  James W. Patton. Raleigh, 1979.
Edmunds, Mary L. R. *Governor Morehead's Blandwood
  and the Family Who Lived There.* Greensboro, 1976.
Epstein, Dena J. *Sinful Tunes and Spirituals: Black Folk
  Music to the Civil War.* Urbana, Ill., 1977.
Franklin, John Hope. *The Free Negro in North Carolina,
  1790–1860.* Chapel Hill, 1943.
Freel, Margaret W. *Our Heritage: The People of Cherokee
  County, North Carolina.* Asheville, 1956.
Gutman, Herbert G. *The Black Family in Slavery and
  Freedom, 1750–1925.* New York, 1976.
Harris, William C. *North Carolina and the Coming of the
  Civil War.* Raleigh, 2000.
Hawkins, William G. *Lunsford Lane: Or, Another Helper
  from North Carolina.* Boston, 1863.
Hodges, J. E. A. *A History of Balls Creek Camp Ground,
  1853–1929.* Maiden, N.C., 1929.
Hunter, Robert, Jr. *Quebec to Carolina in 1785–1786,
  Being the Travel Diary and Observations of Robert
  Hunter, Jr., A Young Merchant of London.* Edited by
  Louis B. Wright and Marion Tinling. San Marino,
  Calif., 1943.
Jackson, George P. *Spiritual Folksongs of Early America.*
  Locust Valley, N.Y., 1953.

Johnson, Guion Griffis. *Ante-Bellum North Carolina: A Social History.* Chapel Hill, 1937.

Knapp, Richard F. *Golden Promise in the Piedmont: The Story of John Reed's Mine.* Raleigh, 1999.

Knapp, Richard F., and Brent D. Glass. *Gold Mining in North Carolina: A Bicentennial History.* Raleigh, 1999.

Knight, Edgar W. *Public School Education in North Carolina.* Boston, 1916.

Konkle, Burton A. *John Motley Morehead and the Development of North Carolina.* Philadelphia, 1922.

Lefler, Hugh T., and Albert R. Newsome. *North Carolina: The History of a Southern State.* 3d ed. Chapel Hill, 1973.

Lemmon, Sarah McCulloh. "Plantation Life at Lake Phelps before the Civil War." Paper presented at the Edenton Symposium, North Carolina Division of Archives and History, 1976.

——, ed. *The Pettigrew Papers.* Vol. 1, *1685–1818.* Raleigh, 1971.

Lossing, Benson J. *The Pictorial Fieldbook of the Revolution.* New York, 1860.

McDaniel, George. "Stagville: Kin and Community." Report, North Carolina Division of Archives and History, 1977.

Marshall, Helen E. *Dorothea Dix.* Chapel Hill, 1937.

Menius, Arthur. "The Bennett Place." Report, North Carolina Division of Archives and History, 1979.

Mobley, Joe A. *James City: A Black Community in North Carolina, 1863–1900.* Raleigh, 2000.

Moore, Mark A. *Moore's Historical Guide to the Wilmington Campaign and the Battles for Fort Fisher.* Mason City, Iowa, 1999.

Muse, Amy. *The Story of the Methodists in the Port of Beaufort.* New Bern, N.C., 1941.

Olmsted, Frederick L. *The Cotton Kingdom.* New York, 1953.

Owens, Leslie H. *This Species of Property: Slave Life and Culture in the Old South.* New York, 1976.

Owsley, Frank L. *Plain Folk of the Old South.* Baton Rouge, 1949.

The Poetical Works of George M. Horton, the Colored Bard of North Carolina. Hillsborough, N.C., 1845.

Powell, William S. *When the Past Refused to Die: A History of Caswell County, North Carolina, 1777–1977.* Durham, 1977.

Robinson, Blackwell P., ed. *The North Carolina Guide.* Chapel Hill, 1955.

Rothman, David J. *The Discovery of the Asylum: Social Order and Disorder in the New Republic.* Boston, 1971.

Rulfs, Donald J. "The Professional Theater in Wilmington." *North Carolina Historical Review* 28 (1951): 119–36.

Shaw, Cornelia R. *Davidson College.* New York, 1923.

Singleton, William Henry. *Recollections of My Slavery Days.* Edited by Katherine Mellen Charron and David S. Cecelski. Raleigh, 1999.

Slave Narratives: A Folk History of Slavery in the United States from Interviews with Former Slaves. Typewritten records prepared by the Federal Writers' Project, Works Progress Administration. Washington, D.C., 1941. Vol. 11 (North Carolina). Microfiche. William R. Perkins Library, Duke University.

Spruill, Julia Cherry. *Women's Life and Work in the Southern Colonies.* Chapel Hill, 1938.

Stick, David. *North Carolina Lighthouses.* Raleigh, 1999.

Stowe, Harriet B. *Dred: A Tale of the Great Dismal Swamp.* Boston, 1856.

Studebaker, Robert B. *History of Eagle Lodge.* Chapel Hill, n.d.

Tarlton, William S. "Somerset Place and Its Restoration." Report, North Carolina Division of State Parks, 1954.

The Thalian Association of Wilmington, North Carolina, with Sketches of Many of Its Members by a Member of the Association. Wilmington, 1871.

Wall, Bennett H. "Ebenezer Pettigrew: An Economic Study of an Antebellum Planter." Ph.D. dissertation, University of North Carolina at Chapel Hill, 1946.

Weatherly, Andrew Earl. *The First Hundred Years of Historic Guilford, 1771–1871.* Greensboro, 1972.

West, John F. *The Ballad of Tom Dula.* Durham, n.d.

Wilson, Peter M. *Southern Exposure.* Chapel Hill, 1927.

Zuber, Richard L. *North Carolina During Reconstruction.* Raleigh, 1996.

NEWSPAPERS AND MAGAZINES

Greensboro Daily News (special edition), 29 May 1971
Hillsborough Recorder
Milton Chronicle
The State

MANUSCRIPT SOURCES

Manuscript Department, William R. Perkins Library,
    Duke University, Durham
      James Bennitt Papers
      Campbell Family Papers
      Joseph F. Fowler Papers
      George Hood Papers
      Thomas C. McNeeley Papers
      Alexander McPheeters Papers
      Officers' and Soldiers' Miscellaneous Letters,
          1861, Confederate States of America,
          Archives, Army, Miscellany
      Tillinghast Family Papers
      John Wilson Papers
      John Wilson and Richard T. Smith Account Book
North Carolina State Archives, Raleigh
      Legislative Documents, Session 1848–49, House
          Document No. 2, "A Memorial Soliciting a
          State Hospital for the Protection and Care of
          the Insane"
      Michaux-Randolph Papers: "A Concise Account of
          the Rise of Camp Meetings"
Southern Historical Collection, Louis R. Wilson
    Library, University of North Carolina, Chapel Hill
      Asa Biggs Papers
      Cameron Family Papers
      Tod R. Caldwell Papers

PART IV. THE QUEST FOR PROGRESS

PRINTED SOURCES

Ashe, Samuel A., ed. *Biographical History of North
    Carolina from Colonial Times to the Present.* 8 vols.
    Greensboro, 1905.

Baltzell, E. Digby. *The Protestant Establishment: Aristocracy
    and Caste in America.* New York, 1964.

Banks, Ann, ed. *First-Person America.* New York, 1980.

Bluestone, Daniel M. "The Southern Railway
    Company." Report, U.S. Heritage Conservation and
    Recreation Service, 1977.

Bobinski, George S. *Carnegie Libraries: Their History and
    Impact on American Public Library Development.*
    Chicago, 1969.

Brawley, James S. *Rowan County: A Brief History.*
    Raleigh, 1974.

Campbell, Helen S. *Household Economics.* New York,
    ca. 1896.

Cash, W. J. *The Mind of the South.* New York, 1941.

Champion, Myra. *The Lost World of Thomas Wolfe.*
    Asheville, 1970.

The City of Raleigh. Raleigh, 1887.

*The City of Raleigh, N.C., and Vicinity: Conditions and
    Resources.* Raleigh, n.d.

Clark, Thomas D. *Pills, Petticoats and Plows: The Southern
    Country Store, 1865–1914.* Indianapolis and New
    York, 1944.

Crow, Jeffrey J., Paul D. Escott, and Flora J. Hatley. *A
    History of African Americans in North Carolina.*
    Raleigh, 2001.

Crum, Mason. *The Story of Lake Junaluska.* Greensboro,
    1950.

Dixon, Roger. *Victorian Architecture.* New York, 1978.

Dowd, Jerome. "Strikes and Lockouts in North
    Carolina." *Gunton's Magazine,* February 1901.

Durden, Robert F. *The Dukes of Durham, 1865–1929.*
    Durham, 1975.

Edmonds, Helen G. *The Negro and Fusion Politics in
    North Carolina, 1896–1901.* Chapel Hill, 1951.

Edwards, Richard. *Contested Terrain: The Transformation
    of the Work Place in the Twentieth Century.* New York,
    1979.

Escott, Paul D. *Slavery Remembered: A Record of
    Twentieth-Century Slave Narratives.* Chapel Hill, 1979.

Fein, Albert. *Frederick Law Olmsted and the American
    Environmental Tradition.* New York, 1972.

Funk, Linda. *The Duke Homestead Guidebook.* Raleigh,
    1978.

Galloway, Dwayne, and Jim Wrinn. *Southern Railway's
    Spencer Shops, 1896–1996.* Lynchburg, Va., 1996.

Gavins, Raymond. "Black Leadership in North
    Carolina to 1900." In *The Black Presence in North
    Carolina,* edited by Rodney Barfield and Jeffrey J.
    Crow. Raleigh, 1978.

Giedion, Sigfried. *Mechanization Takes Command.* New
    York, 1948.

Ginns, Patsy Moore. *Rough Weather Makes Good Timber:
    Carolinians Recall.* Chapel Hill, 1977.

Girouard, Mark. *Sweetness and Light: The Queen Anne
    Movement, 1860–1900.* Oxford, Eng., 1977.

Glass, Brent D. "Southern Mill Hills: Design in a

'Public' Place." In *Carolina Dwelling*, edited by Doug Swaim. Raleigh, 1978.

———. *The Textile Industry in North Carolina*. Raleigh, 1992.

Goodwyn, Lawrence. *Democratic Promise: The Populist Moment in America*. New York, 1976.

Hayden, Harry. *The Wilmington Rebellion*. N.p., 1936.

"Healthful Habits at the Grove Park Inn." *Southern Living*, October 1977.

Hobbs, Peter Burke. "Plantation to Factory: Tradition and Industrialization in Durham, N.C., 1880–1900." Master's thesis, Duke University, 1971.

Holt, Lanier Rand. "'I Had to Like It': A Study of a Durham Textile Community." Honors essay, University of North Carolina at Chapel Hill, 1977.

Hughes, Julian, *Development of the Textile Industry in Alamance County*. Burlington, N.C., 1965.

Janiewski, Dolores. "From Field to Factory: Race, Class, Sex, and the Woman Worker in Durham, 1880–1940." Ph.D. dissertation, Duke University, 1979.

Jolley, Harley E. "The Cradle of Forestry in America." Reprint from *American Forests* 76, nos. 10–12 (October–December 1970).

Johnson, Mary Elizabeth, ed. *Times Down Home: 75 Years with the "Progressive Farmer."* Birmingham, Ala., 1978.

Kelly, Fred, ed. *Miracle at Kitty Hawk: The Letters of Wilbur and Orville Wright*. New York, 1951.

Kraft, Stephanie. *No Castles on Main Street: American Authors and Their Homes*. Chicago, 1979.

Kuhn, Clifford. "Industrialization in Burlington." Report, Southern Oral History Program, University of North Carolina at Chapel Hill, 1978.

Lefler, Hugh T., and Albert R. Newsome. *North Carolina: The History of a Southern State*. 3d ed. Chapel Hill, 1973.

Lincoln, C. Eric. "Black Religion in North Carolina, from Colonial Times to 1900." In *The Black Presence in North Carolina*, edited by Rodney Barfield and Jeffrey J. Crow. Raleigh, 1978.

Little-Stokes, Ruth. "Dilworth Historic District." Report, North Carolina Division of Archives and History, 1978.

Litwack, Leon. *Been in the Storm So Long: The Aftermath of Slavery*. New York, 1979.

Maass, John. *The Victorian Home in America*. New York, 1972.

Martin, Vickie. "Biography of Pearl DeZern Martin." Paper, Duke University, 1980.

McDaniel, George. *Hearth and Home: Preserving a People's Culture*. Philadelphia, 1981.

McDuffie, Jerome A. "Politics in Wilmington and New Hanover County, North Carolina, 1865–1900: The Genesis of a Race Riot." Ph.D. dissertation, Kent State University, 1979.

McMath, Robert C. "Agrarian Protest at the Forks of the Creek." *North Carolina Historical Review* 51 (Winter 1974): 41–63.

Mitchell, Ted. *Thomas Wolfe: A Writer's Life*. Raleigh 1999.

Mobley, Joe A. "In the Shadow of White Society: Princeville, a Black Town in North Carolina, 1865–1915." *North Carolina Historical Review* 63 (1986): 340–84.

Morehouse, H. L. *H. M. Tupper, D.D.: A Narrative of Twenty-Five Years' Work in the South*. New York, 1890.

Morrill, Dan L. "Dilworth: Charlotte's Initial Streetcar Suburb." Paper, in the possession of the author, n.d.

Murphy, Mary. "Burlington." Report, Southern Oral History Program, University of North Carolina at Chapel Hill, 1980.

Murray, Pauli. *Proud Shoes: The Story of an American Family*. New York, 1956.

Newman, Dale. "Work and Community Life in a Southern Textile Town." *Labor History* 19 (Spring 1978): 204–25.

Noblin, Stuart. *Leonidas LaFayette Polk, Agrarian Crusader*. Chapel Hill, 1949.

Parker, Inez Moore. *The Biddle–Johnson C. Smith University Story*. Charlotte, 1975.

Parramore, Thomas C. *First to Fly: North Carolina and the Beginnings of Aviation*. Chapel Hill, 2002.

———. *Triumph at Kitty Hawk: The Wright Brothers and Powered Flight*. Raleigh, 1999.

Perkins, Elsie Wallace. "Reminiscences of a Durham Childhood: The Turn of the Century." In *Durham: A Pictorial History*, edited by Joel A. and Frank A. Kostyu. Norfolk, 1978.

Pierpont, Andrew Warren. "Development of the Textile Industry in Alamance County." Ph.D.

dissertation, University of North Carolina at Chapel Hill, 1953.

Pinehurst, North Carolina. Boston, 1908.

Prince, Richard E. *Southern Railway System Steam Locomotives and Boats.* Green River, Wyo., 1970.

Ransom, Robert L., and Richard Sutch. *One Kind of Freedom: The Economic Consequences of Emancipation.* Cambridge, Mass., 1977.

Robbins, Tyler B. "The Work Experience: The Durham Hosiery Mill, 1898–1976." Paper, Duke University, 1978.

Robinson, Blackwell P., ed. *The North Carolina Guide.* Chapel Hill, 1955.

Rodgers, Daniel T. "Tradition, Modernity, and the American Industrial Worker." *Journal of Interdisciplinary History* 7 (Spring 1977): 655–81.

———. *The Work Ethic in Industrial America, 1850–1920.* Chicago, 1978.

Roper, Laura Wood. *FLO: A Biography of Frederick Law Olmsted.* Baltimore, 1973.

Russ, Peyton F. "A Design History of Reynolda Gardens, 1910–1920." Report, Reynolda House, 1977.

St. Joseph's A.M.E. Church Directory, 1969. N.p., 1969.

Schwarzkopf, S. Kent. *A History of Mt. Mitchell and the Black Mountains: Exploration, Development, and Preservation.* Raleigh, 2000.

Scott, Anne Firor. *The Southern Lady: From Pedestal to Politics, 1830–1930.* Chicago, 1970.

Shackelford, Laurel, and Bill Weinberg, eds. *Our Appalachia: An Oral History.* New York, 1977.

Spencer, Alonzo T., Jr. "The Making of Reynolda House: Learning Center and Museum of American Art." Master's thesis, Wake Forest University, 1978.

Taylor, A. Elizabeth. "The Woman Suffrage Movement in North Carolina." *North Carolina Historical Review* 38 (1961): 45–62, 173–89.

Taylor, Rosser H. *Carolina Crossroads.* Murfreesboro, N.C., 1966.

Terrill, Tom, and Jerrold Hirsch, eds. *Such as Us: Southern Voices of the Thirties.* Chapel Hill, 1978.

Tilley, Nannie May. *The Bright-Tobacco Industry, 1860–1929.* Chapel Hill, 1948.

Tindall, George Brown. *The Emergence of the New South, 1913–1945.* Baton Rouge, 1967.

Tompkins, Daniel A. *History of Mecklenburg County and the City of Charlotte.* 2 vols. Charlotte, 1903.

Turnbull, Andrew. *Thomas Wolfe.* New York, 1967.

Van Noppen, Ina W. and John J. *Western North Carolina Since the Civil War.* Boone, N.C., 1973.

Walls, William J. *The African Methodist Episcopal Zion Church: Reality of the Black Church.* Charlotte, 1974.

Weare, Walter B. *Black Business in the New South: A Social History of the North Carolina Mutual Life Insurance Company.* Urbana, Ill., 1973.

Wiebe, Robert H. *The Search for Order, 1877–1920.* New York, 1967.

Williams, Alexa C. *Raleigh: A Guide to North Carolina's Capital.* Raleigh, 1975.

Wilson, Emily Herring. *George Henry Black, 100 Years.* Winston-Salem, 1979.

Wilson, Peter M. *Southern Exposure.* Chapel Hill, 1927.

Wolfe, Thomas. *Look Homeward, Angel.* New York, 1929.

Woodward, C. Vann. *Origins of the New South, 1877–1913.* Baton Rouge, 1951.

Zimmermann, Hilda Jane. "Penal Reform Movement in the South during the Progressive Era, 1890–1917." *Journal of Southern History* 17 (November 1951): 462–92.

NEWSPAPERS

Alamance *Gleaner,* October and November 1900

Durham *Tobacco Plant,* 22 February 1882, 8 December 1886

Greensboro Daily News (special edition), 29 May 1971

Raleigh *News and Observer,* 5 April 1896

MANUSCRIPT SOURCES

Manuscript Department, William R. Perkins Library, Duke University, Durham
    W. Duke Sons & Co. Papers
    Charles N. Hunter Papers
    Stowe Family Papers, Account Book, 1856–74
    Tillinghast Family Papers
    James King Wilkerson Papers, 1898 Almanac
Southern Historical Collection, Louis R. Wilson Library, University of North Carolina, Chapel Hill
    Thomas Settle Papers

INTERVIEWS

Students affiliated with the Southern Oral History Program (SOHP) at the University of North Carolina at Chapel Hill and the Oral History Program (OHP) at Duke University have recovered remarkable materials on North Carolina since 1900 through interviews with men and women whose memories range back to the early twentieth century. Of the interviews used for this work, the following were of special value:

Bessie Buchanan, interviewed by Lanier Rand, SOHP

Luther Ellis Burch, interviewed by Daniel Ellison, SOHP

Thomas Burt, interviewed by Glen Hinson, SOHP

George Carroll, interviewed by Tyler B. Robbins, OHP

I. L. Dean, interviewed by Richard C. Franck, OHP

Pearl DeZern Martin, interviewed by Vickie W. Martin, OHP

James Dorman, interviewed by Sydney Nathans, OHP

Ethel Faucette, interviewed by Allen Tullos, SOHP

Paul Faucette, interviewed by Allen Tullos, SOHP

Fred Greenhill, interviewed by Tyler B. Robbins, OHP

John Maynard Jones, interviewed by Dolores Janiewski, OHP

Ethel Lovell, interviewed by Julia L. Frey, OHP

Reginald Mitchener, interviewed by Glen Hinson, SOHP

Charles Murray, interviewed by Brent Glass, SOHP

Zelma Montgomery Murray, interviewed by Brent Glass, SOHP

Janie Cameron Riley, interviewed by George McDaniel, OHP

Daisy J. Weadon, interviewed by Mark Weadon, OHP

In addition to these university collections, two independent interviews have also been used:

Elizabeth Williams, interviewed by Elizabeth Turner. Notes of interview in possession of interviewer.

Interview of Fred Loring Seely Jr. In *Our Appalachia: An Oral History*, edited by Laurel Shackelford and Bill Weinberg. New York, 1977.

PART V. EXPRESS LANES AND COUNTRY ROADS

PRINTED SOURCES

Badger, Anthony J. *North Carolina and the New Deal.* Raleigh, 1981.

———. *Prosperity Road: The New Deal, Tobacco, and North Carolina.* Chapel Hill, 1980.

Barefoot, Pamela, and Burt Kornegay. *Mules and Memories: A Photo Documentary of the Tobacco Farmer.* Winston-Salem, 1978.

Bell, John L. *Hard Times: Beginnings of the Great Depression in North Carolina, 1929–1933.* Raleigh, 1982.

Bledsoe, Jerry. *The World's Number One, Flat-Out, All-Time Great Stock Car Racing Book.* Garden City, N.Y., 1975.

Blythe, LeGette. *William Henry Belk.* Chapel Hill, 1950.

Boyd, William K. *The Story of Durham: City of the New South.* Durham, 1925.

Brinton, Hugh Penn. "The Negro in Durham." Ph.D. dissertation, University of North Carolina at Chapel Hill, 1930.

Burlington Industries. *The Spencer Love Story.* Burlington, N.C., 1962.

Carter, Wilmoth. *The Urban Negro in the South.* New York, 1961.

Cecelski, David S. *Along Freedom Road: Hyde County, North Carolina, and the Fate of Black Schooling in the South.* Chapel Hill, 1994.

Chafe, William H. *Civilities and Civil Rights: Greensboro, North Carolina, and the Black Struggle for Freedom.* New York, 1980.

Clay, James W., and Douglas M. Orr Jr. *Metrolina Atlas.* Chapel Hill, 1972.

Clay, James W., Douglas M. Orr Jr., and Alfred W. Stuart. *North Carolina Atlas: Portrait of a Changing Southern State.* Chapel Hill, 1975.

Coates, Albert. *By Her Own Bootstraps: A Saga of Women in North Carolina.* Chapel Hill, 1975.

Cope, Robert F., and Manly Wade Wellman. *The County of Gaston.* Charlotte, 1961.

Cox, William E. *Southern Sidelights.* Raleigh, 1942.

Craig, M. Eleanor. "Recent History of the North Carolina Furniture Manufacturing Industry with Special Attention to Locational Factors." Ph.D. dissertation, Duke University, 1959.

Daniels, Jonathan. "North Carolina." *Holiday*, October 1947.

———. *Tar Heels: A Portrait of North Carolina.* New York, 1941.

Dickey, J. A., and E. C. Branson. *How Farm Tenants Live: A Social-Economic Survey in Chatham County, N.C.* Chapel Hill, 1922.

Federal Writers' Project. *North Carolina: A Guide to the Old North State.* Chapel Hill, 1939.

Gatewood, Willard B., Jr. *Preachers, Pedagogues, and Politics, 1920–1927.* Chapel Hill, 1966.

Ginns, Patsy Moore. *Rough Weather Makes Good Timber: Carolinians Recall.* Chapel Hill, 1977.

Grant, Joanne, ed. *Black Protest History: Documents and Analyses, 1619 to the Present.* New York, 1968.

Hagood, Margaret Jarman. *Mothers of the South: Portraiture of the White Tenant Farm Woman.* Chapel Hill, 1939.

Harden, John. *North Carolina Roads and Their Builders.* Vol. 2. Raleigh, 1966.

Harrill, L. R. *Memories of 4-H.* Raleigh, 1967.

Herring, Harriet L. *Passing of the Mill Village.* Chapel Hill, 1949.

Hill, Michael, ed. *Guide to North Carolina Highway Historical Markers.* Raleigh, 2001.

Hobbs, S. Huntington. *North Carolina: An Economic and Social Profile.* Chapel Hill, 1958.

Hodges, Luther H. *Businessman in the State House: Six Years as Governor of North Carolina.* Chapel Hill, 1962.

Howard, Donald S. *The WPA and Federal Relief Policy.* New York, 1943.

Ireland, Robert E. *Entering the Auto Age: The Early Automobile in North Carolina, 1900–1930.* Raleigh, 1990.

Jackson, Annis Ward. "Reflections of a Moonshiner: The Life and Times of Willard Watson." *Tar Heel,* April 1980.

Kaufman, Naomi. "Minister Hoped to Wreck Segregation." *Durham Morning Herald,* 9 December 1979.

Lefler, Hugh T., and Albert R. Newsome. *North Carolina: The History of a Southern State.* 3d ed. Chapel Hill, 1973.

Marcello, Ronald E. "The North Carolina Works Progress Administration and the Politics of Relief." Ph.D. dissertation, Duke University, 1968.

Marteena, Constance H. *The Lengthening Shadow of a Woman: A Biography of Charlotte Hawkins Brown.* Hicksville, N.Y., 1977.

McKimmon, Jane S. *When We're Green We Grow: The Story of Home Demonstration Work in North Carolina.* Chapel Hill, 1945.

Moore, James L., and Thomas H. Wingate. *Cabarrus Reborn: A Historical Sketch of the Founding and Development of Cannon Mills Company and Kannapolis.* Kannapolis, N.C., 1940.

Murray, Pauli. *Proud Shoes: The Story of an American Family.* New York, 1956.

Myers, James. *Field Notes: Textile Strikes in South.* New York, 1929.

Oakley, Christopher Arris. "Indian Gaming and the Eastern Band of Cherokee Indians." *North Carolina Historical Review* 78 (2001): 133–55.

Parramore, Thomas C. *Carolina Quest.* Englewood Cliffs, N.J., 1978.

Paths toward Freedom: A Biographical History of Blacks and Indians in North Carolina by Blacks and Indians. Raleigh, 1976.

Pierce, Walter H. *Trends in the Development of Agriculture in North Carolina.* Raleigh, 1965.

Poff, Jan-Michael, ed. *Addresses and Public Papers of James Baxter Hunt, Jr., Governor of North Carolina.* Vol 3. Raleigh, 2000.

———. *Addresses and Public Papers of James Grubbs Martin, Governor of North Carolina.* Vol. 1. Raleigh, 1992.

Powell, William S., ed. *Dictionary of North Carolina Biography.* 6 vols. Chapel Hill, 1979–96.

Powledge, Fred. "Going Home to Raleigh." *Harper's Magazine,* April 1970.

Read, Martha Norburn. *Asheville . . . in the Land of the Sky.* Richmond, 1942.

Robinson, Blackwell P., ed. *The North Carolina Guide.* Chapel Hill, 1955.

Rutledge, William E., Jr. *An Illustrated History of Yadkin County, 1850–1965.* Yadkinville, N.C., 1965.

Salmond, John A. *The Civilian Conservation Corps, 1933–1942.* Durham, 1967.

Saunders, W. O. *The Book of Ham.* Elizabeth City, N.C., 1924.

Sewell, Joseph L. "The Only Negro Deaf-Mute Lawyer in the United States." *The Silent Worker*, March 1927.

Shackelford, Laurel, and Bill Weinberg, eds. *Our Appalachia: An Oral History*. New York, 1977.

Sharpe, Bill. *Tar on My Heels*. Winston-Salem, 1946.

Taylor, Rosser H. *Carolina Crossroads*. Murfreesboro, N.C., 1966.

Terrill, Tom E., and Jerrold Hirsch, eds. *Such as Us: Southern Voices of the Thirties*. Chapel Hill, 1978.

Terkel, Studs. *Hard Times: An Oral History of the Great Depression*. New York, 1970.

U.S. Army Corps of Engineers, Board of Engineers for Rivers and Harbors. *The Port of Wilmington, N.C.* Pt. 2. Washington, D.C., 1961.

Wadelington, Charles W., and Richard F. Knapp. *Charlotte Hawkins Brown and Palmer Memorial Institute: What One Young African American Woman Could Do.* Chapel Hill, 1999.

Watson, Helen R. "The Grocery Stores of Yesteryear." *The State*, March 1980.

Waynick, Capus. *North Carolina Roads and Their Builders*. Vol. 1. Raleigh, 1952.

Weare, Walter B. *Black Business in the New South: A Social History of the North Carolina Mutual Life Insurance Company*. Urbana, Ill., 1973.

Wilson: A Special Supplement to the New East Magazine. Greenville, N.C., 1973.

Wilson, Terry P. *The Cart that Changed the World*. Norman, Okla., 1978.

Wolcott, Reed M. *Rose Hill*. New York, 1976.

Wolfe, Tom. "The Last American Hero is Junior Johnson, *Yes!*" *Esquire*, March 1965.

Wolfe, Thomas. *Look Homeward, Angel*. New York, 1929.

NEWSPAPERS AND MAGAZINES

Greensboro Daily News (special edition), 29 May 1971

Research and Farming

The State

Tar Heel: The Magazine of North Carolina

We the People of North Carolina

Clipping File, North Carolina Collection, Louis R. Wilson Library, University of North Carolina, Chapel Hill

MANUSCRIPT SOURCES

Manuscript Department, William R. Perkins Library, Duke University, Durham

    Durham Chamber of Commerce Papers

    Robert P. Harriss Papers

    Hemphill Family Papers

North Carolina Collection, Louis R. Wilson Library, University of North Carolina, Chapel Hill

    Stutz, Carleton, and Peter A. Maxfield. "Tobacco Bag Stringing Operations in North Carolina and Virginia." Richmond, 1939.

Southern Historical Collection, Louis R. Wilson Library, University of North Carolina, Chapel Hill

    Howard W. Odum Subregional Photo Study

Southern Oral History Program, University of North Carolina, Chapel Hill

    Julius Fry, interviewed by William Finger

    Zelma Murray, interviewed by Brent Glass

    Lacy Wright, interviewed by William Finger and Charles Hughes

INDEX

Page numbers in italics refer to illustrations. (When a text reference and an illustration appear on the same page, the page number is given in roman type.)

Caswell, Richard, 154
Caswell County: planters of, 210
Caswell County Courthouse
    (Yanceyville), 292–93
Catawba Indians, 10, 72, 116
Catechna (Indian village), 54, 57
Catholic churches, 279. *See also*
    Roman Catholics
Central Carolina Cooperative
    Exchange, 485
Central Piedmont Community
    College (Charlotte), 579
Cernigliaro, Salvatore, 449
Chambers, Maxwell. *See* Maxwell
    Chambers House
Chapel Hill Weekly, 548
Chapel of the Good Shepherd
    (Warren County), 363, 479
Charles I (king of England), 30
Charles II (king of England), 30
Charles B. Aycock Birthplace (state
    historic site, Wayne County),
    369. *See also* Aycock, Charles B.
Charles Town, 38
Charlotte: map, 538
Charlotte Consolidated Construc-
    tion Company, 419, 421
Charlotte-Douglas International
    Airport, 550, 551
Charlotte Hawkins Brown Museum
    (state historic site, Guilford
    County), 564. *See also* Brown,
    Charlotte Hawkins
Charlotte Motor Speedway, 572
Charlotte Observer, 546
Chatham County, 490–91
Chattoka (Indian town), 49, 54
Cherokee Indians, 14, 19–20, 114,
    116; legend of, concerning early
    migration, 5; Eastern Band of,
    20, 117, 122; and Moravians, 86;
    lifestyle of, 117–20; and white
    society, 121; and slave trade, 121,
    136; lands of, 121, 316; forcibly
    removed from Southeast, 315
Chesapeake Indians, 23, 25
Chesterfield cigarettes, 493, 494
Chicamacomico Lifesaving Station,
    324
Child labor, 394, 397

Chowan County Courthouse
    (Edenton), 39, *40*, 181
Chowan River, 26, 27, 28
Chowanoc Indians, 50
Christ Episcopal Church (New
    Bern), 185
Christ Episcopal Church (Raleigh),
    279, 304, *305*
Chuck Davis Dance Company, 578
Churches: in rural areas, 274–75,
    281, 478–79
Church membership, 566
Church of England, 217
Cigarettes: manufacturing of, 383,
    384–85, 493, 494; marketing of,
    383–84, 494
Civilian Conservation Corps, 508
Civil punishments, 294–95
Civil War: effects of, 336–45; map,
    338
Clay County Courthouse (Hayes-
    ville), 410
Clayton, Eva, 561
Cluck, Earl, 573
Coal Glen disaster, 504
Cobb, Irvin S., 516
Cockfighting, *311*
Cogdell, Ann, 187
Cole, Lavinia, 309
Coleridge (abandoned mill village,
    Randolph County), 388
College basketball, 569–70
College football, 569
Colleton, John, 36
Collins, Edward, 243
Collins, Hugh, 243
Collins, Josiah, 148, 209, 241;
    slaves belonging to, described,
    137, 138, 143
Collins, Josiah, II, 137, 144, 241
Collins, Josiah, III, 137, 241,
    243; and Ebenezer Pettigrew,
    243–44; portrait of, *244*; and
    clothing for slaves, 255–56
Collins, Mary Riggs, 243, 244
Collins, William, 243
Collins family, 259; and life at
    Somerset Place, 241–43, 244–46
Coltrane, John, 578
Columbus, Christopher, 15

Columbus Lodge (Pittsboro), 304
Commodity prices: and Civil War,
    337
Common schools, 237
Community colleges, 579
Computers, 552–53
Concord Presbytery, 334
Cone, Moses, 487
Conestoga wagon, 79
Constitution of 1868 (N.C.), 345–
    48
Continental Furniture Company
    (High Point), 495
"Contrabands" (slaves under Fed-
    eral protection), 342
"Convention of Freedmen" (1865),
    436
Cooper, Anthony Ashley, 36
Coopers, 65, 113
Co-ops, 484, 485–86
Copland, Patrick, 27
Corbin, Francis, 39, 40, 83
Coree Indians, 54
Corn, 34, 113, 248, 265; and
    Cherokee Indians, 117, 118
Corn shuckings (social activity),
    283–84, 446
Cornwallis, Charles, 200
Coronado, Francisco, 18
Cortez, Hernando, 15
Cor Tom (Coree Indian chief), 54
Cotton: cultivation of, 113, 359,
    475, 479; price of, 480
Cotton gin, 113, 207, *209*
Council, Thomas, 409
Country Doctor Museum (Bailey),
    359
Country stores, 366–67, 479; and
    rural life, 269
County commissioner system, 348
County courthouses, 290, 292–93,
    410–11
County courts, 293
County fairs, 446
County seats, 164, 289, 290
"Court week" (in county seats), 295
Coutanch, Michael, 44, 65
Cramer, Stuart W., 497
Cramerton (mill village, Gaston
    County), 497

Eumenian Society/Hall (Davidson College), 334, 335
Evangelicalism, 218, 219, 220, 221, 222, 223, 567, 568
Evans, Henry, 220
Evans, Minnie, 578
Evelina (slave), 157
Everitt, Rebecca, 130, 131, 132
Everitt, Silas, 130, 131, 132, 134, 135
Everitt House (Edgecombe County), 131, 132
Evolution, theory of, 554–55
Exchange rates, 61
Executive Mansion (Raleigh), 419

Factory work/workers, 385, 386, 392–93
Fagensville (predecessor of Carthage), 171
Fanning, David, 153–54, 157
Fanning, Edmund, 92, 92–93, 94, 95, 99, 100, 103; attacked by Regulators, 101
Fanny (slave), 140
Farmer's Advocate, 316
Farmers' Alliance, 373–74
Farmers Cooperative Exchange, 485
Farmers' Union, 484
Farming. See Agriculture
Faucette, Ethel, 393
Fayetteville, 162; origins of, 75, 176; slaves in, 171; population of, 184; as market town, 296, 298; government of, 298
Fayetteville and Western Plank Road, 326
Fayetteville Street (Raleigh), 423
Federal architecture, 212–14
Federal Farm Board, 486
Fenner's Warehouse (Rocky Mount), 364
Ferrell, Rick, 570
Ferrell, Wes, 570
Ferries, 543
Few, James, 102
Few, William, 89, 90, 102
Few, William, Jr., 89, 90–91
Fields, Thomas, 207

Fifteenth Amendment (U.S. Constitution), 345
Fighting, 165, 192, 193, 194
Finlay, Hugh, 177
First Colony Farms, 490
First Presbyterian Church (Fayetteville), 304
First Presbyterian Church (New Bern), 213–14, 215
First Union National Bank, 512
Flour-milling, 113
Floyd, Raymond, 572
Folk medicine, 362
Forbes, William, 74
Fordham's Drug Store (Greensboro), 408
Forestry, 455, 456
Forests, 111–12
Forsyth Savings and Trust Company, 512
Fort Anderson, 65, 339
Fort Barnwell, 57
Fort Bragg, 510
Fort Defiance, 207
Fort Dobbs, 86; reenactors at, 87
Fort Fisher, 339; fortifications at, 340; Union bombardment of, 341
Fort Hancock, 57
Fort Macon, 339
Fort Neoheroka, 57
Fort Raleigh, 21, 22, 516
Fortune (slave), 146
Fourteenth Amendment (U.S. Constitution), 345
Fox, George, 28, 30
Francis McNairy House (Guilford County), 83. See also McNairy, Francis
Franck (Frank), Elizabeth, 191
Franck, Martin, 191
Franklin, Benjamin, 73, 88
Fraternal lodges, 304
Frazier, Leroy, 558
Frazier, Ralph, 558
Free blacks, 300–301
"Freedman's College" (Charlotte), 438
Freedmen (former indentured servants), 27, 28

Freedmen (former slaves), 342
Freedmen's Bureau, 343
Freedom Hill (African American community, Edgecombe County), 356
Friends of the College (N.C. State University), 577
Fries, Francis H., 512
From the Southern Mountains, 575
Front Street Methodist Church (Wilmington), 435
Frosty Morn meatpacking plant (Kinston), 521
Fry, Julius, 498
Frye, Henry E., 560
Fuller, "Blind Boy" (musician), 528
Funeral customs, 186
Furniture industry, 494–96, 503
"Fusion" movement, 376

Gallopade (social event, Rocky Mount), 522
Galloway, Alexander, 436, 437
Gambling, 165, 186, 194, 573
Gardner, O. Max, 500
Gash, Mary, 276
Gaston, William, 164
Gates, Thomas, 26
"Gentleman" class, 190
Geographical barriers, 317–18
George (slave), 146, 147
George I (king of England), 58
George Vanderbilt Hotel (Asheville), 534
Georgian architecture, 159, 212
Germans (from Pennsylvania): migrate to Piedmont, 78, 79, 82–83, 88, 115, 116, 218
Gilbert, Humphrey, 20
Glencoe (mill village), 388, 390, 391, 393; workers' houses at, 390
Gold Hill Mine, 329
Gold mining, 328–31
Goldsboro, 521, 522–23
Golf World, 549
Goodman, Billy, 570
Gordon, William, 34–35
"Gouging," 192

Home Ownership Association, 563
Hood, George, 298
Hood, James W., 437
Hooper, William (grandfather of Rev. William Hooper), 196, *198*
Hooper, Rev. William (grandson of William Hooper), 223
Hope Plantation (Bertie County), 210, 211–12
Horne Creek Farm (Surry County): farmhouse at, *365*; birthday gathering at, *366*; workers at, *367*
Horne Creek Living Historical Farm (state historic site, Surry County), 357
Horn in the West, 517
Horse racing, 313; admission ticket to, *312*
Horseshoe Bend, Battle of, 120
Horton, George Moses, 257, 258
Horton Grove (Historic Stagville, Durham County), 247; slave quarters at, *248*, 253–54; and slave workforce, 250–51; Great Barn at, *254*
Hosiery industry, 502
House in the Horseshoe (state historic site, Moore County), 151–60 passim, 209
Hughes, Hatcher, 575
Hunt, James B., Jr., 579
Hunt, Richard M., 455
Hunter, Charles N., 438
Hunter, Jim ("Catfish"), 570
Hunter, Kermit, 517
Hunter, Robert, Jr.: on Collins canal plan, 137; on Wilmington, 161; on Edenton and its residents, 165, 181
Hunthill (plantation), 150
Hurricanes, 34
Husband, Hermon, 82, 100; protests political abuses by local officials, 95, 99; characterizes goals of Regulators, 99; escapes execution, 103

I-house (Georgian architectural style), 159–60

Immigration: into colony of N.C., 39, 72, 78; to United States, 354
In Abraham's Bosom, 575
Indebtedness: among planters, 63; among yeomen, 264–65, 270
Indentured servants, 27
Indians. *See* American Indians
Indigo, 113, 114, 150
Industrialization, 502–4
Industrial Revolution, 207
Innes, James, 74
Internal improvements, 227
Interstate highways, 543, 546
Iredell, Hannah Johnston, 166, *197*
Iredell, James, 164, 166, 195, *196*, 197, 204
Iredell, James, Jr., 195
Iredell County Courthouse (Statesville), 410
Iredell House (Edenton), 166–68
Ironclads, 339

Jackson, Andrew, 120, 268, 315
Jackson, Franklin, 571
Jackson, Jesse, 558
Jackson, John H., 312
Jackson, Nathaniel, 571
Jamaica Packet (ship), 76
James I (king of England), 26
James K. Polk Memorial (state historic site, Mecklenburg County), 206; dwelling at, *205*, *206*
Jamestown, Va., 25, 26
Jansen, Charles William, 138, 143, 145
Janzen, Christen, 48–49
Jeffcoat, Mrs. Jim, 477
Jefferson, Thomas, 214–16, 225
Jefferson Standard Building (Greensboro), *536*
Jenkins, James, 288
Jessup's Mill (Stokes County), 361
Jews, 280
Joel McLendon House (Moore County), *82*
John Haley House (Guilford County), 132, *133*
John M. Belk Memorial Fund, 514
Johnson, Andrew, 169, 171, 345. *See also* Andrew Johnson House

Johnson, Gerald W., 546
Johnson, Hunter, 575
Johnson, Jacob, 169
Johnson, Junior, 572
Johnson, Mary McDonough, 169
Johnson C. Smith University (Charlotte), 438, 439
John Stevenson House (New Bern), 212–13
Johnston, Gabriel, 63–64, 91
Johnston, Joseph E., 263, 341, *345*
Johnston, Samuel, 91
Johnston, William, 91, 92
John Vogler House (Winston-Salem), 304
John Wright Stanly House (New Bern), 187, *188*. *See also* Stanly, John Wright
Jones, Allen, 155
Jones, Willie, 155
Jonkonnu ceremony, 140, 148; re-creation of, *141*
Jordan Lake, 491
Joseph Bonner House (Bath), 304
Joyce Kilmer Memorial Forest, 19, 111
J. P. Stevens (textile company), 504
Junaluska (Cherokee chief), 120
June German (social event, Rocky Mount), 522
Juno (slave), 157
Justice, Charlie ("Choo-Choo"), 569
Justices of the peace, 293–94, 345
Justice system, 294–95

Kannapolis, 497
Key, V. O., 470
Kilcocanen (Yeopim Indian king), 28
King, John Hoyter, 53
King, Martin Luther, Jr., 558
Kinston, 176, 303, 521
Kiscutanewh (Weapemeoc Indian king), 28
Knights of Labor, 395
Körner, Jules, 416, 417–18
Körner's Folly (Kernersville), 414, 416–18
Kreps, Juanita, 564